CH01657614

The Who's Who of Grantham Town Football Club

by Jon Barnes

ISBN 0-9545031-1-2

Published by Gingerjonny Publications,
39 Severn Drive,
Taunton,
Somerset.
TA1 2PN

First Published July 2005

~

For old Withamenders and young Eaststanders
and all those who proudly support The Gingerbreads

Introduction

This publication was born from the apprehension whilst writing *Grantham Town Football Club ~ The History* that players of importance had been missed. By their nature, team members that tend to remain in the memory are those that either scored the goals or moved on to greater things and with a club like Grantham that tended to be very quickly if they were sufficiently talented! It was always in the back of my mind that there must be players who had trod the London Road turf week in, week out, who had simply merged into the mists of time. So it's with immense pride that the result of that concern is now released. Only a handful of the country's top teams have publications available that goes into this depth on their players, and now there is another one, for Grantham Town. In some respects it has also re-written the history of our club, with a whole host of former star players and Internationals unearthed. Of particular note should be the Cursham brothers of the 1870's, with Arthur being the current England Captain during his time at Grantham. Also the first publication contained 18 individuals that were known to have moved on to Football League prominence. This list would now go into several pages, with particularly the late 1920's players seeming to be of great quality, at a time when the Midland League was considered by some to have been a stronger competition than Division Three.

To the best of my knowledge all facts and figures from the late 1920's onwards are accurate, but as we travel backwards from there, records and team-sheets become more and more scarce, until we're often left with just the goal-scorers, at best. Thankfully, as we get back into the 19th. Century things improve once more. It's for this reason that there simply cannot be a book on *every* Grantham player. This is a book on every Grantham player that there is still evidence of, although I think out of the 1,730 individuals that are listed, only a number in the low double figures are absent.

Some Christian names are missing, but please bare in mind that even only a couple of generations ago match reports were still along the lines of '*Mr* Smith had an excellent game'. As a general rule of thumb I have assumed that if a player had the same surname and played in a similar position from one season to the next, then he was the same individual. Of course this does not guarantee that this was the case, but there are simply no other forms of evidence other than that held by Grantham Library to find out other possible solutions. If I am even slightly unsure as to players' identities then I have listed them twice and noted the possibilities afterwards.

~~~~

It's important in a publication of this nature that matches that are included are *competitive* games. But competitions that have little importance either to a club or supporters today, would have been held in great esteem by those from a different era. Therefore, included in this publication are the following competitions;

All League games relevant to that season, including the abandoned Midland League competition of 1939/40 and the two subsequent 'War-Time' Leagues, plus the Lincolnshire League of 1935/36 (which the first team entered) and the Central Alliance Subsidiary Competition of 1924/25,
All F.A. Cup games,
All F.A. Amateur Cup games,
All F.A. Trophy games,
All League Cup games relevant to that season,
All Lincolnshire Cup games in it's various guises,

Also in the 'Other' section are the following games;
The Redmayne & Todd Cup fixture of 1976/77,
Redmayne Trophy fixtures of 1980/81 and 1981/82,
Northern Premier League President's Cup of 1982/83 and 1984/85,
Midland League Champions V Rest of the League fixtures from 1970/71 and 1971/72,
Midland League Champions V Runners-Up fixture from 1937/38 and 1969/70,
Stamford Nursing Society Cup from 1910/11, 1920/21 and 1937/38,
Spalding Victory Cup from 1937/38,
Grantham Hospital / Charity Cup from 1891/92, 1894/95, 1922/23, 1923/24, 1924/25, 1926/27, 1929/30, 1932/33, 1933/34, 1935/36 and 1936/37,
Wilson Cup from 1935/36 and 1936/37,
Byron Cup from 1933/34,
R.A.F. Shield from 1924/25 and 1926/27,
Grantham Minor Cup from 1893/94, 1894/95, 1904/05, 1906/07, 1907/08 and 1909/10,
Newark Charity Cup from 1889/90, 1890/91 and 1891/92,
~~~~

Kettering Charity Cup from 1888/89, 1889/90 and 1890/91.
And finally, in the same section are the following friendlies;
V R.A.F. XI (twice), Peterborough United (twice), Nottingham Forest, Newark Town and an Army XI from the 1939/40 season,
V Arsenal (1932/33), Boston and West Bromwich Albion (1931/32), Queen's Park (1912/13, 1910/11 & 1909/10),
All Friendlies against *other* teams (i.e. not club matches) prior to League football.
These have been included after using information on whether the full First team played, attendances, press coverage and whether *at the time of play* they would have been classed as competitive.

Acknowledgements

Many thanks to all of the following individuals for assistance in the research for this publication; Monica Aley, Herbert Allen, Jim Allen, Mario Aloi, Barbara Asher, Brian Asher, Ady Barker, John Barker, Caz Barnes, Eric Barnes, Joyce Barnes, Kevin Beck, Steve Beck, Tracey Beeby, Winston Bernard, Malcolm Berridge, Jimmy Bloomer, Darren Bogan, Eric Bond, Mike Bosnell, Sam Branson, Stewert Bratherton, David Bromwich, Cyril Brown, David Brown, Neil Brown, Paul Buckthorpe, Mike Bundy, Dennis Butters, Peter Camm, Graham Capewell, Simon Clark, Kathleen Clay, Ian Coaten, Don Codling, Mick Cole, Kevin Collins, Ned Cooper, Simon Corden, Graham Cowell, Graham Cox, Ged Creane, Jez Creasey, Steve Crome, Chris Curtis, John Dilnot, Bob Don-Duncan, Neil Dorsett, Chris Down, Clive Dyer, Ted Eaglen, Robin Eatch, Gary Elliman, Andy Elsom, Shaughan Farrow, Neil Fleming, Ken Fox, Mick French, Freddie Friend, Chris Gardiner, Bernard Gedney, Dennis Genas, Alf Gibbons, Colin Gibson, Jonny Gilbert, Reg Gilder, Geoff Giles, Jon Godwin, Fred Goodliff, Julian Goulsbra, Andy Graver, Vince Grimes, John Gulson, Edgar Hanson, Ronnie Harbertson, Lloyd Harmston, Steve Harper, Kev Harris, Ronnie Harrison, Maurice Healey, Brent Horobin, Roy Houghton, Dale Igoe, Paul Jacklin, Pete Jackson, David Jerman, Barry Jones, Michael Joyce, Barry Kershaw, Alec King, Sid Lawrence, Joe Lewis, John Little, John Litster, Wayne Manners, Kev Marshall, Neil Marshall, Mick Massingham, Kevin McMenemin, Pete Mogridge, James Morgan, Brian Morley, Crispin Morton, Graham Musson, Ian Nannestad, Graham Neal, Ernie Nixon, Pat Nixon, Craig Norrie, Bob Norris, Julia Ogden, John O'Hare, Alan O'Meara, Stuart Park, Ray Parnham, John Parsons, Barry Pearson, Nick Pearson, Nick Pigott, John Pinchbeck, Tim Preece, John Ramsden, Mick Robinson, Andy Ryder, Rod & Kim Salmine, Steve Saxby, Charlie Scoffield, Gary Scotcher, Barry Shaw, Rob Shippey, Dave Simmons, Dick Skeith, Howard Skeith, Jarrod Smith, Les Stancer, Mark Steptoe, Nick Steptoe, Glynis Sterry, George Stillyards, Marshall Storey, Brian Stubley, John Sutton, Ben Sweet, Tim Thacker, Colin Thompson, Philip Thorn, Ruth Tinley, Pete Tobin, Margeret Toole, Terry Vallance, Michael Ward, Paul Ward, Paul Weston, Craig Whyley, Ralph Wiggington, John Wilkinson, Nick Woodhead, Dave Worthington and James Wright.

Particular note should also go to Mike Koranski for the huge volume of team-sheets made available and to Andy Sutton for his tremendous assistance with player profiles from the modern era. Without these two individuals, this publication would have been impossible to produce.

Thanks to the staff for assistance and use of facilities at Taunton and Grantham libraries.

Thanks to our sponsors; Plaice, Thompson and Richardson ~ Tel; (01476) 562456
and Roger Booth, Michelle Fardell and Helen Reeve for arranging the advertisement.

Scanning by Rod Salmine at MBE Mail Boxes Etc (Taunton), Andy Sutton, Nick Pigott and Paul Jacklin.

Photos courtesy of Grantham Journal, Dean Fardell (Matchday photos available from 01476 568657), Andy Sutton, Grantham Library, Nick Pigott, Simon Clark, Paul Jacklin, Mike Koranski, Kev Marshall, John Pinchbeck, Vic Heppenstall, Sleaford Standard, Boston Standard, Ruth Tinley, Donny On-line, Paul Taylor, Colin Woodcock and Jeff Trice.

Some photographs are direct copies of digital images, some are second generation and others bare little resemblance to what was originally in front of the camera! However, to ensure an unbiased diversification of players represented it was felt essential for these to be included.

Cover design by Jon Barnes, Andy Sutton and Paul Fleming at Zeralynx Printers, Taunton
Printing by MBE Mail Boxes Etc (Taunton) ~ Making Business Easy ~ Tel; (01823) 322263
Binding by Wessex Print Finishers, Wellington
Bar-Codes by Vale Labels, Creech St Michael

Figures quoted are for those games where there is written evidence that the individual concerned played, I have made no assumptions as to whether they did or not. Therefore, as stated before, for players from the early 20th Century and in some instances before this, appearances are the minimum that they played. This does sometimes distort certain player's apparent goalscoring abilities, i.e. if a player scored five times in different games, but *possibly* played in every one, then he is only listed as 5 goals in 5 appearances, as this seemed to be a more accurate way of recording the data than what is little more than guessing.

With Adrian Speed recently breaking the club record of number of appearances made, it seemed interesting to highlight the top ten players in this field and for goal-scorers as well;

	Appearances			*Goals*	
1	Adrian Speed	633+	1	Jack Macartney	416
2	Chris Gardiner	624	2	Bob Norris	188
3	Ronnie Harrison	547	3	Ernie Nixon	179
4	Dennis Benskin	464	4	Mike Bosnell	142
5	Tony Farmer	461	5	Peter Whitehurst	139
6	Jack Macartney	456	6	Mike Alexander	126
7	Gerry Taylor	447	7	Terry Bly	121
8	Bob Norris	444	8=	Dennis Benskin	115
9	Alan Clay	418	8=	Jimmy Rayner	115
10	George Jowett	402	10	Cyril Stocks	103

Places of birth / death could be the registration district, particularly those with just a year figure. In such cases, the event may have occurred in a village covered by that district.

A continually updated version of this publication, maintained by Andy Sutton, will be available on the club's web-site;
www.granthamtownfc.co.uk

Whilst all effort has been taken to ensure that all facts and figures are accurate, no responsibility can be accepted for any errors that may have occurred.

Bibliography

Grantham Town Football Club ~ The History, by Jon Barnes ~ ISBN 0-9545031-0-4
Football League Players' Records, 1946-1992 by Barry J Hugman ~ ISBN 1-869833-20-1
Football League Players' Records, 1888-1939 by Michael Joyce ~ ISBN 1-899468-63-3
The Interlink Express Ultimate Book Of Non-League Players 1997/98, by Steve Whitney ~ ISBN 0-9531258-0-7
Non League Players, by Steve Whitney ~ ISBN 1-869833-30-9
The Non League Footballers Who's Who, by Steve Whitney and Bruce Mith ~ ISBN 1-869833-13-9
Forest Giants, by John McGovern and Rob Jovanovic ~ ISBN 0-9543576-1-2
The Forest Who's Who, by Tony Matthews ~ ISBN 1-904103-20-0
A Who's Who of Grimsby Town AFC, by Douglas Lamming ~ ISBN 0-907033-34-2
Who's Who of Lincoln City 1892-1994, by Donald & Ian Nannestad ~ ISBN 1-874427-90-9
Mansfield Town Who's Who, by Jack Retter and Paul Taylor ~ CD Rom
Peterborough United - The Official History Of The Posh, by Andy Groom and Mick Robinson ~ ISBN 1-874427-15-1
Where Are They Now?, by Andy Pringle and Neil Fissler ~ ISBN 1-897850-92-1
The Grantham Connection, by Jim Allen ~ ISBN 0-9511756-02
Lincolnshire Cricketers 1828-1993, by CJ Bartlett, L King, PR Thorn and KSC Trushell
Alumni Cantabrigienses, by JA Venn
Alumni Oronienses, by Joseph Foster
(Nottingham) Post Football Guide ~ Various editions
Grantham Town Football Club Official Matchday Programme ~ Various editions
Grantham Journal ~ Various Editions

Advance Subscribers

Many thanks to all of the following individuals who once again showed both their dedication to our club, and trust in myself to actually finish the project, by ordering a copy of this publication in advance;

Wayne Ayto	Ken Baptist	Joyce Barnes
Nigel Beck	Rob Bland	Dave Bullock
Mike Bundy	Chris Chambers	Paul Charles
Dennis Christian	Simon Clark	David Coulson
Graham Cowell	Ian De'Ath	Colin Dexter
David Doughty	Mark Fowell	Tony Fraher
George Freeston	Jonny Gilbert	David Graham
Steve Harper	John Hipwell	Ian Hickingbotham
Ian Hullott	Dave Jackson	Sarah Jackson
Mike Koranski	Vicky King	Andy Lambley
Cyril Lambley	Bob Macartney	Paul Manterfield
Nick Marriott	Kev Marshall	Pete Mogridge
Paul Musson	Ted Neville	Richard Panter
Geoff Parnham	John Parsons	Nick Pearson
Nick Pigott	Barry Roberts	Kev Roberts
John Roberts	Jamie Robson	Simon Shaw
Mike Simpson	Jarrod Smith	Andy Sutton
John Tear	Nigel Whittle	

~~~

Grantham Town Supporters Club reformed in 1997 with two main aims; to raise funds for Grantham Town Football Club and to raise funds to benefit supporters. Over the years since, it has been one of the most successful at its level of football.

The dedication and hard work of its' members has produced huge sums of money for The Gingerbreads. Between the years of 1999 and 2004, the Supporters Club raised £45,000 to pay a CVA that hung around the club and threatened to take it under. But that is not all. The club also pay for the First team travel and programme printing costs. All in all, the club now regularly put in over £20,000 a season.

Fortunately the Board of Directors recognise this input. Through exchanging shares in return for donations, Grantham Town Supporters Club is now one of the biggest shareholders in the club. There is a representative invited to every Board meeting and the Supporters Club are in involved in most decisions, even up to the appointment of the manager.

With the CVA now paid, the Supporters Club are looking towards doing more for the supporters as well as the club. To this end, coaches will replace mini-buses for away games and other ways will be looked at to say 'thank-you' to the members who have been through both good times and bad.

Integral to this is the club shop and merchandising efforts. Both this book and Jon's previous, *Grantham Town Football Club ~ The History*, contribute to the work of the Supporters Club. The publication of both books has been a magnificent achievement, one for which I am certainly grateful to Jon.

As with all clubs in non-league football, Grantham Town and it's Supporters Club cannot function without the help of volunteers. It is these people who offer their time and effort to their local side that make the difference. If you would like to join us as we endeavour to ever improve our club, whether it be as a business that would like to be promoted or to an individual who would like to become a bit more involved, then you can contact any official on matchdays or write to either Grantham Town Football Club or Supporter's Club at The Meres Stadium, Trent Road, Grantham , Lincs. Any contribution is welcomed and gratefully received.

Yours in football
Graham Cowell
Chairman
Grantham Town Supporters Club
~~~

Darren Abbott

Seasons Played	League	~	1
	F.A. Cup	~	
1988/89	F.A. Trophy	~	
	League Cup	~	
	Lincs Cup	~	
	Total	~	1

Former Belper Town and Heanor Town winger who came to Grantham on-loan from Eastwood Town, making just one appearance, replacing Spadge Farrow in the March 1989 league game at home to Ashtree Highfield.

Abbott

Seasons Played	League	~	2 (1)
	F.A. Cup	~	
1933/34	Lincs Cup	~	
	Other	~	
	Total	~	2 (1)

Played and scored in the Christmas Day 1933 league fixture against his previous club, Newark Town, as well as the New Year's Eve visit of Gresley Rovers to London Road.

Tony Abrahams

Seasons Played	League	~	15 (2)
	F.A. Cup	~	
1988/89	F.A. Trophy	~	1
	League Cup	~	1
	Lincs Cup	~	
	Total	~	17 (2)

Born 08/12/1969 at Liverpool. Had trials with Manchester United, Liverpool and Everton, then joined local side Stanfield FC, before spending time on the books at Nottingham Forest where he captained their Youth side, including the FAYC Final team. Tony came to Grantham on-loan from The City Ground and made his debut by coming off the bench in the November 1988 match at Atherstone, substituting Danny Anderson. He scored his two goals for the club in consecutive matches against Bilston Town and Rushden Town in the New Year, with his final appearance for Grantham coming at the end of April against Forest Green Rovers. A return to Nottingham was followed by an unsuccessful transfer to Blackpool and then a return to the non-league game with Knowsley United.

Albert Adams

Seasons Played	League	~	3
	Lincs Cup	~	1
1893/94-94/95	Other	~	2 (1)
	Total	~	6 (1)

Born 1873 in Grantham. Brother of John Adams. Albert is known to have played in and scored the consolation goal for the club in the Grantham Minor Cup Final of April 1894, but little is known of other games that he appeared in.

Benny Adams

Seasons Played	League	~	11
	F.A. Cup	~	
1931/32-32/33	Lincs Cup	~	
	Other	~	1
1939/40	Total	~	12

Born circa 1914. Brother of Tom Adams. Benny was only 17 years old on his Grantham debut in January 1932, but by the following year had moved on to play for Grantham Amateurs, followed by Stamford and Newark Town. In March of 1940 he returned to London Road to make three more appearances for the club, against Peterborough United, Newark Town and in a friendly against an Army XI.

John Adams

Seasons Played	League	~	5 (4)
	Lincs Cup	~	1
1893/94-94/95	Other	~	3 (1)
	Total	~	9 (5)

Born 1875 in Grantham. No details are known as to his debut, but is recognised as playing in the same April 1894 Grantham Minor Cup Final as his brother, Albert Adams. The following season John scored a hat-trick in the Grantham League fixture against Spittlegate Victoria as well as single strikes against Rovers Colts and the Charity Cup defeat at the hands of Grantham Rovers in January 1895.

Micky Adams

Seasons Played	League	~	2
	F.A. Cup	~	
1994/95	F.A. Trophy	~	
	League Cup	~	
	Lincs Cup	~	
	Total	~	2

Made only two appearances for Grantham towards the end of the 1994/95 season. His first game came in the April league match at home to Ilkeston Town, followed by the arrival of Moor Green to The Meres at the end of the same month, although Micky's Grantham career ended during that match when he was substituted in favour of Dean Dye.

Tom Adams

Seasons Played	League	~	3
	Lincs Cup	~	
1939/40	Other	~	
	Total	~	3

Centre-Forward who made appearances for the club during the same month, March of 1940, as his brother Benny Adams. He played in two of the corresponding games, at Peterborough and Newark, but had already made his debut in the London Road visit of Newark Town.

Dave Adamson

Seasons Played	League	~	43 (5)
	F.A. Cup	~	1
1983/84-84/85	F.A. Trophy	~	2
	League Cup	~	2
	Lincs Cup	~	3
	Other	~	2
	Total	~	53 (5)

Born 07/05/1951 at Chester-le-Street. Previously played for South Shields, Durham City, Doncaster Rovers, (where he made 28 First team appearances), Hatfield Main, Boston United and Chester-le-Street. Dave was also awarded five appearances for the England semi-professional team during his time at Boston. He made his Grantham debut in the February 1984 Northern Premier League Cup tie at Hyde United and then played in every one of that season's remaining fixtures, scoring his first goal for the club towards the end of the campaign at Rhyl. The following season, one that unfortunately saw Grantham relegated, Dave played in the majority of the club's fixtures, with his final game for Grantham coming in the concluding fixture at Oswestry Town.

Percy Addinall

Seasons Played	League	~	7 (1)
	F.A. Cup	~	1
1920/21-21/22	Lincs Cup	~	1
	Other	~	
	Total	~	9 (1)

Born 1888 at Hull. Half-Back who had previously played for West End (Lincoln) and then Lincoln City in Division 2, making 15 appearances during their 1919/20 season. He joined Grantham in November 1920 and the following March scored his only goal for the club in the league game against New Hucknall Colliery. However, only a year after his debut, records show that Percy had apparently moved on. Died 1932 at Lincoln.

Ku Akeredolu

Seasons Played	League	~	4
	F.A. Cup	~	
1992/93	F.A. Trophy	~	
	League Cup	~	
	Lincs Cup	~	
	Total	~	4

Born circa 1958. Kunle John Akeredolu can safely be labelled as 'much travelled' after previously having two periods at the following clubs, Bedworth United and Shepshed Charterhouse, three at Leicester United, as well as single spells with Anstey Nomads, Corby Town, Rothwell Town, Hinckley Town and Nuneaton

Borough. His Grantham debut came during the December 1992 home fixture against Leicester United when he replaced Adrian Speed. After only a handful of appearances though, his substitution during the March league visit of Redditch United marked the end of his career at the club and he went on to return to Rothwell Town. Ku later became Chairman at Atherstone United, up to the point where they went into liquidation, following which he became Chief Executive of an IT company.

Ken Akers

Seasons Played			
	League	~	120 (3)
	F.A. Cup	~	13
1964/65-66/67	Total	~	133 (3)

Left-Back who was previously on the books at Notts County, before moving to Loughborough United. Ken then made his Grantham debut in the opening game of the 1964/65 season at his former club, Loughborough, and immediately became a near ever-present member of the team. His second season at London Road, in which he played in every competitive match, included the high-light of an appearance against Swindon Town in the FA Cup 2nd Round, as well as goals scored against Spalding United and Loughborough United. In his final season with the club he scored another goal against Lockheed Leamington, before ending his Grantham career in the Testimonial for Ronnie Harbertson and Pim Taylor against a Nottingham Forest side. Little is known of Ken after this, due to him emigrating to Australia in the 1970's.

Keith Alexander

Seasons Played			
	League	~	2
	F.A. Cup	~	
1983/84	F.A. Trophy	~	
	League Cup	~	1
	Lincs Cup	~	
	Total	~	3

Born 14/11/1958 at Nottingham. Began his career as a Junior at Notts County and then moved on to Wisbech Town, Worksop Town, Clifton, Ilkeston Town, Kimberley Town, Alfreton Town, Stamford, (where he played in their 1980 FA Vase Final at Wembley, scoring one of the goals), Boston United, King's Lynn, Corby Town, Spalding United and Boston FC. His Grantham debut, in the opening match of the 1983/84 season at Hyde United, saw him substituted by Stuart Chapman, whilst his other two appearances for the club came in the February 1984 League Cup visit of Hyde United and the April trip up to Gainsborough Trinity. Keith went on to play for Kettering Town, Wisbech, Barnet (and also played for Washingborough in the Lincoln Sunday League at the same time), Grimsby Town, Stockport County, Lincoln City, Mansfield Town, where he also had a spell as Assistant Player/Manager, and Cliftonville, scoring 35 goals in 173 fixtures played during his time with Football League teams. After the end of his playing career, which had also seen him win honours as a St Lucian International, he became Manager at Ilkeston Town, Northwich Victoria, then Lincoln City, where he remains after recovering from life-saving surgery in November 2003.

Mike Alexander

Seasons Played			
	League	~	129 (111)
	F.A. Cup	~	13 (15)
1964/65-68/69	League Cup	~	
	Lincs Cup	~	
	Total	~	142 (126)

Born circa 1941. Originally on the books of Scunthorpe United and then played for Brigg Town (where he scored 120 goals in two seasons) and Gainsborough Trinity. Following a £300 transfer fee Mike came to Grantham and scored on his debut in the February 1965 Midland League game at Worksop Town. By the end of that first season he had notched up 16 strikes in his 16 appearances. Highlights of the following season included scoring all 4 goals in the FA Cup 1st Round defeat of Hendon, equalled in the league game at home to Ashton United, as well as an appearance in the FA Cup 2nd Round game against Swindon Town. By the end of that campaign Mike had amassed another 50 goals in only 48 appearances and his scoring rate continued in the next two seasons, even netting another 4 goals in one match, this time Matlock Town being the victims. At the same time, more FA Cup Proper Round appearances had also occurred, against Wimbledon, Oldham Athletic and Altrincham. However, Mike's Grantham career came to a close after the September 1968 game at Belper Town, with his transfer to Boston United after a £2,000 fee was paid. He was voted the Anglia TV Sports Personality of the year for the 1968/69 season and following a successful couple of years at Boston, he returned to Gainsborough Trinity, even playing at London Road in the late 1970's in a Reserve fixture between two of his clubs.

Charlie Aley

Seasons Played			
	League	~	17
	F.A. Cup	~	
1954/55	Lincs Cup	~	
	Total	~	17

Born 13/09/1933 at Melton Mowbray. Former Holwell Works defender who made his debut at London Road in the November 1954 Midland League match against Scunthorpe United Reserves. Charlie played in many of the remaining games of that season, right up until the last game at Boston United, although he made one further appearance for the club a week later in the Stamford Hospital Cup. He continued to play for his works side at Holwell and then made appearances for Pedigree Petfoods, where his career continued up to his retirement. Died circa 1999 in Grantham.

Bill Allcock

Seasons Played			
	League	~	49 (1)
	F.A. Cup	~	
1929/30	Lincs Cup	~	
	Other	~	
	Total	~	49 (1)

Born 18/07/1907 at Codnor. Half-Back, previously with Heanor Town, who first played for Grantham in the opening fixture of the 1929/30 season at Mansfield Town. End of season statistics show that he missed only one league game during the year and by a process of elimination his only goal for the club must have come either in one of the Christmas fixtures against Newark Town or the season's concluding match at Nottingham Forest Reserves. Bill went on to have a successful Football League career, scoring six goals in his 209 appearances for Bradford Park Avenue and Barrow. Died 1971 at Barrow-in-Furness.

Herbert Allen

Seasons Played			
	League	~	13
	F.A. Cup	~	
1956/57-57/58	Lincs Cup	~	
	Total	~	13

Born 27/10/1924 at Beeston, Nottingham. Full-Back, nick-named 'Tanner', who had previously played for Beeston Boys, Nottingham Forest, Notts County and Corby Town, scoring once in his 34 Football League appearances. Tanner was an industrial draughtsman by trade and played out his football career as a part-time profession, even during his time with the two senior Nottingham sides. After arriving at Grantham he certainly suffered a baptism of fire, making his debut in the January 1957 6-2 defeat against a strong Boston United side. Tanner made a total of 12 appearances during the remainder of that season and was thrown in at the deep end once again the following campaign, making his only appearance of the year at Peterborough United in October. He then spent a season at Heanor Town, before starting his own vending company in Nottingham. Herbert still lives in his home city and despite now being in his 80's, continues to play an active role in the running of that same business.

Horace Allen

Seasons Played			
	League	~	3
	F.A. Cup	~	
1964/65	Total	~	3

Made his debut for the club at London Road in the October 1964 Midland League game against Retford Town. Horace only made two further appearances for Grantham, the first the following week at Goole Town and again in December at Ilkeston Town.

Keith Allen

Seasons Played			
	League	~	1
	F.A. Cup	~	
1946/47	Lincs Cup	~	
	Total	~	1

Made just the one appearance for Grantham, the home league game against Frickley Athletic at the end of May 1947.

T. Allen

Seasons Played			
	League	~	2
	F.A. Cup	~	
1929/30	Lincs Cup	~	
	Other	~	
	Total	~	2

Inside-Right who also played for Scunthorpe & Lindsey United during his career. Unfortunately in an era where individual records are comparatively sparse, there is no data to state which two games he actually played in for Grantham.

Allen

Seasons Played			
	League	~	1
	Lincs Cup	~	
1904/05	Other	~	
	Total	~	1

Available records show just the one appearance for this goalkeeper, in the Midland Amateur Alliance fixture at home to Derby Thornhill in March 1905.

Dick Allman

Seasons Played			
	League	~	1
	F.A. Cup	~	
1910/11	League Cup	~	
	Lincs Cup	~	
	Other	~	
	Total	~	1

Born 1883 at Burslem. Experienced player with clubs previously represented including Burslem Higherhave, Burslem Port Vale, (scoring 11 goals in 26 games), Reading, Portsmouth, Plymouth Argyle, Liverpool, (with one First team appearance there), Wrexham and Ton Pentre. Dick played at least once for Grantham during their Midland Amateur League Championship winning season, but soon returned to The Football League with Leicester Fosse, where he scored three goals in seven matches. His career finished in the London area when he made appearances for Croydon Common, Crystal Palace Reserves and Maidstone United. Died 1943.

Mario Aloi

Seasons Played			
	League	~	2
	F.A. Cup	~	
1987/88	F.A. Trophy	~	1
	League Cup	~	1
	Lincs Cup	~	
	Total	~	4

Born 09/06/1959 at Lincoln. Striker who had scored many goals for the Reserve side and made his senior debut by coming off the bench to replace Peter Whitehurst in the October 1987 FA Trophy defeat at Alvechurch. After a couple of other appearances during the same month, he made an isolated start in the February league game against Coventry Sporting, although he was replaced by Jon Morley during the match. Mario continues to work on the railways, a career which began after leaving school, and he still plays Sunday League football in the Lincoln area, claiming to have scored over 1,000 goals at all levels.

Wally Alsford

Seasons Played			
	League	~	5
	F.A. Cup	~	
1945/46	Lincs Cup	~	
	Total	~	5

Born 06/11/1911 at Edmonton. Former England International, with one cap against Scotland in 1935 which was played in front of a near 130,000 crowd at Hampden Park. At that time, Wally was playing for Tottenham Hotspur, after having had spells on-loan at Cheshunt and Northfleet at the end of the 1920's. In 1937 he moved to Nottingham Forest, finishing with a total of 111 League appearances, and during the War also made guest appearances for Aldershot, Arsenal and Doncaster Rovers. His Grantham debut came in April 1946, at the home league victory against Peterborough United, and was followed by a further four appearances out of the final 5 league games, ending at Frickley Colliery. This was all despite being diagnosed with a bone marrow condition in 1938 when he was told by doctors not to play again. He went on to become a licensee at pubs in Nottingham, Brighton and Bedford. Died 03/06/1968 at Bedford.

Nicky Andersen

Seasons Played			
	League	~	16 (2)
	F.A. Cup	~	
1991/92	F.A. Trophy	~	
	League Cup	~	
1996/97	Lincs Cup	~	
	Total	~	16 (2)

Born 29/03/1969 at Lincoln. Former Mansfield Town, Lincoln City and Nuneaton Borough midfielder who made 21 Football League appearances. Nicky scored on his Grantham debut, the September 1991 league game at Hednesford Town, but after his substitution by Neil Mann in the home game against Alvechurch a week later, he played no further part in Grantham's first season at The Meres. Following spells at Leek Town, Bedworth United, Tamworth, a return to Bedworth, another spell at Nuneaton, and then Corby Town, Nicky returned to Grantham in time for the November 1996 trip to Bilston Town. However, his substitution in the March defeat at the hands of Tamworth marked the end of his Grantham career. Nicky returned once again to Nuneaton, then had a period in management at the helm of Harrowby United and then Spalding United, but is currently Assistant Manager at Bourne Town.

Danny Anderson

Seasons Played			
	League	~	47 (3)
	F.A. Cup	~	2
1987/88-89/90	F.A. Trophy	~	5
	League Cup	~	2
	Lincs Cup	~	1
	Total	~	57 (3)

Born 21/11/1959 at Nottingham. Began his career as an Apprentice at Derby County and then moved on to Long Eaton United, Arnold Town, Ilkeston Town and Shepshed Charterhouse. Danny made his Grantham debut in the January 1988 fixture against Forest Green Rovers and although his appearances were sparse during the rest of the campaign, after the Summer break he had become an important member of the side. That 1988/89 season also saw Danny's three goals for Grantham, scored against Nuneaton Borough, Coventry Sporting and Mile Oak Rovers. He was then appointed player/manager after the departure of Martin O'Neill, bringing Gary Jones to Grantham, although Danny limited himself to just three appearances during December 1989 fixtures. After being substituted for Nigel Vince in the London Road game against Bridgnorth Town, he made no further appearances for the club. Less than two months after that final game, he had also been replaced in the managerial position by a returning John Robertson. Danny was also well known in the Nottingham area for his cricketing skills, playing for many years with Gotham.

John Andrews

Seasons Played			
	League	~	26 (1)
	F.A. Cup	~	
1998/99	F.A. Trophy	~	
	League Cup	~	3
	Lincs Cup	~	
	Total	~	29 (1)

Born 27/09/1978 in Cork, Ireland. Defender who was previously with Ringmahon Rangers (Ireland), Coventry City and Shepshed Dynamo. He made his debut for Grantham in the November 1998 league match at Burton Albion and missed only one of the remaining fixtures, up to the conclusion of the season at Weymouth. John was signed by Mansfield Town in May 1999, scoring one goal in 46 First team appearances, and then went on-loan to Hucknall Town, before a return to his home country with Cork City and then Cobh Ramblers.

Phil Annable

Seasons Played			
	League	~	28 (1)
	F.A. Cup	~	
1982/83-83/84	F.A. Trophy	~	
	League Cup	~	
	Lincs Cup	~	
	Other	~	
	Total	~	28 (1)

Born 1952 at Belper. Previously played for Mansfield Town Reserves, followed by a ten season spell at Burton Albion, making 567 appearances, and then a £6,000 transfer to Boston United. Phil first played for Grantham in the December 1982 league fixture at home to King's Lynn, missing only a handful of that season's games, and also being honoured with appearances for the Northern Premier League representative side. The start of the following season saw Phil's only goal for the club, at home to Worksop Town, but the September visit to Stafford Rangers proved to be his final game for the club. He went on to play for Worksop Town, where he made his 1000th career league appearance.

Anstey

Seasons Played			
	League	~	2 (1)
	Other	~	1
1906/07	Total	~	3 (1)

Known to have played in the 1906/07 league games against Derby Thornhill and Derby YMCA, in which he scored, as well as the Grantham Minor Cup match at Little Gonerby Swifts. He most likely played in many more of that season's games as well.

Appleton

Seasons Played			
	League	~	7
	F.A. Cup	~	
1927/28	Lincs Cup	~	
	Total	~	7

Goalkeeper who made his first appearance for the club in the February 1928 Midland League game against Loughborough Corinthians. However, he played for only a couple of months until the return of Stan Walker, the club's regular 'keeper during this era, which signalled the end of his First team career.

Mark Appleyard

Seasons Played			
	League	~	38 (1)
	F.A. Cup	~	2
1994/95	F.A. Trophy	~	1
	League Cup	~	2
	Lincs Cup	~	1
	Total	~	44 (1)

Former Louth United player who began his Grantham career in the opening match of the 1994/95 season against Grimsby Town in the County Cup. Although naturally a midfielder or defender, in the August league game versus Bedworth United, Mark found himself playing in goal after Grantham's 'keeper, Guy Hardcastle, was sent off. His only goal for the club came in the January 1995 defeat at Armitage and his final appearance came in the closing fixture at Bilston Town, with him leaving the club after missing only four games all season.

Bill Archer

Seasons Played			
	League	~	59
	F.A. Cup	~	1
1938/39-39/40	Lincs Cup	~	3
	Other	~	5
	Total	~	68

Born 05/02/1914 at Scunthorpe. Half-Back who had also played for Gainsborough Trinity, but made his debut for The Gingerbreads in the first game of the 1938/39 season at Shrewsbury Town. Bill only missed a handful of games both that season and the next, right up until his final match at Scunthorpe & Lindsey United in March 1940, the last competitive game until the end of The Second World War. That final season Bill also trained with Lincoln City, whilst in the first two seasons after The War he made a total of 16 appearances for Doncaster Rovers. Died 1992 at Scunthorpe.

Paul Archer

Seasons Played			
	League	~	12
	F.A. Cup	~	3 (1)
1998/99	F.A. Trophy	~	2
	League Cup	~	
	Lincs Cup	~	
	Total	~	17 (1)

Born 25/04/1978 at Leicester. Former Scottish Under-21 International signed from Nottingham Forest. His first game for Grantham came in the club's entry back into the Dr Marten's Premier League, at Worcester City in August 1998. Coming on as substitute in the October FA Cup game at Glossop North End, Paul netted his only goal for the club, with him also playing in the final qualifying round tie at Tamworth. However, the following month saw his last appearance for the club, again coming off the bench, in the home fixture against Atherstone United. He went on to play for Gainsborough Trinity, Spalding United, Leek Town, Hucknall Town, Arnold Town, Gedling Town, Radcliffe Olympic and then Gedling once more.

Armstrong

Seasons Played			
	League	~	3
	F.A. Cup	~	
1891/92	Other	~	
	Total	~	3

Forward who scored in his first game for the club, during a friendly held at Kettering in January 1892, but went on to make only three league appearances, the trip to Notts Olympic and the two encounters against Heanor over the following few weeks.

Armstrong

Seasons Played			
	League	~	
	F.A. Cup	~	
1936/37	Lincs Cup	~	
	Other	~	1
	Total	~	1

Played in just the one game for Grantham, the Wilson Cup defeat at the hands of RAF Cranwell towards the end of the 1936/37 season.

Mark Arnold

Seasons Played			
	League	~	1
	F.A. Cup	~	
1985/86	F.A. Trophy	~	
	League Cup	~	
	Lincs Cup	~	
	Total	~	1

Born 22/06/1962 in Grantham. Midfield player who arrived from Grantham United, at that time the club's 'nursery' side. However, his only appearance for the First team came in the final match of the 1985/86 season at VS Rugby when he came off the bench to replace Chris Moyses. Mark later went on to play for Harrowby United and still lives locally.

Roger Ashby

As a player, Roger made 662 appearances for Kettering Town, a club record, and then started his managerial career at Rushden Town. With the merger of that club and Irthlingborough Diamonds, he was installed as the head of the new club in July 1992. That first season finished with a third place in the league and a year later there were no surprises when the cash rich club won the Beazer Homes League, Midland Division. The 1994/95 season saw Roger lead Rushden & Diamonds to an FA Trophy semi-final, whilst the following campaign saw the club knock Grantham out of the FA Cup, progress to the First Round Proper where they were defeated by Cardiff City, and win the Dr Marten's Premier League. Despite another FA Cup First Round appearance, this time against Boreham Wood, the expected progression into The Football League didn't materialise and in February 1997 Roger was sacked and replaced by Brian Talbot. In November 1999 he was appointed Manager at Bedford Town and in the 2000/01 season he took them to a promotion place in the Ryman League, Division One, whilst a year later the club progressed to the FA Cup First Round, with Peterborough United finally defeating them in a replay. After disagreeing with a change in his contract, Roger was relieved of his duties at Bedford in September 2002. In July of the following year he came to Grantham as Manager and placed the team near the top of the league and got the club to their first FA Cup Proper match since 1975, with *Match of the Day* cameras at The Meres to witness the memorable game against Leyton Orient. However, the club had just begun a disappointing slump in league form that saw them plummet down the table and in February 2004 he resigned as Manager, promptly taking over at Nuneaton Borough where he still remains.

Brian Asher

Seasons Played			
	League	~	34 (18)
	F.A. Cup	~	2
1960/61-61/62	League Cup	~	1
	Lincs Cup	~	4 (1)
	Total	~	41 (19)

Born 27/11/1933 at Helpringham. Centre-Forward with experience at Billingborough, Bourne Town, Boston United, Skegness Town and with a trial at Peterborough United recently behind him. Brian made his debut for Grantham in the first game of the 1960/61 season, at home to Kettering Town Reserves, and finished that Central Alliance campaign as the club's highest scorer, with one hat-trick to his name as well, scored against Derby County 'A' in November 1960. The following season, the club's first back in the Midland League, he scored only three times in ten appearances, the last of which was in April 1962 in the home game against Alfreton Town. Brian went on to finish his career at Holbeach United, then worked as a self-employed plasterer, but is now retired, still living near to Sleaford.

E. Ashton

Seasons Played			
	League	~	1
	F.A. Cup	~	
1945/46	Lincs Cup	~	
	Total	~	1

Played in just the one game for Grantham, the away Midland League fixture at Boston United in October 1945.

Percy Ashton

Seasons Played			
	League	~	90
	F.A. Cup	~	9
1946/47-49/50	Lincs Cup	~	5
	Total	~	104

Born 21/03/1909 at Bolton-on-Dearne. Former West Melton Excelsior goalkeeper with ten years experience at Nottingham Forest, making 189 appearances during his time at The City Ground. Percy made his debut at London Road in January 1947 in a Midland League match against Scarborough and a few months later played in the Lincolnshire County Cup Final draw, and subsequent defeat in the replay, against Gainsborough Trinity. The following season Percy kept goal for the majority of the games and had the perfect view to see Grantham's scoring feats during games like Basford United (7-0) and Ilkeston Town (11-1). He was still the number one choice goalkeeper for the following, perhaps slightly less entertaining season, but made appearances in only the first two league games of the 1949/50 campaign, with the home match against Nottingham Forest Reserves his last, before his position was taken over by Ted Eaglen. Died 19/03/1985 at Nottingham.

Ted Ashton

Seasons Played			
	League	~	33 (1)
	F.A. Cup	~	7 (1)
1945/46-46/47	Lincs Cup	~	2
	Total	~	42 (2)

Born 19/01/1906 at Kilnhurst. Began his career playing for Kilnhurst WMC and Mexborough Town, before spending nine years at Barnsley, scoring 70 goals in 289 appearances there. Ted then moved on to Sheffield United and Carlisle United, before returning to Barnsley, although the outbreak of war meant that he failed to make another First team appearance there. His professional career finished with 353 senior games to his name. Ted scored on his debut for Grantham against Gainsborough Trinity in August 1945, the first Midland League game after the Second World War and also played in every round of that season's FA Cup run, scoring again at Kettering Town, before the club's eventual exit at the hands of Mansfield Town in the Second Round Proper. He was a near ever present member of the team throughout that season, also playing in the Lincolnshire County Cup Final defeat of April 1946, held in front of a 8,500 crowd at Boston United. Ted started with Grantham the following campaign, but played only three games, his last one against Nottingham Forest Reserves in September. Died 1978 at Barnsley.

Richard Atkin

Seasons Played			
	League	~	13
	F.A. Cup	~	
1996/97	F.A. Trophy	~	4
	League Cup	~	
	Lincs Cup	~	
	Total	~	17

Nottingham born player who previously played for his local sides Nuthall and Borrowash Victoria. His Grantham debut came in the first of the epic FA Trophy ties against Blyth Spartans, in January 1997 and he then played a part in the Grantham team right up to the final fixture of the season at Moor Green. After the Summer break, Richard returned to Borrowash, before signing for Long Eaton United and finally having his third spell at Borrowash.

Edwin Atkinson

Seasons Played			
	League	~	1
	F.A. Cup	~	
1937/38	Lincs Cup	~	
	Other	~	
	Total	~	1

Outside-Left, who had also played for Dunkirk, but made just the single appearance for Grantham, the first Midland League game of the 1937/38 season at Gainsborough Trinity.

Atkinson

Seasons Played			
	F.A. Cup	~	
	Other	~	1
1880/81	Total	~	1

Played in the October 1880 5-1 friendly victory at Huntingdon County.

Walter Atmore

Seasons Played			
	F.A. Cup	~	
	Lincs Cup	~	
1885/86	Other	~	4 (1)
1887/88	Total	~	4 (1)

Born 1859 at King's Lynn. Former King's School, Grantham, and Cambridge University student who scored on his debut in the October 1885 friendly against Notts Rangers, but for that season played only once more, the following game at Bourne. He appears two years later playing for the club, around the same time of year, and once more makes just two consecutive appearances, this time against Lincoln Rangers and Notts Rangers again.

Auckland

Seasons Played			
	League	~	5
	F.A. Cup	~	
1920/21-21/22	Lincs Cup	~	
	Other	~	
	Total	~	5

Experienced local player who had also played for the Reserve side, Grantham St. John's and a representative Grantham League side. As for our team, although team-sheets are limited for this period, we know he made at least four league appearances during the 1920/21 season, plus the 1921 New Years Eve fixture at home to Chesterfield Reserves.

Austin

Seasons Played			
	F.A. Cup	~	2
	Lincs Cup	~	4
1884/85	Other	~	20
1886/87-87/88	Total	~	26

Defender who made his Grantham debut in the 7-1 friendly defeat at Newark in November 1884, but played in only one other game during that season. He returned in January 1887 to make another single appearance, in a friendly at Derby County, but the following season he became a near ever-present member of the side. His last game for the club came in April 1888, during a friendly against Grantham Rovers.

Avery

Seasons Played			
	League	~	1
	Lincs Cup	~	
1907/08	Other	~	1
1909/10	Total	~	2

Only two known appearances for this goalkeeper, the Grantham Minor Cup game against Barrowby in November 1907 and the Midland Amateur Alliance league game against West Bridgford Friary played in April 1910.

P. Bacon

Seasons Played			
	League	~	23
	F.A. Cup	~	3
1920/21-21/22	Lincs Cup	~	2
	Other	~	
	Total	~	28

Full-Back who also played for Basford United and was an almost ever present member of the Grantham team for two years at the start of the 1920's. Unfortunately many team-sheets from this period are missing, so it is difficult to acknowledge many specific games that he played a part in.

Jimmy Bagshaw

Seasons Played			
1924/25	League	~	3 (3)
	F.A. Cup	~	
	Lincs Cup	~	
	Other	~	
	Total	~	3 (3)

Born 25/12/1885 at Derby. Former England International player, with one cap awarded in the 1919 draw against Ireland, plus one appearance in the representative England Victory match of the same year. Clubs played for included Fletcher's Athletic, Graham Street Primitives, Derby County from 1906 to 1919, (where he twice won Division Two Championship medals, scoring six goals in 240 appearances), Notts County and Watford. He arrived at Grantham in the Summer of 1924 with a total of 280 senior games to his name, but once again, as far as his Grantham career is concerned, sadly virtually no team sheets are available for this year so we only know of games where Jimmy scored. These included the opening match of the season at Coalville Swifts, plus the Hucknall Byron and Sutton Junction games at London Road. He went on to finish his playing career at Ilkeston United, whilst the late 1930's saw Jimmy become the Trainer at Nottingham Forest, plus spending time scouting for them and Coventry City. Other than football, he also worked as a lace threader and for Raleigh Industries in Nottingham. Died 25/08/1966 at Nottingham.

Nigel Baily

Seasons Played			
1997/98	League	~	31 (1)
	F.A. Cup	~	1
	F.A. Trophy	~	6
	League Cup	~	1
	Lincs Cup	~	1
	Total	~	40 (1)

Born circa 1963 at Nottingham. Previously played for Radcliffe Olympic, Dunkirk, Hucknall Town, Ilkeston Town and Lincoln United with his Grantham debut coming in the County Cup tie at the last of those clubs in August 1997. Nigel played an important part in that season's successful campaign, which finished with him winning a league championship medal. He also appeared in the FA Trophy matches against Hednesford Town and both ties against Southport. His only goal for Grantham came at the end of the season, at Solihull Borough, with only one other game to his name after that, at home to Stourbridge. Nigel went on to play for Stamford Town, before second spells at both Hucknall Town and Lincoln United, followed by a period as Player/Assistant Manager at Gedling Town, with his career finally going full circle as he returned to Radcliffe Olympic, where he still occasionally plays. For many years he has worked for the Royal Mail and is currently a Delivery Office Manager for them, still living in the Nottingham area.

Roy Bain

Seasons Played			
1958/59	League	~	3 (2)
	F.A. Cup	~	1 (1)
	Lincs Cup	~	
	Total	~	4 (3)

Scored in each of his first three games, against North Shields in September 1958, the FA Cup game at home to Gainsborough Trinity, and the league match at Frickley Colliery. Roy made his final appearance only a week later, at Scarborough, and had failed to be on the winning side in any of the games that he had played in..

W. Baker

Seasons Played			
1919/20-20/21	League	~	5 (1)
	F.A. Cup	~	
	Lincs Cup	~	
	Other	~	
	Total	~	5 (1)

After having previously played for Caythorpe and Grantham St John's, he joined Grantham in March 1920, making his debut in the league game at Chesterfield Reserves. He played in several of the remaining matches and then returned the following season to make at least one more appearance, at London Road against Shirebrook in April 1921.

Darren Ball

Seasons Played			
1999/00	League	~	6
	F.A. Cup	~	1
	F.A. Trophy	~	1
	League Cup	~	2 (1)
	Lincs Cup	~	
	Total	~	10 (1)

Former Leicester City Trainee and full-back who was signed on-loan from Ilkeston Town, taking over the position from Lee Rogers in time for the September 1999 league game at Clevedon. This was the first match of the season that Grantham had won a point, after the disastrous start of nine league defeats on the trot. His only goal for the club came in the December League Cup tie against Cambridge City, whilst the following game at home to Margate would prove to be his final one for the club. After returning to Ilkeston, Darren went on to play for Shepshed Dynamo and Anstey Nomads.

Geoff Ball

Seasons Played			
1974/75-75/76	League	~	11 (2)
	F.A. Cup	~	
	F.A. Trophy	~	
	League Cup	~	
	Lincs Cup	~	1
	Total	~	12 (2)

Born 02/11/1944 at Nottingham. After playing for Ericsson's Electronic FC, Geoff made over 100 appearances for Nottingham Forest and Notts County in a professional career spanning 1964 to 1972, and signed for Grantham after spending time as Player/Manager at Ilkeston Town. His debut for the club came in the March 1975 Southern League match at home to Stourbridge and he missed only one of the remaining fixtures, scoring against Weymouth and Atherstone Town on the way. The following season though, he appeared in the opening match against Scunthorpe United in the County Cup and then played no further part in playing for Grantham. Geoff still lives in the Nottingham area.

Ball

Seasons Played			
1893/94-94/95	League	~	
	Lincs Cup	~	
	Other	~	2
	Total	~	2

Defender with only two known appearances, the Grantham Minor Cup Final of April 1894 and the semi-final of the same competition a year later at home to Newark Reserves.

Bampton

Seasons Played			
1936/37	League	~	
	F.A. Cup	~	
	Lincs Cup	~	
	Other	~	1
	Total	~	1

Made just the one appearance for Grantham, in the Wilson Cup defeat at the hands of RAF Cranwell, towards the end of the season.

Roy Banham

Seasons Played			
1965/66-66/67	League	~	45 (1)
	F.A. Cup	~	7
	Total	~	52 (1)

Born 30/10/1936 at Nottingham. Former Hyson Green Boys Club right-back who made 18 appearances for Nottingham Forest and then Peterborough United in the Football League, including their initial all-conquering season in Division Four along with Terry Bly. After spells at Bedford Town and King's Lynn, Roy came to Grantham where he made his debut in the 1965/66 season's opening fixture against Scunthorpe United Reserves. He played in many of the games that year, including every one of the FA Cup matches, culminating in the Second Round Proper tie at home to Swindon and scored his only goal for the club against Goole Town in December 1965. The following season he played in the first four games, but after that appearances became few and far between with the game against Worksop Town in March 1967 his last. Roy was once more in the news during March 2004 when he at long last received his League title winners medal for his period at Peterborough United. A mix up at the time had led all concerned to believe incorrectly that he wasn't entitled to one due to his number of appearances. This led to The Football League commissioning an exact copy for him. Roy is now retired and still lives near to Peterborough.

Gary Banks

Seasons Played			
	League	~	22 (1)
	F.A. Cup	~	2 (1)
1989/90	F.A. Trophy	~	1
	League Cup	~	3
1994/95	Lincs Cup	~	2
	Total	~	30 (2)

Member of the RAF who also had spells at Nuneaton Borough, VS Rugby, Tamworth, Bedworth United and Appleby Frodingham at various times during his career. He made his Grantham debut in the opening match of the 1989/90 season, against Spalding United in the Lincolnshire County Senior Cup. The majority of his appearances during that initial campaign came at the start of the season, with him also scoring his first goal for the club in the October FA Cup tie at Goole Town. He returned to Grantham at the start of the 1994/95 season, a year which saw the club battling against relegation, although Gary scored his other goal for the club in the shock 5-0 win at home to Tamworth. During the January 1995 league fixture at Hinckley Town, Gary was replaced by Player/Manager, Warren Ward, and this was his final appearance for the club. As well as football, Gary was also a useful volleyball player, representing the RAF in international tournaments.

Bannister

Seasons Played			
	League	~	5
	F.A. Cup	~	
1929/30	Lincs Cup	~	
	Other	~	
	Total	~	5

Unfortunately not many details are available on this defender, apart from written evidence that he played in Midland League games against Worksop Town and Scarborough in the Autumn of 1929.

Lee Barber

Seasons Played			
	League	~	5 (1)
	F.A. Cup	~	2 (1)
1988/89	F.A. Trophy	~	1
	League Cup	~	
	Lincs Cup	~	
	Total	~	8 (2)

Former Lincoln United player who progressed through the Reserves to make his First team debut by replacing Tony Simpson in the opening league match of the 1988/89 season at Halesowen Town. Many of Lee's appearances for the club came from the substitute's bench, although his first two starts that he was given resulted in two goals, against Mile Oak Rovers and North Ferriby United. However, the following week's FA Trophy tie at home to Shepshed Charterhouse was his last for the team. He left Grantham to take up a University place in Manchester, but nothing is known about his playing career after this.

Barclay

Seasons Played			
	F.A. Cup	~	
	Lincs Cup	~	
1887/88	Other	~	1
	Total	~	1

Made just one appearance for Grantham, in the 3-0 friendly defeat at Rotherham Town played in March 1888.

Ady Barker

Seasons Played			
	League	~	32
	F.A. Cup	~	1
1993/94-94/95	F.A. Trophy	~	
	League Cup	~	2 (1)
1999/00	Lincs Cup	~	
	Total	~	35 (1)

Born 13/02/1974 at Lincoln. Brother of Baz Barker. Ady began his career on the books of Lincoln City, before moving to Lincoln United, Stamford Town and then Grantham. He made his debut when The Gingerbread's new Player/Manager, Allen Crombie, brought himself off, to be replaced by Ady, in the August 1993 league game against Sutton Coldfield Town. His first goal came in the Dr Marten's League Cup tie at Rushden & Diamonds in September, but after spending many of the games on the bench, he played no further part in the team after the following month. Ady returned to The Meres at the beginning of 1995 for an eleven game consecutive spell in the side, but soon after this he returned once more to Lincoln United. When his Manager, John Wilkinson, was appointed to the top position at Grantham, it signalled Ady's return once more to The Meres, with the home game against Dorchester in December 1999 marking his first game for the club in over four years. He then played in the majority of the remaining fixtures as Grantham ultimately unsuccessfully attempted to steer themselves out of the relegation zone. Sadly for Ady, he missed out on one of the club's biggest games in recent times, the local derby against Boston United, held in front of a 4,000 crowd, whilst his final appearance for Grantham came in the closing fixture of the 1999/00 season when he came off the bench to replace Rick Ranshaw. He still lives in the Lincoln area and currently works as a labourer in the building industry.

Baz Barker

Seasons Played			
	League	~	7 (1)
	F.A. Cup	~	2
1993/94	F.A. Trophy	~	1 (1)
	League Cup	~	1
	Lincs Cup	~	2
	Total	~	13 (2)

Born 02/09/1967 at Lincoln. A former apprentice at Leicester City who then spent time at Boston FC and like his brother Ady Barker, Lincoln United. Baz made his Grantham debut in the shock County Cup victory at Lincoln City at the start of the 1993/94 season, with his first goal for the club in the opening league fixture at Forest Green Rovers. But after the October visit of Hinckley Town, Baz had played his last game for Grantham and he soon returned to Lincoln United. He still lives in his home city and works as a dry-liner in the building industry.

Geoff Barker

Seasons Played			
	League	~	26 (1)
	F.A. Cup	~	4 (1)
1980/81	F.A. Trophy	~	1
	League Cup	~	1
	Lincs Cup	~	3
	Other	~	1
	Total	~	36 (2)

Born 07/02/1949 at Hull. Former Hull City, Southend United, Darlington, Reading and Grimsby Town defender, (with a total of 11 goals scored in 350 League and Cup appearances), who went on to become Player/Manager at Bridlington Trinity before joining Grantham. His first game for the club came in the County Cup victory at home to Boston United at the start of the 1980/81 season and in an interesting few months at London Road, he played in FA Cup games against Long Eaton United, which saw his first goal for the club, and a returning Boston United, which drew a near 1,900 crowd to London Road. Other highlights included the Lincolnshire County Senior Cup Final at Lincoln City and the Redmayne Trophy, when European Champions, Nottingham Forest, came to Grantham. However, a mutual agreement in the Spring of 1981 saw Geoff leave the club, with his substitution in the 7-0 defeat at the hands of Marine marking the end of his playing career. Ronnie Harrison took over the helm at London Road, whilst Geoff soon returned to Bridlington, before taking over at North Ferriby United where he knocked Grantham out of the FA Cup in 1988. He also took them to the FA Vase semi-finals, losing out to eventual winners Tamworth.

Ian Barker

Seasons Played			
	League	~	1
	F.A. Cup	~	
1996/97	F.A. Trophy	~	
	League Cup	~	
	Lincs Cup	~	
	Total	~	1

Goalkeeper who took over the position from the unavailable Peter Bulliman in the March 1997 league game at Shepshed Dynamo.

Peter Barker

Seasons Played			
	League	~	34 (1)
	F.A. Cup	~	3
1983/84	F.A. Trophy	~	7
	League Cup	~	4
	Lincs Cup	~	2 (1)
	Total	~	50 (2)

Former Sheffield Wednesday Schoolboy player who also played for Spalding United and Boston FC. His first game for Grantham came in the August 1983 home fixture against Burton Albion, with his two goals for the club coming in games against Oswestry Town and Scunthorpe United towards the end of that year. Peter was an important member of the side that finished fourth in the Northern Premier League, a prominence in the non-league pyramid that has not been bettered since. His final appearance for the club came in the last home match of the campaign, a 4-0 victory over Marine. After the Summer break, Peter went on to play for Buxton and then Shepshed Charterhouse. He's recently held positions at Ilkeston Town and Lincoln City, but it's not known if he's currently still involved with the game.

Terry Barker

Seasons Played			
	League	~	6
	F.A. Cup	~	
1962/63	Total	~	6

Born 20/07/1943 at Doncaster. Goalkeeper who at only 15 years of age was recommended to Grantham by Jimmy Longworth, but was rejected and soon signed for Arnold Rovers. However, after impressing in a Reserves game at London Road a couple of years later, Terry was offered and duly signed a contract with The Gingerbreads. He replaced Graham Clarke for six matches in November and December of 1962, starting at Ilkeston Town and ending with the visit of Worksop Town to London Road. Unfortunately Grantham were scheduled to play many of the top teams during this time and Terry only managed to be on the winning side once out of those six games. He went on to play for Sutton Town and Ilkeston Town, winning Midland League Select XI and Derbyshire Professionals representative honours. Terry still works in Grantham, in the engineering industry, but lives midway between the town and Nottingham.

Barker

Seasons Played			
	Lincs Cup	~	1
	Other	~	11 (4)
1890/91	Total	~	12 (4)

Played in the first game of the 1890/91 season, a friendly at home to Notts Amateurs United and maintained his place for the majority of that campaign. He could play either forward, or in a more defensive position, and scored in friendlies against Notts St John's, twice in the game with Notts St Luke's, and once against Kettering Town.

Clive Barkes

Seasons Played			
	League	~	6 (6)
	F.A. Cup	~	
1960/61-61/62	League Cup	~	
	Lincs Cup	~	1 (1)
	Total	~	7 (7)

Played for Grantham in Alan Clay's Testimonial against Nottingham Forest in April 1961 and then kept his place in the team for the four remaining league games left, scoring in all but one of those. Clive finished with six goals to his name by the end of the season, but the following year he made only three more appearances, all consecutive in January, against Matlock Town, Holbeach United, (which saw his final goal for the club), and Sutton Town.

Ray Barnard

Seasons Played			
	League	~	84 (2)
	F.A. Cup	~	9
1963/64-65/66	Lincs Cup	~	2
	Total	~	95 (2)

Born 16/04/1933 at Middlesbrough. Former England Schoolboy International who worked his way through the ranks of his local club to make 118 appearances for the First team. In 1960 he was transferred to Lincoln City, where he made another 47 appearances at the heart of the defence, before joining Grantham. His debut for the club came at Alfreton Town, the first game of what would ultimately become Grantham's 1963/64 Midland League Championship winning season. Ray missed only two of that season's matches and even managed to grab a goal in the entertaining 5-5 draw against Goole Town in October. The following year he was once again a near ever present member of The Gingerbreads side that finished runners-up in the league, but by the end of the 1965/66 season Ray had made only another seven appearances, with his other goal for the club coming in the October game at home to Stamford. His final league appearance was in the March 1966 fixture against Alfreton Town although he also played in Cyril Brown's Testimonial against Rotherham at the end of the season. Ray continued to play after the Summer break, signing up for the Lincoln Claytons side.

Eric Barnes

Seasons Played			
	League	~	6
	F.A. Cup	~	
1972/73-73/74	F.A. Trophy	~	
	League Cup	~	1
	Lincs Cup	~	1
	Total	~	8

Born 21/08/1947 at Grantham. Previously played for Wanderers, Old Somerby, Grantham Amateurs, Harrowby United and Grantham Reserves. He stepped up to the First team by coming on as substitute to replace Mick Chambers during the September 1972 league game at home to Kidderminster Harriers, but appearances were limited for Eric that season, with him forced to spectate at many of the fixtures from the bench. This was a trend that was mirrored the following season, although he managed to gain one more appearance to his name, in the August 1973 Southern League Cup tie at Stourbridge. He had a couple of years out of the game due to a serious knee injury, but then returned to Harrowby United, eventually becoming the club's Player/Manager. Eric still lives in Grantham and works for an agricultural company just outside of the town.

H. Barnes

Seasons Played			
	Other	~	1
1876/77	Total	~	1

This individual had been involved with Grantham Football Club from the very beginning and played in many club matches, even being made Captain in a game versus Mr Wyles side. However, he made only the one appearance in a game against another team, the friendly against Retford Rovers in January 1877.

G. Barnett

Seasons Played			
	League	~	1
	F.A. Cup	~	
1930/31	Lincs Cup	~	
	Total	~	1

Made just the one appearance for Grantham, in the November 1930 Midland League visit of Frickley Colliery to London Road.

Harold Barnett

Seasons Played			
	League	~	5 (2)
	F.A. Cup	~	
1945/46	Lincs Cup	~	1 (2)
	Total	~	6 (4)

Born 10/07/1918 at Nantwich. Also played for Whitchurch, Shrewsbury Town, Northwich Victoria and in London Road friendlies during The War. Harold played his first game for the club in the September 1945 Midland League fixture against Shrewsbury Town and then returned for the Boxing Day match at Ransome & Marles, plus the next couple of games as well, scoring against the Reserve sides of Lincoln City and Notts County. Harold returned to the side once more the following March for what would turn out to be his final game, the County Cup semi-final at home to Scunthorpe & Lindsey United, scoring twice in the 7-2 victory. Died 2003 in Grantham.

Micky Adams

Dave Adamson

Mark Appleyard

Paul Archer

Roger Ashby

Brian Asher

Percy Ashton

Gary Banks

Ady Baker

Geoff Barker

Ray Barnard

Jock Basford

Dennis Benskin

Danny Begara

Jimmy Bloomer

Terry Bly

John Barnwell

Born 24/12/1938 at High Heaton, Newcastle. An England Youth International who began his career at Bishop Auckland, before making appearances for Arsenal, (plus winning one England Under-23 cap whilst there), Nottingham Forest and Sheffield United, retiring in June 1971 with a record of 50 goals in 327 senior League games. Just over a year later John had returned to the game as a coach at Hereford United and then Peterborough United, with his promotion to the Manager's seat there in May 1977. Probably his biggest job followed, when he took over at Wolverhampton Wanderers, and he was soon involved in two huge transfers of the time, selling Steve Daly to Manchester City for £1.43m and a week later buying Andy Gray for £1.15m from Aston Villa. At the end of the 1979/80 season he took Wolves to League Cup Final success over his old club, Nottingham Forest, and was voted 'Midland Sports Personality of the Year'. Positions after included time in Saudi Arabia and at AEK Athens, but in June 1987 John returned to England as Manager of Notts County, then Walsall and finally as a consultant to Phil Chard at Northampton Town. Grantham Chairman, Alan Prince, brought John to The Meres at the start of 1996, where he was initially running the club's lottery, but following the departure of Warren Ward and a brief spell with Steve Stoutt as the club's caretaker-manager, he was soon installed at the helm of the club. However, he was in charge for only a few games at the end of the season, which finished with a 14th place in the league, as in July he was awarded the position of Chief Executive of the Football League Manager's Association and had to relinquish ties with any one club. John remains in that position and as such is continually in the sports news, often involved with disputes involving the country's prominent managers.

Percy Barratt

Seasons Played			
1930/31-32/33	League	~	105 (12)
	F.A. Cup	~	6
	Lincs Cup	~	3 (1)
	Other	~	2
	Total	~	116 (13)

Born 06/10/1898 at Annesley. Brother of the Aston Villa player, Nottinghamshire CCC member and England cricketer, Fred Barratt. Percy was a full-back with experience himself at Annesley St Alban's FC, Notts County and Nottingham Forest, making 229 appearances and scoring 17 goals. He scored on his Grantham debut in the first game of the 1930/31 season at Mansfield Town and missed only a few games throughout his three year career at London Road, although unfortunately he was playing in a comparatively poor side that was often struggling at the wrong end of the table. There is no evidence that shows his final appearance for the club, although it is known that his last goal for Grantham came in the February 1933 Midland League match at Bradford Park Avenue Reserves and that he played in the friendly against Arsenal held at London Road the following month. Died 06/07/1974 at Burnley.

Barratt

Seasons Played			
1877/78	F.A. Cup	~	
	Other	~	1
	Total	~	1

Appeared in the final friendly of the 1877/78 season, a 3-1 victory played at Lincoln.

Wayne Barsby

Seasons Played			
1987/88	League	~	1
	F.A. Cup	~	2
	F.A. Trophy	~	
	League Cup	~	2
	Lincs Cup	~	2
	Total	~	7

Nottingham based midfield player who first played for Grantham in the August 1987 County Cup victory over Scunthorpe United. Although he played a part in several of those first few matches under Martin O'Neill's leadership, October saw his last appearance for the club in the 5-0 League Cup defeat against VS Rugby. After leaving London Road, Wayne went on to play for Harrowby United.

Barton

Seasons Played			
1945/46	League	~	1
	F.A. Cup	~	
	Lincs Cup	~	
	Total	~	1

Made just the single appearance for Grantham, in the February 1946 Midland League game at Ollerton Colliery.

Jock Basford

Seasons Played			
1947/48	League	~	2
	F.A. Cup	~	
	Lincs Cup	~	1
	Total	~	3

Born 03/12/1919 at Basford. Christened Walter David Basford but more usually known as 'Jock' or 'John'. He served in the RAF during The War which meant that he played for several clubs, including Brush Sports (Loughborough), Gainsborough Trinity, made guest appearances for Portsmouth, Bournemouth, Southampton, West Ham United, Birmingham and following the end of hostilities joined Bath City and Gloucester City. Somewhere towards the end of that list came his time at Grantham where he played in three games during February of 1948, the fixtures at home to the Reserve sides of Lincoln City and Rotherham United, plus the County Cup semi-final at Boston United. Jock became Player/Manager at Margate in the Summer of 1949 and a year later returned to Lincolnshire to take up a similar role at Holbeach United. Seven years were then spent coaching at Charlton Athletic, before moving to Exeter City were he became Manager for them in the 1966/67 season. What followed then was a long association for Jock with Mansfield Town, which saw various coaching and management positions including the role as Manager for their 1970/71 campaign. He also managed the Notts FA Youth side, taking them to national trophy success in 1974, and it was the younger players that he continued to train with at Mansfield Town right up until his death. Died March 1982 at Mansfield.

Joseph Basker

Seasons Played			
1874/75-75/76	Other	~	7
	Total	~	7

Born circa 1853 in Grantham. Was involved with the club right at the very beginning and played in the very first club match in October 1874 for Mr Gamble's side. He also played in several of the other practice matches along with five appearances in friendlies against other teams, the first of which came in November when the team travelled to Stamford to play a Burghley Park side. He then made two more appearances the following season, with the final one in November 1875 at Bourne. The 1881 census lists his profession as a wine merchant and it also shows that he was related to the Treadgold family, with Arthur later playing for the club. Died December 1914 in Grantham.

Bateman

Seasons Played			
1886/87-87/88	F.A. Cup	~	
	Lincs Cup	~	
	Other	~	3
	Total	~	3

Played in one friendly against Lincoln Lindum in November 1886 and then made another two appearances for the club the following season, firstly during the match against Grantham Volunteers and finally in the visit of Lincoln Rangers, games that took place during October and November 1887 respectively.

Ralph Bateson

Seasons Played			
1952/53	League	~	23 (1)
	F.A. Cup	~	1
	Lincs Cup	~	1
	Total	~	25 (1)

Played in half of the games during the 1952/53 campaign after making his debut in the second Midland League fixture of the season at Peterborough United. Ralph scored in the match against Scunthorpe & Lindsey United Reserves in November 1952 and played his last game for the club the following Spring, in the Lincs County Cup Final against Spalding United which ended in a 1-0 defeat for The Gingerbreads.

Walter Batson

Seasons Played			
	League	~	1 (1)
	F.A. Cup	~	
1935/36	Lincs Cup	~	
	Other	~	
	Total	~	1 (1)

Local player who had also made appearances for Grantham St John's and whose surname is sometimes spelt 'Bateson'. He played and scored the consolation goal for the club in the March 1936 Lincolnshire League game at Boston United.

John Batty

Seasons Played			
	League	~	3
	F.A. Cup	~	
1963/64	Lincs Cup	~	
	Total	~	3

Goalkeeper who stood in for Graham Clarke during Grantham's Midland League Championship winning season. He played in the three Midland League games against Matlock Town, Retford Town and Spalding United, all held during November 1963.

J. Batty

Seasons Played			
	League	~	17 (26)
	FA Amt. Cup	~	
1909/10-10/11	League Cup	~	
	Lincs Cup	~	5 (10)
	Other	~	7 (10)
	Total	~	29 (46)

Centre-Forward who was certainly playing for the club in the first game of the 1909/10 season at Derby YMCA and possibly before this time with no team-sheets available for the previous year. He was one of the first choice members of the team, with appearances quoted above the minimum for each competition. During his confirmed two seasons with the club, he scored hat-tricks in the games against Derby YMCA, South Nottingham, Gonerby Athletic, Old Loughburians, plus 6 goals in the 12-0 demolition of Grantham Swifts in the Stamford Nursery Cup played in November 1910. His final goal for Grantham came in the April 1911 friendly against Queen's Park and after the following week's closing league fixture, he was confirmed as the club's highest scorer in their Midland Amateur League winning season.

John Baverstock

Seasons Played			
	League	~	2
	F.A. Cup	~	
1912/13	Lincs Cup	~	
	Other	~	
	Total	~	2

Born 1880 at Willenhall. Goalkeeper with almost certainly several more appearances to his name than the two games that we have evidence for, the league matches against Ripley Town and Kettering Town in the 1912/13 season. In March 1913 he was transferred to Bolton Wanderers, only a week or so after his team-mate Jabez Cartwright, although he made only two appearances there.

Arthur Bavin

Seasons Played			
	League	~	6 (2)
	F.A. Cup	~	1
1912/13-13/14	Lincs Cup	~	1 (1)
	Other	~	1
1920/21	Total	~	9 (3)

Born 05/02/1887 at Nottingham. Right-Half who had previously played for Lincoln Liberal Club, Lincoln City, (making six appearances as they finished bottom of Division Two in the 1907/08 season), Worksop Town, Grantham Avenue and Mansfield Mechanics. Although no details are known as to his Grantham debut, Arthur was a near ever present member of the side from this era who certainly made many more appearances than those quoted above. We do know that he scored in the County Cup game at Boston Town played in January 1913, followed by the league games against Sutton Town and Gresley Rovers during the 1913/14 season. In 1914 he returned to Lincoln City, although he failed to make another First team appearance there, and went on to play for Ruston Aircraftmen, Barnsley Reserves and Llanelli. He later returned to London Road and made at least one more appearance for Grantham, in the March 1921 Central Alliance game at home to Leicester City Reserves. Arthur was also a well known cricketer, playing for Grantham, Lindum and the Lincolnshire side in the Minor Counties Championship between 1911 and 1926. Died 02/01/1961 at Lincoln.

Bill Baxter

Seasons Played			
	League	~	31
	F.A. Cup	~	2
1954/55	Lincs Cup	~	1
	Total	~	34

Born 06/09/1917 at Nottingham. Wing-Half who began his career at Willson's FC, Vernon Athletic and Berridge Road Institute, before moving to Nottingham Forest and Notts County, making a total of 155 Football League appearances, plus playing in many of the senior matches during World War Two. Bill made his Grantham debut at London Road in the first game of the 1954/55 season against Nottingham Forest Reserves. He missed only one game before his final match for the club, in March 1955 at Mansfield Town Reserves. Died 21/02/1992 at Nottingham.

Marcus Baxter

Seasons Played			
	League	~	2
	F.A. Cup	~	
1996/97	F.A. Trophy	~	4
	League Cup	~	
	Lincs Cup	~	
	Total	~	6

Former Gedling Town forward who made his debut for The Gingerbreads in the October 1996 FA Trophy tie at home to Leek Town. He played in the following rounds against Winsford United and Buxton, as well as two league fixtures, with the December defeat at Dudley Town being his last appearance for the club. Marcus soon returned to Gedling, then had spells at Mickleover Sports, Borrowash Victoria, Belper Town and moved on to Radcliffe Olympic in 2002, before transferring to Cotgrave CW United and then returning once more to Radcliffe in 2005.

Beard

Seasons Played			
	Other	~	1
1879/80	Total	~	1

Just one known appearance for this player, the friendly at Sleaford in March 1880.

Alan Beards

Seasons Played			
	League	~	11 (3)
	F.A. Cup	~	3
1957/58	Lincs Cup	~	
	Total	~	14 (3)

Born 19/10/1932 at Normanton. Outside-Left player who began his career at Whitewood Juniors, before making 40 appearances for Bolton Wanderers, Swindon Town and Stockport County. He made his Grantham debut in the August 1957 Midland League game at Denaby United and completed the majority of his appearances within the first couple of months of the season. Two of Alan's goals came in the September 1957 Midland League victory over York City Reserves played at London Road.

E. Beaumont

Seasons Played			
	F.A. Cup	~	
	Lincs Cup	~	
1885/86	Other	~	1
	Total	~	1

Made just one appearance for the club in the 11-0 friendly victory against Peterborough in March 1886.

F. Beaumont

Seasons Played			
	F.A. Cup	~	
	Lincs Cup	~	
1885/86	Other	~	1
	Total	~	1

Appeared in the following friendly to E. Beaumont, possibly his brother, which was the 4-0 win at home to Notts Waverley played at the end of March 1886.

George Beaumont

Seasons Played			
	F.A. Cup	~	6
	Lincs Cup	~	10
1877/78-81/82	Other	~	63 (4)
1883/84-88/89	Total	~	79 (4)

Born 04/01/1860 in Grantham. Solicitor, Commissioner to Administer Oaths, County Coroner, Magistrates Clerk, Commissioner of Taxes and Hospital Secretary who despite also being one of the original committee members of the club made little impact on the field until the friendly at Stamford in February 1878. George played in many of the club's first games in the FA and Lincolnshire Cups and scored goals against Lincoln, plus a hat-trick in the March 1879 friendly at home to Sleaford. March of 1885 was to be the highlight of his sporting career though, as a member of the first Grantham team to win the County Cup. But by the end of the 1886/87 season his footballing days were becoming limited and he was left with only one or two more appearances earned in the next couple of years. Taking over his interest was cricket. He had already played for the Grantham team and in 1888 became a founder member of the Lincolnshire County side, briefly turning out for them as well. Died 21/07/1904 in Lincoln.

J. Beck

Seasons Played			
	League	~	2
1911/12	Total	~	2

Former Grantham Avenue player with only two known appearances for our club, the Central Alliance games at home to Peterborough Loco and Sutton Junction during the 1911/12 season, although he most likely played a more prominent role in the side than those figures suggest.

Kevin Beck

Seasons Played			
	League	~	34 (1)
	F.A. Cup	~	
1984/85-86/87	F.A. Trophy	~	2
	League Cup	~	1
	Lincs Cup	~	1
	Other	~	
	Total	~	38 (1)

Born 06/11/1962 in Grantham. Cousin of Steve Beck, nephew of Tom Beck and a former Great Gonerby, Gonerby Excelsior and Grantham United player who made two appearances for the First team at the start of the 1984/85 season against Horwich RMI and Worksop Town. A year later Kevin played a more prominent role in the side, playing in about half of that season's games and scoring his one goal for the club against Gloucester City in March 1986. However, the 1986/87 season saw him making a limited amount of appearances again, with his final one at the end of March 1987 against Hednesford Town. Kevin later went on to play for Melton Town and Harrowby United and he still lives locally, running his own roofing company.

Oliver Beck

Seasons Played			
	League	~	9 (6)
	F.A. Cup	~	
1909/10	Lincs Cup	~	1
1914/15	Other	~	1
1921/22-22/23	Total	~	11 (6)

Born 1887 at Spittlegate, Grantham. First played for Grantham during the 1909/10 season, scoring goals against Nottingham University, Derby YMCA and Boots Athletic. Oliver quite possibly played more games during the following few years, but the next written evidence we have of him is scoring a goal in the April 1915 Central Alliance game at home to Mansfield Mechanics. He certainly then played in many of the friendly fixtures for the club during World War 1, scoring several goals in the process, including five in the game against Hornsby No.33 Shop played on Christmas Day 1917. Oliver was still appearing at London Road in the early 1920's and considering the time scale of his career must surely have made substantially more appearances for Grantham than those that are known.

Steve Beck

Seasons Played			
	League	~	10 (3)
	F.A. Cup	~	
1985/86	F.A. Trophy	~	
	League Cup	~	
	Lincs Cup	~	
	Total	~	10 (3)

Born 10/11/1964 at Grantham. Son of Tom Beck and a former Gonerby Excelsior and Grantham Reserves player who had also spent time at Scunthorpe United. He made his full debut in the March 1986 league fixture against Gloucester City by coming off the bench to replace his cousin, Kevin Beck, who had himself just scored what would turn out to be his only goal for the club. Although Steve played a part in several of that season's remaining games, many of those saw him on the substitute's bench. After goals scored against Stourbridge, Leamington and Banbury United, his final appearance for the club came in the April defeat at the hands of Merthyr Tydfil. After returning to local football, a knee injury only a few years after that cut short his playing career. Steve still lives and works in Grantham.

Tom Beck

Seasons Played			
	League	~	2
	F.A. Cup	~	
1945/46	Lincs Cup	~	
	Total	~	2

Born circa 1929. Known by all his friends and colleagues as 'Tidler', he played in two games for Grantham during January 1946, the Midland League games against the Reserve sides of Nottingham Forest and Mansfield Town. His son, Steve, and nephew, Kevin, both went on to play for The Gingerbreads in the 1980's. Died 16/09/1992 in Grantham.

T. Beck

Seasons Played			
	League	~	2 (1)
	F.A. Cup	~	
1912/13	Lincs Cup	~	1 (4)
	Other	~	
1914/15	Total	~	3 (5)

Probably played in many more games than those quoted above as the only two specific games from the 1912/13 season that we know of are the County Cup tie against Grimsby Rovers, where he scored four goals, and an appearance in the Central Alliance fixture at home to Ripley Town. From the final season before The Great War there are records of him scoring in the game at Shirebrook in April 1915 and we then know that he played and scored many times in friendlies played during World War One, including five goals to his name after the match against a Royal Flying Corps XI, played in April 1917.

W. Beck

Seasons Played			
	League	~	2
	F.A. Cup	~	
1921/22-22/23	Lincs Cup	~	
	Other	~	
	Total	~	2

Final member of the Beck family who played in the Central Alliance game at New Hucknall Colliery in April 1922 and the home match against Loughborough Corinthians in January 1923.

Duane Beckett

Seasons Played			
	League	~	5
	F.A. Cup	~	
1999/00	F.A. Trophy	~	
	League Cup	~	
	Lincs Cup	~	1
	Total	~	6

Born 31/05/1978 at Sheffield. Former Barnsley and Doncaster Rovers midfielder who joined Grantham at the start of the 1999/00 season and replaced Darren Bowman in the opening County Cup tie against Scunthorpe United. However, only two of his appearances came from starting games and when he came off the bench in the August league fixture at home to Tamworth it would turn out to be his final one for the club. He soon moved on to play for Frickley Athletic and Stocksbridge Park Steels.

Beckett

Seasons Played			
	League	~	2
	F.A. Cup	~	
1938/39	Lincs Cup	~	1
	Total	~	3

First played for a slightly rearranged 'First' team in the November 1938 friendly against a Chelsea XI, but then was able to make appearances in competitive matches the following Spring when Reg Gregory became unavailable. He played in the County Cup replay against Boston United, Midland League games against Bradford Park Avenue Reserves and Scarborough, plus another friendly against an Arsenal Reserve XI.

Bedford

Seasons Played			
	League	~	6
	F.A. Cup	~	
1930/31	Lincs Cup	~	
	Total	~	6

Also played for Shirebrook and made all his appearances for Grantham towards the end of the 1930/31 season.

Tracey Beeby

Seasons Played			
	League	~	22
	F.A. Cup	~	
1980/81-81/82	F.A. Trophy	~	1
	League Cup	~	
	Lincs Cup	~	2
	Other	~	1
	Total	~	26

Born 27/10/1962 at Nottingham. Full-Back who had previously played for Nottingham Swifts and Clifton All Whites, before progressing through Grantham's Reserve team to make his full debut in the Northern Premier League fixture at Oswestry Town in November 1980. Tracey played in the Redmayne Trophy match against Nottingham Forest the following month, as well as the majority of that season's remaining matches. However, at the end of the campaign he lost his place to Tim Thacker and after the Summer break he made only three more appearances for the First team, with the September 1981 visit of Macclesfield Town to London Road being his final one. After leaving Grantham he joined Hucknall Colliery Welfare and then returned to Clifton. Whilst playing football, Tracey was also employed by the Royal Mail and he still works for them, continuing to live in the Nottingham area. He is also an accomplished ice-hockey player now, regularly appearing for the Ashfield Avalanche team.

Glenn Beech

Seasons Played			
	League	~	83 (34)
	F.A. Cup	~	5 (5)
1985/86-87/88	F.A. Trophy	~	3 (1)
	League Cup	~	10
1991/92	Lincs Cup	~	3
	Total	~	104 (40)

Born 06/12/1960 at Peterborough. Began his career at Aston Villa as a Trainee, before moving to Eye, Yaxley, Spalding United, Bourne Town, Stamford, where he appeared in their 1984 FA Vase Final at Wembley, followed by periods at Wellingborough Town, Rushden Town and Baker Perkins. His first game for Grantham came in the December 1985 match against Oldbury United, with his first goal for the club coming the following month from the penalty spot in the 2-2 draw at home to Bromsgrove Rovers. He missed only a handful of games the following season and a year later, the first under the helm of Martin O'Neill, played in every single match and finished as the club's highest scorer with thirty goals to his name, including a hat-trick in the entertaining 7-3 defeat of Stourbridge in March 1988. Glenn left Grantham in the Summer to go to Boston United, something which still seems to anger O'Neill if the tone of his biography can be believed and then played for Kettering Town's Conference runners-up side, followed by returns to both Boston and Stamford Town. March of 1992 saw Glenn rejoin Grantham, although his appearance in the league fixture at home to Bilston Town would be his only one that season and ultimately his last for the club. He went on to make appearances for Rushden & Diamonds, Sudbury Town and finally Spalding United, then moving into the Assistant Manager's position there.

Beech

Seasons Played			
	League	~	2
	F.A. Cup	~	1
1888/89-90/91	Lincs Cup	~	
	Other	~	8
1892/93	Total	~	11

Defender who made his debut for Grantham in the first friendly of the 1888/89 season at Grimsby Town and continued to appear solely in friendlies for his first three seasons at London Road. He returned to the club a year later and appeared in the first four games of the disastrous 1892/93 season, one which would see the club withdrawing from the league by October. He played in the first two Midland Amateur Alliance fixtures, against Sheffield and Matlock, with his final appearance coming in the FA cup game at home to Belper.

Danny Begara

Began his playing career at the age of 16 in the Uruguyan First Division, before moving to Spain with Seville where he was leading divisional scorer for four consecutive seasons and won two Championship medals. After spells with two other Spanish sides, Danny came to England to begin his managerial career. Reserve Team Manager positions at Luton Town and Sheffield United were followed by First team appointments at Middlesbrough, Rochdale and Stockport County, where he won them promotion and a Wembley appearance. Danny also managed the Brunei National team and the England Under-18 and Under-20 sides, with a World Youth Cup win also to his name. Finally, after Assistant Manager positions at Sheffield Wednesday and Rotherham United, he was installed as Manager at Doncaster Rovers, at the same time as the club were featured in a Channel 4 'fly-on-the-wall' documentary. In the Summer of 1998 he was brought to Grantham by Antrac, who had recently took over the club, and immediately set up what looked to be a promising set of professional players that would take the club to their highest ever level. The dream lasted for only a matter of weeks though, as a string of poor results saw Danny and the club's Chief Scout, Tony Kenworthy, swapping roles.

Bell

Seasons Played			
	F.A. Cup	~	4 (1)
	Lincs Cup	~	7 (2)
1881/82	Other	~	22 (2)
1883/84-86/87	Total	~	33 (5)

Important member of the 1880's side who made his debut at the end of 1881, possibly in the friendly at home to Peterborough. After missing the following season, he became a near permanent member of the team and scored in the November 1883 FA Cup game against Spilsby. The following year he again missed only a few games, although unfortunately for him one of those was the Lincolnshire County Cup Final. This may have been due to the commencement of his 'relegation' from the competitive competitions. In fact all of his future appearances came entirely from friendly fixtures, with his final goal for the club in the September 1886 match against Grantham Volunteers and his last appearance in the following game at Notts Olympic.

Bellamy

Seasons Played			
	League	~	2
1911/12	Total	~	2

Goalkeeper with only two known appearances during the 1911/12 season, the Central Alliance games at home to Peterborough Loco and Sutton Junction. However, those fixtures are the only two where the goalkeeper is listed, so he is most likely to have been that season's number one choice.

Dave Belton

Seasons Played			
	League	~	9 (1)
	F.A. Cup	~	
1984/85-85/86	F.A. Trophy	~	
	League Cup	~	2
	Lincs Cup	~	2 (1)
	Other	~	
	Total	~	13 (2)

Former Skegness Town and Boston FC player who made his debut for The Gingerbreads in the March 1985 Northern Premier League fixture at home to Rhyl, with his first goal for the club coming the following month against Horwich RMI. Dave then played in the first three matches of the new season, scoring against Boston United in the County Cup, but was then awarded only one more appearance, the October league game against Bilston Town. He was known to have later moved down to the Bedford area, but no other information is known on him.

Bennett

Seasons Played			
	League	~	2
	F.A. Cup	~	1
1892/93	Total	~	3

Goalkeeper who played in the first three games, Sheffield, Matlock and Belper, of what would soon turn out to be the disastrous 1892/93 Midland Amateur Alliance season.

Dennis Benskin

Seasons Played			
	League	~	357 (92)
	F.A. Cup	~	19 (7)
1969/70-79/80	F.A. Trophy	~	30 (5)
	League Cup	~	43 (9)
	Lincs Cup	~	11 (2)
	Other	~	4
	Total	~	464 (115)

Born 28/05/1947 at Ruddington, Notts. Made four appearances for the Notts County First team, scoring on his debut, during a five year spell there in the mid-60's, before joining Lockheed Leamington, Bourne Town, Long Eaton United and Stamford. He then scored on his Grantham debut against Boston in August 1969 and immediately became an important member of Terry Bly's side. One of his highlights from that first season was scoring in the FA Cup game against Oldham Athletic. Despite the following year being such a great one for Grantham, Dennis missed several of the league games during the championship winning year and all but one of the FA Cup matches. Compensation arrived though at the end of the year with a Midland League Cup winners medal, with Dennis scoring in the second leg. The season of 1971/72 saw him playing in every single match of what ended as another championship season, plus a Lincolnshire County Cup victory. The following year, Grantham's first in the Southern League, saw another league winners medal for Dennis, plus an appearance in the FA Cup First Round tie at Bradford City. Of course the 1973/74 campaign was one of greatest in the club's history and Dennis played in every round of that year's FA Cup run, including the ties against Rochdale, scoring in the first game, and Middlesbrough, which saw a record attendance at London Road as the club bowed out at the Third Round stage. The next few years were by comparison quite mediocre for the team, although there was a joint testimonial for Dennis in April 1975, along with Bob Norris and Jimmy Bloomer, when Nottingham Forest came to London Road, whilst there was another chance for him to play in the Proper Rounds of the FA Cup when Grantham drew Port Vale in November. April of 1976 saw his first hat-trick as The Gingerbreads defeated Atherstone Town 4-0, but by the time of Grantham's next League Championship victory, at the end of the 1978/79 season, his appearances were starting to become less frequent. As the club entered into the Northern Premier League, it would prove to be his final season playing for the team. It was perhaps fitting that after such an illustrious career it should end on a high note, when September 1979 saw South Liverpool resoundly thrashed 6-2 with Dennis getting one of the goals. After a few appearances for Shepshed Charterhouse and Arnold Town, he soon returned to London Road where he ran the Grantham Reserves side along with John Gulson, before finishing his career with Ruddington. In the 1980's Dennis emigrated to Australia and he still lives there, working on a golf course in Perth.

Bentley

Seasons Played			
	League	~	4
	Lincs Cup	~	2
1904/05-05/06	Other	~	
1909/10	Total	~	6

Played either in defence or midfield and was involved with Grantham from the start of their reformation in 1904, although with comparatively few appearances, he may have been a 'fringe' player.

Bentley

Seasons Played			
	League	~	
	F.A. Cup	~	
1923/24	League Cup	~	
	Lincs Cup	~	
	Other	~	1
	Total	~	1

Played in the Grantham Hospital Cup game at home to Newark Castle Rovers in January 1924. Despite turning out in midfield there is the possibility that he could be the same invididual as the following entry.

Bentley

Seasons Played			
	League	~	3 (1)
	F.A. Cup	~	
1926/27	Lincs Cup	~	
	Other	~	
	Total	~	3 (1)

See previous entry. Forward who played in three games during December 1926, the first of which was the Midland League fixture at Loughborough Corinthians, with his only goal for the club coming the following week against Lincoln City Reserves.

Winston Bernard

Seasons Played			
	League	~	1
	F.A. Cup	~	
1958/59	Lincs Cup	~	
	Total	~	1

Born 05/10/1928 in Jamaica. Member of the RAF and a former Kings Lynn, Corby Town, Peterborough United Reserves and Wisbech Town player who came to London Road after being stationed at Cottesmore. 'Bernie', as he was known, became the first coloured player to represent Grantham when he was promoted from the Reserves after several promising games for them, even scoring seven times in one particular match. He was awarded a place in the line-up for the Midland League game against Scunthorpe United Reserves in January 1959, although this turned out to be his only full appearance for the club. Bernie's employment in the RAF continued right into the early 1990's, but he is now retired and living in Somerset.

Malcolm Berridge

Seasons Played			
	League	~	1
	F.A. Cup	~	
1978/79	F.A. Trophy	~	
	League Cup	~	
	Lincs Cup	~	
	Total	~	1

Born 03/05/1958 in Grantham. Had previously played for several local sides, including Harrowby Villa, Meres Rovers, Aveling Barfords and Woolsthorpe, with trials at Scunthorpe United and Peterborough United behind him. Malcolm made just one full appearance for the club when he came off the bench to replace Collin Chamberlain during the October 1978 league fixture at home to Gloucester City. His football career ended soon after, with the offer of a chance to run a power station in the Caribbean, but he currently lives and works in Jersey, on the engineering side of the local water company.

Bettison

Seasons Played			
	League	~	9
	F.A. Cup	~	6
1912/13-14/15	Lincs Cup	~	
	Other	~	1
1919/20	Total	~	16

Defender who almost certainly played in many more games than those quoted before World War 1, with the 1-0 friendly victory against Queen's Park in March 1913 one of the rare occasions where evidence still exists of his appearance. He returned to London Road after the end of the European conflict to make 10 more appearances, with the November 1919 Central Alliance game against Sutton Junction being his final game for the club.

J. Betts

Seasons Played			
	League	~	2
	F.A. Cup	~	
1927/28	Lincs Cup	~	
	Total	~	2

Goalkeeper who had also played for Grimsby Rovers, Louth Town and at one point had trials with Chelsea. He made two appearances for Grantham, the Midland League games against Scunthorpe & Lindsey United and Mexborough Athletic in November 1927, whilst Walter Fox, the club's first choice 'keeper was unavailable.

Bickerstaff

Seasons Played			
	League	~	1 (3)
	FA Amt. Cup	~	
1910/11	League Cup	~	
	Lincs Cup	~	
	Other	~	
	Total	~	1 (3)

Only one known appearance for this player during the Midland Amateur Alliance Championship winning year, the home game against Notts GNR Clerks played in April 1911, in which he scored a hat-trick.

Joe Bicknell

Seasons Played			
	League	~	3 (1)
	F.A. Cup	~	
1935/36	Lincs Cup	~	
	Other	~	
	Total	~	3 (1)

Centre-Forward who had previously played for Ollerton Colliery and made three appearances for Grantham during September 1935, the Midland League games against Burton Town, Notts County Reserves and finally Bradford Park Avenue Reserves, where he scored his only goal.

Birch

Seasons Played			
	Lincs Cup	~	
	Other	~	3
1890/91	Total	~	3

Played in the first three friendlies of the 1890/91 season, all home games, against Notts Amateurs United, Netherfield and Notts St John's.

Birch

Seasons Played			
	League	~	1
	Lincs Cup	~	
1939/40	Other	~	
	Total	~	1

Made one appearance in goal during the entertaining Midland War-Time League 5-5 draw at home to Newark Town on Boxing Day 1939.

Birchnall

Seasons Played			
	League	~	1
	F.A. Cup	~	
1925/26	Lincs Cup	~	
	Total	~	1

Available records show just the single appearance for Grantham, the Midland League fixture away at Castleford Town, played in September 1925.

Tony Bissett

Seasons Played			
	League	~	2
	F.A. Cup	~	
1967/68	Total	~	2

Played for The Gingerbreads in Midland League games against Skegness Town in September 1967 and Worksop Town a week later.

Blackham

Seasons Played			
	F.A. Cup	~	
	Lincs Cup	~	
1886/87	Other	~	1
	Total	~	1

Made just one appearance for Grantham in the second friendly of the 1886/87 season at Notts Olympic.

Blacknell

Seasons Played			
	League	~	3 (1)
	F.A. Cup	~	
1921/22	Lincs Cup	~	
	Total	~	3 (1)

Inside-Right from the Nottingham area who made his appearances for Grantham in the Spring of 1922. His known games are the Central Alliance fixtures against Long Eaton, Gresley Rovers and the only game in which he scored, the London Road visit of Coalville Swifts.

Steve Blades

Seasons Played			
	League	~	2
	F.A. Cup	~	
1986/87	F.A. Trophy	~	
	League Cup	~	
	Lincs Cup	~	
	Total	~	2

Brother of the former Derby County and Norwich City player, Paul Blades, who himself spent three years on the books at Derby County, before signing for Stamford, playing in their 1984 FA Vase Final appearance at Wembley, and then Rushden Town. His first game for Grantham came in the November 1986 league fixture at home to Gloucester City, with his only other appearance a month later when he came off the bench to replace Larry Burrell in the surprise defeat at lowly Leamington. After the end of his playing career, Steve went on to manage Mirlees Blackstones.

Blood

Seasons Played			
	League	~	1
	F.A. Cup	~	
1932/33	Lincs Cup	~	
	Other	~	
	Total	~	1

Centre-Forward who from *Grantham Journal* archives is known to have made just the single appearance for Grantham. Data exists to show that he also spent time at Notts County at some point in his career, so he may be John Blood (Born 02/10/1914, Nottingham - Died 1992) who played for The Magpies in 1938 and Exeter City after The War.

Brian Bloomer

Seasons Played			
	League	~	1
	F.A. Cup	~	
1974/75	F.A. Trophy	~	
	League Cup	~	
	Lincs Cup	~	
	Total	~	1

Born 03/05/1952 at Cleethorpes. Younger brother of Jimmy Bloomer. Brian previously spent time at Grimsby Town, Barton Town, Grimsby Amateurs, Lincoln United and Lincoln City. His only appearance for Grantham came in the September 1974 defeat at Margate, although he spent the Kettering Town fixture sat on the bench. Soon after this Brian returned to Lincoln United, then moved on to Brigg Town, before making 7 appearances, with one goal to his name, for Scunthorpe United in the 1978/79 season and finally returning to Brigg. Brian still lives in the Cleethorpes area, working with his brother in the fish industry and he is also the father of the current Lincoln City player, Matt Bloomer.

Jimmy Bloomer

Seasons Played			
	League	~	151 (7)
	F.A. Cup	~	15 (1)
1970/71-74/75	F.A. Trophy	~	9
	League Cup	~	15 (1)
	Lincs Cup	~	5
	Other	~	2
	Total	~	197 (9)

Born 22/08/1947 in Glasgow. Brother of Brian Bloomer. Initially followed in his father's foot-steps by playing for Grimsby Town, making 58 appearances and scoring once during the 1960's, before signing for Worksop Town. He made his debut for Grantham in the first Midland League game of the 1970/71 season at Belper and by the end of that first campaign Jimmy had won a Midland League Championship medal, plus made appearances in the League Cup Final and the FA Cup ties against Stockport County and Rotherham United. He had become an important member of probably Grantham's greatest ever side and even managed to net his first goal for the club in the December 1971 league fixture at Worksop Town. Over the next two years he won another two Championship medals, a County Cup winners medal, plus played in the FA Trophy Quarter-Final tie at home to Yeovil Town and the FA Cup First Round encounter at Bradford City. The 1973/74 season saw the club's greatest run in the FA Cup and Jimmy played in all of the rounds, against Kettering Town, Hillingdon Borough, Rochdale and Middlesbrough. Sadly only a week after that Jimmy broke his leg in the Ilkeston Town FA Trophy game, although he was back in the team by the start of the following season. Despite then missing only two games, the January 1975 County Cup tie against Grimsby Town would prove to be his final appearance for Grantham, although he was awarded a joint testimonial a few months later, together with Bob Norris and Dennis Benskin, with a strong Nottingham Forest side coming to London Road. Moving into management, Jimmy took over the helm at Grimsby Amateurs and then spent well over ten years at Louth United. He still lives in the Cleethorpes area and runs his own successful fish wholesale company in Grimsby.

Blundall

Seasons Played			
	League	~	2
	F.A. Cup	~	
1934/35	Lincs Cup	~	
	Total	~	2

Member of the RAF who was stationed near to Grantham and played for the club towards the end of the 1934/35 season in games against Scunthorpe & Lindsey United and Barnsley Reserves.

Terry Bly

Seasons Played			
	League	~	162 (107)
	F.A. Cup	~	19 (10)
1964/65-69/70	F.A. Trophy	~	2
	League Cup	~	12 (4)
	Lincs Cup	~	
	Other	~	
	Total	~	195 (121)

Born 22/10/1935 at Fincham. Footballing legend who was known as 'Billy' to his team-mates and played for Bury Town and Norwich City, making an FA Cup semi-final appearance after the team defeated Spurs and Manchester United, following which national headlines of 'Bly, Bly Babes' was made. He then went on to score 52 goals, a seasonal record in Division 4, during Peterborough United's inaugural Football League campaign, followed by moves to Coventry City and a £13,000 transfer to Notts County. He failed to impress though at The Magpies and after a total of 159 goals in 243 senior appearances during his Football League career, Terry arrived at London Road as Player/Manager for 'a four figure sum', with Jimmy Rayner going in the opposite direction. He achieved the best possible start, scoring on his Grantham debut in the Midland League game against Retford Town in October 1964 and finished this first season at London Road with four hat-tricks to his name. During the next two years he played in the majority of the league games and every FA Cup match, including the ties against Swindon Town, Wimbledon and Oldham Athletic. The following two seasons, 1967/68 and 68/69, Terry was missing for several of the league games but both times he finished as the club's joint highest scorer, firstly with Mike Alexander and then Ernie Nixon. In this time he had added another hat-trick to his name during the September 1967 game at Worksop Town and scored four times in the home games against Loughborough United and Barton Town. Other highlights had included more appearances in the FA Cup Proper, with ties against Altrincham, Chelmsford City and the return of Swindon Town, plus victory in the Midland League Cup. In his final season Terry played only a limited number of games, although he did appear in the highlight of another FA Cup game against Oldham Athletic, before bowing out in the Midland League game at Alfreton Town in April 1970. Of course this was by no means the end of Terry's Grantham career as he then guided them to three consecutive league championships, FA Cup games against Stockport County, (the club's first victory over a Football League side), Rotherham United, Bradford City, the epic victory over Rochdale and a Third Round Proper encounter with Middlesbrough. Those following few years also included an FA Trophy Quarter-Final tie against Yeovil, another Midland League Cup victory and a Lincolnshire County Cup win at Scunthorpe United. If that was not enough, at the pinnacle of his managerial career Terry still found time to run the Mace shop at Morton, but after his departure from the club in the Autumn of 1978, even the youngest of Granthamians will remember him as the man behind Plamore Sports in town. He finally retired in 2002, still lives in the area and is one of Grantham's true greats.

George Blyth

Seasons Played			
	League	~	7
	F.A. Cup	~	
1938/39	Lincs Cup	~	
	Total	~	7

Born 1911 at Motherwell. Goalkeeper who began his career at Scottish clubs Newburgh West End, Hibernian, Perth Rosalea, Perth YMCA and then returned to Hibernian. George was then signed by Notts County, where he went on to make 99 Football League appearances and was considered to be one of the best 'keepers in the Division Three (South) League despite being known to rush out of the penalty area with the view of tackling oncoming strikers! He then played in seven consecutive games for Grantham during October and November of 1938 whilst Maurice Healey was unavailable. The first of these was at Scunthorpe & Lindsey United, with his final game in the home fixture against Mansfield Town Reserves. Died 1984.

Boaler

Seasons Played			
	League	~	3 (1)
	F.A. Cup	~	
1912/13	Lincs Cup	~	1 (1)
	Other	~	
	Total	~	4 (2)

Only played during the 1912/13 season, scoring in the November Lincolnshire County Cup victory over Grimsby Rovers and the March 1913 Central Alliance game against Walsall Reserves.

Boden

Seasons Played			
	League	~	1
	F.A. Cup	~	
1932/33	Lincs Cup	~	
	Other	~	
	Total	~	1

Only one known appearance for this former Mexborough Athletic player, although no details are available as to the actual match.

Darren Bogan

Seasons Played			
	League	~	54 (8)
	F.A. Cup	~	5 (2)
1995/96-96/97	F.A. Trophy	~	5
	League Cup	~	2
1999/00	Lincs Cup	~	1
	Total	~	67 (10)

Born 03/09/1977 at Newcastle. Former Middlesbrough and Hartlepool United Youths player who then joined Billingham Town and after moving down from the North-East, began in the Grantham Reserves side but was soon promoted to the First team. Darren came off the bench to replace Colin Campbell during the November 1995 league match at home to Bury Town and promptly marked his debut with a goal. The following season saw the arrival of Gary Mills as manager and this coincided with Darren's consignment to the bench for many of the fixtures. He left Grantham in 1997 in the search for First team football and soon joined Arnold Town. Darren returned to The Meres for the start of the 1999/00 season and then scored his final goal for Grantham in the 2-2 draw at Clevedon Town, Grantham's first point of that season, and made his final appearance when he replaced Tim Wilkes in the February 2000 defeat at Newport County. He later signed for Scarborough and King's Lynn, but after a short time returned once more to Arnold, before joining Glapwell. Darren still lives in Grantham and works as a Computer Engineer.

Bogg

Seasons Played			
	League	~	3 (1)
	Lincs Cup	~	
1904/05	Other	~	
	Total	~	3 (1)

Played in the Midland Amateur Alliance games against Notts Magdala, Bridgford Athletic, where he scored, and Derby Thornhill during the 1904/05 season.

Frank Bokas

Seasons Played	League	~	31 (1)
	F.A. Cup	~	2
1950/51	Lincs Cup	~	2 (1)
	Total	~	35 (2)

Born 13/05/1914 at Belshill. Began his career with local side Kirkintilloch Rob Roy, before moving to Blackpool and Barnsley, gaining infamy in 1938 when he scored directly from a throw-in. He played for Leeds United during the Second World War and in 1945 moved to Carlisle United, although he failed to make a First team appearance there, finishing with a professional record of 5 goals and 102 games behind him. After time at Gainsborough Trinity, Frank made his debut for Grantham in the September 1950 Midland League fixture at Frickley Colliery and missed only a few games before the end of that campaign. His goals came in the league game at home to Rotherham United Reserves and the 1-1 draw in the February 1951 County Cup semi-final against Gainsborough Trinity, with his final appearance against Doncaster Rovers Reserves in the penultimate league fixture. Died 1996 at Barnsley.

Eric Bond

Seasons Played	League	~	1
	F.A. Cup	~	
1946/47	Lincs Cup	~	
	Total	~	1

Born 02/04/1921 in Grantham. Previously made appearances for Grantham St John's, The Navy and Grantham Reserves. Eric played just the once for the First team, in the October 1946 Midland League game at home to Bradford City Reserves after Jack Hartshorne became unavailable, but was also awarded the honour of joining the Lincolnshire representative side. He then signed for Loughborough Town and after the end of his playing career spent many years at Coles Cranes. Eric is now retired and still lives in Grantham.

Harry Bonshor

Seasons Played	League	~	5
	F.A. Cup	~	
1920/21-21/22	Lincs Cup	~	
	Other	~	
	Total	~	5

Born 1889 at Peterborough. Made appearances for Grantham towards the end of the 1920/21 season and returned to play in one more game a few months later, the 1921 New Year's Eve Central Alliance game at home to Chesterfield Reserves.

Mike Bosnell

Seasons Played	League	~	149 (135)
	F.A. Cup	~	9 (6)
1954/55-57/58	League Cup	~	1
	Lincs Cup	~	8 (1)
1959/60-60/61	Total	~	167 (142)

Born 23/02/1932 at Lincoln. Former Lincoln City Reserves striker who after breaking his leg returned to the game with Holbeach United and then signed for The Gingerbreads. He first played for Grantham in the November 1954 Midland League game at London Road against Scunthorpe & Lindsey United Reserves, scoring a brace on his debut. Mike missed only one of the remaining games from that season, amassing 38 goals to his credit, with the help of six hat-tricks, making him the natural successor to Jack Macartney's position. The following year his scoring skills were even better, with another 53 strikes to his name, including five during the February 1956 game against Goole Town. But in the next two years, Mike only played in approximately half of the season's games, although in that time he scored another 27 goals, including one further hat-trick against Wisbech Town. Mike returned to London Road in February 1960, scoring five goals past Stamford in his first match, and played in all but one of the remaining games of the season. His final appearance for Grantham came in the Lincolnshire County Cup 'A' Final victory over Gainsborough Trinity in April 1961. Mike went on to play for Ashby Institute and March Town United, before giving up the game to concentrate on his own building business. He is now retired, but still lives in the Lincoln area.

Bosworth

Seasons Played	League	~	1
	F.A. Cup	~	
1929/30	Lincs Cup	~	
	Other	~	
	Total	~	1

Made just the single appearance for Grantham, although there are no records to indicate the actual game.

Eric Bott

Seasons Played	League	~	2 (3)
	Lincs Cup	~	
1933/34	Other	~	1
1939/40	Total	~	3 (3)

Born 1916 in Grantham. Young inside-left player who scored three goals for Grantham in the 1933/34 season, two of which came in the Central Combination game at home to Mansfield Town Reserves in March. In 1935 Eric moved to Doncaster Rovers, scoring once in his nine appearances there, but is also known to have spent time with Spittlegate Old Boys, Grantham Loco, Hull City, Peterborough United and Crystal Palace, before his return to London Road in September 1939 to make one more appearance for the club in a friendly against an Army XI.

George Bott

Seasons Played	F.A. Cup	~	
	Other	~	1
1878/79	Total	~	1

Born circa 1847 at Belton. George played in just the one game for Grantham, a friendly at London Road against Notts County on New Year's Day 1879.

Graham Bowater

Seasons Played	League	~	6
	F.A. Cup	~	
2002/03-03/04	F.A. Trophy	~	
	League Cup	~	
	Lincs Cup	~	2
	Total	~	8

Born 1984 at Nottingham. After being released by his local side, Peterborough United, Graham went to Spalding United, but was soon signed up by Grantham. He made his debut in the March 2003 Dr Marten's Premier match at Hinckley United, but during the Summer he looked set to return to Spalding United, although by the start of the new season he was back at The Meres playing in the two Lincolnshire Shield fixtures against Stamford Town and Spalding United. That last game in September 2003 turned out to be Graham's final appearance for The Gingerbreads and after a few more matches which he spent sat on the bench, his return to Spalding finally materialised.

Bowen

Seasons Played	League	~	1 (1)
	Lincs Cup	~	
1931/32	Other	~	
	Total	~	1 (1)

Archives show only one appearance for this individual, in which he scored, although it is not known which actual game it was.

John Bower

Seasons Played	League	~	110 (2)
	F.A. Cup	~	5
1975/76-77/78	F.A. Trophy	~	6
	League Cup	~	13
	Lincs Cup	~	5
	Other	~	1
	Total	~	140 (2)

Born circa 1951. Midfield player signed from Sutton Town, where he helped them become the first side to win the Notts Senior Cup in three consecutive seasons. John made his Grantham debut in the opening match of the 1975/76 season against Scunthorpe United in the Lincolnshire County Senior Cup. His first goal for the club came in the November 1975 Southern League fixture at Dover and only a couple of weeks later he appeared in both matches against Port Vale in the First Round of the FA Cup. The following two seasons John played in the majority of the games, although high points are hard to find as Grantham slid down the table to their eventual relegation spot. His final appearance came in the closing fixture of the 1977/78 season against Minehead, which was actually played at Nuneaton Borough's ground due to work being done on the London Road site.

Bower

Seasons Played			
	F.A. Cup	~	
	Other	~	1
1880/81	Total	~	1

Made just one appearance for Grantham in the February 1881 friendly at home to Notts County.

Bowes

Seasons Played	League	~	10 (1)
	FA Amt. Cup	~	
1905/06-07/08	League Cup	~	
	Lincs Cup	~	3
1909/10-10/11	Other	~	6
	Total	~	19 (1)

Although team-sheets are scarce for this era, he was certainly playing for the club by the November 1905 friendly at Lincoln Lindum, although he seems to have made only a limited number of appearances in this his first season. He became a more permanent member of the squad during the next two years, but unfortunately no records at all are available for the 1908/09 season. By the start of the following season he was playing in every game where data exists, scoring his only known goal in the April 1910 Midland Amateur Alliance game at home to West Bridgford Friary. He was still a valued element of the Championship winning side a year later, although it is impossible to pin-point his final appearance.

Bowler

Seasons Played	League	~	5
	F.A. Cup	~	
1955/56	Lincs Cup	~	
	Total	~	5

Made five consecutive appearances for Grantham in October and November of 1955, starting with the home game against Hull City Reserves, ending in the match versus Gainsborough Trinity and never finishing on the losing side.

Darren Bowman

Seasons Played	League	~	34 (5)
	F.A. Cup	~	2
1998/99-99/00	F.A. Trophy	~	1
	League Cup	~	3
	Lincs Cup	~	2
	Total	~	42 (5)

Born 04/11/1978 at Abergavenny. Recommended by Dave Gilbert after being released by West Bromwich Albion and turned down a move to Chesterfield for the opportunity to come to The Meres. He made his Grantham debut by coming off the substitute's bench in the 1998/99 season's opening match at home to Scunthorpe United and scored his first goal for the club in the September fixture against Merthyr Tydfil. His Grantham career ended soon into the following season though, with his final appearance in the August 1999 game at Halesowen Town. He went on to play for Radcliffe Borough, Leigh RMI, Ramsbottom United, Rossendale United, Stalybridge Celtic, Leek Town and after just one game there, Fleetwood Town.

Edgar Bowmer

Seasons Played	League	~	22 (3)
	F.A. Cup	~	
1928/29	Lincs Cup	~	
	Other	~	
	Total	~	22 (3)

Former Club Captain at Ilkeston United who played in virtually all of the latter half of the 1928/29 season's games, scoring twice in the January 1929 Midland League match at Denaby United, although there are no records to show which other game he scored in.

Ian Bowyer

Seasons Played	League	~	8 (1)
	F.A. Cup	~	
1990/91	F.A. Trophy	~	
	League Cup	~	
	Lincs Cup	~	
	Total	~	8 (1)

Born 06/06/1951 at Ellesmere Port. Began his Football League career at Manchester City, where he won a League Cup winner's medal, then moved to Leyton Orient, before really making his name with two spells at Nottingham Forest, with Sunderland in between. Honours won at The City Ground included medals for victories in the 1979 and 1980 European Cup Finals, the 1978 League Championship, the 1978 and 1979 League Cups, the 1980 Super Cup, (although Ian only played in the first leg victory over Barcelona), plus the 1977 Anglo-Scottish Cup. From an individual point of view though, he is probably best remembered for the header in Cologne that sent Forest through to that important first European Cup Final. With 564 games, he remains Forest's second highest appearance maker and this was followed by the end of his professional career at Hereford United, where he was Player/Manager, finishing with a final tally of over 780 senior appearances to his name. Ian then spent time as Coach at Cheltenham Town and turned out for Grantham during the 1990/91 season as a favour for his old friend and former colleague, John Robertson. The first of those games came in October at Dudley Town, his third, at Hinckley Town, saw Ian score his only goal for the club, whilst his final appearance was when he replaced Dave Swainston during the February 1991 league fixture at Newport AFC. Ian later took up various coaching and management positions, firstly at Plymouth Argyle under Peter Shilton, then Rotherham United and Birmingham, before returning to Nottingham Forest as the club's First Team Coach. However a change in the management structure in November 2004 led to Ian's departure from The City Ground and he moved into the Assistant Manager's position at Milton Keynes Dons.

Alan Boxall

Seasons Played	League	~	1
	F.A. Cup	~	
1984/85	F.A. Trophy	~	
	League Cup	~	
	Lincs Cup	~	
	Other	~	
	Total	~	1

Born 11/05/1953 at Woolwich. Played in the Reserve sides of West Ham and Charlton, before moving to Lincolnshire where he then appeared for Louth United and Barton Town. After this, Alan took over from former Gingerbread, David Dall, at Scunthorpe United, before moving to Chesterfield where he obviously made an impression on their fans. In 1999 he appeared in *4-4-2* magazine after the Chesterfield supporters voted him as their club's worst ever player! This was despite him being renowned for his long throws, having the ability to launch the ball from the half-way line into the penalty area. Grantham fans were hardly given the chance to form their own opinions after his Grantham career lasted just one match, the October 1984 league visit of Southport to London Road.

Boxan

Seasons Played	League	~	3
	F.A. Cup	~	
1930/31	Lincs Cup	~	
	Total	~	3

Originally from the Long Eaton area. There are instances where his surname is listed as 'Poxan' although I am reasonably assured that this is an error. The only definite game that we can establish he played in is the February 1931 Midland League game at Scarborough.

Willie Boyd

Seasons Played			
	League	~	5
	F.A. Cup	~	1
1984/85	F.A. Trophy	~	
	League Cup	~	
	Lincs Cup	~	
	Other	~	
	Total	~	6

Born 18/10/1958 at Bellshill. Former Scottish Youth International goalkeeper who started out as an Apprentice at Hull City, before making over 100 appearances for Doncaster Rovers. He made six appearances for Grantham at the start of the 1984/85 season, replacing Grahame Hempsall, starting at Horwich RMI and ending in the FA Cup tie at home to Halesowen Town in September. Willie was sold to Kettering Town for a £500 fee, but by the end of the decade he had given up the game and moved on to Rugby League, playing in the Doncaster area.

Phil Boyer

Seasons Played			
	League	~	97 (18)
	F.A. Cup	~	7 (1)
1983/84-86/87	F.A. Trophy	~	15 (4)
	League Cup	~	8 (2)
	Lincs Cup	~	5 (1)
	Other	~	
	Total	~	132 (26)

Born 25/01/1949 at Nottingham. Began his career as an Apprentice at Derby County, before making appearances for York City and Bournemouth. He then played over 250 games in Division One for Norwich City and also appeared in their 1975 League Cup Final at Wembley. After a move to Southampton, where he was The League's highest scorer in 1980, Phil transferred to Manchester City, where he suffered the heart-break of missing out on the 1981 FA Cup Final due to injury. His professional career saw a total of 189 goals for him in 612 senior league and cup games. Phil also made one appearance as a full England International, in March 1976 against Wales, held at Wrexham, to go with his two Under-23 caps. After a spell playing for Bulova in Hong Kong, he joined Grantham after returning to the Nottingham area, something of a major coup for new manager, Bob Duncan. His debut came in the September 1983 Northern Premier League game at Horwich RMI, with his first goal coming the following week at home to Mossley. He left Grantham towards the end of their time in the NPL to have short spells at Stamford Town and Shepshed Charterhouse, before Barry Shaw brought him back to Grantham as his assistant during the 1985/86 season. His last goal for Grantham came in the April 1987 league defeat at Brignorth Town, with his final appearance for the club in the closing fixture of the season against Banbury United. Phil briefly followed Barry Shaw in a management role at Harrowby United, but was last known to be working as a bank courier and also scouting for various Football League clubs.

Martyn Boyers

Seasons Played			
	League	~	20 (1)
	F.A. Cup	~	4
1984/85-85/86	F.A. Trophy	~	1
	League Cup	~	8
	Lincs Cup	~	2
	Other	~	
	Total	~	35 (1)

Born 1955 at Grimsby. Previously played for Louth United, Gainsborough Trinity, Skegness Town and was Player/Manager at Boston FC. His first game for Grantham was the March 1985 league fixture at home to Rhyl and Martyn went on to play in most of the remaining games before the Summer break. After missing the opening league game of the 1985/86 season, he scored his only goal for Grantham against Bromsgrove Rovers, but the December FA Trophy defeat at the hands of Burton Albion proved to be his final appearance for the club. He went on to play for King's Lynn and Spalding United, winning a United Counties League winners medal there in 1988, and then returned to King's Lynn as Assistant Manager under his former Gingerbreads team-mate, Shaughan Farrow. Martyn also spent time at the end of the decade as the manager of the Lincolnshire FA representative side. He still lives in the Grimsby area and is Chief Executive of a large company based in the fish industry.

Bradford

Seasons Played			
	League	~	1
	F.A. Cup	~	
1924/25	Lincs Cup	~	
	Other	~	
	Total	~	1

Goalkeeper who according to available records played just the one game in this Championship winning season, the April 1925 Central Alliance fixture at home to Loughborough Corinthians.

John Bradley

Seasons Played			
	League	~	18 (12)
	F.A. Cup	~	
1945/46	Lincs Cup	~	2 (2)
	Total	~	20 (14)

Born 27/11/1916 at Hemsworth. Began his career at Huddersfield Town, before making his Football League debut at Swindon Town, followed by a period at Chelsea just before The War. John made his first appearance for Grantham in the Midland League game at Boston United in October 1945, but it wasn't until the New Year that he became a near permanent member of the side, as he was also turning out for RAF Spittlegate at the same time. This meant that he missed out on the club's FA Cup Rounds at Kettering Town and Mansfield Town. His first two goals for Grantham came in the visit of Ollerton Colliery to London Road at the end of December and over the next couple of months he scored a hat-trick in the 8-0 thrashing of Nottingham Forest Reserves and the consolation goal in the Lincolnshire County Cup Final at Boston United. His final appearance for Grantham came in the 1945/46 closing fixture at Rotherham United Reserves. The following season John signed for Southampton, before moving to Bolton Wanderers and Norwich City, eventually finishing his career with a total of 46 goals scored in 173 Football League games. He is known to have then transferred to Yarmouth Town, but no information is available on his career after this.

Bradley

Seasons Played			
	F.A. Cup	~	
	Other	~	1
1880/81	Total	~	1

Played once for Grantham in the final game of the 1880/81 season, a friendly against Bourne.

Bradley

Seasons Played			
	League	~	2
	F.A. Cup	~	
1919/20	Lincs Cup	~	
	Total	~	2

Appeared in the first two Central Alliance fixtures of the 1919/20 season, away at Long Eaton and Derby County Reserves.

Bradley

Seasons Played			
	League	~	4 (1)
	F.A. Cup	~	
1932/33	Lincs Cup	~	
	Other	~	
	Total	~	4 (1)

Previously with Southwell St Mary's, although unfortunately as far as Grantham is concerned no information is available other than the match in which he scored, the Midland League game at home to Mexborough Athletic in February 1933.

Bramby

Seasons Played			
	League	~	1
	F.A. Cup	~	
1929/30	Lincs Cup	~	
	Other	~	
	Total	~	1

No information available on this player.

Bramhall

Seasons Played	League	~	2
	Lincs Cup	~	
1931/32	Other	~	
	Total	~	2

Also played for Ilkeston United and Notts County Reserves, but once again no information is available on actual Grantham games that he played in.

Bramley

Seasons Played	League	~	35
	F.A. Cup	~	2
1926/27	Lincs Cup	~	1
	Other	~	1
	Total	~	39

Made his debut in the opening fixture of the 1926/27 season at Sutton Town and generally played in midfield. Despite only missing three of that season's Midland League games, he failed to score in any of them.

Ashley Brandy

Seasons Played	League	~	33 (7)
	F.A. Cup	~	4 (1)
1996/97	F.A. Trophy	~	7 (1)
	League Cup	~	1
	Lincs Cup	~	
	Total	~	45 (9)

Born 1973 at Nottingham. Former Arnold Town and Borrowash Victoria striker who made his debut in the opening league match of the 1996/97 season at Redditch United, scoring his first goal for the club a month later against RC Warwick. The highlight of that season had to be the FA Trophy run, with Ashley playing in every round, which ended at The Meres when Heybridge Swifts earned a narrow 1-0 victory. His final appearance for Grantham was in the season's closing game at Moor Green. Ashley still lives in the Nottingham area and currently works for a replacement window company, a position that he has held since the early 1990's.

Mick Brannan

Seasons Played	League	~	34
	F.A. Cup	~	7
1945/46-46/47	Lincs Cup	~	2
	Total	~	43

Born 1911 at Wath-upon-Dearne. Former Rotherham Road FC, Wombwell, Denaby United, Arsenal, Hull City, Barnsley, where he finally made his Football League debut, and Notts County goalkeeper, who despite many years experience had made only 8 senior appearances. However, he was Grantham's first choice 'keeper after the end of the Second World War, making his debut in the opening fixture of the 1945/46 season at home to Gainsborough Trinity. Mick played in every game of that year's FA Cup run, which ended at Mansfield Town at the 2nd Round Proper stage, and the County Cup Final against Boston United in April. The following season though, he lost his place to Tom Gilchrist and made only one more appearance for the club in the September 1946 Midland League match against Lincoln City Reserves. By the start of the 1947/48 campaign, Mick was turning out for Peterborough United, but failed to maintain a place in their First team as well.

Bratley

Seasons Played	League	~	1
	Lincs Cup	~	
1904/05	Other	~	
	Total	~	1

Only one known appearance for this player, during the visit of Notts Magdala Amateurs to the Harlaxton Road ground in March 1905.

Gary Breeden

Seasons Played	League	~	8
	F.A. Cup	~	
1992/93	F.A. Trophy	~	
	League Cup	~	
	Lincs Cup	~	
	Total	~	8

Born circa 1971. Former Harrowby United player and son of Graham Breeden, Benny O'Meara's assistant who came to Grantham after the financial crisis of 1993. Gary's first game for The Gingerbreads came in the January 1993 league fixture at Bedworth United, the first match after the departure of many of that season's players, with his final appearance in the 5-0 defeat at home to Redditch United two months later, when he came off the bench to replace Tony Cook. Gary still lives in town and works for an established local tyre production company.

Brewster

Seasons Played	Other	~	2
1875/76	Total	~	2

Played in the two friendlies against the Third Lincolnshire Rifles and the Conservative Working Mens Club, in November and December of 1875, but for some reason figured in only one of the many club matches from this era.

Briddon

Seasons Played	League	~	2
	F.A. Cup	~	
1952/53	Lincs Cup	~	
	Total	~	2

Born circa 1934. Former Matlock Town player who appeared for Grantham in the first two games of the 1952/53 season, away at Mansfield Town Reserves and Peterborough United.

Bridgman

Seasons Played	F.A. Cup	~	
	Lincs Cup	~	
1884/85	Other	~	2
	Total	~	2

Only made two appearances for Grantham, in the consecutive friendlies against Peterborough and Notts Rangers in October 1884.

Briggs

Seasons Played	Other	~	4
1874/75	Total	~	4

Made his debut appearance in the first ever visit of another team to London Road, the Third Lincolnshire Volunteer Rifles in October 1874, although he had played in club matches preceding this. Other friendlies that he played a part in include Burghley Park, Peterborough and the final match of the season at home to Lincoln.

Briggs

Seasons Played	F.A. Cup	~	
	Lincs Cup	~	
1885/86	Other	~	1
	Total	~	1

Made only one appearance for the club in the friendly against Grantham Volunteers, December 1885.

Briggs

Seasons Played	League	~	4 (1)
	Lincs Cup	~	
1905/06-07/08	Other	~	2
	Total	~	6 (1)

Defender who almost certainly played in considerably more matches than those quoted above and scored at least once, during the Midland Amateur Alliance game at home to Mansfield Amateurs in February 1908.

Briggs

Seasons Played	League	~	17 (3)
	Lincs Cup	~	2
1939/40	Other	~	6 (5)
	Total	~	25 (8)

Scored on his debut in the match at Bradford Park Avenue Reserves in August 1939 and went on to play in all three of the annulled Midland League competition games before the start of the Second World War. He also played in the Lincolnshire County Cup Final against Scunthorpe & Lindsey United, with his final appearance for the club in the closing Midland War-Time fixture against the same side in May 1940.

Darren Bogan

Mike Bosnell

Graham Bowater

Darren Bowman

Ian Bowyer

Phil Boyer

Bill Brindley

Albert Briscoe

Cyril Brown

Fred Brown

Roy Brown

Jack Buckley

Paul Buckthorpe

Gary Bull

Andy Bullimore

Frank Bungay

Bill Brindley

Seasons Played			
	League	~	76 (4)
	F.A. Cup	~	2
1977/78	F.A. Trophy	~	2
	League Cup	~	10 (1)
1981/82-82/83	Lincs Cup	~	1
	Other	~	2
	Total	~	93 (5)

Born 29/01/1947 at Nottingham. Christened John Brindley, but always known as 'Bill'. A former England Schoolboy and Youth International who began his career at Nottingham Forest in 1964, whilst three years later he made headlines by scoring only 10 seconds after coming on as substitute in a match against Southampton. Bill then made over 250 appearances for Notts County, twice being part of promotion winning sides, before joining Gillingham in 1976, finally finishing with 3 goals to his name in a career that had taken in 288 senior fixtures. He signed for Grantham in time for the September 1977 Southern League match at home to Cheltenham Town, but his first period at London Road lasted just into the New Year and after the match against Dartford, Bill moved on to Burton Albion and then Alfreton Town. The arrival of his former team-mate, Jon Nixon, as Player/Manager at Grantham in the Summer of 1981, saw Bill's return to the club and his reinstatement to Grantham's defence for the County Cup tie at home to Boston United. His first goal for The Gingerbreads came at the end of that month in the Northern Premier League fixture at Netherfield and he then played in the majority of that season's games. His final goal for the club came coincidentally again at Netherfield, in April 1983, with his final appearance in the following closing fixture of the season at Matlock Town. Moving into management, Bill took over at Meadows Albion, then Boston FC, taking them to League Championship success, followed by periods at the helm of Heanor Town, Ilkeston Town and Arnold Town, where he has remained for the last few years. Since the end of his playing career Bill has also spent time working for Notts County Lotteries and a fleet car sales company, but is currently Sales Manager for a cleaning and maintenance equipment manufacturer.

Albert Briscoe

Seasons Played			
	League	~	1
	F.A. Cup	~	
1978/79	F.A. Trophy	~	
	League Cup	~	1
	Lincs Cup	~	2
	Total	~	4

Born circa 1957. Previously spent five years at Nottingham Forest, although he failed to make a First team appearance there. His first game for Grantham was in the opening fixture of the 1978/79 season, at Boston United in the Lincolnshire County Senior Cup, but after only four games, the last of which was the 5-0 opening league defeat at Bedford Town, he had moved on.

William Brittain

Seasons Played			
	F.A. Cup	~	1
	Lincs Cup	~	7 (6)
1884/85-88/89	Other	~	38 (5)
1890/91	Total	~	46 (11)

Began his Grantham career in the 1884/85 season, but curiously only played in what would turn out to be the victorious Lincolnshire County Cup competition, including the Final against Gainsborough Trinity in March 1885. This peculiarity was continued the following year, during which he scored four goals in the tie against Gainsborough W.M. As the decade progressed though, he became an increasingly more constant member of the side, with a highlight of playing in the Kettering Charity Cup Final victory at Cambridge Granta in March 1889, and then returning to make a final appearance in the friendly against Langley Mill in March of 1891. William went on to have two spells at Grantham Rovers, with 17 appearances for Lincoln City in the 1894/95 season in-between. He returned to 'The Town' soon after the club's reformation and although no dates are known, by 1911 he was listed as the club's trainer. No information is known of him after this, although he was still alive and well after the Second World War, attending Jack Broadbent's funeral in 1949.

Brittain

Seasons Played			
	F.A. Cup	~	2 (1)
	Other	~	11 (24)
1878/79	Total	~	13 (25)

Even in an age when the emphasis was more on the attacking side of the game, this player was certainly a prolific scorer. He scored five times on his debut, the opening friendly of the 1878/79 season against Sleaford and repeated this feat the following month when Nottingham Law were defeated 12-2. He missed only a couple of games that season and scored a brace in his final appearance, at home to Spilsby in April 1879. Although there is a slight chance that he could be the same player as William Brittain, the following entry should also be noted.

Brittain

Seasons Played			
	F.A. Cup	~	
	Lincs Cup	~	1
1886/87	Other	~	1
	Total	~	2

Although this player could possibly be the same individual as the previous entry, he is definitely not William Brittain as he played in the same games as him, in February 1887 against Notts Waverley and Grimsby Town.

Brittian

Seasons Played			
	League	~	3
	F.A. Cup	~	
1892/93	Total	~	3

Played in all three of the Midland Amateur Alliance games, including the 16-0 defeat at Notts County Rovers in October 1892, before Grantham prematurely resigned from the league.

Brittian

Seasons Played			
	League	~	1
	F.A. Cup	~	
1936/37	Lincs Cup	~	
	Other	~	
	Total	~	1

Made just the one appearance for Grantham in the March 1937 Midland League game at home to Denaby United. His surname is sometimes spelt 'Brittain' in different publications of the time.

Benjamin Broadbent

Seasons Played			
	F.A. Cup	~	
	Lincs Cup	~	
1885/86-87/88	Other	~	9 (2)
	Total	~	9 (2)

Born 1861 at Great Gonerby. Brother of Jack Broadbent. Benjamin scored on his debut in the friendly at Peterborough in October 1885, but played only occasionally over three seasons at London Road, scoring his other goal in December 1886 at Notts County Reserves.

Jack Broadbent

Seasons Played			
	F.A. Cup	~	6
	Lincs Cup	~	11
1883/84-90/91	Other	~	86
	Total	~	103

Born 1864 at Great Gonerby. Brother of Benjamin Broadbent. Jack started with Grantham by making appearances in friendlies, the first of which was the February 1884 defeat at Nottingham Bank. By the start of the 1886/87 season though, he had been 'promoted' to Cup competitions as well. From then on Jack made most of his appearances in the goalkeeping position, but due to his general sporting prowess he also played out-field when a player was unavailable, leaving the 'unimportant' final line of defence to be filled with one of the more minor club players. By the end of the decade he had become a near permanent member of the squad and helped Grantham to win the Kettering Charity Cup in March 1889. During his final season with the club, 1890/91, he became their first professional player and his quality was confirmed when he went on to play for Grantham Rovers and Lincoln City, although his career lasted only two appearances there after he broke his shoulder-blade during an 1894/95 Division Two match at Darwen. Jack continued to live in Grantham after retiring from the game and at the time of the 1901 census was employed as a Turner Fitter in town. Died 22/02/1949 at Grantham.

Bromhead

Seasons Played			
1874/75-75/76	Other	~	2
	Total	~	2

Made only one appearance in the club's initial 1874/75 season, the friendly at Burghley Park in March 1875 and this was equalled the following campaign with another game at Bourne in November. Other than these two games there is no evidence of him playing in any of the numerous club matches that were played during this period.

Bromland

Seasons Played			
1875/76	Other	~	1
	Total	~	1

Played in just the one game for Grantham, the unique match at Peterborough in January 1876 that was played under Rugby Union rules.

Darren Brookes

Seasons Played			
1999/00	League	~	6
	F.A. Cup	~	2
	F.A. Trophy	~	1
	League Cup	~	
	Lincs Cup	~	
	Total	~	9

Born 07/07/1978 at Sheffield. Defender who began his career at local side ABM, before moving to Worksop Town and Doncaster Rovers, where he made nine full appearances. He made his Grantham debut in the August 1999 Dr Marten's Premier League match at home to Newport County, when he came off the bench to replace Lee Rogers. His final appearance for the club though, was only two months later, in the FA Trophy defeat at the hands of Matlock Town. Darren went on to play for Selston and then Alfreton Town, where he was part of their 2002 Northern Counties East League and Cup double winning team and the Unibond Division One Championship winning side a year later. After a brief second spell at Worksop, he joined Stocksbridge Park Steels then Buxton.

Brooks

Seasons Played			
1932/33	League	~	1
	F.A. Cup	~	
	Lincs Cup	~	
	Other	~	
	Total	~	1

Former Notts County goalkeeper who we know from *Grantham Journal* archives played only one game for Grantham, but it is not known which specific match.

Broome

Seasons Played			
1939/40	League	~	2 (1)
	Lincs Cup	~	
	Other	~	
	Total	~	2 (1)

Played in two Midland War-Time League games in December of 1939, against Scunthorpe & Lindsey United and Frickley Colliery, scoring in the first of those.

H. Broughton

Seasons Played			
1905/06-07/08	League	~	8 (1)
	Lincs Cup	~	
	Other	~	2
	Total	~	10 (1)

Brother of Matthew Broughton, with also an A. Broughton playing in friendlies at the start of the 1905/06 season, whilst another sibling, John Jarvis Broughton went on to start a sports shop in Wigan in 1905, later the *JJB Sports* chain. H. Broughton appears on every team-sheet that is available for his first two seasons, scoring in the Midland Amateur Alliance game at home to Derby Thornhill in September 1906. It appears that the following season, 1907/08, saw him making fewer appearances, but with no records at all for the campaign after that, it is impossible to establish the end of his career.

Matthew Broughton

Seasons Played			
1904/05-07/08	League	~	14 (17)
	Lincs Cup	~	1
	Other	~	2 (1)
	Total	~	17 (18)

Born 08/10/1880 in Grantham. Former King's School student and brother of H. Broughton who began his career at either Grantham Rovers or Avenue, before having a successful career at Nottingham Forest, Notts County and Watford, finishing with 6 goals in his 29 Football League appearances. Matthew then returned to his home town to start employment at Ruston & Hornsby's, allowing him to continue football with Grantham FC and cricket with the local club. He scored in his first friendly against Stathern Olympic and almost certainly played many more games than those noted, due to a lack of available records. Matthew probably also scored more goals than are known about, for the same reason, although we do have evidence of five goals scored in the Midland Amateur Alliance match against Derby YMCA in February 1906. Like his sibling, it is not known as to the precise time when his footballing career concluded, although the following entry should be noted. Died 23/01/1957 at Grantham.

Broughton

Seasons Played			
1909/10	League	~	6 (9)
1912/13	F.A. Cup	~	
	Lincs Cup	~	2 (1)
	Other	~	2 (5)
	Total	~	10 (15)

Whilst open to the possibility that this individual could be someone completely different, the natural conclusion is that he is one of the two previous Broughtons. My personally theory is that he is Matthew Broughton, although that is simply due to the similar forward-playing role. Whoever he should prove to be, it seems that he made most of his appearances in the first half of the 1909/10 season, scoring five times in the Midland Amateur League fixture at home to Derby YMCA and a hat-trick in the Grantham Minor Cup game against Gonerby Town. He returned in 1912 to score in three different Central Alliance games, the last of which was the December fixture at home to Ripley Town.

Broughton

Seasons Played			
1923/24	League	~	1 (1)
	F.A. Cup	~	
	League Cup	~	
	Lincs Cup	~	
	Other	~	
	Total	~	1 (1)

Only one known appearance for this member of the Broughton family, scoring the first goal in the April 1924 Central Alliance victory over RAF Cranwell.

Coventry Brown

Seasons Played			
1934/35	League	~	1
	F.A. Cup	~	1 (1)
	Lincs Cup	~	
	Total	~	2 (1)

Member of the RAF who was stationed near to Grantham, allowing him to play, and score, in the FA Cup match against Basford United, and the Midland League match at London Road against Boston United in February of 1935. He also played in a slightly rearranged squad that played a friendly against a Leeds United 'A' side in December 1934.

Cyril Brown

Seasons Played			
1956/57-67/68	League	~	312 (32)
	F.A. Cup	~	29 (4)
	League Cup	~	2
	Lincs Cup	~	9 (3)
	Total	~	352 (39)

Born 28/10/1936 at Sunderland. Former Grantham St Anne's and St John's player who is one of our clubs longest serving players and should receive the highest of acclaim when it is remembered that appearances in secondary competitions like league and county cups were severely limited during this time. Cyril made his debut against Boston United in January 1957 and scored his first goal for Grantham a few months later against Mansfield Town Reserves. He made only a limited amount of appearances during the following two seasons, but by Grantham's entry into the Central Alliance League, he had become a consistent member of the side. He played in the April 1961 Lincolnshire County Cup 'A' Final and scored one of the goals to help secure victory against Gainsborough Trinity. With Grantham's return to the Midland League, Cyril missed many of the games in the latter half of that season, but 1962/63 saw him back and playing in every single game, whilst the following season saw him rewarded with a Midland League Championship medal after one of the clubs most memorable years. For the next three seasons, Cyril became an important member of Terry Bly's new side and he played in most of Grantham's notable FA Cup games including Swindon Town and Wimbledon, whilst in May 1966 he was rewarded with a testimonial when a Rotherham United side were defeated 5-2 by The Gingerbreads. His last season at London Road, 1967/68, saw a final FA Cup Proper encounter in the defeat against Altrincham, before his last goal in the game at Loughborough United and his final competitive match at Retford Town in May 1968. The following week, the conclusion to his long career came in the victorious Bourne Hospital Cup Final, with Grantham earning a 3-0 victory. A few years later his brother-in-law, Colin Skeith, played for the club. Cyril continued to work in the engineering industry in town, plus managed the Great Gonerby team in the early 1980's. He is now retired though, still living close to the town.

David Brown

Seasons Played	League	~	61 (1)
	F.A. Cup	~	4
1956/57-61/62	League Cup	~	
	Lincs Cup	~	2
	Total	~	67 (1)

Born 10/03/1936 at Nottingham. Former Notts County Reserves goalkeeper who took over the slot from Ron Hewitt in the third match of the 1956/57 season at Wisbech Town...and is credited with a goal! A hefty clearance from David saw his opposite number dash out to try and intercept the ball before a surging Alex Gaskell could get onto the end of it. Mis-timing it completely, the ball bounced in front of him, looped over his head and came to rest in the back of the Wisbech goal. David played in the majority of that season's games, with Ron Hewitt returning to deputise when he was unavailable. Unfortunately though, he only played in the first eight games of the following season, before his place was taken by Tony Warrington. Apart from a reasonable run after Christmas 1959, from then until his final game against Alfreton Town in April 1962 he made only a limited amount of appearances, before moving on to Ilkeston Town. David is retired now, having worked for many years as a petroleum engineer, and currently lives in the Birmingham area.

Fred Brown

Seasons Played	League	~	39 (4)
	F.A. Cup	~	5 (2)
1937/38	Lincs Cup	~	2
	Other	~	3
	Total	~	49 (6)

Born 1911 at Birmingham. Inside-Left who had previously played for Hinckley Juniors, Sunderland, Rochdale, Halifax Town, Accrington Stanley and Torquay United, scoring 47 goals in 161 senior appearances. He then moved to Newark Town, before making his Grantham debut in the first game of the 1937/38 season at Gainsborough Trinity. Fred scored in the FA Cup matches against Tevesal & Silverhill Colliery and Boots Athletic, and was a major player in that year's successful side, before his final match for the club in the Winners versus Runners-Up finale to the Midland League season.

James Brown

Seasons Played	League	~	
	F.A. Cup	~	
1998/99	F.A. Trophy	~	
	League Cup	~	
	Lincs Cup	~	1
	Total	~	1

Made only one appearance for Grantham, playing in the opening match of the 1998/99 season, at home to Scunthorpe United in the County Cup.

Ken Brown

Seasons Played	League	~	2
	F.A. Cup	~	
1960/61-61/62	League Cup	~	
	Lincs Cup	~	
	Total	~	2

Came to Grantham from amateur football and played just twice for the First team, the final match of the 1960/61 season at Spalding United, followed nearly a year later with a game at London Road against Bourne Town.

Richard Brown

Seasons Played	League	~	21
	F.A. Cup	~	
1986/87	F.A. Trophy	~	
	League Cup	~	2
	Lincs Cup	~	
	Total	~	23

Born 13/01/1967 at Nottingham. Began his career on Schoolboy forms at Nottingham Forest, before moving to Derby County, Ilkeston Town, Sheffield Wednesday and Grimsby Town. His first game for Grantham came in the December 1986 Bill Dellow Cup tie against Leicester United and he then played in most of the following fixtures, up to the league game at Stourbridge in April 1987. Transfers followed to Boston United, Kettering Town and then a £25,000 move to Blackburn Rovers, where he helped Kenny Dalglish's team into the FA Premier League. Richard also played whilst on loan at Maidstone United and after his return to Ewood Park became Captain of their Reserves team. After being released by Blackburn, he had a spell in America, followed by time at Stockport County and Blackpool, which saw the end of his Football League career and 42 First team games behind him. Richard then briefly returned to Kettering Town, before joining Stalybridge Celtic and Altrincham. He is currently Manager of Monton Amateurs in the Manchester League.

Roy Brown

Seasons Played	League	~	1
	F.A. Cup	~	
1953/54	Lincs Cup	~	
	Total	~	1

Reserves player who made just one First team appearance in October 1953 against Doncaster Rovers Reserves, before being released by the club the following Summer.

Brown

Seasons Played	Other	~	1
1875/76	Total	~	1

Made only one appearance, in the January 1876 match at Peterborough, played under Rugby Union rules.

Brown

Seasons Played	F.A. Cup	~	
	Lincs Cup	~	
1887/88	Other	~	1 (1)
	Total	~	1 (1)

Played, and scored, in the final friendly of the 1887/88 season at home to Grantham Rovers.

Brown

Seasons Played	League	~	1
	F.A. Cup	~	
1921/22	Lincs Cup	~	
	Total	~	1

Outside-Right who also played for Hucknall Byron and was a student at Notts University. He made only one appearance for Grantham, interestingly the Central Alliance game at Hucknall Byron, which raises the question of whether he sportingly offered to play for his 'opponents'. Very sporting if this theory is accurate, especially with Grantham winning the game 3-0.

Brown

Seasons Played			
	League	~	5 (2)
	F.A. Cup	~	1 (3)
1929/30	Lincs Cup	~	
	Other	~	
	Total	~	6 (5)

Centre-Forward who progressed from the Reserves into the First team and scored a hat-trick in the November 1929 FA Cup game against Newark Town, plus goals in league games at Doncaster Rovers Reserves and by deduction, one of the Christmas games against Newark Town again.

Bruce

Seasons Played			
	League	~	2
	Lincs Cup	~	1
1904/05	Other	~	
	Total	~	3

Goalkeeper whose only known appearances in the club's first season after reforming are the Lincolnshire Shield game against Hornsby Engineers, plus Midland Amateur Alliance matches at Notts Magdala and the visit of Notts Magdala Amateurs to the Huntingtower Road ground.

Charles Bryan

Seasons Played			
	F.A. Cup	~	4 (1)
	Lincs Cup	~	
1881/82	Other	~	5
1883/84	Total	~	9 (1)

Born 1864 in Grantham. Brother of Thomas Bryan. Charles' first recorded appearance is in the FA Cup game at home to Brigg Town in November 1881, with his only goal for the club coming in the following round at Staveley. With no games being played by him the following season, he returns in October 1883 against Grantham Volunteers and continues to play in many of that season's remaining games.

Paul Bryan

Seasons Played			
	League	~	
	F.A. Cup	~	
1997/98	F.A. Trophy	~	
	League Cup	~	
	Lincs Cup	~	1
	Total	~	1

Came on as substitute, replacing Dave King, in the July 1997 County Cup game against Gainsborough Trinity.

Thomas Bryan

Seasons Played			
	F.A. Cup	~	2
	Lincs Cup	~	3
1883/84-86/87	Other	~	15 (1)
	Total	~	20 (1)

Born 1866 in Grantham. Brother of Charles Bryan. Thomas played in many of the same games as his sibling during the 1883/84 season and then appeared in the majority of the friendly games the following year, scoring in the match at home to Notts Waverley in January 1885. However, in his final two seasons, appearances became limited, until his last known game at home to Louth in December 1886.

Buck

Seasons Played			
	Other	~	1
1875/76	Total	~	1

Made just the one appearance, in a friendly against the Conservative Working Men's Club in December 1875.

Buckingham

Seasons Played			
	League	~	1
	F.A. Cup	~	
1930/31	Lincs Cup	~	
	Total	~	1

Made only one appearance for Grantham, although there are no records as to the actual game. Local data shows that he was a former Tottenham Hotspur player, although the only individual with that surname who made appearances at White Hart Lane was a Vic Buckingham (Born 23/10/1915 at Greenwich - Died 1995) who made over 200 appearances between 1935 and 1948. Although they could possibly be the same individuals, surely his age would have made him too young for playing at Grantham. I am assuming therefore that we are talking about a namesake that failed to make the Tottenham First team, possibly a relative of Vic.

Buckingham

Seasons Played			
	League	~	1 (1)
	F.A. Cup	~	
1945/46	Lincs Cup	~	
	Total	~	1 (1)

Player who made his only appearance, and scored, in the Christmas Day 1945 fixture at home to Ransome & Marles.

Jack Buckley

Seasons Played			
	League	~	128 (1)
	F.A. Cup	~	14
1935/36-37/38	Lincs Cup	~	10
	Other	~	6
	Total	~	158 (1)

Born 24/11/1903 at Prudhoe. Full-Back who had previously played for Prudhoe Castle, Doncaster Rovers and Lincoln City, making a total of 369 League and Cup appearances, and after becoming landlord at The Malt Shovels public house in Westgate joined the local team. He made his Grantham debut in the first game of the 1935/36 season at Burton Town and immediately became a permanent member of the side. That first season saw him play in the Lincolnshire County Cup Final at Boston United, plus the victorious sides in the Grantham Hospital Cup and Wilson Cup competitions. His only goal for the club came in the September 1937 fixture against Bradford Park Avenue Reserves and by the end of that same season, (which saw Jack win a Midland League runners-up medal), he had missed only six games for Grantham in what amounted to six different competitive competitions. Jack continued to be a licensee in Grantham for several years and later took over a similar position in Doncaster. Died 13/04/1985 at Doncaster.

William Buckley

Seasons Played			
	League	~	46
	F.A. Cup	~	1
1938/39-39/40	Lincs Cup	~	2
1945/46	Other	~	2
1949/50	Total	~	51

Took over Jack Buckley's position for the start of the 1938/39 season at Shrewsbury Town and played in nearly every game of that campaign. William played only occasionally the following year though, but returned for the Christmas 1945 matches at home to Grimsby Town Reserves plus the two games against Ransome & Marles. He made three more appearances for Grantham at the start of the 1949/50 season, with games against Scarborough, Boston United and finally the London Road visit of Worksop Town in September.

Paul Buckthorpe

Seasons Played			
	League	~	1
	F.A. Cup	~	
1993/94	F.A. Trophy	~	
	League Cup	~	
	Lincs Cup	~	
	Total	~	1

Born 19/05/1954 at Lincoln. Former Brigg Town, Ruston Bucyrus, Lincoln City and Lincoln United player who arrived at Grantham as Assistant Manager to Allen Crombie. His only appearance for the club though, came off the substitute's bench in the October 1993 league fixture against Sutton Coldfield Town when he replaced Jeff Potts. Paul still lives in the Lincoln area and works as an engineer in the gas industry, but also coaches the Under-15 side for Lincoln City.

Budge

Seasons Played			
	League	~	1
	F.A. Cup	~	
1891/92	Other	~	
	Total	~	1

There is only one known appearance for this player, in the Midland Amateur Alliance 7-0 defeat at the hands of Notts County Rovers in March 1892, although he did play in a friendly against the same team two days later where Grantham managed to keep the score down to a single goal.

Bugg

Seasons Played			
	League	~	
	F.A. Cup	~	
1934/35	Lincs Cup	~	1
	Total	~	1

Was lucky enough to make his only appearance in the Lincolnshire County Cup Final replay at Boston United in May 1935, but unluckily ended up on the losing side. Quite an unusual name and surely an important game to be making a lone appearance. Another fact is that also playing for the opposition that day was a George Bugg. This makes me wonder whether our own player could possibly have been a brother of the Boston defender that kindly offered to make up the numbers.

Gary Bull

Seasons Played			
	League	~	125 (68)
	F.A. Cup	~	13 (2)
2000/01-02/03	F.A. Trophy	~	7 (1)
	League Cup	~	5 (2)
	Lincs Cup	~	8 (1)
	Total	~	158 (74)

Born 12/06/1966 at Tiptree. 'Bully', the cousin of the former England player, Steve Bull, began his career at Swindon Town and Paget Rangers, before moving to Southampton, although he failed to make a senior appearance there. Appearances did follow though after moves to Cambridge United, Barnet, during their GM Vauxhall Championship winning season, Nottingham Forest and loans to Birmingham City and Brighton, with a free transfer to Birmingham in December 1995. He then spent time at York City, Scunthorpe United and Wolverhampton Wanderers, although he failed to play for the First team with the latter. Gary finished with a career total of 307 senior League and Cup appearances and 78 goals, before his arrival at The Meres in time for the opening match of the 2000/01 season against Gainsborough Trinity in the County Cup. His first goal for Grantham came only two weeks later, in the league game at home to Dartford, with his initial hat-trick the same month against Histon. Gary played in every one of that season's games, including the FA Cup tie at Rushden & Diamonds when The Gingerbreads came so close to causing the shock of the round. He finished that first campaign as the club's highest scorer, netting 32 goals, including another hat-trick at the end of the season as the team defeated Sittingbourne 5-0. Just under a year later he matched this feat in the league fixtures against St Leonards and Chatham Town and as Grantham gained promotion back into Dr Marten's Premier League he finished that year with a tally of 25 goals. Gary's final season at The Meres began with an appearance in the Lincolnshire County Senior Cup Final against Scunthorpe United, whilst October saw him playing in the FA Cup Fourth Qualifying Round tie at Morecambe. His last goal for the club came at Bath City in April 2003, and a month later Gary appeared in the second County Cup Final of the season, this time against Gainsborough Trinity. The conclusion to his Grantham career came in the closing fixture of the 2002/03 season, at home to Moor Green, as the team secured Premier football for another year. Before long though, Manager John Wilkinson departed to Lincoln United, prompting Gary and many of his team-mates to follow.

Bull

Seasons Played			
	League	~	1
	F.A. Cup	~	2
1945/46	Lincs Cup	~	
	Total	~	3

Played for Grantham in the very first match after the Second World War, the Midland League visit of Gainsborough Trinity, as well as the first two FA Cup rounds against Basford United and Ollerton Colliery.

Bull

Seasons Played			
	League	~	1
	F.A. Cup	~	
1952/53	Lincs Cup	~	
	Total	~	1

Made only one appearance for Grantham, in the final game of the 1952/53 season at Lincoln City Reserves. Played in a different position to the previous entry, so doubtful to have been the same individual.

Peter Bulliman

Seasons Played			
	League	~	56
	F.A. Cup	~	5
1996/97-97/98	F.A. Trophy	~	10
	League Cup	~	6
	Lincs Cup	~	2
	Total	~	79

Goalkeeper who had previously played for Cogenhoe, Raunds Town, Wellingborough and Racing Club Warwick. His first game for The Gingerbreads came in the August 1996 league fixture at home to Solihull Borough and he then missed only two of that season's remaining matches. The following campaign he played a vital part in Grantham's domination of the league, although the 6-5 victory at home to Corby Town in December 1997 would turn out to be his final appearance, with Steve Sutton arriving at the club. Peter went on to rejoin Raunds Town and then moved to Ford Sports, Heyford and Sileby Rangers.

Andy Bullimore

Seasons Played			
	League	~	206 (26)
	F.A. Cup	~	12 (4)
1991/92-96/97	F.A. Trophy	~	16 (3)
	League Cup	~	11
	Lincs Cup	~	4
	Total	~	249 (33)

Born 30/11/1968 in Grantham. Started his career at Leicester City, but soon moved on to Pedigree Petfoods and Melton Town, from where he had a month's loan at Kettering Town. Following a supporter's recommendation to John Robertson, 'Bully' made his Grantham debut as a substitute in the February 1992 league fixture at Yate Town and scored his first goal for the club a month later in the home game against Hinckley Town. Despite eventually making so many appearances for the club, highlights for Andy's career are hard to find, as the club embarked upon a barren period. The FA Trophy ties against Witton Albion and Bishop Auckland in the 1993/94 season and the epic Blyth Spartans tie in the same competition three years later are all matches that Andy played a part in. From a personal point of view, he finished the 1995/96 season as the club's highest scorer, with 19 goals, including hat-tricks against Corby Town and Solihull Borough towards the end of the campaign. He scored another three strikes at the start of the following season, as the team started strongly in the FA Cup at Witham Town, but his last goal for Grantham came in the December 1996 FA Trophy tie against Buxton, following which he soon reverted back to his more customary defensive position. His final appearance for the club came in that season's closing fixture at Moor Green and Andy then went on to have two spells at Rothwell Town, with a period at King's Lynn in between. Off the field his claim to fame is that he once appeared on the BBC as 'Roy of the Rovers'!

Wayne Bullimore

Seasons Played			
	League	~	8
	F.A. Cup	~	1
1999/00	F.A. Trophy	~	
	League Cup	~	
	Lincs Cup	~	1
	Total	~	10

Born 12/09/1970 at Sutton-in-Ashfield. Former England Youth International and Manchester United Trainee who went on to sign for Barnsley, followed by a spell at Stockport County, (although he failed to make their First team), then Scunthorpe United, Bradford City, Doncaster Rovers, Peterborough United and Scarborough, amassing a total of 195 appearances and 17 goals to his name. He made his Grantham debut in the opening match of the 1999/00 season at home to Scunthorpe United in the County Cup, but only two months later had played his final game for the club, the 6-0 defeat of Northampton Spencer in the FA Cup. His footballing career soon continued though, and Wayne went on to play for Barrow, Emley & Wakefield, Stalybridge Celtic, Belper Town, Bradford Park Avenue and Stocksbridge Park Steels. In September 2004 he scored a hat-trick of penalties for the last of those clubs within a five minute spell, and yet still ended up on the losing side.

Bullivant

Seasons Played	League	~	16 (27)
	F.A. Cup	~	2 (1)
1912/13-13/14	Lincs Cup	~	1 (2)
	Other	~	1
	Total	~	20 (30)

Although undoubtedly a gifted striker, he was perhaps not as prolific as the above figures first show, due to the fact that many of the reports of this time reveal scorers only. Therefore if a player didn't score then there is no confirmation that he played. We do know though that he netted hat-tricks in 1912/13 league games against Stanton Hill Victoria and Kettering Town, plus four goals against Kettering the following year. Evidence does exist to show that he played in the March 1913 friendly against Queen's Park. With reference to the unusual surname, he could possibly be the former Gainsborough Trinity player, although with three different individuals of that name turning out in Division Two fixtures at The Northolme in the previous few seasons, there is no means of verifying which one.

Robin Bullock

Seasons Played	League	~	7
	F.A. Cup	~	
1956/57	Lincs Cup	~	
	Total	~	7

Made sporadic appearances for Grantham, starting with the opening game of the 1956/57 season at Scarborough and ending with the 6-0 thrashing of Denaby United the following January.

Mike Bundy

Seasons Played	League	~	10 (2)
	F.A. Cup	~	
1951/52-52/53	Lincs Cup	~	
	Total	~	10 (2)

Born 25/01/1928 at Trelewis, South Wales. Began his career playing for Treharris in the Welsh League, Division One, before spending time on the books at Birmingham City and Wolverhampton Wanderers. After representing Army and United Services teams, Mike played for Merthyr Tydfil, before coming to Grantham to take up a teaching position. He made his debut for the First team in the September 1951 Midland League game at Notts County Reserves and scored a week later at London Road when Lincoln City Reserves were defeated. He scored his only other goal for the club in his sole appearance the following season, the home game against Denaby United in April 1953, and following his departure from London Road continued to play for several local sides. Mike, who still lives in Grantham, is probably now more prominently known due to his years service with St Wulfram's School and athletics, both locally and internationally.

Frank Bungay

Seasons Played	League	~	31 (21)
	F.A. Cup	~	4 (5)
1936/37	Lincs Cup	~	2 (2)
	Other	~	
	Total	~	37 (28)

Born 1909 at Ecclesfield, near Sheffield. Frank was a centre-forward who began his career with his local village team, Ecclesfield Red Rose, with considerable success, even scoring fifteen times in one game. He then joined Mexborough Athletic and despite a trial with Bolton Wanderers, was soon signed by First Division side Huddersfield Town. He then played for Southend United, finally finishing with 5 goals in his 20 Football League appearances, before moving to Boston United, where he set a record by scoring in each of nine FA Cup games for them during the 1934/35 season. Frank made his debut for Grantham at the start of the 1936/37 season against Nottingham Forest Reserves and played in the majority of that season's games for the club. Notable achievements during his time at London Road include a hat-trick in the game against Rotherham United Reserves and a goal in the Lincolnshire Senior County Cup Final at home to his old team, Boston United. His final appearance for Grantham came in the April 1937 Midland League fixture at Rotherham United Reserves, meaning that Frank missed out on the replay of the previously mentioned County Final.

Jack Bunting

Seasons Played	League	~	12
	F.A. Cup	~	1
1920/21-21/22	Lincs Cup	~	1
	Other	~	
	Total	~	14

Born 1900 at Bingham. Goalkeeper who was only 16 years of age when he joined Grantham, although he had to wait several years to make his full debut, probably in the Spring of 1921. Later that year he joined Nottingham Forest, although he failed to make a First team appearance there and after a spell with Sneinton and the Nottinghamshire representative side he returned to London Road. In early 1922 he was transferred to Leicester City, but again failed to impress with a senior side, although after time at Boston he finally made eight appearances for Brighton & Hove Albion in the 1924/25 season. After being released by the South coast side, he moved to Mansfield Town, where he was renowned for his immaculate dressing standards, which included a silver tipped cane and his kit carried in a Gladstone bag.

Peter Burdett

Seasons Played	League	~	36 (6)
	F.A. Cup	~	1
1951/52-53/54	Lincs Cup	~	1
	Total	~	38 (6)

Right Winger who had previously played for Melton Town and made his Grantham debut in the September 1951 Midland League game at Scunthorpe & Lindsey United Reserves, missing only one of the remaining games that season. Although due to his position his goals are comparatively few and far between, one of those was the winning goal in the home game against Frickley Colliery. However the following season Peter made only four appearances and for 1953/54 had to wait for the closing game of the season to play in his final game, when Hull City Reserves arrived at London Road.

Archie Burgon

Seasons Played	League	~	34 (13)
	F.A. Cup	~	4 (4)
1931/32	Lincs Cup	~	1 (1)
	Other	~	
1934/35	Total	~	39 (18)

Born 28/03/1912 at Nottingham. Previously spent time at Colwick, Burton Joyce, Nottingham Forest and Newark Town, but unfortunately there is little information on his first spell at Grantham, other than details of his initial goal for the club in the Midland League match against Bradford Park Avenue Reserves in January 1932. Archie was transferred from Grantham to Notts County at the end of that campaign, but returned to London Road for the start of the 1934/35 season. He soon played in probably the high-light of the era, the 13-0 FA Cup victory against Rufford Colliery, scoring four goals himself, and from then on missed only two more matches before his final game for Grantham in December 1934 with the visit of Mexborough Athletic. Within days he had left to play for Tottenham Hotspur, but it was a short career at White Hart Lane as after only four appearances he had moved on to play for Wrexham and then Carlisle, although this last transfer came only two weeks before the outbreak of the Second World War. Archie finished his career with 43 goals in his 172 Football League appearances and notched up another six strikes in 15 cup ties during that time as well. After the end of hostilities he ran pubs in Nottingham and Metheringham, before working as a Highways Inspector up to his retirement. His surname is often spelt 'Burgeon' in Grantham match reports of the time. Died 1994 at Lincoln.

Anton Burke

Seasons Played	League	~	1
	F.A. Cup	~	
2003/04	F.A. Trophy	~	
	League Cup	~	
	Lincs Cup	~	
	Total	~	1

Midfield player who began his career at Notts County as a Trainee, before moving on to Radcliffe Olympic and made just one appearance for Grantham in the April 2004 league defeat at home to Havant & Waterlooville. Injuries during the Summer prevented Anton from joining the team after the break and following the departure of Dave Norton from The Meres, he was soon to follow, moving on to Gedling Town.

Steve Burke

Seasons Played			
	League	~	1
	F.A. Cup	~	
1988/89	F.A. Trophy	~	2
	League Cup	~	
	Lincs Cup	~	
	Total	~	3

Born 29/09/1960 at Nottingham. Former England Youth International who began his career as Nottingham Forest's youngest ever First team player, against Ayr United in the Anglo-Scottish Cup, whilst still attending Gedling School at the age of 16 years and 22 days. At the start of the 1979/80 season, he moved on to Queen's Park Rangers, which was followed by periods at Millwall, Notts County, Lincoln City, Brentford, Doncaster Rovers, West Bromwich Albion and Stockport County. After the end of his professional career, which had seen over 150 Football League appearances, he moved on to Shepshed Charterhouse, before being brought to London Road by his former team-mate, Martin O'Neill. His debut came in the December 1988 FA Trophy tie at home to Matlock Town, but after playing in the replay, his only other appearance for The Gingerbreads was as a substitute in the league game against Coventry Sporting the same month.

Kenny Burns

Seasons Played			
	League	~	18 (5)
	F.A. Cup	~	
1988/89	F.A. Trophy	~	1
	League Cup	~	3
	Lincs Cup	~	
	Total	~	22 (5)

Born 23/09/1953 in Glasgow. Defender who started out on Schoolboy forms with Glasgow Rangers, but began his Football League career at Birmingham City, before really making his name at Nottingham Forest. During his time there, he was part of the side that won the European Cup in 1979 and 1980, the Super Cup in 1980, the Division One Championship in 1978, the League Cup in 1978 and 1979 and Kenny himself was also voted Footballer of the Year in 1978. In fact he was so good that even Brian Clough sometimes failed to find derogatory comments for him. "The ugliest footballer I ever signed, was Kenny Burns", was the best that he could come up with after struggling to find fault with his on-the-field skills! Kenny then moved on to Leeds United, (twice on-loan plus one permanent transfer), Derby County, (on similar terms to his spell at Elland Road), Notts County and finally Barnsley. This saw the end of his professional career and a total of 74 goals in 539 senior fixtures, to go with his Scottish International record of 1 goal in 20 appearances. After time with IF Elfsborg in Sweden, Kenny then continued to play non-league football, firstly with Sutton Town and Stafford Rangers, before signing for his former colleague Martin O'Neill at Grantham. His debut came in the October 1988 league fixture at home to Bridgnorth Town, with his first goal for the club in the January victory over King's Lynn. Kenny even managed to net a hat-trick for Grantham in the 6-0 demolition of Banbury United, only a couple of weeks before his final appearance for the club when he was substituted by Danny Anderson in the league fixture at Hednesford Town. Kenny went on to have short spells at Alfreton Town and Gainsborough Trinity, before having three successful seasons as Player/Coach at Ilkeston Town, one of which saw him finish as the club's highest scorer. His career finally terminated at Oakham United, before he became Assistant Manager at Telford United in the Summer of July 1993. Kenny is currently licensee of a pub in Stoke-on-Trent, plus aiding the corporate department at Nottingham Forest.

Steve Burr

Seasons Played			
	League	~	2
	F.A. Cup	~	
1996/97	F.A. Trophy	~	
	League Cup	~	
	Lincs Cup	~	
	Total	~	2

Born 12/01/1961 at Birmingham. Forward who began his career at Lichfield and Atherstone Town, but it was whilst with Stafford Rangers, Macclesfield Town and after a £12,000 transfer to Hednesford Town, that Steve won medals for the Northern Premier League Championship, Northern Premier League Cup, Southern League Cup, Southern League Midland and Premier Championships, as well as the honour of playing in the 1989 FA Trophy Final. Towards the end of his career he played on loan at Winsford and then moved to Nuneaton Borough, before joining Grantham. However, he made only two appearances during his short stay at The Meres, the April 1997 league games against Bedworth United and Bilston Town, the first of which saw him finish on the bench and the second start on it. After a short spell playing for Shepshed Dynamo, Steve moved into management, taking charge of Nuneaton Borough, Hucknall Town and Northwich Victoria.

Larry Burrell

Seasons Played			
	League	~	151 (29)
	F.A. Cup	~	7 (1)
1985/86-90/91	F.A. Trophy	~	11 (2)
	League Cup	~	23 (3)
	Lincs Cup	~	4
	Total	~	196 (35)

Born 25/04/1963 at Nottingham. 'Buzz', as he was known to his team-mates, joined Grantham from Shepshed Charterhouse, scoring on his debut against Hednesford Town on Boxing Day 1985. He played in many of the games over the next year or so, including the April 1987 match at Bridgnorth Town when he covered for the unavailable goalkeeper, Linden Parslow, with Grantham narrowly losing 2-1. However, it wasn't until the arrival of Martin O'Neill at the beginning of the 1987/88 season that marked the start of Larry's almost permanent place in the side, a year which also saw a hat-trick for him in the March victory over Hednesford Town. After the opening game of the 1989/90 season though, Larry rejoined Shepshed, ending a successful spell at London Road which had even seen him having a trial with Manchester City. He returned to Grantham the following season, playing in virtually every game, including the club's final competitive match at London Road against Dudley Town in September 1990. His last goal for the club came in the April 1991 fixture at Alvechurch, with his final appearance in the season's closing game at Redditch United. He later played for Ilkeston Town, but by the 1996/97 season Larry had become joint-manager, along with his old Gingerbreads team-mate John Humphreys, at Dunkirk. A few gaps in his career commence after that, but at the moment he is still occasionally playing and is also Assistant Manager for the upcoming Santos FC in the Central Midlands League.

Burrows

Seasons Played			
	League	~	7
	F.A. Cup	~	
1905/06-06/07	League Cup	~	1
	Lincs Cup	~	
1910/11	Other	~	1
	Total	~	9

Goalkeeper who played for Grantham in the latter half of the 1905/06 season and was possibly still the number one choice the following year, but very few complete team-sheets are available to verify this. The 1910/11 Championship winning season seems to have seen Chambers as the club's first-choice 'keeper, although Burrows made at least one appearance that year in the League Cup Final defeat at the hands of West Bridgford Albion.

Brian Burton

Seasons Played			
	League	~	163 (13)
	F.A. Cup	~	10 (2)
1956/57-60/61	League Cup	~	3
	Lincs Cup	~	7 (4)
	Total	~	183 (19)

Born 28/12/1932 at Nottingham. Former Basford Boys Club and Nottingham Forest winger, making just three appearances during his six year spell at The City Ground, who made his Grantham debut in the August 1956 Midland League game against Scarborough. He was a prominent member of that season's side and scored his first goal for the club at Grimsby Town Reserves in September. The following year, although only scoring one goal, Brian missed just two games all season and by the end he had been rewarded with a Lincolnshire Senior Cup 'A' runners-up medal after the defeat by Gainsborough Trinity. The season of 1958/59 was a poor one for Grantham as they finished next to bottom in the Midland League and it was also a bad one for Brian as well, who missed several of the year's games. The following two years though, with Grantham in the Central Alliance, Brian was once again a near ever-present member of the side, up until his final match against Gresley Rovers in March 1961, with his career cut short due to an injury sustained in a motoring accident.

Burton

Seasons Played			
	F.A. Cup	~	
	Other	~	1
1878/79	Total	~	1

Played in only one friendly for Grantham, at Lincoln in January 1879.

Burton

Seasons Played			
	League	~	1
	F.A. Cup	~	
1925/26	Lincs Cup	~	
	Total	~	1

Available team-sheets show him making just the one appearance, in the club's first ever game in the Midland League, away at Mansfield Town in August 1925.

Dennis Butters

Seasons Played			
	League	~	43 (15)
	F.A. Cup	~	2
1966/67-67/68	Total	~	45 (15)

Born 21/8/1939 at Grantham. Played for Grantham Reserves in the mid 1950's and then went on to play for Grantham St John's, before returning to London Road. Dennis scored on his First team debut in the September 1966 Midland League game at home to Belper Town, and during that season played in just over half of the total number of matches, including the FA Cup games against Wimbledon and Oldham Athletic. The following year though, he made only 16 appearances, with his Grantham career ending after he was substituted in the March 1968 game against Arnold, following which he joined Boston FC. Dennis currently runs his own electrical contractor's company close to Grantham and is also Secretary of the Newark Alliance Cricket League.

Buttery

Seasons Played			
	League	~	5 (4)
	F.A. Cup	~	
1921/22	Lincs Cup	~	
	Total	~	5 (4)

Centre-Forward from the Lincoln area who it seems played the majority of his Grantham games at the end of 1921. We know that he scored twice in the Central Alliance game at Ilkeston United, plus achieved single strikes against New Hucknall Colliery and Retford Town.

Buxton

Seasons Played			
	League	~	1
	F.A. Cup	~	
1928/29	Lincs Cup	~	
	Other	~	
	Total	~	1

Goalkeeper who also played for the Reserve side as well as Ransome & Marles and made just the one appearance for the First team, when first choice 'keeper Stan Walker was unavailable. No information is available as to the particular match though.

Syd Bycroft

Seasons Played			
	League	~	60 (24)
	F.A. Cup	~	9 (5)
1931/32	Lincs Cup	~	2 (2)
	Other	~	
1934/35-35/36	Total	~	71 (31)

Born 19/02/1912 at Lincoln. Former Notts County player who made his Grantham debut in the Autumn of 1931 and scored his first goal for the club during the Newark Town game on Christmas Day of the same year. At the end of the season Syd was transferred from Grantham to Bradford City, but after time at Hull City and just over two years later, he had returned to London Road, still having failed to make his Football League debut. He took up the role of landlord at the Reaper Inn, only yards from the ground, and was soon playing for Grantham in the 13-0 thrashing of Rufford Colliery in the FA Cup, but also seems to have spent many long periods out of the side that year for some reason. In the 1935/36 season he is again absent from the Grantham side until October, although he had settled into the side once more by the arrival of Notts County in the FA Cup at the end of the following month. Syd scored a hat-trick in his final game for Grantham, the January 1936 match at home to Hull City Reserves, before a brief spell with Newark Town and then signing for Doncaster Rovers, where he also served as a policeman. Remarkably, he spent the next 16 years there and finished with 442 appearances to his name, although with around 100 of those being War-Time fixtures, officially he is not recognised as the club's record appearance holder. We also know that at some point he played for Spalding United, possibly at the end of his career, although he was certainly back at Doncaster Rovers to take up various coaching positions, plus briefly managing them in 1958. Syd continued to scout for the club after this and also ran his own decorating business in the South Yorkshire town. He then continued to work for the family's monumental company until the 1990's. Died 04/10/2004 at Doncaster.

Jason Callaby

Seasons Played			
	League	~	9
	F.A. Cup	~	3
1993/94	F.A. Trophy	~	2
	League Cup	~	2
	Lincs Cup	~	1
	Total	~	17

Born 28/11/1969 at Louth. Previously played for Lincoln United under Allen Crombie and followed his manager to The Meres in the Summer of 1993, making his debut in the County Cup victory over Lincoln City at the start of the season. Jason missed only a couple of games, up until his final appearance in the November league fixture at Bedworth United where he came off the bench to replace Paul Tomlinson. He went on to have the first of two spells at Stamford Town, followed by time at Spalding United, Boston Town and Holbeach United. Jason still turns out for Wiverton, but is heavily occupied with running a shop in Alford.

Peter Camm

Seasons Played			
	League	~	4
	F.A. Cup	~	4
1985/86	F.A. Trophy	~	
	League Cup	~	5
	Lincs Cup	~	
	Total	~	13

Born 24/07/1960 at Doncaster. Began his career in the Youth's side at Barnsley, before playing for Pilkingtons, Bentley Victoria and Goole Town. Peter made his debut for The Gingerbreads by coming on as substitute in the opening league fixture of the 1985/86 season against Sutton Coldfield Town. Although Peter played a part in most of the club's first games back in the Southern League, many of those appearances came from the bench, with the last of those in the Bill Dellow Cup defeat against Corby Town in October. Soon after this he returned to Goole Town and then played for Armthorpe and Doncaster Rovers Reserves. Peter still lives in the Doncaster area and works as an Executive Banking Manager for a national financial company.

Colin Campbell

Seasons Played			
	League	~	36
	F.A. Cup	~	2
1995/96	F.A. Trophy	~	2
	League Cup	~	2
	Lincs Cup	~	2
	Total	~	44

Full-Back who joined Grantham from Nottinghamshire side, Clipstone Miners Welfare, in time for the 1995/96 season's opening match at home to Lincoln City in the County Cup. Colin missed only a few of that season's games, although unfortunately for him it was a mid-table campaign which also saw early exits in the cup competitions. His final appearance for the club came in the closing fixture at Sutton Coldfield Town in May and after the Summer break Colin returned to Clipstone.

F. Campbell

Seasons Played			
1939/40	League	~	2
	Lincs Cup	~	
	Other	~	2
	Total	~	4

Goalkeeper who had previously played for Chesterfield, Walsall and Denaby United. His first game for Grantham came in the opening Midland League fixture of the 1939/40 season at Bradford Park Avenue Reserves, which finished in a 5-2 defeat for the visitors. He offered the club cover whilst Maurice Healey was unavailable and certainly played in some interesting matches, with that initial game being the lowest scoring match that he was involved in. Remarkably the following games included victories by 7-1 and 7-3 scorelines for Grantham, with his final appearance for the club ending after a 7-1 defeat at Peterborough United.

Ray Campbell

Seasons Played			
1988/89	League	~	8 (2)
	F.A. Cup	~	1
	F.A. Trophy	~	3
	League Cup	~	2
	Lincs Cup	~	
	Total	~	14 (2)

Born 03/10//1968 at Downpatrick, Northern Ireland. Former Northern Ireland International at various Youth levels, and Nottingham Forest, including time in their Central League winning side, Cambridge United and Hereford United winger. His Grantham debut came in the September 1988 league fixture at home to Bilston Town, with his goals coming in consecutive matches against Willenhall Town and Atherstone United. It was to be a short career at London Road for Ray though, with his final appearance for the club at the end of November in the home draw against Forest Green Rovers. He later returned to his home country and made appearances for Glentoran in the Irish League.

Steve Cant

Seasons Played			
1979/80	League	~	5 (3)
	F.A. Cup	~	
	F.A. Trophy	~	
	League Cup	~	
	Lincs Cup	~	
	Total	~	5 (3)

Born 16/05/1962 at Derby. Player signed from Nottingham Forest, whose father and grandfather were both Football League players, turning out for Derby County and Bolton Wanderers respectively. Steve scored on his Grantham debut, the October 1979 game at home to Worksop Town and although netting twice more, less than a month later the arrival of Netherfield for a league match signalled his final appearance. Although his career at London Road hadn't been helped with injuries, when he was competing to get in an attacking line that consisted of Robbie Cooke and Dennis Jenas things were never going to be easy. Steve soon left the club and went on to play for Alfreton Town. He still lives in the Nottingham area and currently works in the financial services industry.

Graham Capewell

Seasons Played			
1975/76-77/78	League	~	78 (1)
	F.A. Cup	~	4
	F.A. Trophy	~	5
	League Cup	~	5
	Lincs Cup	~	4 (1)
	Other	~	1
	Total	~	97 (2)

Born 19/08/1955 at Leicester. Twin brother of Martyn Capewell. Graham signed from Leicester City and made his Grantham debut in the October 1975 Southern League match at home to Chelmsford City. The following month he was involved in the club's FA Cup First Round Proper tie against Port Vale, whilst the return trip to Chelmsford City the following February marked Graham's first goal for the club. The following season he missed just one of the games, but the 1977/78 season, although starting with another goal in the County Cup tie at home to Gainsborough Trinity, would soon see the end of his Grantham career. The September 1977 league game at home to Redditch United was his last for The Gingerbreads and Graham went on to play for AP Leamington, Shepshed Charterhouse, Anstey Nomads and Birstall United. He still lives in the Leicester area and works in the printing industry.

Martyn Capewell

Seasons Played			
1975/76-77/78	League	~	76 (12)
	F.A. Cup	~	4
	F.A. Trophy	~	5
	League Cup	~	6
	Lincs Cup	~	2
	Other	~	1
	Total	~	94 (12)

Born 19/08/1955 at Leicester. Twin brother of Graham Capewell. Martyn also arrived at the club from Leicester City, but made his debut just before his sibling in the opening league match of the 1975/76 season at Bath City. His first goal for the club came in the November 1975 trip down to Dover, only a fortnight before he took part in Grantham's FA Cup tie against Port Vale. Although he was still the favoured person for the No 7 shirt the following season, Martyn had also spent several of the games on the substitute's bench and it was coming from this position in the September 1977 defeat at Hastings United that marked his final appearance for the club. No information is available about immediate clubs that he joined, but it is known that Martyn also moved from Anstey Nomads to Birstall Town around the same time as his brother. He also works in the printing industry and continues to live in the Leicester area.

Dave Carlin

Seasons Played			
1987/88	League	~	35
	F.A. Cup	~	2
	F.A. Trophy	~	1
	League Cup	~	5
	Lincs Cup	~	
	Total	~	43

Born 22/02/1969 at Derby. Son of the former Derby County player, Willie Carlin. Dave was a full-back who had spent three years at Nottingham Forest and made his Grantham debut in the August 1987 Westgate Insurance Cup tie against Corby Town. He was an important member of that season's side that came so close to promotion under Martin O'Neill's leadership and played right up until the season's closing fixture against Bilston Town. He moved on to Heanor Town and was still playing in the 2002/03 season for Mickleover Sports.

Matt Carmichael

Seasons Played			
1999/00	League	~	7
	F.A. Cup	~	1
	F.A. Trophy	~	1
	League Cup	~	1
	Lincs Cup	~	
	Total	~	10

Born 13/05/1964 in Singapore. Started his playing career in non-league football with Durrington, Salisbury City, Wycombe Wanderers, Bromley and Basingstoke Town, whilst in the Army, but upon leaving the Forces signed for Lincoln City. Matt then moved on to Scunthorpe United, before making appearances for Barnet, Preston North End, Mansfield Town, Doncaster Rovers and Darlington, including their 1996 Play-Off Final at Wembley. He then returned to non-league football and played for Aylesbury United, Ilkeston Town, in their 1997/98 runner's up spot in the league to Grantham, Stamford and Boston United. Matt came to Grantham as Assistant Manager but was promoted to Caretaker-Manager in September 1999 after Dave Gilbert's dismissal. He awarded himself ten consecutive appearances, starting with the FA Trophy tie against Hitchin Town and ending with the home game against Gloucester City. However, Matt was then sacked himself in December 1999 when Dr Gordon Hotson took over the club and he went on to make appearances for Stamford Town, Lincoln United, Wisbech Town, Little Oakley, Harwich & Parkeston, twice, Wivenhoe Town, Maldon Town and Halstead Town.

Roland Carpenter

Seasons Played			
1930/31	League	~	2
	F.A. Cup	~	
	Lincs Cup	~	
	Total	~	2

Born 16/08/1907 at Fulham. Local Goalkeeper who also played for Grantham St John's, Mansfield Town, Barnsley, Stamford and Ruston & Hornsby. He played in goal for Grantham in the two games when the first choice 'keeper Mobbs was unavailable, the

September 1930 Midland League game at home to Mansfield Town and the March 1931 visit of Bradford Park Avenue Reserves. Died 1992 at Grantham.

Steve Carr

Seasons Played			
	League	~	51 (14)
	F.A. Cup	~	1
1975/76-77/78	F.A. Trophy	~	1
	League Cup	~	3
	Lincs Cup	~	2
	Other	~	
	Total	~	58 (14)

Forward signed from Leicester City whose initial game for Grantham came in the February 1976 league fixture at Wimbledon, with his first goal for the club just under a month later against Stourbridge. After missing the first few games of the following season, he played in the majority of the remaining ones and this trend continued into the following campaign, although only up to the August 1977 defeat at Bedford Town which proved to be his final appearance for Grantham. The last that was known of Steve was in the early 1980's, when he was playing for Shepshed Charterhouse.

Roger Carter

Seasons Played			
	League	~	31 (1)
	F.A. Cup	~	
1958/59	Lincs Cup	~	1
	Total	~	32 (1)

Made his debut in the 1958/59 season's opening match at home to Goole Town and then played in most of that year's games, scoring his only goal for Grantham in the December Midland League game at home to Gainsborough Trinity. Roger's last appearance for Grantham came in the final game of the season away at Ashington.

Steve Carter

Seasons Played			
	League	~	1
	F.A. Cup	~	
1985/86	F.A. Trophy	~	
	League Cup	~	
	Lincs Cup	~	
	Total	~	1

Former Lincoln City Apprentice who made just one appearance for The Gingerbreads by replacing Craig Ramsay during the December 1985 league game against Mile Oak Rovers. Steve went on to play for Spalding United, Boston FC and Lincoln United.

Jabez Cartwright

Seasons Played			
	League	~	3
	F.A. Cup	~	
1911/12-12/13	Lincs Cup	~	
	Other	~	
	Total	~	3

Born circa 1885. Right-Back who would surely have made many more appearances than those quoted above for the club. Towards the end of the 1912/13 season he was transferred to Bolton Wanderers for a £110 fee, a huge sum in those days and yet he failed to make it into their First team. With reference to the unusual Christian name, he may be the same individual as a Jabez Cartwright, member of the Lincolnshire Regiment, formerly residing at Holbeach, who was killed at Flanders in the First World War on 04/10/1917.

Cartwright

Seasons Played			
	League	~	3 (1)
	F.A. Cup	~	
1907/08	Lincs Cup	~	3 (2)
	Other	~	2
1909/10	Total	~	8 (3)

Forward whose first known goal for Grantham is in the February 1908 Midland Amateur Alliance game at home to Mansfield Amateurs, although he had probably been playing for the side before this date. No records are available for 1908/09, but in the following campaign he seems to have played for only the first half of the season.

Cartwright

Seasons Played			
	League	~	1
	F.A. Cup	~	
1914/15	Lincs Cup	~	1 (1)
	Total	~	2 (1)

Defender, who may be a returning Jabez Cartwright, scoring his only known goal for the club in the November 1914 County Cup tie against Boston Swifts.

Matt Carvell

Seasons Played			
	League	~	101 (2)
	F.A. Cup	~	11
1999/00-01/02	F.A. Trophy	~	5
	League Cup	~	4
	Lincs Cup	~	3
	Total	~	124 (2)

Born 25/11/1974 at Burton-upon-Trent. Progressed through Gresley Rovers youth system into their First team, before joining Grantham at the start of the 1999/00 season, making his debut in the opening league game at Gloucester City. Matt missed only one of the remaining games during his first season at The Meres and at the same time scored his only two goals for the club, against Weymouth and Ilkeston Town. The 2000/01 campaign saw Matt play in the FA Cup tie at Rushden & Diamonds, and in his last year at Grantham he was an important member of the side that gained promotion back into the Dr Marten's Premier League. His final appearance came from the substitute's bench in the April 2002 league defeat of Rothwell Town and after the Summer break he joined Wealdstone in time for the start of the 2002/03 season.

Castle

Seasons Played			
	League	~	7 (1)
	Lincs Cup	~	1
1904/05-06/07	Other	~	
	Total	~	8 (1)

Was certainly a member of the reformed Grantham side right from their beginning, with evidence of him scoring in a pre-season friendly in October 1904 despite him generally playing in a defensive position. The following season he seems to have played very few, possibly just the one, match and amongst the very sparse records for 1906/07 we have his only competitive goal, in the first Midland Amateur Alliance game of the season at home to Long Eaton St Lawrence.

Ronald Cattell

Seasons Played			
	League	~	5
	F.A. Cup	~	1
1953/54	Lincs Cup	~	
	Total	~	6

Goalkeeper who played for the First team during September and October of 1953 whilst Ron Hewitt was unavailable, starting at home to Halifax Town Reserves and ending with Bradford Park Avenue Reserves. Ronald had the unfortunate task of picking the ball out of the net seven times when Grantham travelled over to Nottingham Forest Reserves, but he also had an excellent vantage point at that debut London Road game, when the Grantham forwards managed to score eleven goals...and just to keep Ronald busy, the visitors scored three as well!

Charles Cawthorne

Seasons Played			
	League	~	9
	F.A. Cup	~	
1954/55	Lincs Cup	~	
	Total	~	9

Defender who made occasional appearances for Grantham during the 1954/55 season, beginning with the 0-0 draw away at Scarborough in October and ending in the final Midland League game of the season at Boston United.

Martyn Chafer

Seasons Played			
	League	~	1
	F.A. Cup	~	
1987/88	F.A. Trophy	~	
	League Cup	~	1
	Lincs Cup	~	
	Total	~	2

Born 1964 at Nottingham. Midfielder who made just two appearances for Grantham, the October 1987 Westgate Insurance Cup tie at VS Rugby and the league game away at Sutton Coldfield Town the following Saturday. Martyn still lives in the Nottingham area and until the end of 2003 was Coach for Notts Alliance side AC Bulwell.

R. Challis

Seasons Played			
	League	~	7 (6)
	F.A. Cup	~	
1924/25	Lincs Cup	~	
	Other	~	2 (2)
1926/27	Total	~	9 (8)

Very few team-sheets are available for his first season with Grantham, so the first written confirmation is of him scoring twice in the Central Alliance subsidiary competition match at RAF Cranwell in January 1925. At the end of that season he was transferred to Sheffield Wednesday, although he failed to make their First team. He returned to Grantham, scoring in the first match, the RAF Shield game at home to RAF Cranwell in October 1926, but there are no records of him playing for the club after the New Year. He also played for Holwell Works, although at what stage in his career is not known.

Chalmers

Seasons Played			
	League	~	2
	F.A. Cup	~	
1932/33	Lincs Cup	~	
	Other	~	
	Total	~	2

Unfortunately no records are available to indicate which two games he played in during the 1932/33 season.

A. Chamberlain

Seasons Played			
	League	~	11 (3)
	F.A. Cup	~	
1934/35	Lincs Cup	~	1 (1)
	Total	~	12 (4)

Versatile player who had also played for Queen's Park Rangers Reserves and made his Grantham debut in January 1935 at the Bradford City Reserves Midland League match. He played in half of the remaining games of that season, scoring against Frickley Colliery, Gainsborough Trinity and Scunthorpe & Lindsey United, plus netting the equalising goal in the County Cup Final at home to Boston United in April 1935.

Collin Chamberlain

Seasons Played			
	League	~	96 (6)
	F.A. Cup	~	5
1977/78-79/80	F.A. Trophy	~	6
	League Cup	~	7
	Lincs Cup	~	3
	Total	~	117 (6)

Born 1957 at Nottingham. Former Great Britain and England Youth full-back, whose father, Derek Chamberlain, played for Aston Villa and Peterborough United, before moving into management at Stamford Town and Ilkeston Town. Collin started out at Derby County, playing many games in their Reserve side and also turning out for Don Revie's England XI in Peter Daniels Testimonial. His first game for Grantham came in the October 1977 Southern League match at home to Yeovil Town, taking over the defensive position that had recently been vacated by Graham Capewell. He played in the majority of that season's remaining fixtures, scoring his first goal for the club in February against Telford United. After the dejection of that season's relegation, Collin was to play a vital part in the Championship win a year later and appeared in that vital decider against Merthyr Tydfil in May 1979. As Grantham entered into the Northern Premier League it would prove to be his final season at London Road, with his last goal coming in the September victory over Workington Town and his final appearance in the April 1980 trip up to Morecambe. Collin went on to play for Shepshed Charterhouse the following season and is currently a successful businessman, last known to be living in London.

John Chamberlain

Seasons Played			
	League	~	10
	F.A. Cup	~	
1989/90	F.A. Trophy	~	
	League Cup	~	4
	Lincs Cup	~	
	Total	~	14

Born 25/10/1967 at Hucknall. Former Derby County, Shepshed Charterhouse, Eastwood Town and Corby Town player who made his Grantham debut in the Westgate Insurance League Cup tie against Nuneaton Borough in October 1989. After a promising start to his London Road career though, he soon found himself back on the substitute's bench for many of the games and the February 1990 league fixture at home to Sutton Coldfield Town would turn out to be his last with the club.

Chamberlain

Seasons Played			
	F.A. Cup	~	1
	Lincs Cup	~	
1887/88-88/89	Other	~	1 (1)
	Total	~	2 (1)

Scored on his debut in March 1888 during the friendly against Derby Junction, but then made only one other appearance, seven months later in an FA Cup encounter at Horncastle.

Chamberlain

Seasons Played			
	League	~	1
	F.A. Cup	~	
1920/21	Lincs Cup	~	
	Total	~	1

Available team-sheets show him making just the one appearance for Grantham, the final league fixture of the 1920/21 season at Hucknall Byron.

Chamberlain

Seasons Played			
	League	~	1 (1)
	F.A. Cup	~	
1925/26	Lincs Cup	~	
	Total	~	1 (1)

Outside-Right player, originally from the Manchester area, who played and scored in the November 1925 Midland League fixture at Alfreton Town.

J. Chambers

Seasons Played			
	League	~	1
	FA Amt. Cup	~	
1910/11	League Cup	~	
	Lincs Cup	~	1
	Other	~	
	Total	~	2

Goalkeeper, possibly the first choice of that championship winning season, but evidence is only available for two confirmed matches that he played in, the County competition against Gonerby Swifts and the Midland Amateur Alliance game at West Bridgford Albion.

Mick Chambers

Seasons Played			
	League	~	282 (36)
	F.A. Cup	~	22 (3)
1966/67-75/76	F.A. Trophy	~	21 (2)
	League Cup	~	35 (1)
	Lincs Cup	~	10
	Other	~	2
	Total	~	372 (42)

Born 13/06/1946 at Dinnington, Yorkshire. Midfielder, nicknamed 'Squeak' due to his quietness off the field, who had previously spent time on the books of Grimsby Town. He began his Grantham career on Boxing Day 1966, with the 1-1 draw against Gainsborough Trinity, but made only six other appearances before the end of the season. Mick scored his first goal for the club during the September

1967 Midland League match at Arnold, but still only managed a limited number of appearances in that campaign as well, although one of those was in the FA Cup 1st Round match against Altrincham. By the start of the 1968/69 season though, he had become one of the first names to be written down on the team-sheets and despite only adding two more goals to his name, he finished with a high-light of an FA Cup appearance against Swindon Town, plus a Midland League Cup winners medal. Once again Mick missed only a handful of games the following season, giving him another prominent FA Cup game, this time at Oldham Athletic. The early Seventies saw some of Grantham's greatest games and Mick was part of many of these, winning three league championship medals, another Midland League Cup medal, an FA Trophy Quarter-Final appearance against Yeovil Town, plus more FA Cup memories after encounters with Stockport County and Rotherham United. As Grantham entered into The Southern League, Mick's significance in the side continued and the next two seasons included another league title, plus FA Cup Proper ties against Bradford City, Hillingdon Borough and Rochdale, possibly the highlight of his Grantham career as he netted a hat-trick to assist the club to their biggest ever game, at home to Middlesbrough. The 1974/75 season saw Mick miss only two games all year, but it also saw his final goal for the club, in the April victory over Weymouth. Although he played in the first twelve fixtures of the following season, the September 1975 match against Tonbridge would be his last for the club. Mick then moved on to Matlock Town after a £300 transfer, at the time a record fee paid by the Derbyshire club. In April 1993 Mick returned to Grantham, when a team made up of former Gingerbreads played against an 'Entertainers' side at The Meres. Died 17/08/1994 in Rotherham.

Chambers

Seasons Played			
	F.A. Cup	~	
	Other	~	1
1877/78	Total	~	1

Played in just the one game for Grantham, the February 1878 friendly at Nottingham Castle.

Chambers

Seasons Played			
	League	~	2 (1)
	Lincs Cup	~	
1904/05	Other	~	
	Total	~	2 (1)

The only evidence available for this first season back after reforming shows two appearances for this player, in the Midland Amateur fixtures against Notts Magdala Amateurs and Notts Magdala, scoring his only goal in the first of those games.

Chambers

Seasons Played			
	League	~	1 (1)
	F.A. Cup	~	
1925/26	Lincs Cup	~	
	Total	~	1 (1)

No records are available for this player other than the match report that lists him as scoring in the Midland League game at Worksop Town in February 1926.

Chantry

Seasons Played			
	League	~	3
	Lincs Cup	~	1
1893/94-94/95	Other	~	3
	Total	~	7

Goalkeeper who played in the Grantham Minor Cup Final in April 1894 but could have played for Grantham earlier in that season and seems to have played in the majority of the games the following year as well.

Chaplin

Seasons Played			
	League	~	1
	F.A. Cup	~	
1948/49	Lincs Cup	~	
	Total	~	1

Made just the one appearance for Grantham, with the visit of Nottingham Forest Reserves to London Road in September 1948.

Stuart Chapman

Seasons Played			
	League	~	91 (5)
	F.A. Cup	~	10
1979/80-84/85	F.A. Trophy	~	6
	League Cup	~	7 (1)
	Lincs Cup	~	6
	Other	~	4
	Total	~	124 (6)

Born circa 1960 in Aden. Started his career as a Schoolboy at Nottingham Forest, from where he gained his nick-name 'Sammy' after his slightly more illustrious name-sake at the same club. After arriving at Grantham he became Captain of the Youth Team that won the Lincolnshire Inter Cup in 1980, but soon progressed into the First team. His debut came in the April 1980 league victory over Oswestry Town, when he came off the bench to replace Barry Shaw, and by the start of the following season he had become a near permanent member of Grantham's team, scoring his first goal for the club during the opening league fixture at Southport. Stuart played in that season's County Cup Final against Lincoln City, but sadly for him he missed out on the Redmayne Trophy tie against the European Champions. It is doubtful whether Stuart's appearance in the same competition a year later would have been any compensation though, as the November 1981 game against Nottingham Forest saw several of their stars missing and as for Stuart, it was one of the rare appearances that he was offered that year. After playing in the October 1982 Lincolnshire County Senior Cup Final victory over Scunthorpe United and the FA Cup final qualifying round at Telford United, highlights became sparse. Stuart's final goal for Grantham came in the April 1984 league game at home to Marine, with his last appearance the following September, when he came off the bench to replace Mick Daley in the FA Cup tie against Halesowen Town. He went on to play for Heanor Town, but several years later became part of the management team at Harrowby United. Sammy is still involved with local football and lives close to Nottingham.

Chapman

Seasons Played			
	League	~	4
	Lincs Cup	~	
1931/32	Other	~	
	Total	~	4

Local full-back who made his debut in September 1931 during the Midland League game at Mansfield Town Reserves. Unfortunately there are no records to ascertain which other matches he played in.

W. Chappell

Seasons Played			
	League	~	1
	F.A. Cup	~	
1920/21	Lincs Cup	~	
	Other	~	
	Total	~	1

Former Grantham St John's full-back with only one known appearance for our club, the Central Alliance visit of Shirebrook in April 1921.

Arnold Charlesworth

Seasons Played			
	League	~	2
	F.A. Cup	~	
1955/56	Lincs Cup	~	
	Total	~	2

Born 06/07/1930 at Sheffield. Previously played for Penistone Church, Boston United, West Bromwich Albion after a £750 transfer, Rotherham United and York City. Arnold made two appearances for Grantham, against Grimsby Town Reserves and Wisbech Town in December 1955 whilst Alan Clay was unavailable.

Dave Charlesworth

Seasons Played			
	League	~	3
	F.A. Cup	~	1
1989/90	F.A. Trophy	~	1
	League Cup	~	
	Lincs Cup	~	1
	Total	~	6

Made his debut in the opening match of the 1989/90 season against Spalding United in the County Cup, with his final appearance only two months later at Racing Club Warwick. Dave is also known to have spent part of his career at Alfreton Town, although at what point is not known.

Reg Chester

Seasons Played			
1938/39	League	~	18 (7)
	F.A. Cup	~	
	Lincs Cup	~	
	Total	~	18 (7)

Born 21/11/1904 at Long Eaton. Began his career with Long Eaton Rangers and after having trials with Notts County and Mansfield Town went on to Peterborough & Fletton United and Stamford Town. He became the Lincolnshire club's most famous export when he went on to play for Aston Villa, Manchester United, Huddersfield Town and Darlington, finishing his professional career with 52 goals in 162 appearances. He then moved on to Arnold Town and Woodborough United, with his first game for Grantham in a friendly against Grantham St John's in January 1939. Reg's competitive debut came a week later at home to Nottingham Forest Reserves, with his first goal for the club coming in the 9-1 demolition of Denaby United in March. His final appearance for Grantham came in the season's closing fixture at Nottingham Forest Reserves, therefore missing only one game during his short time at London Road. His surname is sometimes spelt 'Chesters'. Died 1977 at Nottingham.

Childs

Seasons Played			
1885/86	F.A. Cup	~	
	Lincs Cup	~	
	Other	~	1
	Total	~	1

Made only one appearance for Grantham, in the November 1885 friendly at Sleaford.

Chilvers

Seasons Played			
1929/30	League	~	1
	F.A. Cup	~	
	Lincs Cup	~	
	Other	~	
	Total	~	1

Only played in the Midland League game at home to Worksop Town in August 1929.

Chivers

Seasons Played			
1932/33	League	~	1
	F.A. Cup	~	
	Lincs Cup	~	
	Total	~	1

Centre-Forward whose single known appearance is the February 1933 Midland League fixture at Frickley Colliery.

Christopher

Seasons Played			
	League	~	
	Other	~	1
1893/94	Total	~	1

With very few records available for this period, the only known game that he played in was the Grantham Minor Cup Final at the end of the 1893/94 season.

Graham Clapham

Seasons Played			
1973/74-76/77	League	~	87 (10)
	F.A. Cup	~	6 (2)
	F.A. Trophy	~	11
	League Cup	~	11
	Lincs Cup	~	4
	Other	~	
	Total	~	119 (12)

Born 23/09/1947 at Lincoln. Began his career as an Apprentice at Newcastle United, before moving on to Sunderland, Shrewsbury Town and Chester City, making 128 appearances in The Football League, scoring ten goals, plus notching up another three strikes in 12 FA Cup and League Cup ties during that time. He joined Grantham at the start of the 1973/74 season, making his debut in the August 1973 League Cup tie against Stourbridge and although he did appear in the FA Cup replay against Rochdale, replacing Ernie Nixon, the rest of the games in that memorable season's competition he was forced to view from the bench. By March of 1974 though, Graham had established himself more in the side, scoring his first goal for the club in the league fixture at Barnet. After the following season, November 1975 saw appearances for Graham in both the First Round of the FA Cup against Port Vale and the replay, whilst a month later, at home to Wealdstone, he scored what would turn out to be his last goal for Grantham. His final appearance came in the opening league game of the 1976/77 season at Redditch United. Graham still lives in the Lincoln area and his son, Jamie, currently has a successful playing career with Birmingham City.

Roly Clapham

Seasons Played			
1938/39	League	~	33
	F.A. Cup	~	1
	Lincs Cup	~	2
	Total	~	36

Midfielder, previously with Boston United and Scarborough, who made his Grantham debut in the first game of the 1938/39 season at Shrewsbury Town. Roly played in every match until a lean spell towards the end of the season, with the April 1939 Midland League visit of Rotherham United Reserves marking his final game. He signed for Gainsborough Trinity after The Second World War and played for them in the first Midland League fixture of the 1945/46 season against Grantham at London Road.

Craig Clark

Seasons Played			
1997/98	League	~	21
	F.A. Cup	~	
	F.A. Trophy	~	8
	League Cup	~	3
	Lincs Cup	~	1
	Total	~	33

Nottingham born defender, formerly with Radcliffe Olympic, Dunkirk, Ilkeston Town and Arnold Town. His first game for Grantham came in the 1997/98 season's opening fixture against Gainsborough Trinity in the County Cup. Craig played in every match of that season's memorable run in the FA Trophy, including the Quarter-Final tie against Southport and also the 6-0 thrashing of their nearest rivals for the Championship, Ilkeston Town. His last game for Grantham was when he came off the bench in the season's closing fixture at home to Stourbridge, a draw which confirmed the Dr Marten's Midland League title. Craig went on to play for Stamford Town, King's Lynn, had second spells at Arnold Town and Radcliffe Olympic, then joined Glapwell and Gedling Town.

Derek Clark

Seasons Played			
1955/56	League	~	3
	F.A. Cup	~	
	Lincs Cup	~	
	Total	~	3

Played in three games during September 1955, the Midland League match at Mansfield Town Reserves and the two games against King's Lynn. Could be the same Derek Clark that was playing for Boston United in the 1945/46 season.

Clark

Seasons Played			
1905/06-07/08	League	~	11 (5)
1909/10	Lincs Cup	~	1 (1)
	Other	~	4 (1)
	Total	~	16 (7)

Player who was certainly evident in the 1905/06 pre-season friendly against Notts Insurance, but it is difficult to pin-point his first competitive game or even goal. Although very few team-sheets are available for this period, his name appears virtually every time, pointing towards him being a principal member of the side right up until his last game for the club. This was in the final Midland Amateur League fixture of the 1909/10 season, at Boots Athletic, during which he scored. Baring in mind that there are no records for 1908/09, he most likely played for five seasons with Grantham.

Clark

Seasons Played			
1931/32	League	~	2
	Lincs Cup	~	
	Other	~	
	Total	~	2

Played twice for Grantham, but no records are available to show which games.

Anton Burke

Syd Bycroft

Jabez Cartwright

Matt Carvell

Mick Chambers

Stuart Chapman

Graham Clapham

E. Clarke

Graham Clarke

Jamie Clarke

Alan Clay

John Cockerill

Andy Cole

David Cole

Allan Collin

Darren Collins

David Clarke

Seasons Played			
	League	~	1
	F.A. Cup	~	
1958/59	Lincs Cup	~	
	Total	~	1

Made just one appearance for The Gingerbreads, in the October 1958 Midland League game at Stockton.

E. Clarke

Seasons Played			
	League	~	3
	F.A. Cup	~	
1919/20-20/21	Lincs Cup	~	1
	Other	~	
	Total	~	4

Goalkeeper who was also in the Army and stationed near to Grantham, making him available to cover Grantham's first choice 'keeper, Albert Humphreys. He played his first game for the club in December 1919 when Leicester City Reserves arrived for a Central Alliance fixture, but made many appearances for that season's Reserves side that won the Grantham League Division One. There is only one known appearance for the First team in the following season, the January 1921 Lincolnshire County Cup tie at home to Scunthorpe & Lindsey United, although he may have played occasionally until the arrival of Bunting in the Spring.

Graham Clarke

Seasons Played			
	League	~	180
	F.A. Cup	~	15
1958/59-64/65	League Cup	~	3
	Lincs Cup	~	10
	Total	~	208

Rotherham based goalkeeper who began his Grantham career by deputising for the unavailable Tony Warrington in the October 1958 game at Frickley Colliery, but by the start of the following season he had made the position his own. In April 1961 he helped Grantham to win the Lincolnshire Senior Cup 'A' at Gainsborough Trinity, whilst the following year, a season in which Graham was missing from only two of the league games, saw highlights of an FA Cup First Round Proper game at Brierley Hill Alliance and another County Cup victory, this time Boston United coming away defeated. After a rather uneventful subsequent season, the Summer 1963 arrival of Jimmy Rayner saw the start of Grantham's first Midland League Championship season. Graham missed the four matches during November but was there for the rest of the season to rightly deserve his medal, despite many games having very little to do! The following year he once again played in every game until what would turn out to be the completion of his Grantham career, the match at Stamford in January 1965. Following this he was replaced with Brian Thompson, but Graham must certainly have had some interesting memories, having played in some Grantham teams that had varied from the woefully poor to the absolute best.

Jamie Clarke

Seasons Played			
	League	~	60 (12)
	F.A. Cup	~	5 (3)
2002/03-04/05	F.A. Trophy	~	5 (2)
	League Cup	~	2 (1)
	Lincs Cup	~	3 (1)
	Total	~	75 (19)

Born 07/03/1982 at Loughborough. Former Ilkeston Town and King's Lynn striker brought to Grantham after a £500 transfer. He made his debut in the August 2002 County Cup tie at Lincoln City and scored his first goal for the club the following month at Tiverton Town. Jamie had a trial at Crewe Alexandra during the Autumn of 2002 and played for The Gingerbreads in the final qualifying round of the FA Cup at Morecambe. But just before another trial, this time at Middlesbrough, he broke his leg in the FA Trophy tie against Hinckley, a game in which he was also being watched by the England Semi-Professional squad selectors. After nearly a year out of the game he returned to the side in September 2003, but after watching the club's FA Cup First Round tie against Leyton Orient from the bench, it became apparent that he needed match fitness and with this in mind he spent a month on loan at Corby Town. He once again returned to The Meres for the Christmas fixtures, but as Grantham dramatically slid down the table, Jamie struggled to find the talent that had made him so feared in the Dr Marten's League, although he did appear, and score, in the first ever Lincolnshire County Shield Final when Grantham beat Gainsborough Trinity in March 2004. Jamie joined up with Grantham's former Manager, John Wilkinson, at Lincoln United for the start of the 2004/05 season, but only months later he had returned to The Meres. Once again though he failed to live up to his previous reputation and he scored his last goal for The Gingerbreads in January 2005 at home to King's Lynn, with his final appearance only days later against the same side in the Southern League Cup. At the end of the month Jamie left the club and went on to play for Harrowby United.

Alan Clay

Seasons Played			
	League	~	370 (10)
	F.A. Cup	~	25 (3)
1946/47-47/48	League Cup	~	1
	Lincs Cup	~	22
1949/50-62/63	Total	~	418 (13)

Born 13/11/1920 at Sleaford. Brother of Jim Clay and a former Sleaford Town player who made his debut for Grantham in January 1947 at home to Barnsley Reserves, scoring his first goal just over two months later at Peterborough United. His first season at London Road ended with Alan appearing in both the Lincolnshire Senior Cup Final games against Gainsborough Trinity, although unfortunately The Gingerbreads were defeated 4-1 in the replay. The following season he made only 13 appearances all year and even after his return in 1949 he still found it difficult to establish a permanent place in the side, although he did manage to force himself into the side that played in the County Cup Final against Boston United. By the start of the 1950/51 season though, Alan had become a significant member of the side, despite missing from several of the early matches a year later. The next two seasons saw Alan appear in consecutive County Cup Finals, the first of which ended in defeat against Spalding United, but finally, in April 1954, The Gingerbreads emerged victorious after beating Gainsborough Trinity 3-0. However, after this he would be playing for a Grantham team that would have precious little to cheer about, until another County Cup Final appearance in April 1958 when Gainsborough Trinity managed to gain revenge, although from a personal level he was obviously chalking up a vast number of games. This figure started to slow during the 1958/59 season, when Alan only made 9 appearances and as Grantham moved into the Central Alliance League the appearances were still stacking up, but obviously at a slower rate. He managed to win a County Cup winner's medal again in April 1961 after another Final against Gainsborough, only days after what would eventually turn out to be his final goal for the club, at home to Spalding United. In a busy time for Alan, the following week saw his testimonial, when Nottingham Forest sent a side over to London Road. Amazingly after the Summer break he finally played in the First Round Proper of the FA Cup, as Grantham travelled over to Brierley Hill Alliance in November 1961 and at the end of that campaign he won yet another Lincolnshire County Cup winner's medal, this time with a Grantham victory over Boston United. Finally Alan made his last, and only appearance of the season, in the December 1962 Midland League game at home to Retford Town. He continued to assist at the club though, generally with the Reserves side, but did make one more appearance in the invitational Bourne Hospital Cup in May 1966, nearly twenty years after that first game, and at the age of 45. Alan continued to live in Sleaford, working in the local government offices, until his retirement. Died circa 1981 at Sleaford.

Jim Clay

Seasons Played			
	League	~	2
	F.A. Cup	~	
1951/52-52/53	Lincs Cup	~	
	Total	~	2

Born 29/01/1927 at Sleaford. Younger brother of Alan Clay and like his sibling had also played for Sleaford. Jim was a defender who made appearances for Grantham in the December 1951 Midland League fixture at Nottingham Forest Reserves and the match at Peterborough United in August of 1952. He went on to become a prominent member of the Sleaford Amateurs team, firstly playing, then eventually moving into the Treasurer's position, which he held for thirty years, with a time as Chairman as well. Jim was a well known and popular figure in his home town, working as a local government officer, and featured in many local events including the popular Festival of Sport and Sleaford Show. He is remembered with the Jim Clay Memorial Trophy which is played annually in the town, generally between veteran teams from Sleaford and Lincoln. Died 25/01/1996 at Sleaford.

Clay

Seasons Played			
	League	~	5 (1)
1912/13-13/14	F.A. Cup	~	2 (1)
	Lincs Cup	~	
	Other	~	
	Total	~	7 (2)

Due to the lack of available records, this individual probably made many more appearances than quoted above. The first recorded goal that we have for him is in the FA Cup game at Notts Rangers in September 1913, followed by another the following month during a Central Alliance match at home to Long Eaton.

Jack Clayton

Seasons Played			
	League	~	28
1934/35	F.A. Cup	~	5 (1)
	Lincs Cup	~	2 (1)
	Total	~	35 (2)

Born 23/04/1907 at Mansfield. Half-Back who had previously played for Loughborough Corinthians, winning a Leicestershire Senior Cup winner's medal whilst there, Chesterfield, Wrexham, where he was part of their 1931 Welsh Cup winning side, Carlisle United and Mansfield Town, finishing with two goals in his 104 senior appearances. Jack made his Grantham debut in the first home game of the 1934/35 season against Notts County Reserves and played in many of that season's matches, including the club's record 13-0 victory in the FA Cup tie against Rufford Colliery, with his first goal for Grantham in the following round at home to Basford United. Jack missed the last couple of games of that season though, including the replay of the County Cup Final, leaving his final match for Grantham as the April Midland League fixture at Rotherham United Reserves. The following season he went on to play for Gainsborough Trinity.

Chris Cleaver

Seasons Played			
	League	~	10 (3)
1998/99	F.A. Cup	~	
	F.A. Trophy	~	
	League Cup	~	
	Lincs Cup	~	
	Total	~	10 (3)

Born 24/03/1979 at Hitchin. Began his career as a Schoolboy at Norwich City, before moving to Peterborough United, where he scored three times in 36 First team appearances. He then joined Grantham after an initial loan period, scoring in his first game in January 1999 at home to Burton Albion. After goals against Gresley Rovers and Rothwell Town his career at The Meres turned out to last less than two months, with the draw against Dorchester Town his final appearance. He went on to play for King's Lynn, Cambridge City, from where he will be forever remembered and despised by Grantham fans due to his unsporting gesture of playing on after an injury, then a move over to Finland with TP Seinajoki, FF Jaro and AC Allianssi.

Clelland

Seasons Played			
	League	~	1
1955/56	F.A. Cup	~	
	Lincs Cup	~	
	Total	~	1

Only made one appearance for Grantham, the September 1955 Midland League game at home to King's Lynn.

Clements

Seasons Played			
	F.A. Cup	~	6
	Lincs Cup	~	8
1885/86-87/88	Other	~	27 (1)
	Total	~	41 (1)

Made his Grantham debut in the October 1885 friendly at Peterborough and immediately became a prominent member of the side. He scored his only known goal for the club in February 1887 during a friendly at home to Notts Waverley, which seems to have been one of his final games.

Clements

Seasons Played			
	Lincs Cup	~	1
	Other	~	2
1889/90	Total	~	3

Could be the same individual as the previous entry, but played a more defensive role. He made appearances in matches against Radcliffe, Lincoln Rangers and Grantham Rovers during the 1889/90 season.

Clements

Seasons Played			
	League	~	1
	F.A. Cup	~	
1923/24	League Cup	~	
	Lincs Cup	~	
	Other	~	
	Total	~	1

Forward who had previously played for Lenton and appeared for Grantham in the April 1924 Central Alliance game at Coalville Swifts.

Clements

Seasons Played			
	League	~	7
	F.A. Cup	~	2
1926/27	Lincs Cup	~	
	Other	~	
	Total	~	9

Possibly the same individual as the previous entry, although doubtful due to him playing in a completely different position. He was certainly playing for Grantham in the opening match of the 1926/27 Midland League season and appeared in every game until the FA Cup match at Newark Town in October, after which he seems to have left London Road.

Mark Clifford

Seasons Played			
	League	~	6
	F.A. Cup	~	
2004/05	F.A. Trophy	~	
	League Cup	~	
	Lincs Cup	~	
	Total	~	6

Born 11/09/1977 at Nottingham. Made five appearances for Mansfield Town, before moving on to Ilkeston Town, Stamford, Ilkeston once more, Boston United, (after a £7,500 transfer), where he helped them to the Conference title and entry into The Football League. Mark gained another nine appearances at York Street during their maiden season in Division Three, played once for Chester City, (on-loan), and then moved to Nuneaton Borough, initially on-loan before a permanent transfer in the Summer of 2003. It was from Nuneaton that Mark came to Grantham on-loan, making six appearances at the start of the 2004/05 season, beginning with the home fixture against Bath City and ending in September at Halesowen Town. Mark returned to Nuneaton, but a month later he had rejoined Ilkeston Town. It was also around this time that he featured in Channel 4's *Property Ladder* television programme, converting a building in Nottingham.

Clifton

Seasons Played			
	League	~	20
	F.A. Cup	~	1
1923/24	League Cup	~	1
	Lincs Cup	~	1
	Other	~	2
	Total	~	25

Former Newark Athletic goalkeeper who played in many, possibly every match of the 1923/24 season.

Roy Clipson

Seasons Played			
	League	~	1
	Lincs Cup	~	
1939/40	Other	~	
	Total	~	1

Born 18/04/1909 at Lincoln. Defender who had previously played for Newark Town, Bury, Bristol City, Altrincham and Rochdale, making 55 Football League appearances. Over two years later he played just once for Grantham against Newark Town in what turned out to be the last Midland League game before the competition was cancelled in September 1939 due to European conflict. His surname is incorrectly spelt 'Clipstone' in the team-sheet. Died 1970 at Sleaford.

Clough

Seasons Played			
	League	~	2 (1)
1894/95	Lincs Cup	~	
	Other	~	
	Total	~	2 (1)

Midfielder who played in the first match of the 1894/95 Grantham League season at Rovers Colts, and scored in the December return match, but there are no records of him playing in any other games.

Clutterbuck

Seasons Played			
	League	~	
	F.A. Cup	~	1
1890/91-91/92	Lincs Cup	~	
	Other	~	3 (2)
	Total	~	4 (2)

Played in three friendly games during the 1890/91 season, against Nottingham Forest Reserves, Notts St George, where he scored twice, and the home game against Langley Mill. However, he made his final appearance for the club only a few months later, in the FA Cup match against Gainsborough Trinity. He was most likely one of the Clutterbuck brothers who were living at West Parade, Grantham, during the 1881 census.

Ian Coaten

Seasons Played			
	League	~	1
	F.A. Cup	~	
1966/67	Total	~	1

Born 04/06/1948 in Grantham. Former Woolsthorpe Rovers and Grantham Youth Centre player who made his only appearance for the First team when he came on as substitute to replace Roy Banham during the September 1966 Midland League game at Lincoln City Reserves. Ian went on to play for Grantham St John's and he still lives locally.

Arthur Cobb

Seasons Played			
	League	~	14
	F.A. Cup	~	
1946/47	Lincs Cup	~	
1951/52	Total	~	14

Played in the Midland League game at Notts County Reserves in January 1947, but then had to wait nearly five years for his next game, at Bradford City Reserves. Although Arthur played in several of that 1951/52 season's games, they were in a wide variety of positions as he invariably filled the place of a more regular player that was out injured. He made his last appearance for the club in February 1952 at Scunthorpe & Lindsey United Reserves.

Cobb

Seasons Played			
	League	~	2 (1)
	Lincs Cup	~	
1904/05	Other	~	
	Total	~	2 (1)

Very little information available on this player, other than that he seemed to play towards the end of the 1904/05 season, in Midland Amateur Alliance games against Derby Thornhill and Burton Casuals, scoring his only goal in the latter.

Cockburn

Seasons Played			
	League	~	1
	F.A. Cup	~	
1927/28	Lincs Cup	~	
	Total	~	1

Goalkeeper who replaced the unavailable Stan Walker in the April 1928 Midland League match at Loughborough Corinthians and managed to keep a clean sheet.

John Cockerill

Seasons Played			
	League	~	3
	F.A. Cup	~	3 (1)
1983/84	F.A. Trophy	~	
	League Cup	~	1
	Lincs Cup	~	
	Total	~	7 (1)

Born 12/07/1961 at Grimsby. Son of the Grimsby Town legend, Ron Cockerill, and a former Boston FC player who signed for Grantham from Lincoln City. He made his debut in the September 1983 league game at home to Mossley and scored his only goal for the club a week later during the FA Cup tie against Rushall Olympic. After six appearances for Grantham, John made a brief return to Lincoln where he still failed to gain a First team place and then returned one more time to London Road to play in the February 1984 League Cup replay against Hyde United. He was soon released from Sincil Bank and went on to make appearances for King's Lynn, Alfreton Town and Stafford Rangers, before making over 100 appearances for Grimsby Town between 1988 and 1992. After the end of his playing career John continued working there and later became the club's Assistant Manager, although his resulting departure in December 2001 led to a lengthy court tribunal to decide whether he had resigned or was dismissed unfairly.

Frank Cockman

Seasons Played			
	League	~	4
1891/92	F.A. Cup	~	
	Other	~	3 (2)
	Total	~	7 (2)

Born circa 1865 in Grantham. An auctioneer's clerk by profession who made his debut for Grantham in the local Charity Cup game at home to Notts St George in November 1891. Frank played infrequently though for the rest of the season, but did score twice in the 12-0 Newark Charity Cup thrashing of Radcliffe in January 1892. Died January 1913 in Grantham.

Codd

Seasons Played			
1878/79-79/80	F.A. Cup	~	
1884/85-85/86	Lincs Cup	~	
1887/88	Other	~	10 (1)
	Total	~	10 (1)

Possibly one of the Arthur or Reuben Codd brothers who were joiners in the town during this period, or Samuel Codd who at one point was the High Bailiff of the Grantham County Court. He first played for Grantham in the February 1879 friendly held at Spilsby, and made appearances in several of the games over the next year until he scored his only goal for the club at Burghley Park in February 1880. There are no records of him playing for the next few years, but he seems to have returned to the club in January 1885 to play in the friendly at home to Notts Waverley. Following this he once again made sporadic appearances although always in friendlies, until his final match against Newark Town in March 1888.

Don Codling

Seasons Played			
	League	~	8 (3)
	F.A. Cup	~	
1954/55	Lincs Cup	~	
	Total	~	8 (3)

Born 06/09/1928 at Leeds. Previously spent 12 years with The Navy, guesting for several teams during that time, including Littlehampton Town and Gravesend & Northfleet. After coming out of service, Don made all his appearances for Grantham in the first few months of the 1954/55 season, starting with the fixture at Denaby United and ending with the home game against Hull City Reserves. By then Don had scored during the visit of Rotherham United Reserves, and a couple of weeks later netted twice when Bradford City Reserves came to London Road. He then moved on to Ransome & Marles and after the end of his playing career worked in the aircraft industry and at Holwell Works. Don is now retired and still lives close to Grantham.

Codling

Seasons Played			
	League	~	29
	F.A. Cup	~	2
1931/32-33/34	Lincs Cup	~	1
	Other	~	1
	Total	~	33

Defender who played one game for Millwall Reserves, as well as making appearances for Boston Town and Newark Town, but it is not known when his actual Grantham debut was, although he is certainly playing at London Road by the end of the 1931/32 season. We know from *Grantham Journal* archives that he made only nine appearances during the following season, but at the start of the 1933/34 campaign he was playing in every game for the first few months. Unfortunately team-sheets then become scarce and we are unable to identify the end of his Grantham career.

Coldron

Seasons Played			
	Lincs Cup	~	
	Other	~	1
1890/91	Total	~	1

Goalkeeper who made just the one appearance for Grantham, a friendly in October 1890 against Notts St Lukes when Jack Broadbent was unavailable.

David Cole

Seasons Played			
	League	~	2
	F.A. Cup	~	
1994/95	F.A. Trophy	~	
	League Cup	~	
	Lincs Cup	~	1
	Total	~	3

Former Motherwell, Scunthorpe United Reserves and Louth United goalkeeper who played in the first three matches of the 1994/95 season, against Grimsby Town, Bridgnorth Town and Tamworth, before Guy Hardcastle arrived at The Meres.

Mick Cole

Seasons Played			
	League	~	1
	F.A. Cup	~	
1960/61	League Cup	~	
	Lincs Cup	~	1
	Total	~	2

Born 26/01/1944 at Osbournby. Started playing football with Osbournby FC, before progressing to Grantham Reserves. Mick made his First team debut in April 1961 at London Road in the Central Alliance game against Spalding United and kept his position a few days later for the victory in the Lincolnshire Senior Cup 'A' Final against Gainsborough Trinity. At just 17 years of age he was the youngest player to have progressed to the final of the competition. He then spent several years back in the Reserves, followed by a trial with Boston United and then made appearances for Grantham Amateurs, Grantham St John's and North Thorsby FC. Mick went on to become a Farm Manager in North Lincolnshire, but currently lives just outside of Melton Mowbray.

Cole

Seasons Played			
	League	~	1
	F.A. Cup	~	
1930/31	Lincs Cup	~	
	Total	~	1

Only made one appearance for Grantham, the November 1930 Midland League match at Frickley Colliery.

Lee Colkin

Seasons Played			
	League	~	1
	F.A. Cup	~	
2003/04	F.A. Trophy	~	
	League Cup	~	
	Lincs Cup	~	
	Total	~	1

Born 15/07/1974 at Nuneaton. Began his career at Northampton Town, making over 100 appearances for them, before moving to Leyton Orient, Hednesford Town, Morecambe, where he played in the side that knocked Grantham out of the FA Cup, and Burton Albion. He made just one appearance for The Gingerbreads in March 2004 at home to Chippenham Town, as a favour to new Manager, Dave Norton, and then went on to play for Tamworth and Hinckley United.

Graham Collier

Seasons Played			
	League	~	51 (8)
	F.A. Cup	~	
1980/81	F.A. Trophy	~	1 (1)
	League Cup	~	3
1982/83	Lincs Cup	~	1
	Other	~	3
	Total	~	59 (9)

Born 12/09/1951 at Nottingham. Previously played for Nottingham Forest, Doncaster Rovers, Scunthorpe United, Barnsley, Buxton, York City, Macclesfield Town and Burton Albion, with 27 goals to his name, scored in 236 games during his time in The Football League. He made his Grantham debut in the October 1980 league game at home to Matlock Town and scored his first goal for the club against South Liverpool at the end of the same month. Graham played in the December Redmayne Trophy game against Nottingham Forest, but at the end of January and the 4-1 defeat at the hands of Gateshead he left London Road. He signed for Boston United after The Pilgrims paid a £500 transfer fee, but later played against them for The Gingerbreads in the opening County Cup tie of the 1982/83 season, plus spent time at Kettering Town. His return to London Road became permanent towards the end of the year and he played in the majority of the remaining matches, scoring in his final appearance for Grantham, the closing fixture of the 1982/83 season at Matlock Town. Graham went on to play for and then manage Eastwood Town, selling Peter Whitehurst to Grantham, briefly turned out for Alfreton Town, before a managerial role at Shepshed Charterhouse. Finally he became assistant to Bill Brindley at Heanor Town.

Alan Collin

Seasons Played			
	League	~	121
	F.A. Cup	~	7
1958/59-61/62	League Cup	~	3
	Lincs Cup	~	10
	Total	~	141

Former Belper Town defender who made his debut for Grantham in the October 1958 Midland League game at Stockton and then missed only one of the remaining matches of that season. As Grantham moved into the Central Alliance League, Alan was an important member of the side that won the County Cup in April 1961 at Gainsborough Trinity. The following year he played in the FA Cup First Round tie at Brierley Hill Alliance and won another Lincolnshire County Cup winner's medal, this time Boston United being the victims. Only a few weeks later Alan turned out for what would be his final game for the club, in the last match of the 1961/62 season at Stamford.

Collingshaw

Seasons Played			
	League	~	12 (1)
	F.A. Cup	~	1
1891/92	Other	~	3
	Total	~	16 (1)

Important member of the first Grantham team to enter a league competition who made his debut in that inaugural Midland Amateur Alliance match at home to Notts County Rovers in September 1891. He scored his only goal for the club in the New Year at Heanor and ended the season having missed only a few of the matches.

Collingwood

Seasons Played			
	Other	~	2
1874/75-75/76	Total	~	2

Made only one appearance for Grantham in their first ever season, the January 1875 friendly played at Bourne under Rugby Union rules and then played once more, against the Conservative Working Men's Club just after Christmas in that year. Bearing in mind the prominent local dignitaries that were playing for the club in these first years, he could easily be Reuben Collingwood (born circa 1852 in Grantham), an auctioneer based in Swinegate.

Collingwood

Seasons Played	League	~	2
	Lincs Cup	~	1
1904/05	Other	~	
1909/10	Total	~	3

Defender who was certainly playing for the club at the start of the 1904/05 season and yet there seem to be no available records of him playing again until the Midland Amateur Alliance game at home to Derby YMCA in October 1909.

Brian Collins

Seasons Played	League	~	2
	F.A. Cup	~	3
1980/81	F.A. Trophy	~	
	League Cup	~	
	Lincs Cup	~	1
	Other	~	
	Total	~	6

Arrived on a free transfer from Grimsby Town after regularly playing for their Reserve side. He first appeared for Grantham in the September 1980 league fixture at Netherfield, but then played only occasionally, until his last game when he came on as a substitute during the October County Cup Final at Lincoln City, replacing Tim Thacker.

Darren Collins

Seasons Played	League	~	11 (4)
	F.A. Cup	~	5 (3)
2003/04-04/05	F.A. Trophy	~	
	League Cup	~	
	Lincs Cup	~	
	Total	~	16 (7)

Born 24/05/1967 at Winchester. Former England Semi-Professional International who previously played for Petersfield United, Northampton Town, scoring 11 times in his 67 League and Cup appearances, Aylesbury United, Enfield and Rushden & Diamonds. He remains the club's record goal-scorer there, after netting 153 goals and won a Dr Marten's League Championship medal with them as well. A £25,000 transfer then took him to Kettering Town, where another league title medal was won, before appearances were made for Cambridge City and Tamworth, which saw a third Southern League medal. He scored on his Grantham debut in September 2004 against Hednesford Town and played an important part in that season's FA Cup run, none more so than when he took over the goalkeeping position in the televised match at home to Leyton Orient when Mario Ziccardi was sent off. Despite bravely attempting to keep The Gingerbreads in the game, he was beaten in injury time. Only a week later he had joined Nuneaton Borough, although it was to be a short spell there, as he returned to The Meres just after Dave Norton arrived. What would turn out to be his final goal for Grantham was scored in September 2004 in the disastrous FA Cup defeat at home to Shepshed Dynamo and with Norton departing The Meres at the end of that game he was quickly followed by Darren who moved on once more, this time to Cogenhoe United.

Jimmy Collins

Seasons Played	League	~	12
	F.A. Cup	~	5
1957/58	Lincs Cup	~	
	Total	~	17

Played for Grantham in the first match of the 1957/58 season at home to Worksop Town and then every game until October, when his appearances abruptly became few and far between. Jimmy then made his final appearance for the club in the April 1958 trip up to York City Reserves.

Kevin Collins

Seasons Played	League	~	21
	F.A. Cup	~	1
1978/79-79/80	F.A. Trophy	~	
	League Cup	~	
	Lincs Cup	~	1
	Total	~	23

Born 16/10/1960 at Nottingham. Signed for Grantham after being released by Nottingham Forest and made his debut in the April 1979 league fixture at home to Banbury United, taking over the position from Jimmy Jackson. Kevin played in every one of the remaining games from that season, including the May victory at home to Merthyr Tydfil which clinched the Southern League, Division One North Championship for The Gingerbreads. After the Summer break he was once again playing in the majority of the games, but the October 1979 game against Worksop Town would prove to be his last for Grantham and he moved on to Long Eaton United. Kevin currently runs his own motor repair company in Nottingham.

Gareth Collinson

Seasons Played	League	~	4
	F.A. Cup	~	1
1998/99	F.A. Trophy	~	
	League Cup	~	
	Lincs Cup	~	
	Total	~	5

Born 1982 at Doncaster. A former Doncaster Rovers Youth Team striker who made his Grantham debut in the opening league match of the Antrac run 1998/99 season at Worcester City and was thought to be a huge prospect for the future. However, his Grantham career ended when he broke his foot whilst on trial at Aston Villa, with his last game for The Gingerbreads being the FA Cup defeat of West Midlands Police at the start of October 1998. After recovering from the injury Gareth went to play for Gainsborough Trinity, Rossington Main, Sheffield FC, Brodsworth Welfare, where he was top scorer for the 2002/03 and 03/04 seasons, Bridlington Town, Buxton and Armthorpe Welfare.

Collyer

Seasons Played	League	~	1
	F.A. Cup	~	
1929/30	Lincs Cup	~	
	Other	~	
	Total	~	1

Centre-Forward who had also played for Sutton Town, but to the best of our knowledge made only one appearance for Grantham, in the first match of the 1929/30 season at Mansfield Town.

Spencer Commons

Seasons Played	League	~	8
	F.A. Cup	~	
2004/05	F.A. Trophy	~	
	League Cup	~	
	Lincs Cup	~	
	Total	~	8

Born ??/01/1985 at Sutton-in-Ashfield. Brother of Nottingham Forest's Kris Commons. Spencer joined The Gingerbreads on work experience from Notts County, making his debut at home to Bath City in August 2004. Soon after this he was released by The Magpies and joined Grantham permanently, but the Southern League fixture against Tiverton Town at the end of the following month would prove to be his final appearance for the club. The arrival of Lee Glover at The Meres saw Spencer's departure and he went on to join Matlock Town.

Jock Comrie

Seasons Played	League	~	1
	F.A. Cup	~	
1911/12	Lincs Cup	~	
	Total	~	1

Born 31/03/1881 at Denny. Had previously played for Third Lanark and Reading, before progressing into The Football League with Glossop, Bradford City and Lincoln City, scoring five goals in a total of 98 appearances. He briefly played for Grantham in their maiden 1911/12 Central Alliance campaign, although no details are known on specific fixtures, and after returning back to Scotland to play for Stenhousemuir, finished his career back at Reading. Died 1916.

Darren Connell

Seasons Played	League	~	8 (1)
	F.A. Cup	~	
2004/05	F.A. Trophy	~	
	League Cup	~	
	Lincs Cup	~	1
	Total	~	9 (1)

Born 03/02/1982 at Blackpool. Began his career with Blackpool, (making three First team appearances), before moving to Macclesfield Town, where he played once more in The Football

League. Transfers followed to Scarborough, Gainsborough Trinity, Barrow, (the last two on-loan), Accrington Stanley and Burscough. He made his Grantham debut coming off the bench in the opening County Shield tie of the 2004/05 season at Brigg Town. Darren scored his only goal for the club in August against Hitchin Town and made his final appearance the following month at Halesowen Town. October 2004 saw the arrival of Lee Glover as the club's Manager and Darren was released from The Meres soon after.

Dick Conroy

Seasons Played			
1957/58	League	~	34
	F.A. Cup	~	2
	Lincs Cup	~	2
	Total	~	38

Born 29/071927 at Bradford. Centre-Half with experience at Swain House, Bradford City, (including a joint benefit match for him in 1952 when Sunderland sent a strong side down to Valley Parade), and Bradford Park Avenue, gaining a total of 227 senior appearances to his name. He made his Grantham debut in the first game of the 1957/58 season at home to Worksop Town and by his last game, at Scarborough in May, had missed very few league matches, mostly during a barren period in the Autumn.. The following season Dick went on to play for Frickley Colliery. Died 1991 at Bradford.

Contrell

Seasons Played			
1934/35	League	~	1
	F.A. Cup	~	
	Lincs Cup	~	
	Total	~	1

Made just one appearance for Grantham in the final Midland League game of the 1934/35 season at Barnsley Reserves.

George Coo

Seasons Played			
1891/92	League	~	5
	F.A. Cup	~	1
	Other	~	
	Total	~	6

Forward who made his debut in Grantham's first ever league game, at home to Notts County Rovers in September 1891, and played in virtually every game for the club until November, with the home fixture against Sheffield being his final one.

Adam Cook

Seasons Played			
1992/93	League	~	19
	F.A. Cup	~	1
	F.A. Trophy	~	1
	League Cup	~	2
	Lincs Cup	~	1
	Total	~	24

Former Ipswich Town central defender who first played for The Gingerbreads in the August 1992 County Cup tie at Lincoln City and despite a promising start to his Grantham career, soon found that his appearances were becoming infrequent. His last game for the club came in the 1992/93 season's closing fixture at home to Bridgnorth Town and he went on to play for Gresley Rovers.

Dave Cook

Seasons Played			
1987/88-88/89	League	~	11
	F.A. Cup	~	2
	F.A. Trophy	~	3
	League Cup	~	1
	Lincs Cup	~	
	Total	~	17

Born 05/02/1969 at Birmingham. Former Lincoln City and Lincoln United player who progressed through the Reserve side into the First team, making his debut in the February 1988 league fixture against Halesowen Town. However, the following season he was called upon by Martin O'Neill to replace those unavailable more often than being a first choice player and his final appearance came in the December 1988 FA Trophy tie at home to Matlock Town when he came off the bench to replace Tony Simpson. He soon left London Road and followed Grantham Reserves manager, Dave Richards, to Bourne Town.

Peter Cook

Seasons Played			
1954/55	League	~	28 (12)
	F.A. Cup	~	3 (2)
	Lincs Cup	~	1
	Total	~	32 (14)

Born 01/02/1927 at Hull. Inside-Left who previously played for local side Kingston Wolves, then Hull City, Scarborough, Bradford City, Crewe Alexandra and Boston United, making over 50 Football League appearances. His Grantham debut came in the opening match of the 1954/55 season at home to Nottingham Forest Reserves, with his first goal in the next game at Notts County Reserves. Despite missing from many of the games after New Year, with his final appearance for Grantham in the April 1955 game at Peterborough United, he still finished the season as the club's second highest scorer behind Mike Bosnell. Died in 1960.

Tony Cook

Seasons Played			
1992/93	League	~	16
	F.A. Cup	~	
	F.A. Trophy	~	
	League Cup	~	
	Lincs Cup	~	
	Total	~	16

Born circa 1966. Local defender and a former Grantham United player who joined the club after the 1992/93 financial crisis, starting with the league game at Bedworth United in January and ending with the season's closing fixture at home to Bridgnorth Town. Tony currently works with Nottingham Forest's Football Academy.

Cook

Seasons Played			
1911/12	League	~	1
	Total	~	1

Only one known appearance for this player, the Central Alliance game at home to Sutton Junction in February 1912.

George Cooke

Seasons Played			
1930/31	League	~	21 (2)
	F.A. Cup	~	
	Lincs Cup	~	
	Total	~	21 (2)

Born 16/04/1902 at Clowne. Brother of Richard Cooke and an outside-left player with experience at Cresswell White Star, Bolsover Town, Bolsover Colliery, Chesterfield, Shirebrook, Norwich City, Portsmouth, Southend United, Wigan Borough, Mansfield Town, where he won a Midland League Championship winner's medal in 1929, Bradford Park Avenue and Connahs Quay. Despite such a long career behind him, he managed only 69 Football League appearances and the majority of those came during his time at Wigan, where he also scored his ten goals. Most of George's games for Grantham came after Christmas 1930, with him scoring in the January Midland League match versus Wombwell, but there are no records to show the location of his other goal, or the end of his London Road career. Died 1976 at Chesterfield.

Richard Cooke

Seasons Played			
1927/28-28/29	League	~	66 (1)
	F.A. Cup	~	10
	Lincs Cup	~	
	Other	~	
	Total	~	76 (1)

Born circa 1903 at Kirkby-in-Ashfield. Brother of George Cooke. A former Kirkby Colliery, Alfreton Town, Mansfield Town, Barnsley and Brentford defender with six Football League appearances to his name, all gained at the final one of those clubs. Richard played for Grantham in the September 1927 Midland League match at Worksop Town and missed very few games during his two season spell, scoring once during that time in September 1928 when Worksop Town came to London Road. Richard went on to return to Mansfield Town, helping them to Byron Cup and Bayley Cup victories in 1930.

Robbie Cooke

Seasons Played			
	League	~	88 (79)
	F.A. Cup	~	6 (3)
1978/79-79/80	F.A. Trophy	~	7 (4)
	League Cup	~	7 (3)
1991/92	Lincs Cup	~	4
	Total	~	112 (89)

Born 16/02/1957 at Rotherham. 'Cookie' was a former Mansfield Town apprentice who joined Grantham at the start of the 1978/79 season, making his debut in the County Cup game against Boston United and perhaps surprisingly only netting his first goal in the sixth game that he took part in, at Stourbridge. Robbie's scoring rate in the second half of the season though, was phenomenal, achieving 31 goals after Christmas, including hat-tricks against King's Lynn, Corby Town and most importantly at home to Merthyr Tydfil in the closing fixture to secure the League title for Grantham. He easily finished as both the club's and the Southern League's highest scorer, with a tally of 43 goals. As Grantham entered into the Northern Premier League, Robbie played in every match of the season and notched up another 39 goals for Grantham, four of which came in the February 1980 thrashing of Tamworth and another hat-trick the following month as the club ventured into Sunday football with a game at home to Gateshead. It wasn't long though before the inevitable happened and he joined Peterborough United after a £12,000 transfer, at the time a record fee for The Gingerbreads. He was soon playing in one of the biggest games for his new club, an FA Cup Fifth Round tie against Manchester City and he finished his first two seasons there as Peterborough's highest scorer. But despite this success, Robbie was then transferred to Cambridge United, before moving to Brentford mid-way through the season. By the end of that campaign Robbie had finished as the club's top scorer, but remarkably he was still the highest scorer with Cambridge. It was only the third time in history that a striker had finished a season in the top spot for two different clubs. As well as this near unique achievement, he also scored his club's consolation goal in the Final of the Freight Rover Trophy at Wembley in 1985 and after a £30,000 fee was paid, Robbie then moved to Millwall, where he won a Second Division Championship medal. This was his final transfer in The Football League and at the end of his professional career he had 155 goals to his name in 386 senior League and Cup appearances. Robbie then signed for Kettering Town and whilst there was soon awarded England Semi-Professional honours, playing for a club that finished runners-up in the GM Vauxhall Conference, with Robbie himself finishing as the top goalscorer in the league. He rejoined Grantham at the start of the 1991/92 season as Player/Coach, playing in the club's first ever match at The Meres, against Ilkeston Town in the FA Cup, although it was to be a short spell back with the team. His last goal for Grantham came in the November 1991 league fixture against Newport AFC, with his final appearance in the same month, at home to Sutton Coldfield Town. Robbie went on to play for Northampton Spencer, where he won a United Counties League winners medal and Bourne Town. After the end of his playing career he became manager of Warboys Town and Assistant Manager at Kettering Town, plus worked for several years at the Thomas Cook headquarters at Peterborough, but is currently Chief Scout at Everton.

Alan Cooper

Seasons Played			
	League	~	3
	F.A. Cup	~	
1961/62-62/63	Lincs Cup	~	
	Total	~	3

Forward who played for the First team in two away games at the end of the 1961/62 season, at Gainsborough Trinity and Stamford Town and made one more appearance the following season when Holbeach United came to London Road in December 1962.

Cyril Cooper

Seasons Played			
	League	~	4 (1)
	F.A. Cup	~	
1919/20-20/21	Lincs Cup	~	
	Other	~	
	Total	~	4 (1)

Born circa 1896. Known as 'Whip' due to his speed, Cyril played twice for Grantham at the end of the 1919/20 season, with confirmed appearances against Mansfield Town and Loughborough Corinthians. There are only two known appearances during the next season as well, with the December 1920 home game against Chesterfield Reserves seeing his only goal for the club. Cyril also turned out for Spittlegate United during his career and his son, Ned, later played for the club. Died 1950 in Grantham.

Ned Cooper

Seasons Played			
	League	~	1
1948/49	F.A. Cup	~	
	Lincs Cup	~	
	Total	~	1

Born 22/03/1925 in Grantham. Son of Cyril Cooper. Ned began his career at Nottingham Forest and Lincoln City, before returning to his home club after the War. He made just the one appearance for the First team in the Midland League game against Nottingham Forest Reserves in September of 1948 and soon after joined Ransome & Marles. Ned is retired now, but still lives in Grantham.

Neil Cooper

Seasons Played			
	League	~	25 (1)
	F.A. Cup	~	4
1988/89-90/91	F.A. Trophy	~	3
	League Cup	~	4
	Lincs Cup	~	2
	Total	~	38 (1)

First played for Grantham by coming off the bench to replace Spadge Farrow in the 1988/89 season's opening league fixture at Halesowen Town, but was only infrequently called upon again that year. This trend continued the following season, although the October 1989 fixture at Racing Club Warwick saw Neil score the consolation goal. His final appearance for Grantham was in the September 1990 FA Cup defeat at Hinckley Athletic, during which he was replaced by substitute, Dennis Jenas. Neil did however make it onto the front of the club's official matchday programme from the first season at The Meres, the first mosaic cover used in the industry.

James Cope

Seasons Played			
	League	~	12
	F.A. Cup	~	2
1998/99	F.A. Trophy	~	2
	League Cup	~	
	Lincs Cup	~	1
	Total	~	17

Born 04/10/1973 at Birmingham. A former Stafford Rangers player who also made 4 appearances for Shrewsbury Town during the season preceding signing for Grantham. His first game for The Gingerbreads was in the opening league fixture of the 1998/99 season at Worcester City and whilst he made an appearance for the club in the October FA Cup final qualifying round tie at Tamworth, James unfortunately managed to get himself sent off during that important match. Despite playing in many of the early games that season, appearances soon became sparse as new Manager, Tony Kenworthy, searched for a team that was worthy of the professional hype. James played his final game for Grantham in the season's closing fixture at Weymouth and after the Summer went on to play for Redditch United, then Moor Green, Stourbridge, Studley BKL and Sutton Coldfield Town.

Copley

Seasons Played			
	League	~	6 (6)
	F.A. Cup	~	
1925/26	Lincs Cup	~	
	Total	~	6 (6)

Appearances from this season are derived from a list of Grantham scorers, so very little information is available for this player other than his first goal for the club, against Lincoln City Reserves in November 1925, and his last goal, against Scunthorpe & Lindsey United the following March.

Copson

Seasons Played			
	F.A. Cup	~	3
	Lincs Cup	~	11 (2)
1884/85-86/87	Other	~	21 (1)
	Total	~	35 (3)

Played his first competitive game for Grantham in the October 1884 FA Cup tie against Grimsby Town and then turned out in virtually every other game that season, including the Lincolnshire Senior Cup Final, the scene of Grantham's first ever trophy victory. The following season his talents seem to have been saved for the competitive matches only, but by the end of 1886 he was only playing occasionally and made his last appearance for the club in a friendly against Derby County in March 1887. He may be the same 'Copson' who was registered as secretary of the Grantham Rovers club just over ten years later, plus most likely to be William Copson (born 1866 in Grantham) who by the time of the 1901 census was working as a solicitor's clerk in town.

Corben

Seasons Played			
	League	~	7
	Lincs Cup	~	2
1904/05-06/07	Other	~	
	Total	~	9

Player who most likely made many more appearances for Grantham than those quoted above, due to the lack of team-sheets available today. However records that are still obtainable show a quite versatile player who covered virtually every position from Goalkeeper to Centre-Forward during his time with the club.

Mark Corbett

Seasons Played			
	League	~	5
	F.A. Cup	~	2
1997/98	F.A. Trophy	~	
	League Cup	~	2
	Lincs Cup	~	1
	Total	~	10

Midfielder who previously played for Arnold Town, Hucknall Town and Shepshed Dynamo. His Grantham debut came in the August 1997 Lincolnshire County Senior Cup defeat at Lincoln United and although he played a part in Grantham's record league start to a season, many of the above figures arose from appearances from the substitute's bench. His final game for Grantham came in the November Dr Marten's League Cup tie against Wisbech Town.

Corcoran

Seasons Played			
	League	~	1
	F.A. Cup	~	
1925/26	Lincs Cup	~	
	Total	~	1

Available records show him playing just one game for Grantham, the Midland League fixture against Loughborough Corinthians in the Autumn of 1925.

Simon Corden

Seasons Played			
	League	~	16
	F.A. Cup	~	1
1989/90	F.A. Trophy	~	1
	League Cup	~	
1994/95	Lincs Cup	~	
	Total	~	18

Born 26/12/1969 at Grantham. Started off playing for Gonerby Excelsior and then moved on to Grantham United, Harrowby United and Grantham Reserves. Simon was promoted to the First team for the September 1989 FA Cup tie against Louth United, but it would be five years later before he pulled on a Grantham shirt again. He had a good spell in the side over the Winter of 1994/95, but played his last game for the club in April when he came off the bench to replace Steve Daly in the league defeat at Newport AFC. Simon still lives in Grantham and continues to play football with Gonerby.

Cottam

Seasons Played			
	League	~	4
	F.A. Cup	~	
1946/47	Lincs Cup	~	
	Total	~	4

Played in the first two games of the 1946/47 season at Lincoln City Reserves and Boston United, but made only two more appearances for the First team, on Christmas Day against Ransome & Marles and the final match of the season at Notts County Reserves.

Alan Coulbeck

Seasons Played			
	League	~	8
	F.A. Cup	~	
1956/57	Lincs Cup	~	
	Total	~	8

Made his First team debut in the September 1956 game at Grimsby Town Reserves, but appeared only infrequently then until his final match, the Midland League game at Denaby United in January.

Fred Coulson

Seasons Played			
	League	~	14 (5)
	F.A. Cup	~	1
1951/52	Lincs Cup	~	
1955/56	Total	~	15 (5)

Born 04/03/1922 at Thetford. Corporal in the RAF who scored on his debut in October 1951 during the Midland League match at Halifax Town Reserves, but from then on seems to have only played when Dan Hellings was unavailable. After spending time as a Drill Instructor at Hednesford, he returned in September 1955 when Alan Clay was out of the match at Goole Town and following a slight change to the side, Fred not only started the game but scored the winning goal as well. Died 1996 at Bury St Edmunds.

Cowen

Seasons Played			
	Other	~	1
1879/80	Total	~	1

Forward who played in the 7-0 thrashing of Notts County in the January 1880 friendly, but there are no records that show him making any other appearances for the team.

Graham Cox

Seasons Played			
	League	~	98
	F.A. Cup	~	8
1977/78-82/83	F.A. Trophy	~	4
	League Cup	~	8
1985/86	Lincs Cup	~	3
	Other	~	3
	Total	~	124

Born 10/08/1958 in Grantham. A former King's School pupil who previously played in goal for Grantham Amateurs and Grantham St John's. His first game for The Gingerbreads was in the February 1978 Southern League Cup tie at Banbury, but the next few years saw Graham make only limited appearances for the First team due to the consistency of Chris Gardiner. By the start of the 1981/82 season though, Graham's patience had been rewarded when he became the club's first choice 'keeper and in October 1982 he played in the victorious County Cup Final against Scunthorpe United and the final qualifying round of the FA Cup at Telford United. At the end of that season he left London Road and went on to play for Sleaford Town, Bourne Town and Wellington Diamonds in New Zealand, but returned to Grantham in the Autumn of 1985. Graham then missed only three games up until the end of that season at VS Rugby. He later returned to play for Sleaford Town and then Boston FC, even playing some of the games in spectacles, and finally Wiverton FC. Graham now lives just north of Sleaford and is a Sales & Marketing Director in the food industry.

Mark Cox

Seasons Played			
	League	~	18 (3)
	F.A. Cup	~	
1984/85	F.A. Trophy	~	
	League Cup	~	5 (1)
	Lincs Cup	~	
	Other	~	1
	Total	~	24 (4)

Born 04/10/1959 at Birmingham. Began his career at Lincoln City and Doncaster Rovers, making a total of 20 Football League appearances, before moving on to Boston FC, Shepshed Charterhouse, Alfreton Town and Boston United. His Grantham debut came in the December 1984 President's Cup match at Matlock Town, with his first goal for the club in the February league victory over Bangor City. Despite his experience, Mark's addition to the team failed to elevate them out of the Northern Premier League relegation zone and his final appearance came in their last NPL fixture at Oswestry Town. Mark moved on to Spalding United and also had a second spell with Boston FC.

Cox

Seasons Played			
1874/75-79/80	F.A. Cup	~	5 (1)
1881/82	Lincs Cup	~	
1883/84	Other	~	52 (33)
	Total	~	57 (34)

Appeared in three matches during Grantham's inaugural season, including the match at Bourne which was played under Rugby Union Rules. He also turned out in several of the club matches, even captaining one side in January 1875, and scored his first goal during a friendly at home to Newark in November 1875. Appearances were awarded to him in many games for Grantham right up until the end of the decade, including the first ever FA Cup match when Clapham Rovers came to London Road in October 1877. By then he had become one of the club's first renowned strikers after several hat-tricks and even putting five goals past the Nottingham Law side in November 1878. Finally he returned to London Road to make a few more appearances towards the end of 1881 and once again two years later for what seems to be his final game, a friendly at home to Grantham Volunteers in October 1883.

Cox

Seasons Played			
	League	~	2
	F.A. Cup	~	
1936/37	Lincs Cup	~	1
	Other	~	
	Total	~	3

Goalkeeper who had previously made appearances for RAF Cranwell and played for Grantham whilst Arthur Jepson was unavailable. He appeared in two Midland League games, against Scarborough in February 1937 and Hull City Reserves a month later, which was only two days after his appearance in the County Cup replay at home to Scunthorpe & Lindsey United.

Cragg

Seasons Played			
	Lincs Cup	~	
	Other	~	3
1890/91	Total	~	3

Played in goal when Jack Broadbent became unavailable for the friendlies against Boston NE and Notts St George, plus the Newark Charity Cup tie at home to Grantham Rovers Colts.

Bernard Crapper

Seasons Played			
	League	~	4 (2)
	F.A. Cup	~	
1935/36	Lincs Cup	~	
	Other	~	
	Total	~	4 (2)

Centre-Forward, previously with Ecclesfield and Leeds United, who made four appearances for Grantham during March of 1936, scoring in the Lincolnshire League game at home to Gainsborough Trinity and also during his final match at home to Scarborough in the Midland League.

Dean Craven

Seasons Played			
	League	~	5
	F.A. Cup	~	
2003/04	F.A. Trophy	~	
	League Cup	~	
	Lincs Cup	~	
	Total	~	5

Born 17/02/1979 at Shrewsbury. Left-sided player who began his career as a Trainee at West Bromwich Albion, before spending three years at Shrewsbury Town, making 11 League appearances during that time. He went on to play for Merthyr Tydfil, Stafford Rangers, Hednesford Town, Bilston Town, Bridgnorth, following which he was voted 2002/03 Player of the Year for the Midland Football Alliance League. Dean then joined Hereford United and came to Grantham on-loan towards the end of the 2003/04 season, playing in five league games, starting with the home draw against Tiverton Town at the start of April and ending against Havant & Waterlooville. At the end of the season Dean joined the 'new' club AFC Telford United, helping them to promotion in their first year.

George Craven

Seasons Played			
	League	~	105 (2)
	F.A. Cup	~	2
1949/50-51/52	Lincs Cup	~	7
	Total	~	114 (2)

Centre-Half from Lincoln, with experience at Boston United, who made his Grantham debut on New Year's Eve 1949 in the Midland League game at Scunthorpe & Lindsey United. George then played in nearly every one of the remaining matches of that season, including the Lincolnshire Senior Cup 'A' Final against Boston United and the replay. During the next two years George once more missed very few matches and even managed to score in the games at Rotherham United Reserves and the Boxing Day 1951 encounter at Peterborough United. He made his final appearance for the club in the last league game of the 1951/52 season at Goole Town.

Andy Crawford

Seasons Played			
	League	~	162 (8)
	F.A. Cup	~	10
1970/71-74/75	F.A. Trophy	~	12
	League Cup	~	14
	Lincs Cup	~	6
	Other	~	1
	Total	~	205 (8)

Born circa 1946 at Ketton, near Stamford. Defender who had previously spent time on the books at Peterborough United, before moving to Spalding United and Stamford Town. Andy first played for Grantham in the opening Midland League match of the 1970/71 season at Belper and in October scored his first goal for the club during the home match against Heanor Town. However, he then missed many of the remaining games of that season, including the important FA Cup ties, although he had returned in time to feature in the second leg of the Midland League Cup final. The following year though, Andy was able to play a more noticeable role in the Grantham championship winning team. He also managed to play in the February 1972 FA Trophy Quarter-Final game against Yeovil Town and won a Lincolnshire County Cup winner's medal after the game against Scunthorpe United. As Grantham moved into the Southern League, Andy appeared in the FA Cup First Round tie against Bradford City and won another League Championship medal, whilst the following year he played in the FA Cup ties against Hillingdon Borough, Rochdale and Middlesbrough. He finished the 1974/75 season by scoring in his last match for the club, the April league defeat of Guildford City. Andy then returned to Stamford and played for them in the 1976 FA Vase Final at Wembley, before moving to Bourne Town and Mirlees Blackstone. He was last known to be running a pub in the Stamford area.

George Crawford

Seasons Played			
	League	~	29
	F.A. Cup	~	2
1966/67-67/68	Total	~	31

Born circa 1941. Former Skegness Town and Worksop Town goalkeeper, nick-named 'The Cat' due to his tremendous agility, who shared his role throughout the 1966/67 season with John Small, playing in the important FA Cup victories over Boston United and Wimbledon, but missing out on the 2nd Round Proper game at home to Oldham Athletic. The following year he only managed eight more appearances, with the Midland League fixture in March 1968 at home to Scunthorpe United Reserves being his final game. George went on to play for Boston FC and currently lives near to Skegness, working as a self-employed joiner.

Gerard Creane

Seasons Played			
	League	~	6 (1)
	F.A. Cup	~	
1991/92	F.A. Trophy	~	
	League Cup	~	
	Lincs Cup	~	
	Total	~	6 (1)

Born 02/02/1962 at Lincoln. 'Ged', as he is better known, previously played for Witham Wanderers (Lincoln), Lincoln City, making seven League appearances, Tsun Wan (Hong Kong), FC Jaro (Finland), Stafford Rangers, Boston United, including an FA Trophy Final appearance at Wembley in 1985, Kettering Town and King's Lynn. He played for Grantham in six of the final seven fixtures of the 1991/92 season, starting against Hinckley Town, scoring his only goal at King's Lynn and ending in the closing game at Solihull Borough. Ged later played for Lincoln United and then moved into the management position there towards the end of the decade, but returned to Grantham at the start of John Wilkinson's period, as a scout for the club. Ged still lives in the Lincoln area and works as a roofing contractor.

Jez Creasey

Seasons Played			
	League	~	
	F.A. Cup	~	
1988/89	F.A. Trophy	~	
	League Cup	~	1
	Lincs Cup	~	
	Total	~	1

Born 13/02/1966 at Lincoln. Previously played for several local sides in the Lincoln area, before joining Grantham Reserves in the 1986/87 season. However, Jez made just one full appearance for

The Gingerbreads, in the November 1988 Westgate Insurance League Cup tie at home to Atherstone United, although he also gained another start in the friendly against Nottingham Forest, arranged as part of Gary Crosby's transfer. He went on to play for Bourne Town and Nettleham United. Jez still lives in Lincoln and works as a surveyor for a national telecommunications company.

Cyril Creed

Seasons Played			
	League	~	7 (2)
	F.A. Cup	~	
1926/27	Lincs Cup	~	1
	Other	~	1 (2)
1932/33	Total	~	9 (4)

Coming from Melton Mowbray, Cyril was a centre-forward who had also played for Holwell Works and scored twice on his Grantham debut in the October 1926 RAF Shield tie at home to RAF Cranwell. But after the end of the following month he seems to have made only a few more appearances before the end of the season. Cyril returned to London Road six years later to play in a single game, but there are no records to indicate which one.

Creighton

Seasons Played			
	League	~	1 (1)
	F.A. Cup	~	
1935/36	Lincs Cup	~	
	Other	~	1 (2)
	Total	~	2 (3)

Centre-Forward, possibly a serviceman based near to the town bearing in mind that he also played for Grantham RAF, who scored in both the games he played in. The first of those was the Lincolnshire League fixture at home to Lincoln City Reserves in April 1936 and then the Wilson Cup match at the end of the year where he scored twice against the Lincoln League XI to help secure the trophy.

Kevin Cresswell

Seasons Played			
	League	~	1
	F.A. Cup	~	
1990/91	F.A. Trophy	~	
	League Cup	~	
	Lincs Cup	~	1
	Total	~	2

Former Ilkeston Town striker who made appearances for Grantham against Grimsby Town and Tamworth at the start of the 1990/91 season.

Crews

Seasons Played			
	League	~	6 (1)
	F.A. Cup	~	2
1919/20	Lincs Cup	~	
	Total	~	8 (1)

Lieutenant in the Armed Forces who played in the centre-half position and made his debut for Grantham in the October 1919 Central Alliance match at home to Shirebrook. He played most of his games before Christmas, but it is not known during which fixture he scored his only goal for the club.

Brian Croft

Seasons Played			
	League	~	7 (1)
	F.A. Cup	~	
1988/89	F.A. Trophy	~	
	League Cup	~	
	Lincs Cup	~	
	Total	~	7 (1)

Born 27/09/1967 at Chester. Former Chester City and Cambridge United player who made his Grantham debut in the April 1989 league fixture at home to Dudley Town and scored his only goal for the club in the following match, the 6-0 thrashing of Banbury United. His short career with The Gingerbreads included many of the subsequent games up to the May trip to Gloucester City. The following season Brian returned to Chester City and then went on to play for Queen's Park Rangers, Shrewsbury Town, Torquay United, Southport and Stockport County, before finally returning back to Chester for the 1999/00 season. During his time in The Football League, Brian scored 8 goals in a total of 198 games, plus made one substitute's appearance in the League Cup.

Allen Crombie

Seasons Played			
	League	~	10 (1)
	F.A. Cup	~	
1984/85	F.A. Trophy	~	1
	League Cup	~	3 (2)
1993/94	Lincs Cup	~	2 (1)
	Other	~	
	Total	~	16 (4)

Born 16/10/1961 at Lincoln. Former Lincoln City player who made five appearances for Grantham towards the end of the 1984/85 season, starting at Workington and scoring in both the League Cup tie against Rhyl and the subsequent replay. He returned to his home town to play for Lincoln United, before a £2,500 transfer took him to Boston United in July 1988. Allen then returned to Lincoln United, this time as their manager, taking them to the Central Midlands League title and the First Round of the FA Cup, before taking over the manager's position at Grantham in time for the start of the 1993/94 season. After playing in several of the early games of the year, his role became more as cover, with his last goal in the March 1994 league fixture at Redditch United and his final appearance for the club at the end of the same month against Newport AFC. He did however name himself as a substitute for many of the closing games, as Grantham finished the season in a disappointing mid-table position. After the Board promoted player, Warren Ward, to the helm, Allen went on to become Player/Coach at Nettleham United and later returned to Lincoln United once more as manager, but resigned in December 2001 and took up a coaching position at Lincoln Moorlands.

Steve Crome

Seasons Played			
	League	~	4
	F.A. Cup	~	1
1988/89	F.A. Trophy	~	
	League Cup	~	
	Lincs Cup	~	1
	Total	~	6

Born 03/11/1961 at King's Lynn. Signed from his home club and first played for Grantham in the 1988/89 season's opening fixture at home to Gainsborough Trinity in the Lincolnshire County Senior Cup. However, after playing in six consecutive games for The Gingerbreads, the September FA Cup tie against Borrowash Victoria proved to be his final appearance for the club. Steve soon returned to King's Lynn to play for local side Northend United and he still lives in the town.

John Crompton

Seasons Played			
	League	~	2
	F.A. Cup	~	
1948/49-49/50	Lincs Cup	~	
	Total	~	2

Goalkeeper who covered for the unavailable Percy Ashton in the last away match of the 1948/49 season, an entertaining 5-5 draw at Mansfield Town Reserves. The following season he then deputised for Ted Eaglen at the home fixture against Frickley Colliery in March 1950, once again a high-scoring game, which ended with a 3-3 result.

Bob Crookes

Seasons Played			
	League	~	29 (11)
	F.A. Cup	~	1
1958/59	Lincs Cup	~	1
	Total	~	31 (11)

Born 29/02/1924 at Retford. Forward who began his career at North Leverton and Retford Town, before making over 200 appearances for Notts County between 1949 and 1955. Following a spell at Worksop Town, Bob made his Grantham debut in the first game of the 1958/59 season, the home Midland League match against Goole Town and scored his first goal two weeks later at Denaby United. He played in most of that season's games, where Grantham finished next to bottom in the league, and after ending with a tally of 11 goals, was the second highest scorer of the year, only one behind Bernard Weakley. Despite retiring from the game after leaving London Road, Bob was persuaded to play again for his home team, Retford Town, in 1961, where he also worked as a schoolmaster for many years.

Darren Crookes

Seasons Played			
	League	~	4
	F.A. Cup	~	
1994/95	F.A. Trophy	~	
	League Cup	~	
	Lincs Cup	~	
	Total	~	4

Lincoln based player who appeared in four fixtures during the 1994/95 season when Mark Appleyard was unavailable, starting with the New Year's Eve game at home to Newport AFC and ending less than two months later at Rothwell Town. Unfortunately for Darren a recurrence of a knee injury forced him to quit the club, although he still plays both football and cricket at local levels around the Lincoln area.

Cropper

Seasons Played			
	League	~	1
	F.A. Cup	~	
1925/26	Lincs Cup	~	
	Total	~	1

Half-Back from the Manchester area who played in the away Midland League fixture at Alfreton Town in November of 1925.

Gary Crosby

Seasons Played			
	League	~	8 (2)
	F.A. Cup	~	
1987/88	F.A. Trophy	~	
	League Cup	~	1
	Lincs Cup	~	
	Total	~	9 (2)

Born 08/05/1964 at Sleaford. Former Lincoln City and Ruston Sports player who was left languishing in the local league with Lincoln United after it was decided that he was lacking in both height and skills. He was signed by Martin O'Neill though, after being spotted in a County Representative match held at London Road and made his debut for Grantham in the October 1987 Westgate Insurance League Cup tie against Wellingborough Town, scoring his first goal at home to Atherstone United the following Saturday. Four weeks later he scored again, this time the winning goal at Mile Oak Rovers, but O'Neill was well on the way to sending him on to bigger and better things. The December 1987 league fixture against Banbury United would be his last for the club and Gary signed for Nottingham Forest for what remains a club record fee of £20,000, after cancelling a trial for Manchester United due to be held only days later, prompting a rather irate phone call from a certain Mr Ferguson! Crosby's rise to fame had been dramatic and from a personal point of view this was simply emphasised when the first trip with his new colleagues, simply as a squad member, saw Forest come away with a victory and Gary's sudden realisation that the subsequent win bonus would be more than his previous month's salary working as a joiner for Simon's at Lincoln! His inclusion into football's elite was soon complete when he made national headlines, controversially heading the ball out of Manchester City goalkeeper, Andy Dibble's hands to score a goal. In November 1988 Crosby returned to London Road with Forest to take part in a friendly, agreed as part of the transfer. Whilst with The Reds, Gary won a League Cup winner's medal in 1990, three ZDS Cup winner's medals and also played in the 1991 FA Cup Final at Wembley, a match which should have seen Brian Clough finally get his hands on the elusive trophy, but which is now better remembered for Paul Gascoigne's tackling. Gary went on to play for Grimsby Town, on loan, and Huddersfield Town, on a free transfer, which frustratingly scuppered any hopes of further funds coming Grantham's way with a 20% clause in the initial contract. By the end of his professional career, Gary had notched up 34 goals in a total of 282 League and Cup matches. He then joined Rushden & Diamonds, briefly returned to Lincoln United, before joining Nigel Clough as Assistant Manager at Burton Albion, although work commitments forced his resignation from there at the start of 2005.

Fred Crossley

Seasons Played			
	League	~	1
	F.A. Cup	~	
1962/63	Total	~	1

Made just the one appearance for the First team, playing in the August 1962 Midland League game at home to Boston United.

Arthur Crouch

Seasons Played			
	League	~	10 (4)
	F.A. Cup	~	1
1946/47	Lincs Cup	~	
	Total	~	11 (4)

Scored twice on his debut during the September 1946 game against Lincoln City Reserves at London Road, but although Arthur played in the next few games, he then had to wait until the following Spring before making any more First team appearances. The visit of Frickley Colliery in May was his last game for the club, a season which had also seen him play for a Lincolnshire representative side.

Cullen

Seasons Played			
	League	~	6 (6)
	F.A. Cup	~	
1925/26	Lincs Cup	~	
	Total	~	6 (6)

The only information we have on this individual is the games where he scored. He netted a brace in the second match of the 1925/26 season at Sutton Town, and the last recorded goal for him is in January 1926 during the 4-1 victory at Ilkeston United.

Carl Cunningham

Seasons Played			
	League	~	2
	F.A. Cup	~	
1997/98	F.A. Trophy	~	
	League Cup	~	
	Lincs Cup	~	
	Total	~	2

Derby born striker who was a regular in the Derby County Reserves side before being released at the end of the 1995/96 season. He joined Gresley Rovers and played in their Championship winning side, before moving to Alfreton Town and then Grantham. Carl made only two appearances for The Gingerbreads though, the November 1997 league fixtures against Sutton Coldfield Town and Solihull Borough. He later went on to play for Belper Town, where he was the club's top goalscorer in the 2001/02 season, Mickleover Sports, a return to Belper, then Long Eaton United.

Cunningham

Seasons Played			
	League	~	1 (1)
	F.A. Cup	~	
1932/33	Lincs Cup	~	
	Other	~	
	Total	~	1 (1)

Played and scored in just one game for Grantham, the April 1933 defeat at Barnsley Reserves.

Terry Curran

Seasons Played			
	League	~	2
	F.A. Cup	~	
1987/88	F.A. Trophy	~	
	League Cup	~	
	Lincs Cup	~	
	Total	~	2

Born 20/03/1955 at Kinsley, Yorkshire. Former prominent Football League player with experience at Doncaster Rovers, Nottingham Forest, Bury, Derby County, Southampton, Sheffield Wednesday, Sheffield United, Everton, Huddersfield Town, Panionis of Greece, Hull City and Sunderland. In that time he had made over 450 appearances in senior football, scoring 72 goals in the League alone. Terry made two appearances for Grantham in September 1987, as a favour for the club's new Manager, Martin O'Neill, against Moor Green and Bridgnorth Town. He returned to The Football League in November 1987 by signing for Grimsby Town, but only a few months later moved on to Chesterfield and after a lone substitute's appearance there, his final senior career figures finished at 84 League and Cup goals in 477 fixtures. Following this, he became Manager of Goole Town and then Mossley, but was last known to be running a newsagents shop in Bradford.

Gareth Collinson

Darren Connell

Robbie Cooke

James Cope

Simon Corden

Graham Cox

Andy Crawford

Darren Crookes

Gary Crosby

Arthur Crouch

Chris Curtis

Mick Daley

Simon Dakin

Brett Darby

Craig Davis

F. Dicks

Steve Curry

Seasons Played			
	League	~	8
	F.A. Cup	~	
2000/01	F.A. Trophy	~	
	League Cup	~	
	Lincs Cup	~	
	Total	~	8

Yorkshire born goalkeeper, previously with Bridlington Trinity, Hatfield Main and Goole Town, who arrived on-loan from Gainsborough Trinity as cover for Mario Ziccardi during his lengthy suspension in the Spring of 2001. The first of those fixtures was the March league game at home to Wisbech Town, until the 5-0 victory over Hastings United the following month. After his release from Gainsborough Trinity, Steve went on to play for Lincoln United and Matlock Town.

Arthur Cursham

Seasons Played			
	F.A. Cup	~	
	Other	~	5
1876/77-78/79	Total	~	5

Born 14/03/1853 at Wilford. Colliery proprietor and the first of two brothers who both played for England, with Arthur being a *current* International during his time at Grantham. He also played for Oakham School, Nottingham Law Club, Notts County and Sheffield, making his Grantham debut in a friendly at home to Bourne just before Christmas 1876, but then made only occasional guest appearances until his last game in March 1879, the 13-0 thrashing of Sleaford at London Road. His England career had seen him score twice in six appearances between 1876 and 1883, at home to Scotland in 1878 and at the end of his career in the 5-0 win over Wales, plus captaining two of the games as well. Although Arthur came from a notable Nottinghamshire family, by the 1880's his financial position had become somewhat precarious, to such a point that some club appearances he made under the alias of R. H. Venables in an attempt to stave off any of his creditors. Arthur also played for the Nottinghamshire and Derbyshire County cricket teams between 1876 and 1880, before emigrating to Florida in 1884. However, within months of arriving in America he had succumbed to yellow fever and malaria. Died 24/12/1884 in Pera, Florida.

Harry Cursham

Seasons Played			
	F.A. Cup	~	
	Other	~	2 (1)
1876/77-77/78	Total	~	2 (1)

Born 27/11/1859 at Wilford. Christened 'Henry', but was more often known as 'Harry'. A former Repton School, Notts County and Corinthians player who appeared for Grantham in the same two games as his brother in the previous entry. He scored in the first of those, a friendly at Notts Castle in March 1877 and then played against the same team nearly a year later. Harry went on to play for Thursday Wanderers (Sheffield), before returning to Notts County, during which time he scored five goals in eight England International games between 1880 and 1884. The first of those was on his debut against Ireland in a 13-0 victory and was followed by a goal at home to Wales and a hat-trick, again versus Ireland in February 1884. Harry continued to play for County and holds the pre-War record for most FA Cup goals, with 48 to his name, including six during an 11-1 win against Wednesbury Strollers in 1882. He also scored three goals in 12 appearances during the initial two seasons of the Football League at the end of the decade. Like his brother, Harry was also an accomplished cricketer, playing for the Nottinghamshire County side in 1880 and then again in 1904, a 24 year gap which is a world record for first class cricket. He stayed in the Nottingham area after the end of his sporting career and worked as a solicitor and insurance broker. Died 06/08/1941 at Holme Pierrepoint.

Curshaw

Seasons Played			
	F.A. Cup	~	4
	Lincs Cup	~	
1880/81-81/82	Other	~	
	Total	~	4

Played in the three FA Cup matches at the end of 1880 and seems to have made only one appearance for the club the following year, in the Cup replay at Staveley in November 1881.

Chris Curtis

Seasons Played			
	League	~	29
	F.A. Cup	~	4
1987/88-88/89	F.A. Trophy	~	1
	League Cup	~	6
	Lincs Cup	~	1
	Total	~	41

Born 02/01/1963 in Grantham. Full-Back who previously played for Sleaford Town and Harrowby United and then progressed through the Reserves to make his senior debut in the opening league fixture of the 1987/88 season at Merthyr Tydfil. He was an important member of that year's side, until the arrival of the experienced Mick McGuire the following Spring saw Chris relegated to the side for many of the remaining fixtures. Although he was back in the team after the Summer break, nine consecutive appearances and the FA Cup defeat at North Ferriby United marked the end of his career at London Road. Chris soon returned to Harrowby, then joined Stamford Town and later became Assistant Manager to Barry Nash back at Harrowby United. He also worked for the local water authority in the customer services department and at the start of 2005 was the focal point of a friendly between Harrowby and Grantham, due to an illness which he was sadly soon to succumb to. Died 12/03/2005 in Grantham.

G. Curtis

Seasons Played			
	F.A. Cup	~	7 (2)
	Lincs Cup	~	13 (11)
1883/84-86/87	Other	~	6 (6)
	Total	~	26 (19)

Forward who scored a hat-trick in the first game that we have definite evidence of him playing, the November 1883 friendly at home to Lincoln Rovers. The following season he continued to score many important goals, including another hat-trick against Lincoln Lindum, although he failed to score himself in the triumphant final of the Lincolnshire Senior Cup against Gainsborough Trinity in March 1885 that he played in. For the next two seasons he seems to have appeared mainly in competitive competitions only and after Grantham were knocked out of the County Cup by Grimsby Town in February 1887, he played no more for the club.

H. Curtis

Seasons Played			
	F.A. Cup	~	1
	Lincs Cup	~	
1885/86	Other	~	2
	Total	~	3

Possible brother of the previous entry. Played in the FA Cup match at Gainsborough Trinity in October 1885 along with two friendlies at the beginning of the season.

R. Curtis

Seasons Played			
	League	~	1 (1)
	F.A. Cup	~	
1921/22	Lincs Cup	~	
	Other	~	1 (1)
1926/27	Total	~	2 (2)

Also played for the Reserve side and Grantham St John's, but the only details of his Grantham career that we have are the goal in April 1922 during the Central Alliance match at New Hucknall Colliery and once again five years later in the 12-0 win over his old side Grantham St John's in the local charity competition.

Westgarth Cuthbert

Seasons Played			
	League	~	54 (2)
	F.A. Cup	~	7
1939/40	Lincs Cup	~	4
	Other	~	7
1945/46	Total	~	72 (2)

Born 1913 at Morpeth. Former South Elmsall, Rotherham United, Hull City, Carlisle United, Accrington Stanley and Frickley Colliery defender with eight Football League appearances behind him. 'Wes', as he was better known, made his Grantham debut in the first Midland League match of the 1939/40 season at Bradford Park Avenue Reserves and in a year when obviously many players were used, Westgarth finished as the player with the second highest number of appearances. In April 1940 he scored his only two goals for the club, during the Midland War-Time League match at

Gainsborough Trinity. He returned after the end of The War and played in every FA Cup game during the 1945/46 season's run, including Kettering Town and Mansfield Town. Wes also missed only a few of the league games, before making his final appearance in the April 1946 Midland League game at Mansfield Town Reserves.

Cutt

Seasons Played			
	League	~	
	F.A. Cup	~	
1912/13	Lincs Cup	~	
	Other	~	1
	Total	~	1

Defender who played in the March 1913 friendly against Queen's Park, but no other team-sheets available for that season show him as playing.

George Cutts

Seasons Played			
	League	~	1
	F.A. Cup	~	
1925/26	Lincs Cup	~	
	Total	~	1

Born 11/03/1900 at Nottingham. Goalkeeper previously with New Hucknall Colliery, Arnold Town, Mansfield Town, during their 1919/20 Central Alliance winning side, Watford, gaining six senior appearances, and Sutton Town. George played for Grantham in the club's first ever Midland League game, at Mansfield Town in August 1925, but no other evidence of games played exists. He went on to play for Hucknall Byron, Hucknall British Legion, Loughborough Corinthians and Raleigh Athletic, although he also made a guest appearance for a Nottingham Forest side during World War Two at the age of 41.

Cutts

Seasons Played			
	Lincs Cup	~	
	Other	~	2 (1)
1889/90	Total	~	2 (1)

Forward who played in two friendlies during December 1889, firstly in the home game against Mapperley, where he scored, and then a week later at Newark.

Simon Dakin

Seasons Played			
	League	~	134 (11)
	F.A. Cup	~	7
1996/97-98/99	F.A. Trophy	~	15 (3)
	League Cup	~	7
2003/04	Lincs Cup	~	3
	Total	~	166 (14)

Born 30/11/1974 at Nottingham. Defender who began his career as a Trainee at Derby County and then gained Football League experience at Hull City, scoring once in 42 First team appearances, before moving into non-league football with Arnold Town. His first game for Grantham was in the October 1996 league fixture at home to Ilkeston Town, with his initial goal for the club in the following match against Raunds Town. After establishing himself as an important member of Gary Mills' team, the following season he won a Dr Marten's Midland Division Championship medal after playing in virtually all of the games, including the FA Trophy ties against Hednesford Town and Southport. As Grantham moved into the Premier Division and professional contracts, Simon not only became one of the few to make the transition, but also finished as the player to make the most appearances for the club as more individuals were used than was either planned or hoped. In the Summer of 1999 though, he moved on to King's Lynn and then Hinckley United, before returning to The Meres at the start of the 2003/04 season. Once again he was a near constant member of the side, playing in the FA Cup First Round tie against Leyton Orient, although missing out on the inaugural Lincolnshire Shield Final against Gainsborough Trinity. His last goal for the club came in the April 2004 league fixture at home to Worcester City, with his final appearance a week later at Weymouth. He retired from the game to concentrate on his profession as a Solicitor in Nottingham, but by the end of the year he had been tempted to come back by Gedling Town.

Billy Dale

Seasons Played			
	League	~	12
	F.A. Cup	~	
1955/56	Lincs Cup	~	1
	Total	~	13

Midfielder who made his debut in February of 1956 in the Midland League match at home to Goole Town. Billy then missed only three of the remaining matches and played in the final league game at York City Reserves, although he did appear in a friendly against Peterborough United a week later.

Dale

Seasons Played			
	League	~	2 (3)
	FA Amt. Cup	~	
1910/11	League Cup	~	
	Lincs Cup	~	
	Other	~	
	Total	~	2 (3)

The only information available on this player is for the two games in which he scored, the February 1911 Midland Amateur Alliance match at Old Loughburians, where he netted a brace, and a few weeks later during the home game against Notts GNR Clerks.

Mick Daley

Seasons Played			
	League	~	45
	F.A. Cup	~	4
1983/84-84/85	F.A. Trophy	~	6 (1)
	League Cup	~	3
	Lincs Cup	~	3
	Other	~	1
	Total	~	62 (1)

Born circa 1952 in Yorkshire. Started his career on the books at Sheffield Wednesday, before making appearances for Scarborough and then serving seven successful years at Boston FC, most of which where spent as Club Captain. Honours won there included a Midland League Championship, Midland League Cup, Lincolnshire Senior Cup 'A' winner's medal and an appearance in Boston's maiden game in the First Round of the FA Cup against Barnsley, with Mick opening the scoring in the 3-1 defeat and still being remembered by many for his cartwheel celebrations! He then moved to Gainsborough Trinity, where he helped the team win the Northern Premier Challenge Shield, before joining Grantham in the Summer of 1983. Mick made his debut in the opening fixture of the new season at Hyde United and played in defence for the Grantham side that would finish 4th in the Northern Premier League, also netting his only goal for the club in the February 1984 FA Trophy replay against Bishop Auckland. The following season, despite playing many games for the club during the Autumn, the Boxing Day fixture at Goole Town was to be Mick's last for Grantham and he soon moved on to become Assistant Manager at Buxton. He currently lives near to Sheffield and is the Mechanical Clerk of Works for the local government architects.

David Dall

Seasons Played			
	League	~	10 (2)
	F.A. Cup	~	1
1979/80	F.A. Trophy	~	
	League Cup	~	1
	Lincs Cup	~	2
	Total	~	14 (2)

Born 10/10/1957 at St Andrews, Scotland. After spending time at Levan Royals, Nottingham Forest and Cowdenbeath, David joined Corby Town, from where he signed for Grantham after a then record £1,500 transfer which was financially assisted by one of the club's sponsors. His first game for The Gingerbreads was in the County Cup tie against Boston United at the end of July 1979. After only 14 appearances though, and goals in the matches against Workington and South Liverpool, David was sold to Scunthorpe United for £7,500 in October. He scored twice in his 85 appearances there and after losing his place to future Gingerbread, Alan Boxall, David went on to play for Falkirk and East Fife in the Scottish League.

Tim Dalton

Seasons Played	League	~	5
	F.A. Cup	~	2
1987/88	F.A. Trophy	~	
	League Cup	~	1
	Lincs Cup	~	2
	Total	~	10

Born 14/10/1965 at Waterford, Ireland. Goalkeeper who previously played for Coventry City Youths, Notts County, where he made a sole First team appearance, Boston United, Bradford City Reserves and Tranmere Rovers, with another Football League start during his loan spell there. His debut for Grantham came in the 1987/88 season's opening fixture against Scunthorpe United in the County Cup. But it was a short career for Tim at London Road, with his final game in September at Bridgnorth Town and Cameron Miles then taking over the position. Tim went on to play for Shepshed Charterhouse, Derry City, where he played against Benfica in a European competition, Airdrie and Gillingham.

Steve Daly

Seasons Played	League	~	7
	F.A. Cup	~	
1994/95	F.A. Trophy	~	
	League Cup	~	
	Lincs Cup	~	
	Total	~	7

Former Lincoln United player who made seven appearances for Grantham towards the end of the 1994/95 season. The first of those was the league fixture at home to Forest Green Rovers in March, with his last game the home defeat against Ilkeston Town only six weeks later when he came off the bench to replace Mark Appleyard.

Danby

Seasons Played	F.A. Cup	~	2
1875/76-76/77	Other	~	3
1878/79	Total	~	5

Played only occasionally for Grantham, with his first game in a friendly at home to Nottingham Castle in 1876. He made only one appearance the following season, and then in 1878 played in the two FA Cup games against Sheffield, before making his last appearance for the club the following March in a friendly at Southwell.

Brett Darby

Seasons Played	League	~	12
	F.A. Cup	~	1
2004/05	F.A. Trophy	~	
	League Cup	~	
	Lincs Cup	~	1
	Total	~	14

Born 10/11/1983 at Leicester. Began his career at local side Ratby & Groby, before spending time at Leicester City, then making ten Football League appearances at Southend United and finally joining Tamworth. Brett joined Grantham in the Summer of 2004, making his debut in the opening Lincolnshire County Shield game of the season at Brigg Town. He played in every match at the start of the season, but following the October trip down to Cirencester Town, where he came off the bench, he was released by the club and signed for Corby Town.

Jimmy Darroch

Seasons Played	League	~	25 (5)
	F.A. Cup	~	1
1958/59	Lincs Cup	~	1
1961/62	Total	~	27 (5)

Right-winger who scored in his first game for Grantham, the opening match of the 1958/59 season at home to Goole Town and played in many of that season's games, apart from the months of November and December when Brian Burton took over his role. After a spell at Boston United, Jimmy helped out the club a few years later when he made one final appearance in November 1961 during the home league game against Heanor Town, a week after impressing in a friendly against Worksop Town.

Craig Davis

Seasons Played	League	~	9
	F.A. Cup	~	
1998/99	F.A. Trophy	~	
	League Cup	~	
	Lincs Cup	~	1
	Total	~	10

Born 12/10/1977 at Rotherham. Young goalkeeper, previously with Rotherham United and Gateshead, who signed from Doncaster Rovers after notching up 16 league and cup appearances during his time there. His first game for Grantham came in the 1998/99 season's opening fixture at home to Scunthorpe United in the Lincolnshire County Senior Cup, but his final appearance for the club soon arrived, after the September league fixture against Crawley Town. Craig went on to play for Telford United and Barrow.

Darren Davis

Seasons Played	League	~	5
	F.A. Cup	~	1
1995/96	F.A. Trophy	~	
	League Cup	~	
	Lincs Cup	~	2
	Total	~	8

Born 05/02/1967 at Sutton-in-Ashfield. Former England Youth International who made over 240 league appearances for Notts County, Lincoln City and Maidstone United. Darren then moved into non-league football to play for Boston United, Eynesbury Rovers and Frickley Athletic, before returning to The Football League with Scarborough. Darren joined Grantham in time to make his debut in the August 1995 County Cup tie against Lincoln City, although after only seven consecutive appearances he had left The Meres and rejoined The Imps again. It was to be a short spell though at Sincil Bank and he finally finished his professional career with a total of 15 goals to his name in 334 senior league and cup fixtures. Darren came back to Grantham in the same season, but was sent off on his return against King's Lynn in October, in what turned out to be his final appearance for the club. He went on to play for Leicester United, Malaysian side, FB, Woodland Wellington in Singapore and then after coming back to England made appearances for VS Rugby, Hucknall Town and Arnold Town, followed by his managerial appointment at Gedling Town in 2002.

Davis

Seasons Played	League	~	2 (1)
	F.A. Cup	~	
1885/86-91/92	Lincs Cup	~	
	Other	~	16 (2)
	Total	~	18 (3)

Made his Grantham debut in the December 1885 friendly against Lincoln City and for some reason over the next few years made only occasional appearances, always either at the beginning or the end of the season. Finally he broke this routine during Grantham's first ever league season, 1891/92, when he made three appearances during November, scoring in the Midland Amateur Alliance game against Sheffield.

Davis

Seasons Played	League	~	1
	F.A. Cup	~	
1922/23	Lincs Cup	~	
	Other	~	
	Total	~	1

Former Ilkeston United player who made one appearance for Grantham in the first game of the 1922/23 season away at Leicester City Reserves.

Davis

Seasons Played	League	~	4 (2)
	F.A. Cup	~	
1946/47	Lincs Cup	~	1 (1)
	Total	~	5 (3)

Made his debut by scoring twice in the Midland League game at home to Gainsborough Trinity in February 1947, but then appeared only four more times for the club, scoring his only other goal in the County Cup Final replay against Gainsborough Trinity. His final appearance for Grantham came three days later at home to Scunthorpe & Lindsey United.

Simon Daws

Seasons Played			
	League	~	18 (1)
	F.A. Cup	~	1
1987/88	F.A. Trophy	~	1
	League Cup	~	7
1990/91	Lincs Cup	~	2
	Total	~	29 (1)

Born 25/03/1964 at Nottingham. Local player who came through the Reserve side to come on as substitute in the opening County Cup tie of the 1987/88 season against Scunthorpe United. Despite a positive start in the First team, including a goal in the September league fixture at Buckingham Town, Simon soon found himself spending much of the time back on the bench. He returned to local football around the Nottingham area, including making appearances for John Player, before returning to the club as they began their temporary stay at Spalding United. His final appearance for Grantham came in the April 1991 league match against Stroud and he went on to play for Southwell City, where he won a Notts Senior Cup runners-up medal, followed by Corby Town, Stamford, Spalding United and Bottesford. Simon has also spent time as Player/Manager for Cottesmore Amateurs in the Leicestershire Senior League and currently lives midway between Grantham and Nottingham.

Dawson

Seasons Played			
	League	~	5 (1)
	Lincs Cup	~	
1904/05	Other	~	
	Total	~	5 (1)

Defender who probably made more appearances for Grantham in this first season back after reforming. He scored just one goal as far as we know, during the initial Midland Amateur Alliance game of the season at home to Bridgford Athletic.

Day

Seasons Played			
	League	~	4
1905/06	Total	~	4

Played in either defence or midfield and seems to have made appearances for Grantham during the Spring of 1906. He was certainly playing in the last game of the 1905/06 season at home to Loughborough Corinthians.

Deacon

Seasons Played			
	F.A. Cup	~	3
	Lincs Cup	~	
1880/81-81/82	Other	~	2
	Total	~	5

Forward who played in the two FA Cup ties against Stafford Road, Wolverhampton, in December 1880 and at least two of the remaining friendlies from that season. Very few team-sheets are available for the following year, but once again he is evident in the FA Cup, this time in the November 1881 Second Round game at Staveley.

Jack Dean

Seasons Played			
	League	~	20 (7)
	F.A. Cup	~	
1957/58-58/59	Lincs Cup	~	2
	Total	~	22 (7)

Jack made his First team debut in the September 1957 Midland League home fixture against Bradford Park Avenue Reserves, but then had to wait until New Year's Day to begin a decent run of games for the club. However, those matches were to include a hat-trick in what must have been one of the biggest upsets of the season, the 7-3 defeat of Peterborough United, plus an appearance in the Lincolnshire Senior Cup 'A' Final against Gainsborough Trinity in April 1958. The following season Jack had to once again wait until the New Year to make his mark in the team, but this time he was only able to add another five appearances to his name, with the league game at South Shields in April 1959 being his final match for Grantham.

Tommy Deans

Seasons Played			
	League	~	20
	F.A. Cup	~	1
1959/60	League Cup	~	2
	Lincs Cup	~	1
	Total	~	24

Born 07/01/1922 at Shieldhill. Left-Back who began his career at Armadale Thistle and Clyde, where he gained Scottish League Representative honours, before joining Notts County in 1949 after a £6,000 transfer fee. Tommy was soon awarded the captaincy there and made over 250 appearances in their successful side which included England International, Tommy Lawton. He then moved into the non-league game with Boston United, followed by Wisbech Town, before joining The Gingerbreads. Tommy made his Grantham debut in the first game of the club's return to the Central Alliance League, the visit of Ely City to London Road and played in many of that season's league runners-up games, apart from a period during the Winter where he went nearly three months with just one appearance. He played his last game for the club at Rugby Town Reserves in April 1960. Died 30/10/2000 at Nottingham.

Andy Deardon

Seasons Played			
	League	~	2
	F.A. Cup	~	
1982/83	F.A. Trophy	~	
	League Cup	~	
1985/86	Lincs Cup	~	
	Other	~	
	Total	~	2

Prolific striker for Grantham Reserves who was promoted to the First team for the April 1982 Northern Premier League match at Mossley and the December 1985 fixture against Stourbridge, with appearances also made in-between for Grantham United.

Billy Death

Seasons Played			
	League	~	22 (11)
	F.A. Cup	~	2
1932/33	Lincs Cup	~	1
	Other	~	1
	Total	~	26 (11)

Born 13/11/1900 at Rotherham. As a young footballer Billy was discovered kicking a salmon tin around the back streets of his Rotherham home. He became an outside-left player at Broome Athletic, Rotherham Town and Notts County, playing in the official opening fixture at Barcelona's new Les Cortes stadium, their home before the Nou Camp, against St Mirren in 1922, and winning a Division Two Championship a year later whilst still at Meadow Lane. Dropping back into non-league football, Billy signed for Mansfield Town, where he was part of their Midland League winning side in 1924, before moving to Sunderland, Exeter City, Gillingham and then returning to Mansfield Town as they entered The Football League. Billy scored 32 goals in a professional career lasting 140 Football League games, plus netted another seven strikes in 10 FA Cup games. He then joined Grantham, scoring his first goal for the club in the September 1932 draw at Boston and his last in the January visit of Scunthorpe & Lindsey United. He probably left London Road soon after this, possibly to join Heanor Town, where it is known he spent some of his playing career. By the middle of the decade though, he was playing for Sutton Town and City Transport, Nottingham, where he worked as a driver up to his retirement. Died 03/07/1984 at Rotherham.

Brian Deehan

Seasons Played			
	League	~	1
	F.A. Cup	~	
1959/60	League Cup	~	
	Lincs Cup	~	
	Total	~	1

Made only one appearance for Grantham, the September 1959 Central Alliance League game at Corby Town Reserves.

DeGroot

Seasons Played	League	~	2
	F.A. Cup	~	
1946/47	Lincs Cup	~	
	Total	~	2

Dutch goalkeeper who played twice for Grantham after the end of Tom Gilchrist's career, the home games against Doncaster Rovers Reserves and Ollerton Colliery in January 1947, .

Harold Dennis

Seasons Played	League	~	101 (28)
	F.A. Cup	~	9 (6)
1922/23	Lincs Cup	~	1 (1)
	Other	~	4 (1)
1927/28-29/30	Total	~	115 (36)

Born 1903 at Newark. Forward who had previously spent time at Newark Athletic and played for Grantham in many of the 1922/23 season's games, scoring his first goal for the club in the September 1922 game at home to Coalville Swifts. After a return to his home club, in 1925 he moved to Huddersfield Town, making just one appearance, followed by Southend United, but with two goals in only eleven senior games there, he came back to Grantham for the start of the 1927/28 season and soon scored his only known hat-trick in the FA Cup tie at home to Newark Town. Available records show that he was still a principal member of the side the following season, playing in the FA Cup Proper matches against Rhyl Athletic and Wigan Borough, but by the end of the 1929/30 season he had made only eight more appearances, with his final goal for the club coming in the September 1929 Midland League game at home to Worksop Town. We do know that during his time at Grantham he was awarded the honour of a place in the Midland League representative side, whilst by the end of his career he had won Central League and West Riding Championship medals, probably with the Reserve side of Huddersfield Town, and an Escritt & Bennett winner's medal. Harold also made appearances for Ancaster and Newark Town at some point.

Dennis

Seasons Played	League	~	
	Lincs Cup	~	
1909/10	Other	~	1
	Total	~	1

Only one known appearance for this player, the Grantham Minor Cup tie at home to Little Gonerby Swifts in November 1909.

A. Derrick

Seasons Played	League	~	129
	F.A. Cup	~	5
1926/27-29/30	Lincs Cup	~	1
	Other	~	
	Total	~	135

Full-Back who also played for Sneinton and Mansfield Town, before making his Grantham debut in the Spring of 1927. He seems to have made the position his own by the following year and played in the FA Cup Proper encounters with Rhyl Athletic and Wigan Borough towards the end of 1928. He continued to play for the club right up until the end of the 1929/30 season.

Derwy

Seasons Played	League	~	1
	Other	~	
1906/07	Total	~	1

Forward, who due to available records is only known to have played in one game for Grantham, the September 1906 Midland Amateur Alliance match at home to Derby Thornhill.

Dexter

Seasons Played	League	~	3
	F.A. Cup	~	
1933/34	Lincs Cup	~	
	Other	~	
	Total	~	3

Forward who had also played for Long Eaton and is known to have appeared in the first three Central Combination League games for Grantham, against Loughborough Corinthians, Bolsover and Ripley Town, but appears to have played no other part in the team after that.

Geoff Dibble

Seasons Played	League	~	
	F.A. Cup	~	
1980/81	F.A. Trophy	~	
	League Cup	~	
	Lincs Cup	~	
	Other	~	1
	Total	~	1

Possible Nottingham based player who made only one game for Grantham, but what a match to appear in, the December 1980 Redmayne Trophy tie against the European Champions, Nottingham Forest, when he came on as a substitute.

Bill Dickinson

Seasons Played	League	~	5 (3)
	F.A. Cup	~	
1960/61	League Cup	~	
	Lincs Cup	~	
	Total	~	5 (3)

Forward from Ruskington who had previously made appearances for Sleaford Amateurs and Boston United. He played for Grantham in three games at the start of the 1960/61 season when Mike Bosnell was unavailable and scored in the matches against Rothwell Town and Long Eaton United. Bill was again able to play for the First team over the Christmas period, to cover Brian Asher, and scored in his final game at Wellingborough on New Year's Eve.

Cecil Dickinson

Seasons Played	League	~	38 (17)
	F.A. Cup	~	
1937/38	Lincs Cup	~	3 (2)
	Other	~	5 (4)
1939/40	Total	~	46 (23)

Forward who made his debut in the September 1937 Midland League game at Boston United, but had to wait until December to score for the club, eventually netting twice in the game at Newark Town. It was a disappointing end of season for Grantham, finishing in the runners-up position to Shrewsbury Town in the league and as far as Cecil was concerned, I doubt if there was much compensation for him by scoring one of the goals in the Spalding Victory Cup match. He returned in September 1939 with a goal in a friendly against an RAF XI, but it wasn't until the Christmas period that Cecil was once again turning out for the club week in, week out. After playing in the Lincolnshire Senior Cup Final against Scunthorpe & Lindsey United, he made his final appearance in the Midland War-Time match at Peterborough United in May 1940.

Cyril Dickinson

Seasons Played	League	~	33 (12)
	F.A. Cup	~	
1938/39	Lincs Cup	~	2 (3)
	Total	~	35 (15)

Player who had previously turned out for the beautifully titled Rauceby Mental Hospital FC and scored twice on his Grantham debut during the visit of Boston United to London Road in September of 1938. Cyril played and scored in many entertaining matches during that campaign, including a 5-5 draw with Boston United in the County Cup and the 9-1 demolition of Denaby United. He made his final appearance for the club in May 1939, during a Midland League match at Nottingham Forest Reserves.

R. Dickinson

Seasons Played	League	~	2
	F.A. Cup	~	
1938/39	Lincs Cup	~	
	Total	~	2

Forward who played in the first two games of the 1938/39 season, away at Shrewsbury Town and Barnsley Reserves.

Syd Dickinson

Seasons Played	League	~	98 (10)
	F.A. Cup	~	12 (2)
1935/36-37/38	Lincs Cup	~	8 (1)
	Other	~	3
	Total	~	121 (13)

Born 17/08/1906 at Nottingham. Left-sided player with experience at Dale Rovers, Nottingham Forest, Mansfield Town, Bradford Park

Avenue, where he won a Division Three (North) Championship medal, Port Vale and Lincoln City, with a total of 24 goals scored in his 182 Football League appearances, plus two more strikes in 14 FA Cup ties. Syd made his debut for Grantham in the first game of the 1935/36 season at Burton Town and a few months later played in the FA Cup First Round match against Notts County, followed by appearances in the County Cup Final against Boston United and the Grantham Hospital Cup victory over Doncaster Rovers. The following season he received a Lincolnshire Senior Cup winner's medal after the eventual defeat of The Pilgrims, but in the 1937/38 season, when Grantham finished runner's-up in the league to Shrewsbury Town, Syd was missing from most of the games after the Christmas period, although he returned to play in the Stamford Nursing Society Cup match at the end of April. After his playing career was over, Syd continued working in the game as a scout for Aston Villa and Notts County, with the last of those posts reaching well into the 1960's. Died 02/02/1984 at Rushcliffe.

Dickinson

Seasons Played			
	League	~	9 (1)
	Other	~	
1931/32	Lincs Cup	~	
	Other	~	1
1933/34	Total	~	10 (1)

There is very little information available on this player's particular games, other than we know that he scored his only goal for the club during the March 1931 Midland League game against Nottingham Forest Reserves. He returned though in October 1933 to play in the Grantham Hospital Cup tie against St John's, with his final match a week later when the team travelled over to Heanor for a league fixture. Of course there is the possibility that with him being a local player, (we know he also played for Grantham Amateurs), that he could be a younger character of one of the previous Dickinson entries.

F. Dicks

Seasons Played			
	League	~	36 (1)
	F.A. Cup	~	2
1919/20	League Cup	~	
	Lincs Cup	~	3
1923/24	Other	~	
	Total	~	41 (1)

Centre-Forward who also played for Hucknall Byron and made his debut for Grantham in the FA Cup replay against Boots Athletic, which was held on Notts County's ground in October 1919. After his first couple of games though, he had to revert to a more defensive position, possibly due to the quality of strikers already at the club during this time, like Ernie Eatch and Sid Howard, plus several others. It was a rare occasion then for him to play up front and this meant that he only scored once for Grantham, during the Central Alliance game at Gresley Rovers in January 1920. He returned to London Road in September 1923 and made irregular appearances until his last recorded match in April 1924 at Heanor Town.

John Dilnot

Seasons Played			
	League	~	1
	F.A. Cup	~	
1998/99	F.A. Trophy	~	
	League Cup	~	
	Lincs Cup	~	
	Total	~	1

Born 19/11/1977 at Nottingham. Defender who began his career on the books of Lincoln City and Chesterfield, before making appearances for Alfreton Town and Gresley Rovers. After joining Grantham on-loan he made just one appearance for the club, in the October 1998 Dr Marten's Premier League fixture at Halesowen Town. Clubs represented after that include Heanor Town, Clipstone Welfare, Ripley Town (on-loan), Radford and Sandiacre Town, where he currently plays.

Clive Dixon

Seasons Played			
	League	~	26 (11)
	F.A. Cup	~	
1973/74-75/76	F.A. Trophy	~	1
	League Cup	~	3 (1)
	Lincs Cup	~	1
	Total	~	31 (12)

Forward from the Lincoln area who made his debut in the March 1974 league fixture at home to Weymouth and scored his first goal for the club in the following match at Wimbledon. He had a good run in the side at the end of that season, with Ernie Nixon out, but made only 8 appearances and 13 over the next two years, with the October 1975 trip down to Dunstable his final game for the club. Clive was last known to be still living in the Lincoln area, working for the County Council.

F. Dixon

Seasons Played			
	League	~	6 (2)
	F.A. Cup	~	
1929/30	Lincs Cup	~	
	Other	~	
	Total	~	6 (2)

Outside-Left player who had previously made appearances for Thursday Wolves and scored in the two games against Denaby United in December 1929, but there is no information available on the other four matches that he played in.

Harry Dixon

Seasons Played			
	Other	~	2
1874/75	Total	~	2

Born circa 1855 at West Retford, Nottinghamshire. Brother of Percy Dixon and educated at The King's School in Grantham where his name can still be seen etched under one of the windows in the Old School, although unlike the town's other famous juvenile offender, Isaac Newton, Harry managed to get away with the misdemeanour twice! He was involved with Grantham Football Club from their conception, playing in the very first club match, the first visit of another team, when the Third Lincolnshire Volunteer Rifles arrived at London Road in October 1874, but made no other appearances for the club after the friendly at Lincoln just over a month later. Nothing is known of him over the next few years, but by the time of the 1901 census he was working as a solicitor in Paddington, London.

Percy Dixon

Seasons Played			
	F.A. Cup	~	1
1874/75-75/76	Other	~	16 (3)
1877/78	Total	~	17 (3)

Born circa 1853 at West Retford, Nottinghamshire. Brother of Harry Dixon. Percy also attended The King's School and was a member of the original committee whose aim was to start a football club in the town. He played in the first club match, captained several of the following games, and appeared in the first competitive fixture versus the Third Lincolnshire Volunteer Rifles. The following season he is notable by his absence, until he returns in February of 1876 and scores goals against Bourne and Sleaford. Finally, the following October he scores his last goal for the club in a friendly against Stamford, plays in the club's inaugural FA Cup match against Clapham Rovers, but makes his final appearance for Grantham at Retford Rovers only days later. Like his brother, Percy was also working as a solicitor in 1901, this time in Tonbridge.

Dixon

Seasons Played			
	League	~	2 (2)
	F.A. Cup	~	2 (2)
1911/12-12/13	Lincs Cup	~	1 (1)
	Other	~	
	Total	~	5 (5)

Unfortunately only the goals are recorded for this player, with his first in March 1912 during a Central Alliance game at home to Ilkeston United and his last in October of the same year during the 7-1 thrashing of Grimsby Rovers in the County Cup.

Dixon

Seasons Played			
1925/26	League	~	1
	F.A. Cup	~	
	Lincs Cup	~	
	Total	~	1

Previously played for Nottingham Forest Reserves, but made only one appearance for Grantham, at London Road against Lincoln City Reserves in November 1925.

Dobbs

Seasons Played			
1879/80-81/82	F.A. Cup	~	5 (1)
1883/84	Lincs Cup	~	
	Other	~	15 (13)
	Total	~	20 (14)

Made his debut in a friendly against Newark at the start of the 1879/80 season and played in every game from that campaign where full records are available. He scored several times over the next few years, including a tally of five after the game against Sleaford in February 1880 and possibly finished at least one of the seasons as the club's highest scorer. Grantham Football Club played no matches during 1882/83 and he seems to eventually return for just one more game, a friendly against Grantham Volunteers in October 1883.

J. Donaldson

Seasons Played			
1932/33-33/34	League	~	34 (30)
1939/40	F.A. Cup	~	2 (1)
1945/46	Lincs Cup	~	3 (4)
	Other	~	4 (7)
	Total	~	43 (42)

Records show that he played in only a few games from the 1932/33 season, but we do know that they included hat-tricks in the matches against Mansfield Town Reserves and Boston. By the following season though, he was playing in nearly every game and finished as the club's highest scorer, helped by further hat-tricks against Newark Town, Worksop Town and a single strike in the Grantham Hospital Cup Final against TW Rust & Co. He was certainly absent from London Road at the start of the next campaign and it was presumably during this era that he played for Halifax Town, Crystal Palace and Newark Town, achievements we know that he secured at some point during his career. However, he returned to Grantham just before the Second World War and played at London Road in the final two Midland 'War-Time' League fixtures, as well as making many appearances for the club in the friendly matches during The War. He made his last appearance for the club on Christmas Day 1945 in the League encounter against Ransome & Marles.

Willie Donaldson

Seasons Played			
1952/53-54/55	League	~	128 (15)
	F.A. Cup	~	6 (2)
	Lincs Cup	~	5 (2)
	Total	~	139 (19)

Born 20/01/1920 in Edinburgh. A former Desert Rat during The War, and winger who had previously played for Leith Athletic, Bradford Park Avenue and Mansfield Town, earning a total of 97 Football League appearances. He still holds the distinction of being the shortest player, at 5' 2", to have played for Bradford Park Avenue, although it is not known whether he also holds this record for any other clubs he represented. Willie first played for Grantham in the opening match of the 1952/53 season at Mansfield Town Reserves, and scored his first goal for the club the following month during the FA Cup victory at Bourne Town. He played in the County Cup Final at Spalding United at the end of that season, whilst a year later in the same competition he scored a goal to help achieve victory over Gainsborough Trinity. The following year he made it the third season where he had played in virtually every game for The Gingerbreads, but it was a poor year for the team with precious little to cheer about. The term petered out with Willie scoring his last goal in the game against Doncaster Rovers Reserves and his final appearance for the club in the closing fixture at Boston United. At the end of his playing career he returned to Bradford and became a publican. Died 1977 at Bradford.

Doncaster

Seasons Played			
1913/14	League	~	1 (1)
	F.A. Cup	~	1
	Lincs Cup	~	
	Total	~	2 (1)

Defender who played in the September 1913 FA Cup tie against Grantham Avenue, scored in the Central Alliance match at home to Notts County Reserves two days later and may have appeared in other games for the club at the start of that season.

George Dooley

Seasons Played			
1934/35-37/38	League	~	61 (25)
	F.A. Cup	~	12 (6)
	Lincs Cup	~	7 (3)
	Other	~	1
	Total	~	81 (34)

Former Codnor Park and Newark Town centre-forward who scored twice during his first match for Grantham, the March 1935 Midland League draw against Gainsborough Trinity. George missed only one of the remaining games during the following few months and appeared in both the Lincolnshire Senior County Cup Final and the replay at Boston United. The following season George missed many of the games, but luckily managed to play in some of the year's highlights, including the FA Cup match against Notts County and the County Cup Final, again versus The Pilgrims. By the start of the 1936/37 season, George's appearances were becoming limited and with both Frank Bungay and Harry Siddall playing up front, many of those appearances came from the midfield position that he was allocated. This didn't stop him from scoring goals though and at the end of the season he had forced himself into the side for another Lincolnshire Senior Cup Final replay against Boston once more. Of course the following year saw Grantham finish runners-up in the Midland League, but George had to accept a somewhat secondary role covering unavailable players. He scored his last goal for the club in the April 1938 draw at home to Grimsby Town Reserves, followed by his final appearance in that crucial match at Shrewsbury Town a few weeks later.

Neil Dorsett

Seasons Played			
1991/92	League	~	14 (4)
	F.A. Cup	~	
	F.A. Trophy	~	
	League Cup	~	4 (1)
	Lincs Cup	~	
	Total	~	18 (5)

Born 03/10/1963 at Derby. Midfielder who began his career with Borrowash Victoria and Burton Albion, before having a spell playing in New Zealand with Claudland Rovers, Whitenata City, Massey AFC and Mount Mangamui. Signed by John Robertson, Neil made his Grantham debut in the September 1991 league fixture at Hednesford Town and scored a brace in the following game against Bedworth United. After scoring twice again in the February 1992 fixture at home to Tamworth, the following game against RC Warwick saw him replaced by substitute Chris Grocock and he made no further appearances for the club. Neil went on to play for Leicester United, Shepshed Charterhouse and Ilkeston Town. He still lives in Derby and runs his own carpet shop in the city.

Pete Down

Seasons Played			
1970/71-73/74	League	~	22
1977/78	F.A. Cup	~	3
	F.A. Trophy	~	2
	League Cup	~	10
	Lincs Cup	~	
	Other	~	1
	Total	~	38

Born 11/09/1948 at Bottesford. Local player with experience at Ropsley and Harrowby United who began his Grantham career in the October 1970 Midland League draw at Arnold, but made only another four appearances by the end of that season. This trend continued the following year, although Pete managed to score in a Bancroft Invitation Cup tie against Wisbech when several of the First team players were rested. Grantham's first two seasons in the Southern League saw Pete once more called upon as and when needed, but the 1975/76 season saw him playing for Stamford

Town, culminating in a Wembley appearance in the FA Vase Final. He returned once more to London Road towards the end of the 1977/78 season and played in the two legs of the Southern League Cup Semi-Final against Gravesend & Northfleet, with his final appearance for Grantham in the April 1978 league game at Worcester City. Pete continued to play in local football and then as a manager took Melton Town to a league title, before returning to Harrowby United. He later assisted The Gingerbreads by running the Social Club, around the same time as his sons, Simon and Chris Down, played for the club. Pete is currently landlord of a public house near to Barnsley.

Simon Down

Seasons Played			
	League	~	7
	F.A. Cup	~	
1994/95-95/96	F.A. Trophy	~	
	League Cup	~	1
	Lincs Cup	~	2
	Total	~	10

Born 12/08/1974 in Grantham. Son of Pete Down and a defender who had previously played for Croxton Kerrial and Grantham Reserves. He made his First team debut in the December 1994 league fixture at Buckingham Town and had his best run in the side at the end of the campaign, with four consecutive appearances. The following year he was awarded another four games for the First team, with the October 1995 match at home to Bedworth United his final one for the club. Simon went on to play for Cottesmore Amateurs, Bourne Town and Harrowby United. He still lives in Grantham, works for a distribution company opposite The Meres stadium and is Assistant Manager for the Harrowby Villa team.

Downham

Seasons Played			
	League	~	16 (2)
	F.A. Cup	~	
1929/30	Lincs Cup	~	
	Other	~	
	Total	~	16 (2)

Former Loughborough Corinthians player who was certainly playing at London Road by November 1929 and scored in the Midland League games against Scunthorpe & Lindsey United and Notts County Reserves.

George Downing

Seasons Played			
	F.A. Cup	~	1
	Other	~	34
1874/75-77/78	Total	~	35

Born 1854 at Barrowby. Brother of William Downing and probably also related to the other 'Downings' who were playing for Grantham in those early years. George played in that very first competitive match when the Third Lincolnshire Volunteer Rifles came to London Road and continued to represent Grantham in many of those early games, including the club matches, even captaining one side on occasions. During his final season with Grantham he played in the club's first FA Cup match against Clapham Rovers, before making his last appearance in a friendly at Lincoln towards the end of the season. By the 1881 census George was working on his father's farm at Barrowby, whilst he was also a Captain in the Royal South Lincoln Militia, but twenty years later he had retired to Warwickshire.

John Downing

Seasons Played			
1875/76	F.A. Cup	~	
	Other	~	4
1877/78	Total	~	4

Born circa 1853 at Casthorpe. Almost certainly a brother of George and William Downing. John made his debut in January 1876 when Grantham travelled over to Nottingham Castle for a friendly. However, he seems to have appeared only once more for the club during that season, again over at Nottingham when the team played against Nottingham Lace. He finally played in two more games for Grantham over a year later, in both the matches against Stamford. In the 1881 census John was working his own farm at Weston in Lincolnshire, whilst 1901 saw his profession listed as Baker, in Abingdon.

Mick Downing

Seasons Played			
	League	~	32 (3)
	F.A. Cup	~	
1984/85	F.A. Trophy	~	3
	League Cup	~	3
	Lincs Cup	~	2 (1)
	Other	~	2 (1)
	Total	~	42 (5)

Born circa 1958. Previously spent time at Barnsley and Grimsby Town and scored on his Grantham debut in the opening fixture of the 1984/85 season at Boston United in the County Cup. Mick played in most of the games that year, but in a campaign which finished with a league relegation, highlights are hard to find. His final goal for Grantham came in the Boxing Day defeat at Goole Town, with appearances coming right up until the club's last Northern Premier League game at Oswestry Town. The following season Mick signed for Goole Town and then moved to Harrogate Town.

T. Downing

Seasons Played			
	Other	~	1
1874/75	Total	~	1

Despite playing in many club matches during that maiden season, he made only one appearance against another side, the first game versus the Third Lincolnshire Volunteer Rifles in October 1874.

William Downing

Seasons Played			
	F.A. Cup	~	1
	Other	~	24
1874/75-77/78	Total	~	25

Born 1855 at Casthorpe. Brother of George Downing and the fourth and hopefully final member of the Downing family (see following entry). William joined the club at the start of 1875 and played in his first friendly in February when a Sleaford side came to London Road. He played in many of the games during the following two seasons and during some of the club matches from this period was able to captain one of the sides. Surely the most interesting of these must have been when he captained a side against George Downing's team in a game played in January 1876 under Rugby Union Rules. Later that year William played in Grantham's first ever FA Cup game, when Clapham Rovers came to London Road, and was still appearing regularly up until the match at Sleaford in February 1878. According to the 1881 census, along with the other 'Downings' from this era, William was farming, although at a separate location at Barrowby to his father.

Downing

Seasons Played			
	F.A. Cup	~	2
	Other	~	21 (1)
1878/79-80/81	Total	~	23 (1)

Most probably one of the previous 'Downing' entries, but from the opening friendly of the 1878/79 season at Sleaford only one appears, so no initial was used which we could now use to verify his identity. There is simply no means available to substantially narrow the task down, bearing in mind that three 'Downing's' made appearances the year before and players didn't even adhere to a particular position. Anyway, whoever he might have been, he scored the only known goal of his Grantham career during the April 1879 friendly against Burghley Park and played right up until the final game of the 1880/81 season, when Bourne visited London Road.

Downs

Seasons Played			
	League	~	
	F.A. Cup	~	
1914/15	Lincs Cup	~	1 (1)
	Total	~	1 (1)

There is only one known appearance for this individual, discovered due to his opening goal during the November 1914 County Cup replay against Boston Swifts.

Fred Doyle

Seasons Played			
	League	~	9 (5)
	F.A. Cup	~	
1956/57	Lincs Cup	~	
	Total	~	9 (5)

Forward who scored on his debut for Grantham during the November 1956 game at home to Peterborough United and then played in the following month's games as well. Fred had another spell in the First team during February, which saw his final goal for the club against Doncaster Rovers Reserves, with his last appearance in the home game against Gainsborough Trinity at the beginning of March 1957.

Drake

Seasons Played	Other	~	4
1875/76-76/77	Total	~	4

First played for Grantham in December 1875 when the team appeared in a friendly at home to Nottingham Lace. Apparently he only played during that month and the following one, although he made one further appearance in November 1876 at Sleaford.

Drew

Seasons Played	League	~	1
	Lincs Cup	~	1
1904/05	Other	~	
	Total	~	2

Played in two games towards the beginning of the 1904/05 season, the County competition tie against Hornsby Engineers and the Midland Amateur Alliance game the following week at home to Notts Magdala.

Dave Drinkell

Seasons Played	League	~	10
	F.A. Cup	~	4 (1)
1985/86	F.A. Trophy	~	
	League Cup	~	6
	Lincs Cup	~	2
	Total	~	22 (1)

Born 1959 at Grimsby. Former Boston FC midfielder and brother of the former Grimsby Town, Norwich City and Coventry City player, Kevin Drinkell. Dave made his Grantham debut in the 1985/86 season's opening fixture against Boston United in the County Cup and scored his only goal for the club in the September FA Cup tie against Oldbury United. After playing in every single one of the early games though from that campaign, the November league fixture at Leamington saw Dave come off the bench to replace Kevin Beck and this turned out to be his final appearance for Grantham. He went on to play for Appleby Frodingham, King's Lynn and Lincoln United.

J. Driver

Seasons Played	League	~	9 (13)
	F.A. Cup	~	
1924/25-25/26	Lincs Cup	~	1 (1)
	Other	~	4 (7)
	Total	~	14 (21)

Former Hucknall Byron and Shirebrook forward who was considered to be a tremendous signing for Grantham, but unfortunately the club was fined after playing him before the actual transfer was completed. The only information valid to his Grantham career consists of the games where he scored, starting with the Central Alliance fixture at home to his old club, Hucknall Byron, in December 1924. He was obviously an accomplished striker with the fact that he netted hat-tricks over the next few months against RAF Cranwell and Sutton Junction and finished the championship winning season as the club's top scorer. It seems certain that he departed the club soon after the start of the new season as his name disappears from the list of scorers after the abandoned game against Alfreton Town in September of 1925.

Scott Drury

Seasons Played	League	~	20
	F.A. Cup	~	2
1994/95-95/96	F.A. Trophy	~	2
	League Cup	~	1
	Lincs Cup	~	1
	Total	~	26

Former Spalding United and Wyberton goalkeeper who first played for Grantham when he replaced the injured Guy Hardcastle in the January 1995 league fixture at Hinckley Town and then appeared in the final three matches of the season. The majority of his games for the club came at the start of the following season, but the return of Hardcastle in the Autumn after recovering from a broken arm, saw his appearances limited once more. Scott's final game for Grantham came in the April 1996 defeat at Rothwell Town.

J. Dudley

Seasons Played	League	~	1
	Lincs Cup	~	
1931/32	Other	~	
	Total	~	1

Brother of W. Dudley and an Inside-Forward who had also played for Lenton Gregory. Unfortunately no information is available to denote which game he played in for Grantham.

W. Dudley

Seasons Played	League	~	43 (35)
	F.A. Cup	~	3
1931/32-32/33	Lincs Cup	~	2 (1)
	Other	~	3 (4)
	Total	~	51 (40)

Centre-Forward who, like his brother, also played for Lenton Gregory, and scored his first goal for Grantham in the Midland League game at Scunthorpe & Lindsey United just after the 1932 New Year. He scored hat-tricks in the next few months during a friendly against West Bromwich Albion and the league game at home to Hull City Reserves, but was missing from the team at the start of the 1932/33 season for some reason. When he returned in November though, he continued to make his mark within the Midland League and finished the season with another 20 league goals to his name, aided by three strikes during the home fixture against Barnsley Reserves and one more when Wombwell left London Road after a 10-0 defeat. There is no confirmation as to his last game for the club, but he was certainly scoring well into April of 1933.

Ayden Duffy

Seasons Played	League	~	3
	F.A. Cup	~	
2004/05	F.A. Trophy	~	1
	League Cup	~	
	Lincs Cup	~	
	Total	~	4

Born 16/11/1986 at Kettering. Apprentice goalkeeper with Lincoln City, who had also made appearances for Bourne Town. Ayden joined The Gingerbreads as cover for Mario Ziccardi and played three times in November 2004, against Hednesford Town, Chippenham Town and Havant & Waterlooville. He went back to Lincoln and a few weeks later to Bourne Town on work experience, but returned to The Meres in April 2004 to play once more for the club, against Halesowen Town.

Duggon

Seasons Played	League	~	2
	F.A. Cup	~	
1920/21	Lincs Cup	~	
	Other	~	
1925/26	Total	~	2

Local player who had previously played for A&J Shaw, Grantham St John's and Grantham Pensions Hospital, but available team-sheets only show two appearances for our club. First was the April 1921 Central Alliance game against Shirebrook, but there are then no records of another appearance for him until the 1925/26 season and even then it doesn't indicate the particular fixture.

J. Dulson

Seasons Played	League	~	18 (11)
	F.A. Cup	~	
1926/27	Lincs Cup	~	1 (1)
1929/30	Other	~	
1934/35	Total	~	19 (12)

Centre-forward who made his Grantham debut in the September 1926 Midland League game at home to York City. He scored a hat-trick two days later when Sutton Town were thrashed 12-3, but then apparently departed London Road almost straight after this. He returned at the end of the decade though, to make two more appearances, but it wasn't until November 1934 that he spent his longest period with Grantham, a three month spell that netted him nine goals including a hat-trick in the match against Rotherham United Reserves. Press reports from the time state that he was a former Accrington Stanley striker. There was a Joe Dulson (born 31/01/1913 at Basford, Notts) who played for them and Nottingham Forest, but take another look at his date of birth and it can't be the same player who made his Grantham debut in 1926. Therefore we are either talking about two 'Dulson's' who played for Grantham around this time or the local press simply assumed incorrectly that he was the former League player.

Bob Duncan

Seasons Played			
	League	~	9
	F.A. Cup	~	1
1983/84-85/86	F.A. Trophy	~	2
	League Cup	~	3
	Lincs Cup	~	
	Other	~	
	Total	~	15

Born 14/01/1949 at Wigan. Christened Robert Don-Duncan but was more commonly known without the double-barrelled surname during his time at Grantham. He began his footballing career at the helm of Queen's University in Northern Ireland, before returning to England and playing for Loughborough Universities, Boston United and Holbeach United. Whilst at the latter, Bob became Player/Manager and then moved on to the helm of Boston FC. He came to Grantham as Player/Manager at the start of the 1983/84 season, although he made only infrequent appearances himself, the first of which was the FA Trophy tie and replay against Leicester United. The season finished with Grantham in fourth position in the Northern Premier League, a place in the non-league pyramid that has not been bettered since. The following season though, saw an almost complete reversal of fortunes as wage restrictions led to the club's eventual relegation. As Grantham returned to the Southern League, wages were still a problem and Bob was forced to play in defence for many of the early games, although the October draw against Bridgnorth Town was his last for the club. Soon after this Bob was relieved of his duties, to be replaced by Barry Shaw and he went on to assist at Skegness Town, before taking over at Spalding United where he guided them to the United Counties Championship. Bob returned to Grantham as Manager after the departure of John Robertson in March 1992 and the following season he took The Gingerbreads to third place in the league, before a financial crisis in the New Year led to Bob and many of the players leaving the club. He returned once more to Boston FC, now re-named Boston Town, and is still at the helm there, plus teaches at the local High School.

Duncan

Seasons Played			
	League	~	1
	Lincs Cup	~	
1907/08	Other	~	
	Total	~	1

Only one known appearance for this goalkeeper, the February 1908 Midland Amateur Alliance game against Mansfield Amateurs, although it is quite probable that he played in other matches that season.

S. Dunn

Seasons Played			
	League	~	3
	F.A. Cup	~	
1929/30	Lincs Cup	~	
	Other	~	
	Total	~	3

Defender who had also played for Sneinton and made appearances for Grantham against Worksop Town and Loughborough Corinthians at the start of the 1929/30 season, but no records are available to show his final appearance.

Dave Durham

Seasons Played			
	League	~	26 (1)
	F.A. Cup	~	1
1989/90-91/92	F.A. Trophy	~	2
	League Cup	~	6
	Lincs Cup	~	2
	Total	~	37 (1)

Progressed through the Reserves to make his senior debut in the November 1989 Westgate Insurance League Cup tie at Atherstone United, with his first goal in the March 1990 league victory at Bridgnorth Town. The following season he played in nearly half of the games, one of which was Grantham's last ever match at London Road, when Dudley Town arrived for a league fixture in September 1990. Grantham's first season at The Meres saw Dave struggling to command a regular place and the October 1991 Beazer Homes League Cup tie against Atherstone United, when he came on as substitute, was his last for the club, coincidentally the same ground that his Gingerbread's career had started on. Dave then moved to Harrowby United, but little is known of him after that.

DuRose

Seasons Played			
	League	~	1 (2)
	F.A. Cup	~	1 (1)
1920/21	Lincs Cup	~	
	Other	~	
	Total	~	2 (3)

Inside-Right who had previously played for Lincoln Robey and scored on his Grantham debut during the October 1920 FA Cup tie at home to Shirebrook. He netted a brace a week later in the 8-0 thrashing of RAF Cranwell, but there are no records of him playing for the club after this game.

Darren Dye

Seasons Played			
	League	~	135 (6)
	F.A. Cup	~	13
1995/96	F.A. Trophy	~	8 (1)
	League Cup	~	5
2000/01-02/03	Lincs Cup	~	5
	Total	~	166 (7)

Born 15/09/1967 at Lincoln. Brother of Dean Dye. Defender who began his career at Lincoln Moorlands, before moving to Nettleham United and then Lincoln United. His first game for Grantham came in the October 1995 league fixture against Stourbridge, with his initial goal for the club the following month at home to Bury Town. Darren played in every one of that season's remaining games, but moved on in the Summer to play for firstly Worksop Town and then Lincoln United. He returned to The Meres at the start of the 2000/01 season and was an important member of Grantham's defence, playing in the FA Cup tie at Rushden & Diamonds, whilst a year later he missed only one of the league games that eventually saw Grantham promoted back into the Dr Marten's Premier League. Darren played in the August 2002 Lincolnshire County Senior Cup Final against Scunthorpe United, the culmination of the previous year's competition, and the final qualifying round tie in the FA Cup against Morecambe. His last goal for the club came just after Christmas at Weymouth, with his final appearance in the March 2003 league fixture at home to Crawley Town. Darren still lives at Lincoln and works as a Maintenance Technician.

Dean Dye

Seasons Played			
	League	~	32 (5)
	F.A. Cup	~	2
1994/95-95/96	F.A. Trophy	~	1
	League Cup	~	
	Lincs Cup	~	1
	Total	~	36 (5)

Born 05/03/1969 at Lincoln. Brother of Darren Dye. Previously played for Nettleham United, Lincoln United, twice, with Boston FC and Sutton Town in-between, Charlton Athletic, Lincoln City, then had two more spells at Lincoln United, once again with Boston FC in the middle. He made his Grantham debut by replacing Kasi Oseni during the November 1994 league match at home to Armitage and scored his first goal only four weeks later against Nuneaton Borough. For the rest of the season Dean played in every game for The Gingerbreads and after the Summer break scored a brace in the September 1995 game at Bury Town. These would turn out to be his last goals for the club though, as the following Saturday he broke his leg in the FA Cup tie against Rushden & Diamonds. Following his recovery from this injury, Dean returned yet again to Lincoln United, before transferring to Worksop Town and finally going full circle by signing for Nettleham United.

Reg Dyer

Seasons Played			
	League	~	61 (4)
	F.A. Cup	~	10 (1)
1948/49-50/51	Lincs Cup	~	2
	Total	~	73 (5)

Born 1917 at Filey. Centre-Half who began his career with Filey and Bradford Park Avenue, before going on to score one goal in ten First team appearances for Torquay United. After The War Reg signed for Peterborough United and then Grantham, making his debut in the opening match of the 1948/49 season at Scarborough and scoring his first goal for the club only two weeks later during the home game against Boston United. Reg played in many of those first matches until he lost his position after the arrival of Joe Parr at the end of the year. But by the start of the 1949/50 season, a few departures from the club allowed both players to become secure in the Grantham defence. Reg played in the highlight of the season, when the team travelled to Wrexham for an FA Cup First Round tie, and the following week netted a brace in the league fixture at Mansfield Town Reserves for what would ultimately be his last goals for the club. Reg unfortunately missed out on the County Cup Final at the end of the season, whilst the 1950/51 campaign saw him playing in only a handful of matches, with his last game for the club when Halifax Town Reserves came to London Road in October 1950. This was also the end of his playing career. He went into the haulage business with a Peterborough company and then, after moving back to the Torquay area, continued driving up to his retirement. Died 04/10/2004 at Torquay.

William Dyson

Seasons Played			
	League	~	6
	F.A. Cup	~	
1929/30	Lincs Cup	~	
	Other	~	
	Total	~	6

Born circa 1904 at Gedling. Former Gedling Colliery, Mansfield Town, Ilkeston United and Grantham Reserves player who, sadly, we are unable to highlight First team games in which he played. After his spell at London Road though, he moved on to Sutton Town, Heanor Town and Ilkeston Town.

Eagle

Seasons Played			
	League	~	7 (5)
	FA Amt. Cup	~	
1905/06-06/07	League Cup	~	
	Lincs Cup	~	2 (1)
1909/10-10/11	Other	~	2
	Total	~	11 (6)

Made his Grantham debut in the final game of the 1905/06 season at home to Loughborough Corinthians, but little is known about his work the following year, other than a goal in the February 1907 game against Derby YMCA. There are no records of him playing during the next two seasons, although of course it is quite possible that he may have made occasional appearances. Certainly by the start of the 1909/10 season he seems to have become a consistent member of the side and he was making regular appearances during the following league championship winning season, until the last recorded instance of his name, scoring twice in the February 1911 defeat of Notts Grosvenor.

Ted Eaglen

Seasons Played			
	League	~	41
	F.A. Cup	~	6
1949/50	Lincs Cup	~	4
	Total	~	51

Born 07/07/1924 at Swineshead. Former Parachute Regiment Sergeant during World War Two who had previously played in goal for Boston United. He took over the role from Percy Ashton at the start of the 1949/50 season and although occupying the role for only one season, it did allow him to play in the FA Cup First Round against Wrexham and both the Lincolnshire Senior Cup 'A' final and replay at Boston United. Ted played his last game for the club in May 1950 at York City Reserves and went on to join Spalding United and March Town United. He also spent many years playing cricket and worked as a celebrity minder at The Gliderdrome in Boston, which at the time was hosting the premier acts from the entertainment industry. Ted is retired now, but still lives in the Boston area.

George Eales

Seasons Played			
	League	~	13 (4)
	F.A. Cup	~	
1935/36	Lincs Cup	~	1
	Other	~	
	Total	~	14 (4)

Local player who had also played for Lee & Grinling, Grantham St John's and first played for our club in the December 1935 draw at home to Doncaster Rovers Reserves, managing to score two of the goals himself. However, less than three months later he had played his last game for Grantham, the Midland League match at home to Boston United, meaning he had not only missed out on the FA Cup tie against Notts County, but also the local cup finals at the end of the season.

Eales

Seasons Played			
	League	~	1
	FA Amt. Cup	~	
1910/11	League Cup	~	
	Lincs Cup	~	
	Other	~	
	Total	~	1

Only one recorded appearance for this player, the important victory at West Bridgford Albion in January 1911, during Grantham's league title winning season.

Paul Eason

Seasons Played			
	League	~	1
	F.A. Cup	~	
1986/87	F.A. Trophy	~	1
	League Cup	~	1
	Lincs Cup	~	
	Total	~	3

Born 03/09/1960 at Leicester. Former Apprentice Goalkeeper at Leicester City who arrived at Grantham on-loan from Shepshed Charterhouse to cover Linden Parslow's suspension. He played in the League Cup fixture against Leicester United, the FA Trophy defeat at home to Blyth Spartans and finally the Boxing Day match against Leicester United.

Jock Eastmead

Seasons Played			
	League	~	4 (2)
	F.A. Cup	~	1
1914/15	Lincs Cup	~	
1919/20	Total	~	5 (2)

Player who was previously with Grantham Avenue, but very little information exists as to the games he played in for Grantham during the final Central Alliance competition until after the end of The Great War. Jock returned to play at London Road in 1919, after a period at Lincoln City, but made only two more appearances, with the league fixture at Ilkeston United in November being his final game.

Edgar Eatch

Seasons Played			
	League	~	67 (34)
	F.A. Cup	~	3 (7)
1919/20-22/23	Lincs Cup	~	3 (2)
	Other	~	3 (2)
1926/27	Total	~	76 (45)

Born May 1899 at Wainfleet. Younger brother of Chairman, Arthur Eatch. Edgar's debut is difficult to pinpoint due to his other sibling, Ernie, playing for the club at the same time. By the Central Alliance game at home to Sutton Junction in November 1919 though, the surname Eatch appears twice on the team-sheet and although the difficulty persists throughout that season, (the local reporter sometimes tries to help the reader by writing 'E.Eatch'!) we know that he scored twice during this first term. The following season he was playing more regularly for the club and he scored his first hat-trick in the December 1920 victory over Kettering Town and matched this achievement a year later when New Hucknall Colliery came to London Road, a year where he finished as Grantham's highest scorer. Although the following season, 1922/23, was a poor one for the team, Edgar still finished as the club's second highest scorer, but he decided to move on and went to start a successful period at Peterborough & Fletton United. Edgar returned at the end of 1926 though, to help out his home club, but after the January 1927 defeat at Long Eaton there is no record of his name appearing on team-sheets again. After this period, he went on to play for Stamford.

Ernie Eatch

Seasons Played			
	League	~	98 (34)
	F.A. Cup	~	12 (5)
1912/13-14/15	League Cup	~	1
	Lincs Cup	~	8 (3)
1919/20-24/25	Other	~	8 (3)
	Total	~	127 (45)

Born 04/09/1891 at Newark. Brother of Arthur and Edgar Eatch. Ernie was playing for Grantham during the 1912/13 season, but really made a name for himself with his debut goal, scored in a friendly against the mighty Queen's Park in March 1913. Up until the outbreak of the First World War he was then a near permanent member of the side. The first Central Alliance game after the end of the European conflict, at Long Eaton in September 1919, saw Ernie back in the team and he finished that season as Grantham's highest scorer. He was soon having to battle with his brother for the starring role at the club and although it wouldn't be long before his sibling was scoring the goals, Ernie still had his moments, including scoring five past a Boots Athletic side in an FA Cup tie in October 1921. During the next few years Grantham achieved little in the league, so one of the few highlights for Ernie would have been an appearance in the April 1923 Grantham Hospital Cup Final against Boston. By the start of 1924 though, he was only making occasional appearances for the club and although his last game unfortunately cannot be found, his final goal came in the January 1925 Grantham Hospital Cup tie against Ruston & Hornsby's. Died 02/02/1971 at Grantham.

Paul Edmunds

Seasons Played			
	League	~	64 (13)
	F.A. Cup	~	7 (2)
1983/84-85/86	F.A. Trophy	~	7 (1)
	League Cup	~	8 (2)
	Lincs Cup	~	2 (2)
	Other	~	2
	Total	~	90 (20)

Born 02/12/1957 at Doncaster. Winger who began his career with local Suffolk side Troston, before moving to Leicester City and Bournemouth. Appearances were limited though, with only 22 in total in The Football League, with two goals to his credit for both clubs, with another four appearances in various cup competitions. He joined Grantham after periods playing for Guiseley and Bentley Victoria, where he was the club's top scorer, and after turning down an offer from Hull City. He made his debut in the 1983/84 season's opening game at Hyde United and scored his first goal for the club a week later at Chorley. Paul played in approximately half of that season's league matches, a year where the team finished fourth in the Northern Premier League. Although he was a much more prominent member of the team the following season, Grantham finally suffered the indignity of relegation. As the club moved back to the Southern League, Paul continued to play in most of the games, although his final goal for Grantham came in the October 1985 league fixture against Bridgnorth Town, with his concluding appearance only days later in the FA Cup tie at home to Atherstone United. During his time at Grantham he was awarded appearances for the Northern Premier League representative side and a dream move to Aston Villa was sadly thwarted by an injury. Paul went on to play for Burton Albion, Goole Town, Armthorpe Welfare and then managed the Doncaster Belles ladies team, for whom his wife played. He still lives in the Doncaster area and currently works as a teacher.

Neil Edwards

Seasons Played			
	League	~	1
	F.A. Cup	~	
1989/90	F.A. Trophy	~	
	League Cup	~	
	Lincs Cup	~	
	Total	~	1

Born 14/03/1966 in Rowley Regis. Began his career with Oldwinsford, before scoring seven goals in his 29 appearances for Wolverhampton Wanderers. After suffering injuries that cut short his professional career he moved to Kettering Town from where he made his one appearance for Grantham, on loan, in the January 1990 fixture at Sutton Coldfield Town after Gary Jones was transferred in the opposite direction. Following his release from Kettering Town, Neil went on to make appearances for Corby Town and Rothwell Town, before returning to Corby.

Mark St Clair Edwards

Seasons Played			
	League	~	97 (3)
	F.A. Cup	~	4
1985/86-87/88	F.A. Trophy	~	6
	League Cup	~	12 (1)
	Lincs Cup	~	2
	Total	~	121 (4)

Born 23/09/1957 at St Kitts, West Indies. Central defender, nick-named 'Piper', who previously played for Basford United and then had nine seasons at Arnold Town. His first game for Grantham was in the Bill Dellow League Cup tie against King's Lynn in October 1985, with his initial goal a fortnight later in the same competition at home to Corby Town. St Clair was a major player for Grantham for those first two seasons back in the Southern League, although they were depressing times at London Road, with some of the lowest ever crowds watching mid-table mediocrity. Things did change significantly though in the 1987/88 season with the arrival of Martin O'Neill, but St Clair had several periods out of the team and his final appearance came in the April 1988 defeat at Atherstone United. After his release in the Summer, he went on to play for Eastwood Town.

Edwards

Seasons Played			
	League	~	3
	F.A. Cup	~	
1936/37	Lincs Cup	~	
	Other	~	
	Total	~	3

Goalkeeper who covered the unavailable Arthur Jepson in the March 1937 visit of Grimsby Town Reserves and the two matches against Mansfield Town Reserves in the same month.

Justin Elkington

Seasons Played			
	League	~	1
	F.A. Cup	~	
1994/95	F.A. Trophy	~	
	League Cup	~	
	Lincs Cup	~	
	Total	~	1

Born 1971 at Lincoln. Began his career spending time on Schoolboy forms at Mansfield Town, Lincoln City, Sheffield Wednesday, Tottenham Hotspur, Ipswich Town and Notts County. He then went on to play for King's Lynn and Spalding United, before joining Grantham, although it was only the one game that he played in, the Boxing Day 1994 5-0 loss at home to King's Lynn. Justin is currently Director of Coaching for a soccer club in Oklahama, USA.

Gary Elliman

Seasons Played			
	League	~	52 (2)
	F.A. Cup	~	3
1983/84-84/85	F.A. Trophy	~	6
	League Cup	~	3
	Lincs Cup	~	4
	Other	~	1
	Total	~	69 (2)

Born 07/04/1959 at Sheffield. Began his career on the books of Sheffield United and Sunderland, before moving on to Boston United, Boston FC, Skegness Town, Buxton and Burton Albion. He joined Grantham at the start of the 1983/84 season, making his debut in the opening fixture at Hyde United. Gary missed only one league game during that campaign, scoring goals against Buxton and Macclesfield Town, as The Gingerbreads finished fourth in the NPL. The following season though, Gary struggled to maintain his place in the side and the November league fixture at Rhyl was his last for the club. He went on to play for Long Eaton United, Gainsborough Trinity, Armthorpe Welfare, Belper Town, Worksop Town and continues to turn out in the Grantham League. Gary still lives locally and works as a Pharmaceutical Sales Manager.

Dave Elliott

Seasons Played			
	League	~	59 (13)
	F.A. Cup	~	3
1986/87-87/88	F.A. Trophy	~	6 (2)
	League Cup	~	7 (3)
1996/97-97/98	Lincs Cup	~	3
	Total	~	78 (18)

Born 10/03/1963 at Nottingham. Previously played for Burton Albion and Clifton All Whites, where he was the club's top scorer during the 1985/86 season. His first game for Grantham came in the August 1986 County Cup tie against Scunthorpe United, with his opening goal a week later in the Bill Dellow League Cup tie against Leicester United. Despite playing in the majority of the games, in March 1987 he left London Road for the chance to play in Finland, although he returned to Grantham a few months later to make a 14 match consecutive run during the Winter of 1987/88. Dave went on to play for Shepshed Charterhouse and Harrowby United, amongst others, before returning to the club again towards the end of the 1996/97 season, scoring once more in the final home match of the season against Bilston Town. His final term with The Gingerbreads was a struggle for Dave as Gary Mills had put together a formidable side that led the Dr Marten's Midland Division from start to finish. He was awarded only five more appearances, the last of which came in the January 1998 League Cup defeat at Raunds Town.

Ray Elliott

Seasons Played			
	League	~	14
	F.A. Cup	~	
1982/83	F.A. Trophy	~	
	League Cup	~	
	Lincs Cup	~	
	Other	~	
	Total	~	14

Former Mansfield Town Reserves player and King's Lynn Assistant Player/Manager who first appeared for Grantham in the February 1983 fixture at home to Marine. Ray then missed only two of the remaining league matches, until the season's closing game at Matlock Town where he was substituted off the field. The following campaign saw him appearing for Burton Albion, but he was sadly killed in a car crash during his time there. Died circa 1984.

Raymond Elliott

Seasons Played			
	League	~	5
	F.A. Cup	~	
1957/58	Lincs Cup	~	
	Total	~	5

Previously played for Bognor Regis, Millwall, Headington United (now Oxford United) and then returned to Bognor, before signing for Grantham. He played in five games towards the end of 1957, starting at Goole Town and ending at Gainsborough Trinity, when a replacement for the departing Jimmy Collins was needed. It is also known that his father played for Grantham, presumably the following 1920/21 entry, assuming that he did make First team appearances.

Elliott

Seasons Played			
	League	~	1
	Lincs Cup	~	
1904/05	Other	~	
	Total	~	1

Only one known appearance for this player, the Midland Amateur Alliance game at home to Notts Magdala Amateurs in March 1905.

Elliott

Seasons Played			
	League	~	4 (5)
	F.A. Cup	~	1
1920/21	Lincs Cup	~	1 (1)
	Other	~	
	Total	~	6 (6)

Centre-Forward who had also played for Billingborough, Spalding United and scored on his Grantham debut in the league game against Mansfield Town in September 1920. However, there seems to be no mention of his name after the goal little more than two months later in the County Cup tie at Stamford Town.

Neil Ellis

Seasons Played			
	League	~	1
	F.A. Cup	~	
1985/86	F.A. Trophy	~	
	League Cup	~	1
	Lincs Cup	~	
	Total	~	2

Former Louth United player who made two appearances for The Gingerbreads at the end of October 1985, the Bill Dellow League Cup defeat against VS Rugby and the league fixture at Hednesford Town, with him moving on to Ross Sports soon after.

Ellis

Seasons Played			
	League	~	1
	F.A. Cup	~	1
1919/20	Lincs Cup	~	
	Total	~	2

Played in two games at the start of the 1919/20 season, the Central Alliance match at Derby County Reserves and the FA Cup victory over Arnold St Mary's the following week.

Albert Ellswood

Seasons Played			
	League	~	3
	F.A. Cup	~	
1948/49	Lincs Cup	~	
	Total	~	3

Goalkeeper who covered for the unavailable Percy Ashton during the two games against Shrewsbury Town and the match at Grimsby Town Reserves in January of 1949.

Elmore

Seasons Played			
	F.A. Cup	~	
	Other	~	1
1878/79	Total	~	1

Made only one appearance for Grantham when the team travelled over to Boston for a friendly in November 1878.

Andy Elsom

Seasons Played			
	League	~	20
	F.A. Cup	~	3
1984/85-87/88	F.A. Trophy	~	1
	League Cup	~	6
	Lincs Cup	~	3
	Other	~	
	Total	~	33

Born 01/03/1962 in Grantham. Former Gonerby Excelsior and Grantham United defender who also played many games for the Reserves during his time with the club. He made his debut in the February 1985 league fixture at home to Bangor City and then played in the following four games, plus the club's last ever Northern Premier League match at Oswestry Town in May. The following season Andy was called upon only a handful of times, but the 1986/87 season was his best at London Road with 18 appearances to his name. He then played in five of the opening six games in the new season, but the arrival of Martin O'Neill soon coincided with the completion of Andy's First team career, with the surprise FA Cup replay defeat against Chatteris Town in September 1987 his last appearance for the club. He went on to play for Stamford Town, Harrowby United, York RI, Selby Town and Pickering Town. Andy still lives in the York area and works as a joiner.

Emery

Seasons Played			
	League	~	1
	F.A. Cup	~	
1925/26	Lincs Cup	~	
	Total	~	1

Played in the club's first ever Midland League game, away at Mansfield Town at the start of the 1925/26 season and also made appearances for Newark Town and Boston during his career.

Emmett

Seasons Played			
	F.A. Cup	~	
	Other	~	1
1877/78	Total	~	1

Possibly one of the Peregrine or William Emmett brothers who were bakers in town during this time. He played in just one match for Grantham, the February 1878 friendly at Nottingham Castle.

W. Errington

Seasons Played			
	League	~	1
	F.A. Cup	~	
1936/37	Lincs Cup	~	
	Other	~	
	Total	~	1

Left-Back who had previously played for West Stanley and made just the single appearance for Grantham in the October 1936 fixture at home to Frickley Colliery when Harry Wilbourne was rested.

Willie Donaldson

Bob Don-Duncan

Simon Down

Dave Drinkell

Darren Dye

Edgar Eatch

Ernie Eatch

Paul Edmunds

Gary Elliman

Mick Farmer

Ron Farmer

Tony Farmer

Neil Featherstone

Harold Flowers

Colin Foster

Mark Foster

Eustace

Seasons Played			
	League	~	4 (3)
	FA Amt. Cup	~	
1907/08	League Cup	~	1 (1)
	Lincs Cup	~	1
1910/11	Other	~	1
	Total	~	7 (4)

Little information is known about this player apart from his first recorded goal for the club in the November 1907 league game against Notts Magdala and the evidence that he was probably a valuable member of the 1910/11 Midland Amateur League winners team. The last game where he managed to get on the score-sheet was when he put a brace past the Notts GNR Clerks side in April 1911.

Albert Evans

Seasons Played			
	League	~	29 (15)
	F.A. Cup	~	1 (1)
1929/30	Lincs Cup	~	1 (1)
	Other	~	
	Total	~	31 (17)

Born 17/01/1901 at Camberwell. Forward who had previously played for Woking and Tottenham Hotspur, making five Football League appearances in a two year spell at White Hart Lane. Albert made his Grantham debut in the first game of the 1929/30 season at Mansfield Town, with his first goal for the club two weeks later against Staveley. His last goal for Grantham was in the January 1930 defeat of Barnsley Reserves, but no information is known about his final appearance. Died 1969.

Dion Evans

Seasons Played			
	League	~	5 (1)
	F.A. Cup	~	
1995/96	F.A. Trophy	~	
	League Cup	~	
	Lincs Cup	~	
	Total	~	5 (1)

Born 07/10/1976 at Nottingham. Former Lincoln City Apprentice who first played for Grantham in the February 1995 league defeat at Nuneaton Borough, but made all but one of his future appearances coming off the bench. One of those was the victory at home to Leicester United where Dion scored the only goal of the game, a month before his final appearance in the April league fixture at Rothwell Town.

Jamie Evans

Seasons Played			
	League	~	5
	F.A. Cup	~	1
1992/93	F.A. Trophy	~	
	League Cup	~	1
	Lincs Cup	~	1
	Total	~	8

Born 05/10/1973 at Sheffield. Began his career as a Trainee at Sheffield United, before moving to Grantham, where he made his debut in the 1992/93 season's opening fixture at Lincoln City in the County Cup. After playing in the first seven games Jamie made just one more appearance after this, when he replaced Adam Cook during the October 1992 BCS League Cup tie at Sutton Coldfield Town. Jamie soon moved on to play for Matlock Town, followed by Leek Town's Championship winning side.

Steve Evans

Seasons Played			
	League	~	6 (1)
	F.A. Cup	~	
2004/05	F.A. Trophy	~	
	League Cup	~	
	Lincs Cup	~	1
	Total	~	7 (1)

Born 12/11/1980 at Coventry. Began his career at Aston Villa, although he failed to make their First team. Steve then joined Burton Albion, followed by on-loan spells at Moor Green and Tamworth, with the move to the last of those being made permanent in February 2003, just in time to assist The Lambs to Dr Marten's Premier League success. That Summer he moved to Hednesford Town and at the end of the 2003/04 season won an FA Trophy winner's medal, poignantly for Steve with the Final held at Villa Park. He began the 2004/05 season at Rugby United, but joined Grantham the following March, making his debut in the Southern League local derby at Stamford. Steve's first goal for the club came the following week at home to Dunstable Town and just to complete a busy few weeks in his career, he played in the April 2005 Lincolnshire County Shield victory at Gainsborough Trinity, coming off the bench to replace Jason White. Steve has rapidly become an important member of Grantham's team and remains with the club.

Jack Fahy

Seasons Played			
	League	~	44 (13)
	F.A. Cup	~	1
1938/39-39/40	Lincs Cup	~	2
	Other	~	7 (7)
	Total	~	54 (20)

Former Sproxton forward who scored on his Grantham debut during the Midland League clash against Boston United in September 1938, but after Cyril Dickinson's arrival the following month only managed infrequent appearances. The following season though he appeared in every single match, (no doubt helped by six goals scored in a pre-season friendly at Newark Town), the only player to do so during the cancelled Midland League competition and subsequent War-Time League. Some of those games Jack even deputised in goal, and also included amongst those fixtures was the 7-1 defeat in the Lincolnshire Senior Cup Final against Scunthorpe & Lindsey United at the end of April 1940. His final match for the club came a few weeks later and saw an equally disappointing result against the same team, albeit with only a five goal defeat this time.

Fahy

Seasons Played			
	League	~	1
	F.A. Cup	~	
1912/13	Lincs Cup	~	
	Other	~	
	Total	~	1

Only one recorded appearance for this player, the Central Alliance fixture at home to Kettering Town in February 1913.

Fahy

Seasons Played			
	League	~	1
	F.A. Cup	~	3 (1)
1919/20	Lincs Cup	~	1
	Total	~	5 (1)

Inside-Right who we know also spent time at Coventry City, but could possibly be the same individual as the previous entry. He played for Grantham in the September 1919 FA Cup tie against Arnold St Mary's, scoring one of the goals, but appeared in only a handful of other games during that season, with no instances of him after the County Cup tie at home to Humber Craving Dock in December of that year.

George Falconbridge

Seasons Played			
	League	~	7
	F.A. Cup	~	
1929/30	Lincs Cup	~	
	Other	~	
	Total	~	7

Former Ilkeston United and Southend United player who scored twice in 19 Football League appearances in the preceding two seasons before arriving at London Road. George was certainly making appearances for Grantham towards the start of the 1929/30 season, but no other information is available on him.

Ronald Faries

Seasons Played			
	League	~	5 (2)
	F.A. Cup	~	
1955/56	Lincs Cup	~	
	Total	~	5 (2)

Forward who scored in both of his first two games for Grantham, against King's Lynn and Bradford City Reserves in September 1955. He only made another two appearances though, in December, before his final game at Hull City Reserves in April of the following year.

Paul Farley

Seasons Played			
	League	~	1
	F.A. Cup	~	
1999/00	F.A. Trophy	~	
	League Cup	~	
	Lincs Cup	~	
	Total	~	1

Born 25/12/1976 at Wolverhampton. Son of the ex-Wolves player, John Farley, and himself a former Hull City Trainee, Brigg Town and North Ferriby United full-back who signed for Grantham on-loan from Lincoln United. Paul made just one appearance for The Gingerbreads in the January 2000 defeat at Worcester City when Jim Neil was unavailable. Following his release from Lincoln he moved to Matlock Town, then returned to North Ferriby, joined Bridlington Trinity and finally went back to North Ferriby again, where he remains.

Stan Farley

Seasons Played			
	League	~	15 (1)
	F.A. Cup	~	
1983/84-84/85	F.A. Trophy	~	
	League Cup	~	
	Lincs Cup	~	2
	Other	~	
	Total	~	17 (1)

Midfield player signed from Harworth Colliery who first played for Grantham in the March 1984 league fixture at Burton Albion, with his only goal for The Gingerbreads at Rhyl towards the end of the season. The following campaign though, saw Stan make only four further appearances, the last of which came in the final Northern Premier League home fixture against Marine. He later became Coach at Harworth Welfare and Manager at Armthorpe Welfare.

Mick Farmer

Seasons Played			
	League	~	105 (3)
	F.A. Cup	~	6
1970/71-74/75	F.A. Trophy	~	9 (1)
	League Cup	~	14
	Lincs Cup	~	6
	Other	~	2
	Total	~	142 (4)

Born 22/11/1944 at Leicester. Started out as an Apprentice at Birmingham City, making one First team start, before signing for Lincoln City at the end of the 1964/65 season where he made another 22 appearances. Mick then moved into non-league football, playing for Skegness Town and Arnold Town, before joining Grantham. He made his debut in the first game of the 1970/71 season at Belper and scored the first of his four goals for the club a week later at Retford. Mick played in Grantham's maiden victory over a Football League side in the FA Cup, when Stockport County came to London Road in November 1970, and by the end of his first season had won Midland League and Midland League Cup winners medals as well. The following season Mick once again played in the majority of the games, with some of the highlights including an FA Trophy Quarter-Final tie against Yeovil, a County Cup Final victory over Scunthorpe United and, of course, another league title. As The Gingerbreads moved into the Southern League, he played in the FA Cup First Round tie at Bradford City and was finally awarded with his third consecutive league winner's medal. The season of 1973/74 was one of the most memorable in the club's history, but Mick's appearances were becoming limited. In fact he played no part in Grantham's famous FA Cup run during that season and spent time playing for Oadby Town. He returned to London Road though, but his last appearance came in October 1974 when Grantham defeated Yeovil Town at London Road. Mick was last known to be working for a Building Society, having been in the financial sector for many years, although there is the possibility that he moved on to employment as a Greeting Card Salesman.

Ron Farmer

Seasons Played			
	League	~	2
	F.A. Cup	~	
1969/70	F.A. Trophy	~	
	League Cup	~	
	Lincs Cup	~	
	Other	~	
	Total	~	2

Born 06/03/1936 at Guernsey, Channel Islands. Forward who previously spent time at Nottingham Forest, (along with his goalkeeping brother Bill), Coventry City, seeing their dramatic rise from the Fourth to the First Division in 315 senior appearances, and Notts County. His professional career finished with 57 goals to his name in 396 League, FA Cup and League Cup fixtures. However, Ron only played for Grantham in the first two games of the 1969/70 season, at Belper Town and two days later the home game against Boston FC. He later became the Youth Team Coach at Coventry City and worked for Massey Ferguson.

Tony Farmer

Seasons Played			
	League	~	391 (11)
	F.A. Cup	~	35 (1)
1958/59-69/70	F.A. Trophy	~	5
	League Cup	~	14
	Lincs Cup	~	15 (1)
	Other	~	1
	Total	~	461 (13)

Born circa 1939. Began his long Grantham career at Skegness in September 1958 and missed only one of the remaining games from that first season. As the club moved into the Central Alliance League, it wasn't until the end of 1960 that the team had to suffer a lengthy spell without Tony and soon after returning he scored his first goal for the club in the league game at home to Spalding United. Only a few days later, in April 1961, he appeared in the triumphant County Cup Final game, with The Gingerbreads defeating Gainsborough Trinity by a single goal. The following season Tony played in every Grantham game, including the FA Cup First Round encounter at Brierley Hill Alliance, and whilst he missed only a handful of matches from the 1962/63 season it was the following Midland League Championship winning season that would prove to be one of the highlights of his career as, once again, he failed to miss a single game. Tony continued to be a valuable member of the Grantham team upon the arrival of Terry Bly, and in May 1965 he was rewarded with a joint Testimonial, along with George Jowett, when a side made up of Peterborough United and Notts County players, including the great Derek Dougan, came to London Road. Of course there would still be many great moments to come for Tony in the next few years, including FA Cup Proper appearances against Hendon, Swindon Town, Wimbledon, Oldham Athletic, Altrincham, Chelmsford City, the return of Swindon Town and finally, a repeat of the Oldham Athletic clash, this time played at Boundary Park. In April 1969 he scored his last goal for the club, in the home game against Belper Town, but a few weeks later Tony won a medal in the inaugural Midland League Cup, when the Grantham team nervously lost to Arnold by two goals in the second leg of the final after securing a 3-0 victory at London Road. Tony still had a full season to play though, and right up until the end of his Grantham career he continued to play in virtually every game. His final match for Grantham came in the April 1970 Midland League Champions versus Runners-Up trophy game, although with Alfreton Town and Grantham already assured of their positions this was actually held a week before the end of the season and John Woolley took Tony's position for the final league game. Died in 2002.

Farnsworth

Seasons Played			
	League	~	1
	F.A. Cup	~	
1920/21	Lincs Cup	~	
	Other	~	
	Total	~	1

Full-Back with just the one recorded appearance, the Central Alliance fixture away at Long Eaton in January 1921.

Robert Farrow

Seasons Played			
1986/87-90/91	League	~	100 (23)
	F.A. Cup	~	7 (4)
	F.A. Trophy	~	7 (4)
	League Cup	~	11 (1)
	Lincs Cup	~	4
	Total	~	129 (32)

Born 30/07/1966. Former Arnold Town and Eastwood Town player who was better known by his nickname of 'Spadge'. He made his Grantham debut in the March 1987 league fixture against Mile Oak Rovers, with his first goal for the club two weeks later at Stourbridge. He played in many of the games over the next few years, scoring a hat-trick on Boxing Day 1987 as The Gingerbreads beat King's Lynn 4-1, but the 1989/90 season was his most consistent when he missed only six games all year. The final away fixture of that season, at Barry Town, also saw Spadge's final goal for the club, with his last appearance in the club's concluding game at London Road in September 1990 against Dudley Town. In fact he was to be the final substitute to come on in a competitive game at the ground, when he replaced Craig Weston in that match.

Shaughan Farrow

Seasons Played			
1985/86	League	~	10
	F.A. Cup	~	1
	F.A. Trophy	~	1
	League Cup	~	4
	Lincs Cup	~	
	Total	~	16

Born 13/09/1956 at Grimsby. Former Grimsby Town Reserves defender who also had periods at Louth United, Brigg Town, Skegness Town, Boston FC and Spalding United. His first game for The Gingerbreads was in the 1985/86 season's opening league fixture at Sutton Coldfield Town, but the November draw against Rushden Town proved to be his last for the club. After a brief spell back at Spalding coaching, Shaughan soon moved into management at Brigg Town and King's Lynn, but returned to Grantham as Assistant Manager to Bob Duncan in March 1992. Since departing The Meres in the 1993 New Year he has held a management position at Boston Town, coached at Grimsby Town and more recently spent time at the helm of Lucarlys in the Lincolnshire League. Shaughan is currently a Marketing Consultant, covering the Humberside region.

Neil Featherstone

Seasons Played			
1999/00	League	~	10 (2)
	F.A. Cup	~	2 (1)
	F.A. Trophy	~	1
	League Cup	~	
	Lincs Cup	~	
	Total	~	13 (3)

Played in Boston United's Reserve side, before moving into their First team and then arriving at The Meres in time to make his debut in the 1999/00 season's opening league match at Gloucester City. He scored his first goal for the club in the August defeat at Halesowen Town, but his thirteenth consecutive appearance, at home to Matlock Town in the FA Trophy, marked the end of his Grantham career and he moved on to Spalding United. Neil currently works for a printing company and still lives in the East of the county.

Ferrall

Seasons Played			
1886/87	F.A. Cup	~	
	Lincs Cup	~	2 (1)
	Other	~	
	Total	~	2 (1)

Only played in the two County Cup matches from the 1886/87 season, firstly scoring in the game at Market Rasen on New Year's Day and then playing the following month at Grimsby Town.

George Fillingham

Seasons Played			
1889/90-92/93	League	~	12
	F.A. Cup	~	1
	Lincs Cup	~	2
	Other	~	15 (3)
	Total	~	30 (3)

Born 1874 at Spittlegate. An auctioneer by profession who first played for Grantham in a friendly against Boston NE in November 1889 and continued to make appearances in several of the remaining friendlies of that season. After the Summer break he was promoted to appearances in the competitive fixtures as well and scored his first goal for the club in the September 1890 friendly at home to Notts Amateurs United. The following season, 1891/92, he played in Grantham's first ever league game when Notts County Rovers came to London Road and by now he had become a constant member of the team. This continued into the disastrous 1892/93 season, until his concluding game and the club's final fixture before disbanding, the 16-0 defeat at Notts County Rovers in October. George was also an proficient cricketer, playing for the Grantham team and the Lincolnshire County side in 1894.

Firth

Seasons Played			
1933/34	League	~	
	F.A. Cup	~	1
	Lincs Cup	~	
	Other	~	
	Total	~	1

There is just one known appearance for this player, in the FA Cup replay at Sutton Town in October 1933.

Fisher

Seasons Played			
1890/91	Lincs Cup	~	3
	Other	~	11
	Total	~	14

Played in many of the 1890/91 season's games, beginning with the friendly against Notts Amateurs United at London Road in September, with his final recorded appearance during the home game against Langley Mill the following March.

Neil Fleming

Seasons Played			
1974/75-75/76	League	~	18
	F.A. Cup	~	2
	F.A. Trophy	~	
	League Cup	~	1
	Lincs Cup	~	1
	Total	~	22

Born 09/01/1950 at Felixstowe. Defender, previously with Lincoln United, Gainsborough Trinity and Lincoln Claytons, with several seasons also playing for Sunday League side, Swiss Cottage. Neil then joined Lincoln City, where he made one First team appearance during the 1973/74 season, before coming to London Road. His Grantham career began with the December 1974 Southern League fixture at Guildford, but despite playing in the following five matches as well, Neil soon began to struggle to maintain a place in the team. This course continued during the 1975/76 season, with only ten further appearances, although two of those came in the November FA Cup First Round matches against Port Vale. Neil's final game for the club came in January 1976 at home to Burton Albion and his career continued at Gainsborough Trinity, Ruston Bucyrus, Gainsborough United and then a return back to Lincoln Claytons. He still lives in Lincoln and currently works as an inspector in the engineering industry and in the last few years has spent time coaching at Lincoln United and Lincoln Moorlands.

Jason Fletcher

Seasons Played			
1988/89-89/90	League	~	30 (1)
	F.A. Cup	~	2
	F.A. Trophy	~	1
1991/92	League Cup	~	3
	Lincs Cup	~	
	Total	~	36 (1)

Born 24/10/1969 at Nottingham. Defender who joined the club from Nottingham Forest, initially on-loan, with his Grantham debut in the league fixture at home to Willenhall Town at the end of October 1988. His first season at London Road finished with 25 appearances to his name and one goal in the April 1989 6-0 thrashing of Banbury United. The following season saw Jason alternating several times between Grantham and Forest, to make appearances for their Reserve side, an arrangement which continued in the 1991/92 season as well. His final appearance for The Gingerbreads came in the New Year's Day 1992 defeat at Nuneaton Borough. His career finished prematurely due to injury, but he continued to work for Forest in their Football in the Community programme. After returning to University, Jason qualified as a physiotherapist and he currently works in hospitals and clinics around the Chesterfield area.

Paul Fletcher

Seasons Played	League	~	4
	F.A. Cup	~	
1986/87	F.A. Trophy	~	
	League Cup	~	
	Lincs Cup	~	
	Total	~	4

Full-Back who came on-loan from Eastwood Town and made four appearances for Grantham towards the end of the 1986/87 season, starting with the March league fixture against Buckingham Town and ending a month later at home to Banbury United. Paul turned down the offer of a permanent move to London Road though and returned to Eastwood Town, where he was still playing at the end of the decade.

Harold Flowers

Seasons Played	League	~	11 (10)
	F.A. Cup	~	1 (1)
1919/20	Lincs Cup	~	1
1922/23	Other	~	
1924/25	Total	~	13 (11)

Born 01/10/1896 in Grantham. Local player who also turned out for the interestingly titled Grantham Glue Works, as well as Ransome & Marles, Grantham St John's, Grantham Pensions Hospital, New Somerby United and the Grantham Reserves side. Harold made his First team debut in the November 1919 Lincolnshire Senior Cup tie at Boston, but made very few further appearances until the start of the 1924/25 season. He scored all of his goals for Grantham during that season, with his final strike coming in the Central Alliance game at home to Matlock Town in April 1925. Died 24/12/1989 at Grantham.

Flowers

Seasons Played	League	~	2
	F.A. Cup	~	
1892/93	Total	~	2

His Grantham career started well, with a victory in the league game at home to Matlock Town in October 1892, but ended two weeks later with the 16-0 defeat at Notts County Rovers and the club's subsequent dissolvement.

Fluck

Seasons Played	League	~	10 (5)
	F.A. Cup	~	
1922/23-23/24	League Cup	~	
	Lincs Cup	~	1
	Other	~	5 (2)
	Total	~	16 (7)

Player who began his Grantham career soon after the 1923 New Year, with his first recorded goal for the club coming in the March Central Alliance fixture at home to Shirebrook. The following month he scored again in the Grantham Hospital Cup Final against Boston Reserves, but after the Summer break he appears to have made only a few appearances for the club, with the last record of his name coming in the Grantham Hospital Cup tie against Grantham St John's in February 1924.

Andy Foden

Seasons Played	League	~	1
	F.A. Cup	~	
1999/00	F.A. Trophy	~	
	League Cup	~	1
	Lincs Cup	~	
	Total	~	2

Born 1974 at Stoke-on-Trent. Former Mansfield Town and Lincoln City Trainee who signed on-loan from Lincoln United. He played for Grantham in the December 1999 defeat at Salisbury City and the following Dr Marten's Cup tie at home to Cambridge City. After his release from Lincoln United, Andy went on to make appearances for Harrowby United.

Footitt

Seasons Played	League	~	2 (2)
	Lincs Cup	~	
1904/05	Other	~	
	Total	~	2 (2)

Played and scored in a friendly against Lincoln Lindum in March 1905 and was then given the chance to play in the final two league games of the season, at home to Derby Thornhill and Burton Casuals, and promptly scored against them as well.

Footitt

Seasons Played	League	~	1
	F.A. Cup	~	
1928/29	Lincs Cup	~	
	Other	~	
	Total	~	1

Only one known appearance for this individual, but no information is available to indicate the game that he played in.

Footlitt

Seasons Played	League	~	4 (1)
	Lincs Cup	~	
1894/95	Other	~	2 (1)
	Total	~	6 (2)

Made his debut in the opening Grantham League fixture of the 1894/95 season against Grantham Rovers Colts and scored his first goal a week later in the match at Spittlegate Victoria. He most probably played in many of that season's fixtures, with his name still evident in the Grantham Minor Cup tie against Newark Reserves the following April.

Forbes

Seasons Played	F.A. Cup	~	
	Lincs Cup	~	1
1884/85	Other	~	
	Total	~	1

Made only one appearance for Grantham, in the Lincolnshire Senior Cup semi-final replay against Horncastle in February 1885.

Ford

Seasons Played	League	~	1
	F.A. Cup	~	
1945/46	Lincs Cup	~	
	Total	~	1

Defender who played in the final Midland League game of the 1945/46 season at Rotherham United Reserves.

Foreman

Seasons Played	League	~	1
	F.A. Cup	~	
1945/46	Lincs Cup	~	
	Total	~	1

Made only one appearance for Grantham in the home game against Bradford Park Avenue Reserves in February 1946.

Rob Forman

Seasons Played	League	~	37
	F.A. Cup	~	
1979/80-81/82	F.A. Trophy	~	
	League Cup	~	2
1983/84	Lincs Cup	~	2 (1)
	Other	~	1
1985/86	Total	~	42 (1)

Defender who progressed through the Reserves and made his First team debut in the December 1979 Northern Premier League Cup tie at South Liverpool, a match that was replayed due to Grantham's hosts previously fielding an ineligible player. The following season was Rob's best for The Gingerbreads, as he played in about half of the year's games, including the October 1980 County Cup Final defeat against Lincoln City and the December game against Nottingham Forest in the Redmayne Trophy. The 1981/82 season saw only a few appearances for Rob, whilst he returned to the First team two years later after a spell at Boston FC for a single league game and four more as Grantham returned to the Southern League. His final appearance for the club came in the February 1986 league defeat at home to Rushden Town. During this period Rob also worked as a pig farmer in the Sleaford area, but no details are known as to his current location or profession.

Pascal Formann

Seasons Played			
	League	~	1
	F.A. Cup	~	
2003/04	F.A. Trophy	~	
	League Cup	~	
	Lincs Cup	~	
	Total	~	1

Born 16/11/1982 in Werne, Germany. Nottingham Forest's third choice goalkeeper who was signed on-loan to cover Mario Ziccardi's suspension for the November 2003 Dr Marten's Premier League trip down to Tiverton Town. He was released by Forest at the end of that season and after trials at Notts County, Doncaster Rovers and Oldham Athletic, he joined Scarborough.

Forrester

Seasons Played			
	League	~	46
	Lincs Cup	~	1 (1)
1931/32	Other	~	
	Total	~	47 (1)

Played his first game for Grantham in the opening match of the 1931/32 season at Loughborough Corinthians and then appeared in every game during that campaign, scoring in the County Cup tie against Scunthorpe & Lindsey United in February 1932.

Dave Forsey

Seasons Played			
	League	~	
	F.A. Cup	~	1
1995/96	F.A. Trophy	~	
	League Cup	~	
	Lincs Cup	~	
	Total	~	1

Made only one appearance for Grantham in the August 1995 FA Cup tie against Shepshed Dynamo when he came off the bench to replace Dean Dye.

Jose Fortes

Seasons Played			
	League	~	3
	F.A. Cup	~	
1996/97	F.A. Trophy	~	1
	League Cup	~	2
	Lincs Cup	~	
	Total	~	6

Swedish student with experience at Gothenburg who signed on-loan from Leicester City and made all his appearances for Grantham during October 1996, starting with the league fixture at Paget Rangers and finishing at The Meres when he came on as substitute during the Dr Marten's League Cup tie against Corby Town.

Bertie Foster

Seasons Played			
	League	~	1
	F.A. Cup	~	
1911/12	Lincs Cup	~	
	Total	~	1

Born 1885 at Sleaford. Former Grantham Avenue and Lincoln City player, with two goals to his credit in 73 games during his time at Sincil Bank, who was brought to Grantham in an attempt to strengthen the side after their promotion into the Central Alliance League. No details are known as to the amount of games that he played, but he may have been at London Road for two seasons, with him returning to Lincoln City in the 1914/15 season, although he made no more First team appearances there. Died 1959 at Sleaford.

Bob Foster

Seasons Played			
	League	~	66 (27)
	F.A. Cup	~	7 (2)
1961/62-62/63	Lincs Cup	~	4 (3)
	Total	~	77 (32)

Born 19/07/1929 at Sheffield. Forward and former England 'B' International with over 100 appearances for Chesterfield, Preston North End, including their First Division runners-up side in 1953, and Rotherham United. He came to Grantham as the club's Captain and began his career in the opening match of the 1961/62 season, the home game against Worksop Town, scoring his first goal for the club the following week at Skegness. Bob continued to play in nearly every game during that season, including the FA Cup First Round game at Brierley Hill Alliance and the victorious Lincolnshire Senior Cup 'A' Final against Boston United where he scored two of the goals. The following season he only missed two of the matches and scored his last two goals for the club in the April 1963 game at Retford, followed by his final appearance in the penultimate league fixture at Gainsborough Trinity. Bob left London Road in the Summer and returned to Rotherham United to become Trainer for their Reserves side.

Colin Foster

Seasons Played			
	League	~	61 (7)
	F.A. Cup	~	7
1981/82-82/83	F.A. Trophy	~	2
	League Cup	~	7 (1)
	Lincs Cup	~	5
	Other	~	5
	Total	~	87 (8)

Born 26/12/1952 at Bulwell. Former Mansfield Town defender, with Division Four and Division Three honours won there in 1975 and 1977. After a transfer to Peterborough United, Colin's professional career finished with over 300 senior appearances to his name. He was one of the first signings by his former colleague and new manager at Grantham, Jon Nixon, with his debut in the County Cup match against Boston United at the start of the 1981/82 season. Colin's first goal for The Gingerbreads came in the October 1981 Northern Premier League Cup game at Matlock Town, whilst a year later he played in the Lincolnshire County Senior Cup Final victory over Scunthorpe United and the FA Cup Fourth Qualifying Round tie at Telford United. The following month saw his final goal for the club, at Oswestry Town, with the closure of his Grantham career in the first leg of the NPL Cup semi-final at Burton Albion in March 1983. Colin was also well known in the Nottinghamshire area for his cricketing skills, but as far as football is concerned he went on to play for Rushden Town and Shepshed Charterhouse, before moving into management at King's Lynn, Corby Town, Peterborough City and Stamford Town. He was last known to be working as a painter and decorator in the Peterborough area and his son, Steve Foster, currently plays in The Football League for Doncaster Rovers.

Harry Foster

Seasons Played			
	League	~	17 (2)
	F.A. Cup	~	1
1923/24	League Cup	~	1
	Lincs Cup	~	1
1933/34	Other	~	1
	Total	~	21 (2)

Born circa 1903 at Newark. Local player who made his Grantham debut in the Central Alliance League Cup tie at home to RAF Cranwell in November 1923 and scored his first goal for the club a month later during the league fixture against Heanor Town. He seems to have left the club soon after though, but in 1930 he had joined Doncaster Rovers, where he made 34 appearances. Harry returned to Grantham ten years after his first spell and most likely played in many of the 1933/34 season's games, but scored only one other known goal for the club, in April 1934 at Matlock Town.

Mark Foster

Seasons Played			
	League	~	15
	F.A. Cup	~	5
2000/01-02/03	F.A. Trophy	~	2
	League Cup	~	3
	Lincs Cup	~	3
	Total	~	28

Born 12/04/1981 at Sheffield. Former Lincoln City Schoolboy midfielder and Lincoln United player who progressed through the Reserve side. He made a lone appearance for the First team in the 2000/01 season by replacing Tim Wilkes during the September league match at Bashley. The following season saw another 20 appearances for Mark, with many of those coming from the substitute's bench, although he was awarded a rare start in the biggest game of the year at home to Canvey Island in the FA Trophy. The 2002/03 season began for Mark with an appearance in the Final of the County Cup at home to Scunthorpe United, although all but one of his remaining games were once again from the bench, the last of which came during the Dr Marten's Cup victory over Shepshed Dynamo in December 2002. He went on to play for

Gainsborough Trinity, had a second spell at Lincoln United, followed by Harrowby United, helping them to United Counties Division One honours.

Foster

Seasons Played			
	League	~	1 (1)
	Lincs Cup	~	1
1904/05	Other	~	
	Total	~	2 (1)

Player who is known to have made appearances for Grantham at the start of this first season back after reforming, with his only known goal in the November 1904 Midland Amateur Alliance fixture at home to Notts Magdala.

Foster

Seasons Played			
	League	~	1
	F.A. Cup	~	
1919/20	Lincs Cup	~	
	Total	~	1

No information is available on this player other than his appearance in the December 1919 game at Sutton Town.

Foulkes

Seasons Played			
	League	~	1
	F.A. Cup	~	
1930/31	Lincs Cup	~	
	Total	~	1

Available records show just one appearance for this player, away at Denaby United in November 1930.

J. Fowell

Seasons Played			
	League	~	1
	F.A. Cup	~	
1920/21	Lincs Cup	~	
	Other	~	
	Total	~	1

Just the single recorded appearance for this player, the away April 1921 Central Alliance fixture at Ilkeston United.

Leigh Fox

Seasons Played			
	League	~	1
	F.A. Cup	~	
2004/05	F.A. Trophy	~	
	League Cup	~	1
	Lincs Cup	~	1
	Total	~	3

Born circa 1987. Young Grantham Reserves winger who was brought into the First team squad by Lee Glover. Leigh made his debut by coming off the bench to replace Adam Sturgess in the January 2005 Southern League Cup defeat at King's Lynn and remains with the club.

Martin Fox

Seasons Played			
	League	~	29
	F.A. Cup	~	3
1999/00	F.A. Trophy	~	1
	League Cup	~	1
2003/04	Lincs Cup	~	2
	Total	~	36

Born 21/04/79 at Sutton-in-Ashfield. Young player that began his footballing career at Leicester City and after being released by them joined Grantham. Martin started with the opening league fixture of the 1999/00 season at Gloucester City, but ended his first spell with the club at Rothwell just over a month later. Playing in eight games of that disastrous start of the season meant that he held the record of being The Gingerbread with the longest career that involved losing in every game. He perhaps wisely moved on, firstly to Chesham United, then Cambridge City and Hinckley United, before returning to The Meres for the start of the 2003/04 season. This time it was a more prosperous period at the club and he gained an FA Cup First Round appearance when Leyton Orient came to town in November 2003. However, after the January 2004 league victory at home to Crawley Town he was released by the club and moved to Coalville Town, then joined Leicestershire Senior League side Ellistown, but rejoined Coalville at the start of 2005.

Walter Fox

Seasons Played			
	League	~	16
	F.A. Cup	~	5
1927/28	Lincs Cup	~	
	Total	~	21

Goalkeeper who had previously played for Matlock Town, Alfreton Town and made one appearance for his home team, Derby County, in their 1925/26 Division Two runners-up season. Walter made his debut for Grantham in the opening match of the 1927/28 season at York City and was the club's first choice 'keeper until the start of 1928 when the return of Stan Walker marked the end of his London Road career.

Dale Foxcroft

Seasons Played			
	League	~	27
	F.A. Cup	~	2
1989/90-90/91	F.A. Trophy	~	1
	League Cup	~	8
	Lincs Cup	~	
	Total	~	38

Born 28/03/1964 at Newmarket. Former Spalding United, Gainsborough, Boston United and Bourne Town goalkeeper who made his debut in the September 1989 FA Trophy game at Newtown, taking over the role from Linden Parslow. It was a game which must have impressed the club's new debutante, with the team bus breaking down and the players arriving late in a fleet of taxis! Perhaps unsurprisingly then, after only 13 appearances, he returned for a second spell at Spalding, but then came back to Grantham in November 1990 to play his first game for the club at their new stadium. Dale then appeared in every game for The Gingerbreads, until the March 1991 defeat at home to Sutton Coldfield Town.

Chris Francis

Seasons Played			
	League	~	20
	F.A. Cup	~	2
1986/87	F.A. Trophy	~	4
	League Cup	~	6
	Lincs Cup	~	1
	Total	~	33

Born 07/07/1963 in London. Former Arnold Town and Long Eaton United full-back who came on as substitute to make his debut in the 1986/87 season's opening fixture against Scunthorpe United in the County Cup. Chris played in the majority of the following games, up to his last appearance for the club in February 1987 against Halesowen Town, and he then moved to Finland to pursue his footballing career.

Willis Francis

Seasons Played			
	League	~	50 (3)
	F.A. Cup	~	1
2003/04-04/05	F.A. Trophy	~	3
	League Cup	~	
	Lincs Cup	~	3
	Total	~	57 (3)

Born 26/07/1985 at Nottingham. Young midfielder who came from Notts County on work experience, (with 13 appearances for their First team behind him), after former Grantham manager, Gary Mills, took over at Meadow Lane. His first game for The Gingerbreads came in the February 2004 league fixture at Newport County and although he had a brief return to Notts County, he soon joined Grantham in a permanent move. Willis scored his initial goal for the club in the January 2005 win over King's Lynn, whilst three months later he played in the Lincolnshire County Shield victory over Gainsborough Trinity. A tremendous prospect for the future, Willis remains at the club.

Francis

Seasons Played			
	League	~	1
	F.A. Cup	~	
1925/26	Lincs Cup	~	
	Total	~	1

Available team-sheets show just the single appearance for this Serviceman, at home to Boston in February 1926.

Francis

Seasons Played			
	League	~	
	F.A. Cup	~	
1936/37	Lincs Cup	~	
	Other	~	1 (1)
	Total	~	1 (1)

Played and scored one of the goals in the Wilson Cup game against RAF Cranwell at the end of the 1936/37 season.

Stuart Franklin

Seasons Played			
	League	~	80 (4)
	F.A. Cup	~	3
1983/84-84/85	F.A. Trophy	~	10 (2)
	League Cup	~	9 (1)
	Lincs Cup	~	4
	Other	~	2
	Total	~	108 (7)

Born circa 1961, possibly at Sheffield. Former Chesterfield Youth team full-back with experience at Alfreton Town and Belper Town, where he had the distinction of appearing in every position during one season, including goalkeeper. He made his debut for Grantham in the 1983/84 season's opening game at Hyde United and scored his first goal for the club in the FA Trophy replay at Leicester United in October 1983. Stuart missed only two games during that season, whilst the following campaign saw him once again top the club's appearance charts despite missing the final three league fixtures. His last goal for Grantham came in the April 1985 league match at Gainsborough Trinity, with the end of his Gingerbreads career only days later at Morecambe. Stuart went on to play for Matlock Town the following season and was last known to be working for a local government, with him still living in the Sheffield area.

Andy Frawley

Seasons Played			
	League	~	13 (1)
	F.A. Cup	~	4
1996/97	F.A. Trophy	~	3 (1)
	League Cup	~	2
	Lincs Cup	~	
	Total	~	22 (2)

Born 1975 at Nottingham. Former Notts County Trainee who had also appeared for Crewe Alexandra, Ilkeston Town and Dunkirk. His first game for Grantham came in the August 1996 league fixture at Raunds Town and the closure of his time at The Meres arrived the following March, when he came off the bench to replace Ashley Brandy in the game against Shepshed Dynamo. In that time Andy had scored in the matches against Bilston Town and Winsford United. After leaving the club he went on to captain the Gedling Town team, but more recently has been making appearances for Pelican FC in the Central Midlands League.

Levi Freeman

Seasons Played			
	F.A. Cup	~	
	Lincs Cup	~	
1887/88	Other	~	1
	Total	~	1

Born 1871 in Grantham. Made only one appearance for the club, a friendly against Derby Junction in March 1888, lining up alongside his brother, Walter Freeman. At the time of the 1901 census Levi was still living in Grantham, working as a Blacksmith's Stoker.

Walter Freeman

Seasons Played			
	League	~	10 (2)
	F.A. Cup	~	2
1885/86	Lincs Cup	~	3
1887/88-88/89	Other	~	18
1890/91-92/93	Total	~	33 (2)

Born 1869 in Grantham. Brother of Levi Freeman. Walter first played for Grantham in the January 1886 friendly at Notts Rangers, but only appeared in a few games each season, including the same match as Levi in March 1888, until the start of the 1890/91 season. From then on he became quite a regular player for the team, playing in the club's first ever league game, at home to Notts County Rovers in September 1891, and scoring two goals the following month in the 5-1 defeat over Sheffield. Walter made his last appearance for the club in the October 1892 FA Cup tie at home to Belper. Just under ten years later, during the National Census, Walter was listed as an Iron Moulder, living at Little Gonerby.

Mick French

Seasons Played			
	League	~	1
	F.A. Cup	~	
1966/67	Total	~	1

Born 20/09/1944 at Mexborough. Former Skegness Town winger who spent two months at London Road, playing just once for the First team in the opening Midland League game of the 1966/67 season at Goole Town. He then returned to Skegness and later played for Croft United and Spilsby Town. Mick is currently a football programme dealer and still lives in Skegness.

Sammy Fretwell

Seasons Played			
	League	~	18 (1)
	F.A. Cup	~	1
1923/24-24/25	League Cup	~	1
	Lincs Cup	~	1
	Other	~	2
	Total	~	23 (1)

Defender who made his Grantham debut in the first match of the 1923/24 season at Gresley Rovers and played in the majority of that season's games. However, information for the following campaign consists of goalscorers only, so the only data that we know of is that he scored his sole goal for the club in the February 1925 league subsidiary competition fixture at home to Newark Town.

Steven Friend

Seasons Played			
	League	~	9 (2)
	F.A. Cup	~	
1980/81-81/82	F.A. Trophy	~	
	League Cup	~	1
1985/86	Lincs Cup	~	2
	Other	~	
	Total	~	12 (2)

Born 30/04/1960 at Newark. Always known by the name of 'Freddie', he started out playing for Rutlanders, Balderton Old Boys and Worthington Simpson. Freddie then progressed through the Reserves side to make his debut in the March 1981 game at home to Goole Town and scored a brace in the following match against Worksop Town. After that promising start he made only three appearances at the start of the new season though, but returned to the First team in 1985 to play in another three games. However, the Boxing Day match against Hednesford Town saw Freddie come on as substitute and promptly break his leg. He was awarded a benefit match soon after, with Grantham sending a team over to Newark to play Hoval Farral works side. After a lengthy recovery he eventually returned to the game with Worthington Simpson, at the same time as they had a successful run in the FA Sunday Cup, and also followed Barry Shaw to Harrowby United, before finishing his playing career with the Three Gables. He still lives in the Newark area and works for the Royal Mail.

Tony Frisby

Seasons Played			
	League	~	3
	F.A. Cup	~	
1961/62-62/63	Lincs Cup	~	
	Total	~	3

Defender who played in the Midland League matches against Gainsborough Trinity in April 1962, and the two games during October of that year at Goole Town and Loughborough United.

Frisby

Seasons Played			
	League	~	3
	Lincs Cup	~	1
1894/95	Other	~	2
	Total	~	6

Most likely played in many of the 1894/95 season's Grantham League games, starting with the away fixture against Grantham Rovers Colts in September 1894.

E. Frith

Seasons Played			
	F.A. Cup	~	
	Other	~	1
1880/81	Total	~	1

Played alongside his namesake, possibly members of the same family, in the final friendly of the 1880/81 season against Bourne.

Frith

Seasons Played			
1878/79	F.A. Cup	~	5 (2)
1880/81-81/82	Lincs Cup	~	6 (2)
1883/84-84/85	Other	~	6 (1)
1886/87	Total	~	17 (5)

Made his debut for Grantham in the January 1879 friendly at Lincoln, but apparently didn't play again for the club until the start of the 1880/81 season. He scored his first goal for the club in the FA Cup tie against Calthorpe, Birmingham in November 1880 and from then on his appearances seem to predominantly occur during either the FA Cup or the County competition, culminating in his goal during Grantham's first ever Lincolnshire Senior Cup Final win in March 1885 against Gainsborough Trinity. He returned to make one last appearance for the club in the February 1887 County Cup tie at Grimsby Town.

Bob Fry

Seasons Played			
1963/64	League	~	7 (5)
	F.A. Cup	~	4 (1)
	Lincs Cup	~	
	Total	~	11 (6)

Scored on his Grantham debut at Alfreton Town in the first match of what would turn out to be a title winning 1963/64 season. Despite an impressive scoring record in the first couple of months, after the Midland League home fixture in October against Long Eaton United Bob lost his place to the returning Charlie Scoffield.

Andy Furnell

Seasons Played			
2000/01	League	~	28 (3)
	F.A. Cup	~	3
	F.A. Trophy	~	1 (1)
	League Cup	~	2 (1)
	Lincs Cup	~	1
	Total	~	35 (5)

Born 13/02/1977 at Peterborough. Former England Youth International who began his career with his home club at the age of sixteen and had the highlight of playing in the 1993/94 FA Cup tie against Tottenham Hotspur, but sadly missed one of the penalties as The Posh went out of the competition in the shoot-out. He made a total of 23 appearances there and also had on-loan spells with VS Rugby and Chertsey Town, before moving to Rushden & Diamonds, Nuneaton Borough, Stamford Town, Wisbech Town and then having a spell playing in the USA. He made his Grantham debut in the September 2000 FA Cup tie at home to Bedworth, with his first goal for the club the following month when the team demolished Corby Town 5-1. Andy spent a period on-loan at Wisbech Town towards the end of the season, but returned to Grantham and made his final appearance in the closing fixture against St Leonards. He joined Wisbech Town once more during the Summer of 2001 and moved to Soham Town three years later.

Furniss

Seasons Played			
1909/10	League	~	
	Lincs Cup	~	
	Other	~	1
	Total	~	1

Goalkeeper who occupied the last line of defence during the 2-0 friendly defeat against Queen's Park in March 1910. He may have played in this position during other games from that season, although at the start of that campaign a player by the name of Lee was the club's first choice.

Chris Gaffney

Seasons Played			
1989/90-90/91	League	~	51 (1)
	F.A. Cup	~	1
	F.A. Trophy	~	1
	League Cup	~	6
	Lincs Cup	~	
	Total	~	59 (1)

Born 30/01/1971 at Sheffield. Former Spalding United, Shepshed Charterhouse, Worksop Town, Goole Town, Denaby United and Gainsborough Trinity defender. His first game for Grantham came in the Boxing Day 1989 fixture at home to Tamworth, with his only goal for the club only days later against Hednesford Town. Chris played in the majority of the remaining games from that season, whilst the following year he appeared in the last ever competitive match at London Road, against Dudley Town. He continued to play a vital role in the team as they spent time lodging at Spalding United, up to the 1990/91 season's closing fixture at Redditch United, and he then moved on to Burton Albion.

Tim Gale

Seasons Played			
1982/83	League	~	6 (1)
	F.A. Cup	~	5 (1)
	F.A. Trophy	~	1
	League Cup	~	1 (1)
	Lincs Cup	~	1
	Other	~	1
	Total	~	15 (3)

Born circa 1963. After three seasons at Peterborough United, Tim was released by them and was playing in the Peterborough League when he signed for Grantham. Tim made his debut in the September 1982 President's Cup tie at Marine, with his first goal coming the following Saturday against Hinckley Athletic in the FA Cup. He played in the October County Cup Final victory over Scunthorpe United and the FA Cup final qualifying round at Telford United, but after 15 consecutive appearances the November defeat at home to Tamworth was to be his last for the club. Tim went on to play in Sweden with Bralanda, before returning to England with Wisbech Town, King's Lynn, Corby Town, Stamford and Mirlees Blackstone.

Jackie Gallagher

Seasons Played			
1991/92	League	~	1
	F.A. Cup	~	
	F.A. Trophy	~	
	League Cup	~	
	Lincs Cup	~	
	Total	~	1

Born 06/04/1958 at Wisbech. Forward who spent much of his career seemingly alternating between the professional game and non-league football. He started out at March Town, before moving to Lincoln City, King's Lynn, Peterborough United and then spent a period playing football in Hong Kong. He returned to England and signed for Torquay United, had a second spell at Peterborough United and then joined Wolverhampton Wanderers, but in-between each move he also had periods at his home team, Wisbech Town. Following the end of his professional career, with 31 goals in 165 Football League appearances, Jackie stayed in non-league with first Boston United, followed by his single appearance for Grantham when he came on as substitute in the April 1992 league fixture at King's Lynn, replacing Neil Gardner. After this he played for Diss, had a fourth spell at Wisbech Town and not surprisingly eventually became their Manager, spending just over a year at the helm there between 2003 and 2004.

Randolph Galloway

Seasons Played			
1929/30	League	~	2
	F.A. Cup	~	
	Lincs Cup	~	
	Other	~	
	Total	~	2

Born 22/12/1896 at Sunderland. Centre-Forward who had a prestigious career behind him, scoring 42 goals in 128 senior appearances for Sunderland Tramways, Derby County, Nottingham Forest, Luton Town, Coventry City and Tottenham Hotspur. However, he made just two appearances for Grantham, against Gainsborough Trinity and Staveley Town in October 1929. Died 1964.

Gamage

Seasons Played			
1946/47	League	~	1
	F.A. Cup	~	
	Lincs Cup	~	
	Total	~	1

Defender who made only one appearance for Grantham, although it was one of the biggest league games of the season, the April 1947 clash against Peterborough United. He was most likely related to the club's Treasurer from the previous year, S. Gamage, although of course he could be the same individual.

Arthur Gamble

Seasons Played			
1874/75-75/76	F.A. Cup	~	
1878/79-80/81	Other	~	17
	Total	~	17

Born 1857 in Grantham. The first of three members of the Gamble family who were part of the club in those very early years. In fact this player was the Captain of that inaugural football game at London Road against Arthur Hutchinson's team. For some reason he missed out on appearing in the match against the Third Lincolnshire Volunteer Rifles, so the maiden competitive game for him is the friendly against Burghley Park in November 1874. He then played in many of the friendlies during those first two seasons, but following this he seems to have suspended his playing career until the end of the decade when he made occasional appearances once more, with the October 1880 friendly at Huntingdon County being his final game. In the next few years Arthur progressed in his political career and in 1892 became Mayor of Grantham, whilst 1901 saw him listed as a chemist in the town.

Ernest Gamble

Seasons Played			
1875/76	F.A. Cup	~	
1878/79-80/81	Other	~	10
	Total	~	10

Born 1856 in Grantham. The first recorded instance of Ernest playing is in the December 1875 friendly at home to Nottingham Lace, but he then seems to have made only a few appearances each season with his final game being in a November 1880 game against Nottingham Park.

Sidney Gamble

Seasons Played			
	F.A. Cup	~	
	Other	~	14 (3)
1874/75-78/79	Total	~	14 (3)

Born 1854 in Grantham. One of the original committee members, but although he played in one of the first club matches, Sidney didn't make his debut for the full Grantham team until the beginning of December 1874 in a friendly against Lincoln. He then started to play more regularly for the side in the 1876/77 season and in January we have the first recorded goal for him during a friendly held at Retford Rovers. However, after the Summer break he made only two more appearances for the club, with the October 1878 home fixture against Lincoln being his last game. Sidney unquestionably had plenty to keep him active after the end of his footballing career though, as he was an important Granthamian whose posts included Borough Treasurer and Grantham Town Fire Chief alongside his joint professions of architect and sanitary engineer, whilst somewhere in between he managed to fit in his other hobby of amateur photography. By 1901 though, Sidney had apparently moved to Southwark, London, although he was still working as a civil engineer.

Willie Gamble

Seasons Played			
	League	~	13 (9)
	F.A. Cup	~	
1987/88	F.A. Trophy	~	
	League Cup	~	
	Lincs Cup	~	
	Total	~	13 (9)

Born 05/03/1968 at Cottam. Lincoln City striker, scoring 14 goals in his 64 appearances there, who came to Grantham on-loan and played in the final thirteen fixtures of the 1987/88 season. The first of those was the February match against Halesowen Town, with his maiden goal a week later at home to Buckingham Town. Willie formed a terrific striking partnership with Peter Whitehurst and Grantham won eleven of the games whilst he was at London Road, with the club agonisingly missing out on promotion by a single point. Willie scored in that closing fixture against Bilston Town and after a brief return to Lincoln City, moved on to play for Boston United, Shepshed Albion, Harworth Colliery Institute, Brigg Town, Armthorpe Welfare, Glapwell, Collingham and until recently, Retford Town, where he remains as Assistant Manager for their Reserves side.

Chris Gardiner

Seasons Played			
	League	~	477
	F.A. Cup	~	32
1968/69-81/82	F.A. Trophy	~	33
	League Cup	~	55
1984/85	Lincs Cup	~	22
	Other	~	5
	Total	~	624

Born 22/12/1946 at Brownhills, Staffordshire. Started out in local football as a striker, scoring 70 goals in one season for Colsterworth Mines, but began goalkeeping with Sunday League side, Beedon Park. At the end of the 1966/67 and 1967/68 season's, with appearances also made for Grantham St John's, he played in goal for Grantham sides that appeared in the Bourne Hospital Cup. Chris played his first genuine competitive game for the club after taking over the goalkeeping role from John Small for the first game of the 1968/69 season at Sutton Town. In this first season, he played in every game and whilst Grantham was still in the Midland League, he began to notch up appearances in some of the club's important games. Amongst those were the FA Cup ties against Chelmsford City, Swindon Town, Oldham Athletic, Stockport County and Rotherham United, an FA Trophy Quarter-Final tie against Yeovil Town, along with the achievements of two Midland League Championship winners medals, two for the Midland League Cup and one for the Lincolnshire County Cup. The first two campaigns after Grantham's entry into the Southern League saw appearances for Chris in FA Cup ties against Bradford City, Hillingdon Borough, Rochdale and the club's biggest ever game, at home to Middlesbrough in the January 1974 Third Round Proper game, not to mention another league winner's medal as Grantham swept their new opponents aside. The following four seasons saw precious little for the supporters to cheer about, other than an FA Cup tie against Port Vale, which obviously Chris played in as well as the majority of the other games as well. Grantham briefly dipped down a level in the non-league pyramid in the Summer of 1978, but a year later Chris had won his fourth league winner's medal, when Grantham clinched the Southern League Division One North Championship by a single point, with Chris playing in that all important decider at home to Merthyr Tydfil in May 1979. Grantham moved into the Northern Premier League and his ability soon became noticed by the England Semi-Professional selectors although unfortunately Chris never made the starting line-up. More highlights continued with The Gingerbreads though. He played in the October 1980 County Cup Final against Lincoln City and only two months later faced his most formidable opponents when Nottingham Forest came to London Road, with Trevor Francis putting three past him. The following Summer marked the end of his secure career at London Road, although the 1981/82 season did see four more appearances for Chris, but his under-study for several years, Graham Cox, was finally awarded the coveted Number 1 shirt. He then spent two seasons at Bourne Town and had a brief spell at Stamford Town, before a surprise return as cover to London Road, although the February 1985 league fixture at home to Bangor City was his lone and final appearance. Other than football, Chris was also a reputable cricketer, winning a Daily Mirror award for performances in the Haig Cup and well known on the local darts scene. Chris spent over 25 years at the top of Grantham's list of record appearance makers, but lost the lead in February 2005 to Adrian Speed, sportingly being at The Meres to see his record equalled. For many years Chris worked for a steel business on the outskirts of town, but is now an inspector at a local tyre production company and he still lives close to Grantham.

Neil Gardner

Seasons Played			
	League	~	3
	F.A. Cup	~	
1991/92-92/93	F.A. Trophy	~	
	League Cup	~	
	Lincs Cup	~	
	Total	~	3

Local goalkeeper who became a regular in the Reserves side before moving on to Harrowby United. He played outfield though in the April 1992 league fixture at King's Lynn, but was replaced by Jackie Gallagher, another player who was making a lone appearance that season. Neil then played in goal for two fixtures a year later when Jon Godwin was unavailable, against Sutton Coldfield Town and King's Lynn once more.

John Garland

Seasons Played			
	League	~	2
	F.A. Cup	~	
1967/68	Total	~	2

Made just two appearances for Grantham, firstly coming on as substitute for Mick Chambers during the September 1967 game against Skegness Town and then starting in the January fixture at home to Ilkeston United.

Jack Garnham

Seasons Played			
	League	~	24 (9)
	F.A. Cup	~	
1929/30-30/31	Lincs Cup	~	
	Other	~	
	Total	~	24 (9)

Born circa 1907 at Clipstone. Former Clipstone Colliery, Mansfield Town and Sutton Junction player who progressed from the Reserve side into the First team, although at what point in the 1929/30 season is not known apart from the evidence that shows his first goal in the March fixture against Doncaster Rovers Reserves. He seems to have played a more prominent role in the side the following year, with his final goal for the club coming in the March 1931 Midland League defeat of Scunthorpe & Lindsey United.

Robert Gash

Seasons Played			
	Lincs Cup	~	
	Other	~	3
1889/90	Total	~	3

Private in the Lincolnshire Regiment who played in three of the 1889/90 season's first four friendlies, beginning with Leicester Fosse Reserves and ending with the home game against Boston NE. Robert went on to play for Grantham Rovers, Lincoln City, Gainsborough Trinity, Grantham Avenue and Hornsby's Engineers (Lincoln), scoring four goals in a total of 27 appearances for the two Lincolnshire sides that were at that time battling in Division Two of The Football League.

Alex Gaskell

Seasons Played			
	League	~	38 (28)
	F.A. Cup	~	4 (4)
1956/57	Lincs Cup	~	
	Total	~	42 (32)

Born 30/07/1932 at Leigh. Started his career at Hindsford, Blackburn Rovers and Manchester United, before making First team appearances for Southport, Newcastle United and Mansfield Town. He began his Grantham career in the opening match of the 1956/57 season at Scarborough and scored his first goal a week later at Wisbech. Alex finished the season as the club's highest scorer, aided by four goals in the return encounter against Scarborough and the 11-0 demolition of Denaby United in the New Year. He scored a brace in the April match at Gainsborough Trinity, his last goals for the club, and made his final appearance for Grantham in the season's closing league fixture at Lincoln City Reserves. Alex then returned to the North-West and made six appearances for Tranmere Rovers the following season, bringing his Football League totals to 41 goals in 93 appearances, before returning to non-league football with Rhyl, Wigan Rovers, Mossley and Winsford United, where he retired from the game in 1962 after breaking his wrist.

Craig Gaunt

Seasons Played			
	League	~	3
	F.A. Cup	~	
1998/99	F.A. Trophy	~	
	League Cup	~	
	Lincs Cup	~	
	Total	~	3

Born 31/03/1973 at Nottingham. Came through The FA's Centre of Excellence, before becoming a Trainee at Arsenal. Moves then followed to Telford United, Scarborough, Bromsgrove Rovers, (where he won a Bob Lord Trophy winner's medal), a £6,000 transfer to Kettering Town, then Ilkeston Town, New Orleans in America and Woodlands Wellington in Singapore. In a three week career at The Meres, beginning in February 1999, he played for Grantham against Hastings Town, Burton Albion and Bath City. After a brief return to Singapore, Craig went on to play for Chester City, Moor Green, Hucknall Town, where he became Club Captain, Leigh RMI and finally returned to Ilkeston.

Geddes

Seasons Played			
	League	~	1
	F.A. Cup	~	
1919/20	Lincs Cup	~	
	Total	~	1

Half-Back who had previously played for Arnold St. Mary's, but apparently appeared for Grantham in only the opening league game of the 1919/20 season at Long Eaton.

Bernard Gedney

Seasons Played			
	League	~	
	F.A. Cup	~	1
1949/50	Lincs Cup	~	
	Total	~	1

Born 03/08/1924 at Bicker. Previously spent three years at Boston United, before coming to London Road, but made just one appearance for the First team, taking over from the unavailable Len Thorpe for the September 1949 FA Cup match at Linby Colliery. Bernard went on to play for Bicker, helping them to success in the Lincolnshire Junior Cup. He later became a prominent Bowls player, representing England at the Flat Green variation, for which he still plays. A farmer all his life, Bernard is retired now, but still lives in the same house in which he was born.

Alan Gee

Seasons Played			
	League	~	50 (1)
	F.A. Cup	~	6
1957/58-58/59	Lincs Cup	~	2
	Total	~	58 (1)

Born 16/03/1932 at Chesterfield. Former Rotherham United right-back who played in every remaining game of the 1957/58 season for Grantham after making his debut in the September fixture at Doncaster Rovers Reserves. He scored his only goal for the club soon after, during Bradford Park Avenue Reserves visit to London Road, and later managed to play in that season's County Cup Final against Gainsborough Trinity in April 1958. The following season he missed only one of the first few games, but after the October fixture at Frickley Colliery he made no more appearances for the club.

Russ Gee

Seasons Played			
	League	~	9
	F.A. Cup	~	1
1989/90	F.A. Trophy	~	
	League Cup	~	
1992/93	Lincs Cup	~	1
	Total	~	11

Born 12/10/1963 at Keyworth. Former Shepshed, Keyworth and Oakham United defender who made his debut for Grantham in the August 1989 league fixture at Bedworth United and appeared for The Gingerbreads in times of crisis, none more so than when he played in goal during that season's FA Cup tie against Louth United! The New Year of 1993 was also a case in point when Bob Duncan and several of the players left due to financial problems and Russ returned after having spells with Long Eaton United and Sandiacre Town amongst others. He made another six appearances for the club, ending with the March 1993 game at home to RC Warwick.

Gee

Seasons Played			
	F.A. Cup	~	
	Lincs Cup	~	
1884/85	Other	~	3
	Total	~	3

Played in three of the 1884/85 season's friendlies, starting with the game at Peterborough in October and ending with their return to London Road the following February.

Fred Geeson

Seasons Played			
	F.A. Cup	~	5
	Lincs Cup	~	5 (1)
1883/84-89/90	Other	~	59 (9)
	Total	~	69 (10)

Born 23/08/1862 at Redmile. The first recorded instance of Fred's name is in the match report for the February 1884 friendly at Nottingham Bank and although the following year saw him play in both of the FA Cup matches and many of the season's friendlies, for some reason he played no part in the successful County Cup side. For the next couple of season's he appears to have played comparatively little for the club, but by the end of the decade he had found a more attacking role and was both appearing, and scoring, more regularly, with his first recorded goal in the December 1887 County Cup tie at home to Grimsby Humber Rovers. Fred continued playing for the club until his final appearance in the January 1890 Kettering Charity Cup clash against local rivals Grantham Rovers. His career is also known to have taken him to Grantham Vics and Boston Town, whilst he also played cricket for Grantham, Boston, Skegness, Marylebone (Lord's, London) and the Leicestershire and Lincolnshire County sides. Died 02/05/1920 at Johannesburg, South Africa.

Domenico Genovese

Seasons Played			
	League	~	1 (1)
	F.A. Cup	~	
1986/87	F.A. Trophy	~	
	League Cup	~	
	Lincs Cup	~	
	Total	~	1 (1)

Born 02/02/1961 at Peterborough. Striker who previously played for Stamford, including their 1984 FA Vase Final win at Wembley, Boston United and Kettering Town. He came to Grantham just after the club had beaten Rushden Town 8-0 and made his debut in the January 1987 league fixture against Bilston Town. With The Gingerbreads going into the half-time break five goals up, one of which came from Domenico, it was a double anti-climax when the team failed to capitalise on their domination, finishing with 'only' a 5-0 victory, and Genovese failing to make another appearance. He went on to play for Cambridge City, Peterborough United, scoring once in his 8 games, and then returning to Kettering and Cambridge before finally joining Holbeach United. He started his managerial career at Mirlees Blackstone and then moved to Kettering Town, firstly as Youth Team coach, before progressing to the First team.

Danny George

Seasons Played			
	League	~	57 (3)
	F.A. Cup	~	4
2001/02-02/03	F.A. Trophy	~	3
	League Cup	~	4 (1)
	Lincs Cup	~	4
	Total	~	72 (4)

Born 22/10/1978 at Lincoln. Began his career as a Trainee at Nottingham Forest, before moving on to Doncaster Rovers, Burton Albion and Hinckley United, where he helped the Leicestershire side gain promotion to the Dr Marten's Premier League. He made his Grantham debut in the opening league fixture of the 2001/02 season against Tonbridge Angels and scored his first goal for the club a week later at Burnham. Despite battling that first season for his position with Matt Carvell, a year that saw promotion for The Gingerbreads, the following campaign he played a more prominent role in the side. It was a year that saw a Lincolnshire County Senior Cup Final appearance for Danny at the start of the season, at home to Scunthorpe United, but at the end, soon after he had played what would turn out to be his final game for the club in the May 2003 fixture at home to Moor Green, Danny followed his manager, John Wilkinson, and several of his colleagues to Lincoln United.

George

Seasons Played			
	F.A. Cup	~	
	Other	~	1
1877/78	Total	~	1

Played just the once for Grantham in the 6-0 thrashing of Retford Rovers in February 1878.

Gary Germaine

Seasons Played			
	League	~	30
	F.A. Cup	~	
1998/99	F.A. Trophy	~	
	League Cup	~	4
	Lincs Cup	~	
	Total	~	34

Born 02/08/1976 at Birmingham. Former Scottish U-21 International Goalkeeper signed from West Bromwich Albion after loan spells with Telford United, Scunthorpe United, Shrewsbury Town and Leek Town. He made 12 Football League appearances during his time with the two senior loan clubs and remarkably he features in an internet supporter's poll from the former team to find their greatest ever players, despite such a short stay. Gary first played for Grantham in the November Dr Marten's Premier League game at home to Cambridge City. He missed out on the surreal start to that Antrac run season, but played in every one of the remaining games, ending in the season's closing fixture at Weymouth. He left Grantham to play in America and was last known to be making appearances for Tennessee FC and coaching for two NCAA Universities.

Donovan Gethfield

Seasons Played			
	League	~	18 (2)
	F.A. Cup	~	
1995/96	F.A. Trophy	~	2
	League Cup	~	
	Lincs Cup	~	
	Total	~	20 (2)

Born 1967 at Coventry. Much travelled defender with appearances for Coventry City, Atherstone, VS Rugby, Coventry Sporting, Banbury United, Tamworth, Bedworth United, Bromsgrove Rovers, Leicester United, Racing Club Warwick and Arnold Town behind him. He made his debut for The Gingerbreads in the October 1995 FA Trophy tie against Harrogate Town and then missed out on only a handful of games until the following March. He scored a brace in the victory over Tamworth at the start of that month, but the following fixture at Redditch United was his last match for the club. Donovan moved on to Ilkeston Town, before making appearances for Raunds Town, Shepshed Dynamo and Long Eaton United. He currently lives in Mansfield, works for an international energy company and is also Manger of Ollerton Town FC.

Alfie Gibbons

Seasons Played			
	League	~	28 (14)
	F.A. Cup	~	3
1963/64-64/65	Lincs Cup	~	
	Total	~	31 (14)

Born 28/09/1943 at Grimsby. Former Grantham Amateurs and St John's player who made his First team debut in March 1964 at Long Eaton when Brian Storrow was unavailable. Alfie kept his place for the rest of the season and finished with ten goals to his name after only 16 appearances, as Grantham won the Midland League title for the first time in their history. He began the following season starting in many of the games, but scored his last goal for the club in the home game against Matlock Town, with his final appearance in the Midland League fixture at Stamford just after the New Year. Alfie went on to make appearances for Spalding United, Loughborough United, a return to Grantham St John's, before continuing to play for several local sides. Alfie still lives in Grantham and currently works for a local food manufacturing company.

Colin Gibson

Seasons Played			
	League	~	7
	F.A. Cup	~	
1974/75-77/78	F.A. Trophy	~	
	League Cup	~	3
	Lincs Cup	~	1
	Other	~	
	Total	~	11

Born 24/08/1948 in Grantham. Former Foster's Builders, Grantham St John's and Grantham Reserves player who made a lone appearance for the First team during the 1974/75 season against Grimsby Town in the January County Cup tie. Colin played only a handful of times over the following few years, culminating in three appearances during March 1978, the last of which was the home fixture against Weymouth. He went on to play for the Stamford side that completed the United Counties League and Cup double, before ending his career with Sleaford Town. Colin still lives in the Grantham area, is holder of a local milk franchise, and is also a Squash Coach.

Gibson

Seasons Played			
	F.A. Cup	~	
	Lincs Cup	~	
1883/84	Other	~	2
	Total	~	2

Played in the first friendly of the 1883/84 season at home to Grantham Volunteers, followed by the game at Gainsborough Trinity and may have made a few other appearances as well.

Martin Fox

Willis Francis

Stuart Franklin

Sammy Fretwell

Andy Furnell

Chris Gardiner

Domenico Genovese

Danny George

Alfie Gibbons

Dave Gilbert

Neil Glasser

Lee Glover

Joby Gowshall

Gerry Graham

Alf Graver

Andy Gray

Gibson

Seasons Played			
1927/28	League	~	12 (10)
	F.A. Cup	~	1
	Lincs Cup	~	1 (1)
	Total	~	14 (11)

Outside-Left from Loughborough who made his Grantham debut in the October 1927 FA Cup game against Sutton Town and scored his first goal the following month in the league match at home to Scunthorpe & Lindsey United. He played in several of the following games, although his name cannot be found in match reports after the game against Boston in April.

Giddling

Seasons Played			
1906/07	League	~	
	Other	~	1
	Total	~	1

Defender who played in the November 1906 Grantham Minor Cup clash against Little Gonerby Swifts, but in a season when very few team-sheets are available there is no means of telling whether this was his only game or just one of many.

Keith Gifford

Seasons Played			
1958/59-59/60	League	~	3
	F.A. Cup	~	
	League Cup	~	
	Lincs Cup	~	
	Total	~	3

Played in the Midland League fixture at Blyth Spartans in April 1959 and the following season played twice more, with his final appearance in the November league match at Stamford, meaning that all three of his appearances were away from London Road.

Dave Gilbert

Seasons Played			
1998/99-02/03	League	~	103 (12)
	F.A. Cup	~	9 (1)
	F.A. Trophy	~	8 (1)
	League Cup	~	7 (1)
	Lincs Cup	~	3
	Total	~	130 (15)

Born 22/06/1963 at Lincoln. 'Diddy', as he was affectionately known, previously played for Lincoln City, Scunthorpe United and Boston United, where he made an FA Trophy Final appearance at Wembley. Moving back into The Football League, appearances then followed for Northampton Town, where he won a Fourth Division League winners medal, Grimsby Town, where he twice was part of their promotion winning side, West Bromwich Albion, with on-loan spells at York City and a return to Grimsby Town. Dave scored a total of 70 goals in 486 Football League appearances, with 12 more strikes to his name in 87 cup competition games. He joined Grantham as the club's full-time Player/Coach at the start of the 1998/99 season, making his debut in the opening fixture of that season against Scunthorpe United in the County Cup. Dave scored his initial goal for the club from the penalty spot in the first home league game against Bromsgrove Rovers, whilst October saw him playing in the club's FA Cup final qualifying round tie at Tamworth. The following season began with Dave's promotion into the manager's chair, but it was only to last a matter of months after Grantham lost every league game, although his final match in charge, in September 1999, saw a 6-0 victory in the FA Cup over Northampton Spencer. Dave then moved on to become Player/Coach at Spalding United, before returning to Grantham during the 2000/01 season. He was an important member of the side that won promotion back to the Dr Marten's Premier League in the Summer of 2002, but his final season at The Meres saw Dave make only 20 appearances, although one of those was in the October FA Cup final qualifying round match at Morecambe, when he came off the bench to replace Brendan McDaid. His last game came in the March 2003 league fixture at home to Hastings United, but at the end of that campaign he moved to Lincoln United, following John Wilkinson and several of his team-mates.

Gilbert

Seasons Played			
1889/90	Lincs Cup	~	
	Other	~	6 (2)
	Total	~	6 (2)

Forward who scored twice on his debut against Leicester Fosse Reserves in October 1889 and then played in many of the first games from that season, until his last appearance just before Christmas when Beeston Town came to London Road.

Gilbert

Seasons Played			
1923/24	League	~	1
	F.A. Cup	~	
	League Cup	~	
	Lincs Cup	~	
	Other	~	
	Total	~	1

There is only one known appearance for this forward, the March 1924 Central Alliance fixture against Heanor Town.

Tom Gilchrist

Seasons Played			
1945/46-46/47	League	~	17
	F.A. Cup	~	1
	Lincs Cup	~	
	Total	~	18

Former Swansea City Reserves goalkeeper who took over from the unavailable Mick Brannan in the March 1946 Midland League game against Rotherham United Reserves. At the start of the following season though he made the position his own, although only until the New Year, with his final game against Ransome & Marles, when Percy Ashton took over the goalkeeping role. Tom was renowned for the size of his hands and could hold two balls (those old heavy leather ones as well!) by his fingertips, with his arms down by his sides.

Gilchrist

Seasons Played			
1919/20	League	~	3
	F.A. Cup	~	2 (1)
	Lincs Cup	~	
	Total	~	5 (1)

Inside-Right who was a Lieutenant in the Armed Forces and first played for Grantham in the October 1919 Central Alliance game at London Road against Shirebrook. He scored his sole goal for the club a few weeks later in the FA Cup tie against Sutton Town, but only a month later he had played his last game when the team travelled over to Hucknall Byron.

Gilden

Seasons Played			
1932/33	League	~	1
	F.A. Cup	~	
	Lincs Cup	~	
	Other	~	
	Total	~	1

Made only one appearance for Grantham in the 1932/33 season, although no information is available to show the actual match.

Reg Gilder

Seasons Played			
1945/46	League	~	12
	F.A. Cup	~	5
	Lincs Cup	~	
	Total	~	17

Born 06/02/1921 at Broadway, Worcestershire. Defender who was stationed at Belton Park just after The War and played in the first Midland League game of the 1945/46 season against Gainsborough Trinity. Reg made appearances in both legs of the FA Cup encounters against Kettering Town and Mansfield Town, but after that played only infrequently, with his final game for the club at Peterborough United the following Easter, although his career then continued at Gonerby. After coming out of The Forces, Reg worked for the local gas company for many years, but he is now retired, still living in Grantham.

Jack Gilding

Seasons Played			
1931/32	League	~	9
	Lincs Cup	~	
	Other	~	
	Total	~	9

Was certainly playing in the first fixture of the 1931/32 season, at Loughborough Corinthians, but no data exists to show the other matches that he played in.

Ernie Gillatt

Seasons Played			
	League	~	2
	F.A. Cup	~	1
1926/27	Lincs Cup	~	
	Other	~	1
	Total	~	4

Born 1900 at Wensley. Centre-Forward who had previously played for Hartshay Colliery, Matlock Town, Clapton Orient, Burnley, Mansfield Town, (during their 1924 and 1925 Midland League winning years), and Barnsley, scoring seven times in his 75 Football League appearances. Ernie made his Grantham debut in the October 1926 FA Cup defeat at Newark Town, but only played in the following three games and left without scoring a single goal. Died at Sheffield.

Willie Gillison

Seasons Played			
	League	~	5 (2)
	F.A. Cup	~	1
1933/34-34/35	Lincs Cup	~	
	Other	~	1 (1)
	Total	~	7 (3)

Centre-Forward from Ropsley who had also played for Grantham Amateurs and Grantham St. John's. He scored on his September 1933 debut at London Road in the Central Combination game against Loughborough Corinthians, but made only six other appearances over the next 18 months, with the March 1935 fixture at Scunthorpe & Lindsey United his final game for the club. Willie was also noted for his ability at cricket and darts, even showing Laurel & Hardy his skills with 'the arrows' when they stayed at The Red Lion Hotel in 1947 during a tour of the country.

Gilmore

Seasons Played			
	Other	~	1
1876/77	Total	~	1

There is only one known appearance for this player, the 1-1 draw against Lincoln in November 1876.

Girdham

Seasons Played			
	League	~	6 (1)
	F.A. Cup	~	1
1947/48	Lincs Cup	~	
	Total	~	7 (1)

Scored his only goal for the club on his debut, the first Midland League game of the 1947/48 season at Scarborough and although he played the majority of his games in the first few matches of that season, his final appearance was on Boxing Day in the fixture at Ransome & Marles.

Chris Giscombe

Seasons Played			
	League	~	4 (1)
	F.A. Cup	~	
1980/81	F.A. Trophy	~	
	League Cup	~	
	Lincs Cup	~	
	Other	~	
	Total	~	4 (1)

Possible Nottingham based forward who scored on his Grantham debut in the November 1980 league match at home to Mossley when he came off the bench to replace Player/Manager, Geoff Barker. This led to appearances in the following two games, but Chris played only once more for The Gingerbreads, at Lancaster City just before Christmas. He went on to play for Bulwell Villa, but nothing is known about him after this.

Neil Glasser

Seasons Played			
	League	~	95 (7)
	F.A. Cup	~	7
1996/97-98/99	F.A. Trophy	~	15 (2)
	League Cup	~	8
	Lincs Cup	~	4
	Total	~	129 (9)

Born 17/10/1974 at Nottingham. A former Nottingham Forest and Notts County midfielder who had also played for Bromsgrove Rovers and Ilkeston Town. His first game for Grantham came in the opening match of the 1996/97 season against Grimsby Town, with his first goal in the home fixture against Solihull Borough the same month. He played a significant role in Gary Mill's successful side, appearing in the Spring 1998 memorable games against Hednesford Town and Southport, plus the 6-0 thrashing of Ilkeston Town in the league. After winning a Dr Marten's League, Midland Division Championship medal at The Meres only months later, Neil was rewarded with a professional contract when the side moved up to the Premier Division and scored in the opening league victory at Worcester City. However, it would ultimately become his last goal for Grantham and after playing in the FA Cup final qualifying round tie at Tamworth, his concluding appearance came in the April match at Atherstone United. Neil went on to play for Burton Albion, where he won a Unibond Premier League Championship medal, before signing for Worksop Town.

Lee Glover

Seasons Played			
	League	~	21 (4)
	F.A. Cup	~	
2004/05	F.A. Trophy	~	
	League Cup	~	
	Lincs Cup	~	1
	Total	~	22 (4)

Born 24/04/1970 at Kettering. Began his career with Kettering Town, but in July 1986 moved to Nottingham Forest, where he made 105 appearances, one of which was the 1991 FA Cup Final against Tottenham Hotspur. He was also a non-playing substitute in the 1989 League Cup success, won a Simod Cup winner's medal a year later and helped The Reds to promotion back into The Premiership in 1994. He had already been capped by Scotland at Youth level and during his time at The City Ground Lee was also awarded three appearances in the Under-21 set-up. On-loan spells at Leicester City, Barnsley and Luton Town were followed by a permanent move to Port Vale in August 1994 and two years later Rotherham United, where he was part of the team that won promotion back into the Second Division. After a spell on-loan at Huddersfield Town, Lee joined Macclesfield Town in July 2000 and then made appearances for Mansfield Town. His professional career finished with more than 80 goals in over 400 senior appearances. Moving into the non-league game, Lee joined Burton Albion, with his path crossing that of Gary Crosby's for the third time and in December 2002 was appointed Player/Manager at Corby Town. But both his seasons there finished with The Steelmen struggling at the wrong end of the table. Following Dave Norton's departure from The Meres, Lee was brought to Grantham, holding a full UEFA 'B' coaching certificate to go with his BSc (Honours) degree in Sports Science. His debut was delayed for a couple of weeks due to illness, but he brought himself off the bench in the December 2004 Southern League fixture at home to Cirencester Town and scored his first goal a month later in the 5-1 win over King's Lynn. In April 2005 Lee steered the team to a Lincolnshire Shield Final victory over Gainsborough Trinity and he remains with the club, having assembled a squad which seems capable of challenging for Conference entry in the 2005/06 season.

Fred Goddard

Seasons Played			
	League	~	13 (2)
	F.A. Cup	~	3 (2)
1935/36	Lincs Cup	~	
	Other	~	
	Total	~	16 (4)

Fred at one time played for Lincoln Corinthians, the 'nursery' side for Lincoln City, but began his Grantham career in September 1935 with the Midland League trip up to Bradford City Reserves. He played in every game over the next couple of months and even managed two goals in the FA Cup encounter at home to Newark Town. But by the end of the year his place had been taken, firstly by George Eales and then by Harry Pringle, although he made a few more appearances until his final one in the February 1936 Lincolnshire League clash against Grimsby Town Reserves.

Godson

Seasons Played			
	F.A. Cup	~	
	Other	~	1
1878/79	Total	~	1

Made just one appearance for Grantham in the November 1878 5-0 friendly defeat of Boston.

Jon Godwin

Seasons Played			
	League	~	86
1991/92-93/94	F.A. Cup	~	4
	F.A. Trophy	~	6
	League Cup	~	4
	Lincs Cup	~	3
	Total	~	103

Born 20/09/1973 at Sheffield. Young goalkeeper signed from Sheffield United on the recommendation of their Youth Team Coach and former Gingerbread, Keith Mincher, after having had trials with Sheffield Wednesday and Manchester United. He played in five games for Grantham at the end of the 1991/92 season, starting at Redditch United, and missed only a few of the fixtures in the following two seasons, although there are precious few highlights to comment on, bar the FA Trophy ties against Witton Albion and Bishop Auckland at the beginning of 1994. He made his final appearance for the club in the May 1994 league trip over to Dudley Town and went on to play for Buxton, Matlock Town, Long Eaton United and Arnold Town, before a knee injury forced an early retirement. Jon now lives in the Nottingham area and works for a Chesterfield based architectural company.

George Goften

Seasons Played			
	League	~	3 (1)
	F.A. Cup	~	
1935/36	Lincs Cup	~	
	Other	~	
	Total	~	3 (1)

Born 28/02/1912 at Hartlepool. Centre-Forward with experience at Newcastle United Reserves, Queen's Park Rangers, scoring eight times in his seven senior appearances, and Dunkirk United. He played in only three games for Grantham during February of 1936, starting at home to Scunthorpe & Lindsey United, scoring in the match against Grimsby Town Reserves and ending at Gainsborough Trinity. Died 1990.

Craig Goldsmith

Seasons Played			
	League	~	13 (4)
	F.A. Cup	~	
1992/93	F.A. Trophy	~	
	League Cup	~	
	Lincs Cup	~	
	Total	~	13 (4)

Born 27/08/1963 at Peterborough. Former Raunds Town, Mirlees Blackstone, Peterborough United, Carlisle United, Rushden Town and Stamford Town winger with seven goals to his name during his 76 Football League appearances. His first game for Grantham came in the February 1993 fixture at Evesham United with his four goals for the club coming in consecutive matches a month later. He played for The Gingerbreads up until that season's closing game at home to Bridgnorth Town and then went on to play for Harrowby United and Eye United.

Gooderson

Seasons Played			
	League	~	1 (1)
	FA Amt. Cup	~	1 (1)
1910/11	League Cup	~	
	Lincs Cup	~	1
	Other	~	
	Total	~	3 (2)

Seems to have played predominantly at the start of the 1910/11 Midland Amateur League title winning season, scoring in the league game against Derby YMCA and then during the club's only match in the FA Amateur Cup at home to Loughborough Corinthians in October 1910.

Goodley

Seasons Played			
	League	~	
	F.A. Cup	~	
1936/37	Lincs Cup	~	
	Other	~	1 (1)
	Total	~	1 (1)

Played and scored in his only appearance for Grantham, the Wilson Cup fixture against RAF Cranwell at the end of the 1936/37 season.

Colin Goodwin

Seasons Played			
	League	~	5
	F.A. Cup	~	
1979/80	F.A. Trophy	~	1
	League Cup	~	1
	Lincs Cup	~	1
	Total	~	8

Born circa 1958. Defender who previously spent time at Mansfield Town and Notts County, making his Grantham debut in the August 1979 County Cup tie at Gainsborough Trinity and then playing in all seven games during December, ending at Goole Town.

Scott Goodwin

Seasons Played			
	League	~	22 (1)
	F.A. Cup	~	
1998/99	F.A. Trophy	~	
	League Cup	~	2
	Lincs Cup	~	
	Total	~	24 (1)

Born 13/09/1978 at Hull. Full-Back who was released by Coventry City and then moved on to Shepshed Dynamo, before coming on as substitute in Grantham's November 1998 game at home to Atherstone United. Scott played in many of the remaining matches from that season, scoring his only goal in the return to Atherstone, two weeks before his final game at Weymouth. He went on to play for Hednesford Town, Hereford United, Kettering Town, Gravesend & Northfleet and Tamworth, before returning to Hednesford. A busy 2004/05 season for Scott saw him join Canvey Island in September, but moves soon followed to Bishop's Stortford and Nuneaton Borough, although he was released by them in May 2005.

Goodwin

Seasons Played			
	League	~	15 (3)
	F.A. Cup	~	2
1890/91-92/93	Lincs Cup	~	
	Other	~	8
1894/95	Total	~	25 (3)

Made his debut in the January 1891 friendly at home to Nottingham Forest Reserves, but only played twice more before the end of that season. The following campaign though, he appeared in the majority of the competitive fixtures, scoring his first goal against Mansfield Town in October. However, he was also unfortunate enough to play in every league match of the disastrous 1892/93 season, including the 16-0 defeat at Notts County Rovers. He returned to the club in the 1894/95 season and finally made his last appearance for the club in the local Charity Cup tie against Grantham Rovers in January.

Goodyear

Seasons Played			
	League	~	
	F.A. Cup	~	1
1921/22	Lincs Cup	~	
	Total	~	1

Centre-Forward who had previously played for Gainsborough Trinity, but was brought in from the Reserves side to play in the October 1921 FA Cup game against Mansfield Town.

Mark Gore

Seasons Played			
	League	~	23 (9)
	F.A. Cup	~	
1992/93-93/94	F.A. Trophy	~	
	League Cup	~	
	Lincs Cup	~	1
	Total	~	24 (9)

Born 05/12/1965 at Aldershot. Centre-Forward with experience at Boston United and German side, Bundersperd, who came to Grantham from Notts Alliance side, Worthington & Simpson. Mark made his debut by coming off the bench to replace Barratt Noble in the February 1993 league fixture at home to Newport AFC and scored the winning goal. He was seen as a tremendous prospect after scoring nine goals by the end of the season, including a hat-trick in the 3-3 draw against Stourbridge. However after only six more appearances at the start of the following campaign, five of which came from the bench, he finished his Grantham career in the September 1993 game at Yate Town.

Andy Gould

Seasons Played			
	League	~	26 (2)
	F.A. Cup	~	1
1976/77-77/78	F.A. Trophy	~	1
	League Cup	~	4
	Lincs Cup	~	2
	Other	~	
	Total	~	34 (2)

Midfield player signed from Leicester City who made his debut in the February 1977 Southern League game at Yeovil Town, but played his last match for the club less than a year later at Nuneaton Borough in the FA Trophy. In that time Andy had scored against Redditch United and Barnet and although no information is available about his subsequent club, it is known that he was making appearances for Shepshed Charterhouse in the early 1980's. Andy is thought to be still living in the Leicester area.

Rob Gould

Seasons Played			
	League	~	33 (1)
	F.A. Cup	~	4 (2)
2003/04-04/05	F.A. Trophy	~	1
	League Cup	~	1
	Lincs Cup	~	2
	Total	~	41 (3)

Born 07/07/1975 at Northampton. Former Cogenhoe United, Racing Club Warwick, Raunds Town, Rothwell Town, Ilkeston Town, where he was the club's leading scorer during the 2000/01 season, Tamworth, St Albans and Bishops Stortford defender. He made his debut for Grantham in the club's inaugural Lincolnshire County Shield tie against Stamford at the start of the 2003/04 season and scored his first goal for the club later that month at home to Cambridge City. Rob played in every game until the New Year, including the FA Cup First Round Proper tie against Leyton Orient, but as the team slipped down towards the relegation zone, questions began to be asked about the team's defence and Rob was singled out by some of the supporters for particular criticism. He played in the February 2004 fixture against Nuneaton Borough, Dave Norton's first in charge, but then went on to play for Brackley and Kettering Town. After a short spell on-loan at Stamford, he was brought back to The Meres in March 2005 on a similar arrangement, playing in five consecutive fixtures. The last of those was at Stamford at the end of the month and Rob then returned to Kettering.

Joby Gowshall

Seasons Played			
	League	~	17
	F.A. Cup	~	
2002/03	F.A. Trophy	~	
	League Cup	~	2
	Lincs Cup	~	
	Total	~	19

Born 07/08/1975 at Louth. Defender who had previously played for Grimsby Town, Lincoln City, Boston United, where he helped the club win the Dr Marten's Premier League, Gainsborough Trinity and King's Lynn. He played his first game for Grantham in the November 2002 league game at Welling United as well as most of the remaining fixtures of that season, until the closing game at home to Moor Green, where a 4-0 win secured Dr Marten's Premier football for another year. Only weeks later though, the departure of John Wilkinson to Lincoln United prompted a mass following of Grantham players to the same club, Joby included.

Gerry Graham

Seasons Played			
	League	~	17 (3)
	F.A. Cup	~	
1969/70	F.A. Trophy	~	5
	League Cup	~	2
	Lincs Cup	~	
	Other	~	
	Total	~	24 (3)

Born 31/01/1941 at Aspatria, Cumbria. Began his career with Blackpool and then played for Peterborough United in their first seasons in The Football League, before moving to Mansfield Town in 1964. Games followed for Cambridge United, Worcester City, where he was the club's top scorer in the 1967/68 season, Workington and Nuneaton Borough, before he joined The Gingerbreads. He made his first appearance by replacing Jimmy Jackson during the October 1969 victory over Belper Town and then scored twice at the end of the month to secure a 3-2 victory at Arnold. Despite spending many of the games sat on the substitutes bench, Gerry certainly played his part in that season's success and had the highlight of playing in front of nearly 7,000 supporters in the FA Trophy match at Worcester City, no doubt swelled by the home fans chance to see their former favourite in action once more. He made his final appearance in the April 1970 draw at home to Warley.

Milton Graham

Seasons Played			
	League	~	9
	F.A. Cup	~	
1992/93	F.A. Trophy	~	1
	League Cup	~	2
	Lincs Cup	~	
	Total	~	12

Born 02/11/1962 at Hackney. Started his Football League career with Bournemouth and in January 1984 was on the back pages of every Sunday newspaper after scoring one of the goals that helped the Division Three strugglers knock holders, Manchester United, out of the FA Cup. Milton also won an Associate Members Cup medal during his time there and then moved on to Chester City and Peterborough United, finally making a total of 264 appearances, with 31 goals to his name. His career continued in non-league football with Spalding United, King's Lynn and Poole Town, before his arrival at The Meres. He made his debut for Grantham by coming off the bench to replace Chris Grocock during the September 1992 FA Trophy defeat against Congleton Town, but after the January home game against Barri Town, the disclosure of financial problems within the club led to the departure of Milton and several of his team-mates. After leaving The Mere's, he made appearances for Bourne Town, Holbeach United, Corby Town and Stamford, where he won a United Counties League Championship winner's medal. He began his managerial career with Peterborough League side Pearl, before taking over as Assistant Manager at Holbeach United, where he remains.

Paul Grainger

Seasons Played			
	League	~	17 (3)
	F.A. Cup	~	
1982/83	F.A. Trophy	~	
	League Cup	~	3
	Lincs Cup	~	
	Other	~	
	Total	~	20 (3)

Former Burton Albion and Shepshed Charterhouse player who began his Grantham career in the January 1983 league fixture against Buxton and scored the first of three goals for the club later that month at Worksop Town. He played in the majority of the remaining games from that season, up to the closing match at Matlock Town, during which Paul replaced Ray Elliott. After leaving London Road he went on to play for Ilkeston Town.

Ossie Grant

Seasons Played			
	League	~	61 (9)
	F.A. Cup	~	4 (1)
1978/79-80/81	F.A. Trophy	~	3 (1)
	League Cup	~	3
	Lincs Cup	~	4
	Other	~	1
	Total	~	76 (11)

Born circa 1959. Former England Youth International forward who began his career as an Apprentice at Notts County, followed by a brief spell at Boston United. He joined Grantham towards the end of the 1978/79 season, making his debut in the March defeat of Enderby Town and scoring his first goal for the club the following month at home to Cambridge City. Although he played his part in that season's Championship win, the deciding fixture against Merthyr Tydfil saw Player/Manager, Bob Norris, stick to an experienced side and it was a game that Ossie missed out on. As Grantham moved up to the Northern Premier League, Ossie was still struggling to maintain his place in a side that consisted of a first-choice of Robbie Cooke and Dennis Jenas up front. In the Summer of 1980 though, Cookie's departure to Peterborough United promoted Ossie to an almost permanent place in the side, including games against Lincoln City in the County Cup Final and Nottingham Forest in the Redmayne Trophy. His final goal for the club had come in the November 1980 fixture against Mossley, with his last game in the season's closing match at Runcorn. Ossie currently lives in London, where he is an international diamond dealer.

Rob Grant

Seasons Played			
	League	~	6
1992/93	F.A. Cup	~	
	F.A. Trophy	~	
	League Cup	~	
	Lincs Cup	~	
	Total	~	6

Former Melton Town player who appeared in the final six fixtures of the 1992/93 season, four of which came from the substitute's bench. The first of those was the April league game at Sutton Coldfield, with the last match of the campaign at home to Bridgnorth Town ending Rob's time at The Meres.

Grant

Seasons Played			
	League	~	1 (1)
1913/14	F.A. Cup	~	
	Lincs Cup	~	
	Total	~	1 (1)

Player that is known to have scored in the Central Alliance game against Mansfield Mechanics in November 1913, but no data exists to show whether he played in any other games.

W. Grantham

Seasons Played			
	League	~	4 (1)
1904/05-05/06	Lincs Cup	~	
	Other	~	
	Total	~	4 (1)

Scored in the first league game after the club's reformation, the October 1904 game at home to Bridgford Athletic, but from then only played infrequently, with the previously mentioned club's return to Grantham his last known appearance in November 1905.

Alf Graver

Seasons Played			
	League	~	75 (26)
1952/53-54/55	F.A. Cup	~	
	League Cup	~	
	Lincs Cup	~	5 (4)
1960/61	Total	~	80 (30)

Born 19/05/1933 at Bloemfontein, County Durham. Brother of the Lincoln City legend, Andy Graver. After spells with Annfield Plain and Lincoln City Reserves, Alf made his Grantham debut in the December 1952 fixture at Gainsborough Trinity when John Mulholland became unavailable. He scored his first goal for the club in the 4-4 draw against Corby Town on Boxing Day and made several more appearances before the end of the season, including the County Cup Final against Spalding United. After Mulholland's final game the following October, Alf was able to make the position his own. In April 1954 he scored one of the goals to give Grantham victory in the Lincolnshire Senior Cup 'A' Final against Gainsborough Trinity, but for the following season he played in only a few of the games. However, Alf returned to the club nearly five years later, after a spell with Boston United, and scored 15 more goals for Grantham in only 14 appearances during that 1960/61 season, the last coming at Rushden Town, before his final game for the club in April 1961 at Stamford. Alf finished his career with the Ruston Bucyrus works team, where he was also employed. Died 1981 at Lincoln.

S. Graves

Seasons Played			
	League	~	4 (1)
1939/40	Lincs Cup	~	1
	Other	~	
	Total	~	5 (1)

Service-man who had also played for Ruston Bucyrus and made his Grantham debut in the November 1939 fixture at Scunthorpe & Lindsey United. He made most of his appearances though in the second of the 'War-Time' leagues, but played his last game for the club in the April 1940 Lincolnshire Senior Cup Final defeat.

Andy Gray

Seasons Played			
	League	~	28 (6)
1999/00-00/01	F.A. Cup	~	6 (2)
	F.A. Trophy	~	
	League Cup	~	
	Lincs Cup	~	1
	Total	~	35 (8)

Born 08/08/1975 at Sheffield. Began his career in local Sheffield football before being signed by Boston United and despite having had trials at Sheffield Wednesday and Coventry City, then moved on to Lincoln United. The arrival of John Wilkinson at The Meres soon saw Andy following him, where he made his debut in the December 1999 fixture against Dorchester Town and scored his first two goals for the club in the 5-1 victory over Salisbury City a month later. Andy missed only one of that season's remaining games as The Gingerbreads gallantly attempted to escape relegation. After the Summer break though, he scored a brace against Borrowash Victoria, as the club began their FA Cup run, but these would prove to be his last strikes for the club. He made his final appearance when he came on as substitute in the final qualifying round match at Rushden & Diamonds and went on to play for Worksop Town. However it's thought that he is now in the South-East of the country, working in the earth-moving industry.

Gray

Seasons Played			
	Other	~	21
1874/75-75/76	Total	~	21

Played in many of the earliest club matches, plus the very first game against another team when the Third Lincolnshire Volunteer Rifles came to London Road in October 1874. He made his final appearance in the closing friendly of the following season at Nottingham Lace.

Graydon

Seasons Played			
	F.A. Cup	~	
1883/84-84/85	Lincs Cup	~	
	Other	~	5
	Total	~	5

The first instance of his name appearing in match reports comes in the December 1883 friendly at Spilsby. He also played in some of the friendlies at the start of the following season, but the 7-1 defeat at Newark in November 1884 was his final game for Grantham.

Phil Greaves

Seasons Played			
	League	~	13
1984/85-86/87	F.A. Cup	~	1
	F.A. Trophy	~	1
	League Cup	~	2
	Lincs Cup	~	1
	Other	~	
	Total	~	18

Born circa 1964. Goalkeeper who arrived from Grantham United to make two First team appearances during the 1984/85 season, starting with the opening game at Boston United in the County Cup. The following season saw Phil covering for Graham Cox in three league games during March, whilst the 1986/87 season proved to be his best for the club, making several appearances up to his final one in the season's closing fixture at Banbury United. At the end of the decade he was playing for Harrowby United, but no other information is known on clubs that he played for, although it is thought that he still lives locally.

Eddie Green

Seasons Played			
	League	~	32
1981/82-83/84	F.A. Cup	~	3
	F.A. Trophy	~	
	League Cup	~	2
	Lincs Cup	~	
	Other	~	2
	Total	~	39

Born circa 1960. Former England Schoolboy and Under-18 International goalkeeper who had also played for the British Universities side that toured America. He covered for Graham Cox in the October 1981 league fixture at home to Burton Albion and the visit of Nottingham Forest to London Road the following month. The 1982/83 season saw Eddie's promotion to the club's first-choice 'keeper, a position he held for the first 14 games of the next season as well. The October 1983 defeat at Marine was his last for Grantham and the following week Grahame Hempsall had taken over the role. Eddie went on to play for Stamford Town, Retford Town, Worksop Town, Ilkeston Town and Heanor Town.

Haydn Green

Seasons Played			
	League	~	5 (1)
	F.A. Cup	~	
1922/23	Lincs Cup	~	
	Other	~	
	Total	~	5 (1)

Born circa 1890 in Nottinghamshire. Former Nottingham Forest, Chesterfield, where he scored five goals in 21 First team appearances, Ilkeston United, Manchester United, Aston Villa and Reading centre-forward. He played for Grantham during the first few months of the 1922/23 season, but scored only once, in the September Central Alliance fixture at home to Hucknall Byron. In 1931 Haydn became Manager of Hull City, then took charge at Swansea City, both before and after The Second World War and in 1951 spent a short spell at the helm of Watford. Died 1957.

Mark Green

Seasons Played			
	League	~	1
	F.A. Cup	~	
1996/97	F.A. Trophy	~	
	League Cup	~	
	Lincs Cup	~	
	Total	~	1

Spent time on the books of Nottingham Forest and joined Grantham from Kimberley Town. It was a short career with The Gingerbreads though, as his debut for the club in the March 1997 fixture against Tamworth abruptly came to an end when he was substituted.

Valentine Green

Seasons Played			
	Other	~	4
1874/75-75/76	Total	~	4

Born 1851 at Knipton, Leicestershire. An architect, land agent and diocesan surveyor who was the club's original secretary and treasurer. His father will be known to many proficient chess players as he was the founder of the 'Green Variation' move. Valentine made his debut in the January 1875 friendly at Newark, but appears to have only played in a few matches the following season, with the game against Bourne in February 1876 his last known appearance for the club. At the end of the century Valentine designed the Dysart Road workhouse, which many older Granthamians will remember as it became the Hill View Hospital.

Green

Seasons Played			
	League	~	4 (2)
	Lincs Cup	~	1
1904/05	Other	~	
	Total	~	5 (2)

Forward who plays in many of the games where full reports are available for the 1904/05 season and scored in the league fixtures against Notts Magdala and Notts Magdala Amateurs.

Green

Seasons Played			
	League	~	1
	FA Amt. Cup	~	
1910/11	League Cup	~	
	Lincs Cup	~	
	Other	~	
	Total	~	1

Very few team-sheets are available for this season, so the only game that we know for certain that he played in was the January 1911 fixture at West Bridgford Albion.

Ernest Greenberry

Seasons Played			
	League	~	5
	F.A. Cup	~	
1949/50-50/51	Lincs Cup	~	
	Total	~	5

Made his First team debut in March 1950 when Reg Dyer became unavailable for the Midland League fixture at Goole Town, but played only three more times that season and then had to wait until December to make his last appearance in the league game against Bradford City Reserves.

Greenhalgh

Seasons Played			
	Other	~	1 (1)
1876/77	Total	~	1 (1)

Scored in his only known appearance for Grantham in the December 1876 match against Bourne.

Reg Gregory

Seasons Played			
	League	~	319 (15)
	F.A. Cup	~	32 (4)
1934/35-39/40	Lincs Cup	~	23 (2)
	Other	~	12 (2)
1945/46-48/49	Total	~	386 (23)

Scored on his debut at Mexborough Athletic in September 1934 and the following Saturday netted a hat-trick in the record 13-0 defeat of Rufford Colliery in the FA Cup. By the end of the season Reg had settled into the side and had also appeared in both the Final and replay of the County Cup competition against Boston United. The following season, a year where he missed only one of the matches, included the highlights of an FA Cup First Round encounter against Notts County and another Lincolnshire Senior Cup Final appearance, along with team victories in the Grantham Hospital and Wilson Cups. April of 1937 saw Reg finally win a County Cup winners medal as Grantham at long last managed to defeat Boston United, whilst the following season saw Grantham finish as runners-up in the Midland League. As the decade came to a close there was little cheer for the Grantham supporters, although obviously Reg was continuing to accumulate those appearances and just before the end of competitive fixtures, he played in another County Cup Final, this time against Scunthorpe & Lindsey United. Reg returned to London Road after The War and although he missed some of the games from that season, these didn't include the important two legs in the FA Cup games against Kettering Town and Mansfield Town. However, he must have felt that feeling of deja-vu as another Boston United victory left Reg with his fourth County Cup runners-up medal. The following season he was back as a near permanent member of the side as the team worked their way to the seemingly predestined outcome in the Lincolnshire County Cup Final, although a few months later he once more appeared in the FA Cup First Round as Grantham made the trip up to Stockton. Reg made his final appearance for Grantham in September 1948 when Nottingham Forest Reserves drew at London Road and perhaps surprisingly his final goal for his club was still back in March 1940 during the friendly against an Army XI.

Tim Gregory

Seasons Played			
	League	~	5
	F.A. Cup	~	2
1933/34	Lincs Cup	~	
	Other	~	
	Total	~	7

Centre-half who had also played for Shirebrook and Bolsover and made appearances in the first seven games of the 1933/34 season for Grantham, beginning at Loughborough Corinthians and ending in the FA Cup replay at Sutton.

Gregory

Seasons Played			
	League	~	10 (11)
	F.A. Cup	~	3 (5)
1911/12-12/13	Lincs Cup	~	
	Other	~	
1914/15	Total	~	13 (16)

Made his Grantham debut in the latter half of the 1911/12 season, with his first recorded goal coming in the Central Alliance fixture at home to Sutton Junction in April. The following September he scored a hat-trick in the FA Cup replay against Sneinton, but at a time when many of the match reports consisted simply of a list of the goalscorers, there is no means of knowing just how many appearances he was making. He certainly seemed to be a more prominent member of the side at the start of the final league competition before the end of World War One and he was scoring right up until the January 1915 fixture at home to Ilkeston United.

Grey

Seasons Played			
	League	~	1 (1)
	FA Amt. Cup	~	
1910/11	League Cup	~	
	Lincs Cup	~	1
	Other	~	
	Total	~	2 (1)

Scored in the opening 1910/11 league game against Notts GNR Clerks, but his only other confirmed appearance is the following month in a County competition match against Gonerby Athletic.

Steve Grice

Seasons Played			
	League	~	5
	F.A. Cup	~	
1980/81	F.A. Trophy	~	
	League Cup	~	
	Lincs Cup	~	
	Other	~	
	Total	~	5

Born circa 1964. Former Nottingham Forest Schoolboy and Ruddington player who appeared in five games for Grantham at the end of the 1980/81 season, starting as a substitute in the March fixture at home to Worksop Town and ending in the closing game at Runcorn.

Griffen

Seasons Played			
	League	~	1
	F.A. Cup	~	
1919/20	Lincs Cup	~	
	Total	~	1

Forward who made only one appearance for Grantham, in the November 1919 league match at Ilkeston United.

Griffith

Seasons Played			
	Other	~	5
1875/76-76/77	Total	~	5

Played his first game for the club in the December 1875 friendly against the Conservative Working Men's Club and made his last known appearance in the January 1877 benefit match against Nottingham Castle, when the gate receipts were forwarded to Grantham Hospital.

Stan Griffiths

Seasons Played			
	League	~	3
	F.A. Cup	~	
1938/39	Lincs Cup	~	
	Total	~	3

Born 1911 at Pentre, Wales. Forward with experience at Cardiff City, Swansea City, Chester City, Gillingham, where he made his Football League debut, before returning to Cardiff City, and then making appearances for Bangor City and Dundalk, where he won a Dublin Cup medal along with a runners-up medal in the Irish Free State League. As far as his Grantham career is concerned, he played in only three games during the Autumn of 1938, the Midland League games against the Reserve sides of Doncaster Rovers and Grimsby Town, plus the match at Peterborough United.

Griffiths

Seasons Played			
	F.A. Cup	~	
	Other	~	3
1878/79	Total	~	3

Made his debut in the January 1879 match against Notts County, but played his final game for the club only the following month in the friendly at Spilsby.

Vince Grimes

Seasons Played			
	League	~	17 (2)
	F.A. Cup	~	1
1984/85	F.A. Trophy	~	3 (1)
	League Cup	~	
	Lincs Cup	~	
	Other	~	2
	Total	~	23 (3)

Born 13/05/1954 at Scunthorpe. Midfielder with over 250 appearances for Hull City, Bradford City and Scunthorpe United behind him. He made his debut for Grantham in the September 1984 FA Cup tie at home to Halesowen Town and scored his first goal for the club at the end of the same month against Morecambe. However, Vince played his final game for the club only a few weeks into the New Year, at home to Buxton, and with the club's league position becoming more and more precarious as each week went by, he went on to play for Gainsborough Trinity and then Bottesford Town. Vince still lives in the Scunthorpe area and works for North Lincolnshire District Council.

Chris Grocock

Seasons Played			
	League	~	187 (24)
	F.A. Cup	~	9 (1)
1989/90-93/94	F.A. Trophy	~	15 (3)
	League Cup	~	21 (2)
1996/97-97/98	Lincs Cup	~	7
	Total	~	239 (30)

Born 30/10/1968 at Grimsby. Former England Schoolboy International who began his career at Grimsby Town, scoring once in his 43 appearances, before a short spell at Boston United where supporters later voted him the 51st most popular player in the club's history, which I think is a compliment! He scored on his debut for Grantham in the April league fixture against Hednesford Town and played in all six of the final games from that season, whilst the 1990/91 campaign saw Chris play in the final league game at London Road in September against Dudley Town and finally miss just one of the matches. Grantham's first season at The Meres saw him still playing in virtually every fixture, including the opening match at the new stadium against Ilkeston Town in the September 1991 FA Cup tie. The club was rocked with the loss of several players in January 1993 due to financial problems, but although Chris stayed at The Meres at that time, only a few weeks later he had moved on to Bridlington Town where he won an FA Vase winners medal at Wembley at the end of the season. Chris was back with Grantham after the Summer break though and it was that season's FA Trophy that many supporters will remember him by, as his goal against Witton Albion caused one of the shocks of the day, to send The Gingerbreads into the Second Round. At the start of the 1994/95 season Chris was playing for Boston Town, where he later won a United Counties League winner's medal, before being brought back to Grantham by the club's new Manager, Gary Mills, during the Summer of 1996. He played an important part in the side that came so close to awarding Mills promotion at his first attempt, scoring what would be his final two goals for the club in the March 1997 fixture at Stourbridge. After only four appearances in the 1997/98 season, the last of which came from the substitute's bench during the August league match at home to Paget Rangers, he went back to Boston Town, before making appearances for Brigg Town, Louth United and Grimsby Borough. Chris is currently a solicitor in Grimsby.

Ted Guest

Seasons Played			
	League	~	42 (17)
	F.A. Cup	~	
1949/50-51/52	Lincs Cup	~	3 (1)
	Total	~	45 (18)

Forward who scored on his debut in the February 1950 league game against Scarborough and played in several of the remaining fixtures, including the Lincolnshire Senior Cup 'A' Final against Boston United where he scored one of the consolation goals. Ted played in many of the following season's games and even managed a hat-trick in the December visit of York City Reserves to London Road, but he made only two more appearances for the club towards the start of the 1951/52 season, with the game at Notts County Reserves being his final match.

John Gulson

Seasons Played			
	League	~	48 (4)
	F.A. Cup	~	
1976/77-79/80	F.A. Trophy	~	4
	League Cup	~	8 (1)
	Lincs Cup	~	2 (1)
	Other	~	
	Total	~	62 (6)

Born 24/09/1946 in London. PT Instructor with experience at Wycombe Wanderers, Sutton Town, Loughborough Colleges, Chesham United, Newhall United and Ilkeston Town, with a trial at Nottingham Forest recently behind him. He played in defence for The Gingerbreads in the November 1976 fixture at home to

Redditch United and scored his first goal for the club just after Christmas against Margate. Despite playing at London Road for four years, his appearances were limited, with the final one coming in the November 1979 Northern Premier League game at home to Runcorn. John stayed on at London Road for a while as the club's coach and joint manager of the Reserves, along with Dennis Benskin. He was also well known for his cricketing skills, playing for Grantham and Belvoir at various times. John still lives close to Grantham, but works for a college in Slough, which limits his time spent in the area.

Alec Guyan

Seasons Played	League	~	12 (4)
	Lincs Cup	~	2 (2)
1939/40	Other	~	1
	Total	~	15 (6)

Originally from Scotland, Alec had also played for Grantham St John's after moving to the area, and scored on his debut for our club in the November 1939 game at Denaby United. He played in many of the games after Christmas and scored Grantham's only goal in the 7-1 County Cup Final defeat at the hands of Scunthorpe & Lindsey United. He made his last appearance for the club two weeks later at Peterborough United.

Darren Gwyther

Seasons Played	League	~	39 (8)
	F.A. Cup	~	4 (1)
1995/96-96/97	F.A. Trophy	~	3
	League Cup	~	4
1998/99-99/00	Lincs Cup	~	2
	Total	~	52 (9)

Born 09/11/1979 in Grantham. Progressed through the Reserves side to make his full debut in the April 1996 match at Dudley Town, scoring his first goal for the club only weeks later against RC Warwick. However, after only two appearances the following season, it was the 1998/99 campaign that saw Darren's emergence as a noticeable member of the First team, although several of the games that he was involved in began from the substitute's bench. This was a role that continued the following year, with his last goal for Grantham in the club's final match of the Millennium, an exciting nine goal game at Ilkeston Town with The Gingerbreads losing by the odd strike. His last appearance for the club came in the February 2000 fixture at home to Weymouth, when he came off the bench to replace Tim Wilkes. He would undoubtedly have made many more appearances for the club had he not suffered from a serious illness and several injuries, including suffering from broken legs twice. Darren later went on to play for Spalding United and Harrowby United and is hopeful that he will be able to restart playing local football in the near future. He now lives at Sleaford and works as a welder.

Christopher Hackett

Seasons Played	League	~	7 (3)
	F.A. Cup	~	1 (1)
1924/25	Lincs Cup	~	
	Other	~	
1927/28-28/29	Total	~	8 (4)

Born 09/02/1903 at Mansfield. Outside-Right who had previously played for Mansfield Town, Bitterlings, Langwith Colliery and Newark Town. Although his exact debut date is not known, Chris was playing for Grantham towards the start of the 1924/25 season and scored his first goal for the club in the September FA Cup tie against Newark Town. At some point during that season he was transferred to Leicester City, although he failed to make their First team, and then went on to play for Caernarvon Town before returning to London Road towards the closing stages of the 1927/28 season. However, he appears to have made only a couple of appearances over the next year, a period which also saw him playing for Bury and Scunthorpe & Lindsey United, and his final game for Grantham came in April 1929 when the team travelled over to Shirebrook. The following season he joined Bristol Rovers, making just one appearance, before moving to Loughborough Corinthians and Accrington Stanley, where he played seven games in The Football League. Died January 1983 at Leicester.

Len Hague

Seasons Played	League	~	22
	F.A. Cup	~	
1958/59	Lincs Cup	~	1
	Total	~	23

Len made his Grantham debut against Goole Town in the first match of the 1958/59 season, with his final appearance the following March in the Midland League game against Horden Colliery, after which Alan Clay took over his position.

Paul Haig

Seasons Played	League	~	6 (3)
	F.A. Cup	~	
1919/20	Lincs Cup	~	2 (1)
	Total	~	8 (4)

Nottingham born forward with experience at Eastwood Rangers, Leicester Fosse, Mansfield Mechanics and Notts County, scoring twice in his 13 Football League appearances. Paul scored on his Grantham debut in the October 1919 fixture against Shirebrook and made several appearances in the games over the Christmas period, but played no other part in that season after the January County Cup tie at Gainsborough Trinity.

Dave Hailwood

Seasons Played	League	~	62 (6)
	F.A. Cup	~	1
1977/78-79/80	F.A. Trophy	~	5 (1)
	League Cup	~	7
	Lincs Cup	~	1
	Total	~	76 (7)

Born 17/10/1954 at Nottingham. Made one appearance for Mansfield Town during the 1973/74 season and signed for Grantham from Long Eaton United. His first game for The Gingerbreads was in the February 1978 league fixture at Redditch United, with his maiden goal for the club coming at the end of the following month against AP Leamington. Dave played in many of the games in the 1978/79 Championship winning season, including the crucial deciding match against Merthyr Tydfil at the end of the campaign. Dave's final two goals for the club came in the 6-0 thrashing of Tamworth in February 1980 and his last appearance was at the end of the following month at home to Macclesfield Town. He went on to play for Arnold Town and then returned to Long Eaton. Dave still lives in the Nottingham area and works for a large sports wholesale company.

Len Hainsworth

Seasons Played	League	~	33 (1)
	F.A. Cup	~	4
1955/56	Lincs Cup	~	
	Total	~	37 (1)

Born 25/01/1918 at Rotherham. Centre-Half with over 150 Football League appearances behind him whilst at Rotherham United, Doncaster Rovers and Workington. Len first played for Grantham in the opening match of the 1955/56 season at Boston United and scored his one and only goal two days later against Frickley Colliery at London Road. He played an important role in that season's side and made his final appearance in the last league game of the season at Denaby United, although he did also appear in a friendly played at Peterborough United the following day.

Chris Hall

Seasons Played	League	~	27 (1)
	F.A. Cup	~	2
2001/02-02/03	F.A. Trophy	~	2
	League Cup	~	3
	Lincs Cup	~	4
	Total	~	38 (1)

Born 03/03/1983 at Lincoln. Former Leeds United Trainee who progressed through the Reserves side to make his First team debut by replacing Jon Hawley during the September 2001 league game at Rugby United. The majority of his appearances came from the bench that year and this was a trend that continued the following season as well, although Chris did play in the County Cup Final against Scunthorpe United and at the end of that campaign scored his only goal for the club at Bath City. His last appearance for Grantham was in the April 2003 County Cup Final defeat at Gainsborough Trinity, with Chris sitting out the closing league fixture at home to Moor Green the following Saturday. Along with

Manager, John Wilkinson, and many of his colleagues, he went on to play for Lincoln United, before moving to Burton Albion despite coming close to a dream move to Leicester City in the Spring of 2004.

Mark Hall

Seasons Played			
	League	~	52 (3)
	F.A. Cup	~	5 (1)
1989/90-90/91	F.A. Trophy	~	2
	League Cup	~	8
	Lincs Cup	~	1
	Total	~	68 (4)

Born 11/05/1970 at Doncaster. Former Doncaster Rovers defender, with just two senior appearances during his time there, who made his debut for Grantham in the August 1989 match at Bedworth United and scored his first goal for the club the following month in the FA Cup tie against Louth United. Although not renowned for his scoring, he does hold the distinction of netting the final competitive goal at London Road, when he stroked the ball home from the penalty spot in the September 1990 fixture against Alvechurch. Mark also appeared in the last ever game, against Dudley Town, at the end of the same month. He scored once more for the club in the November fixture against Stroud, before his final appearance in the March 1991 league defeat at home to Nuneaton Borough. Mark went on to play for Worksop Town, Frickley Colliery and Armthorpe Miners Welfare.

Hall

Seasons Played			
	F.A. Cup	~	
	Lincs Cup	~	
1883/84-84/85	Other	~	2
	Total	~	2

Records show an appearance in the first friendly of the 1883/84 season against Grantham Volunteers, but there are no other instances of his name until a year later when, interestingly, Grantham played in a friendly against the same team.

Hall

Seasons Played			
	League	~	2 (1)
	F.A. Cup	~	
1923/24	League Cup	~	
	Lincs Cup	~	
1925/26	Other	~	
	Total	~	2 (1)

Forward who had also played for Newark Town and appeared for Grantham against Ilkeston United in March 1924, but there are no records of another appearance until his goal in the September 1925 Midland League game at home to Alfreton Town.

Hall

Seasons Played			
	League	~	7 (1)
	F.A. Cup	~	
1934/35	Lincs Cup	~	2
	Total	~	9 (1)

Could play in either midfield or as a striker and made his debut in the March 1935 home game against Gainsborough Trinity. He scored his only goal for Grantham in the penultimate league fixture of the season at Lincoln City Reserves, but his final appearance came a week later in the replay of the Lincolnshire Senior Cup Final at Boston United.

Henry Hallams

Seasons Played			
	League	~	1
1911/12	Total	~	1

Born circa 1890 at Sleaford. Defender whose only known Grantham appearance is in the Central Alliance fixture at home to Peterborough GN Loco in December 1911. The opponents that day were a team that Henry went on to play for, whilst he also made two appearances for Lincoln City in the 1913/14 season.

Wayne Hallcro

Seasons Played			
	League	~	90 (2)
	F.A. Cup	~	10
1992/93	F.A. Trophy	~	5
1997/98	League Cup	~	8
1999/00-02/03	Lincs Cup	~	7
	Total	~	120 (2)

Born 13/01/1973 at Peterborough. Began his career as a Trainee at Northampton Town, before moving on to Cotgrave and then making a lone appearance for Grantham in the January 1993 league fixture at Bedworth United following the departure of many of that season's players due to financial constraints. Wayne returned to the club at the start of the 1997/98 season after playing for Dunkirk and Arnold Town, but made only 13 appearances all year, although one of those was in the memorable fight-back at Bath City that set up the club's great run in the FA Trophy. He moved on to Stamford Town and King's Lynn, but returned to The Meres again in the Autumn of 1999 as part of a swap deal involving Emeka Nwadike. Wayne played in the majority of that season's remaining matches, which saw the club come so close to escaping what seemed a doomed relegation position, with his first goal for the club in the closing fixture at home to Crawley Town. The following season saw many appearances for Wayne, including the October trip to Rushden & Diamonds in the FA Cup and his only other goal for the club in the 5-2 victory over Histon. The 2001/02 promotion winning season saw only 18 appearances for him though, whilst the following year he was only awarded 12. However, he did play in the Lincolnshire County Senior Cup Final against Scunthorpe United at The Meres in August 2002 and the October FA Cup final qualifying tie at Morecambe. Wayne's final appearance for the club came in the Dr Marten's League Cup defeat at King's Lynn in February 2003 and he then spent a couple of months at Arnold Town. After the Summer break, he went on to play for Harrowby United, where he was appointed Club Captain and is now Assistant Manager.

Dominic Hallows

Seasons Played			
	League	~	96 (3)
	F.A. Cup	~	4
2002/03-04/05	F.A. Trophy	~	4
	League Cup	~	5
	Lincs Cup	~	7 (1)
	Total	~	116 (4)

Born 14/03/1983 at Leicester. Began his career at Nottingham Forest, but signed for The Gingerbreads after being released by Leicester City. He scored on his Grantham debut when he came off the bench in the 2002/03 season's opening league fixture at Folkestone Invicta. Dom played in many of that year's games, including the October FA Cup tie at Morecambe and the April 2003 County Cup Final at Gainsborough Trinity. The following season continued with many of his appearances coming from the substitute's bench, including the March 2004 Lincolnshire County Shield Final victory over Gainsborough Trinity, although he did manage to covert the crucial fifth penalty to secure the win for Grantham. For the 2004/05 season Dom became an almost permanent presence in the Grantham defence, with another Lincolnshire Shield winner's medal won when he came off the bench to replace Jason Turner in the culmination of the competition, again versus Gainsborough Trinity. However, this would turn out to be Dom's final appearance for The Gingerbreads as only a week into the close season he was released by the club.

Simon Hammans

Seasons Played			
	League	~	1
	F.A. Cup	~	
1989/90	F.A. Trophy	~	
	League Cup	~	
	Lincs Cup	~	1
	Total	~	2

Born 1966 at Arnold. Full-Back, and thought to be a member of the RAF, who played in the August 1989 County Cup tie against Spalding United and the opening league fixture of the season at Dudley Town.

Hancock

Seasons Played			
	Other	~	1
1875/76	Total	~	1

Made only one appearance for Grantham in the December 1875 friendly against the Conservative Working Mens Club.

Eddie Green

Reg Gregory

Chris Grocock

Dave Hailwood

Len Hainsworth

Chris Hall

Mark Hall

Wayne Hallcro

Dominic Hallows

Barry Harbershon

Ronnie Harbertson

Mark Harbottle

Jamie Hardwick

Ronnie Harrison

Walter Harrison

Paul Hart

Reg Handley

Seasons Played			
	League	~	22
	F.A. Cup	~	
1931/32-32/33	Lincs Cup	~	
	Other	~	
	Total	~	22

Local player who had previously played for Grantham Amateurs and at one time had a trial with Leicester City. End of season data shows that Reg played in about a quarter of the matches during the two seasons he spent at London Road, but with no goals scored we unfortunately cannot pinpoint any of the specific matches.

Cyril Hanson

Seasons Played			
	League	~	22 (3)
	F.A. Cup	~	2
1931/32-34/35	Lincs Cup	~	
	Other	~	1 (2)
	Total	~	25 (5)

Former Central School pupil who also played for Grantham Amateurs, Nottingham Forest Reserves, Newark Town and Grantham St John's. Cyril only played a couple of games during his first two seasons at London Road, but by the start of the 1933/34 term he was playing a more prominent role in the side and scored his first goal for the club in the fixture against Ilkeston United just a couple of days before Christmas. He played his last game for Grantham a year later in the Midland League game at Bradford Park Avenue Reserves, his only appearance of that 1934/35 season.

Edgar Hanson

Seasons Played			
	League	~	5 (2)
	F.A. Cup	~	
1965/66	Total	~	5 (2)

Born 02/06/1936 at Cranwell. Experienced player who began his career with Grantham Reserves, before moving on to Brush Sports, Loughborough United, Bourne Town, Long Eaton United, (all of these club's he was leading goal-scorer), Ilkeston Town and Boston United. Edgar came to Grantham as a Player/Coach for the Reserves side, but First team injuries saw five appearances for him in a three week spell just before Easter 1966, starting at Lockheed Leamington and scoring in the league games against Sutton Town and Ashton United, the latter being his final game for Grantham. His footballing career finished with Colsterworth and BMarco's, although he later went on to set up the Plamore League in town along with Terry Bly. Edgar is now retired and living in Banbury.

Barry Harbershon

Seasons Played			
	League	~	83
	F.A. Cup	~	7 (1)
1960/61-62/63	League Cup	~	1
	Lincs Cup	~	7
	Total	~	98 (1)

Left-sided player with experience at Lincoln City who made his first appearance for Grantham in the September 1960 league game against Derby County 'A', taking over the position from George Stafford. Barry then played in every match, not only for the remainder of that season but the following one as well. In that time he played in the two County Cup Final victories over Gainsborough Trinity and Boston United, plus after scoring his only goal for the club in an earlier round against Louth United, the FA Cup First Round tie at Brierley Hill Alliance in November 1961. Once again Barry played in the majority of the games during the 1962/63 season, right up until his final appearance for the club in the April league fixture at Sutton Town.

Ronnie Harbertson

Seasons Played			
	League	~	136 (63)
	F.A. Cup	~	7 (3)
1962/63-67/68	Lincs Cup	~	2
	Total	~	145 (66)

Born 23/12/1929 at Redcar. Experienced forward who began his career at North Shields and Newcastle United, before making a total of 251 appearances, with 83 goals to his name, for Bradford City, Brighton & Hove Albion, Grimsby Town, (followed by a spell with Ashington), Darlington, Lincoln City and Wrexham, where he won a Welsh Cup winner's medal in 1960. Ronnie scored twice in his first Grantham game, the opening match of the 1962/63 season at Holbeach United, netted a hat-trick the following month against Sutton Town and at the end of his first campaign with the club finished as their top scorer. The following season was Grantham's first Midland League Championship year and although only missing one of the games, needless to say Ronnie finished somewhat behind the record scoring of Jimmy Rayner, although he still managed a respectable 23 more goals to his name and none probably more important than in the game at Scarborough which secured the title. During the 1964/65 season he missed several of the games during December and January, but worse was to come the following year when he missed every single one of the FA Cup games which ended in a Second Round tie at home to Swindon Town. For his last two seasons with Grantham, Ronnie's appearances came infrequently and he scored his last two goals in the January 1967 game at home to Stamford, a few months before his joint Testimonial, along with Pim Taylor, against Nottingham Forest. Ronnie then had to wait nearly a year for his next and ultimately final competitive appearance for Grantham, in the April 1968 Midland League fixture at Gainsborough Trinity, although he did appear once more at the end of the season in the Bourne Hospital Cup Final. Ronnie went on to become a Prison Officer and then caretaker at a sheltered housing scheme and during 2003 was guest of honour as Darlington FC left the Feethams Stadium for their new home. He is retired now, but still lives in the Lincoln area.

Dave Harbottle

Seasons Played			
	League	~	33 (11)
	F.A. Cup	~	2 (1)
1997/98	F.A. Trophy	~	5 (1)
	League Cup	~	3
	Lincs Cup	~	
	Total	~	43 (13)

Born 13/10/1969 at Nottingham. Midfield player and brother of Mark Harbottle. Dave was previously with Notts County, Scarborough, Dunkirk, Sutton Town, Gedling Town, Ilkeston Town and Lincoln United. He played his first game for Grantham in the 1997/98 season's opening league fixture at Brackley Town and scored his maiden goal for the club only days later at home to Paget Rangers. Dave played an important role in that year's Championship winning season, but by the Spring of 1998 he was struggling to maintain his place and as Grantham played in many memorable matches, Dave was only rewarded with one appearance, as a substitute in the FA Trophy replay against Southport. April saw his final goal for the club at Ilkeston Town, with his last appearance at Moor Green the same month, when he replaced Dave King. He went on to play for Stamford Town, Hucknall Town and Woollerton, before the start of his managerial posts which returned him to Gedling Town, Dunkirk, then time at Barwell, before returning to Dunkirk once more, along with another former Gingerbread, Wayne Manners.

Mark Harbottle

Seasons Played			
	League	~	51 (12)
	F.A. Cup	~	2
1997/98	F.A. Trophy	~	7 (1)
	League Cup	~	3 (1)
1999/00-00/01	Lincs Cup	~	1
	Total	~	64 (14)

Born 26/09/1968 at Nottingham. A former England Youth International who like his brother, Dave Harbottle, began his career at Notts County, which was followed by an on loan spell at Doncaster Rovers, then Scarborough, before moving into non-league football. Clubs represented, often more than once, include Oakham United, Shepshed Charterhouse / Albion / Dynamo, Burton Albion, Ilkeston Town, Leicester United and Tamworth, where he won a Dr Marten's Midland League Championship medal. He then followed his brother to The Meres, making his debut in the same August 1997 fixture at Brackley Town, but Mark had to wait until the following month for his first goal when the home victory over Blakenall saw him score from the penalty spot. It was these spot-kicks that Mark will be best remembered for, as he netted a hat-trick of penalties in the 6-0 victory over Ilkeston Town, plus the important kicks that secured a draw against Southport in the FA Trophy and against Stourbridge that won the league title for Grantham. He went on to play for Stamford Town, Hinckley United, King's Lynn and Woollerton, before returning to The Meres for the final 14 league fixtures of the 1999/00 season, with his brace in the February game at Cambridge City ultimately turning out to be his final goals for the club. Despite playing in the first four matches of the 2000/01 season, Mark returned to the side on New

Year's Day to make one more appearance for The Gingerbreads, as the team drew 1-1 at home to Spalding United. He then moved back to Shepshed, before making appearances for Barwell, which included time as Assistant Manager, Ilkeston Town again, Hucknall Town and Dunkirk.

Guy Hardcastle

Seasons Played			
	League	~	58
	F.A. Cup	~	2
1994/95-95/96	F.A. Trophy	~	1
	League Cup	~	2
	Lincs Cup	~	
	Total	~	63

Born 1971 at Huddersfield. Goalkeeper who first played for the club in the August 1994 FA Cup tie against Leicester United and was promptly sent off only two days later in the league game at home to Bedworth United. It was a poor season for the club, but it got even worse for Guy when April of 1995 saw him break his arm. He tentatively returned to the side in the October Dr Marten's League Cup draw at Ilkeston Town, but by the end of the following month he had regained his place permanently. Guy's last appearance for Grantham came in the 1995/96 season's closing fixture at Sutton Coldfield Town, following which he moved to Wisbech Town.

Jamie Hardwick

Seasons Played			
	League	~	31 (4)
	F.A. Cup	~	2
1994/95-95/96	F.A. Trophy	~	2
	League Cup	~	2
	Lincs Cup	~	2
	Total	~	39 (4)

Born circa 1972. Former Lincoln City Reserves and Boston United winger who made his debut for Grantham in the March 1994 league fixture at Nuneaton Borough and then scored his first goal in the April defeat at Newport AFC. His last game for the club came just before Christmas 1995 in the home match against Evesham United, with Jamie therefore playing in every single game during his career with The Gingerbreads. He went on to play for Gainsborough Trinity and Clipstone Welfare.

Fred Hardy

Seasons Played			
	League	~	11
	F.A. Cup	~	
1934/35-35/36	Lincs Cup	~	2
	Other	~	1 (1)
	Total	~	14 (1)

Born circa 1917. Right-Back who was only 18 years of age on his Grantham debut in the final league match of the 1934/35 season at Barnsley Reserves. The following campaign though, his appearances were generally limited to those fixtures where Harry Wilbourn was unavailable, but in his final game for Grantham he managed to score one of the goals in the Wilson Cup victory over a Lincoln League XI, played at Sincil Bank in May 1936. Following his departure from London Road he went on to play for Alfreton Town and Ripley Town.

John Hardy

Seasons Played			
	League	~	1
	F.A. Cup	~	
1959/60	League Cup	~	
	Lincs Cup	~	
	Total	~	1

Defender who made just one appearance for the First team in the September 1959 defeat at Bourne Town.

William Hardy

Seasons Played			
	League	~	4
	F.A. Cup	~	
1946/47	Lincs Cup	~	
	Total	~	4

Born 25/10/1915 at Denaby. Forward who had played for Rotherham United, Nottingham Forest and Gainsborough Trinity before The War, netting 11 goals in his 47 Football League appearances. He played in four of the final league games of the 1946/47 season for Grantham, commencing with the London Road visit of Denaby United and ending with the Midland League fixture at Doncaster Rovers Reserves. Died 1990 at Gainsborough.

Hardy

Seasons Played			
	F.A. Cup	~	1
1884/85	Lincs Cup	~	
	Other	~	
	Total	~	1

Played only once for Grantham, in the FA Cup tie at home to Grimsby Town in October 1884.

Hardy

Seasons Played			
	F.A. Cup	~	
	Lincs Cup	~	
1888/89	Other	~	8 (4)
	Total	~	8 (4)

Made his debut in the opening friendly of the 1888/89 season at Grimsby Town and scored his first goal a week later at Notts Olympic. He then played in nearly every friendly for Grantham until his final appearance less than three months later when a team from Boston came over to London Road.

Hardy

Seasons Played			
	League	~	5
	F.A. Cup	~	1 (1)
1891/92-92/93	Other	~	
	Total	~	6 (1)

Could possibly be the same player as the previous entry, although this individual played a much more defensive role. His name first appears in the match reports for the February 1892 league fixture against Long Eaton Athletic, although he had played in friendlies for the club the previous month. He appeared in every match of the following season, (scoring in the October 1892 FA Cup defeat at home to Belper), up to the club's disbandment after the 16-0 defeat at Notts County Rovers.

Steve Hare

Seasons Played			
	League	~	42 (2)
	F.A. Cup	~	2
1990/91	F.A. Trophy	~	4
	League Cup	~	4 (3)
1996/97-97/98	Lincs Cup	~	1
	Total	~	53 (5)

Signed from Hucknall Town in time for the opening league fixture of the 1990/91 season against Bridgnorth Town, but returned there after only four games for Grantham. He later played for Arnold Town and Shepshed Dynamo, before coming back to Grantham in February 1997. Despite then earning several of his appearances from the substitute's bench, the following Championship winning season saw Steve play in about half of the games, with his first two goals for the club in the November 1997 Dr Marten's League Cup tie at Wisbech Town. He played in the FA Trophy tie against Hednesford Town and came on as substitute in the 6-0 win over Ilkeston Town and the FA Trophy replay at Southport. His final appearance for the club was in the April 1998 league victory at Solihull Borough and after the end of the season Steve retired from the game.

Mel Harnwell

Seasons Played			
	League	~	39 (7)
	F.A. Cup	~	3 (1)
1967/68	Total	~	42 (8)

Made his Grantham debut in the first Midland League match of the 1967/68 season at Belper Town and scored his first goal for the club a few days later in the game at Stamford. Mel played in the FA Cup First Round tie against Altrincham as well as the majority of the other games, until his final appearance in April 1968 when Skegness Town came to London Road. He actually finished the season as the club's third highest scorer, although somewhat behind Mike Alexander and Terry Bly. Mel went on to become Player/Manager at Spalding United, whilst his career also took him at some point to a similar position at Wisbech Town.

Lee Harriman

Seasons Played			
	League	~	
	F.A. Cup	~	
1995/96	F.A. Trophy	~	
	League Cup	~	
	Lincs Cup	~	2
	Total	~	2

Born 18/04/1969 at Leicester. Midfielder who previously played for Lutterworth Town, Highfield Rangers, Hinckley Athletic, Houghton Rangers, Hinckley Town and VS Rugby. He played for Grantham in the two County Cup games at the start of the 1995/96 season against Lincoln City and Boston United, but found himself substituted in both matches. Lee then continued his travels around the non-league circuit by returning to Hinckley Town, before moving on to Barwell, Corby Town, a return to Hinckley Athletic, Shepshed Dynamo, second spells at both Corby and Rugby, Thringstone United as Player/Manager, Gresley Rovers and Coalville Town, again as a Player/Manager, taking them to the FA Cup First Round in 2004.

Cecil Harris

Seasons Played			
	League	~	1
	F.A. Cup	~	
1920/21	Lincs Cup	~	
	Total	~	1

Born 01/09/1896 in Grantham. Generally played in the Reserves side, but certainly made at least one full appearance for Grantham in the 1920/21 season. The following year he moved on to Aston Villa, where he made 26 First team appearances over a four year period and then spent two seasons at Grimsby Town, scoring once in 48 matches, before moving on to Gainsborough Trinity. Died 1976 at Lincoln.

Errol Harris

Seasons Played			
	League	~	1
	F.A. Cup	~	
1963/64	Lincs Cup	~	
	Total	~	1

Goalkeeper who stood in for the unavailable Graham Clarke in the November 1963 league game at Arnold, keeping a clean sheet during the 3-0 win.

'Ginger' Harris

Seasons Played			
	League	~	48 (2)
	F.A. Cup	~	6
1946/47-48/49	Lincs Cup	~	1
	Total	~	55 (2)

Defender, always known by his nick-name, although it is thought that his actual name may have been Jimmy. He made just one appearance for Grantham during the 1946/47 season, at Grimsby Town Reserves towards the end of the league campaign, but after the Summer period he became a near permanent member of the side. Ginger played in every round of that year's FA Cup run, including the 11-1 defeat of Ilkeston Town and the First Round tie at Stockton. He also scored his only two goals for the club that season, in the games against the Reserve sides of Grimsby Town and York City. In the 1948/49 season he made only 11 more appearances for the club, all coming after Christmas, with his final start in the April fixture against Rotherham United Reserves. Ginger is also known to have played for Boston United at some point during his career.

Kevin Harris

Seasons Played			
	League	~	1
	F.A. Cup	~	
1983/84	F.A. Trophy	~	
	League Cup	~	
	Lincs Cup	~	1
	Total	~	2

Born 17/02/1960 at Boston. Local player who had previously spent time at Boston FC and appeared for The Gingerbreads in the October 1983 league match at home to Hyde United and the December County Cup tie against Scunthorpe United. Kev's Grantham career ended infamously with his sending off during that game, when he threatened one of the opposition with a corner-flag. He went on to play for Melton Town, Pedigree Petfoods, Harrowby United, Great Gonerby and then several local sides. Kev still lives locally and works in the timber building construction industry.

Terry Harris

Seasons Played			
	League	~	43 (14)
	F.A. Cup	~	3 (1)
1992/93-93/94	F.A. Trophy	~	4 (3)
	League Cup	~	2
	Lincs Cup	~	2
	Total	~	54 (18)

Born circa 1966 in London. Striker who began his career at Enfield at the same time as playing for his local amateur side, Norseman, and then after a fifteen month spell at Sheffield United returned to Enfield. Appearances followed for Kettering Town, Bridlington Town and Worksop Town, before joining Grantham Town, where he made his debut in the October 1992 league game at Redditch United, scoring his first goal for the club the following week at home to Gresley Rovers. The January 1993 financial problems which led to the departure of many of the players, saw only a temporary halt to Terry's Grantham career, with his return to the side after only a few weeks. He was then a prominent member of Allen Crombie's side the following season, with his last goal for the club coming in the April 1994 league match at Rushden & Diamonds and his final appearance in the closing fixture at Dudley Town. Thanks to the club's fanzine Terry became synonymous with bins during his time at The Meres, due to a game where he scored and turned round to see that none of his team-mates were celebrating with him. Seemingly without a hint of concern he carried on running to continue his jubilation with a blue bin at the edge of the pitch!

Harris

Seasons Played			
	F.A. Cup	~	2
	Other	~	
1880/81	Total	~	2

Player who interestingly only appears in the two December 1880 FA Cup encounters against Stafford Road, Wolverhampton, and not in any other of the season's matches, even friendlies.

Jack Harrison

Seasons Played			
	League	~	26 (2)
	F.A. Cup	~	
1950/51-51/52	Lincs Cup	~	
	Total	~	26 (2)

First played for Grantham towards the end of the 1950/51 season at Peterborough United and scored one of his only two goals for the club a few days later in Peterborough's return match. Jack played in many of the games at the start of the following season, but coincidentally his last two matches for Grantham were once again against Peterborough United, on Christmas Day and Boxing Day of 1951.

J. Harrison

Seasons Played			
	Other	~	7 (11)
1875/76	Total	~	7 (11)

Scored twice in his first game against Newark in November 1875 and played in many of the same fixtures as his namesake W. Harrison, possibly his brother. But he really inflated his scoring ratio though in his last two games, scoring four times in a friendly against Lincoln and then twice during his and the club's last game of the 1875/76 season at Nottingham Lace.

Ronnie Harrison

Seasons Played			
	League	~	422 (32)
	F.A. Cup	~	33 (1)
1966/67-78/79	F.A. Trophy	~	27 (2)
	League Cup	~	45 (6)
	Lincs Cup	~	17 (3)
	Other	~	3 (1)
	Total	~	547 (45)

Born May 1945 at Antrim, Northern Ireland. Central defender who previously played in the Grantham League for Navenby and Fulbeck. He made his debut for Grantham in the opening Midland League match of the 1966/67 season at Goole Town, scoring his first goal for the club in October against Loughborough United. He played in many of that season's games, including the FA Cup ties against Wimbledon and Oldham Athletic and over the next few years also made appearances in FA Cup Proper rounds against

Altrincham, Chelmsford City, Swindon Town, the second match against Oldham Athletic, Stockport County and Rotherham United. Towards the end of the decade Ronnie and the team began to start putting together some trophies and medals and by the club's entry into the Southern League he had played his part in the two Midland League Championships and the two Midland League Cup victories. Also, within the FA Trophy competition there were the highlights of playing in front of 6,714 spectators at Worcester City and a London Road Quarter-Final tie against Yeovil Town. Elsewhere he scored one of the goals that secured the Lincolnshire County Cup victory over Scunthorpe United and he had already been awarded a joint Testimonial, along with Mick Chambers, when a Leicester City side came to London Road in May 1971. As Grantham moved into the Southern League, there was soon another FA Cup Proper appearance for Ronnie when the club played Bradford City and this was followed only months later with another league championship winner's medal. The 1973/74 season was one of the greatest seasons in the club's history and Ronnie played his part in every round of that year's FA Cup run, including the ties against Rochdale and Middlesbrough. The following two seasons still saw Ronnie as an important member of the side and he was rewarded with another FA Cup memory when the club played Port Vale in November 1975. After a fairly uneventful following campaign, the 1977/78 season unfortunately saw Grantham battling at the foot of the table all year. It was also a year which saw Ronnie's final goal for the club when he scored in the April 1978 fixture at home to Dover, a game which saw a rare victory for The Gingerbreads. Despite playing in the side for many of the games after the Summer break, his appearance in the October 1978 FA Cup tie at Boston FC was to be his last for the team, with the imminent departure of Terry Bly just around the corner. However, he continued to be involved with the club and even went on to have two spells as Grantham manager, first midway through the 1979/80 season after Bob Norris left the club, and then towards the end of the following season with the departure of Geoff Barker. Ronnie still lives in the Grantham area and works in the engineering industry.

Walter Harrison

Seasons Played			
	League	~	79 (3)
	F.A. Cup	~	9 (1)
1955/56-57/58	Lincs Cup	~	2
	Total	~	90 (4)

Born 16/01/1923 at Coalville. Former Coalville Town and Leicester City right-half who had played in the 1949 FA Cup Final at Wembley against Wolverhampton Wanderers, plus was awarded England 'B' team International honours. Following a move to Chesterfield, Walter finished his professional career with a record of 17 goals in 220 appearances. He made his debut for Grantham in the opening match of the 1955/56 season at Boston United and scored his first goal for the club against Notts County Reserves the following month. Walter missed only a handful of matches both that season and the next, but in the 1957/58 season he made only two appearances for Grantham, with his last game coming in the October FA Cup replay at home to Brigg Town, and he then moved on to Hinckley Athletic.

W. Harrison

Seasons Played			
	Other	~	10 (1)
1875/76	Total	~	10 (1)

The first definite evidence of him playing for Grantham comes in the November 1875 match report for the Third Lincolnshire Volunteer Rifles game and by the end of that month he is joined by what seems to be his brother, J. Harrison. In fact their first game together, at home to Newark, saw them both scoring in the 5-0 win. He made his last appearance for the club in the final friendly of the season at Nottingham Lace.

Harrison

Seasons Played			
	League	~	1 (1)
	Lincs Cup	~	
1904/05	Other	~	
	Total	~	1 (1)

Scored in his only know appearance for Grantham, the March 1905 Midland Amateur Alliance game at home to Derby Thornhill.

Paul Hart

Seasons Played			
	League	~	5
	F.A. Cup	~	
1990/91	F.A. Trophy	~	
	League Cup	~	2
	Lincs Cup	~	
	Total	~	7

Born 04/05/1953 at Manchester. Defender who began his career at Stockport County and Blackpool, before becoming the £300,000 replacement for Gordon McQueen at Leeds United. He then signed for Nottingham Forest, where he is still remembered for the 'goal that never was' during that infamous UEFA Cup semi-final against Anderlecht. Paul had what seemed a perfectly legal goal disallowed in the match, following which Brian Clough stated that the tie had been 'crooked'. It was only many years later, after the referee had died, that Anderlecht admitted that they had bribed the official. Transfers then ensued to Sheffield Wednesday, Birmingham City and Notts County, culminating in a total of 39 goals in 567 Football League appearances, plus nine more strikes in 97 various cup ties. After a spell as Manager at Chesterfield, Paul came to Grantham at the start of 1991 as a favour for his former colleague, John Robertson, and made his debut in the Larchimage Windows League Cup tie against King's Lynn. He played seven games in all for the club whilst they shared Spalding United's ground, with his last appearance in March against Sutton Coldfield Town. After coaching positions at Nottingham Forest, Notts County and Sheffield Wednesday, Paul then worked wonders with the Youth Teams of Leeds United and Forest. Following the departure of David Platt from the managerial seat at The City Ground, he was promoted to the position and had an excellent start that stabilised the cash ravaged club. However, after a poor run that saw Forest plunge into a relegation battle during the 2003/04 season, he was sacked, but soon moved on to Barnsley. On the first anniversary of his time there though, a mutual decision was made for him to move on.

Hart

Seasons Played			
	F.A. Cup	~	
	Other	~	6 (2)
1878/79	Total	~	6 (2)

Made his debut in the February 1879 friendly at Spilsby and then played in every match during the remainder of that season, scoring in the home games against Sleaford and Boston.

Aiden Harte

Seasons Played			
	League	~	
	F.A. Cup	~	
1999/00	F.A. Trophy	~	
	League Cup	~	
	Lincs Cup	~	1
	Total	~	1

Former Bradford City and Millwall striker who made just one appearance for Grantham in the opening fixture of the 1999/00 season at home to Scunthorpe United in the County Cup.

Jack Hartshorne

Seasons Played			
	League	~	30
	F.A. Cup	~	1
1946/47-47/48	Lincs Cup	~	1
	Total	~	32

Born 25/03/1907 at Willenhall. Defender who began his career at local side Short Heath, before spending time at Stoke City and Macclesfield Town. In 1936 Jack moved to Lincoln City and made exactly 100 appearances before the commencement of war stalled his career. He first played for Grantham in the opening league match of the 1946/47 season against the Reserve team of his former club, Lincoln City, but he had a long lay-off at the end of that season, missing the Final of the Lincolnshire Senior Cup. After the Summer break he only played twice more for the club, with the September league game at Grimsby Town Reserves his last appearance, following which he moved to Boston United. Died 1971 at Stoke-on-Trent.

Harvey

Seasons Played			
	F.A. Cup	~	
	Lincs Cup	~	2
1884/85-87/88	Other	~	18 (6)
	Total	~	20 (6)

Made his debut in November 1884 in the friendly held at Newark, but only played twice more that season. He scored his first goal for Grantham the following October, against Notts Rangers, and whilst he was often called upon to play in the friendly fixtures, his appearances in competitive competitions were severely limited. He played his last game for Grantham against Lincoln Rangers in November 1887.

Haslem

Seasons Played			
	League	~	1
	F.A. Cup	~	
1928/29	Lincs Cup	~	
	Other	~	
	Total	~	1

End of season records show that he made just one appearance for Grantham, although the specific game is not known.

Cyril Hatton

Seasons Played			
	League	~	63 (10)
	F.A. Cup	~	5 (5)
1954/55-56/57	Lincs Cup	~	2
	Total	~	70 (15)

Born 14/09/1918 at Bulwell. At a very early age his family moved to Grantham and he played in the same Boy's Central team as Aubrey Southwell. Cyril began his career playing for Notts Corinthians and Grantham Co-op, but was soon signed by Notts County. Transfers followed to Queen's Park Rangers and Chesterfield and he finished with 100 goals scored in a professional career that saw 286 senior League and Cup games, plus two appearances in the 1948/49 FA XI team. Cyril then returned to his home town and became Player/Manager for Grantham, scoring on his debut in the opening match of the 1954/55 season at home to Nottingham Forest Reserves. Although he played in approximately half of those first two season's matches, in an era of mid table mediocrity, individual highlights are hard to find other than his hat-trick in the April 1956 game at home to Scarborough. The 1956/57 season saw Cyril playing only occasionally, although he scored in his final appearance against Bradford City Reserves in April 1957. He resigned from his Grantham position due to the offer of a representative's job from a Nottingham based company, although he later returned to town and ran a newsagents shop on Dudley Road. Died 03/07/1987 in Grantham.

Hawker

Seasons Played			
	League	~	2
	F.A. Cup	~	
1926/27	Lincs Cup	~	
	Other	~	
	Total	~	2

Played in two Midland League games for the First team, but also made many appearances for the Reserves side as well as Ilkeston United and Long Eaton.

Hawkes

Seasons Played			
	League	~	
	F.A. Cup	~	
1891/92	Other	~	1
	Total	~	1

Only one known appearance for this player, in the Grantham Charity Cup tie against Derby County Reserves in December 1891.

Shaun Hawkey

Seasons Played			
	League	~	
	F.A. Cup	~	
1991/92	F.A. Trophy	~	
	League Cup	~	
	Lincs Cup	~	1
	Total	~	1

Born 10/12/1969 at Grimsby. Defender who played just once for Grantham in the opening match of the 1991/92 season at Grimsby Town in the Lincolnshire County Senior Cup. His career also took in time at Grimsby Town, both senior Boston sides, Holbeach United and college football in America for Pennsylvania.

Jon Hawley

Seasons Played			
	League	~	83 (9)
	F.A. Cup	~	7 (3)
1999/00-02/03	F.A. Trophy	~	4
	League Cup	~	6 (1)
	Lincs Cup	~	5
	Total	~	105 (13)

Born 23/01/1978 at Lincoln. Former Portsmouth and Lincoln City player who came on as substitute in the April 2000 league fixture at home to Burton Albion to make his debut. He scored his first goal for the club a fortnight later in the 6-0 mauling of Atherstone United. Jon played in the majority of the games during the 2000/01 season, including the disappointing 4-5 defeat at Rushden & Diamonds in the FA Cup, although during Grantham's following promotion winning season he only played in approximately half of the games, several of which came from the bench. He then left The Meres in an attempt to join the Fire Brigade, but soon returned to the club, with his last goal for Grantham coming during the March 2003 league game at home to Hastings United. He then played in the County Cup Final at Gainsborough Trinity, only days before his final appearance in the season's closing fixture at home to Moor Green. He left soon after, along with many of his team-mates and John Wilkinson, for Lincoln United.

Mark Hawthorne

Seasons Played			
	League	~	7
	F.A. Cup	~	
1998/99	F.A. Trophy	~	
	League Cup	~	1
	Lincs Cup	~	1
	Total	~	9

Born 21/08/1979 at Sunderland. Former Ipswich Town and Doncaster Rovers player, (where he made eight First team appearances), who made his debut for The Gingerbreads in the 1998/99 season's first match against Scunthorpe United in the County Cup. Unfortunately Mark was injured in the game against Cambridge City in September and never really regained his full fitness, despite making two more appearances in December, the last of which was against Rothwell Town in the League Cup. Mark was then released by the club at the end of the season and was last known to be living back up in the North-East.

L. Hayes

Seasons Played			
	League	~	1
	F.A. Cup	~	
1925/26	Lincs Cup	~	
	Total	~	1

Available team-sheets indicate just one appearance for this player, the October 1925 Midland League game at Lincoln City Reserves.

Alan Haynes

Seasons Played			
	League	~	42
	F.A. Cup	~	4
1963/64	Lincs Cup	~	2
	Total	~	48

Defender who played in every game of the 1963/64 Midland League Championship winning season, starting at Alfreton Town and ending with the last match at Skegness Town, with the title well and truly sewn up by then.

Cyril Haynes

Seasons Played			
	League	~	14
	F.A. Cup	~	
1954/55-55/56	Lincs Cup	~	
	Total	~	14

Defender who began his Grantham career in March 1955 with the Midland League game at Rotherham United Reserves and played in several of the remaining fixtures, plus the Stamford Hospital Cup at the end of the season. Cyril played only a few more times for the club after the Summer break and his final appearance came in the September 1955 game at Worksop Town.

Peter Haynes

Seasons Played	League	~	3
	F.A. Cup	~	
1991/92	F.A. Trophy	~	
	League Cup	~	
	Lincs Cup	~	
	Total	~	3

Goalkeeper who covered for the unavailable Jon Godwin in the March 1992 league games against Hednesford Town, Nuneaton Borough and King's Lynn.

R. Haynes

Seasons Played	League	~	2
	F.A. Cup	~	
1919/20	Lincs Cup	~	2
	Other	~	
1926/27	Total	~	4

Defender who made his First team debut in the December 1919 County Cup tie at home to Humber Craving Dock, but made only a couple of other appearances, generally when 'Tiny' Yaldren was unavailable. He was, however, the Captain of the Reserves side which won the Grantham League Division One title at the end of the 1919/20 season. He returned to help out the club several years later, when he made his final appearance in the February 1927 Lincolnshire Senior Cup match against Stamford Town.

Paul Haywood

Seasons Played	League	~	5
	F.A. Cup	~	
1994/95	F.A. Trophy	~	
	League Cup	~	
	Lincs Cup	~	
	Total	~	5

Born 04/10/1975 at Barnsley. Defender signed on-loan from Nottingham Forest, after having had a period at Doncaster Rovers, as the club desperately tried to escape the relegation zone. He first played for Grantham in the January 1995 league fixture at home to Hinckley Town and finished a month later against Dudley Town. After his release from The City Ground, Paul went on to play for Emley, Frickley Athletic, Brodsworth Welfare and Stocksbridge Park Steels.

Dave Heal

Seasons Played	League	~	32 (2)
	F.A. Cup	~	2 (1)
1980/81-81/82	F.A. Trophy	~	1
	League Cup	~	3
	Lincs Cup	~	1
	Other	~	1
	Total	~	40 (3)

Born November 1962. Started out on Schoolboy forms at Notts County and after coming to Grantham progressed through the Reserves. He played in the final two league games of the 1980/81 season, starting with a substitution to replace Jimmy Jackson in the home match against Netherfield. The following season Dave maintained his place in the side and scored his first goal for the club in the September 1981 FA Cup victory over Eastwood Town. His final appearance came in that season's closing fixture at Macclesfield Town and he then left the club to train for a career in the Armed Forces.

Maurice Healey

Seasons Played	League	~	46
	F.A. Cup	~	
1938/39-39/40	Lincs Cup	~	3
	Other	~	4
	Total	~	53

Goalkeeper who at one time was on an amateur contract with Fulham and also made appearances for Stamford Town. He took over the role after Arthur Jepson left London Road, making his debut in the first game of the 1938/39 season at Shrewsbury Town. Bar a two month spell at the end of the year, Maurice was a permanent member of the team, even having to face the Arsenal forwards in a friendly held in February 1939. The following season, with the outbreak of World War Two, Grantham used no fewer than nine goalkeepers and Maurice's final appearance came in the March 1940 Midland War-Time League fixture at home to Newark Town.

Maurice Healey

Seasons Played	League	~	9 (4)
	F.A. Cup	~	2
1956/57	League Cup	~	
1959/60-61/62	Lincs Cup	~	
1963/64-65/66	Total	~	11 (4)

Born 25/06/1940 at Wilsford. Former Nottingham Forest Youths player who made his Grantham First team debut in the November 1956 game at the Reserves team of his old club, but due to sparse appearances had to wait until April 1964 to score his first goal for the team. However, Maurice then turned it into a hat-trick as Denaby United came away from London Road with a 12-2 defeat. He finally made his last appearance for the club in the March 1966 league fixture at Stamford, taking nearly ten years for him to make only eleven appearances. Maurice went on to play for Harrowby United, Sleaford Town, Wilsford and Foster's Builders. He is now retired but still lives near to the town.

Heaney

Seasons Played	Lincs Cup	~	
	Other	~	1
1890/91	Total	~	1

Made just one appearance for Grantham in the January 1891 friendly at home to Nottingham Forest Reserves.

Trevor Hebberd

Seasons Played	League	~	11
	F.A. Cup	~	2
1995/96	F.A. Trophy	~	1
	League Cup	~	2
	Lincs Cup	~	2
	Total	~	18

Born 19/06/1958 at Alresford. Experienced midfielder with 71 goals scored in a total of 685 appearances at Southampton, (plus Washington Diplomats on-loan), Bolton Wanderers, Leicester City, Oxford United, Derby County, Plymouth, Chesterfield and Lincoln City. He first appeared for Grantham in the opening County Cup game of the 1995/96 season at home to Lincoln City and played a part in the majority of the games over the next couple of months, up to the November trip to Solihull Borough.

Leslie Heelbeck

Seasons Played	League	~	13
	F.A. Cup	~	
1930/31	Lincs Cup	~	
	Total	~	13

Born 13/05/1911 at Scarborough. Left-sided player who had previously played for Scarborough, Newark Town and made thirteen appearances for Grantham towards the end of the 1930/31 season. The following campaign saw him playing for Carlisle United and successful moves followed to Wolverhampton Wanderers and Rotherham United, where he became Club Captain. He finished his professional career at the end of the 1936/37 season with seven goals in his 122 League appearances. Leslie's Surname is sometimes spelt 'Heelbrook'. Died 1998.

Heil

Seasons Played	League	~	1
	F.A. Cup	~	
1925/26	Lincs Cup	~	
	Total	~	1

Full-Back with only the single known appearance, at home to Wombwell in October 1925.

Dan Hellings

Seasons Played	League	~	88 (34)
	F.A. Cup	~	10 (3)
1949/50-51/52	Lincs Cup	~	3 (3)
	Total	~	101 (40)

Born 09/12/1923 at Lincoln. Former Lincoln Rovers, Ransome & Marles and Lincoln City right-winger, with three Football League appearances to his name, who made his debut for Grantham in the initial Midland League game of the 1949/50 season at Scarborough and scored his first goal for the club four weeks later at Boston United. At the end of that month Dan netted all four goals in the match against Halifax Town Reserves and there would be more highlights in that first season, including playing in front of 8,302 spectators in the FA Cup First Round encounter against Wrexham and scoring one of the consolation goals in the County Cup Final replay against Boston United. The following two seasons saw Dan playing in about half of the matches and he scored during his final appearance for Grantham, in the April 1952 league game at Gainsborough Trinity. He went on to play for Skegness Town, Alford United and Ransome & Marles. Died 1996 at Leicester.

Tony Hemmings

Seasons Played			
	League	~	7
	F.A. Cup	~	
2003/04	F.A. Trophy	~	
	League Cup	~	
	Lincs Cup	~	
	Total	~	7

Born 21/09/1967 at Burton-on-Trent. Former Burton Albion, Rochester and Northwich Victoria winger who gained one England Semi-Professional cap against Finland in 1993. A £25,000 transfer then took him to Wycombe Wanderers and this was followed by moves to Macclesfield Town, where he played in the 1996 FA Trophy Final at Wembley, Hednesford Town, Gloucester City, Altrincham and Ilkeston Town. A second progression into The Football League followed after a £10,000 fee was paid by Chester City and then appearances were made for Carlisle United, Ilkeston Town again, before Gary Mills paid £7,500 to take him to Tamworth. Another spell at Ilkeston was followed by his move to Alfreton Town, from where Tony joined Grantham on-loan. He played in the final seven fixtures of the 2003/04 season for The Gingerbreads, starting at home to Tiverton Town and ending at Weymouth in May.

Grahame Hempsall

Seasons Played			
	League	~	65
	F.A. Cup	~	
1983/84-84/85	F.A. Trophy	~	10
	League Cup	~	9
	Lincs Cup	~	3
	Other	~	2
	Total	~	89

Born 1962 at Doncaster. Goalkeeper who joined Grantham from Yorkshire Main and took over the role from Eddie Green in time for the October 1983 game at Macclesfield Town. He played in every single one of the remaining fixtures, in a season which saw Grantham finish fourth in the Northern Premier League. Although he missed a few games in the 1984/85 season, fortunes had declined and his final appearance for the club, against Oswestry Town in May 1985, was played with The Gingerbreads already doomed to a relegation zone finish. Grahame currently lives in Derbyshire and is the Area Manager for one of the national water companies.

Charles Hemsley

Seasons Played			
	Other	~	6
1874/75-75/76	Total	~	6

Born 1851 at Harlaxton. Brother of Henry Hemsley. Charles appeared in Grantham's very first club match, turning out for Arthur Hutchinson's side, but didn't play in a game against another team until December 1874 when Grantham went over to Sleaford for a friendly. His last game for the club came just over a year later in the friendly at Nottingham Castle. Charles was later ordained as a Reverend and occupied several church positions in Bedfordshire, plus spent many years as Assistant Master at Bedford School. Died 22/09/1933 at Bedford.

Henry Hemsley

Seasons Played			
	Other	~	18
1874/75-76/77	Total	~	18

Born circa 1850 at Harlaxton. Played along with his brother, Charles Hemsley, in the first club match, although on the opposite side as he lined up for Arthur Gamble's team. Henry made his first 'competitive' appearance in a match against Burghley Park in November 1874 and played in many of the same games as his sibling, but also made extra appearances during the same period as well. Finally he made his last known appearance for the club in the November 1876 friendly at home to Lincoln and by the 1881 census was farming in Cotham, Nottinghamshire.

Nigel Hemstock

Seasons Played			
	League	~	9 (1)
	F.A. Cup	~	
2002/03	F.A. Trophy	~	
	League Cup	~	
	Lincs Cup	~	1
	Total	~	10 (1)

Began his career as a Trainee at Scunthorpe United, before moving to Frickley Athletic and then scoring on his debut for Grantham in the March 2003 league fixture at Havant & Waterlooville. Despite playing in only ten games, the last of which came in April at home to Hinckley United, Nigel holds the club record for the most career appearances *all* earned from the substitute's bench. By the following season he was playing for Wakefield & Emley and later moved to Gateshead and Ashington.

Damien Henderson

Seasons Played			
	League	~	5 (2)
	F.A. Cup	~	
1998/99	F.A. Trophy	~	
	League Cup	~	
	Lincs Cup	~	
	Total	~	5 (2)

Born 12/05/1973 at Leeds. Began his career at Leeds United, but failed to make their First team, and after a loan spell at Yeovil Town moved to Scarborough to gain his Football League debut. Appearances then followed for Scunthorpe United, Hereford United, Hartlepool United and Blyth Spartans, from where he arrived at Grantham on-loan, with a record of 16 goals to his name in 125 senior games. He scored a brace on his debut at The Meres in the Boxing Day 1998 clash at home to Ilkeston Town and played in the next four games, up to his last appearance a month later at Gloucester City. Damien returned to Blyth Spartans and then moved to Farsley Celtic and Harrogate Railway.

Jason Hendry

Seasons Played			
	League	~	1
	F.A. Cup	~	
1992/93	F.A. Trophy	~	
	League Cup	~	
	Lincs Cup	~	
	Total	~	1

Made just one appearance in the January 1993 league game at Bedworth United after the departure of several of the club's players.

Walter Henshaw

Seasons Played			
	League	~	6 (2)
	FA Amt. Cup	~	
1910/11-13/14	League Cup	~	1 (1)
	Lincs Cup	~	1
	Other	~	2 (1)
	Total	~	10 (4)

Born circa 1886. An engineer's gauger who was a member of the 1910/11 Championship winning team, with his first recorded goal coming in the November 1910 Stamford Nursery Cup tie against Grantham Swifts. He almost certainly played in many matches over the next few seasons, considerably more than the figures quoted, with his name last appearing as a scorer in the match report from the February 1914 Central Alliance fixture at home to Gresley Rovers. Died 13/09/1918 at Grantham.

Hensley

Seasons Played			
	League	~	1 (1)
	F.A. Cup	~	
1914/15	Lincs Cup	~	
	Total	~	1 (1)

Only one known appearance for this player, the league match against Derby County Reserves in November 1914, during which he scored.

Jack Hartshorne

Jon Hawley

Mark Hawthorne

Alan Haynes

R. Haynes

Paul Haywood

Tony Hemmings

Tony Hepburn

Mark Hesk

Ron Hewitt

Bill Hill

Maurice Hilton

Rob Himsworth

Stu Hodson

Brent Horobin

Roy Houghton

E. Henson

Seasons Played			
	League	~	1
	Lincs Cup	~	
1939/40	Other	~	
	Total	~	1

Made one appearance for Grantham in the very last Midland 'War-Time' League match, against Scunthorpe & Lindsey United in May 1940.

Tony Hepburn

Seasons Played			
	League	~	3 (1)
	F.A. Cup	~	
1957/58	Lincs Cup	~	
	Total	~	3 (1)

Born 22/05/1932 in Scotland. Outside-Right with experience at Clydebank, Glasgow Celtic, Dumbarton, Ayr United, Distillery and Greenock Morton. Tony played in three Midland League games for Grantham during April 1958, against Denaby United, King's Lynn, which saw his only goal, and finally Boston United, where his career was to continue the following season.

Malcolm Herd

Seasons Played			
	League	~	2
	F.A. Cup	~	
1977/78	F.A. Trophy	~	
	League Cup	~	
	Lincs Cup	~	
	Total	~	2

Played in the October 1977 league fixture at Maidstone United and the April 1978 match against Wealdstone, which despite being a home fixture was played at Kettering because of ongoing work at the London Road ground.

Herrington

Seasons Played			
	League	~	1
	F.A. Cup	~	
1945/46	Lincs Cup	~	
	Total	~	1

Played only once for Grantham in the December 1945 fixture at home to Grimsby Town Reserves.

Ernest Heseltine

Seasons Played			
	League	~	1
	F.A. Cup	~	
1983/84	F.A. Trophy	~	
	League Cup	~	
	Lincs Cup	~	
	Total	~	1

Defender who joined Grantham from Barnsley, but made just one appearance for the club in the September 1983 league game at home to Horwich RMI.

Mark Hesk

Seasons Played			
	League	~	9
	F.A. Cup	~	1
1983/84	F.A. Trophy	~	1
	League Cup	~	
	Lincs Cup	~	
	Total	~	11

Born 1958 at Ormskirk, Lancashire. Full-Back who began his career on Schoolboy forms at Liverpool and then had spells with Marine and South Liverpool. His first game for Grantham came in the September 1983 match at home to Mossley and despite playing in many games over the next month or so, the November defeat against Matlock Town was his last for the club. Mark then went on to play for Shepshed Charterhouse and at the end of the decade was appointed Player/Coach at Burnham after moving down to the area.

Harry Hewitt

Seasons Played			
	League	~	12 (2)
	F.A. Cup	~	
1946/47	Lincs Cup	~	
	Total	~	12 (2)

Born 24/06/1919 at Chesterfield. Former Chesterfield and Mansfield Town player, with a guest appearance for Notts County during The War, who made his Grantham debut in the April 1947 league fixture against Scunthorpe & Lindsey United after the departure of Rawlinson. He then played in every one of the remaining fixtures, bar the concluding match, in the mean time scoring against Frickley Colliery and Denaby United.

Ron Hewitt

Seasons Played			
	League	~	191
	F.A. Cup	~	10
1947/48	Lincs Cup	~	6
1952/53-56/57	Total	~	207

Born 21/01/1924 at Chesterfield. Former Youlgreave FC, Sheffield United and Lincoln City goalkeeper who made four appearances for Grantham in the 1947/48 season, beginning at Bradford City Reserves in September, playing for the club in a midfield position. After a spell at Worksop Town, his return to Grantham saw him take over the goalkeeping role from Horace Hinton for the first match of the 1952/53 season against Mansfield Town Reserves, but for some reason he failed to turn up for the next game at Peterborough United. This resulted in 'Pim' Taylor having to take over the role, a position which he kept the following week! But after two defeats Ron's misdemeanour was forgiven and he returned to the starting line-up. These first two seasons in this role for Ron, saw him play in both the Lincolnshire Senior Cup 'A' Finals, firstly against Spalding United and then the 3-0 victory over Gainsborough Trinity. He also made widespread headlines himself when he defied the national engineers strike, which singled him out for some particular abuse from some supporters. Up until the start of the 1956/57 season Ron had played in nearly every match for the club, but during that final season he was replaced for many of the games by David Brown, and ultimately Ron's final appearance for the club came in the last league game of the season at Lincoln City Reserves. He went on to play for Spalding United, whilst at some point during his career, probably at the start, Ron also made appearances for Staveley Works and Chesterfield Reserves.

Hewitt

Seasons Played			
	League	~	1
	Lincs Cup	~	
1907/08	Other	~	
	Total	~	1

Midfielder who played in the February 1908 league game against Mansfield Amateurs, but no evidence exists for any other appearances he may have made.

Hewn

Seasons Played			
	League	~	1
1911/12	Total	~	1

Only one known appearance for this individual, in the December 1911 Central Alliance game at home to Peterborough Loco.

Hibbitt

Seasons Played			
	League	~	1
	F.A. Cup	~	
1924/25	Lincs Cup	~	
	Other	~	
	Total	~	1

Available records show just a single appearance for this centre-forward, the second game of the 1924/25 season away at Long Eaton. We do know however that he also played for Worksop Town at some point in his career.

Bill Hill

Seasons Played			
	League	~	118 (61)
	F.A. Cup	~	9 (6)
1961/62-64/65	Lincs Cup	~	6 (3)
	Total	~	133 (70)

Born 06/01/1936 at Sheffield. Began his career at Rawmarsh Miners Welfare, before scoring three goals in 29 League games for York City, and then moving on to Scarborough. Bill first played for Grantham in the opening match of the 1961/62 season at home to Worksop Town and scored his initial goal for the club two weeks later at Spalding United. In his debut season at London Road he played in the FA Cup First Round tie at Brierley Hill Alliance and the County Cup Final victory over Boston United, whilst the following season, although a quiet one for the club, saw Bill and Ronnie Harbertson battling all year for the status as club's highest scorer, with Ronnie finally just nicking it in the penultimate league game. Bill was also a valuable member of the 1963/64 Midland League title winning side and whilst the following season was his last for the club, and saw him miss many of the games, it did include one of his personal highlights. With Terry Bly unavailable, Bill was asked to perform a more central role in the January 1965 game at home to Denaby United and by the final whistle Grantham had won 9-1 with Bill scoring seven of the goals. It obviously didn't help his career though, as the next game against Worksop Town was his final appearance for the club! No definite details are known as to his following club, although data exists to show that by October 1966 he was playing for Matlock Town.

Steve Hill

Seasons Played	League	~	2
	F.A. Cup	~	
1991/92-92/93	F.A. Trophy	~	
	League Cup	~	
	Lincs Cup	~	
	Total	~	2

Played in the final match of the 1991/92 season at Solihull Borough and then covered for the unavailable Jon Godwin in goal for the April 1993 league game at Leicester United.

Hill

Seasons Played	League	~	4
	Lincs Cup	~	
1931/32	Other	~	
	Total	~	4

Centre-Forward who had previously scored 110 goals in one season for Sneinton Whiteheads and yet failed to find the net for Grantham in his four appearances.

Hills

Seasons Played	League	~	1
	F.A. Cup	~	
1927/28	Lincs Cup	~	
	Total	~	1

Only one known appearance for this player, the November 1927 Midland League game at Mexborough Athletic.

Maurice Hilton

Seasons Played	League	~	7 (1)
	F.A. Cup	~	1
1998/99	F.A. Trophy	~	
	League Cup	~	1
	Lincs Cup	~	
	Total	~	9 (1)

Born 14/03/1979 at Stockton-on-Tees. Former Blackpool and Doncaster Rovers player who made 10 league and one FA Cup appearance whilst in Division Three, before joining Grantham. He made his debut in the opening match of the 1998/99 season at home to Scunthorpe United in the County Cup and scored his only goal in September against Dorchester Town. His last appearance for Grantham was in the October league fixture at Halesowen Town and he later went on to sign for Gateshead, but was last known to be playing for Seaham Red Star a couple of years ago.

Rob Himsworth

Seasons Played	League	~	4 (1)
	F.A. Cup	~	
1983/84	F.A. Trophy	~	
	League Cup	~	
	Lincs Cup	~	
	Total	~	4 (1)

Born circa 1956. 'Curly' was a former Holbeach United and Boston FC player who scored on his debut in the opening fixture of the 1983/84 season at Hyde United. However, after only four appearances the September match at Stafford Rangers turned out be his final game for the club. He went on to play for Boston United, but his career there was cut short when he broke his leg playing in a Reserves fixture at York Street. Rob still lives in the Boston area and maintains a heavy involvement in local football, especially Boston Town, whose Reserve team he continues to occasionally turn out for.

Hind

Seasons Played	Lincs Cup	~	
	Other	~	1 (3)
1890/91	Total	~	1 (3)

Scored a hat-trick in his sole appearance for the club, the March 1890 friendly against Notts St George. See following entry.

Hinde

Seasons Played	Lincs Cup	~	
	Other	~	1
1890/91	Total	~	1

With reference to the previous entry, two players that had very similar surnames, made only one appearance for Grantham, and in the same game against Notts St George. One has to wonder whether we are talking about two brothers, with a typing error in the team sheet.

Steve Hines

Seasons Played	League	~	87 (13)
	F.A. Cup	~	7
1981/82-83/84	F.A. Trophy	~	3
	League Cup	~	8
	Lincs Cup	~	3
	Other	~	5 (1)
	Total	~	113 (14)

Born 23/08/1963 at South Shields. Former Nottingham Forest Schoolboy player who made his debut for Grantham in the club's opening league game of the 1981/82 season at Mossley, scoring his first goal a month later at home to Macclesfield Town. He was a constant member of the 1981/82 season's team, whilst the following year he played in the County Cup Final victory over Scunthorpe United and the final FA Cup qualifying round at Telford United. However, October of 1983 saw Steve's final goal for Grantham, against Witton Albion, with his last appearance less than two weeks later at Southport. Transfers followed to Kettering Town, King's Lynn and Corby Town, although his main profession kept him working in Grantham for many years after leaving London Road.

Horace Hinton

Seasons Played	League	~	79
	F.A. Cup	~	4
1950/51-51/52	Lincs Cup	~	3
	Total	~	86

Goalkeeper who made his debut in the September 1950 league fixture at York City Reserves, after William Mowl had played in the first couple of matches of the season. Horace missed only two games during his time with the club and made his last appearance in the closing fixture of the 1951/52 season at Goole Town, following which he went on to play for Corby Town.

V. Hitchbourne

Seasons Played	League	~	53 (1)
	F.A. Cup	~	6
1931/32-33/34	Lincs Cup	~	3
	Other	~	3
	Total	~	65 (1)

Listed as a former Welsh International defender, but certainly didn't appear for the full national side. He had previously had two spells at Stamford, as well as playing for Bourne Town, Heanor Town and Spalding United. As for his time with Grantham, he made just one appearance in the 1931/32 season, the opening fixture at Loughborough Corinthians, but the following year was playing in virtually every game, including the friendly against Arsenal and the last match of the season at Wombwell, where he scored his only goal for the club. He was certainly playing well into 1934 for Grantham, but the date of his final appearance is not known.

Hobury

Seasons Played	League	~	1
	F.A. Cup	~	
1934/35	Lincs Cup	~	
	Total	~	1

Defender who was able to make one appearance for Grantham in the last game of the 1934/35 season at Barnsley Reserves, when Jack Clayton became unavailable.

Frank Hoddinott

Seasons Played			
1931/32	League	~	27 (12)
	Lincs Cup	~	1 (1)
	Other	~	
	Total	~	28 (13)

Born 29/11/1894 at Brecon, Wales. Forward with a long footballing career behind him, with clubs represented including Aberdare Athletic, Watford, Chelsea after a £3,500 transfer, a £1,000 move to Crystal Palace where he became the Club Captain, Rhyl Athletic, New Brighton, Ilkeston United and Newark Town. He finished his professional career with 57 goals in 189 senior games and during this time had also managed to attain 6 caps for the Welsh International team. Frank made his Grantham debut in the first match of the 1931/32 season at Loughborough Corinthians and scored his first goal for the club the following week at Mansfield Town Reserves. He made the majority of his appearances during the first half of the season and scored his last Grantham goal in the January 1932 London Road visit of Chesterfield Reserves. Died 1980 at Southend.

Hodgkin

Seasons Played			
1881/82	F.A. Cup	~	
	Lincs Cup	~	
	Other	~	1
	Total	~	1

Just one known appearance for this player, in the 6-1 friendly victory over Peterborough in December 1881.

Vincent Hodgkinson

Seasons Played			
1928/29-30/31	League	~	118 (17)
	F.A. Cup	~	4 (1)
	Lincs Cup	~	1 (2)
	Other	~	1 (1)
	Total	~	124 (21)

Born 01/11/1906 at Wollaton. Previously played for Magdala Amateurs, Nottingham Forest, scoring once in his nine First team appearances, and Blackpool. His exact debut date for Grantham is not known, but his first two goals for the club came in the January 1929 Lincolnshire Senior Cup tie at home to Stamford Town. The following season he played in nearly every match and scored a hat-trick in the league game against Wombwell and a goal in the Grantham Hospital Cup victory over Mansfield Town. In his final season at London Road, Vincent played in every single match, leaving his final appearance for the club against Rotherham United Reserves. He went on to play for Loughborough Corinthians, Lincoln City, making just one appearance in Division Two, and Lysaght's Sports, where he was Club Captain. Despite such a long footballing career, Vincent had made only 10 appearances in The Football League and was probably more successful with the cricket ball. He took 162 wickets for Lincolnshire in the Minor Counties League between 1936 and 1952, plus also played for the Lysaght's and Appleby-Froddingham clubs. Died 28/06/1990 at Scunthorpe.

Hodgson

Seasons Played			
1888/89	F.A. Cup	~	
	Lincs Cup	~	
	Other	~	2
	Total	~	2

Played in goal during the December 1888 friendlies against Boston and Basford United when Jack Broadbent was unavailable.

Stu Hodson

Seasons Played			
1977/78-80/81	League	~	113 (4)
	F.A. Cup	~	8
	F.A. Trophy	~	7 (1)
	League Cup	~	12 (2)
	Lincs Cup	~	7
	Other	~	1
	Total	~	148 (7)

Born 05/11/1950 at Peterborough. Former Chatteris Town, Ely City and Peterborough United defender who made his debut for Grantham in the opening match of the 1977/78 season at home to Gainsborough Trinity in the Lincolnshire County Senior Cup. Stu scored his first two goals for the club in the November 1977 League Cup tie against King's Lynn, but it was a disappointing season as Grantham finished bottom of the league. However, he played in many of the games the following year as the club bounced back to win the Southern League, Division One North title, including the classic deciding match against Merthyr Tydfil in May. He was also a prominent member of the first two Northern Premier squads and during that time played in the October 1980 County Cup Final against Lincoln City, only days after what would turn out to be his final goal against Matlock Town, and the December game against the European Champions, Nottingham Forest. His final game for The Gingerbreads was in that season's closing fixture at Runcorn, although the following year his playing career continued when he moved to Bourne Town. He became their Assistant Manager in the 1983/84 season and later moved onto the helm at Spalding United and Stamford Town. Stu still lives in the Peterborough area and until comparatively recently was still playing football in Veteran tournaments.

Michael Hoe

Seasons Played			
1995/96	League	~	10
	F.A. Cup	~	
	F.A. Trophy	~	
	League Cup	~	
	Lincs Cup	~	
	Total	~	10

Born 1969 at Worksop. Striker who began his career as a Trainee at Rotherham United and first played for Grantham in the March 1996 league game at home to Tamworth. He then appeared in most of the remaining fixtures, up to the closing match at Sutton Coldfield Town. His career is also known to have taken him to Hereford United, Worksop Town, Guiseley, Stalybridge Celtic, Alfreton Town, Sheffield FC (the world's oldest football club), Parkgate, Denaby United and Ossett Albion.

Hogg

Seasons Played			
1939/40	League	~	10
	Lincs Cup	~	1
	Other	~	
	Total	~	11

Full-Back who also played for Newark Town, Ballymena, Partick Thistle and first played for Grantham in the December 1939 Midland 'War-Time' fixture at home to Boston United. He missed only a couple of the fixtures, until his last appearance for the club the following March against Newark Town.

Fred Holbeach

Seasons Played			
1932/33	League	~	17 (3)
	F.A. Cup	~	
	Lincs Cup	~	2
	Other	~	2 (1)
	Total	~	21 (4)

Born 17/03/1910 at Mansfield. Inside-Right who had previously played for Welbeck Colliery, but very little is known about his Grantham career. Available records show that he played in the March 1933 friendly against Arsenal and scored all four of his goals in the second half of the season, but little else is known on specific matches that he was involved in. The following season he made two appearances for Luton Town and then moved to Yeovil and Petters United.

Derek Holland

Seasons Played			
1948/49	League	~	12 (1)
	F.A. Cup	~	
	Lincs Cup	~	1
	Total	~	13 (1)

Forward who made his Grantham debut in the November 1948 fixture against Nottingham Forest Reserves and scored his only goal for the club a fortnight later at home to Mansfield Town Reserves. Derek had two spells in the First team and made his final appearance for the club in the March 1949 league game at home to Doncaster Rovers Reserves.

Andy Holmes

Seasons Played			
1992/93	League	~	
	F.A. Cup	~	
	F.A. Trophy	~	
	League Cup	~	2
	Lincs Cup	~	
	Total	~	2

Melton Mowbray based player who made several appearances on the substitute's bench towards the end of 1992, but was actually brought on in only the two League Cup ties against Sutton Coldfield Town in October.

Geoffrey Holmes

Seasons Played			
1959/60	League	~	8 (2)
	F.A. Cup	~	
	League Cup	~	2 (1)
	Lincs Cup	~	
	Total	~	10 (3)

Made his First team debut in the September defeat at Corby Town Reserves and scored his first goal for the club only three weeks later in the rather surprising 7-0 victory when the same team returned to London Road. Geoffrey played in several of those early season games, but his final appearance came only two months later against Long Eaton United.

Holmes

Seasons Played			
1874/75	Other	~	2
	Total	~	2

Played in Grantham's very first club match, turning out for Arthur Hutchinson's team, the October 1874 friendly against the Third Lincolnshire Volunteer Rifles and the next match versus Burghley Park. He also played in a club match two days later, but after this his name no longer appears in club records.

Holt

Seasons Played			
1885/86-86/87	F.A. Cup	~	
	Lincs Cup	~	
	Other	~	2
	Total	~	2

Player who appeared in the December 1885 friendly at Newark and the match against Notts County Reserves a year later, but there are no records that show any other games that he was involved in.

Gary Hooley

Seasons Played			
1983/84	League	~	2
	F.A. Cup	~	
	F.A. Trophy	~	
	League Cup	~	
	Lincs Cup	~	
	Total	~	2

Born 1957 at Barnsley. Striker who had previously played in the Yorkshire League and twice joined Grantham on-loan from Frickley Athletic to make appearances in the February 1984 fixture at Morecambe and the April match at home to Gainsborough Trinity. The following season Gary was the second highest scorer in the Conference, during Frickley's short stay in non-league's top flight, whilst the 1985/86 season saw him move on to Scarborough.

Hone

Seasons Played			
1905/06	League	~	4
1907/08	Lincs Cup	~	
	Other	~	1
	Total	~	5

Forward who made his Grantham debut towards the end of the 1905/06 season and certainly made occasional appearances a couple of years later. But without any records of him actually scoring for Grantham it is difficult to predict whether he played in the season between.

Harry Hopewell

Seasons Played			
1924/25	League	~	1 (1)
	F.A. Cup	~	
	Lincs Cup	~	
	Other	~	2 (2)
	Total	~	3 (3)

Born 12/08/1896 at Basford. Right-Half who had previously spent time at Bagnall Rovers, Basford United, Nottingham Forest, Bulwell, Norwich City, where he played 27 times in the early 1920's, Ilkeston United and Newark Town, where he was Club Captain. Harry is known to have scored for Grantham against Hucknall Byron, Lincoln Robeys and RAF Spittlegate, but is most likely to have made other appearances for the club during that 1924/25 season. Died 1968 at Nottingham.

Frank Hopkins

Seasons Played			
1957/58	League	~	7 (1)
	F.A. Cup	~	1
	Lincs Cup	~	
	Total	~	8 (1)

First played for Grantham in the October 1957 FA Cup defeat at Alford and scored in his next game for the club in November at home to Notts County Reserves. That game was the start of Frank's main period in the First team, but he did return for one more game the following April at Grimsby Town Reserves.

T. Hopkinson

Seasons Played			
1874/75-77/78	F.A. Cup	~	
	Other	~	29 (1)
	Total	~	29 (1)

Played for Mr Gamble's side in the club's maiden game, the first visit of another team when the Third Lincolnshire Volunteer Rifles came to London Road and appeared in many of the ensuing friendlies as well. He scored his only known goal for the club in the November 1877 match at home to Lincoln, a few months before his final appearance in the closing fixture of the season, again at Lincoln.

Hopkinson

Seasons Played			
1922/23	League	~	
	F.A. Cup	~	
	Lincs Cup	~	
	Other	~	1
	Total	~	1

Goalkeeper who to the best of our knowledge played just the one game, the Grantham Hospital Cup semi-final against Spalding United in March 1923.

Alf Hornsby

Seasons Played			
1956/57	League	~	3
	F.A. Cup	~	
	Lincs Cup	~	
	Total	~	3

Played in the opening two games of the 1956/57 season at Scarborough and Frickley Colliery, but by the end of August he had made his final appearance for the club, in the first home game of the season when Frickley Colliery played their return match.

Brent Horobin

Seasons Played			
1967/68-74/75	League	~	283 (56)
1976/77-77/78	F.A. Cup	~	22 (5)
	F.A. Trophy	~	21 (4)
	League Cup	~	36 (6)
	Lincs Cup	~	8 (1)
	Other	~	3 (1)
	Total	~	373 (73)

Born 09/01/1947 at Melton Mowbray. Former Notts County player, who also had trials with Nottingham Forest and then joined Scunthorpe United, playing with Kevin Keegan and Ray Clemance at The Old Show Ground. Brent then came to Grantham and scored on his debut in the October 1967 Midland League game against Long Eaton United, but made only nine appearances in his first season at London Road. In the following campaign Brent played in the majority of the fixtures, although in the Proper rounds of the FA Cup he had to settle for a substitution appearance in the tie against Chelmsford City, whilst the following round at home to Swindon Town saw him sitting on the bench for the whole of the game. However, Brent did play in every match of the inaugural Midland League Cup and even managed a goal in the first leg of the final. The 1969/70 season saw appearances for him in the FA Cup at Oldham Athletic, whilst the final seasons that Grantham spent in the Midland League included more highlights in the same competition against Stockport County and Rotherham United. In that time, Brent was also rewarded with medals for two Midland League Championships, another Midland League Cup and the Lincolnshire Senior Cup victory over Scunthorpe United. In Grantham's first season in the Southern League he missed only two league games all year and played in the FA Cup match against Bradford City. A year later he scored the final goal in the dying minutes of extra time to secure victory in the FA Cup Second Round against Rochdale and of course played in the next game against Middlesbrough. After an uneventful 1974/75 season, Brent became Player/Manager at Melton Town, taking them to League title success, but came back to London Road for two more seasons with The Gingerbreads. His final goal for the club came in April 1978 against Dover, with his last game in the season's closing fixture against Minehead, which was played at Nuneaton due to work on Grantham's ground. He went on to manage Holwell Works and then returned to Melton Town once more, around the same time as he began tennis coaching. In the 1990's he was one of the people behind the newly formed Melton Mowbray FC and he still lives in the town, coaching tennis for several of the sports clubs in that area.

Jack Horsley

Seasons Played			
	League	~	24 (1)
	F.A. Cup	~	3
1919/20	Lincs Cup	~	3 (1)
	Total	~	30 (2)

Born 1887. Former Grantham Avenue and Newark Town player who moved to Leeds City and made 29 appearances for them in Division Two during their 1909/10 and 1910/11 seasons. He scored on his Grantham debut in October 1919 against Long Eaton and played in many of the season's games right up until the closing fixture at Shirebrook. In January 1921 he was appointed Apprentice Coach for the Reserves side and later became Trainer for Newark Town.

Alan Horton

Seasons Played			
	League	~	9 (4)
	F.A. Cup	~	
1955/56	Lincs Cup	~	
	Total	~	9 (4)

Scored in his first two games for Grantham, beginning with the February 1956 game against Scunthorpe & Lindsey United Reserves. Alan played in about half of the fixtures over the next couple of months, until his final appearance in the Midland League fixture at home to Scarborough in April.

Neil Horwood

Seasons Played			
	League	~	22 (1)
	F.A. Cup	~	5 (2)
1985/86	F.A. Trophy	~	2
	League Cup	~	8 (1)
1991/92	Lincs Cup	~	1
	Total	~	38 (4)

Born 04/08/1964 at Peterhead. Young player who arrived at London Road from Grimsby Pelham and made his debut in the opening league fixture of the 1985/86 season against Sutton Coldfield Town. He scored his first goal for the club a month later at Banbury United, but soon after the December defeat at Oldbury United he left London Road. He went on to play for Appleby Frodingham, Kettering Town, King's Lynn, Grimsby Town, Halifax Town, Tranmere Rovers and Cambridge United, scoring three times in his 22 Football League appearances. Neil then returned to non-league football with Welling United, Spalding United and then, after a £10,000 transfer, Kettering Town. By the start of the 1991/92 season though, he had returned to Grantham and played in the first match at The Meres against Ilkeston Town in the FA Cup, before his final game for the club against Alvechurch in October after 13 consecutive appearances. Following his departure from The Meres, Neil went on to play for Gainsborough Trinity and Hyde United.

Mick Hoskins

Seasons Played			
	League	~	21 (1)
	F.A. Cup	~	
1989/90	F.A. Trophy	~	
	League Cup	~	4
	Lincs Cup	~	
	Total	~	25 (1)

Born 03/11/1966 at Chesterfield. Former Chesterfield, Goole Town, Matlock Town and Belper Town player who first appeared for Grantham in the October 1989 league fixture at RC Warwick. Mick scored his only goal for Grantham against Stroud, a couple of weeks before his final appearance for the club in March 1990 at home to Barry Town, following which he returned to Belper.

Roy Houghton

Seasons Played			
	League	~	1
	Lincs Cup	~	
1939/40	Other	~	1 (1)
	Total	~	2 (1)

Born 31/03/1921 at Billingborough. Brother of the Aston Villa and England player, Eric Houghton. Roy was a former Notts County player, with eight First team appearances, who scored in his first game for Grantham against Newark Town in October 1939 and then played in the initial Midland 'War-Time' League game at home to Denaby United. After The Second World War Roy went on to join Boston United and then Peterborough United, before returning to Billingborough to help with the family bakery business. He is now retired, but still lives in the village.

A. Howard

Seasons Played			
1874/75-76/77	F.A. Cup	~	5 (1)
1878/79-80/81	Other	~	39 (7)
	Total	~	44 (8)

First of a long list of 'Howard's' who played for Grantham during this period. This individual appeared in the very first match in October 1874 against the Third Lincolnshire Volunteer Rifles and although playing in many of the club matches from that first season, for some reason he made no other appearances in friendlies against other teams. This curiosity was redressed the following season though and he scored his first goal for the club against Newark in November 1875, as well as captaining one of the club games. He continued to be a prominent member of the team, apart for a lull during the 1877/78 season, right up until his final appearance in the April 1881 friendly at home to Bourne.

A.J. Howard

Seasons Played			
1879/80	Other	~	1
	Total	~	1

Made only one appearance for Grantham in the October 1879 friendly at home to Newark. This is definitely a different player to the previous entry, due to the fact that they played alongside each other in that particular game.

I. Howard

Seasons Played			
1874/75	F.A. Cup	~	3
1876/77-80/81	Other	~	14 (2)
	Total	~	17 (2)

Played in Grantham's first ever match against another side, the Third Lincolnshire Volunteer Rifles, and like the previously mentioned A. Howard this was his only game from that season. He returned a year later but it wasn't until the start of the new decade that he began to play more regularly. Finally he scored his first known goal for the club in November 1880 against Gainsborough, although this was only a month before what would turn out to be his final appearance, in the FA Cup replay at Stafford Road, Wolverhampton.

J. Howard

Seasons Played			
	F.A. Cup	~	
	Other	~	14 (2)
1875/76-80/81	Total	~	14 (2)

Made his debut in the November 1875 friendly at Bourne, but for the next couple of years played only occasionally for the club. He scored his first goal in the February 1878 match at Nottingham Castle, but his appearances were restricted to friendlies only and although he scored his next goal in the opening match of the 1880/81 season at Huntingdon County, this proved to be his last game.

Mick Howard

Seasons Played			
	League	~	10 (4)
	F.A. Cup	~	4 (4)
1982/83	F.A. Trophy	~	1
	League Cup	~	
	Lincs Cup	~	2 (1)
	Other	~	1
	Total	~	18 (9)

Former Ilkeston Town striker who scored within 45 seconds of his debut for Grantham in the August 1982 County Cup tie at home to Gainsborough Trinity. He returned to the side at the end of the following month and scored seven more times within the next three weeks, including an 18 minute hat-trick during the FA Cup replay against Winterton Rangers. Mick played in the October Lincolnshire County Cup Final victory at Scunthorpe United and the final qualifying round of the FA Cup against Telford United, but after such a brilliant start to his Grantham career it was unfortunate that his goals soon dried up, as did his appearances, with his final game for the club just after Christmas at home to King's Lynn. Mick returned to Ilkeston Town and then moved on to Eastwood Racing FC and Borrowash Victoria.

M. Howard

Seasons Played			
	Other	~	12
1874/75-76/77	Total	~	12

Final member of what could quite possibly be five brothers playing for the club during the same period. This Howard made his debut in the December 1874 friendly at Sleaford and whereas his previous namesakes had been more prominent towards the end of the decade, this individual made all of his appearances during the club's first three seasons. His last known game came in January 1877 when the team travelled over to Bourne.

Sid Howard

Seasons Played			
	League	~	77 (32)
	F.A. Cup	~	11 (8)
1912/13-14/15	League Cup	~	1 (1)
	Lincs Cup	~	9 (6)
1919/20-21/22	Other	~	3 (1)
1923/24	Total	~	101 (48)

Forward whose first known Grantham goal came in the October 1912 league game against Leicester Fosse Reserves, but little is known about other matches that he played in that season apart from those that he scored in and the friendly fixture against Queen's Park. He was a near constant member of the side for five league seasons, as well as the whole period during the First World War, but by the start of the 1921/22 season Sid's appearances were becoming more infrequent. For the following campaign there is no evidence of him playing in any games, although a year later Sid was back in the team and still scoring, right up until the March 1924 Central Alliance fixture at home to Ilkeston United. He is often credited with the fact that he is one of the players to have made a record number of appearances for Grantham, due to not missing a single match for six years and making 300 consecutive appearances. However, a significant proportion of those matches must have been friendlies played during the First World War, meaning that although he undoubtedly made many more appearances than those shown above, perhaps the figure for competitive games is not quite as large as the legend would have us believe.

Howard

Seasons Played			
	F.A. Cup	~	2 (2)
	Lincs Cup	~	
1881/82	Other	~	3
1884/85	Total	~	5 (2)

Most probably one of the previous 'Howard' entries, (surely not a sixth brother!), but with no initial attributed to his surname it's impossible to tell which one. Whoever he may prove to be, he scored twice in the FA Cup game against Brigg Town in November 1881 and returned for the first two friendlies of the 1884/85 season with the game against Sleaford marking his final appearance.

Reg Howlett

Seasons Played			
	League	~	27 (4)
	F.A. Cup	~	1 (1)
1951/52-52/53	Lincs Cup	~	1
	Total	~	29 (5)

Born 28/04/1932 at Cleethorpes. Made his Grantham debut in the January 1952 Midland League game against Nottingham Forest Reserves and played in all the remaining matches bar the final one, scoring in the fixture with Halifax Town Reserves and netting a brace against Gainsborough Trinity. After the Summer break Reg still had a secure place in the team, but after October his appearances became few and far between, although he did manage to score in his final appearance for the club at Nottingham Forest Reserves in March 1953. Reg is also known to have spent time at Nottingham Forest and Southampton at some point in his career and by the mid 1950's he was playing for Boston United, including their record 6-1 victory in the FA Cup over Derby County, but by the end of the decade he had moved on to Wisbech Town. In 2003 Reg returned to York Street as Guest of Honour when The Pilgrims reunited several of their famous Fiftie's side.

Ernest Hoyland

Seasons Played			
	League	~	10 (2)
	F.A. Cup	~	
1945/46	Lincs Cup	~	1
	Total	~	11 (2)

Born 17/01/1914 at Thurnscoe. Winger previously with Thurnscoe Victoria, Halifax Town, Blackpool, West Bromwich Albion and Lincoln City, who scored a total of eight goals in his 33 Football League appearances, with one more goal to his name in four cup matches during the second half of the 1930's. Ernest made all of his appearances for Grantham in the Spring of 1946, beginning with the home game against Rotherham United Reserves. He scored in the matches against Barnsley Reserves and Boston United, but although he only missed two games during his short time at London Road, unluckily for him one of those was the County Cup Final match. Ernest made his final appearance in the April 1946 league match at Mansfield Town Reserves.

Hubbard

Seasons Played			
	League	~	1
	F.A. Cup	~	
1922/23	Lincs Cup	~	
	Other	~	
	Total	~	1

Records show just the one appearance for this player, the home game against Gresley Rovers in January 1923.

Clifford Hubberd

Seasons Played			
	League	~	19 (3)
	F.A. Cup	~	5 (3)
1947/48	Lincs Cup	~	
	Total	~	24 (6)

Born 1911 at Worksop. Experienced player who began his career with Manton Colliery and Scunthorpe United, before scoring 56 goals in 183 games for Hull City. The final two seasons before The War saw Clifford playing for West Ham United, although he was only awarded four appearances, despite scoring three times during them. He went on to play for Ransome & Marles, Goole Town and Worksop Town, before arriving at London Road. He first played for Grantham in the league game against Hull City Reserves at the end of August 1947 and six weeks later he scored in his next game for the club at Rotherham United Reserves. This was the start of his best run in the First team, which included two goals in the FA Cup demolition of Ilkeston Town and an appearance in the First Round Proper against Stockton. Clifford also made occasional appearances the following Spring, but the April 1948 match at Denaby United would prove to be his final one.

Scott Huckerby

Seasons Played			
	League	~	21 (3)
	F.A. Cup	~	1
2003/04-04/05	F.A. Trophy	~	2
	League Cup	~	
	Lincs Cup	~	1
	Total	~	25 (3)

Born 09/08/1977 at Nottingham. Brother of the Norwich City striker, Darren Huckerby. Scott started his career on the books at Lincoln City, before joining Ilkeston Town, playing against Grantham in the 1997/98 League Championship battle. Following a £10,000 transfer to Telford United, moves then followed to Woking, Hinckley United, Hinckley Town, Eastwood Town and Kidsgrove Athletic. He scored on his debut for Grantham in the March 2004 league fixture at home to Weymouth and missed only two of the remaining games from that season. However, with just one goal in the 2004/05 season, at home to Hemel Hempstead in August, the arrival of Lee Glover a few months later prompted Scott's relegation to the substitute's bench. In December 2004 he was released by the club and went on to play for Glapwell and Arnold Town.

Chris Hudson

Seasons Played			
	League	~	
	F.A. Cup	~	
1991/92	F.A. Trophy	~	
	League Cup	~	
	Lincs Cup	~	1
	Total	~	1

Goalkeeper who made just one appearance for Grantham in the opening County Cup tie of the 1991/92 season at Grimsby Town.

John Hudson

Seasons Played			
	League	~	10
	F.A. Cup	~	
1987/88	F.A. Trophy	~	1
	League Cup	~	2
	Lincs Cup	~	
	Total	~	13

Born 24/11/1964 at Manchester. Started his career at Manchester City, although he failed to make a First team appearance there, before moving on to Oldham Athletic and Rochdale, with a period playing in the Swedish League in-between. His first game for Grantham came in the September 1987 league match at Bridgnorth Town, but John made only twelve more appearances, including his final game against Halesowen Town at the end of February 1988. John is now back up in the North-West where he works as the Regional Director for the PFA's Football in the Community programme.

Hughes

Seasons Played			
	League	~	15 (4)
	F.A. Cup	~	1
1889/90-92/93	Lincs Cup	~	1
	Other	~	11 (5)
	Total	~	28 (9)

Played in the first friendly of the 1889/90 season at home to Leicester Fosse Reserves and scored his first goal for the club towards the end of the year against Mapperley. The following campaign he can only be found playing in the one game, but by the start of the 1891/92 season and Grantham's first ever league fixture at home to Notts County Rovers, he once more consistently appears in the side. He was still playing for Grantham at the start of the following season, but seems to have perhaps wisely departed before the 16-0 record defeat and subsequent club disbandment.

Hughes

Seasons Played			
	League	~	5
1905/06	Total	~	5

Most likely a consistent member of the 1905/06 season as he appears in pre-season friendlies, right the way through to league games the following April.

Hughes

Seasons Played			
	League	~	
	F.A. Cup	~	
1912/13	Lincs Cup	~	
	Other	~	1
	Total	~	1

Forward who is known to have played in the March 1913 friendly against Queen's Park, but no evidence exists of any other appearances that he may have made.

Albert Humphreys

Seasons Played			
	League	~	41
	F.A. Cup	~	9
1913/14-14/15	Lincs Cup	~	4
	Other	~	
1919/20-21/22	Total	~	54

Goalkeeper who joined the First team at the start of the 1913/14 season and was soon playing in the huge FA Cup derby at home to Grantham Avenue. Played in front of a 4,000 crowd, the team were sadly knocked out after a 1-0 defeat. Albert remained the club's first choice 'keeper for the years spanning the First World War, up until the end of the 1919/20 season, although he still made occasional further appearances for Grantham in the following two years as well. After the end of his playing career he became Trainer at Hucknall Byron.

John Humphreys

Seasons Played			
	League	~	128 (23)
	F.A. Cup	~	5 (1)
1985/86-88/89	F.A. Trophy	~	11 (1)
	League Cup	~	16 (1)
1997/98	Lincs Cup	~	4
	Total	~	164 (26)

Born 23/08/1965 at Nottingham. Midfield player who started out on the books at Notts County, before moving on to Rainworth Miners Welfare, Eastwood Town, Arnold Town and Shepshed Charterhouse. He made his debut for The Gingerbreads in the March 1986 league fixture against Stourbridge and scored his first goal for the club in that season's closing fixture at VS Rugby. John missed only a few of Grantham's matches over the next three seasons, two of which were under the guidance of Martin O'Neill, and he even had a trial with Nottingham Forest in the same game as Gary Crosby. He went on to play for Spalding United, Telford United, Ilkeston Town and Dunkirk, where he became joint-manager along with his old team-mate, Larry Burrell. John returned to Grantham though in the Summer of 1997 and played in the first six league matches, which all ended in victories for The Gingerbreads in their Championship winning season. His last game for the club was in the September 1997 match against VS Rugby and he went on to play for Borrowash Victoria for a short while, before returning to Dunkirk once more and then making appearances for Wollaton. In the Summer of 2004 John was appointed Manager of Radcliffe Olympic, although a shortage of playing staff has forced him to turn out on occasions.

Eric Hunt

Seasons Played			
	League	~	229
	F.A. Cup	~	22
1947/48-53/54	Lincs Cup	~	9
	Total	~	260

Left-Back who had also played for Worthington Simpson, Ransome & Marles and made his Grantham debut at the start of the 1947/48 season at Scarborough. Eric then played in every round of that season's FA Cup run, which included the 11-1 thrashing of Ilkeston Town and the First Round encounter at Stockton. Over the next few years he played in most of Grantham's matches and was rewarded with another FA Cup First Round appearance in November 1949 against Wrexham, whilst the end of the same season saw the first of two Lincolnshire Senior Cup 'A' Final's that he played in. Unfortunately Eric was on the losing side both times, firstly after Boston United's victory and then in March 1953 after a shock win by Spalding United. In the Autumn of 1953 he lost his place to John Little, although he made one more appearance for Grantham the following January in a league match at Worksop Town. He finished his Grantham career with a total of 260 appearances and yet not once was he in the right place at the right time to get his name on the score-sheets.

Hunt

Seasons Played			
	Other	~	1
1875/76	Total	~	1

Made just one appearance for Grantham in the January 1876 friendly against Peterborough which was played under Rugby Union rules.

Hunt

Seasons Played			
	League	~	1
	F.A. Cup	~	
1959/60	League Cup	~	
	Lincs Cup	~	
	Total	~	1

Played just once for Grantham at home to Derby County 'A' in an April 1960 Central Alliance fixture.

Ronald Hunter

Seasons Played			
	League	~	8 (1)
	F.A. Cup	~	1
1938/39	Lincs Cup	~	1
	Total	~	10 (1)

Outside-Left player who had also made appearances for Fulham as an amateur and played all but one of his games for Grantham at the start of the 1938/39 season, beginning with the first league game at Shrewsbury which pitted the previous season's top two teams together. Ronald scored his only goal for the club at home to Barnsley Reserves and returned to make his final appearance for the club in the March 1939 County Cup replay against Boston United.

Steve Hunter

Seasons Played			
	League	~	1
	F.A. Cup	~	
1987/88-88/89	F.A. Trophy	~	
	League Cup	~	
	Lincs Cup	~	1
	Total	~	2

Reserves player and member of the RAF who stepped up to appear in the February 1988 league match against Halesowen Town and then came on as substitute in the 1988/89 season's opening County Cup tie at home to Gainsborough Trinity.

Mark Hurst

Seasons Played			
	League	~	48 (15)
	F.A. Cup	~	1 (1)
1991/92	F.A. Trophy	~	1
	League Cup	~	11 (4)
1997/98	Lincs Cup	~	1
	Total	~	62 (20)

Born 18/08/1970 at Derby. Striker who began his career at Nottingham Forest, before having two years at Huddersfield Town, followed by time at Telford United. He made his debut for Grantham in the 1991/92 season's opening game at Grimsby Town and scored his first goal for the club in the initial league fixture against Bridgnorth Town. At the end of that month Mark scored the first ever Grantham goal at The Meres, in the opening game against Ilkeston Town in the FA Cup, and by the end of that campaign he had missed only one game and easily finished as the club's highest scorer with 20 goals to his name. Although he was watched by several Football League scouts, it was Leicester United that he surprisingly moved to, followed by Gresley Rovers, where he was a member of their Dr Marten's League title winning side in the 1996/97 season. Mark was brought back to The Meres by Gary Mills to play in the January 1998 Dr Marten's Cup tie at Raunds Town and seven of the final league games. He made his last appearance for the club in that season's final fixture at home to Stourbridge, as the team nervously secured the draw that was needed for the league championship title. Mark then went on to play for Blakenall and Hinckley United, before a return to Gresley, followed by a spell at Mickleover Sports. He currently works as a painter and decorator in the Derby area.

Hutchins

Seasons Played			
	League	~	29 (6)
	F.A. Cup	~	2
1925/26-26/27	Lincs Cup	~	1
	Other	~	1
1932/33	Total	~	33 (6)

Full-Back who had previously played for Nottingham Forest and scored his first goal for Grantham in the March 1926 Midland League game against York City. He left London Road just after the 1927 New Year, but returned sometime during the 1932/33 season to make eight more appearances. His surname is quite often also spelt 'Hutchings'.

Arthur Hutchinson

Seasons Played	F.A. Cup	~	11 (1)
1874/75-78/79	Lincs Cup	~	18 (8)
1883/84-87/88	Other	~	115 (44)
1889/90	Total	~	144 (53)

Born 06/04/1855 in Grantham. Owner of a Wines & Spirits shop on Finkin Street who was a member of the Grantham Corps of Volunteers and the Oddfellows Society, but more importantly was the man who created Grantham Football Club by requesting a meeting for any other interested sporting parties. He was an original committee member, Captain of the very first club game against Mr Gamble's side and Club Captain from the very first match against another team in October 1874 when The Third Lincolnshire Volunteer Rifles came to London Road. Obviously Arthur played in nearly every Grantham match from this initial period and scored his first known goal for the club in the February 1875 friendly against Sleaford. He went on to play in the club's maiden FA Cup tie, in October 1877 against Clapham Rovers, and became the first Grantham captain to lift a trophy when Gainsborough Trinity were defeated in the March 1885 Lincolnshire Senior Cup Final. At the end of that season Arthur was rewarded with a complimentary dinner at The Guildhall to mark his tenth year as Club Captain, during which it was stated that 'prior to the previous season he missed only one match'. However, this simply does not tally with the match reports and team-sheets of the period, although this statement could possibly have meant in trophy related fixtures like the FA Cup and County competition. He was still a prominent member of the side right up until the end of the 1887/88 season and then returned for two more matches in November 1889 with his final appearance coming in the match against Boston NE. Off the field, Arthur was elected as a Town Councillor in November 1885 and he progressed in local politics to occupy the post of Grantham Mayor in both 1893 and 1901. He was also Managing Director of the local brewery, a Director in several of the town's principal companies, rose to the rank of Major in the 2nd Volunteer Battalion of the Lincolnshire Regiment and was one of the town's leading magistrates up to the 1920's. Died 09/07/1930 at Grantham.

Hutchinson

Seasons Played			
	League	~	1
	F.A. Cup	~	
1925/26	Lincs Cup	~	
	Total	~	1

Half-Back with just one known appearance, the Midland League game at Boston in December 1925.

Hutt

Seasons Played			
	League	~	7 (5)
	F.A. Cup	~	4
1936/37	Lincs Cup	~	
	Other	~	
	Total	~	11 (5)

Outside-Left player who had also spent time at Goole Town and was able to gain his first Grantham appearance in the October 1936 FA Cup draw against Ollerton Colliery after George Rudkin became unavailable. He kept his place in the team for the next seven matches, but was then forced to make up the rest of his appearances individually, with his last game coming in March of the following year against Doncaster Rovers Reserves.

Chris Hyam

Seasons Played			
	League	~	2
	F.A. Cup	~	
2004/05	F.A. Trophy	~	
	League Cup	~	
	Lincs Cup	~	
	Total	~	2

Young Grimsby Town Youth player who joined Grantham on work experience in March 2005, playing against Solihull Borough and Team Bath.

Hyde

Seasons Played			
	League	~	3
	F.A. Cup	~	
1928/29	Lincs Cup	~	
	Other	~	
	Total	~	3

Goalkeeper who played at the end of the 1928/29 season for Grantham due to the regular 'keeper, Stan Walker, being unavailable.

Dale Igoe

Seasons Played			
	League	~	23 (4)
	F.A. Cup	~	
1991/92	F.A. Trophy	~	
	League Cup	~	5
	Lincs Cup	~	
	Total	~	28 (4)

Born 25/02/1964 at Derby. Tall central defender who previously played for Bromsgrove Rovers and made his debut for Grantham in the September 1991 league game at Hednesford Town. Dale scored his first goal for the club in November at Stourbridge, but made his final appearance the following February at home to Bridgnorth Town. He went on to make appearances for Nuneaton Borough, Leicester United, Ilkeston Town, Shepshed Dynamo and Mickleover Sports. Dale still lives in the Derby area and is Managing Director of his own paving and driveway construction company.

Niall Inman

Seasons Played			
	League	~	27
	F.A. Cup	~	1
2003/04	F.A. Trophy	~	
	League Cup	~	1
	Lincs Cup	~	3 (2)
	Total	~	32 (2)

Born 06/02/1978 at Wakefield. Former Republic of Ireland Youth and Under-21 International with experience at Norwich City, Peterborough United, Stevenage Borough and Kettering Town, with the latter two being on-loan. After a trial with American side Charleston Battery in 2001, Niall moved on to Dover Athletic, followed by a return to Kettering, where he won a Dr Marten's Premier League Championship medal. He scored on his debut for The Gingerbreads in the County Cup tie at home to Stamford at the start of the 2003/04 season and played in many of the season's games, including the Lincolnshire Shield Final against Gainsborough Trinity where he came off the bench to score his only other goal for the club. This turned out to be his last appearance for the club and in April 2004 he went on to play for Mildenhall Town.

Sidney Iremonger

Seasons Played			
	League	~	7 (2)
	F.A. Cup	~	1
1921/22	Lincs Cup	~	1
	Total	~	9 (2)

Half-Back whose surname is sometimes spelt 'Ironmonger'. He had previously played for Newark Athletic and Lincoln City, scoring once in his three First team appearances there. Sidney first scored for Grantham in the September 1921 Central Alliance fixture at home to Loughborough Corinthians and was a regular player in the first half of that season. He went on to play for Newark Town, but died after an accident on the football field, although no further details are known.

Ison

Seasons Played			
	League	~	1
	F.A. Cup	~	
1924/25	Lincs Cup	~	
	Other	~	
	Total	~	1

Leicester based Grantham Reserves centre-forward who made just one appearance for the First team, although no information is available on the specific game.

Jimmy Jackson

Seasons Played			
	League	~	257 (39)
	F.A. Cup	~	20 (2)
1969/70-70/71	F.A. Trophy	~	15 (1)
	League Cup	~	26 (6)
1975/76-81/82	Lincs Cup	~	13 (1)
	Other	~	3
	Total	~	334 (49)

Born November 1948 at Bourne. After signing from Bourne Town, Jimmy started out as a striker at Grantham and scored on his debut in the first home game of the 1969/70 season against Boston FC. Although he fitted well into the team straight away, Jimmy had to settle with substitute appearances in both of that season's FA Cup games against Gainsborough Trinity and Oldham Athletic. On Boxing Day 1969 he netted his first hat-trick for the club, with Stamford being the unfortunate victims, but by the start of the following season, Grantham's first of what would be three consecutive Championships, Terry Bly was spoilt for choice with quality strikers and Jimmy was forced to sit out many of the games. In fact, after the January FA Trophy defeat at Yeovil Town, Jimmy played no further part in the season other than the League's final Champion's versus Rest of the League game. After a return to Bourne, he came back to London Road, this time in his favoured centre-half position. He played in the November 1975 FA Cup First Round tie against Port Vale, but the next few years saw precious little to cheer about, until the 1978/79 Championship winning season, although Jimmy missed out on the final six league fixtures. The first couple of years that Grantham spent in the Northern Premier League continued with him as a valuable asset to the team, although he scored his final goal for the club on Boxing Day 1979 at Marine and, unluckily for Jimmy, often seemed to miss out on some of the biggest games. His final appearance for Grantham came in the August 1981 County Cup defeat against Boston United, following which he returned again to Bourne Town and also spent a period of time in the managerial position there. He came back to Grantham towards the end of the club's time in the Northern Premier League, but his only First team appearances were limited to those in the Midland Floodlit League. This period was followed by a final return to Bourne in a board-room capacity. He continues to live in the Bourne area, works as a plasterer and is still an avid follower of his home team.

Kirk Jackson

Seasons Played			
	League	~	16 (7)
	F.A. Cup	~	2
1998/99	F.A. Trophy	~	2
	League Cup	~	3
	Lincs Cup	~	1
	Total	~	24 (7)

Born 16/10/1976 at Barnsley. Former Sheffield Wednesday, Scunthorpe United and Chesterfield striker who signed for Grantham on a free transfer after a spell on-loan at Gainsborough Trinity. He made his debut in the 1998/99 season's opening match at home to Scunthorpe United in the County Cup and scored his first goal in the August league fixture against Bromsgrove Rovers. He was undoubtedly a quality player, but his last appearance for Grantham came in January 1999 at Rothwell Town in the Dr Marten's League Cup. He went on to play with Chris Waddle at Worksop Town and after a season which saw him score 40 goals, he moved on to Darlington for a £20,000 fee. Transfers then followed to Stevenage Borough, Yeovil Town after another £20,000 move, where he helped them win the Conference and entry into The Football League, plus appeared in their televised FA Cup tie at home to Liverpool. An on-loan spell at Dagenham & Redbridge was followed by a move to Hornchurch in the Summer of 2004, but financial problems there only a few months later led to his transfer to Weymouth in November. Kirk has scored seven goals during his time in The Football League, which saw 58 appearances, plus played in another 13 cup fixtures as well. He has also been awarded six caps at England Semi-Professional level and was picked for a representative National Game XI versus the USA in March 2002.

Pete Jackson

Seasons Played			
	League	~	7 (1)
	F.A. Cup	~	
1977/78	F.A. Trophy	~	2
	League Cup	~	1
	Lincs Cup	~	
	Total	~	10 (1)

Born 20/03/1954 at Leicester. A former regular scorer in the Football Combination for both Cardiff City and Leicester City who made his debut for Grantham in the November 1977 league fixture at home to Nuneaton Borough. His only goal for the club came on Boxing Day in the derby against Kettering Town, only a couple of weeks before his final appearance, again versus Nuneaton Borough, but this time in the FA Trophy. He went on to play for Birstall United, Melton Town and Thringstone Miners Welfare, whilst he is currently Assistant Manager back at Birstall.

Jackson

Seasons Played			
	League	~	1 (2)
	Lincs Cup	~	
1904/05	Other	~	
	Total	~	1 (2)

Centre-Forward who scored twice in the Midland Amateur Alliance game against Notts Magdala Amateurs in March 1905, but no records exist to show any other appearances for him.

Roy Jacobs

Seasons Played			
	League	~	32 (1)
	F.A. Cup	~	3
1967/68	Total	~	35 (1)

Defender who first played for Grantham in the opening match of the 1967/68 season at Belper Town. Roy played in the FA Cup First Round tie against Altrincham and only missed one game before his final appearance in April against Alfreton Town. In the mean time he had scored his only goal for the club in the March fixture at Matlock Town and he went on to play for Boston FC.

Sid Howard

Scott Huckerby

Albert Humphreys

Arthur Hutchinson

Niall Inman

Jimmy Jackson

Kirk Jackson

Nicky Jarvis

Arthur Jepson

Gary Jones

George Jowett

Jamie Kearns

Alex Kirby

Guy Last

Seamus Lawless

Eddie Lawrence

Paul James

Seasons Played			
	League	~	
	F.A. Cup	~	
1996/97	F.A. Trophy	~	
	League Cup	~	
	Lincs Cup	~	1
	Total	~	1

Made just one appearance by coming off the bench to replace Brendan McDaid in the opening County Cup tie of the 1996/97 season at home to Grimsby Town.

James

Seasons Played			
	League	~	13 (1)
	F.A. Cup	~	1
1890/91-91/92	Lincs Cup	~	1
	Other	~	4
	Total	~	19 (1)

Played only one game during the 1890/91 season, the County Cup match against Grantham Rovers in January 1891, but appeared in virtually every game the following season, including the club's first ever league match at home to Notts County Rovers. His only goal for Grantham came a year after his debut, in the Midland Amateur Alliance fixture at Heanor.

H. Jarratt

Seasons Played			
	F.A. Cup	~	
	Lincs Cup	~	
1885/86	Other	~	1
	Total	~	1

Made only one appearance, playing in the same game as his namesake in the following entry (albeit with a spelling error), the January 1886 friendly against Notts Rangers.

Rev. Beaumont Jarrett

Seasons Played			
	F.A. Cup	~	8
	Lincs Cup	~	13
1878/79-80/81	Other	~	19 (2)
1883/84-86/87	Total	~	40 (2)

Born 18/07/1855 in London. Former Harrow School, Cambridge University, Old Harrovians and England player who had been awarded three International caps for the matches against Scotland in the consecutive years between 1876 and 1878. He made his Grantham debut in the December 1878 friendly at London Road against Southwell, but for his first three seasons with the club he seems to have made only one or two appearances each year, most likely due to his ministerial duties in other parts of the County. He was certainly known to be the Parson at Coningsby in the 1881 census. Upon returning to the club at the start of the 1883/84 season, he was a more noticeable member and in the following campaign he played in every round of the Lincolnshire Senior Cup which culminated in victory against Gainsborough Trinity. His last known appearance comes in the December 1886 friendly against Notts Olympic, but unfortunately no team-sheet is available for the following weeks FA Cup Third Round tie against Horncastle, so we are unable to verify whether he also played in this game. His name is sometimes spelt 'Jarratt' in Grantham's team-sheets. Died 11/04/1905 at Louth.

Steve Jarrett

Seasons Played			
	League	~	
	F.A. Cup	~	
1979/80	F.A. Trophy	~	
	League Cup	~	1
	Lincs Cup	~	
	Total	~	1

Made only one appearance for Grantham in the December 1979 Northern Premier League Cup tie at South Liverpool. This was a replay of the original September fixture, due to the hosts fielding an ineligible player.

Nicky Jarvis

Seasons Played			
	League	~	166 (11)
	F.A. Cup	~	12
1978/79-79/80	F.A. Trophy	~	14 (1)
	League Cup	~	13 (1)
1981/82-85/86	Lincs Cup	~	9
	Other	~	5
	Total	~	219 (13)

Born 19/09/1955 at Mansfield. Son of Don Jarvis, the former Lightweight professional boxer. Nicky started out on the books of Derby County and after trials with Notts County and Chesterfield joined Ilkeston Town. He made his Grantham debut in the first game of the 1978/79 season at Boston United in the County Cup and scored his maiden goal for the club only weeks later at Corby Town in the first round of the Southern League Cup. Nicky was the only member of that season's Championship winning side who played in every single game, whilst Grantham's entrance into the Northern Premier League continued with his near constant appearance. He was transferred to Scunthorpe United in the Summer of 1980 after a £2,000 fee was paid, and following 26 appearances that season moved to Shepshed Charterhouse, before returning to Grantham in September 1981. He briefly left London Road in 1982 to join Long Eaton United, but was back in time to play in the County Cup Final victory over Scunthorpe United and the final FA Cup qualifying round tie at Telford United. Nicky continued to play in the majority of the games for Grantham, up to the Autumn of 1984 when he joined Matlock Town. However, he was back once more at London Road just over a year later, but made only four more appearances for Grantham, the last of which came in the March 1986 league game against Coventry Sporting. Nicky now runs his own civil engineering company and lives mid-way between Nottingham and Derby.

Jarvis

Seasons Played			
	League	~	2
	Lincs Cup	~	1 (1)
1894/95	Other	~	1
	Total	~	4 (1)

Scored in the November 1894 Lincolnshire Shield game against Grantham Rovers Colts and is most likely to have played in more games from the 1894/95 season than those shown above.

Jarvis

Seasons Played			
	League	~	1 (2)
	F.A. Cup	~	
1934/35	Lincs Cup	~	
	Total	~	1 (2)

Centre-Forward who was in the RAF and unfortunately only able to play once for Grantham. However, he scored twice in the April 1935 5-0 drubbing of Scunthorpe & Lindsey United.

A. Jefferies

Seasons Played			
	League	~	2
	Lincs Cup	~	1
1939/40	Other	~	
	Total	~	3

Goalkeeper who made three appearances for Grantham in the second Midland 'War-Time' League, with an impressive debut in the 4-1 defeat of Gainsborough Trinity. But he was the unfortunate victim to have to pick the ball out of the net seven times in the County Cup Final against Scunthorpe & Lindsey United and made his final appearance a fortnight later at Peterborough United.

Jeffery

Seasons Played			
	Lincs Cup	~	
	Other	~	1
1889/90	Total	~	1

Player who made just one appearance for Grantham in the December 1889 friendly at home to Beeston Town.

Dennis Jenas

Seasons Played			
	League	~	55 (26)
	F.A. Cup	~	6 (2)
1979/80-80/81	F.A. Trophy	~	4 (2)
	League Cup	~	3 (1)
1985/86	Lincs Cup	~	3 (1)
	Other	~	
1990/91	Total	~	71 (32)

Born 09/05/1960 at Nottingham. Dennis was actually christened *Genas*, but changed his name as he wanted to be known as DJ at school. He was a former Clifton All Whites and Ajax, Nottingham, striker who had previously had trials with Nottingham Forest. Dennis made his debut for Grantham in the August 1979 league match at Southport and scored his first goal for the club a week later in the 5-0 thrashing of Workington. He immediately formed an impressive forward partnership with Robbie Cooke and this continued the following season with the arrival of Dave Leadbeater. Dennis played in the October 1980 County Cup Final at Lincoln City, but soon after this he left London Road to move to Burton Albion. Transfers then followed to Buxton, Matlock Town, Shepshed Charterhouse, Kettering Town, Wellingborough Town and Eastwood Town, before he returned to Grantham in November 1985 to make a lone appearance in the game against Rushden Town. His playing career continued at Arnold Town and Alfreton Town, where he finished for both clubs as the season's top scorer, winning two league championship medals. A brief period was then spent with Kallsi in the Finnish Division Three, as their Player/Coach, after he had become only the third coloured player to achieve the FA's full coaching licence. In the 1988/89 season he was appointed Player/Manager at Ilkeston Town and following a brief spell at Tamworth, Dennis returned once more to Grantham. However, he made just five more appearances, the last of which came in October 1990 at home to Atherstone United in the FA Trophy, just a week before the club left London Road. In the early 1990's, Dennis played for Sutton Town, Highfield Rangers, Harrowby United and Forest Athletic amongst others. During that time he was also a coach for the Nottingham Forest Academy, which of course is where his son, the current Newcastle United and England star, Jermaine Jenas, began his career. Dennis has had to revert to his original name now after remarrying in the United States, where he works as a Football Coach in New Mexico and is President of Elite FC.

Bob Jenkins

Seasons Played			
	League	~	14
	F.A. Cup	~	1
1947/48-48/49	Lincs Cup	~	
	Total	~	15

Goalkeeper who made his debut in the August 1947 game at home to Hull City Reserves when Percy Ashton was unavailable. He was also able to have a six match run in the First team at the end of the season, but obviously after the Summer break appearances became infrequent once more and his final games came in the Christmas 1948 fixtures against Ransome & Marles.

J. Jenkinson

Seasons Played			
	League	~	1
	F.A. Cup	~	
1930/31	Lincs Cup	~	
	Total	~	1

His only known appearance is in the November 1930 Midland League fixture at home to Frickley Colliery.

Roy Jenkinson

Seasons Played			
	League	~	2
	F.A. Cup	~	1
1959/60	League Cup	~	
	Lincs Cup	~	
	Total	~	3

Made his First team debut in the August 1959 league game at home to Bourne Town, but following a match at Rothwell Town made his final appearance less than a month later in the First qualifying round of the FA Cup against Skegness Town. It is also known that Roy made appearances for Boston United at some point during his career.

Jenkinson

Seasons Played			
	F.A. Cup	~	
	Lincs Cup	~	1
1885/86-87/88	Other	~	13
	Total	~	14

First played for Grantham in the November 1885 match at Bourne, but appearances were always infrequent and limited to friendlies, until he was awarded a place in the County Cup semi-final side against Gainsborough Trinity in March 1888. He played only once more for the club though, in a friendly at Rotherham Town towards the end of the same month.

John Jennings

Seasons Played			
	League	~	1
	F.A. Cup	~	
1968/69	League Cup	~	
	Lincs Cup	~	
	Total	~	1

Born circa 1949. Former Kiveton Park player who started the Midland League fixture against Matlock Town at the end of August 1968, but was then substituted during the match. John sat on the bench for the next couple of games, but was not given another chance to play.

Arthur Jepson

Seasons Played			
	League	~	124
	F.A. Cup	~	12
1935/36-37/38	Lincs Cup	~	9
	Other	~	7
	Total	~	152

Born 12/07/1915 in Selston, Nottinghamshire. Former Newark Town and Mansfield Town goalkeeper who made his debut in the first match of the 1935/36 season at Burton Town and then played in every game, bar two Lincolnshire League fixtures, in his first season. Highlights from that campaign included an FA Cup First Round tie against Notts County, a County Cup Final against Boston United, plus victories in the Grantham Hospital Cup and the Wilson Cup. The following season Arthur played in another Lincolnshire Senior Cup Final and was then a huge asset to the 1937/38 side that finished as runners-up in the Midland League to Shrewsbury Town. His last two games for the club came in the Spalding Victory Cup and the traditional Champions versus Runners-Up game at the end of the season. During his time at London Road Arthur was lodging at The Maltshovels public house in Westgate and for many of his games at least one scout would be watching him from the terraces. Serious offers came from Notts County and Burnley, but he eventually moved to Port Vale on a free transfer in June 1938. After serving in the RAF during The War and making guest appearances for Nottingham Forest, a move to First Division Stoke City followed, Stanley Matthews' side, for a £3,750 fee, £50 of which was sent back to Grantham. He finished his Football League career at Lincoln City, with a total of 148 senior appearances to his name and went on play for Northwich Victoria, Gloucester City and Hinckley United, where he became their Player/Manager. Arthur's career then took him into scouting positions with Coventry City and Middlesbrough, before he returned to management, taking over the helm at Hinckley Athletic in 1963. Other than football, he was a successful member of Nottinghamshire County Cricket Club and in his later life was also one of the country's top cricketing umpires, officiating in many top games, including Test Matches between 1960 and 1969. By all accounts he was considered to be somewhat of a character. In 1971 Arthur was officiating the Gillette Cup semi-final between Lancashire and Gloucestershire, a match which carried on until 8:50pm. A worried Lancashire Captain commented, "It's getting dark 'Ump', there's the moon", to which Arthur retorted, "You can see the moon...how bloody far do you want to see!". Died 17/07/1997 at Kirkby-in-Ashfield.

Jervis

Seasons Played			
	Other	~	1
1875/76	Total	~	1

Played in many of that 1875/76 season's club matches, but as far as friendlies were concerned only appeared in the final one at Nottingham Lace in April.

Jessop

Seasons Played			
1877/78	F.A. Cup	~	
1879/80	Other	~	2
	Total	~	2

Played for Grantham in friendlies against Bourne in March 1878 and Nottingham Law in November 1879.

Jilder

Seasons Played			
1945/46	League	~	1
	F.A. Cup	~	
	Lincs Cup	~	
	Total	~	1

Midfielder who made one appearance for Grantham in the April 1946 Midland League game at Barnsley Reserves, although there is the possibility that he could be a mis-spelt Reg *Gilder*, although if this is true, then he was playing out of position.

George Johnson

Seasons Played			
1956/57	League	~	26 (4)
	F.A. Cup	~	4 (1)
	Lincs Cup	~	1
	Total	~	31 (5)

Born 06/10/1932 at Esh, Durham. Forward who previously played for Langley Park Juniors and Lincoln City, scoring once in his three Football League appearances. George made his Grantham debut in the August 1956 game at Frickley Colliery and scored his first two goals for the club the following month against Grimsby Town Reserves. He then had several good runs in the team, right up until the final fixture at Lincoln City Reserves. Died 2002.

Paul Johnson

Seasons Played			
1991/92	League	~	21 (1)
	F.A. Cup	~	
	F.A. Trophy	~	
	League Cup	~	6
	Lincs Cup	~	1
	Total	~	28 (1)

Local player who progressed through the Reserves to make his debut by coming off the bench in the 1991/92 season's opening County Cup tie at Grimsby Town. His next game came in October and this was soon followed by a goal in the match at home to Rushden Town. Paul then continued to play in many of Grantham's fixtures until his last appearance in February 1992 when Tamworth came to The Meres. He went on to play for Notts Alliance side, Greenwood Meadows.

Steve Johnson

Seasons Played			
1988/89	League	~	16 (3)
	F.A. Cup	~	
	F.A. Trophy	~	
	League Cup	~	
	Lincs Cup	~	
	Total	~	16 (3)

Born 18/02/1961. Former Stratford Town, Dulwich Hamlet, Hendon, Leamington, Gloucester City and Bilston Town striker who arrived at Grantham after a £500 transfer. He made his debut in the February 1989 defeat at Stourbridge and scored his first goal for The Gingerbreads a week later against Mile Oak Rovers. Steve played in many of the remaining fixtures from that season, up to the closing game at Nuneaton Borough, and went on to play for Willenhall Town and Tamworth.

Johnson

Seasons Played			
1929/30	League	~	1
	F.A. Cup	~	
	Lincs Cup	~	
	Other	~	
	Total	~	1

Former Grimsby Town player who made a single appearance at London Road in the November 1929 Midland League match against Scunthorpe & Lindsey United.

S. Johnston

Seasons Played			
1936/37-37/38	League	~	3
1939/40	F.A. Cup	~	
	Lincs Cup	~	
	Other	~	
	Total	~	3

Inside-Right who had also played for Mowbray's Sports, Spittlegate Old Boys and Grantham Reserves. He made three appearances for the First team, against Chesterfield Reserves in April 1937, Frickley Colliery in March 1938 and Scunthorpe & Lindsey United in November 1939.

Johnston

Seasons Played			
1874/75-77/78	F.A. Cup	~	1
1879/80	Other	~	14 (2)
	Total	~	15 (2)

Captain of one of the sides in Grantham's second ever club match and played in three of that first season's friendlies, starting at home to Bourne in January 1875 and scoring in a replay of the same fixture a couple of months later. The following season he only played in one friendly, but by the start of the 1877/78 he was more evident in the team and appeared in the club's first ever FA Cup tie against Clapham Rovers in October. His last known game for Grantham comes on New Year's Day 1880 when the team beat Horbling & District 4-1.

Johnston

Seasons Played			
1904/05	League	~	
	Lincs Cup	~	1
	Other	~	
	Total	~	1

Played in the County Shield competition against Hornsby Engineers in November 1904, although it is not known if he made any other appearances for the club.

Alan Jones

Seasons Played			
1981/82	League	~	24
	F.A. Cup	~	
	F.A. Trophy	~	
	League Cup	~	2
	Lincs Cup	~	
	Other	~	1 (2)
	Total	~	27 (2)

Former Frickley Athletic midfielder who had a dream debut for Grantham by scoring a brace against Nottingham Forest in the November 1981 Redmayne Trophy, although The Reds managed to put five past Eddie Green as well. He missed only a handful of games up to the April 1982 league fixture at Bangor City.

Barry Jones

Seasons Played			
1965/66	League	~	5
1968/69	F.A. Cup	~	
	League Cup	~	
	Lincs Cup	~	
	Total	~	5

Born 03/12/1944 in Grantham. Began his career with Grantham Colts and then had trials with Southampton, Nottingham Forest and Leicester City, before returning to the town to play for Earlesfield FC. Barry then made four appearances in the Grantham First team, with Ronnie Harbertson unavailable during the Spring of 1966, beginning with the short trip over to Spalding United. His final appearance for The Gingerbreads came from the substitute's bench when he replaced Ronnie Webster in the September 1968 league game at Heanor Town and after leaving London Road went on to play for Grantham St John's and Gonerby. Barry still lives close to the town and works as an Importer / Agent.

David Jones

Seasons Played			
1996/97	League	~	
	F.A. Cup	~	
	F.A. Trophy	~	1
	League Cup	~	
	Lincs Cup	~	
	Total	~	1

Made only one appearance for Grantham in the January 1997 FA Trophy second replay at home to Blyth Spartans, although he was replaced during the game by Ashley Brandy.

Gary Jones

Seasons Played			
	League	~	14 (13)
	F.A. Cup	~	
1989/90	F.A. Trophy	~	
	League Cup	~	2 (1)
	Lincs Cup	~	
	Total	~	16 (14)

Born 06/04/1969 at Huddersfield. Striker who previously played for Rossington Main, Doncaster Rovers and scored on his debut for Grantham in the November 1989 league match at home to Willenhall Town after coming off the bench. He soon earned the nickname 'Goal-a-game-Gary' due to his scoring exploits, which included a hat-trick on Boxing Day against Tamworth, but the January 1990 fixture at home to Dudley Town was to be his last for the club. He signed for Kettering Town after a £17,500 transfer and despite having trials with Newcastle United and Manchester United, then moved to Boston United, before finally making his Football League debut at Southend United. Gary was even offered back to Grantham in the early 1990's, but the club felt that at the time the forwards that they currently had were more than adequate. Moves then followed to Lincoln City (on-loan), Notts County after a £140,000 transfer, where he won a Division Three Championship medal, Scunthorpe United (on-loan) and he then became Hartlepool United's record signing after a £60,000 fee was paid for him. Gary finally had a spell at Halifax Town and by the end of his professional career had scored 94 goals in 394 senior League and cup fixtures. Gary then returned to the non-league game with Nuneaton Borough, Hucknall Town, Gainsborough Trinity and Armthorpe Welfare.

George Jones

Seasons Played			
	League	~	34 (2)
	F.A. Cup	~	1 (1)
1922/23-23/24	League Cup	~	1
	Lincs Cup	~	1
	Other	~	4 (1)
	Total	~	41 (4)

Born 30/11/1896 at Carlton. Half-Back who had also played for Nottingham Forest and Mansfield Town, gaining a total of 41 senior appearances. George made his Grantham debut at the start of the 1922/23 season, but had to wait until the following February to score his first goal for the club in the Grantham Hospital Cup tie against A&J Shaw. He continued to play in many games the following season, although his final appearance is not known.

Glyn Jones

Seasons Played			
	League	~	2 (1)
	F.A. Cup	~	1 (2)
1965/66	Total	~	3 (3)

Born 08/04/1936 at Rotherham. Former England Youth International who made over 100 appearances whilst at Sheffield United, Rotherham United and Mansfield Town. Following a spell with Cheltenham Town, he first played for Grantham in the September 1965 Midland League fixture against Skegness Town and scored twice against the same team three weeks later in the FA Cup. Glyn scored once again for Grantham in his final appearance the following week at home to Spalding United.

Kris Jones

Seasons Played			
	League	~	
	F.A. Cup	~	
1997/98	F.A. Trophy	~	
	League Cup	~	1
	Lincs Cup	~	
	Total	~	1

Born 28/12/1980 at Wisbech. Former Wales U-17 International player, previously with Wisbech Town, King's Lynn, Kettering Town, Bourne Town and Sleaford Town. He made only one appearance for The Gingerbreads though, in the November 1997 Dr Marten's League Cup tie at Wisbech Town. Kris went back to Sleaford Town, then transferred to Bourne Town, Spalding United, Harrowby United, before signing for Shepshed Dynamo at the end of 2003 and then returning to Bourne Town.

Mike Jones

Seasons Played			
	League	~	1
	F.A. Cup	~	
1985/86	F.A. Trophy	~	
	League Cup	~	1
	Lincs Cup	~	2
	Total	~	4

Former England U-19 player and Apprentice at Sheffield United who after a spell in Finland, (which had seen him play for the National FA in a representative game), returned to England where he made appearances for Kiveton Park. He made his debut for Grantham in the opening County Cup tie of the 1985/86 season against Boston United, but less than a month later had played his final game, at Corby Town in the Bill Dellow League Cup, and moved to Spalding United.

Thomas Jones

Seasons Played			
	League	~	3
	F.A. Cup	~	1 (2)
1919/20	Lincs Cup	~	2
	Total	~	6 (2)

Born 1884 at Aberaman, Glamorgan. A former Welsh International who gained one cap in the match against Ireland in 1908 and had previously played for Aberaman Athletic, Aberdare Town, playing in their Welsh Cup runners-up sides, Nottingham Forest, earning two appearances, before a return to Aberdare. Tom was naturally a left-sided player and the star of the Welsh valleys in the early part of the 20th. century, being described by one local reporter as a "brilliant runner and tricky dribbler". At the end of his playing career he came to Grantham and although some of his appearances came via defensive positions, he also played up front for the club and consequentially scored twice on his debut in the October 1919 FA Cup encounter at home to Sutton Town. He played in the following five games, but left the club after the league match at Hucknall Byron just over a month after his debut. In the Summer of 1923 he became Secretary/Manager at Merthyr Town, who at that time were in Division Three (South) of the Football League, and then scouted for Cardiff City up to the end of the decade. Tom was also a qualified solicitor, spent time as secretary of Aberdare Town and was Vice-President of the FA of Wales. Died 1958 at Porthcawl, Glamorgan.

Jones

Seasons Played			
	F.A. Cup	~	
	Lincs Cup	~	1
1886/87	Other	~	
	Total	~	1

Played only one game for Grantham in the 1887 New Year's Day County Cup tie held at Market Rasen Town.

Jones

Seasons Played			
	League	~	10 (2)
	Lincs Cup	~	1 (1)
1904/05-05/06	Other	~	
1907/08	Total	~	11 (3)

Prominent member of the first Grantham team after the club reformed, scoring his initial goal in the November 1904 County tie against Hornsby Engineers. He played for two consecutive seasons and may have also appeared in the 1906/07 season as there are very few team-sheets available for this period. Because of this, his final appearance cannot be detected, but he was certainly evident in Spring 1908 matches.

Jorden

Seasons Played			
	League	~	1
	F.A. Cup	~	
1929/30	Lincs Cup	~	
	Other	~	
	Total	~	1

Former Bulwell player who made just one appearance for Grantham, although details of the particular game are not known.

George Jowett

Seasons Played			
	League	~	362 (26)
	F.A. Cup	~	26 (1)
1957/58-67/68	League Cup	~	3
	Lincs Cup	~	11 (1)
	Total	~	402 (28)

Born 1937 at Rotherham. Signed from Denaby United and played one game for Grantham in the 1957/58 season, the 7-0 defeat at Wisbech Town on Christmas Day, but following his next game at Stockton the following October, which marked his first time on the score-sheet, George became a near ever present member of the team for the next decade. Whilst Grantham were playing in the Central Alliance (South) League, he made appearances in the County Cup victories over Gainsborough Trinity and Boston United, as well as the FA Cup First Round at Brierley Hill Alliance. As Grantham returned to the Midland League he managed to play for the second season running in every single match, an achievement which was matched in the 1963/64 campaign, but obviously with the reward of a League Championship medal at the end of it. At the end of the following season, in May 1965, George was awarded a joint Testimonial along with Tony Farmer, as a combined Peterborough United and Notts County team defeated Grantham in an entertaining 7-3 match at London Road. After the Summer break the highlights continued as the FA Cup brought games against Hendon and Swindon Town for George and this trend continued for his final two seasons at London Road as he played in FA Cup Proper matches against Wimbledon, Oldham Athletic and Altrincham. He scored his last goal for the club in the March 1968 league game at Alfreton Town, a few weeks before his final appearance in the closing fixture of the 1967/68 season at Lockheed Leamington. Since that first full season back in 1958/59, George had missed only nine games in all competitions during the subsequent ten years. He went on to manage Kiveton Park FC, run a public house in Rotherham and also became a successful race horse owner. Died in 2002.

Tony Joynes

Seasons Played			
	League	~	3
	F.A. Cup	~	1
1988/89-89/90	F.A. Trophy	~	
	League Cup	~	1
	Lincs Cup	~	
	Total	~	5

Born 1970 at Ashton-under-Lyne. Won a Midland Regional Alliance League winners medal at the age of 16 whilst with the Reserves and progressed into the First team the following season. His first game came in the opening league fixture of the 1988/89 season at Halesowen Town, but he was awarded only three more appearances that season, whilst a lone game in the League Cup match against Nuneaton Borough in October 1990 was his last for the club. Tony had a spell on-loan to Bourne Town, but nothing is known of him after that.

Jubb

Seasons Played			
	League	~	1 (1)
	Lincs Cup	~	
1931/32	Other	~	
	Total	~	1 (1)

Played and scored in one game for Grantham, although unfortunately details of the actual match are not known.

A. Julian

Seasons Played			
	League	~	2
	F.A. Cup	~	
1937/38	Lincs Cup	~	
	Other	~	
	Total	~	2

Born circa 1919. 18 year old Army Serviceman who was based near to the town and played in the Midland League games against the Reserve sides of Doncaster Rovers at the end of March 1938 and Grimsby Town just over a week later.

Steve Julian

Seasons Played			
	League	~	21
	F.A. Cup	~	
2004/05	F.A. Trophy	~	
	League Cup	~	
	Lincs Cup	~	2
	Total	~	23

Born 23/05/1983 at Kettering. Began his career at Corby Town, making his First team debut at the age of 16, before joining Oadby Town, helping to the FA Vase semi-final. In the Summer of 2003 he rejoined Corby and later followed his Manager, Lee Glover, to Grantham, making his debut in the December 2004 Southern League fixture at Hednesford Town. Steve has consistently played in the side since, including the April 2005 Lincolnshire Shield Final victory over Gainsborough Trinity, and remains with the club.

Gordon Kaile

Seasons Played			
	League	~	3
	F.A. Cup	~	
1956/57	Lincs Cup	~	
	Total	~	3

Born 07/12/1924 at Blandford Camp. Previously made appearances for RAOC Chilwell, Nottingham Forest, scoring nine times in his 66 games, Preston North End, (where he deputised for Tom Finney), and Exeter City, before becoming Player/Coach at St Luke's College. He played on the wing for Grantham in the first three games of the 1956/57 season at Scarborough, Frickley Colliery and Wisbech Town. Died 1988 in North Dorset.

Archie Kean

Seasons Played			
	League	~	1 (2)
	F.A. Cup	~	
1925/26	Lincs Cup	~	
	Total	~	1 (2)

Born 30/09/1895 at Parkhead. Centre-Forward who began his career with local sides Parkhead and Croy Celtic, before making a total of 87 Football League appearances at Clapton Orient, Lincoln City and Blackburn Rovers, scoring 11 goals, all of which came during his spell at Sincil Bank. Data exists to show only one definite game that he played in for Grantham though, scoring twice in the 4-2 defeat of Alfreton Town towards the end of September 1925. This game came a few days after the original league fixture had been abandoned with the score-line at 1-1. His surname is sometimes spelt 'Keen'.

Jamie Kearns

Seasons Played			
	League	~	32 (1)
	F.A. Cup	~	4
2003/04	F.A. Trophy	~	1
	League Cup	~	1
	Lincs Cup	~	3 (1)
	Total	~	41 (2)

Born 1980 at Northampton. Began his career as a YTS player at Aston Villa, playing with future England stars Darius Vassell and Gareth Barry, followed by Northampton Town as a Trainee. Jamie was released to Reading on-loan and then made appearances for Raunds Town, Tamworth, Paget Rangers, Gainsborough Trinity, Rothwell Town and Cambridge City, before returning to Rothwell. He made his debut for Grantham in the club's inaugural Lincolnshire Shield tie against Stamford Town at the beginning of the 2003/04 season. Jamie scored his first goal for the club in the following round at Spalding United and a few weeks later played in the FA Cup First Round game at home to Leyton Orient. His other goal came in the New Year victory over Crawley Town, with an appearance for him in the County Shield Final victory at home to Gainsborough Trinity, shortly before his final game in April 2004 against Stafford Rangers. Jamie went on to join Kettering Town in the Summer, but his spell there lasted only a couple of months.

Harry Keeling

Seasons Played			
	League	~	1 (1)
	F.A. Cup	~	
1925/26	Lincs Cup	~	
	Total	~	1 (1)

Born 10/02/1906 at Huthwaite. Inside-Left player who had previously spent time at Sutton Town, Mansfield Town and scored for Grantham in the December 1925 victory over Denaby United. Harry went on to play for Luton Town, Wolverhampton Wanderers and Notts County, although each time he failed to break into the First team. He finally made his Football League debut in the 1929/30 season at Torquay United and then moved to Swindon Town, Norwich City, a return to Mansfield Town, who by then had been elected to Division Three (South), Bath City, Hereford United, Tamworth, Brierley Hill Alliance and Hereford once more. Harry finished his playing career with a total of 18 goals scored in 63 Football League appearances. In 1995 he was known to be retired and living in Weston-Super-Mare.

Walter Keeton

Seasons Played			
	League	~	151 (57)
1926/27-30/31	F.A. Cup	~	13 (4)
	Lincs Cup	~	6 (8)
	Other	~	5 (6)
1933/34	Total	~	175 (75)

Born 30/04/1905 at Shirebrook. Made his Grantham debut in the February 1927 Midland League game at home to Alfreton Town and scored his first goal for the club the following week against his home team, Shirebrook. Near the end of that season Walter netted his first hat-trick as Grantham demolished St John's 12-0 in the local Charity Cup Final. Needless to say, by the start of the following season Walter's name was one of the first to go down on the team-sheet and in November 1928 he appeared in the FA Cup First Round tie against Rhyl Athletic and the next round at Wigan Borough. Although he was certainly scoring some tremendous goals, it wasn't until the end of the 1929/30 season that he managed to finally catch up with the club's centre-forward, James Sullivan, as they both finished joint highest scorers. After only nine appearances at the start of the 1930/31 season he was transferred to Sunderland in the First Division for a fee of around £450, before moving on to Nottingham Forest two years later and then returning to Sunderland, finishing with only one goal in a total of 17 Football League appearances. He came back to Grantham during the 1933/34 season and although no details are available to indicate his final appearance, he was still scoring up to the March 1934 Central Combination fixture at home to Matlock Town. After a disappointing campaign which saw the club finish next to bottom in the league, he received high praise in the end of season round-up in the *Grantham Journal*. "Walter Keeton was easily the most capable player in the Grantham side. It was no fault of his that the team so regularly went down". He also made appearances for Mansfield Colliery, Mansfield Shoe Co, Watford Reserves, Notts County Reserves and Loughborough Corinthians during his footballing career. However, he was also a first class cricketer and set a batting record for Nottinghamshire CCC that still stands today of 312 N.O. against Middlesex. Walter was also awarded two England caps after playing Test Matches in 1934 against Australia and 1939 versus the West Indies and was the Wisden Cricketer of the Year in 1940. Died 10/10/1980 at Forest Town, Nottinghamshire.

Kelk

Seasons Played			
	League	~	3 (1)
	F.A. Cup	~	1
1933/34	Lincs Cup	~	
	Other	~	
	Total	~	4 (1)

Born circa 1916. Inside-left player who was only 17 years old when he scored on his Grantham debut in the September 1933 league fixture at home to Loughborough Corinthians. His final appearance came the following month, most likely in the game against Heanor Town.

Chris Kelly

Seasons Played			
	League	~	1
	F.A. Cup	~	1
1987/88	F.A. Trophy	~	
	League Cup	~	
	Lincs Cup	~	
	Total	~	2

Born 06/11/1962 at Glasgow. Reserves player who turned out for the First team in the August 1987 league fixture against Rushden Town and the FA Cup replay defeat at Chatteris Town a couple of days later. After being released by Grantham, he moved to Mirlees Blackstone, but a back injury forced an early retirement from the game. Chris still lives in Grantham and works as a self-employed tiler.

Jim Kelly

Seasons Played			
	League	~	5 (5)
	F.A. Cup	~	3
1963/64	Lincs Cup	~	
	Total	~	8 (5)

Former Preston North End player who scored twice on his Grantham debut at Boston United in August 1963 and then played in the following seven matches for Grantham. After the FA Cup tie at home to Stamford, Bill Hill took his place and Jim failed to make another appearance.

Haydn Kemp

Seasons Played			
	League	~	41 (2)
	F.A. Cup	~	4 (2)
1932/33	Lincs Cup	~	1
	Other	~	1
	Total	~	47 (4)

Born 17/01/1897 at Mosborough, near Sheffield. 'Hady' began his career at New Bolsover Wesleyans, Staveley West End, Anston United, Bolsover Colliery, Bolsover Town and Chesterfield Municipal, before having ten successful years at Notts County, where he scored 6 goals in 286 appearances. In 1931/32 he played for the ill-fated Thames side that was relegated out of The Football League, scoring two goals in 28 games. Haydn then joined Grantham in the Summer of 1932 and missed only a handful of that season's games, scoring his first goal for the club in the 8-1 thrashing of Sutton Junction in the FA Cup. No details are known as to the end of his Grantham career, but by December 1933 he had joined Heanor Town and two years later he was Club Captain. After the end of his playing days, Haydn returned to Meadow Lane where he scouted for the club. Died 01/04/1982 at Nottingham.

Alan Kennedy

Seasons Played			
	League	~	3
	F.A. Cup	~	
1987/88	F.A. Trophy	~	
	League Cup	~	
	Lincs Cup	~	
	Total	~	3

Born 31/08/1954 at Sunderland. Started his career at Newcastle United, playing in the 1974 FA Cup Final and 1976 League Cup Final, before moving to Liverpool where he became a major player in one of the games great sides and also earned his nick-name of 'Barney Rubble'. He was part of the European Cup winning sides of 1981 and 1984 and remains the only British player to score two winning goals in the Final of that competition. His domestic honours include five First Division Championship medals and four for successes in the League Cup, all during his time at Anfield which finally finished after 359 appearances. He also won two England caps during that time, against Northern Ireland and Wales in the 1983/84 Home Internationals Championship. Transfers then followed to Sunderland, Ashington, Huskvana of Sweden, Beerschot in Belgium, Denmark's Club 1903, before returning to England with Hartlepool. He was brought to Grantham by Martin O'Neill for three games during December 1987, against Dudley Town, Rushden Town and Banbury United. Alan then spent a brief time at Northwich Victoria, before returning to The Football League with Wigan Athletic, followed by moves to Colne Dynamoes and Wrexham. This would be Alan's final spell in the League and at the end, he had scored 26 goals in 506 appearances, plus netted five more strikes in 185 various cup games. But this wasn't the end of his playing career and periods then followed with Morecambe, Netherfield, where he was the club's Player/Manager, Radcliffe Borough and Barrow. Alan currently runs a corporate entertainment company, is an accomplished after-dinner speaker and conducts his own radio programme.

Charles Kennedy

Seasons Played			
	League	~	26 (3)
	F.A. Cup	~	1
1958/59	Lincs Cup	~	1
	Total	~	28 (3)

Made his Grantham debut in the opening game of the 1958/59 season at home to Goole Town and scored twice in the league match against Sutton Town and once in the home game against Denaby United. Charles played in about half of the season's fixtures, until his final appearance in the closing game at Ashington.

Tony Kenworthy

Born 30/10/1958 at Leeds. Former England Youth International, who had twelve seasons with Sheffield United, making a total of 286 appearances which saw a Division Four Championship in 1982 and a Division Three promotion two years later. In 1986 he moved to Mansfield Town to help secure their own promotion into the Third Division, whilst a year later he scored the winning penalty for The Stags in the Freight Rover Trophy Final at Wembley. He then had trials with Huddersfield Town and Chesterfield, before dropping into the non-league game with Ashfield United and Oakham United. After a spell coaching at Darlington, Tony was brought to Grantham by Antrac in the Summer of 1998 as the club's Chief Scout, but within a few weeks he was promoted into the manager's seat at the expense of Danny Begara. Results failed to turn around though, apart from an FA Cup run which saw Grantham falter at the final qualifying hurdle against Tamworth. The final ten games of the season even finished with Grantham failing to win a single game and the club worryingly finished only two points off the relegation zone. It was no surprise when the 1999/00 season began without Tony at the helm, when he was replaced by Dave Gilbert. At present he works for the company responsible for collating the Carling Opta stastical information on Premiership games.

Jock Kerr

Seasons Played			
	League	~	2
	F.A. Cup	~	
1952/53-53/54	Lincs Cup	~	
	Total	~	2

Goalkeeper who played in the November 1952 league game at Boston United and the April 1954 match against York City Reserves, both times when Ron Hewitt was unavailable. He let in six goals during those two games but still ended up on the winning side after the Lincolnshire derby.

Barry Kershaw

Seasons Played			
	League	~	2
	F.A. Cup	~	
1969/70	F.A. Trophy	~	
	League Cup	~	
	Lincs Cup	~	
	Other	~	
	Total	~	2

Born 15/11/1943 at Rochdale. Previously played for Grantham St Anne's and St John's, before coming to London Road. Barry made First team appearances in the games against Worksop Town and Alfreton Town in the Spring of 1970 and in a season which saw Grantham finish in the runners-up spot in the league, was unlucky to have to play in two games that the team lost. He went on to play for Woolsthorpe, before switching sports and joining the Kesteven Rugby Club. He is now semi-retired and still lives in the Grantham area.

Kershaw

Seasons Played			
	Other	~	1
1875/76	Total	~	1

Made just one appearance for Grantham in the November 1875 friendly against the Third Lincolnshire Volunteer Rifles.

Kettle

Seasons Played			
	League	~	2
	F.A. Cup	~	
1930/31	Lincs Cup	~	
	Total	~	2

Former Grimsby Haycroft Rovers player who made just two appearances for Grantham, although details on those games are not available.

Kettleborough

Seasons Played			
	F.A. Cup	~	
	Lincs Cup	~	
1886/87	Other	~	3 (1)
	Total	~	3 (1)

Scored on his debut, the first friendly of the 1886/87 season at home to Grantham Volunteers and then went on to play in games against Boston and finally a repeat match against The Volunteers the following January.

Kew

Seasons Played			
	League	~	
	Lincs Cup	~	
1894/95	Other	~	1
	Total	~	1

According to available records, only played in the local Charity Cup tie against Grantham Rovers in January 1895.

Kilgallon

Seasons Played			
	League	~	7 (2)
	F.A. Cup	~	2
1933/34	Lincs Cup	~	1
	Other	~	1
	Total	~	11 (2)

Centre-Forward who also played for Stockport County and scored on his Grantham debut against Bolsover in September 1933. However, he seems to have left the club by the New Year, possibly with the league match against Chesterfield 'A' being his final appearance.

Ian Kilgour

Seasons Played			
	League	~	12 (1)
	F.A. Cup	~	
1992/93	F.A. Trophy	~	
	League Cup	~	
	Lincs Cup	~	
	Total	~	12 (1)

Former Stamford Town player who joined Grantham for the January 1993 league match at Bedworth United after the departure of many of the players due to financial constraints. He scored in the March fixture at home to Nuneaton Borough and played in most of the games after that, up to the April match against Stourbridge.

Alec King

Seasons Played			
	League	~	10
	F.A. Cup	~	
1964/65	Total	~	10

Born 18/02/1942 in Rhodesia. Started his career on the books at Peterborough United, before joining Grantham St John's. Alec first played for The Gingerbreads in the October 1964 Midland League fixture at Goole Town and then completed his Grantham career in two short spells, culminating in the April 1965 game at Long Eaton. Following a spell playing in Canada for Vancouver, he returned to London Road, although his appearances were limited to those in the Reserves side, and he finished his career with Great Gonerby. Alec still lives in the area and is now retired, having worked as a National Account Manager.

Cecil King

Seasons Played			
	League	~	4
	F.A. Cup	~	
1931/32-32/33	Lincs Cup	~	
	Other	~	
	Total	~	4

Born 04/04/1908 in Grantham. 'Cis', as he was better known, was a local player who had also turned out for Grantham Amateurs, but no information is available on the games that he played in for our club. Died April 1997 in Grantham.

Dave King

Seasons Played			
	League	~	49 (28)
	F.A. Cup	~	2
1996/97-97/98	F.A. Trophy	~	8 (3)
	League Cup	~	4 (2)
	Lincs Cup	~	2
	Total	~	65 (33)

Previously played for Gresley Rovers, Heanor Town, Sutton Town, Ilkeston Town, Sandiacre Town, Shepshed Albion, Rochester and Shepshed Dynamo. He made his debut for Grantham in the March 1997 league fixture at home to Tamworth and scored a brace in the following game against Moor Green. He almost immediately formed a deadly strike partnership with Dave Taylor, originally an on-loan player from Ilkeston Town, and the success continued the following season as Grantham headed the league table from start to finish. Dave also scored the winner in the FA Trophy tie at Bath City, the first goal in the 2-1 victory at home to Hednesford Town in the following round and the consolation goal at Southport in the quarter-finals. He came on as substitute in the season's closing fixture at home to Stourbridge, as Grantham secured the draw for the League Championship, but this was to be his final appearance for the club. He went on to play for Hinckley United and then returned to Gresley Rovers. Dave became the joint manager of Long Eaton United in the Summer of 2002, but two years later moved on to Gedling Town, although that position lasted only a matter of weeks.

Mike King

Seasons Played	League	~	1
	F.A. Cup	~	
1960/61	League Cup	~	
	Lincs Cup	~	
	Total	~	1

Defender who made only one appearance for the club in the January 1961 league match at home to Potton United.

Simon King

Seasons Played	League	~	4 (1)
	F.A. Cup	~	
1986/87-87/88	F.A. Trophy	~	
	League Cup	~	
	Lincs Cup	~	1
	Total	~	5 (1)

Played Youth football for Borussia Moenchengladbach in Germany and then made appearances for Lincoln United and Grantham United, before progressing through the Reserves. His First team debut came at the end of March 1987 against Hednesford Town, with his only goal for the club coming days later as Grantham defeated Bilston Town. However, Simon was awarded only two more appearances that season and his final game came in the August 1987 County Cup defeat against Boston United. After departing London Road, he went on to play for Harrowby United.

Alex Kirby

Seasons Played	League	~	3
	F.A. Cup	~	
1999/00-00/01	F.A. Trophy	~	
	League Cup	~	1
	Lincs Cup	~	
	Total	~	4

Reserves team full-back who played in the January 2000 Dr Marten's League Cup tie at King's Lynn and three league fixtures during the 2000/01 season, the last of which was at home to Baldock Town in March. No details are known on immediate following clubs, but Alex signed for Long Eaton United at the start of the 2004/05 season.

Jack Kirk

Seasons Played	League	~	18 (1)
	F.A. Cup	~	1
1955/56	Lincs Cup	~	1
	Total	~	20 (1)

Right-winger who played in the first three games of the 1955/56 season, beginning with the trip over to Boston United. Jack then played in many of the following games, scoring his only goal for the club against Hull City Reserves, until his final appearance the following March in the County Cup tie, coincidentally once again at Boston United.

William Kirk

Seasons Played	League	~	44 (11)
	F.A. Cup	~	5
1932/33	Lincs Cup	~	2
	Other	~	1 (1)
	Total	~	52 (12)

Born 1914 in Grantham. Former Caythorpe and Lincoln City Reserves player who made his Grantham debut in the first match of the 1932/33 season at Scarborough and went on to play in every game of that campaign, scoring his first goal for the club in the September Midland League defeat at home to Loughborough Corinthians. He also scored Grantham's only goal during the famous friendly against Arsenal in March 1933, which ended in a 4-1 defeat for the hosts. The following season he joined Mansfield Town, scoring once in his eight First team appearances, then Gainsborough Trinity, before moving to West Ham United Reserves, Yeovil & Petters United and Worcester City. Other clubs he spent time at include Grantham Amateurs and the Reserve team of Plymouth Argyle, although at what point in his career is not known. Died January 1991 in Mansfield.

Kirk

Seasons Played	F.A. Cup	~	3
	Other	~	15 (3)
1874/75-78/79	Total	~	18 (3)

Scored on his debut in the November 1874 friendly at home to Peterborough, but went on to play only once more during that season for Grantham. He became more evident in the side over the next couple of years and played in Grantham's first ever FA Cup tie when Clapham Rovers came to London Road in October 1877. He made his final appearance for Grantham a year later, in the same competition, in the First Round replay at home to Sheffield.

Kirk

Seasons Played	F.A. Cup	~	
	Lincs Cup	~	
1887/88	Other	~	1
	Total	~	1

Played in goal during the 3-0 friendly defeat at home to Notts Jardine in March 1888.

Kirk

Seasons Played	League	~	6 (3)
	F.A. Cup	~	
1945/46	Lincs Cup	~	
	Total	~	6 (3)

First played for Grantham in the December 1945 league game at home to Grimsby Town Reserves and scored his initial goal just over a week later in the 5-1 defeat of Ollerton Colliery. He also scored in his next two games, but had to wait until March before he made his final appearance, against Rotherham United Reserves.

Peter Kirkham

Seasons Played	League	~	19
	F.A. Cup	~	
1998/99	F.A. Trophy	~	
	League Cup	~	3
	Lincs Cup	~	
	Total	~	22

Born 28/10/74 at Newcastle. Began his career as a Trainee at Newcastle United, but made his Football League debut after moving to Darlington. He then joined Gretna, Blyth Spartans and South Shields, before returning to Darlington and then signing for Grantham. He made his debut for The Gingerbreads in the November 1998 league trip down to Salisbury City, but by the end of that campaign many of Peter's appearances were coming from the bench, although his last game, in the closing fixture at Weymouth, saw him start the match. By the beginning of the following season, he had returned to the North-East to play for Chester-le-Street, followed by time at Dunstan FB, Jarrow, Hebburn, Consett and Whitby Bay.

Kirrage

Seasons Played	League	~	1
	F.A. Cup	~	
1920/21	Lincs Cup	~	
	Other	~	
	Total	~	1

Midfielder who also played for the Reserves side and Newark Athletic, but has only one known appearance for the First team in the March 1921 league game against Leicester City Reserves. Could possibly be Frank Kirrage (born 03/03/1893 at Bromley) who played for Nottingham Forest and Ilkeston United just after The First World War.

Kneightley

Seasons Played	League	~	1
	F.A. Cup	~	
1919/20	Lincs Cup	~	1
	Total	~	2

Half-Back who made several appearances for the Reserves side as well as Grantham St John's and played in the November 1919 Central Alliance fixture at Ilkeston United and the County Cup tie two weeks later at Boston.

Ian Knight

Seasons Played	League	~	12 (2)
	F.A. Cup	~	3 (1)
1993/94	F.A. Trophy	~	3
	League Cup	~	2
	Lincs Cup	~	2
	Total	~	22 (3)

Born 26/10/1966 at Hartlepool. Former England Under-21 International who had previously played for Barnsley, Sheffield Wednesday, Scunthorpe United, Grimsby Town and Boston United, with a total of two goals in 45 Football League appearances to his name. He joined Grantham at the start of the 1993/94 season, making his debut in the County Cup victory at Lincoln City and scored his first goal for the club at the end of September in the FA Cup replay at home to Telford United. Ian played in many of the games in the first half of that season, but the league defeat at King's Lynn just after Christmas proved to be his final appearance. Little is known of his subsequent clubs, but he later became Director of Youth Football at Grimsby Town.

Charles Knott

Seasons Played	League	~	8 (5)
	F.A. Cup	~	1
1920/21	Lincs Cup	~	3 (8)
	Other	~	
1922/23	Total	~	12 (13)

Born 1899 at Billinghay. Former Billinghay midfielder who made his Grantham debut in the October 1920 league game against Sutton Junction and scored his first goal for the club a month later in the first round of the Lincolnshire Senior Cup at Stamford Town. In the following round at home to Ruston & Hornsby's (Lincoln) he managed to score an incredible seven times in the 10-1 annihilation, but for some reason appeared to play only infrequently after that. He returned to the club to make his final appearance in the January 1923 Central Alliance fixture at Welbeck Colliery.

W. Lacey

Seasons Played	League	~	28 (4)
	F.A. Cup	~	2
1920/21-21/22	League Cup	~	1
1923/24	Lincs Cup	~	2 (1)
1925/26	Other	~	2
	Total	~	35 (5)

Midfielder who had previously played for Basford United and whose first known appearance for Grantham came in the December 1920 game against Chesterfield Reserves, with his initial goal the following February at home to Hucknall Byron. He played in the majority of the following season's games and once again in the 1923/24 season. Although his last appearance is not known, evidence shows that he scored his final two goals for the club in the October 1925 defeat at home to Mansfield Town.

Martyn Lakin

Seasons Played	League	~	1
	F.A. Cup	~	
1995/96	F.A. Trophy	~	
	League Cup	~	
	Lincs Cup	~	1
	Total	~	2

Born 25/08/1973 at Sheffield. Goalkeeper who started out on the books at Sheffield United and Huddersfield Town, also playing for the British Colleges representative side and taking part in the World Student Games held at his home city. Appearances then followed for Spalding United, Boston United, Alfreton Town, Maltby Miners Welfare and Ashfield United, before turning out for Grantham. He made only two appearances though for The Gingerbreads, as cover for Scott Drury in the August 1995 County Cup tie at Lincoln City and the league fixture at home to Nuneaton Borough the following month. He went on to play for Pershore Town, Cheltenham Town, Moor Green, Evesham United, Studley BKL, Boston Town, Holbeach United, Yaxley and Bourne Town, but is currently goalkeeping coach for Boston United's Youth team.

Ray Lambert

Seasons Played	League	~	3
	F.A. Cup	~	
1945/46	Lincs Cup	~	
	Total	~	3

Born 18/07/1922 at Bagillt, Flintshire. At the time of his appearances for Grantham, Ray was also a contemporary Liverpool defender. Arriving at London Road on-loan, he played in the final three games of the 1945/46 season, both the fixtures against Frickley Colliery and the closing game at Rotherham United Reserves. Ray went on to become one of Anfield's greats over the next few years, playing a senior role in the club's 1946/47 Division One Championship win, appeared in the 1950 FA Cup Final against Arsenal at Wembley and won five International caps for Wales. He retired from the game in 1956 having spent all of his professional career at Liverpool, accumulating 341 appearances.

Lane

Seasons Played	F.A. Cup	~	2 (1)
	Lincs Cup	~	3 (1)
1886/87-87/88	Other	~	14 (1)
	Total	~	19 (3)

Initially played for Grantham in the penultimate friendly of the 1886/87 season against Lincoln Lindum and then scored his first goal for the club in the final game, a 3-2 victory over Derby County. He continued to play in many games after the Summer break, right up until his last match in February 1888 at home to Notts County Reserves.

Lane

Seasons Played	League	~	5
	F.A. Cup	~	2 (2)
1921/22	League Cup	~	
	Lincs Cup	~	
1923/24	Other	~	
	Total	~	7 (2)

First scored for the club in September 1921 after Grantham travelled over to Shirebrook for an FA Cup tie and then played a handful of games both that season and in the 1923/24 one as well, with his last known appearance coming in the April 1924 game at Coalville Swifts.

Large

Seasons Played	F.A. Cup	~	
	Other	~	3
1877/78	Total	~	3

Played in three games during the Winter of 1877/78 against Sleaford, Stamford and Retford Rovers.

Guy Last

Seasons Played	League	~	5
	F.A. Cup	~	
2002/03	F.A. Trophy	~	
	League Cup	~	
	Lincs Cup	~	1
	Total	~	6

Born 1984 at Rhuddlan, North Wales. Midfielder and former Welsh U-19 International who was released by Peterborough United after having trials with Southend United. He made his debut for Grantham in the April 2003 league fixture at home to Tiverton Town and played in most of the remaining games over the next month, albeit with many of the appearances starting from the bench. Guy played in the Lincolnshire County Senior Cup Final against Gainsborough Trinity, but this turned out to be his final game for the club and he moved to Cirencester Town in October 2003 without playing again for the First team. However, his spell there was short and after touring Australia Guy returned home, then joined Deeping Rangers, although recently he has had trials with Sheffield United.

Latter

Seasons Played	F.A. Cup	~	
	Lincs Cup	~	
1887/88	Other	~	3
1889/90	Total	~	3

Goalkeeper who covered for Jack Broadbent when he was unavailable for the games against Gainsborough Trinity in

December 1887, Rotherham Town during March 1888 and finally the friendly at home to Newark in January 1890. Unfortunately all three times he ended up on the losing side.

Lavis

Seasons Played			
	League	~	4 (3)
	Lincs Cup	~	1
1893/94-94/95	Other	~	2
	Total	~	7 (3)

Forward, whose surname is sometimes spelt 'Larvis', who played in the Grantham Minor Cup Final in April 1894 and many of the Grantham League fixtures the following season, scoring goals against Spittlegate Victoria and twice at home to Grantham Rovers Colts in December 1894.

Law

Seasons Played			
	League	~	1
	F.A. Cup	~	
1929/30	Lincs Cup	~	
	Other	~	
	Total	~	1

Made just one appearance for Grantham during the 1929/30 season, although it is not known during which actual game.

Seamus Lawless

Seasons Played			
	League	~	1
	F.A. Cup	~	
2002/03	F.A. Trophy	~	
	League Cup	~	
	Lincs Cup	~	
	Total	~	1

Former Lincoln United goalkeeper who signed for The Gingerbreads during the 2000/01 season, but following games back at Lincoln and also with Brigg Town, made his Grantham First team debut in April 2003 when he replaced the suspended Mario Ziccardi for the match at Worcester City. He was released by the club soon after this and returned to Lincoln United and later Brigg Town. Seamus still lives in the Lincoln area, working in the building industry, but is hopeful of starting a football management career in the near future.

Eddie Lawrence

Seasons Played			
	League	~	68
	F.A. Cup	~	2
1946/47-48/49	Lincs Cup	~	3
	Total	~	73

Born 24/08/1907 at Cefn Mawr, Wales. Experienced player who began his career with Cefn Druids, before transfers to Wrexham, Clapton Orient, Notts County, Bournemouth & Boscombe Athletic and then a return to Clapton. He finished his professional career in 1938 having scored four goals in 319 Football League appearances and was also awarded two Welsh International caps against Ireland in 1930 and Scotland in 1932, plus was part of the Welsh FA's representative side that toured Canada in 1929. His career continued in Nottingham with Players Athletic, although he returned to Meadow Lane around the outbreak of The War to play in club friendlies. Eddie made his debut for Grantham in the opening match of the 1946/47 season at Lincoln City Reserves and then played in nearly all of that year's games, including both the Lincolnshire Senior Cup Final against Gainsborough Trinity and the replay. The following seasons though, he only played in about half of the matches and missed out on the FA Cup First Round game at Stockton after suffering a suspected fractured skull in the game against Nottingham Forest Reserves. Eddie made his final appearances in the Christmas 1948 fixtures against Ransome & Marles. Died 20/07/1989 at Nottingham.

Sid Lawrence

Seasons Played			
	League	~	26 (8)
	F.A. Cup	~	
1958/59-60/61	League Cup	~	2
	Lincs Cup	~	3 (2)
	Total	~	31 (10)

Born 15/12/1939 in Grantham. Previously spent time at Mansfield Town, with a trial at Blackpool before he joined his home club. Sid started his Grantham First team career with three appearances during April 1959 and scored in the first of those against Spennymoor United. The following season he played in several of the matches, but in the 1960/61 campaign he had to wait until February for his first game and then made only one other appearance before his final match in April 1961 against Spalding United. Sid went on to play for Ransome & Marles and he still lives in Grantham, working as a plumber.

George Laxton

Seasons Played			
	League	~	3 (5)
	F.A. Cup	~	
1925/26	Lincs Cup	~	
	Total	~	3 (5)

Born 1896 in Brazil. Centre-Forward who had previously spent time at Netherfield Rangers, Nottingham Forest and then 'Grantham' around the time of The First World War, although this may have been Grantham Avenue. He then moved to Notts County and Norwich City, making 16 appearances during their 1920/21 season, before joining Bohemians. He returned to the town a few years later and scored for Grantham in the games against Boston and Sutton Town during the 1925/26 season and netted a hat-trick in the April 1926 fixture against Long Eaton at London Road. Died 1961.

Layton

Seasons Played			
	Other	~	1
1874/75	Total	~	1

Played only once for Grantham, in the March 1875 friendly at Burghley Park. Of course at this time, as well as Association Rules, Rugby Union rules were sometimes played. But in this game it was worryingly played under "Own Rules"!

Dave Leadbeater

Seasons Played			
	League	~	179 (77)
	F.A. Cup	~	13 (5)
1980/81-84/85	F.A. Trophy	~	12 (4)
	League Cup	~	13 (3)
	Lincs Cup	~	10 (6)
	Other	~	7 (5)
	Total	~	234 (100)

Born 22/01/1957 at Barnsley. Nick-named 'Legsy' and a former top-scorer with the Hull City Reserves team who followed new Grantham manager, Geoff Barker, from Bridlington Trinity after a record £2,500 transfer. He made his debut in the opening County Cup game of the 1980/81 season at Boston United and surprisingly had to wait until his fifth match, at Morecambe, to score his first goal. The next few months saw appearances for Dave in the County Cup Final against Lincoln City and against the European Champions in the Redmayne Trophy. He played in every game that year and finished as the club's top scorer, a feat that was equalled over the next three seasons as well. In October 1982 Dave scored the winning goal in the Lincolnshire County Senior Cup Final at Scunthorpe United, whilst the following Saturday he played in the final qualifying round of The FA Cup against Telford United. After the highlight of a fourth place in the league at the end of the 1983/84 season, a year which saw hat-tricks for him in the games against Scunthorpe United and Rhyl, the following campaign was a disappointing one for both the club and Dave. After netting only six strikes in the first few months of the season, he scored his 100th goal in his final game at Runcorn during an FA Trophy replay in January 1985. 'Legsy' went on to play for Alfreton Town, before having a couple of spells at both Ossett Town and North Ferriby United, during the latter time rejoining Geoff Barker. He then moved into management himself on his return to Ossett. Dave currently lives in the Barnsley area and after several years scouting for Middlesbrough, has moved on to work for Crystal Palace.

T. Lee

Seasons Played			
	League	~	5 (2)
	F.A. Cup	~	
1926/27	Lincs Cup	~	
	Other	~	1 (1)
	Total	~	6 (3)

Reserves forward who played in some of the First team fixtures during the latter half of the 1926/27 season, scoring in the games against Long Eaton, Boston and his former club, Shirebrook.

Lee

Seasons Played			
	F.A. Cup	~	2 (1)
	Lincs Cup	~	1
1879/80	Other	~	11 (1)
1883/84-86/87	Total	~	14 (2)

Known to have played in the 1880 New Year's Day friendly against Horbling & District, but there are no further records of appearances until the start of the 1883/84 season. He scored his first goal for the club in the November 1883 FA Cup tie at home to Spilsby, but after the end of that season he seems to have been 'relegated' to friendly games only and played in his last match during November 1886 at Boston.

Lee

Seasons Played			
	League	~	3
	Lincs Cup	~	2
1909/10	Other	~	3
	Total	~	8

First choice goalkeeper during the 1909/10 season who made his debut in the opening Midland Amateur League game at Derby YMCA, but may have missed the final few matches of the season.

Harold Leek

Seasons Played			
	League	~	2
	Lincs Cup	~	
1939/40	Other	~	
	Total	~	2

Defender who played in the difficult last two Midland 'War-Time' League games at Peterborough United and Scunthorpe & Lindsey United. By the early 1950's, Harold was the Landlord at The Barley Mow public house opposite the ground, although it is not known if he held this position during his short playing career with the club.

F. Leeson

Seasons Played			
	League	~	1
	F.A. Cup	~	1
1919/20	Lincs Cup	~	
	Total	~	2

Played twice for Grantham during October 1919, firstly in the home game against Long Eaton and then the FA Cup replay at Boots Athletic. He was also a member of the Reserves side which successfully won the Grantham League Division One that same season.

Pete Lehair

Seasons Played			
	League	~	2
	F.A. Cup	~	
1999/00	F.A. Trophy	~	
	League Cup	~	1
	Lincs Cup	~	
	Total	~	3

Joined Grantham from the RAF, but made just three appearances during December 1999 against Cambridge City in the Dr Marten's League Cup, plus Margate and Ilkeston Town in the league.

Alec Leonce

Seasons Played			
	League	~	15 (5)
	F.A. Cup	~	1
1995/96	F.A. Trophy	~	2 (1)
	League Cup	~	
	Lincs Cup	~	
	Total	~	18 (6)

Born 1962 at Islington. RAF serviceman who had previously played for Elgin City and made his Grantham debut in the September 1995 league game at home to Bilston Town, scoring his first goal for the club the following month at Harrogate Town in the FA Trophy. He then missed only a handful of games until his final appearance in December against Leicester United. Alec is still in the RAF and currently lives in the Oxford area.

Leverton

Seasons Played			
	Lincs Cup	~	
	Other	~	1
1890/91	Total	~	1

Made just one appearance for Grantham in the January 1891 friendly at Langley Mill.

Levesly

Seasons Played			
	Lincs Cup	~	
	Other	~	2
1890/91	Total	~	2

Played in the October 1890 friendly against Nottingham Forest Reserves, but then had to wait until the following March to make his next and ultimately final appearance in the home tie against Notts Olympic in the Newark Charity Cup. Possibly John Levesly (or Lievesley) who was born in Grantham circa 1873.

John Levick

Seasons Played			
	F.A. Cup	~	
	Lincs Cup	~	2
1885/86	Other	~	6
	Total	~	8

Born 1864 at Tuxford. Made his Grantham debut in the November 1885 friendly at Bourne and then played in the next seven matches, with the game against Gainsborough W.M. in the County Cup his last game for the club. John went on to become an inn-keeper in the town. Died December 1902 in Grantham.

Levy

Seasons Played			
	League	~	5 (1)
	F.A. Cup	~	
1934/35	Lincs Cup	~	
	Total	~	5 (1)

Played three games for Grantham in February 1935, beginning with the visit of Boston United and scoring his only goal against Barnsley Reserves in the following fixture. He then made two more consecutive appearances in April, with the Midland League game against Scunthorpe & Lindsey United his final one.

Joe Lewis

Seasons Played			
	League	~	2
	F.A. Cup	~	
1967/68	Total	~	2

Born 14/07/1941 in Grantham. Former Grantham St John's and Grantham Reserves defender who played in the final two matches of the 1967/68 season at Retford Town and Lockheed Leamington. Unluckily for Joe, that first game, a 6-0 loss, was Grantham's worst defeat since the match against Peterborough United in 1958. He later moved on to Boston FC, before returning to Grantham Reserves and finally Harrowby United, where he became Manager there in the mid 1970's. Joe still lives in Grantham and works as a fitter in one of the town's premier engineering companies.

Lewis

Seasons Played			
	League	~	1
	F.A. Cup	~	
1935/36	Lincs Cup	~	
	Other	~	2
	Total	~	3

Centre-Half who also played for Grantham RAF and as far as our team is concerned must have some sort of a record, with only three appearances to his name, two of which were in trophy finals. He played his first match in the April 1936 league game at Mexborough, but then went on to play in the victorious Grantham Hospital Cup and Wilson Cup finals against Doncaster Rovers and a Lincoln League XI respectively.

Ben Lilywhite

Seasons Played			
	League	~	
	F.A. Cup	~	
1996/97	F.A. Trophy	~	2
	League Cup	~	
	Lincs Cup	~	
	Total	~	2

Reserves player who broke through into the First team to play in the two FA Trophy games against Buxton during December 1997, the last game coming off the bench to replace Andy Bullimore.

Lincoln

Seasons Played	F.A. Cup	~	
	Lincs Cup	~	
1888/89-89/90	Other	~	2 (2)
	Total	~	2 (2)

Forward who scored on his debut in the February 1889 friendly against Sphinx and then in his next, and final appearance, in November at home to Notts Amateurs United.

Albert Linnecor

Seasons Played	League	~	70 (10)
	F.A. Cup	~	6
1967/68-68/69	League Cup	~	8
	Lincs Cup	~	2 (1)
	Total	~	86 (11)

Born 30/11/1933 at Birmingham. Former Birmingham City and Lincoln City player who finished his professional career with 300 appearances to his name, the majority of those coming from his eight seasons at Sincil Bank. After a spell with Boston United, he scored on his Grantham debut in the opening match of the 1967/68 season at Belper Town and then went on to play in all but one of that campaign's fixtures. One of the highlights was an FA Cup First Round appearance against Altrincham, but the team went one better the following year, as after defeating Chelmsford City they played Swindon Town in a Second Round tie. Bert's final game for the club was in the second leg of the Midland League Cup Final at Arnold, which earned him another medal to add to those earned in the Football League. He went on to play for Bourne Town, Boston FC, Worksop Town and was then associated for many years with Ruston Sports as both a player and Manager. Bert is now retired though, but still lives in the Lincoln area.

Bert Lister

Seasons Played	League	~	107 (23)
	F.A. Cup	~	11 (1)
1946/47-49/50	Lincs Cup	~	4 (1)
	Total	~	122 (25)

Left-winger with experience at Stoke City and Halifax Town who made his Grantham debut in the opening fixture of the 1946/47 season at Lincoln City Reserves and scored his first two goals for the club a few weeks later in the 6-0 thrashing of Boston United. Bert played in the majority of that season's games, including the County Cup Final against Gainsborough Trinity, whilst after the Summer break he appeared in every round of Grantham's FA Cup run, which saw the 11-1 demolition of Ilkeston Town and the First Round tie at Stockton. Whilst Bert still occupied a secure position within the team during the 1948/49 season, the September 1949 league game in front of 7,000+ Scunthorpe & Lindsey supporters proved to be his final appearance for Grantham and he soon moved on to Peterborough United.

Lister

Seasons Played	F.A. Cup	~	
	Lincs Cup	~	
1887/88	Other	~	1
	Total	~	1

Made just one appearance for Grantham in the February 1888 friendly against Notts Olympic.

John Little

Seasons Played	League	~	73 (1)
	F.A. Cup	~	9
1952/53-57/58	Lincs Cup	~	4
	Total	~	86 (1)

Born 26/08/1932 at Swindon. Former Grantham St Anne's left-back who made his debut in the January 1953 Midland League fixture at Wisbech Town. Over the next two seasons John played in about half of the games for the club, although one of those was the Lincolnshire Senior Cup 'A' Final victory over Gainsborough Trinity. As the seasons passed by though, John's appearances became more infrequent, although he managed to finally get his name on the score-sheet in the February 1955 game against Frickley Colliery. His last appearance came in the April 1958 league fixture at King's Lynn and he went on to spend time at Scunthorpe United and Burnley. Other than football, John also played cricket for Grantham CC, ran a sports shop on London Road and later a model shop in town. He is now retired and still lives in the Grantham area.

Robert Littledyke

Seasons Played	League	~	11 (3)
	F.A. Cup	~	3 (2)
1937/38	Lincs Cup	~	
	Other	~	1
	Total	~	15 (5)

Born 05/07/1913 at Chester-le-Street. Centre-Forward who had previously played for City of Durham, Lincoln City and Mansfield Town, scoring twice in a total of 20 senior appearances whilst in The Football League. Robert first played for Grantham in the opening match of the 1937/38 season at Gainsborough Trinity and scored his initial goal for the club in October when the team travelled up to Scarborough. However, with a formidable forward line-up that helped The Gingerbreads to a runners-up spot in the Midland League, Robert's appearances were scarce. He played his last game in the Stamford Nursing Society Cup at the end of April 1938 and although no details are known as to his following club, he is known to have made guest appearances for Northampton Town during The Second World War.

Derrick Liversidge

Seasons Played	League	~	1
	F.A. Cup	~	
1959/60	League Cup	~	
	Lincs Cup	~	
	Total	~	1

Made only one appearance for Grantham in the September 1959 Central Alliance (South) fixture at Bourne Town.

Liversidge

Seasons Played	Other	~	1 (1)
1876/77	Total	~	1 (1)

Scored on his debut in the January 1877 friendly at Retford Rovers, although no records exist to show any other appearances.

Llewellyn

Seasons Played	League	~	2
	F.A. Cup	~	
1936/37	Lincs Cup	~	
	Other	~	
	Total	~	2

Forward who made two appearances around Easter 1937 in the Midland League games against Mansfield Town Reserves and Denaby United.

Chris Logan

Seasons Played	League	~	9 (1)
	F.A. Cup	~	
1999/00	F.A. Trophy	~	
	League Cup	~	2 (1)
	Lincs Cup	~	
	Total	~	11 (2)

Former Boots Athletic striker who made his Grantham debut in the October 1999 league game at Burton Albion and scored in the match against Rothwell Town, plus his final appearance in December at home to Margate.

A. Logsden

Seasons Played	League	~	1
	F.A. Cup	~	
1934/35	Lincs Cup	~	
	Total	~	1

Made just one appearance for Grantham in the April 1935 league game against Hull City Reserves.

Logsden

Seasons Played	League	~	12 (2)
	F.A. Cup	~	2 (1)
1919/20-20/21	Lincs Cup	~	2
	Other	~	1 (1)
1922/23	Total	~	17 (4)

Forward who also played for Grantham Reserves, Newark Athletic and whilst it is not known whether or not he made his debut on Boxing Day 1919, certainly the following day he scored twice in the game at home to Welbeck Colliery. Due to the fact that he was only covering matches when Sid Howard was unavailable, he only managed occasional appearances during the rest of the season. The following year though, he moved into the midfield position but still failed to make an impact on the side. He did return in the 1922/23 season, but no records can be found of any appearance after the September 1922 fixture at home to New Hucknall Colliery.

Long

Seasons Played			
	League	~	1
	F.A. Cup	~	
1935/36	Lincs Cup	~	
	Other	~	
	Total	~	1

Made just one appearance for the club at Scunthorpe & Lindsey United in the February 1936 Lincolnshire League fixture. This was the season that the First team competed in both that and the Midland League competition.

Jimmy Longworth

Seasons Played			
	League	~	30 (19)
	F.A. Cup	~	4
1954/55-55/56	Lincs Cup	~	
	Total	~	34 (19)

Brother of Walter Longworth. Jimmy signed from Ransome & Marles and first played for Grantham in the September 1954 draw at Denaby United, scoring his initial goal for the club a few days later against Wisbech Town at London Road. He managed only a handful of further appearances that year, but after the Summer break put together a record of 18 goals in his 22 league appearances, aided by four strikes in the November 1955 Midland League game at home to Lincoln City Reserves. His final game for Grantham came the following February at Scarborough. He was then transferred to Peterborough United, whilst at the start of the 1960's was known to be playing for Boston United. In the 1990's Jimmy was thought to be still living in the Peterborough area, but he may have moved down to Milton Keynes a few years ago.

Walter Longworth

Seasons Played			
	League	~	24 (4)
	F.A. Cup	~	2 (4)
1954/55	Lincs Cup	~	1
	Total	~	27 (8)

Also a former Ransome & Marles player who made his Grantham debut two weeks after his brother Jimmy, against Frickley Colliery in September 1954, and put his sibling to shame somewhat by managing to score four goals in the FA Cup tie against Barton Town at the end of that month. Walter played in many of the remaining fixtures, up to the April 1955 league fixture at Wisbech Town although he did appear, and score twice, in the Stamford Hospital Cup match at the end of the season.

Lovlee

Seasons Played			
	League	~	2
1905/06	Total	~	2

Defender with only two known appearances, the February 1906 league games against Bridgford Athletic and Derby YMCA. He was most probably either John, or Wilfred Lovlee (Born circa 1886 - Died September 1917 in Grantham), brothers who at that time were residing at Railway Terrace in Grantham.

Harry Lowe

Seasons Played			
	League	~	33
	Lincs Cup	~	
1931/32	Other	~	
	Total	~	33

Born 20/03/1886 at Whitwell, Derbyshire. Half-Back who had previously played for Whitwell St Lawrence, Gainsborough Trinity, Liverpool, making 120 appearances, Nottingham Forest, helping them to success in the Victory Shield in 1919, Mansfield Town and Newark Town. Harry had scored six goals in 231 Football League appearances and despite being 45 years of age made his Grantham debut in the first Midland League game of the 1931/32 season at Loughborough Corinthians. Unfortunately there are no details as to other games that he played in, although with 33 appearances he obviously played in the majority of the matches that season. Died 25/10/1958 at Worksop.

Lowe

Seasons Played			
	League	~	
	Lincs Cup	~	
1909/10	Other	~	1
	Total	~	1

Forward whose only known appearance is in the March 1910 friendly against Queen's Park.

Glyn Lumb

Seasons Played			
	League	~	24 (1)
	F.A. Cup	~	1
1978/79-79/80	F.A. Trophy	~	
	League Cup	~	2
	Lincs Cup	~	2
	Total	~	29 (1)

Member of the RAF who also made appearances for the Combined Services Representative side. His first game for Grantham came in the January 1979 Southern League Cup tie at Weymouth and he played in the majority of the matches over the next couple of months, although he missed out on the final few fixtures of that Championship winning season. Glyn played in the first 16 games of the following campaign, scoring his only goal in the September match at Workington, but his last appearance came in the October 1979 match at Tamworth. He is still involved with the RAF, currently working as a PT Instructor in the East Midlands.

Jim Lumby

Seasons Played			
	League	~	14 (6)
	F.A. Cup	~	
1984/85	F.A. Trophy	~	
	League Cup	~	5 (2)
	Lincs Cup	~	
	Other	~	
	Total	~	19 (8)

Born 02/10/1954 at Grimsby. Jim had previously played for Grimsby Town, Boston United, including their FA Cup Second Round tie against Sheffield United, Gainsborough Trinity, Brigg Town, Scunthorpe United, Carlisle United, Tranmere Rovers and Mansfield Town, making over 200 appearances in The Football League. After a return to Boston and a spell playing in Hong Kong, he scored on his debut for Grantham in January 1985 against Buxton and then missed just one game up to his final appearance in the season's closing fixture and the club's last ever Northern Premier League match, at Oswestry Town. During his career, he also played for Gainsborough Trinity and Ross Sports, although no details are known to indicate at what point. He was last known to be running a pub in Cleethorpes, close to the home of Grimsby Town FC.

W. Lunn

Seasons Played			
	League	~	2
	F.A. Cup	~	
1938/39	Lincs Cup	~	1 (2)
	Total	~	3 (2)

Local player who also played for Grantham St. John's and replaced Gorden Stimpson for the January 1939 games against Scarborough, Boston United, where he scored twice in the 5-5 County Cup draw, and Frickley Colliery.

Lunn

Seasons Played			
	F.A. Cup	~	
	Lincs Cup	~	1
1886/87	Other	~	10
	Total	~	11

Made his debut in the second match of the 1886/87 season at Notts Olympic and although playing in many of the other friendlies during that season, was only able to gain one place in a competitive competition when he lined up at Market Rasen Town in the Lincolnshire Senior Cup tie. He made his final appearance in February 1887 at home to Lincoln Lindum.

Dave Leadbeater

Harold Leek

F. Leeson

Albert Linnecor

John Little

Bert Lister

Jimmy Longworth

Jack Macartney

Neil Mann

Jamie March

Jeff Marchant

Bill Marriott

Marriott (1912/13)

Everton Marsh

Lee Marshall

Freddie Martin

Lunn

Seasons Played			
	League	~	1
	F.A. Cup	~	
1934/35	Lincs Cup	~	
	Total	~	1

Centre-Forward who also played for Lincoln Burton Road and made just a single appearance for Grantham in the November 1934 league game against Hull City Reserves.

George Lyall

Seasons Played			
	League	~	5
	F.A. Cup	~	
1980/81	F.A. Trophy	~	
	League Cup	~	
	Lincs Cup	~	
	Other	~	
	Total	~	5

Born 04/05/1947 at Wick. Midfield player who made appearances for Kingskettle Amateurs (Fife), Raith Rovers, Preston North End, Nottingham Forest and Hull City, finishing his professional career with 54 goals to his name in 306 Football League and cup games. He will be best remembered, perhaps unfortunately, for his converted penalty for Forest in the 1974 FA Cup Quarter-Final against Newcastle United. This was followed by a huge Geordie pitch invasion which led to the tie being abandoned and replayed, with Newcastle being banned from staging Cup matches for a year. After a spell at Scarborough, where George failed to make a First team appearance, and Goole Town as Player/Manager, he joined Grantham. He played only five games though for The Gingerbreads, starting in February 1981 at home to Morecambe and ending a month later against Worksop Town. He continued to play for Bridlington Town and North Ferriby United up to the end of the 1981/82 season. George is still self-employed, but can be found more often than not on one of the golf courses near Derby.

John Lyne

Seasons Played			
	F.A. Cup	~	
	Other	~	1
1878/79	Total	~	1

Born 1857 in Grantham. Stationer and Printer who worked for the family business in Westgate and made just one appearance for Grantham against Burghley Park in October 1878. Died October 1907 in Grantham.

C. Mabbott

Seasons Played			
	Lincs Cup	~	3
	Other	~	11 (6)
1890/91	Total	~	14 (6)

First of three players with this surname, most likely to have been brothers, who made appearances for Grantham during the 1890/91 season. This individual made his debut in the October friendly against Notts St John's, scored his first goal for the club at the start of the following month against Boston NE and then played right up until the end of the season.

R. Mabbott

Seasons Played			
	Lincs Cup	~	
	Other	~	1
1890/91	Total	~	1

Made just one appearance for Grantham in the September 1890 friendly against Netherfield.

W. Mabbott

Seasons Played			
	League	~	13 (3)
	F.A. Cup	~	1
1890/91-91/92	Other	~	11 (5)
	Total	~	25 (8)

Made his debut in the opening friendly of the 1890/91 season against Notts Amateurs United and scored his first goal for the club the following month at home to Notts St John's. He was certainly the most evident of the three Mabbotts and his career progressed into the following season, Grantham's first ever league campaign. He played in the initial Midland Amateur Alliance fixture at home to Notts County Rovers and was still a prominent member of the team by the following Spring.

F. Mableson

Seasons Played			
	League	~	2 (1)
	F.A. Cup	~	
1921/22	Lincs Cup	~	
	Total	~	2 (1)

Local player with experience in the Reserves side and with Grantham St John's who made at least two appearances during the 1921/22 season, scoring his only goal for the club in the February 1922 Central Alliance fixture at Hucknall Byron.

Jack Macartney

Seasons Played			
	League	~	403 (364)
	F.A. Cup	~	25 (28)
1937/38-39/40	Lincs Cup	~	20 (15)
	Other	~	8 (9)
1945/46-55/56	Total	~	456 (416)

Born 21/10/1918 at Stamford. The 'Local Legend' and Grantham's record goal-scorer. An 18 year old Jack arrived at Grantham from Spalding United, after previously being with Stamford Town and Grantham Thursday, when he was offered a £1 a week contract together with a £2 a week job at Mowbray's Brewery in town. He scored twice on his Grantham debut at home to Rotherham United Reserves in December 1937 after taking over the position from Robert Littledyke. He played in every one of the remaining fixtures, scoring 17 goals to help Grantham to their runners-up position in the Midland League and that was a figure only four behind the season's highest scorer, Cyril Stocks. The end of that first season had also seen Grantham compete in the Spalding Victory Cup, which had been agreed during Jack's transfer, and although Grantham won the tie 5-1, he failed to get on the score-sheet that day. In October 1938 he scored his first hat-trick for the club against Doncaster Rovers Reserves, but things got even better when later in the season he put five past the Denaby United goalkeeper. The final campaign of the decade saw Grantham playing in the two Midland 'War-Time' Leagues, although Jack was missing from many of these games. The first season after World War 2 saw him still missing from his Grantham position due to being stationed abroad, although he did manage to score four hat-tricks and play in his first Lincolnshire County Cup Final, against Boston United. Jack was reaching the pinnacle of his career and began the 1946/47 season with four goals in the first game at Lincoln City Reserves and incredibly equalled that at Frickley Colliery plus netted eight hat-tricks as well. It was around this time that the stories began of his shots "breaking goal-keeper's fingers and the opposition's cross-bars". Notts County Reserves and England 'B' 'keeper, Gordon Bradley, was the unfortunate victim as he got a couple of fingers to one of Jack's penalties, but the other part of the statement seems to sadly be a myth as the Lincoln City Reserves 'keeper, Parkins, assisted the break with his own weight! A book could be written on Jack's exploits in the following season alone, but unfortunately we have to be concise. He began with a hat-trick at Scarborough and helped Grantham into the First Round of the FA Cup with all four goals in the First Qualifying Round at Spalding United, a single strike at Basford United and six goals in the 11-1 thrashing of Ilkeston United. Surprisingly Jack failed to find the net in either the Fourth Qualifying Round tie at home to Goole Town, the replay, and even the First Round Proper encounter at Stockton. Back in the league the highlights continued though and towards the end of the season in a fixture against Bradford Park Avenue Reserves, Jack was being marked by the England 'B' player and future England manager, Ron Greenwood. He scored eight times in the entertaining 9-6 victory and finished the season with 64 goals in his 44 appearances. The goals continued to go in after the Summer break, although the best record that he could manage in that 1948/49 season was 'only' four in the league game at home to Scarborough. In March of 1949 Jack, along with Alf Sams and Reg Gregory were awarded a benefit game and over 3,000 supporters came to London Road to support the players in a friendly against a Representative XI. The end of the decade saw another FA Cup First Round appearance for Jack, as he scored Grantham's consolation goal in the tie at Wrexham, whilst in the league he scored five past Frickley Colliery and after the New Year netted four in the County Cup semi-final replay against Gainsborough Trinity. As we move into the 1950s Jack's scoring prowess was starting to diminish, although that statement can only be viewed against his own standards. The 1950/51 season finished with 28 goals, including three hat-tricks to Jack's name and that level of finishing continued over the next couple of years. Finally in April 1954 Jack won his first Lincolnshire County Cup winner's medal after the team defeated Gainsborough Trinity. He had played in three previous finals and been on the losing side every time, although during his Grantham career he had also missed two others, but even then the team had lost. Jack played in only 7 games during the 1954/55 season, scoring his final goal for the club in September at Corby Town. The following season he returned to the side one final time and although it was perhaps fitting that it should be in front of a huge 10,800 crowd at London Road it was a shame that it was London Road, Peterborough, in the Christmas Midland League fixture. During his career Jack had been watched by Football League scouts many times, but even Granthamian, and then Notts County Captain, Aubrey Southwell, could not tempt him away from London Road. His loyalty to the club even continued after his career had finished and he carried on in various capacities including Reserve team Player/Coach and First Team Trainer right up until 1966. His retirement was marked before the Sutton Town fixture in September, when Terry Bly presented him with a clock on behalf of the club. Died February 1992 in Grantham.

Billy Macdonald

Seasons Played			
	League	~	7
	F.A. Cup	~	2
1926/27	Lincs Cup	~	
	Other	~	
	Total	~	9

Born 1882 at Quebec, County Durham. Midfielder who had previously played for Craghead United, Hull City, Chesterfield, Fulham and Durham City, scoring seven goals in 151 Football League appearances during a professional career spanning the years from 1911 to 1925. He then had two spells at Shirebrook, playing for Alfreton Town in-between, before his Grantham debut in the opening game of the 1926/27 season at Sutton Town. Billy played in every game up to the end of October, but then made only one other appearance for the club, in January, at Ilkeston United, by which time he was well into his forties. Died 1948.

Tony Macek

Seasons Played			
	League	~	23 (2)
	F.A. Cup	~	
1995/96	F.A. Trophy	~	2 (2)
	League Cup	~	
	Lincs Cup	~	
	Total	~	25 (4)

Born 1969 at Oldham. Former Lincoln United player who made his debut for Grantham by coming off the bench during the September 1995 league match at Paget Rangers and scored his first two goals for the club during the FA Trophy defeat of Harrogate Town the following month. He stayed at The Meres for the rest of the season and scored his last goal in the May 1996 closing fixture at Sutton Coldfield Town. No information is known on following clubs, but in the last couple of years Tony has made appearances for Wootton Bassett in the Hellenic League.

John Machin

Seasons Played			
	League	~	
	F.A. Cup	~	
2001/02	F.A. Trophy	~	
	League Cup	~	
	Lincs Cup	~	1
	Total	~	1

Reserves midfielder who made one appearance for the First team in the opening County Cup tie of the 2001/02 season at Gainsborough Trinity when he came off the bench to replace Dave Taylor.

Jim MacLachan

Seasons Played			
	League	~	15 (2)
	F.A. Cup	~	3
1982/83	F.A. Trophy	~	1
	League Cup	~	2
	Lincs Cup	~	
	Other	~	3 (1)
	Total	~	24 (3)

Former Burton Albion midfielder who made his debut for Grantham in the September 1982 league fixture at Hyde United and scored his first goal for the club at the end of the same month against Worksop Town. He came on as substitute during the October FA Cup final qualifying round tie at Telford United, replacing Player/Manager Jon Nixon, but his last game for Grantham came in the January 1983 President's Cup semi-final at King's Lynn, following which he went on to play for Ilkeston Town.

Craig Maddison

Seasons Played			
	League	~	24
	F.A. Cup	~	1
1996/97-97/98	F.A. Trophy	~	1
	League Cup	~	1
	Lincs Cup	~	
	Total	~	27

Born 1974 at Nottingham. Midfield player who started out at GPT Plessey, before moving to Grimsby Town, although he failed to earn a First team place there. Craig then made appearances for Arnold Town and Ilkeston Town, before joining Grantham after a period playing in Australia. His first game came in the February 1997 league match at home to Paget Rangers and although he played in every remaining game of that season, the 1997/98 Championship winning campaign began with a limited amount of appearances for Craig, the last of which came in October at Stourbridge. He left The Meres to join Hucknall Town, before returning to Arnold and then moving to Gedling Town, where he became their joint manager in February 2004, although only months later, at the end of the season, he had left.

Malcouranne

Seasons Played			
	League	~	8
	Other	~	
1905/06-06/07	Total	~	8

Defender who was certainly evident in the 1905/06 pre-season friendlies and then in every league game from that year where full team-sheets are available. He also played at the beginning of the following season, but no details are known about the end of his career.

Aubrey Malim

Seasons Played			
	Other	~	3
1874/75	Total	~	3

Born 01/05/1848 in Grantham. Played in the club's first ever game, against the Third Lincolnshire Volunteer Rifles in October 1874, followed by the match against Peterborough and finally the December friendly at Lincoln. Based in Westgate, he went on to become a prominent dignitary in the town, as Borough Coroner, Clerk to the Local Health Board, Town Clerk and solicitor. Died 10/05/1929 at Grantham.

Maltby

Seasons Played			
	Other	~	1
1879/80	Total	~	1

Made only one appearance for the team in the November 1879 friendly against Nottingham Law.

Manees

Seasons Played			
	League	~	1
	Lincs Cup	~	
1904/05	Other	~	
	Total	~	1

Just one known game which this individual played in, the March 1905 Midland Amateur Alliance fixture against Derby Thornhill.

Herbert Mann

Seasons Played			
	League	~	34 (7)
	F.A. Cup	~	
1930/31	Lincs Cup	~	
	Total	~	34 (7)

Born 30/12/1907 at Nuneaton. Winger who had previously played for Griff Colliery and Derby County, making six appearances as The Rams finished runners-up to Sheffield Wednesday in the First Division Championship. Bert first played for Grantham in the Autumn of 1930 and then must have appeared in virtually all of that season's remaining fixtures, with his first known goal in the December match at home to Hull City Reserves. In the 1931 close season he signed for Manchester United and seemed to have a promising future ahead of him. However, a broken collar bone ended his career at Old Trafford two years later, after two goals in 13 appearances, and he moved on to Ripley Town.

Neil Mann

Seasons Played			
	League	~	53 (9)
	F.A. Cup	~	2
1991/92-92/93	F.A. Trophy	~	1
	League Cup	~	8
	Lincs Cup	~	1
	Total	~	65 (9)

Born 19/11/1972 at Nottingham. Son of the former Manchester City player and Grimsby Town Assistant Manager, Arthur Mann. Neil had previously played for Grimsby Town Reserves and Spalding United, after having periods on the books at Notts County and Nottingham Forest. He scored on his debut for Grantham in the opening fixture of the 1991/92 season at Bridgnorth Town and two weeks later played in the first ever game at The Meres when Ilkeston Town arrived for an FA Cup tie. Neil played in the majority of that season's matches and the following year as well, up to his final appearance in the March 1993 game at home to Nuneaton Borough. He then moved to Hull City, where he became a regular in their side for the rest of the decade, but went on-loan to Scarborough and Gainsborough Trinity towards the end of his career. With 12 goals to his name in 209 First team appearances for Hull, he was awarded a Testimonial in July 2003 against a Grimsby Town team, and remains at the club as a Youth Team Coach.

Wayne Manners

Seasons Played			
	League	~	4
	F.A. Cup	~	
1991/92	F.A. Trophy	~	
	League Cup	~	2
	Lincs Cup	~	
	Total	~	6

Born 24/09/1969 at Nottingham. Began his career as a Trainee at Halifax Town, before signing for Stanton, Alfreton Town and Sutton Town. He played in most of the games during February 1992, starting against Yate Town in the league and ending at the beginning of March at RC Warwick. After leaving Grantham, Wayne went on to play for Greenwood Meadows, Heanor Town, Dunkirk, Ruddington, Ilkeston Town, Hinckley United, Gedling Town and Arnold Town, before returning to Dunkirk as a member of the management team, along with another former Gingerbread, Dave Harbottle.

Mantle

Seasons Played			
	League	~	1
	Lincs Cup	~	
1904/05	Other	~	
	Total	~	1

Known to have played in the January 1905 league game at Notts Magdala, but no evidence exists of any other appearances he may have made.

Alan Maples

Seasons Played			
	League	~	1 (1)
	F.A. Cup	~	
1961/62	Lincs Cup	~	
	Total	~	1 (1)

Scored in his only appearance, the opening match of the 1961/62 season at home to Worksop Town. His surname may be spelt 'Marples'.

Harold March

Seasons Played			
	League	~	49 (4)
	F.A. Cup	~	6 (1)
1932/33-33/34	Lincs Cup	~	2
	Other	~	1
	Total	~	58 (5)

Born 30/01/1904 at Gamston. Spent most of his early life in The Army, but joined Hull City in 1929, where he made eight First team appearances. A year later he moved to Lincoln City and was the highest scorer for their Reserves side during his time there, plus scored five goals in 11 matches for the senior side. Although his Grantham debut is not known, his first goal came in the October 1932 FA Cup tie against Sutton Junction. The following season he played infrequently and once again no details are known as to the end of his career. His surname is sometimes spelt 'Mach' in Grantham team-sheets. Died 22/07/1977 at Lincoln.

Jamie March

Seasons Played			
	League	~	14 (2)
	F.A. Cup	~	
2003/04	F.A. Trophy	~	
	League Cup	~	
	Lincs Cup	~	1
	Total	~	15 (2)

Born 21/03/1976 at Leicester. Defender who previously played for Friar Lane Old Boys, Leicester City, Kettering Town, Stevenage Borough, where he played in the FA Cup Third Round tie against Newcastle United, Leek Town, Nuneaton Borough, Burton Albion, King's Lynn, Hinckley United, Tamworth and Halesowen Town, before his return to King's Lynn. He made his debut for Grantham in the February 2004 league match at Newport County, with his first goal a month later against Worcester City. Jamie played in all but two of the remaining fixtures from that season, including the Lincolnshire Shield victory over Gainsborough Trinity. He played his last game for Grantham in the closing fixture at Weymouth and went on to play for Bedworth United the following season.

Jeff Marchant

Seasons Played			
	League	~	12
	F.A. Cup	~	
1968/69-69/70	F.A. Trophy	~	
	League Cup	~	3
	Lincs Cup	~	
	Other	~	
	Total	~	15

Defender who made his debut in the September 1968 league fixture at Heanor Town. He had a good run in the First team at the end of that season, after replacing Paddy Phelan, and was able to play in both legs of the Midland League Cup Final. However, he made his final appearance soon after the Summer break in the Midland League game at home to Ilkeston United. Jeff went on to play for Stamford Town, including their 1976 FA Vase Final appearance at Wembley and rejoined Grantham towards the end of the decade but failed to gain another First team appearance.

Marks

Seasons Played			
	League	~	3 (1)
	Lincs Cup	~	
1927/28	Other	~	
1931/32	Total	~	3 (1)

Made two appearances for Grantham in February 1928 against Shirebrook and Mansfield Town, plus the only game where he scored, the January 1932 league game at Barnsley Reserves. Quite possibly made more appearances for the club than those figures above.

Geoff Marlow

Seasons Played			
	League	~	44 (8)
	F.A. Cup	~	6 (1)
1949/50	Lincs Cup	~	4
	Total	~	54 (9)

Born 13/12/1912 at Worksop. Former Dinnington Athletic, Lincoln City and Newark Town winger, with 32 goals scored in 89 League and cup appearances whilst at Sincil Bank. Geoff first played for Grantham in the opening league game of the 1949/50 season at Scarborough and then scored his first two goals for the club a week later at London Road in the 3-2 defeat by Nottingham Forest Reserves. Geoff played in all but two of that season's games, including the FA Cup First Round tie at Wrexham and the County Cup Final at Boston United. He played his last game for Grantham in the closing fixture at York City Reserves and later made appearances for Stalybridge Celtic and Skegness Town. Geoff was also an accomplished cricketer, playing for the Lincolnshire County side from 1946 to 1957 as well as the Ruston Bucyrus club team. Died 08/11/1978 at Lincoln.

Bill Marriott

Seasons Played			
	League	~	100 (20)
	F.A. Cup	~	14 (4)
1965/66-68/69	League Cup	~	5
	Lincs Cup	~	2
	Total	~	121 (24)

Born circa 1933. Previously spent time on the books at Lincoln City, Boston United and signed for Grantham from Lockheed Leamington. He made his debut in August 1965 when the team travelled over to Worksop Town for a league game, and scored his first goal for the club the following weekend at Gainsborough Trinity. He played in every game until Christmas, including the FA Cup matches at home to Hendon and Swindon Town, but then made only a few more appearances before the end of the campaign. Bill became the first ever Grantham player to be substituted, when Neil Marshall took over his place during the August 1966 league fixture at Spalding United. That season and the following one he played in about half of the matches, but sadly for him missed out on all three of the FA Cup Proper ties. Finally in November 1968 he was again able to appear at that stage in the national competition, against Chelmsford City, but even then he was substituted in favour of Brent Horobin. His last game for Grantham came in the April 1969 fixture at home to Belper Town, although in both the legs of the Midland League Cup Final he sat on the bench, but was unable to come on to the field of play. Died 2004 at Lincoln.

Dale Marriott

Seasons Played			
	League	~	2
	F.A. Cup	~	
1996/97	F.A. Trophy	~	
	League Cup	~	
	Lincs Cup	~	1
	Total	~	3

Former Holwell Sports defender who played in three of the first four matches of the 1996/97 season against Grimsby Town, Redditch United and Raunds Town.

Frank Marriott

Seasons Played			
	League	~	2 (2)
	F.A. Cup	~	
1925/26	Lincs Cup	~	1 (1)
	Total	~	3 (3)

Born 26/10/1893 at Sutton-in-Ashfield. Left-Back who had previously played for Sutton Junction, Notts County, Swansea City and Lincoln City, scoring one goal in a total of 99 Football League fixtures, with 17 more appearances to his name in FA Cup ties. Frank scored for Grantham in the December 1925 County Cup tie at home to Boston, plus the league games against Denaby United and Ilkeston United just after the Christmas period, and almost certainly played in many more games that season.

Geoff Marriott

Seasons Played			
	League	~	29 (11)
	F.A. Cup	~	2 (1)
1919/20-20/21	Lincs Cup	~	4 (3)
	Other	~	1 (1)
	Total	~	36 (16)

Inside-Right with experience at Newark Athletic who made his Grantham debut in the opening match of the 1919/20 season at Long Eaton and scored his first goal at the end of the same month during the FA Cup draw against Boots Athletic. Geoff played in many of that season's games, but the following year seemed to play more infrequently and the last known instance of his name appearing in the team-sheet occurs in March 1921 against Leicester City Reserves.

W. Marriott

Seasons Played			
	League	~	2 (1)
	F.A. Cup	~	2 (1)
1919/20	Lincs Cup	~	1
	Total	~	5 (2)

Made his debut in the October 1919 FA Cup tie against Boots Athletic, the same game as the previous entry's first goal, and then scored himself in the replay. He played only a handful of games though for the club and his goal in the January league fixture at home to Chesterfield Reserves is the last time his name appears.

Marriott

Seasons Played			
	League	~	13 (12)
	F.A. Cup	~	1
1912/13-13/14	Lincs Cup	~	1 (1)
	Other	~	1
	Total	~	16 (13)

Most probably played in many of the games during his two year spell with the club, which definitely includes the March 1913 friendly against Queen's Park, but evidence from this era is generally only of those players who scored.

Tony Marsden

Seasons Played			
	League	~	86 (8)
	F.A. Cup	~	5 (1)
1989/90-91/92	F.A. Trophy	~	2
	League Cup	~	15 (4)
	Lincs Cup	~	1
	Total	~	109 (13)

Born 03/12/1969 at Derby. Former Burton Albion and Belper Town player who made his Grantham debut in the August 1989 league fixture at Bedworth United, with his first goal for the club coming at the end of September in the FA Cup game at Boston FC. Tony played in many games during his three season spell with The Gingerbreads, including the club's first match at The Meres against Ilkeston Town in August 1991. His last goal for the club came in the February 1992 Beazer Homes League Cup tie against VS Rugby and his final appearance in March at home to Hednesford Town. Tony was transferred to Gresley Rovers, winning a Dr Marten's League Championship winning medal during his five seasons there, before his return to Burton Albion, followed by appearances at King's Lynn and Mickleover Sports. Tony is back now living in his home city of Derby and works as a builder.

Everton Marsh

Seasons Played			
	League	~	60 (11)
	F.A. Cup	~	2
1985/86-86/87	F.A. Trophy	~	6
	League Cup	~	6 (3)
	Lincs Cup	~	
	Total	~	74 (14)

Born 07/01/1963 at Nottingham. Signed from Ruddington and scored on his debut for Grantham in the November 1985 league match against Leamington. Everton played in the majority of the club's games up to his final appearance in the April 1987 game at Leicester United, with his last goal coming a few months previously at home to Buckingham Town. He went on to play for Worksop Town, Stafford Rangers and Matlock Town and by the mid-90's was a member of the management team at Gedling Town.

Lee Marshall

Seasons Played			
	League	~	128 (16)
	F.A. Cup	~	13 (1)
1994/95	F.A. Trophy	~	6
	League Cup	~	5 (1)
2000/01-02/03	Lincs Cup	~	8 (2)
	Total	~	160 (20)

Born 02/08/1977 at Nottingham. Began his career as a Trainee at Nottingham Forest and was picked out by Brian Clough as a star for the future. After arriving on-loan, he scored a brace on his debut for Grantham in January 1995 at home to Hinckley Town, but it was to be a short six match initial career at The Meres before he moved on to Stockport County. However, Lee was released by them at the end of the 1994/95 season after only one First team appearance and despite being offered a contract by Darlington, then decided to move on to Eastwood Town, before a £5,000 transfer took him to Scunthorpe United. In three seasons there he scored twice in 54 matches, many of those starting from the substitute's bench, and rejoined Grantham at the start of the 2000/01 season. Lee played in every game for The Gingerbreads during that campaign, including the October FA Cup tie at Rushden & Diamonds. Once again, he played in every league match of the 2001/02 promotion winning season, whilst his final season at The Meres included appearances in the August 2002 County Cup Final at home to Scunthorpe United, the final FA Cup qualifying round tie at Morecambe and the April 2003 Lincolnshire County Senior Cup Final at Gainsborough Trinity. Only days after that defeat, Lee scored in his final game for The Gingerbreads at home to Moor Green and along with many of his colleagues went on to play for Lincoln United and then joined Harrowby United.

Neil Marshall

Seasons Played			
	League	~	1
	F.A. Cup	~	
1966/67	Total	~	1

Born 11/02/1948 at Sleaford. Former Ancaster and Grantham Reserves winger who played in the Bourne Hospital Cup Final at the end of May 1966, but his only competitive appearance came in the August fixture at Spalding United when he replaced Bill

Marriott, therefore becoming Grantham's first ever substitute. Neil went on to play for Sleaford Town and Sleaford Rangers, but a broken leg stalled his career at an early age. He still lives close to Grantham and runs his own engineering supply company at Peterborough.

Marshall

Seasons Played			
	F.A. Cup	~	
	Lincs Cup	~	1
1886/87-90/91	Other	~	24
	Total	~	25

Made his debut in the January 1887 friendly against Grantham Volunteers, but it wasn't until the end of the decade that he had progressed into the competitive games, playing in the November 1889 County Cup tie against Lincoln Rangers and the same season's Kettering Charity Cup. His last appearance comes in January 1891, when Nottingham Forest Reserves came to London Road for a friendly.

Marshall

Seasons Played			
	League	~	2
	F.A. Cup	~	1
1892/93	Total	~	3

Played in the Midland Amateur Alliance fixture at home to Matlock, the FA Cup tie against Belper and unfortunately the 16-0 record defeat at Notts County Rovers. Could possibly be the same player as the previous entry.

Marshall

Seasons Played			
	League	~	3
	F.A. Cup	~	
1935/36	Lincs Cup	~	
	Other	~	
	Total	~	3

Centre-Forward who had also played for Sutton Town and as far as Grantham is concerned played in the two February 1935 Lincolnshire League fixtures against Scunthorpe & Lindsey United and Grimsby Town Reserves, followed by the Midland League game at home to Boston United.

Marsland

Seasons Played			
	F.A. Cup	~	3
	Other	~	2 (2)
1877/78-78/79	Total	~	5 (2)

Made his debut in the club's first ever FA Cup tie against Clapham Rovers in October 1877 and then scored his first goal against Sleaford three weeks later. The following season he only appeared in the two FA Cup games, with the London Road replay of the Sheffield tie in November 1878 his final game.

Freddie Martin

Seasons Played			
	League	~	175 (14)
1952/53-56/57	F.A. Cup	~	7
	Lincs Cup	~	6
	Total	~	188 (14)

Born 14/04/1925 at Nottingham. Former Sutton Town, Ipswich Town and Blackburn Rovers player who finally gained his Football League debut after a transfer to Accrington Stanley. He made a total of 64 league appearances there and after relocating back to his home town joined Grantham, making his debut in the opening match of the 1952/53 season at Mansfield Town Reserves and scoring his first goal against Doncaster Rovers Reserves the following month. Freddie played in nearly all of that season's games, including the County Cup Final at Spalding United, as he did the following year which finished with a medal in the County competition after Grantham defeated Gainsborough Trinity. By now he had reverted to a more defensive role within the team, meaning his final goal came in the Midland League fixture against Bradford City Reserves in October 1954, although he continued to play in the team right up to his final appearance at Goole Town in January 1957.

Jae Martin

Seasons Played			
	League	~	8 (2)
	F.A. Cup	~	
1998/99	F.A. Trophy	~	
	League Cup	~	
	Lincs Cup	~	
	Total	~	8 (2)

Born 05/02/1976 at Hampstead. Midfielder who began his career at Southend United, before moving to Leyton Orient, Birmingham City, Lincoln City and Peterborough United, from where he joined Grantham on-loan. He made his debut in March 1999 against Dorchester Town and scored in his final two matches against Tamworth and Hastings Town the following month. After another spell on-loan, at Welling United, he was released by Peterborough at the end of the 2000/01 season, finishing with Football League totals of 6 goals in 79 games and one more strike to his name in 16 cup matches. Jae then moved on to Woking, followed by Moor Green a few months later.

Martin

Seasons Played			
	League	~	1
	F.A. Cup	~	
1928/29	Lincs Cup	~	
	Other	~	
	Total	~	1

Centre-Half who had previously played for Huddersfield Town Reserves and made just one appearance for Grantham in the January 1929 Midland League fixture at home to Frickley Colliery.

Mick Massingham

Seasons Played			
	League	~	6
	F.A. Cup	~	
1963/64-65/66	Lincs Cup	~	
	Total	~	6

Born 20/02/1946 at Helpringham. Started his career on Schoolboy forms with Lincoln City, at the same time as playing for Sleaford Rangers. After being brought to London Road by Alan Clay, Mick played for Grantham in the three league games around Christmas 1963, the home fixtures against Skegness and Lockheed Leamington, plus the Boxing Day trip over to Heanor Town. He then joined Sleaford Town, but returned to Grantham a year or so later, with the April 1965 fixture his next appearance, once again versus Heanor Town, before his final two games for the club in September against Worksop Town and Skegness. Mick finished his career with Gonerby Rovers, where he also coached and managed, before turning to refereeing. He is a Class 1 official, appointed to the Central Midlands League, a National Licensed Instructor, Chairman of Grantham Referees Society, yet despite all this he still manages to find time to run his own roofing business in the area.

Matkin

Seasons Played			
	F.A. Cup	~	
	Other	~	20 (2)
1876/77-80/81	Total	~	20 (2)

First played for Grantham in the opening friendly of the 1876/77 season at Peterborough, but it wasn't until the following year that he became a regular in the team, scoring his first goal for the club at Stamford in February 1878. Progressing towards the end of the decade though, appearances became infrequent once more and his final game came in November 1880 at home to Nottingham Park.

Mattews

Seasons Played			
	F.A. Cup	~	
	Lincs Cup	~	
1885/86	Other	~	6
1887/88	Total	~	6

Made one appearance for the club in the Christmas 1885 fixture against Grantham Volunteers, but no records exist of any more games played until the start of the 1887/88 season. He then appears in the team right up until the following Spring.

Nick Matthews

Seasons Played			
	League	~	3
	F.A. Cup	~	
2004/05	F.A. Trophy	~	
	League Cup	~	
	Lincs Cup	~	1
	Total	~	4

Born 14/09/1985 at Leicester. Began his career at Leicester City and then moved to Oadby Town, Boston United Reserves, King's Lynn and Rugby United. Nick joined Grantham on the transfer deadline day in March 2005 and made his debut by coming off the bench to replace Adam Sturgess in the home fixture against Dunstable Town at the start of the following month. Only weeks later he had secured his first honours with the club, helping The Gingerbreads to a Lincolnshire Shield Final victory against Gainsborough Trinity. The following Saturday saw the conclusion to the season, at home to Bedford Town, and it also marked the end of Nick's short Grantham career when he was released by the club soon after.

Maule

Seasons Played			
	F.A. Cup	~	4 (2)
	Lincs Cup	~	
1880/81-81/82	Other	~	2
	Total	~	6 (2)

His Grantham debut came in the November 1880 FA Cup tie at Calthorpe, Birmingham, with his first goal in the following round's replay at Stafford Road, Wolverhampton. His last known appearance comes once again in the national Cup competition, a year later, where he also scores his final goal, at London Road against Brigg Town.

Mawer

Seasons Played			
	League	~	1
	Lincs Cup	~	
1939/40	Other	~	
	Total	~	1

Army soldier who was based near to Grantham and played in one game against Denaby United in March 1940.

Maws

Seasons Played			
	League	~	
	Lincs Cup	~	
1894/95	Other	~	1
	Total	~	1

Only one appearance known for this player, in the January 1895 local Charity Cup tie against Grantham Rovers.

Jason Maxwell

Seasons Played			
	League	~	8 (1)
	F.A. Cup	~	2
1994/95	F.A. Trophy	~	
	League Cup	~	1
	Lincs Cup	~	
	Total	~	11 (1)

Born 01/09/1972 at Lincoln. Previously played for Scunthorpe United, Appleby Frodingham and made his Grantham debut in the 1994/95 season's opening league fixture at home to Bridgnorth Town. He scored his only goal against Bedworth United and missed just one game, amazingly the 7-2 victory over Stourbridge, before his last game at RC Warwick in October. Jason moved to Buxton and then Gainsborough Trinity, where he finished his first season there as the club's highest scorer and represented the Unibond League in 1996, before signing for Bradford Park Avenue, a return to Gainsborough, then Belper Town.

McAllister

Seasons Played			
	League	~	1
	F.A. Cup	~	
1934/35	Lincs Cup	~	
	Total	~	1

Midfielder who played for Grantham in the final Midland League fixture of the 1934/35 season at Barnsley Reserves.

Matt McCaul

Seasons Played			
	League	~	11
	F.A. Cup	~	
2003/04	F.A. Trophy	~	
	League Cup	~	
	Lincs Cup	~	1
	Total	~	12

Born 20/10/1982 at Derby. Began his career at Notts County as a Trainee, before moving to Central Midlands side, Graham St Prims, and Nuneaton Borough. He followed new Grantham manager, Dave Norton, to The Meres, where he made his debut against his former club in the February 2004 league fixture. Matt played in many of the remaining games from that season, including the victorious Lincolnshire Shield Final at home to Gainsborough Trinity, before his last appearance in the closing match at Weymouth. He left the club in the Summer of 2004 to concentrate on his University studies, but by the start of the subsequent season he had rejoined Graham St Prims.

Micky McClung

Seasons Played			
	League	~	1
	F.A. Cup	~	
1979/80	F.A. Trophy	~	
	League Cup	~	
	Lincs Cup	~	
	Total	~	1

Grantham Youth and Reserves player who came on as substitute in the 1979/80 season's final game at South Liverpool, replacing Nicky Jarvis. After leaving London Road, he went on to play for Arnold Town.

Paddy McConnall

Seasons Played			
	League	~	4
	F.A. Cup	~	
1936/37	Lincs Cup	~	
	Other	~	
	Total	~	4

Born 05/02/1900 at Rasharkin. A former Northern Ireland International who played against Wales in 1928 and England in 1932. Clubs represented included Belshill Athletic, Larkhall Thistle, Bathgate, Bradford City, Doncaster Rovers, Southport, Shelbourne, Boston United and Spalding United, with a tally of 36 goals in 201 matches played during his time in The Football League. Paddy made his debut for Grantham at the end of August 1936 against Gainsborough Trinity, but only a fortnight later, and following two games against Boston United plus the home fixture against Peterborough United, he had left the club to join Scottish side Hibernian. Died in 1971.

Tom McCreedy

Seasons Played			
	League	~	2
	F.A. Cup	~	
1951/52	Lincs Cup	~	
	Total	~	2

Born 28/09/1923 at Port Glasgow. Former Clyde, Cowdenbeath, Hartlepools United and Lincoln City player who had scored 4 goals in his 47 senior appearances. Tom played in just two games for Grantham, the Midland League fixture at Denaby United in September 1951 and the London Road visit of Goole Town a month later, before joining Spalding United. His surname is sometimes spelt 'McCreadie'. Died 19/02/2004.

Brendan McDaid

Seasons Played			
	League	~	188 (39)
	F.A. Cup	~	16 (2)
1995/96-96/97	F.A. Trophy	~	10 (1)
	League Cup	~	9 (1)
1999/00-02/03	Lincs Cup	~	9 (1)
	Total	~	232 (44)

Born 02/06/1974 at Lincoln. Began his career at Lincoln Moorlands, before moving to Boston FC and Lincoln United. He made his debut for The Gingerbreads in the December 1995 league fixture at home to Dudley Town and played in every one of the remaining games from that season, scoring his first goal in the February 1996 match against Corby Town. Brendan was a near permanent member of Gary Mills' new side as well at the start of the 1996/97 season, but he returned to Lincoln United in January 1997.

He rejoined Grantham though in December 1999 when he followed new manager, John Wilkinson, to The Meres and missed only a handful of matches over the next couple of years, scoring a hat-trick in the opening league game of the 2000/01 season at home to Dartford and playing in the October FA Cup tie at Rushden & Diamonds. Brendan appeared in every single match during the 2001/02 promotion winning season, netting the crucial goal at Banbury in April that sealed Dr Marten's Premier football for the following campaign. The 2002/03 season saw appearances for Brendan in the County Cup Final against Scunthorpe United, the FA Cup Fourth Qualifying Round tie at Morecambe and the second County Cup final of the year, in April 2003 at Gainsborough Trinity. His final goal came in the season's closing fixture at home to Moor Green and soon after this he once more returned to Lincoln United, along with his manager and many of his team-mates.

Seamus McDonagh

Seasons Played			
1990/91-91/92	League	~	22
	F.A. Cup	~	1
	F.A. Trophy	~	1
	League Cup	~	7
	Lincs Cup	~	1
	Total	~	32

Born 6/10/1952 at Rotherham. Goalkeeper, also known as 'Jim', who began his career at Rotherham United, before moving to Manchester United, although he failed to make any First team appearances there. Other clubs that he then played for included Bolton Wanderers, twice, during which he won a League Division Two winners medal, Everton, Notts County, twice, Birmingham City, Gillingham, Sunderland, Wichita (USA), Scarborough, Huddersfield Town and Charlton Athletic. The end of his professional career had seen Seamus make over 500 senior appearances and he even had a goal credited to his name during his time at Bolton. He also won 24 caps as an Irish International, although as a youngster he had been a former England Youth International. Seamus then moved to Galway Rovers and spent time as Manager of Derry City, before returning to England and playing once more for Spalding United and Telford United. He made two appearances for Grantham at the start of the 1990/91 season, against Grimsby Town and Bridgnorth Town, and then had two spells in the side during the following season. He played for Grantham in the club's first game at The Meres against Ilkeston Town in the August 1991 FA Cup tie and made his last appearance in the March 1992 league fixture at RC Warwick. He then returned to Telford, where he also spent time as their Reserve Team Manager, before playing for Arnold Town and Ilkeston Town Veterans. Since then Seamus has had coaching positions at Nottingham Forest, Leicester City and Coventry City, where he remains, and he also scouts for the Irish FA.

McDougal

Seasons Played			
1909/10	League	~	
	Lincs Cup	~	
	Other	~	1
	Total	~	1

Midfielder who played in the March 1910 friendly against Queen's Park, but it is not known whether he also appeared in any other of that season's games as well.

Jim McDowall

Seasons Played			
1965/66-66/67	League	~	40
	F.A. Cup	~	7
	Total	~	47

Born 25/10/1940 in Glasgow. Goalkeeper who started his career at Scottish club Baillieston, before moving to Notts County, Boston United, Scunthorpe United and Grantham Reserves. He took over the role from Brian Thompson in time for the August 1965 league game at Worksop Town and then played in every round of that season's FA Cup run. That included the First Round Proper match against Hendon and the following round when Swindon Town came to London Road, although, of course, Jim was forced to pick the ball out of the net six times during that game. The following season, with the arrival of George Crawford, Jim was limited to making only seven appearances and the April 1967 fixture at Scarborough was to be his final match for the club. Following the Summer break, Jim moved on to Heanor Town and at some point his career also took him to Brigg Town, although at what point is not known.

McGin

Seasons Played			
1891/92	League	~	1
	F.A. Cup	~	
	Other	~	
	Total	~	1

Known to have played in the March 1892 league game at Notts County Rovers, but no information exists to show any other appearances that he may have made.

Jamie McGowan

Seasons Played			
2004/05	League	~	5
	F.A. Cup	~	
	F.A. Trophy	~	
	League Cup	~	
	Lincs Cup	~	
	Total	~	5

Born 1985 at Mansfield. Former Hucknall Town, Eastwood Town and Kidsgrove Athletic midfielder who made his Grantham debut in the September 2004 game at Bedford Town. Jamie appeared in all but one of the games over the next few weeks, but following the October defeat at Cirencester Town he was released by The Gingerbreads new Manager, Lee Glover.

Bill McGrath

Seasons Played			
1952/53	League	~	34
	F.A. Cup	~	2
	Lincs Cup	~	2
	Total	~	38

Defender from Bradford who first played for Grantham in the opening league game of the 1952/53 season at Mansfield Town Reserves. Bill played in many of that season's games, including the Lincolnshire Senior Cup 'A' Final against Spalding United and the closing fixture at Lincoln City Reserves. Bill's surname is often seen spelt in various different ways, including MacGrath or MaGrath.

Mick McGuire

Seasons Played			
1987/88-90/91	League	~	63 (3)
	F.A. Cup	~	
	F.A. Trophy	~	2
	League Cup	~	
	Lincs Cup	~	
	Total	~	65 (3)

Born 04/09/1952 at Blackpool. Former England Youth International who began his career at Coventry City, before a £60,000 transfer took him to Norwich City in January 1975. He was Captain of the side that gained promotion into the First Division and eventually made over 200 appearances in his seven years with The Canaries, plus spent time on-loan to Tampa Bay Rowdies in America. Clubs represented after this period included Barnsley, Oldham Athletic and Blackpool, although he failed to make a First Team appearance in his short spell there. After a total of 422 League and cup appearances, plus 24 goals to his name, Mick's former Norwich lodger, Martin O'Neill, brought him to Grantham where he made his debut in the January 1988 league fixture against Stourbridge, although he had become disillusioned with the game and needed some persuasion from his friend to come to London Road. He played in about half of the games the following season, scoring in consecutive April fixtures against Coventry Sporting and Forest Green Rovers, eight games in the 1989/90 campaign and sixteen times during Grantham's spell at Spalding United. Mick scored in his final game for the club in the April 1991 league draw against Hinckley Town. After many years being associated with the PFA, he was appointed their Deputy Chief Executive in July 2002.

McGuire

Seasons Played			
1939/40	League	~	1
	Lincs Cup	~	
	Other	~	
	Total	~	1

Inside-Left player with Scottish League experience at King's Park, who made just one appearance for Grantham in the December 1939 Midland 'War-Time' fixture at home to Boston United.

Pete McGurk

Seasons Played			
	League	~	5
	F.A. Cup	~	
1980/81	F.A. Trophy	~	
	League Cup	~	
	Lincs Cup	~	1
	Other	~	
	Total	~	6

Joined on-loan from Long Eaton United, where he had spent nine seasons, after impressing Geoff Barker during the epic FA Cup tie against them earlier in the season. His first game was in October 1980 versus Buxton and he appeared in the County Cup Final against Lincoln City, before his final appearance for Grantham at home to Mossley in November. The following month he moved on to Ilkeston Town, but returned to Long Eaton two years later, eventually moving into a managerial position there. After time in charge at Slack & Parr and Borrowash Victoria, in February 2004 Pete was awarded the position of Manager at Shepshed Dynamo.

Alan McIlwain

Seasons Played			
	League	~	3
	F.A. Cup	~	
1984/85	F.A. Trophy	~	
	League Cup	~	
	Lincs Cup	~	
	Other	~	
	Total	~	3

Born 1956 at King's Lynn. Former Corby Town and Desborough Town player who then played for Stamford Town, including their 1984 FA Vase Final appearance at Wembley. He played for Grantham in the two October 1984 league fixtures against Hyde United, the final home match of the season against Marine and then went on to make appearances for Kettering Town and Rushden Town.

McIntosh

Seasons Played			
	League	~	1
	F.A. Cup	~	
1925/26	Lincs Cup	~	
	Total	~	1

Half-Back who also played for Crewe Alexandra and whose only known appearance for Grantham came in the December 1925 Midland League match at Boston.

Robert McKenzie

Seasons Played			
	League	~	1
	F.A. Cup	~	
1998/99	F.A. Trophy	~	
	League Cup	~	
	Lincs Cup	~	1
	Total	~	2

Born 22/03/1979 at Hexham. Former Rotherham United midfielder, who made 11 appearances for their First Team, but played just twice for Grantham in the opening County Cup match at home to Scunthorpe United and the September 1998 league fixture at Bromsgrove Rovers.

Steve McLoughlin

Seasons Played			
	League	~	25
	F.A. Cup	~	
1991/92	F.A. Trophy	~	
	League Cup	~	5
	Lincs Cup	~	
	Total	~	30

Former Brighton & Hove Albion, Notts County and Nottingham Forest player who made his debut for Grantham in the November 1991 Barclays Commercial Services League Cup tie at home to Atherstone United. Apart from a brief spell out of the side at the beginning of February, Steve played in every game up to his last appearance in April 1992 at home to Nuneaton Borough. He went on to play for Ilkeston Town and Leicester United.

Kevin McMenamin

Seasons Played			
	League	~	1
	F.A. Cup	~	
1975/76	F.A. Trophy	~	
	League Cup	~	
	Lincs Cup	~	
	Total	~	1

Born 05/08/1956 at Nottingham. Young player previously with Clifton All Whites and Mansfield Town on Schoolboy forms, who joined Grantham after being released by Notts County. However, he made just one appearance for the club in the February 1976 league game at home to Tonbridge, although he was a non-playing substitute in two other games during that year. He went on to spend time at Ilkeston Town, Loughborough United, Clifton and then continued to play Veteran's football until only a few years ago. Kevin is now a successful businessman based in Nottingham, handling pensions for some of the countries top football managers and players.

John McPherson

Seasons Played			
	League	~	10
	F.A. Cup	~	4
1984/85-85/86	F.A. Trophy	~	
	League Cup	~	6
	Lincs Cup	~	2
	Other	~	
	Total	~	22

Experienced goalkeeper who had previously represented the British Polytechnics XI, Midland League XI and Lincolnshire FA XI, with clubs he played for including Spalding United, Holbeach United, Eastwood Town, Boston FC, Skegness Town, King's Lynn and Boston United. He covered for the unavailable Grahame Hempsall in the April 1984 league fixture at home to Witton Albion and after a brief spell at Long Eaton United, came back to Grantham as the club's first choice 'keeper upon their return to the Southern League. His last game for The Gingerbreads came in October 1985 against Hednesford Town, before he was replaced by a returning Graham Cox and he then moved on to Eastwood Town.

Dave McVay

Seasons Played			
	League	~	3
	F.A. Cup	~	
1981/82	F.A. Trophy	~	
	League Cup	~	
	Lincs Cup	~	
	Other	~	
	Total	~	3

Born 05/03/1955 at Workington. Former England Schoolboy International Captain who previously played for Ilkeston Town, Notts County, making his debut just weeks after leaving school, Torquay United, Peterborough United and Lincoln City, amassing 219 senior appearances and scoring three goals whilst in The Football League. He joined Grantham after a month's trial at Boston United and played in three games during November 1981 against Lancaster City, Goole Town and South Liverpool, all of which saw victories for The Gingerbreads. He returned to Boston United, but was forced to retire from the game after breaking his leg during a match there. Dave then went into journalism, firstly as a Sports Reporter with the *Nottingham Evening Post*, before joining *The Times* as the writer behind the 'Old Pro' column. He has also co-written the biography of Tommy Lawton, published work on Notts County and released his own humorous diaries which he wrote during his playing career. Titled *'Steak,,,Diana Ross ~ Diary of a Football Nobody'*, it is hoped that it will soon be turned into either a television series or film.

Walter Mears

Seasons Played			
	League	~	5 (5)
	F.A. Cup	~	
1914/15	Lincs Cup	~	
1920/21	Other	~	2 (1)
1922/23	Total	~	7 (6)

Born circa 1890, possibly at Peterborough. Local centre-forward who made several appearances for the Reserves side, but also played for Thursday Wolves, Old Comrades, Wakefield and Wisbech. Many of his appearances have only been discovered from score-sheets, with his first known goal for Grantham coming in the March

1915 Central Alliance fixture at home to Notts County Reserves. He returned to the club in the Spring of 1921, but made only a few more appearances and the February 1923 local Hospital Cup tie against A&J Shaw is his last known game for Grantham. Died 25/01/1937 at Grantham.

Medhurst

Seasons Played	League	~	2
	Lincs Cup	~	1
1904/05-06/07	Other	~	
	Total	~	3

Midfielder who made occasional appearances for the club in the first three seasons after their reformation.

Mee

Seasons Played	League	~	6 (2)
	F.A. Cup	~	3 (3)
1932/33-33/34	Lincs Cup	~	
	Other	~	
	Total	~	9 (5)

Former Peterborough & Fletton United player who first scored for Grantham in the September 1932 league fixture at Rotherham United Reserves and only a couple of days later netted a hat-trick in the 8-1 FA Cup thrashing of Sutton Junction at London Road. He most likely played in many more games that season and certainly, at the start of the 1933/34 campaign, he was lining up for the team nearly every week. However, after his goal against Ilkeston United in November there are no more records of his name appearing in the team-sheets.

Mellor

Seasons Played	League	~	2
	F.A. Cup	~	
1926/27	Lincs Cup	~	
	Other	~	
	Total	~	2

Former Shirebrook full-back who made just two appearances for Grantham during February 1927 against Denaby United and Alfreton Town.

Melson

Seasons Played	League	~	6 (1)
	F.A. Cup	~	2
1926/27	Lincs Cup	~	
	Other	~	
	Total	~	8 (1)

Forward who had also played for Boston, Lincoln City Reserves and made his Grantham debut in the first league game of the 1926/27 season at Sutton Town, scoring his only goal for the club during Sutton's return match at London Road a month later. After playing in those first eight games though, he left the club, with the October 1926 home fixture against Worksop Town being his final one.

Alfred Middleton

Seasons Played	League	~	38 (16)
	F.A. Cup	~	3 (3)
1922/23-24/25	League Cup	~	1 (1)
	Lincs Cup	~	1
	Other	~	6 (5)
	Total	~	49 (25)

Born 1890. Previously with Mansfield Wesleyans, Mansfield Town, Mansfield Mechanics, Stockport County, playing two games in The Football League, a return to Mansfield Town, where he was part of their 1919/20 Central Alliance winning team, and then Sutton Junction. Alfred usually played in the centre-forward position, but was also very effective at half-back as well. He made his Grantham debut in October 1922 at London Road against New Hucknall Colliery and scored his first goal at the end of the year against Long Eaton. It was a poor Grantham team that season though and even finishing the campaign with only twelve goals to his name, Alfred still finished as the club's top scorer. Unfortunately he played in an era where many match reports list only goal scorers, so he most likely made many more appearances than those shown above. He scored twice for Grantham in the March 1925 Grantham Hospital Cup tie against Lincoln Robey's, but after that his final appearance is not known. Even today, Alfred is still held in high esteem at Mansfield Town, where he remains the fourth highest scorer in the club's history.

Billy Middleton

Seasons Played	League	~	37 (1)
	F.A. Cup	~	
1934/35-35/36	Lincs Cup	~	5 (4)
	Other	~	
	Total	~	42 (5)

Scottish RAF man who was based near to Grantham and although Billy first played for the club in the December 1934 friendly against a Leeds United side, he had to wait until the end of the month to make his first competitive debut in the league fixture at home to Mexborough Athletic. He played in many of that season's remaining games, including the County Cup Final and replay against Boston United, whilst a year later, although his four goals in the same competition helped Grantham defeat Lysaght's Sports in the semi-final, he was sadly forced to miss out on another Lincolnshire Senior Cup Final appearance. Billy played his final game for Grantham in the closing 1935/36 league fixture of the season at Lincoln City Reserves.

Cameron Miles

Seasons Played	League	~	18
	F.A. Cup	~	
1987/88	F.A. Trophy	~	1
	League Cup	~	3
	Lincs Cup	~	
	Total	~	22

Born circa 1965 in Scotland. Goalkeeper who joined Grantham after playing local league football and made his debut in the September 1987 fixture against Banbury United. Cameron missed many of the games during October and November, but was then a member of the team right up to the February 1988 league defeat at Coventry Sporting, played in front of only 45 spectators. Despite attracting interest from several of the local Football League sides, it was Corby Town he eventually moved to, followed by appearances for Ilkeston Town and Heanor Town.

Paul Miles

Seasons Played	League	~	4
	F.A. Cup	~	
2002/03	F.A. Trophy	~	1
	League Cup	~	3
	Lincs Cup	~	
	Total	~	8

Born 21/09/1983 at Bangor. Former Grantham Youth team player who progressed into the First team for the October 2002 Dr Marten's League Cup tie at home to Histon and then made all of his appearances before the end of the year, with the trip down to Weymouth just after Christmas his last game for the club. Paul left soon after this to tour around Australia.

Miles

Seasons Played	League	~	1
	F.A. Cup	~	
1935/36	Lincs Cup	~	
	Other	~	
	Total	~	1

Centre-Forward who also played for Annersley Colliery and made just one appearance for Grantham in the December 1935 fixture against Doncaster Rovers Reserves when Sid Bycroft was unavailable.

C. Miller

Seasons Played	F.A. Cup	~	
	Lincs Cup	~	
1883/84-84/85	Other	~	6 (1)
	Total	~	6 (1)

Made just two appearances for our club at the start of the 1883/84 season, beginning with the friendly against Grantham Volunteers and then scored his only goal a year later against the same team. He played his final game in February 1885 when Sleaford came over to London Road for a friendly.

Mick Massingham

Matt McCaul

Brendan McDaid

Jim McDowell

Jamie McGowan

Robert McKenzie

John McPherson

Paul Miles

Gary Mills

Jason Minett

Geoff Morley

Percy Moulding

Bob Mountain

Graham Neal

Jim Neil

Willie Neil

W. Miller

Seasons Played			
	F.A. Cup	~	
	Lincs Cup	~	
1874/75-75/76	Other	~	7 (1)
1883/84-84/85	Total	~	7 (1)

Played in Grantham's initial club match and the first ever competitive game, against the Third Lincolnshire Volunteer Rifles, but it was to be his only appearance for the team that season. After the Summer break he played in a handful of games, scoring his only goal for the club in March 1876 at London Road against Lincoln, but surprisingly returned to the side in November 1883 against Gainsborough Trinity and twice at the start of the following season, with the friendly at Peterborough being his last match for the club.

Gary Mills

Seasons Played			
	League	~	67 (3)
	F.A. Cup	~	6
1996/97-97/98	F.A. Trophy	~	16
	League Cup	~	5
	Lincs Cup	~	3
	Total	~	97 (3)

Born 11/11/1961 at Northampton. Former England Schoolboy Rugby Union International, who in football also gained International honours at Schoolboy, Youth and Under-23 levels. Gary made his Football League debut for Nottingham Forest against Arsenal as a 16 year old and earned himself a European Cup winner's medal at the age of 18 after replacing the injured Trevor Francis for the 1980 Final. He also played for Derby County and Seattle Sounders in America, on-loan, Notts County and Leicester City, before returning to Meadow Lane where he won an Anglo-Italian Cup winner's medal in 1995. After accumulating a total of 577 League and cup appearances, with 42 goals to his name, he came to Grantham as the club's Player/Manager following the departure of John Barnwell, making his debut in the 1996/97 season's opening match at home to Grimsby Town in the County Cup. He scored his first goal for the club the following month against Evesham United and following a successful campaign came within two points of taking the club to promotion at his first attempt. Of course that disappointment was soon forgotten with the success of the 1997/98 season. Gary took Grantham on a record start in the league, with 11 straight wins, the quarter-finals of the FA Trophy, with Gary playing in every round including the final two ties against Conference sides, Hednesford Town and Southport. The whole town was right behind the club once more and this fact was emphasised with the 2,191 attendance for the league fixture against rivals Ilkeston Town in March 1998, whilst The Gingerbreads sent everybody home happy after an unbelievable 6-0 win. The league title was secured in the final game of the season against Stourbridge, a fixture which saw Gary come off the bench to make what would turn out to be his last appearance. The biggest surprise of the year came only a week or so after the title celebrations, as differences with the Board of Directors led to his departure from the club. He soon moved on to Gresley Rovers, followed by time at the helm of King's Lynn, a short playing spell at Boston United, before taking over the Manager's role at Tamworth. Gary joined his former team-mate, Gary McAllister, as First team Coach at Coventry City in August 2002 and in January 2004 he became the Manager of Notts County. But only months later, at the beginning of November, he had been relieved of this position and became Assistant Manager for their Youth side whilst the issue of a settlement payment was resolved.

Mills

Seasons Played			
	F.A. Cup	~	
	Lincs Cup	~	
1883/84-84/85	Other	~	2
	Total	~	2

Played in goal during the 7-1 defeat at Nottingham Bank in February 1884 and then in the November friendly at Newark which resulted in an identical score-line. He failed to make any more appearances for the side after those two games.

Jason Milner

Seasons Played			
	League	~	
	F.A. Cup	~	
1992/93	F.A. Trophy	~	
	League Cup	~	
	Lincs Cup	~	1
	Total	~	1

Former Mansfield Town and Gainsborough Trinity player who made only one appearance for Grantham in the opening County Cup tie of the 1992/93 season at Lincoln City. He went on to play for Glapwell and Arnold Town, amongst others.

Keith Mincher

Seasons Played			
	League	~	41 (17)
	F.A. Cup	~	
1966/67-68/69	League Cup	~	5 (1)
	Lincs Cup	~	1
	Total	~	47 (18)

Scored on his First team debut in February 1967 against Lincoln City Reserves, but then had to wait until April for his next game, although he also scored in that fixture and incredibly continued this trend over the following two matches as well. The next two seasons Keith played in about half of the league games, with a short spell at Loughborough United and a trial at Rotherham United in the middle, but sadly for him none of the FA Cup ties. He scored his last goal for the club in the March 1968 game at Ashby, two days before his final appearance when Skegness Town came over to London Road, and despite suffering from a serious cartilage injury, coincidentally that was Keith's next footballing destination. In the early 1990's he was known to be running Sheffield United's Youth team.

Jason Minett

Seasons Played			
	League	~	58 (2)
	F.A. Cup	~	5
2001/02-03/04	F.A. Trophy	~	3 (1)
	League Cup	~	1
	Lincs Cup	~	6
	Total	~	73 (3)

Born 12/08/1971 at Peterborough. Previously played for Norwich City, (making one appearance in the Premiership), Exeter City, twice, and Lincoln City, accumulating a total of 10 goals in 182 senior matches. Jason then moved into the Conference with Doncaster Rovers, before making appearances for Boston United, King's Lynn and Stocksbridge Park Steels on loan. He made his debut for Grantham in the April 2002 league fixture at Rothwell Town and played in the final six matches, which all ended in victories for Grantham, confirming the club's promotion. Jason's first full season at The Meres included appearances in the County Cup Final against Scunthorpe United, the final qualifying round FA Cup tie at Morecambe, his first goal for the club in the November 2002 FA Trophy tie at home to Hinckley United and another Lincolnshire County Senior Cup Final, this time at Gainsborough Trinity at the end of the campaign. He also played in the November 2003 FA First Round tie against Leyton Orient and the March 2004 Lincolnshire Shield victory over Gainsborough Trinity. His last goal for The Gingerbreads had come in the league fixture at Chippenham Town, with his final appearance in the April 2004 match against Havant & Waterlooville. He left Grantham in the Summer of 2004 for Lincoln United.

A. Mitchell

Seasons Played			
	League	~	12
	F.A. Cup	~	1
1889/90	Lincs Cup	~	
	Other	~	11
1891/92-92/93	Total	~	24

Made his debut in the December 1889 friendly at home to Mapperley and then played in several of that year's remaining games. He returned to the club at the start of the 1891/92 season and played in the club's first ever league fixture, at home to Notts County Rovers, and was then a virtual permanent member of that season's team. But after the Summer break he made only one other appearance for the club, at Sheffield, only weeks before Grantham Football Club's demise. Possibly the brother of Robert Mitchell.

F. Mitchell

Seasons Played			
	League	~	29 (11)
	F.A. Cup	~	1 (1)
1920/21-21/22	League Cup	~	1
	Lincs Cup	~	1 (2)
1923/24	Other	~	2 (3)
	Total	~	34 (17)

Centre-Forward who had previously played for Grantham St John's, Newark Athletic, as well as the Reserves side, and scored on his First team debut in November 1920 against Sutton Town when Edgar Eatch was unavailable. Because of the quality of the team's strikers, appearances were limited, although one of those from the same season saw him score all three goals in the 3-2 victory over Kettering Town. In the 1923/24 season he was able to gain a more noticeable place in the side, possibly due to the loss of Edgar Eatch. Even though he wasn't able to get close to the club's top scorer, Stanley Streets, he did finish second and managed to score twice in the Grantham Hospital Cup Final at home to Woolsthorpe.

Mark Mitchell

Seasons Played			
	League	~	8 (2)
	F.A. Cup	~	2 (1)
1984/85-85/86	F.A. Trophy	~	
	League Cup	~	4
	Lincs Cup	~	3
	Other	~	
	Total	~	17 (3)

Born 13/08/1961 at Cleethorpes. Former Grimsby Town Apprentice, with experience at Bourne Town and Stamford Town. Mark made one appearance for Grantham at the start of the 1984/85 season, coming on as substitute in the County Cup match against Lincoln City to replace Mick Downing. He was more noticeable though in the following season, scoring against Mile Oak Rovers and Bromsgrove Rovers, but his last appearance came in the November 1985 league fixture against Wellingborough Town, a match which also saw his final goal as well. Mark moved on to play for Wisbech Town, Spalding United and then went back to Bourne Town, where he became their Player/Manager. A few years ago he returned once more to Bourne as Manager, then spent time as their Director of Football, before returning to his initial role at the helm in October 2003. Mark also currently works as a Manager at a Spalding food manufacturing company.

Robert Mitchell

Seasons Played			
	Lincs Cup	~	3
	Other	~	17 (2)
1889/90-90/91	Total	~	20 (2)

Born circa 1861. Possible brother of A. Mitchell. Robert first played for Grantham in the opening friendly of the 1889/90 season at home to Leicester Fosse Reserves and then appeared in many of the season's remaining fixtures, scoring two goals in the Boxing Day encounter against Notts Rangers. He continued to be a constant member of the team the following season as well, but unfortunately details of his final appearance are not known. Died March 1918 at Grantham.

Mitchell

Seasons Played			
	League	~	1
	Other	~	
1906/07	Total	~	1

Forward who is known to have played in the September 1906 league game against Derby Thornhill, but no information is available to show any other games that he might have played in.

Mitchell

Seasons Played			
	League	~	5
	Lincs Cup	~	2
1909/10	Other	~	4
	Total	~	11

Defender who made his debut in the opening Midland Amateur League fixture of the 1909/10 season at Derby YMCA and then continued to make many more appearances during that year, including the March 1910 friendly against Queen's Park.

Mitchell

Seasons Played			
	League	~	6 (3)
	F.A. Cup	~	
1933/34	Lincs Cup	~	1
	Other	~	1
	Total	~	8 (3)

Played in the first league game of the 1933/34 season at Loughborough Corinthians and then scored a hat-trick in the next game at Bolsover. He played in many of that season's early games, but no evidence appears for matches played in after the December fixture at Gresley Rovers.

Mitchell

Seasons Played			
	League	~	9 (3)
	F.A. Cup	~	7 (2)
1945/46-46/47	Lincs Cup	~	
	Total	~	16 (5)

Forward who scored on his debut in the initial league game after the end of World War Two, at home to Gainsborough Trinity, and then missed just three matches played in those first couple of months. He appeared in every tie of that season's FA Cup run, including the two legs against Kettering Town and Mansfield Town in the Proper Rounds, but the Christmas Day fixture at home to Ransome & Marles was his last of the season. He returned to Grantham though in November 1946 to make one more appearance against Gainsborough Trinity in the Midland League.

Fred Mobbs

Seasons Played			
	League	~	44
	F.A. Cup	~	2
1930/31	Lincs Cup	~	
	Total	~	46

Born 29/07/1904 at Gainsborough. Goalkeeper who had previously made appearances for Gainsborough Trinity, Blackpool, where he played in 24 games during their 1927/28 Division Two season, Aldershot and Newark Town. He played for Grantham in the first game of the 1930/31 season at Mansfield Town and then missed just two league fixtures during the whole season. Died 1973 at Gainsborough.

Andy Moore

Seasons Played			
	League	~	16 (1)
	F.A. Cup	~	
1992/93	F.A. Trophy	~	1
	League Cup	~	2
	Lincs Cup	~	
	Total	~	19 (1)

Born 14/11/1965 at Cleethorpes. Defender who made 65 League appearances whilst at Grimsby Town, plus spent time on-loan at Wigan Athletic, before helping Lincoln City to win the Conference Championship in 1987/88. After periods playing at Blackpool, Shamrock Rovers, Hong Kong and Western Suburb in Australia, Andy signed for Boston United and then came to Grantham. His first game was in the September 1992 FA Trophy tie against Congleton Town and he then played in every match, scoring his only goal for the club on Boxing Day against King's Lynn, until his last appearance in January 1994 at home to Barri Town. Andy later played for Gainsborough Trinity, Wisbech Town, Fakenham Town, Brigg Town, Lincoln United and Spalding United.

Christian Moore

Seasons Played			
	League	~	8 (2)
	F.A. Cup	~	
1996/97	F.A. Trophy	~	
	League Cup	~	
	Lincs Cup	~	
	Total	~	8 (2)

Born 04/11/1972 at Derby. Began his career as a Trainee at Leicester City, before making one appearance for Stockport County, albeit from the substitute's bench. Moves then followed to Sandiacre Town, Leicester United, Burton Albion and Forest Green Rovers, from where he came to Grantham on-loan in November 1996. His first game for The Gingerbreads was in the league match at Sutton Coldfield Town and after goals against Evesham United and Dudley Town, his last appearance for the club came in the February 1997 league defeat of Paget Rangers. Chris went on to play for Ilkeston Town, before a £20,000 return to Burton, a transfer to Telford United and following their demise, a move to Worcester City.

Tony Moore

Seasons Played			
1986/87	League	~	7
	F.A. Cup	~	2
	F.A. Trophy	~	3
	League Cup	~	3
	Lincs Cup	~	1
	Total	~	16

Born 19/09/1957 at Wolverhampton. Full-Back who previously played for Burton Albion, Sheffield United, Crewe Alexandra, Worksop Town, Rochdale, Belper Town and Gainsborough Trinity, scoring twice in his 49 Football League appearances. His first game for Grantham came in the opening County Cup tie of the 1986/87 season at Scunthorpe United, with his final appearance at the end of November against Sutton Coldfield Town. Tony then returned to Gainsborough, followed by a brief spell at York City, before his return once more to Gainsborough as Assistant Manager.

Moore

Seasons Played			
1939/40	League	~	1
	Lincs Cup	~	
	Other	~	
	Total	~	1

Full-Back who had previously played for Grimsby Town and made just one appearance for Grantham in the April 1940 Midland 'War-Time' League game against Scunthorpe & Lindsey United. He must have been kept busy by the soon to be champion's forwards, when you consider the 8-0 final score-line against Grantham.

Gerald Morgan

Seasons Played			
1929/30-30/31	League	~	54 (1)
	F.A. Cup	~	1
	Lincs Cup	~	
	Other	~	
	Total	~	55 (1)

Born 25/07/1899 at Belfast. Centre-Half who had previously played for Cliftonville, Linfield, Nottingham Forest, scoring six times in 219 games, and Luton Town, where he made another four senior appearances. Gerry was also a former Irish International player who was awarded eight caps for his country, starting against England in 1922 and was described at the time as "a perfect wizard with the head". Gerry came to Grantham for an undisclosed fee, but one that was described at the time as 'the largest ever given by a Midland League club'. He made his debut in the October 1929 league fixture at Lincoln City Reserves and then scored his only goal for the club in the December match at Denaby United. Sadly, little is known about other games that he played in, but data from the end of the season shows that he was a near constant member of the side, as he was at the start of the following campaign as well. Gerry appears to have left the club soon after the 1931 New Year, with possibly the January match at Chesterfield Reserves his final game. The following season he played for Cork and then spent two years at Ballymena, finally finishing with well over 400 senior appearances to his name, half of which came in Irish League and Cup competitions. Gerry continued to be involved with Irish football and later in life became the trainer of the National side. Died 1959 in Ireland.

James Morgan

Seasons Played			
2000/01	League	~	1
	F.A. Cup	~	
	F.A. Trophy	~	
	League Cup	~	1
	Lincs Cup	~	
	Total	~	2

Born 11/09/1975 at Lincoln. Former Lincoln City Youth, Boston Town, Sleaford Town and Lincoln United goalkeeper who joined the club as cover for Mario Ziccardi. He played in the November 2000 games against Wisbech Town and Rothwell Town, but soon after returned to Lincoln United, then had a brief spell at Lincoln Moorlands, before returning to United once more. James still lives in the Lincoln area and currently works as a plumber.

Morgan

Seasons Played			
1927/28	League	~	1
	F.A. Cup	~	
	Lincs Cup	~	
	Total	~	1

Goalkeeper who played in one game, the October 1927 Midland League fixture at home to Scarborough when Walter Fox was unavailable. Perhaps he should have played more often, as the team pulled off a surprising 2-1 win over the title contenders.

Morgan

Seasons Played			
1947/48	League	~	1
	F.A. Cup	~	
	Lincs Cup	~	
	Total	~	1

Goalkeeper who made just one appearance to cover Percy Ashton in the January 1948 fixture at Gainsborough Trinity, an interesting game to say the least as Grantham lost 10-6! Even though goalkeepers tend to have a longer career than their outfield team-mates, surely this individual must be a different player to the previous entry.

Brian Morley

Seasons Played			
1963/64-65/66	League	~	12 (5)
	F.A. Cup	~	1
	Lincs Cup	~	
	Total	~	13 (5)

Born 10/10/1942 in Grantham. 'Nip', as he was known, began his career at Nottingham Forest, playing in the 'A' side, before joining his home team. For the First team he played in the final two league fixtures of the 1963/64 season as a replacement for Cyril Brown and scored in the first of those against Gainsborough Trinity. Brian made another two appearances the following season and then had his best run in the First team at the start of the 1965/66 season. His final competitive appearance came in the February 1966 fixture at home to Arnold, although he played and scored in the Bourne Hospital Cup Final at the end of the season. After also playing for the Lincolnshire representative side during his time at London Road, moves followed to Stamford Town and Spalding United. Brian is now retired and still lives in Grantham.

Geoff Morley

Seasons Played			
1951/52	League	~	208 (28)
1953/54-58/59	F.A. Cup	~	14 (1)
	Lincs Cup	~	5
	Total	~	227 (29)

Former Nottingham Forest Reserves midfielder who made his debut in the opening game of the 1951/52 season at home to Worksop Town and although only missing two games in that first campaign, had to wait until the following February to score his first goal which came in the match at Scunthorpe & Lindsey United. Geoff returned at the start of the 1953/54 season and played in about half of that year's games, whilst in the following campaign he once more became a consistent member of the team. This trend continued over the next few years, although sadly for Geoff it was at a time when the team as a whole was having little to cheer about. It was to get even worse though during the 1957/58 season as he was left to make many of his appearances when either Dick Conroy or Alan Clay were injured and with Grantham at long last reaching the County Cup Final once more, neither of the two previously mentioned players were out of the team. Geoff scored his final goal for the club in the November 1958 Midland League game at Spennymoor United, a few weeks before his last appearance in the home match against Stockton.

Jon Morley

Seasons Played			
1987/88	League	~	17 (1)
	F.A. Cup	~	1
	F.A. Trophy	~	
	League Cup	~	2
	Lincs Cup	~	
	Total	~	20 (1)

Defender who progressed through the Reserves side to make his debut in the October 1987 league fixture at London Road against Coventry Sporting. Jon had a good run in the side over the Winter, scoring his only goal in November against Mile Oak Rovers, but made his final appearance in the return league game at Coventry Sporting in February 1988.

Morley

Seasons Played			
	League	~	2
	F.A. Cup	~	1
1892/93	Total	~	3

Defender who joined the club at the start of the ill-fated 1892/93 season, playing in the league games against Sheffield, Matlock and finally the FA Cup tie at home to Belper.

Ernie Morris

Seasons Played			
	League	~	11 (7)
	F.A. Cup	~	3
1950/51-51/52	Lincs Cup	~	
	Total	~	14 (7)

Born 11/05/1921 at Stocksbridge. Former Nottingham Forest, (with one goal to his name after four appearances), and York City centre-forward who made his debut for Grantham in the first Midland League game of the 1950/51 season at Bradford City Reserves. He then had to wait until the end of October to score his first goal for the club, but made it three in the game at home to Halifax Town Reserves and amazingly on the return fixture only a fortnight later scored another hat-trick. Perhaps unsurprisingly then, Ernie soon moved on to Halifax Town, but failed to impress there and after making just one First team appearance returned to London Road just under a year later. However, Ernie was to play only one more game for Grantham, with the October 1951 fixture against Goole Town being the last one for the club.

Harold Morris

Seasons Played			
	League	~	35 (4)
	Lincs Cup	~	1 (1)
1931/32	Other	~	
	Total	~	36 (5)

Born 02/09/1902 at Bolsover. Experienced player who had started his career in goal at Bolsover Town, before changing to the striker's role after a move to Bolsover Colliery. Transfers followed to Worksop Town, where he was the club's top scorer, a short return to Bolsover Colliery, then Watford, (with four goals to his name in 50 mid 1920's appearances), and Mansfield Town. Whilst there he was an important member of the Midland League Championship and Mansfield Hospital Cup winning team that also had a tremendous run in the 1928/29 FA Cup, finally losing to Arsenal in the Fourth Round at Highbury. Harry then signed for Barnsley, making a lone First team appearance, and Shirebrook, before coming to Grantham. He made his debut in the opening league fixture of the 1931/32 season at Loughborough Corinthians, with his first goal for the club a fortnight later at Boston. Although end of season data shows that he played in most of the year's matches, it is not known which was his final game. The following season he went on to play for Shirebrook Supporters. Died 1976 at Bolsover.

Stuart Morris

Seasons Played			
	League	~	3
	F.A. Cup	~	
1999/00	F.A. Trophy	~	
	League Cup	~	2
	Lincs Cup	~	
	Total	~	5

Midfielder who signed for the club after a period playing football in Finland and started his first game in the October 1999 league fixture at Burton Albion. Stuart then became an almost permanent member of the substitute's bench over the next couple of months, from where he made all his other appearances, the last of which came in December at home to Margate.

John Morton

Seasons Played			
	League	~	1
	F.A. Cup	~	
1992/93	F.A. Trophy	~	
	League Cup	~	
	Lincs Cup	~	
	Total	~	1

Born 27/11/1966 in Grantham. Local player who made one appearance in the April 1993 league match at Leicester United. He went on to play for Cottesmore, Mirlees Blackstone and Bourne Town.

Ken Moseley

Seasons Played			
	League	~	3
	F.A. Cup	~	
1948/49	Lincs Cup	~	
	Total	~	3

Centre-Forward who had the almost impossible task of covering for Jack Macartney whilst he was out of the January 1949 league fixtures against Grimsby Town Reserves, Denaby United and Gainsborough Trinity. Sadly for Ken he failed to score in any of the matches.

Percy Moulding

Seasons Played			
	League	~	
	F.A. Cup	~	
1919/20	Lincs Cup	~	1
	Total	~	1

Born 1895 in Grantham. Inside-Right who had also played for Grantham St John's, but made just one appearance for the Grantham First team in the November 1919 Lincolnshire Senior Cup tie against Boston. He did however play many games for that season's successful Reserves side that won the Grantham League Division One. Died 15/07/1974 at Grantham.

Ryan Moulds

Seasons Played			
	League	~	1
	F.A. Cup	~	3
1998/99-99/00	F.A. Trophy	~	2
	League Cup	~	1
	Lincs Cup	~	
	Total	~	7

Born 1976 at Melton Mowbray. Step-son of the club's then Chairman, Alan Prince, and Reserves goalkeeper who covered the position in between the Grantham careers of Craig Davis and Gary Germaine. Ryan's first game came in October 1998 against West Midlands Police in the FA Cup, with an appearance in the final qualifying round tie at Tamworth as well. He made one more lone appearance the following season in the December 1999 Dr Marten's League Cup tie at home to Cambridge City.

J. Moulsher

Seasons Played			
	League	~	2
	Lincs Cup	~	1
1894/95	Other	~	
	Total	~	3

Either John or Joseph, who were both older brothers of William Moulsher and born in Grantham. Whichever one, he is known to have played in many of the 1894/95 Grantham & District League fixtures.

William Moulsher

Seasons Played			
	League	~	3
	Lincs Cup	~	1
1893/94-94/95	Other	~	3
	Total	~	7

Born 1872 in Grantham. Known to have played in the Grantham Minor Cup Final of April 1894 and like his brother, the previous entry, played in many of the following season's matches as well.

Moulsher

Seasons Played			
	Lincs Cup	~	
	Other	~	1
1890/91	Total	~	1

Most likely one of the two previous entries, who played in the October 1890 friendly at home to Notts St Luke's, but with no initial listed it is impossible to specify which one he is.

Bob Mountain

Seasons Played			
	League	~	32 (14)
	F.A. Cup	~	2
1980/81-81/82	F.A. Trophy	~	
	League Cup	~	1 (1)
	Lincs Cup	~	2
	Other	~	2
	Total	~	39 (15)

Born 11/09/1956 at Wombwell. Started his career at Bolton Wanderers and then made one appearance for Huddersfield Town during the 1973/74 season, before joining Frickley Athletic,

Mexborough Town and Bridlington Trinity. He was signed for Grantham by his former Manager, Geoff Barker, making his debut in the December 1980 league match at home to Runcorn and only days later was playing against Nottingham Forest in the Redmayne Trophy. Despite already missing half of the league fixtures, as the season finished Bob came close to over-hauling the club's top goalscorer, Dave Leadbeater, aided by hat-tricks against Buxton and Netherfield. The following campaign he made another 15 appearances, but surprisingly only scored twice more, the last of which was against Matlock Town in the first round of the Northern Premier League Cup. Bob made his final appearance for Grantham in Nottingham Forest's return game in November 1981 and he then went on to play for Alfreton Town, Matlock Town, where he finished as the Northern Premier League's leading scorer during the 1982/83 season, and Stafford Rangers.

William Mowl

Seasons Played	League	~	5
	F.A. Cup	~	
1949/50-50/51	Lincs Cup	~	
	Total	~	5

Born 23/06/1922 at Bulwell. Former Notts County and Mansfield Town goalkeeper who covered for Ted Eaglen at the Bradford Park Avenue Reserves league fixture at the end of the 1949/50 season and then kept the position after the Summer break until the arrival of Horace Hinton. William then made one further appearance for the club at Doncaster Rovers Reserves in the penultimate league fixture of the 1950/51 season.

Chris Moyses

Seasons Played	League	~	26
	F.A. Cup	~	
1985/86	F.A. Trophy	~	
	League Cup	~	
	Lincs Cup	~	
	Total	~	26

Born 01/11/1965 at Lincoln. Former Lincoln City, Halifax Town, Boston United and Shepshed Charterhouse player who made his Grantham debut in the October 1985 league fixture against Hednesford Town and appeared in most of the games up to the season's closing match at VS Rugby. Chris went on to play for Spalding United and King's Lynn.

John Mulholland

Seasons Played	League	~	39 (10)
	F.A. Cup	~	4 (1)
1952/53-53/54	Lincs Cup	~	1
	Total	~	44 (11)

Born 07/12/1928 at Dumbarton. Former Renton Boys Guild, Plymouth Argyle, Grimsby Town and Scunthorpe United right-winger who made his Grantham debut in the September 1952 Midland League fixture at home to Peterborough United and then scored his first goal for the club less than three weeks later when Scarborough came to London Road. Despite having to fight for his place with Alf Graver, John managed to gain the ascendancy and finished the season with 32 appearances to his name. He seemed to have secured his place in the side the following season, but after playing in every one of the first 12 games, the October FA Cup tie against Ashby Institute proved to be his final match for the club.

Darren Munton

Seasons Played	League	~	5 (1)
	F.A. Cup	~	
1996/97	F.A. Trophy	~	4 (1)
	League Cup	~	
	Lincs Cup	~	
	Total	~	9 (2)

Born 19/09/1967 at Melton Mowbray. Forward who began his career at Oakham United, before moving to Melton Town, Pedigree Petfoods, Bourne Town, where he helped the club win the United Counties Championship, and then the first of three spells at Boston United. Darren spent a couple of months at King's Lynn and came to Grantham in time to make his debut in the December 1996 league fixture at Hinckley United. His two goals were scored in the matches against Redditch United and Blyth Spartans, but after nine consecutive appearances the February 1997 match at home to RC Warwick turned out to be his last for the club. He later played for Lincoln United and Spalding United, during which a second United Counties League winners medal was won. Darren then moved into management, firstly at Cottesmore Amateurs, before his return to Bourne where he spent just over a year as Player/Manager.

Graham Musson

Seasons Played	League	~	2
	F.A. Cup	~	
1961/62-62/63	Lincs Cup	~	
	Total	~	2

Born 02/04/1938 at Corby Glen. Son of Harry Musson and a former Corby Glen defender who made just two appearances for the First team, the September 1961 Midland League fixture at Sutton Town and the match at Ilkeston Town just over a year later. Graham currently runs a farm near to Grantham.

Harry Musson

Seasons Played	League	~	13 (2)
	F.A. Cup	~	2
1919/20-20/21	Lincs Cup	~	1 (2)
	Other	~	
	Total	~	16 (4)

Born 18/05/1895 at Corby Glen. Father of Graham Musson and a centre-forward who also played for Corby Glen and Spalding United. Harry scored twice during his first game for Grantham in November 1919 at Hucknall Byron, but with such quality in Grantham's forward line he was struggling to command a regular place in the team. By the start of the following season he had reverted to a more defensive role to try and play more often, although it seems as though this worked for only a few months as there is no information that shows him playing after November 1920, with the Central Alliance fixture at home to Sutton Town possibly his last match for the club.

Musson

Seasons Played	F.A. Cup	~	
	Lincs Cup	~	
1886/87	Other	~	3 (1)
	Total	~	3 (1)

The first known game for this player comes in November 1886 when Grantham played Newark in a friendly at London Road. He is recognised as scoring in the 4-1 win over Louth and his last game was against Grantham Volunteers the following January.

Musson

Seasons Played	League	~	1
	Lincs Cup	~	
1893/94-94/95	Other	~	1
	Total	~	2

Possibly the same player as the previous entry, who is known to have played in the April 1894 Grantham Minor Cup Final and the first Grantham & District League fixture after the Summer interval against Rovers Colts.

Mycroft

Seasons Played	League	~	1
	F.A. Cup	~	
1934/35	Lincs Cup	~	
	Total	~	1

Played in the April 1935 Midland League fixture at home to Chesterfield Reserves. My apologies to the individual if the following theory is wrong. At the time, Sid *Bycroft* was playing for the club, but according to the match report not in that particular game. Could this be an example of a typing error in the team-sheet that was not picked up by those who calculated end of season statistics?

Colin Myers

Seasons Played	League	~	3
	F.A. Cup	~	1 (2)
1925/26	Lincs Cup	~	
1930/31	Total	~	4 (2)

Born 1894 at Chapeltown. Vastly experienced left-sided player who had previously played for Northfleet, Crystal Palace, Hickleton Main Colliery, Bradford City, Southend United, Aberdare Athletic, Northampton Town, Queen's Park Rangers and Exeter City. He appeared for Grantham in the April 1926 league game against Sutton Town, but this may have been just a single trial for the club that he played in at that time. In the Summer he moved to Hartlepools United and finally finished his professional career in 1927 having scored 60 goals in a total of 186 Football League fixtures, plus netted 12 more times in ten FA Cup games. Colin then joined Gainsborough Trinity, but returned to Grantham in 1930, scoring twice in October against Ransome & Marles in the FA Cup. However, he then made only a few other appearances for the club, although details of his final game are not known and he went on to play for King's Lynn. Died 1984.

Barry Nash

Seasons Played	League	~	5
	F.A. Cup	~	
1976/77-77/78	F.A. Trophy	~	
	League Cup	~	
1985/86	Lincs Cup	~	
	Other	~	
	Total	~	5

Born circa 1961. Former Grantham United player who made occasional appearances for the side, starting against Nuneaton Borough in May 1977. He played twice for The Gingerbreads the following season and returned to help out Barry Shaw at the end of the 1985/86 campaign, with his last appearance for the club at VS Rugby. His career ended due to an injury whilst playing for Mirlees Blackstone during the 1988/89 season, which led to his return to London Road as the club's Reserves Team Manager. Following this, Barry went on to take over the helm at Harrowby United, and he still lives locally.

Eric Naylor

Seasons Played	League	~	30 (11)
	F.A. Cup	~	
1958/59-60/61	League Cup	~	1
	Lincs Cup	~	
1962/63	Total	~	31 (11)

Forward who had a tremendous start to his Grantham career by scoring in his first game against Scarborough in November 1958 and netted a brace the following week at Gainsborough Trinity. Even so, by January his place had been taken by Bernard Weakley and the following season he was only able to make six further appearances. However, Eric had his best run in the First team during the Winter of 1960/61 as he made 15 consecutive appearances, but then had to wait until Christmas two years later to play once more, a match at London Road against Holbeach United that saw his final goal in what turned out to be the conclusion to his Grantham career.

Naylor

Seasons Played	League	~	1
	F.A. Cup	~	
1930/31	Lincs Cup	~	
	Total	~	1

Half-Back who had also played for Butler's Hill, Bulwell and made just the one appearance for Grantham in the February 1931 away fixture at Scarborough.

Graham Neal

Seasons Played	League	~	54 (1)
	F.A. Cup	~	7
1983/84-85/86	F.A. Trophy	~	8
	League Cup	~	11 (1)
	Lincs Cup	~	3
	Other	~	2
	Total	~	85 (2)

Born 06/03/1960 at Boston. Former Spalding United and Boston FC defender who made his debut for Grantham in the 1983/84 season's opening league fixture at Hyde United, with his first goal for the club in the New Year's Eve Bass Challenge League Cup tie against Gainsborough Trinity. Although Graham missed out on many of that season's games after this, he was back in the side for the 1984/85 season. He scored his other goal for Grantham in October 1985 against Merthyr Tydfil, but the following month made his final appearance in the game at home to Coventry Sporting. After being released by Grantham, he returned to Spalding, then played for Wyberton, before joining up with his home side once more. Graham finally retired from the game at the age of 42 having won various County honours to go with a United Counties Championship medal. He still lives in Boston, working as a Store Manager for a fruit and vegetable packing company.

John Neal

Seasons Played	League	~	1
	F.A. Cup	~	
1992/93	F.A. Trophy	~	
	League Cup	~	
	Lincs Cup	~	
	Total	~	1

Former Cottesmore player who made just one appearance for Grantham in the April 1993 league fixture at Leicester United. He went on to play for Holwell, Bourne Town, Mirlees Blackstone and Corby Town.

Grant Neil

Seasons Played	League	~	9
	F.A. Cup	~	2
1996/97-97/98	F.A. Trophy	~	3
	League Cup	~	1
	Lincs Cup	~	1
	Total	~	16

Born 03/09/1973 at Bury St Edmunds. Brother of Jim Neil. Grant progressed through the Reserves to make his First team debut in the August 1996 FA Cup tie at Witham Town and played in 14 other games during that season, plus the opening County Cup tie of the 1997/98 season at Gainsborough Trinity. After leaving The Meres, he went on to play for Bourne Town, Bedworth United, Cottesmore, Long Buckby and Lutterworth Town.

Jim Neil

Seasons Played	League	~	127 (21)
	F.A. Cup	~	13 (3)
1996/97	F.A. Trophy	~	9
1999/00-02/03	League Cup	~	5 (1)
2004/05	Lincs Cup	~	7 (2)
	Total	~	161 (27)

Born 28/02/1976 at Bury St Edmunds. Brother of Grant Neil. Jim originally began his career at Grimsby Town, before joining Grantham on-loan from Scunthorpe United. He made four appearances during October 1996, starting with the league game at Paget Rangers and scoring his first goal for the club at home to Raunds Town. After returning to Scunthorpe and with a total of nine appearances in The Football League, Jim went on to play for Burton Albion and Gainsborough Trinity, before rejoining Grantham at the start of the 1999/00 season. He then missed only one game during that campaign, but missed several matches in the 2000/01 season, although he played and scored in the FA Cup tie at Rushden & Diamonds which ended with a 5-4 defeat for Grantham. Once more Jim played in about half of the games the following season, the club's promotion winning year, whilst the 2002/03 camapign saw appearances for him in the County Cup Final against Scunthorpe United and Morecambe in the final qualifying round of the FA Cup. He joined Stamford on-loan during January 2003 and made three more appearances upon his return to Grantham, the last of which was in March 2003 at Havant & Waterlooville. Jim moved to Harrowby United for the start of the following season, but returned to The Meres once more in September 2004, signed by Caretaker/ Manager, Adrian Speed. However, work commitments forced the end of his Grantham career and Jim's final goal came in his closing appearance for the club, in March 2005 against Stamford in the Lincolnshire Shield.

William Neil

Seasons Played	League	~	30 (5)
	F.A. Cup	~	1
1953/54	Lincs Cup	~	2 (1)
1957/58	Total	~	33 (6)

Born 20/04/1924 at Lanark. Former Morton and Bradford Park Avenue player who made his Grantham debut in the October 1953 FA Cup replay against Ashby Institute and then scored his first goal a month later at Lincoln City Reserves. That fixture was at the start of William's best run in the side, as he then played in every single game until April, including the County Cup Final victory where he managed to score one of the goals against Gainsborough Trinity. William returned to the side at the beginning of the 1957/58 season to make two more appearances, against Denaby United and finally in the visit of Scunthorpe & Lindsey United Reserves to London Road in September.

F. Nelson

Seasons Played			
	League	~	6
	F.A. Cup	~	
1946/47	Lincs Cup	~	3
	Total	~	9

First played for Grantham in the January 1947 league game at home to Barnsley Reserves and then made all of his appearances for the club over the next couple of months. He played in that season's Lincolnshire Senior Cup Final against Gainsborough Trinity and his last appearance for Grantham came in the replay.

Nelson

Seasons Played			
	F.A. Cup	~	
	Lincs Cup	~	
1883/84	Other	~	1
	Total	~	1

Individual with only one known appearance for the club in December 1883 against Spilsby.

Paul Neville

Seasons Played			
	League	~	14 (2)
	F.A. Cup	~	
1989/90	F.A. Trophy	~	
	League Cup	~	4
	Lincs Cup	~	
	Total	~	18 (2)

Born 19/07/1963 at Stepney. Signed from Eastwood Town and made his Grantham debut in the Westgate Insurance League Cup tie against Nuneaton Borough in October 1989. He scored a brace in the February league fixture against Willenhall Town, but made his final appearance the following month at Bridgnorth Town.

Harry Newby

Seasons Played			
	League	~	3 (1)
	F.A. Cup	~	
1938/39	Lincs Cup	~	
	Total	~	3 (1)

Former Grimsby Town and Boston United defender who played in the friendly against Chelsea in November 1938 and was then able to keep the place for the following week's game against Mansfield Town Reserves when William Buckley was unavailable. Harry played in two more games, again as cover for the same player, against Frickley Colliery and then in March at home to Hull City Reserves where he got one of the goals in the 6-2 defeat.

Marcus Newell

Seasons Played			
	League	~	11
	F.A. Cup	~	1
1991/92-92/93	F.A. Trophy	~	
	League Cup	~	
	Lincs Cup	~	
	Total	~	12

Began his career as a YTS player at Grimsby Town, before moving on to Spalding United, King's Lynn and Immingham Town. His first game for Grantham came in March 1991 at Redditch United, but despite playing in all of the remaining fixtures from that season, plus several at the start of the 1992/93 campaign, the September match at Newport was his last for the club. Marcus went on to play for Winterton Rangers, Wisbech Town, Bedworth United and at the end of the decade returned to Winterton.

Harry Newey

Seasons Played			
	League	~	6 (2)
	F.A. Cup	~	1
1948/49	Lincs Cup	~	
	Total	~	7 (2)

Made his debut in the September 1948 game against Notts County Reserves and then had five more occasional appearances over the next few months, scoring against Scarborough. Harry made a lone and final appearance at London Road against Doncaster Rovers Reserves the following March, a game which also saw his final goal.

Rob Newham

Seasons Played			
	League	~	11
	F.A. Cup	~	
1990/91	F.A. Trophy	~	
	League Cup	~	
	Lincs Cup	~	
	Total	~	11

Goalkeeper who signed from Sunday League side, Greyhounders, to play in the final 11 league matches of the 1990/91 season, starting at Bridgnorth Town and ending against Redditch United. Rob continued to play local football, including spending time at Harrowby United.

Victor Newman

Seasons Played			
	League	~	8 (5)
	F.A. Cup	~	1
1928/29	Lincs Cup	~	1
	Other	~	3 (3)
1932/33-34/35	Total	~	13 (8)

Local player who also made appearances for Grantham Amateurs, Grantham St John's and played just once for our club during the 1928/29 season, although the specific game is not known. Victor made another single appearance during the 1932/33 season, scoring in the Grantham Hospital Cup tie against Ransome & Marles and then finally was given a reasonable run in the side when he appeared in many of the games in the latter half of the following campaign, culminating in one of the goals during the victorious local Hospital Cup Final against T.W. Rust & Co. His final appearance for the club came in the October 1934 Midland League game at Doncaster Rovers Reserves.

Newson

Seasons Played			
	League	~	2
	F.A. Cup	~	
1933/34	Lincs Cup	~	
	Other	~	
	Total	~	2

Played in the December 1933 fixtures against Chesterfield Reserves and Gresley Rovers, but it is not known whether they were his only appearances during that season.

Newton

Seasons Played			
	F.A. Cup	~	
	Lincs Cup	~	
1885/86	Other	~	1
	Total	~	1

Played just once for Grantham in the November 1885 friendly at Bourne.

Newton

Seasons Played			
	League	~	2
	F.A. Cup	~	
1920/21	Lincs Cup	~	
	Other	~	
	Total	~	2

Half-Back from the Lincoln area who appeared for Grantham in the two March 1921 Central Alliance fixtures against Kettering Town and Welbeck Colliery.

J. Nicholls

Seasons Played			
	League	~	2
	F.A. Cup	~	
1932/33	Lincs Cup	~	
	Other	~	
1936/37	Total	~	2

Local player who had also made appearances for Grantham Amateurs and Mowbray Sports but had just a single appearance for our club during the 1932/33 season and then one more nearly four years later in January 1937 against Bradford City Reserves.

F. Nelson

Ernie Nixon

Jon Nixon

Bob Norris

Dave Norton

Kris Nurse

Emeka Nwadike

Derek Oliver

Martin O'Neill

Kasi Oseni

Steve Parkinson

Ray Parnham

Jeff Parry

Glenn Pearson

Roger Peck

Robert Pell

Ernie Nixon

Seasons Played			
1968/69-76/77	League	~	246 (137)
	F.A. Cup	~	24 (11)
	F.A. Trophy	~	22 (9)
	League Cup	~	32 (17)
	Lincs Cup	~	9 (5)
	Other	~	2
	Total	~	335 (179)

Born 20/10/1947 at Newark. Forward who previously spent time at Nottingham Forest, (captaining their Youth side in a tour of Holland), and briefly, Lincoln City. Ernie made his Grantham debut in the September 1968 Midland League match at Long Eaton United, scoring his first goal for the club only three days later against Warley. In his first season with Grantham he played in the FA Cup First Round against Chelmsford City, the next round at home to Swindon Town, scored four times in the league match at Lockheed Leamington and at the end of the campaign won a winner's medal in the Midland League Cup. Grantham's final three seasons in the Midland League saw two Championship winner's medals for Ernie, another in the League Cup, one in the Lincolnshire County Cup, appearances in the FA Cup Proper against Oldham Athletic, Stockport County and Rotherham United, where he netted the consolation goal, plus, finally, an FA Trophy Quarter-Final appearance in the match against Yeovil Town. As for his scoring, the same time-scale had seen four more hat-tricks credited to him and even another instance where he managed to find the target four times, with the poor Stamford 'keeper being the unfortunate victim, this time in April 1972. Grantham's first season in the Southern League ended with another League Championship, the Merit Cup after the club's 113 goals, 23 of which came from Ernie, (including four in the match at Bury Town), plus an appearance in the FA Cup First Round Proper at Bradford City. The 1973/74 season will of course be best remembered for the FA Cup run and Ernie played in every round, including the ties against Rochdale and Middlesbrough. It was to be an early finish to the season though, as he played no further part in the matches after the start of February, but still finished as the club's joint highest scorer along with Bob Norris. Although Grantham finished as runners-up to Dartford in the Southern League Premier and eight points adrift, when faced with the fact that The Gingerbreads lost six of the games following Ernie's departure from the side, one can only wonder whether the outcome would have been any different had he played. He was back in the side the following season though, scoring another hat-trick in September at home to Telford United, although it was a comparatively indifferent year for the club, whilst November 1975 saw another appearance in the FA Cup First Round, this time against Port Vale. Ernie scored in the opening match of the 1976/77 season, but his career was tragically cut short when he broke a leg in the match against Maidstone United in 1976, which was also the first ever floodlit game at London Road. Ernie currently works as a Prison Officer and is now based in the south-west of the country.

Jon Nixon

Seasons Played			
1981/82-82/83	League	~	46 (5)
	F.A. Cup	~	6 (2)
	F.A. Trophy	~	2
	League Cup	~	6 (2)
	Lincs Cup	~	3 (1)
	Other	~	2
	Total	~	65 (10)

Born 20/01/1948 at Ilkeston. Began his career at Derby County and Ilkeston Town, before scoring 65 times in a total of 420 appearances for Notts County, Peterborough United, where he scored the winning goal in the FA Cup match against Nottingham Forest that sent The Posh to Old Trafford, Shrewsbury Town, Barnsley and Halifax Town. After spells at Long Eaton United and Burton Albion, Jon came to Grantham as Player/Manager, making his debut in the opening County Cup tie of the 1981/82 season at home to Boston United and scoring his first goal in the October league fixture against Buxton. He played in many of the games during that season, whilst the following campaign saw appearances for him in the October 1982 County Cup Final victory at Scunthorpe United and the final qualifying round of the FA Cup against Telford United, with what would turn out to be his last goal for the club in the previous round at home to Armitage. Jon missed many of the games in the latter half of that campaign, but played in the closing fixture at Matlock Town. He went on to join the management teams at Shepshed Charterhouse and then Kettering Town, but by the mid 1990's was working with his old team-mate, Dave Needham in a company supplying personalised number plates.

Nixon

Seasons Played			
1931/32	League	~	1 (1)
	Lincs Cup	~	
	Other	~	
	Total	~	1 (1)

Centre-Forward who during the three previous seasons at Bulwell had amassed an impressive tally of 124 goals and then scored on his debut at London Road against Hull City Reserves in April 1932. Sadly for Grantham though, that game was his one and only appearance for the club.

Barratt Noble

Seasons Played			
1992/93	League	~	9
	F.A. Cup	~	
	F.A. Trophy	~	
	League Cup	~	
	Lincs Cup	~	
	Total	~	9

Born 1974 at Sheffield. Signed from Nottingham Forest and made his debut for Grantham in the January 1993 league fixture at Bilston Town, but even with many of the seasons players having departed The Meres, leaving the club with a depleted squad, Barratt soon found himself being restricted to substitution appearances. However, he did start in his final game for Grantham, the season's closing fixture at home to Bridgnorth Town.

Craig Norrie

Seasons Played			
1984/85	League	~	4 (1)
	F.A. Cup	~	1
	F.A. Trophy	~	
	League Cup	~	
	Lincs Cup	~	
	Other	~	
	Total	~	5 (1)

Born 22/07/1960 at Hull. Previously made 31 appearances for Hull City, before playing football for Wagenincen, Holland, and then spent a period in the Belgian League with Winterslag. Unfortunately, this led to Grantham being fined £50 and a one point deduction in the league after it was discovered that the club had failed to get International clearance for him before his debut in the August 1985 league game at Marine. As if to compound the problem, Craig played only four more times for the club, scoring against Matlock Town and making his final appearance in the September FA Cup tie against Halesowen Town. He went on to play for Gainsborough Trinity, Bishop Auckland and then rejoined his Grantham team-mate, Dave Leadbeater, at North Ferriby United, before turning out for Mazda in the Japanese League. Craig finished his career back at North Ferriby, although after moving to Belgium he continued to play in local leagues. He still lives there, works as a bricklayer and also manages one of the local football sides.

Bob Norris

Seasons Played			
1970/71-79/80	League	~	339 (155)
	F.A. Cup	~	24 (7)
	F.A. Trophy	~	26 (8)
	League Cup	~	38 (14)
	Lincs Cup	~	15 (4)
	Other	~	2
	Total	~	444 (188)

Born circa 1949 at Nottingham. Former England Youth International who like his father and grandfather had spent time at Nottingham Forest, before moving to Mansfield Town Reserves and Ilkeston Town. He made his Grantham debut in the opening fixture of the 1970/71 season at Belper Town and along with Ernie Nixon immediately forged one of the most deadly striking partnerships that the Midland League had ever seen. Bob scored his first goal for the club in the home match against Boston FC and that first season at London Road brought highlights including the winning goal in Grantham's maiden victory over a Football League side, when Stockport County were defeated in November, a Second Round appearance against Rotherham United, plus five goals in the league fixture against Ashby that helped him finish as the club's top scorer. Just to top it off, there was obviously the Midland League Championship winner's medal, which was matched in the League

Cup competition as Bob scored two of the goals in the first leg at Arnold. It was going to be difficult to surpass those achievements the following season, but Bob certainly tried and knocked in 37 goals during the year, including all four goals in the Midland League fixture against Boston. The year finished with another League title and a goal for Bob as Grantham defeated Scunthorpe United in the County Cup Final. With Grantham moving into the Southern League, he found the defences no more difficult to penetrate, as his 33 goals, including four against Atherstone Town and a hat-trick at home to Bury Town, helped Grantham to both the Southern League Merit Cup and another league title. Bob also played in the November 1972 FA Cup First Round Proper tie at Bradford City, whilst a year later he appeared in every round of the Cup run, scoring the fourth goal against Rochdale that finally put Grantham ahead in the match, and playing in the Third Round Proper tie against Middlesbrough in front of London Road's biggest ever attendance. He continued to play in the majority of the games for the club over the next couple of years, scoring another hat-trick at home to Margate in March 1975, whilst a month later Nottingham Forest came to London Road for a joint testimonial for Bob, along with Jimmy Bloomer and Dennis Benskin. The November 1975 FA Cup tie against Port Vale saw goals for him in both the original match and the replay, but that season actually ended with Jimmy Jackson as the club's highest scorer, the first time that Bob hadn't finished with the honour, although after the departure of David Platt he was back at the top after the 1977/78 relegation season. Soon after the start of the following campaign Bob took over the managerial role after Terry Bly departed, and turned the team around to win the Southern League, Division One (North) Championship, also playing in that crucial closing match against Merthyr Tydfil. His last game for Grantham came in the October 1979 league fixture at home to Witton Albion and after little over a year at the helm, he had left the club, initially for a short playing spell at Arnold Town, followed by another period in the manager's chair as he initiated Shepshed Charterhouse's rise up the non-league pyramid. Bob finished his playing career in the mid 1980's by making appearances for Radcliffe. After many years involvement with the Redmayne & Todd sports shop in Nottingham, Bob currently runs his own textile firm in the city, that manufactures, amongst other things, football kits. He is still involved with the Radcliffe Veterans football team as well.

Bill Northgraves

Seasons Played			
	League	~	14 (2)
	Lincs Cup	~	
1938/39-39/40	Other	~	4
	Total	~	18 (2)

Played in the closing seven league fixtures of the 1938/39 season, beginning at London Road against Lincoln City Reserves, and many of the following season's first games as well, both in the abandoned Midland League competition and the 'War-Time' tournament. Bill's final appearance for Grantham came in the December 1939 fixture at home to Boston United.

Dave Norton

Born 1965 in Cannock. Spent nineteen years playing in a football career that began at Aston Villa, before moves to Notts County, Rochdale and Hull City, both on-loan, followed by a permanent move to Hull in August 1991. Transfers followed to Northampton Town, Hereford United, Cheltenham Town, in their Conference winning season, Yeovil Town and then Forest Green Rovers. In November 2000, Dave and fellow player, Nigel Spink, were appointed joint-managers and at the end of that season they took the club to an FA Trophy Final, poignantly for them both, back at Villa Park. Soon after the Summer break though, Spink was appointed as sole Manager, prompting Norton to join Gainsborough Trinity and the following campaign, 2002/03, Tamworth as Assistant Manager to Darron Gee. In the Summer of 2003 Dave made the short trip across to Nuneaton Borough, as Assistant to Alan Lewer, but he resigned from Manor Park around the Christmas period following cut-backs that forced the departure of Darren Collins from the club. After unsuccessfully applying for the Grantham position the previous Summer, he was invited to take over The Gingerbreads following the shock departure of Roger Ashby to Nuneaton in February 2004. He made his debut in a potentially explosive encounter with Nuneaton Borough, but any thoughts of gaining revenge on Ashby were soon abandoned with the visitors finally trouncing Grantham 5-0. With the team already falling down the table, Norton failed to halt the decline and the club not only missed the cut for the new Conference set-up, but finished bottom of the league. Results in the new campaign were not as good as was hoped for and he resigned after a shock FA Cup defeat at the hands of Shepshed Dynamo in September 2004. In November he was appointed Assistant Manager at Stafford Rangers, where he remains.

Ben Nower

Seasons Played			
	League	~	23
	F.A. Cup	~	2
1999/00	F.A. Trophy	~	1
	League Cup	~	1
	Lincs Cup	~	1
	Total	~	28

Born 1981 at Horsham. Goalkeeper who was signed from Lincoln City and made his debut in the opening match of the 1999/00 season at home to Scunthorpe United in the County Cup. Ben missed just one match at the start of December, but the imminent arrival of Mario Ziccardi saw the end of his Grantham career, with his final appearance in the January 2000 victory at Atherstone United. He briefly joined Stamford Town, before returning to The Meres as cover, although he failed to make another First team appearance. Ben went on to play for King's Lynn and AFC Sudbury, but left in 2003 after seeking work in the Peterborough area, although he had returned to Sudbury in time for the start of the 2004/05 season.

Nugee

Seasons Played			
	Other	~	6 (3)
1874/75	Total	~	6 (3)

Played in Grantham's first ever game, against the Third Lincolnshire Volunteer Rifles in October 1874 and earned the distinction of becoming the first Grantham player to score a goal. He then became the first player to score a brace, as the team ran out 2-0 winners in the game. He made a few other appearances during that initial season, right up until the final friendly at home to Lincoln in March. His surname is sometimes spelt 'Nujee' in match reports of the time. Despite his importance in the history of our club, the lack of a Christian name in match reports of the time has impeded the search for definite details of him, even with such an unusual surname. According to the 1881 census there were no individuals with the name of Nugee or Nujee, although that is known to be an error. However, the census twenty years later lists just one family with that surname in the whole of the country, living at Croxton Kerrial. Therefore I am reasonably convinced that the head of that household, Francis Nugee (born 1855 at Wymering, Hants), a local clergyman educated at Eton and Oxford, is the same character that scored the first goal for Grantham.

David Nurse

Seasons Played			
	League	~	2
	F.A. Cup	~	
1998/99	F.A. Trophy	~	
	League Cup	~	
	Lincs Cup	~	
	Total	~	2

Born 12/10/1976 at King's Lynn. Goalkeeper who spent time at Manchester City, Millwall, gaining a single League Cup appearance, Brentford, Barry Town, where he played in their Champions League tie at Dynamo Kiev, and York City. He made just two appearances for Grantham though, covering for Craig Davis in the September 1998 league fixtures against Bath City and Bromsgrove Rovers.

Kris Nurse

Seasons Played			
	League	~	4
	F.A. Cup	~	
2003/04-04/05	F.A. Trophy	~	
	League Cup	~	
	Lincs Cup	~	
	Total	~	4

Born 24/10/1985 at Leicester. Forward who had previously played for Notts County Youth and Reserves and joined The Gingerbreads on work experience from Meadow Lane, playing for new Grantham Manager, Dave Norton, in his first game for the club in February 2004 at home to Nuneaton Borough. This mutual benefit arrangement worked well for both clubs and he went on to a similar agreement at Gresley Rovers and Stamford Town. Kris returned to

The Meres at the start of the following season and played for The Gingerbreads in the first three league games, closing his time at the club with the home fixture against Bath City.

Emeka Nwadike

Seasons Played	League	~	43 (3)
	F.A. Cup	~	5
1998/99-99/00	F.A. Trophy	~	3
	League Cup	~	3
	Lincs Cup	~	2
	Total	~	56 (3)

Born 09/08/1978 at Camberwell. Christened Chukwuemeka Ibezimife Nwadike and soon became known as Emeka, whilst upon starting football gained the nick-name 'Macca'. He was a former Wolverhampton Wanderers and Shrewsbury Town player, with four First team appearances there, who first played for Grantham in the 1998/99 Lincolnshire County Senior Cup game at home to Scunthorpe United. He scored his initial goal for the club the following month at Bromsgrove Rovers and played in many of the games during the Antrac run period, including the FA Cup final qualifying round tie at Tamworth in October 1998. Emeka played in the first 14 games of the following campaign, with his final appearance in the October FA Trophy defeat at home to Matlock Town. He went on to play for King's Lynn, Ilkeston Town, after a £5,000 transfer, Hednesford Town and Alfreton Town.

Oakley

Seasons Played	League	~	1 (1)
	F.A. Cup	~	
1954/55	Lincs Cup	~	
	Total	~	1 (1)

Played in the final league game of the 1954/55 season at Boston United in Peter Cook's usual position, and managed to score Grantham's goal in the 1-1 draw.

Alan O'Donnall

Seasons Played	League	~	7
	F.A. Cup	~	
1964/65	Total	~	7

Defender who replaced the unavailable Ray Barnard for the September 1964 fixture at Denaby United, but only made a handful of other appearances until his final game for the club at London Road the following February against Goole Town.

O'Dowda

Seasons Played	F.A. Cup	~	3 (1)
	Other	~	9 (2)
1879/80-80/81	Total	~	12 (3)

Made his debut in the first friendly of the 1879/80 season at home to Newark and then appeared in every game from that season where team-sheets still exist, scoring twice against Sleaford the following February. The importance of this player was shown the following season with his appearance in all three of the club's FA Cup ties, with his last known game coming in the final one of those matches at Stafford Road, Wolverhampton.

Charles Offord

Seasons Played	F.A. Cup	~	
	Lincs Cup	~	1
1886/87-87/88	Other	~	24 (2)
1889/90-90/91	Total	~	25 (2)

Born circa 1865. A confectioner by trade who played in the November 1886 friendly at Boston, but then made only one other appearance during that season and the following one as well. Finally at the end of the decade he became a more prominent member of the side and even progressed from the friendlies to play in the County Cup for his final game, against Boston in November 1890. Died November 1918 at Grantham.

Ogden

Seasons Played	F.A. Cup	~	
	Lincs Cup	~	
1883/84-84/85	Other	~	4
1886/87	Total	~	4

For some reason only played for our club in matches against the Grantham Volunteers. For all three seasons quoted above, Grantham would play them as their opening friendly and this individual appeared in each one, as well as his final appearance for the club when the Volunteers came to London Road once more in January 1887.

John O'Hare

Seasons Played	League	~	27 (1)
	F.A. Cup	~	
1991/92	F.A. Trophy	~	
	League Cup	~	7
	Lincs Cup	~	
	Total	~	34 (1)

Born 22/07/1966 at Sunderland. Son of the former Scottish International of the same name. John junior began his career as a Trainee at Nottingham Forest, before having a spell in New Zealand with Rotua City and then returning to England where he played for Grimsby Town Reserves. He made his Grantham debut in the October 1991 league fixture at home to Solihull Borough, scored his only goal against Yate Town and made his final appearance in the closing match and return fixture at Solihull Borough. John went on to play for Leicester United, Stapenhill, Heanor Town and then returned to Stapenhill. He now runs his own recruitment consultancy in Burton-upon-Trent.

Oldfield

Seasons Played	F.A. Cup	~	
	Other	~	2 (1)
1878/79	Total	~	2 (1)

Scored on his debut against Boston in November 1878, but then made only one other appearance for the club at the end of the season against Spilsby.

Derek Oliver

Seasons Played	League	~	4 (1)
	F.A. Cup	~	
1973/74	F.A. Trophy	~	
	League Cup	~	
	Lincs Cup	~	
	Total	~	4 (1)

Played four First team games during the 1973/74 season, starting at home to Dartford in December 1973 and then made three more appearances the following April, scoring against Chelmsford City and ending at Kettering Town. Derek currently lives in the Lincoln area, but no details are known as to his profession.

Alan O'Meara

Seasons Played	League	~	10 (1)
	F.A. Cup	~	2
1978/79	F.A. Trophy	~	
1986/87	League Cup	~	1
1992/93	Lincs Cup	~	
	Total	~	13 (1)

Born 15/12/1958 in Grantham. Known by all his colleagues as 'Benny' and played in goal for Grantham Amateurs, before spending time on the books at Sheffield Wednesday, then joining Scunthorpe United, making 41 senior appearances there in the mid 1970's. He made five appearances for The Gingerbreads in the 1978/79 season, starting as cover for Chris Gardiner in the September league match at home to Bromsgrove Rovers and then played in four of the next five games in an out-field position. In April 1986, with Everton Marsh out of the side, Benny returned to help out the club once more and scored in the league game against Wellingborough Town. He then spent several seasons at Mirlees Blackstone, before joining Stamford Town in the early 1990's and then Harrowby United. He unexpectedly rejoined Grantham once more, this time as Manager, after the 1992/93 financial crisis led to Bob Duncan's departure. With the loss of many of the players as well, Benny was forced to play in seven of the games, the last of which was in April 1993 at Leicester United. He returned to Harrowby in the Summer and took them to the United Counties, Division One championship. Benny still lives in the area and works for a local tyre production company.

Martin O'Neill

Born 01/03/1952 at Kilrea, Northern Ireland. Originally played Gaelic football, before joining Distillery where he won an Irish Cup winner's medal in 1971 and played against Barcelona in the ensuing European competition. In October 1971 he was signed by Nottingham Forest, but it was only upon the arrival of Brian Clough that his career really took off. Medals were won in the Anglo-Scottish Cup, the League Championship, two occasions in the League Cup, plus the European Cup and the European Super Cup. Despite the success, Martin continually clashed with his manager and was dropped for the first of Forest's European finals, against FF Malmo in 1979, something that he still regards as the biggest disappointment of his career. In 1981 he moved to Norwich City and after a brief spell at Manchester City, plus a return to Norwich, his career finished whilst at Notts County following a serious leg injury in February 1985, with a total of 106 goals scored in just short of 600 senior career games. Martin had also made 64 appearances as a Northern Ireland International, with nine goals to his name, in a 13 year period which included captaining the squad that reached the 1982 World Cup Finals in Spain. Whilst there he played in every game, including the memorable 1-0 win over the hosts that sent Northern Ireland unexpectedly through to the second round. Just to complete an almost perfect period, Martin was awarded the MBE that year as well. In 1984 he also captained his country to a Home International Championship and with the disbandment of the tournament soon after, he remains the last player to have lifted that trophy. Following time selling insurance he was enticed back into the game by Grantham Chairman, Tony Balfe, and took up the position of Manager in time for the first league game of the 1987/88 season at Merthyr Tydfil. Martin transformed the side, bringing in some quality new players, including Gary Crosby, coupled with some of the former greats of the game like Mick McGuire, Alan Kennedy, Terry Curran, with his former Forest team-mate John Robertson also a recent addition to the London Road team. Despite early defeats in the FA competitions, Martin took The Gingerbreads to within a point of promotion and the season finished with an appearance in the Final of the Evans Halshaw Floodlit Cup, along with Alfreton Town. The following season Grantham were installed as favourites for the league title and yet despite the arrival of former Forest legend, Kenny Burns, the club could only finish fifth in the league and also suffered another shock FA Cup defeat, this time at North Ferriby United. After a disagreement about the following campaign's playing budget, Martin left London Road in the Summer of 1989. He spent a couple of months at Shepshed Charterhouse, but soon took Wycombe Wanderers to two FA Trophy successes and guided them from the GM Vauxhall Championship to League entry and then Division Two via the play-offs. Martin then moved into the Manager's seat at Leicester City and returned them to The Premiership and in 1997 and 2000 took them to League Cup Finals. His first season at Celtic was nothing short of spectacular. Martin led The Bhoys to the Scottish treble in 2000/01, finally ending their rivals, Glasgow Rangers, strangle-hold on the game north of the border, whilst the following season ended with a record haul of points for another title and an appearance in the Scottish Cup Final once more. Despite missing out on Scottish honours in the 2002/03 season, Celtic managed a UEFA Cup Final appearance, but by the following campaign things were back to normal with a Scottish League and Cup double and on a personal note, an OBE in the New Year's Honours list for Martin in December of 2003. The 2004/05 season saw Celtic gain another Scottish Cup Final appearance and at the time of going to press were in a prime position to secure Martin's fourth league title. Grantham fans can be rightfully proud that such a prominent player cut his managerial teeth at our club and went on to become one of the best leaders in the sport.

Orson

Seasons Played			
	F.A. Cup	~	5 (2)
	Lincs Cup	~	10 (5)
1883/84-87/88	Other	~	35 (11)
	Total	~	50 (18)

First played for the club in the November 1883 friendly at Gainsborough Trinity and by the following season had become a regular in Grantham's games. He even scored a hat-trick in the Lincolnshire Senior Cup replay against Grantham Victoria a year after his debut, although for some reason he missed both the semi-final replay and the Final itself. The next few years he continued to be not only a near constant member of the side, but one of the leading scorers as well, right up until his final appearance for the club in the opening fixture of the 1887/88 season against Grantham Volunteers.

O'Shea

Seasons Played			
	League	~	
	Lincs Cup	~	
1907/08	Other	~	1
	Total	~	1

Midfielder who is known to have played in the November 1907 Grantham Minor Cup tie at home to Barrowby, although no information is available to show any other appearances for him.

Kasi Oseni

Seasons Played			
	League	~	33 (1)
	F.A. Cup	~	2
1994/95-95/96	F.A. Trophy	~	
	League Cup	~	2
	Lincs Cup	~	1
	Total	~	38 (1)

Previously with Lincoln City and made his Grantham debut in the 1994/95 season's opening County Cup tie at home to Grimsby Town. Kasi scored his only goal the following January against Hinckley Town and after becoming a regular player during that campaign, returned to the side in April 1996 to make a lone appearance at RC Warwick. He went on to play for several Lincolnshire League sides and is thought to be still living in the Lincoln area.

Over

Seasons Played			
	F.A. Cup	~	
	Lincs Cup	~	
1887/88	Other	~	6
	Total	~	6

Made his debut for the club in the December 1887 friendly at home to Lockwood and then played in many of the games during the next couple of months, until his last match against Derby County in February the following year.

Owen

Seasons Played			
	F.A. Cup	~	
	Other	~	1
1878/79	Total	~	1

Played only one game for Grantham in the November 1878 friendly at Boston.

Frank Oxspring

Seasons Played			
	League	~	16
	F.A. Cup	~	
1966/67-67/68	Total	~	16

Defender who made his First team debut in the January 1967 fixture at home to Stamford and then made seven more appearances over the next couple of months. The following season he doubled the amount of games that he played in, spread throughout the year, with his final appearance coming in April 1968 against Retford Town.

Pacey

Seasons Played			
	League	~	1
	Lincs Cup	~	1
1907/08	Other	~	2
1909/10	Total	~	4

With very few team-sheets available for this period, there is no means of telling just how common his appearances actually were at the start of his Grantham career. We do know though that they were quite infrequent during the 1909/10 season with his last known game for the club in the November 1909 County competition against Grantham Avenue.

E. Palfreyman

Seasons Played			
	League	~	3
	F.A. Cup	~	
1937/38-38/39	Lincs Cup	~	
	Other	~	
	Total	~	3

Full-Back who also played for Grantham St John's, Northern Rubber Works FC (Retford) and Ransome & Marles, but made just one appearance for Grantham in the 1937/38 season, the September Midland League game at Boston United when Harry Wilbourn became unavailable. He faired little better in the next season, as Harry missed only two games, giving Palfreyman the option to play only against Shrewsbury Town and Barnsley Reserves at the start of the campaign.

Dave Palmer

Seasons Played			
1985/86	League	~	1
	F.A. Cup	~	
	F.A. Trophy	~	
	League Cup	~	
	Lincs Cup	~	
	Total	~	1

Reserves team player who made just one appearance for the senior side in the November 1985 league fixture against Leamington.

Alan Park

Seasons Played			
1994/95	League	~	13 (5)
	F.A. Cup	~	1 (1)
	F.A. Trophy	~	1
	League Cup	~	1
	Lincs Cup	~	
	Total	~	16 (6)

Born 08/05/1961 at Greenock, Scotland. Former Hykeham Town and Lincoln United player, known by his colleagues as 'Alfie', and brother of Stuart Park. Alan made his debut in the August 1994 league draw at Tamworth and then scored his first *four* goals in the extraordinary 7-2 Grantham win at Stourbridge less than two weeks later. To the best of knowledge this is the biggest away win, in the modern era, by a side in the Southern League that eventually finished in a relegation zone. He made all but one of his appearances before December, with a lone substitution in the March 1995 league game at home to Stourbridge with Manager, Warren Ward, no doubt hoping for a reproduction of Alan's scoring skills to get the club out of trouble. Of course Grantham lost this return fixture! Alan returned to Lincoln United and he still lives in the city today, where he works for the Royal Mail.

Stuart Park

Seasons Played			
1994/95	League	~	1
	F.A. Cup	~	
	F.A. Trophy	~	
	League Cup	~	
	Lincs Cup	~	
	Total	~	1

Born 25/07/1958 at Greenock, Scotland. Previously played for Hykeham Town, Lincoln Claytons, Boston FC and like his brother, Alan Park, Lincoln United. Stuart then played in the same game for Grantham as his sibling, the March 1995 league fixture at home to Stourbridge. After returning to Lincoln United, Stuart went on to play for Heanor Town and Lincoln Moorlands. He still lives in Lincoln and works as a clerk in the manufacturing industry.

David Parker

Seasons Played			
1988/89	League	~	4
	F.A. Cup	~	
	F.A. Trophy	~	1
	League Cup	~	1
	Lincs Cup	~	
	Total	~	6

Born 17/11/1969 in Grantham. Full-Back who was previously with Mansfield Town and first played for Grantham in the November 1988 league fixture at home to Gloucester City. He made a total of six appearances over the next couple of months, the last of which was against King's Lynn just after the New Year. David went on to play for Harrowby United, Stamford Town and currently works as a sports teacher.

Parker

Seasons Played			
1876/77	Other	~	2
	Total	~	2

Played in the 0-0 draw against Nottingham Castle in January 1877 and the friendly at Retford Rovers two weeks later.

Parker

Seasons Played			
1883/84	F.A. Cup	~	1
	Lincs Cup	~	
	Other	~	
	Total	~	1

Only one known appearance for this player, in the November 1883 FA Cup tie against Spilsby.

Parker

Seasons Played			
1888/89	F.A. Cup	~	
	Lincs Cup	~	1
	Other	~	18 (1)
	Total	~	19 (1)

First played for the club in October 1888 against Notts Jardines and then appeared in virtually every one of the remaining matches of that season, scoring his only goal for the club in February when the Sphinx team came to London Road. His last appearance came in the local derby against Grantham Rovers in April 1889.

Parker

Seasons Played			
1905/06	League	~	4 (1)
	Total	~	4 (1)

Made several appearances for the club in the latter half of the 1905/06 season, with his only known goal coming in the March 1906 Midland Amateur Alliance fixture at Notts University.

Parker

Seasons Played			
1926/27	League	~	4
	F.A. Cup	~	
	Lincs Cup	~	
	Other	~	1
	Total	~	5

Former Matlock Town player who was given his debut in the October 1926 RAF Shield match against RAF Cranwell after Melson had left the club, but only a month later he had also made his final appearance for the club, when Wath Athletic came to London Road for a league fixture.

Parker

Seasons Played			
1936/37	League	~	
	F.A. Cup	~	
	Lincs Cup	~	
	Other	~	1
	Total	~	1

Made just one appearance for Grantham in the Wilson Cup Final against RAF Cranwell at the end of the 1936/37 season.

Ian Parkes

Seasons Played			
1996/97	League	~	37 (6)
	F.A. Cup	~	4
	F.A. Trophy	~	4
	League Cup	~	2
	Lincs Cup	~	1
	Total	~	48 (6)

Previously played for Dunkirk, Bedworth United and made his Grantham debut in the opening County Cup match of the 1996/97 season at home to Grimsby Town. His first goal came in the same month at Raunds Town and Ian appeared in the majority of Grantham's games that campaign, ending at Moor Green in the closing fixture. After the Summer interval he went on to play for Arnold Town.

David Parkin

Seasons Played			
1988/89	League	~	5
	F.A. Cup	~	1
	F.A. Trophy	~	1
	League Cup	~	
	Lincs Cup	~	1
	Total	~	8

Born 02/05/1970 at Lincoln. Signed from Lincoln City after making just one First team appearance for them in a minor cup competition and made his Grantham debut in the opening County Cup tie of the 1988/89 season against Gainsborough Trinity. After coming on as substitute in the shock FA Cup defeat at North Ferriby United a month later though, he played no further part in playing for The Gingerbreads and soon moved on to Lincoln United, Nettleham United and then returned to Lincoln United.

Mark Parkinson

Seasons Played			
1996/97-97/98	League	~	14 (1)
	F.A. Cup	~	1
	F.A. Trophy	~	6
	League Cup	~	3
	Lincs Cup	~	2
	Total	~	26 (1)

Local player who progressed through the Reserves and stepped up to the senior side by making his debut in the August 1996 FA Cup tie at Witham Town. Mark played in a total of 16 games that year and 10 the following season, scoring his only goal against VS Rugby in October 1997 and making his last appearance in December at home to Raunds Town in the Dr Marten's League Cup. Although he was named as a substitute in several of the following games, he soon left The Meres and went on to play for Cottesmore and Long Buckby.

Steve Parkinson

Seasons Played			
1994/95-96/97	League	~	57 (5)
	F.A. Cup	~	1
	F.A. Trophy	~	3 (1)
	League Cup	~	3 (1)
	Lincs Cup	~	3
	Total	~	67 (7)

Born 27/08/1974 at Lincoln. Former Horncastle Town and Lincoln City player, with five Football League appearances to his name, who made his Grantham debut in the February 1994 league fixture at Sutton Coldfield Town, with his first goal coming the following month at Moor Green. Steve played in most of the games from both the remainder of that season and the following year as well. However, the arrival of Gary Mills coincided with Steve's demise from the side and he made his last appearance in the October 1996 Dr Marten's League Cup tie at Corby Town, before moving on to Boston Town.

Parkinson

Seasons Played			
1875/76 1877/78-78/79 1880/81	F.A. Cup	~	4
	Other	~	10
	Total	~	14

Played once for Grantham towards the end of the 1875/76 season against Lincoln, but then didn't turn out again for the club until over a year later. He then appeared in the club's first ever FA Cup match against Clapham Rovers in October 1877 and many of both that and the following season's games. His last appearance for Grantham came in the November 1880 FA Cup tie at Calthorpe, Birmingham.

Parkinson

Seasons Played			
1912/13	League	~	
	F.A. Cup	~	
	Lincs Cup	~	
	Other	~	1
	Total	~	1

Known to have appeared in the March 1913 friendly against Queen's Park, but no information is available to show any other matches that he may have played in.

Ray Parnham

Seasons Played			
1939/40	League	~	2
	Lincs Cup	~	
	Other	~	
	Total	~	2

Born 24/01/1922 at Chippenham. Local goalkeeper who also played for the Aveling Barfords works team and appeared for Grantham in the January 1940 Midland 'War-Time' League draw against Gainsborough Trinity. Ray then played in the next fixture at home to Denaby United, but after the team suffered a 7-1 defeat he made no other appearances for the club. Following time in the Royal Navy, he played for Grantham St John's, Stamford Town, Bourne Town and Wisbech Town, with other games for the Barfords team where he continued to work as an electrical engineer. Ray is now retired but still lives in the town.

Parnham

Seasons Played			
1922/23-23/24 1926/27	League	~	18 (1)
	F.A. Cup	~	
	League Cup	~	
	Lincs Cup	~	
	Other	~	3 (1)
	Total	~	21 (2)

Midfielder who had also played for Carlton Scroop and made his Grantham debut sometime in the Winter of 1922/23, scoring his first goal for the club in the closing league fixture at Shirebrook. He only made a few appearances during the next season, netting his second goal for the club in the Grantham Hospital Cup tie at home to Newark Castle Rovers and returned to London Road to finish his Grantham career in the 1926/27 campaign, although his final appearance is not known.

Joe Parr

Seasons Played			
1948/49-51/52	League	~	123 (5)
	F.A. Cup	~	7
	Lincs Cup	~	8
	Total	~	138 (5)

Right-sided player with experience at Ransome & Marles and Newark Town who took over Reg Dyer's defensive position for the 1949 New Year's Day fixture at home to Shrewsbury Town. Joe then missed only one of the remaining matches from that season, as well as scoring his first goal for the club against Gainsborough Trinity in April. The following season he appeared in the FA Cup First Round tie against Wrexham, and both the County Cup Final and replay against Boston United. Despite missing many of Grantham's matches during the Autumn of 1950, Joe returned to the side to then play almost constantly until his final appearance for the club in the closing fixture of the 1951/52 season at Goole Town, a match that also marked his final goal for Grantham.

Parr

Seasons Played			
1876/77	Other	~	2
	Total	~	2

Individual who is known to have played in the January 1877 friendly at home to Nottingham Castle and the return fixture at the end of March.

Jeff Parry

Seasons Played			
1978/79	League	~	4 (1)
	F.A. Cup	~	1 (4)
	F.A. Trophy	~	
	League Cup	~	3
	Lincs Cup	~	2
	Total	~	10 (5)

Born circa 1960. Former Notts County Youth and Boston United player who first played for Grantham in the opening County Cup tie of the 1978/79 season at Boston United. His first goal for the club came at the beginning of September at Stourbridge, but two weeks later he netted four in the 5-3 FA Cup victory at home to Ashby Institute. His final appearance came at the end of that same month, against Bromsgrove Rovers, and he went on to play for Ilkeston Town. Jeff was later transferred to Nottingham Forest for a £2,000 fee, but despite scoring many goals for their Reserve side failed to make a First Team appearance at The City Ground. After his release from Forest he dropped down to the Midland League with Kimberley Town.

Linden Parslow

Seasons Played			
1986/87-89/90	League	~	88
	F.A. Cup	~	5
	F.A. Trophy	~	8
	League Cup	~	8
	Lincs Cup	~	3
	Total	~	112

Born 28/10/1963 in Australia. RAF serviceman and goalkeeper who spent time at Peterborough United, before making appearances for Stamford, where he played in their FA Vase runners-up side at Wembley in 1984, and Rushden Town. He made his Grantham debut in the 1986/87 season's opening Lincolnshire County Senior Cup game at Scunthorpe United, but left London Road towards the end of that first campaign for a spell at Mirlees Blackstone. He returned to Grantham in February 1988 to play in the final 13 league fixtures of Martin O'Neill's side, ending up on the losing side only twice as the club came close to promotion. Linden played in every game during the 1988/89 season, plus several of the minor Floodlit League games, even coming on as a substitute in one match and playing on the wing, helping Grantham to a 3-1 win, but sadly failing to appear on the score-sheet. He made seven more appearances in the following season, with his last game against Rushden Town in September 1989. He left to play for Nuneaton Borough, Atherstone United, Kettering Town, Boston Town, Spalding United and was last known to be playing for Dhahran in Saudi Arabia only a couple of years ago.

James Parton

Seasons Played			
	League	~	20
	F.A. Cup	~	2
1926/27	Lincs Cup	~	
	Other	~	1
	Total	~	23

Born 03/12/1902 at Barrow. Full-Back who had previously played for Barrow Submarine Engine Athletic and Barrow in Division Three (North). He came to Grantham from them on-loan and made his debut in the opening Midland League fixture of the 1926/27 season at Sutton Town. He then appeared in nearly every match until the end of January, with the game at Long Eaton possibly his final appearance for the club. James returned to Barrow and in 1929 joined Rochdale, finally finishing his League career with two goals scored in a total of 54 appearances. Died 1981 at Barrow-in-Furness.

Pattison

Seasons Played			
	League	~	1
	F.A. Cup	~	
1925/26	Lincs Cup	~	
	Other	~	
	Total	~	1

Outside-Left player with just one known appearance for Grantham, the 6-2 Midland League victory over Sutton Town in April 1926.

Peach

Seasons Played			
	League	~	3
	F.A. Cup	~	
1951/52	Lincs Cup	~	
	Total	~	3

Forward who played for the First team in the January 1952 league game at home to Notts County Reserves and the March fixtures against the Reserve sides of Halifax Town and Bradford Park Avenue.

Peake

Seasons Played			
	F.A. Cup	~	
1875/76	Other	~	5
1878/79	Total	~	5

Made at least four appearances for the club in the 1875/76 season and then returned one more time in February 1879 to play in a friendly at Spilsby.

William Pearce

Seasons Played			
	League	~	184 (8)
	F.A. Cup	~	7
1927/28-31/32	Lincs Cup	~	
	Other	~	
	Total	~	191 (8)

Born 24/04/1889 at Ilkeston. Half-Back who had previously played for Ilkeston United, twice, Long Eaton, Norwich City, (scoring twice in 19 appearances), and Loughborough Corinthians. William made his Grantham debut in November 1927, with his first goal for the club coming in the January fixture at home to Mexborough Athletic. By then he was a near permanent member of the side and the following season he played in the FA Cup First Round against Rhyl Athletic and the next tie at Wigan Borough. He continued to notch up the appearances well into the new decade, despite being over 40 years of age by then. Although no details are known as to the end of his career, the 1931/32 season saw him play 34 times, so it would certainly have been well into the New Year at the very least. There are close to 200 games where we have evidence that he played and I have little doubt that he must surely have easily surpassed that double century. Other than football, William was also an accomplished cricketer as well and won 3 medals with the Derbyshire County side in his time there.

Curtis Pearson

Seasons Played			
	League	~	44 (22)
	F.A. Cup	~	4 (4)
1932/33	Lincs Cup	~	2 (2)
	Other	~	1
	Total	~	51 (28)

Prolific centre-forward whose first goal for Grantham came in the September 1932 Midland League fixture at Loughborough Corinthians, and his quality was shown by the fact that he scored 22 league goals in a poor Grantham team that could only finish 17th in the table. His final goal for the club came in April 1933 at Barnsley Reserves and the following season he joined Birmingham City, although he failed to make their First team. In the 1935/36 season, Curtis played nine games for Walsall, whilst it is also known that at some point in his career he also had spells with Derby County and Lenton, although no information is available to indicate when.

Glenn Pearson

Seasons Played			
	League	~	50 (5)
	F.A. Cup	~	4
1992/93-94/95	F.A. Trophy	~	2
	League Cup	~	3
	Lincs Cup	~	2
	Total	~	61 (5)

Born 1973 at Lincoln. Former Lincoln United and Boston FC midfielder who first played for Grantham in the March 1993 league fixture at Weston-Super-Mare, with his maiden goal the following Saturday at home to Hinckley Town. Glenn played in just over half the games the following year, whilst his final appearance came in January 1994, again during Hinckley Town's visit to The Meres. Glenn returned to Lincoln United, then signed for Sleaford Town, once more went back to Lincoln United, this time as Player/Manager in 2002, before joining Harrowby United at the start of the 2004/05 season.

Ian Pearson

Seasons Played			
	League	~	
	F.A. Cup	~	1
1996/97	F.A. Trophy	~	
	League Cup	~	
	Lincs Cup	~	1
	Total	~	2

Reserves team member who played for the First team in the 1996/97 season's opening County Cup tie at home to Grimsby Town and the FA Cup tie at Witham Town at the end of the same month, both times coming off the substitute's bench.

Pearson

Seasons Played			
	League	~	
	F.A. Cup	~	
1912/13	Lincs Cup	~	
	Other	~	1
	Total	~	1

Goalkeeper who played for Grantham after John Baverstock left the club, but unfortunately, although evidence shows that he played in the March 1913 friendly against Queen's Park, no data is available for the surrounding league games.

Pearson

Seasons Played			
	League	~	1
	F.A. Cup	~	
1925/26	Lincs Cup	~	
	Other	~	
	Total	~	1

Available records show just one appearance for this player, the home fixture against Shirebrook in December 1925.

Roger Peck

Seasons Played			
	League	~	13 (1)
	F.A. Cup	~	
1969/70	F.A. Trophy	~	
	League Cup	~	4
	Lincs Cup	~	
	Other	~	1
	Total	~	18 (1)

Defender who replaced Kelvin Yeomans in the January 1970 Midland League match against Barton Town and then kept the position for most of the remaining fixtures, scoring his only goal for the club in March against Worksop Town. His last appearance for Grantham came in the finale to the season as the Champions, Alfreton Town, drew 2-2 with Grantham.

David Peet

Seasons Played			
	League	~	1
	F.A. Cup	~	1
1996/97	F.A. Trophy	~	
	League Cup	~	
	Lincs Cup	~	1
	Total	~	3

Former Aston Villa Trainee goalkeeper who made his debut for Grantham in the 1996/97 season's opening County Cup tie against Grimsby Town, played in the first league game at Redditch United, but made only one more appearance after the arrival of Peter Bulliman, at home to Boston Town in the September FA Cup tie. David went on to play for Holwell Sports and Warboys.

Robert Pell

Seasons Played			
	League	~	35 (3)
	F.A. Cup	~	2
1998/99	F.A. Trophy	~	1
	League Cup	~	4 (1)
	Lincs Cup	~	1
	Total	~	43 (4)

Born 05/02/1979 at Leeds. Started his career on Schoolboy forms at Sheffield United, before moving on to Rotherham United and Doncaster Rovers, scoring once in a total of 12 senior appearances. He came to Grantham at the start of the 1998/99 season, making his debut in the County Cup tie at home to Scunthorpe United at the end of July and scoring his first goal in the opening league fixture at Worcester City. He played in most of the games during that season, including the October 1998 final qualifying round FA Cup tie at Tamworth. His last appearance for The Gingerbreads was in the closing match at Weymouth and he went on to play for FC Jaro in Finland, followed by Northwich Victoria, Southport, Droylsden, Guiseley and then had a spell playing in Norway for Larvik. Robert returned to England in January 2003 and to Southport, before joining Worksop Town, Wakefield & Emley on-loan, Harrogate Town and finally rejoining Wakefield in a permanent move.

Mark Pennant

Seasons Played			
	League	~	24
	F.A. Cup	~	1
1997/98	F.A. Trophy	~	6
	League Cup	~	4
	Lincs Cup	~	
	Total	~	35

Born 04/05/1966 at Nottingham. Left-Back, known to his colleagues as 'Budgie', previously with Oakham United, Sutton Town, Eastwood Town, Corby Town, Ashfield United, Gainsborough Trinity and Ilkeston Town. After spending a couple of games spectating from the bench, he made his Grantham debut in the September 1997 FA Cup tie at Solihull Borough and played in some of the great games the following Spring, including the 6-0 thrashing of his old team, Ilkeston Town and the FA Trophy quarter-final against Southport. He also played in the closing fixture at home to Stourbridge, a game that confirmed the Dr Marten's, Midland Division Championship for Grantham. After the Summer break though, Mark went on to play for Stamford Town, then Hinckley United and Gedling Town.

Chris Penny

Seasons Played			
	League	~	3
	F.A. Cup	~	
1991/92	F.A. Trophy	~	
	League Cup	~	
	Lincs Cup	~	
	Total	~	3

Born 16/02/1973 at Rochford. Former Brigg Town full-back who went on to make one appearance for Doncaster Rovers, before joining Grimsby Town Reserves. It was also a short career at The Meres as well, with just three appearances during March 1992 at home to Bilston Town, Hednesford Town and Nuneaton Borough. Chris later emigrated to America, where he played for Philadelphia Kixx, Hampton Roads Mariners and Hershey Wildcats, before coaching in various schools and colleges, culminating in the Pennsylvania State University where he remains. Chris is also Director of a soccer camp and has written several theses in teaching studies.

Perkins

Seasons Played			
	F.A. Cup	~	
	Other	~	4
1875/76-78/79	Total	~	4

Made his debut in the March 1876 friendly against Nottingham Castle, but rarely played for the club, with his last appearance coming in February 1879 when the team travelled over to Spilsby.

Perkins

Seasons Played			
	League	~	1
	F.A. Cup	~	
1930/31	Lincs Cup	~	
	Total	~	1

Centre-Forward who made just one appearance for Grantham in the March 1931 league game against Scunthorpe & Lindsey United.

Perry

Seasons Played			
	League	~	51 (9)
	F.A. Cup	~	
1930/31-31/32	Lincs Cup	~	
	Other	~	
	Total	~	51 (9)

Former Goole Town and Scunthorpe & Lindsey United player who scored on his Grantham debut in September 1930 against Boston. Whilst being a prominent member of the team in his first season at London Road, the following year he made only 14 appearances.

Paddy Phelan

Seasons Played			
	League	~	30
	F.A. Cup	~	4
1968/69	League Cup	~	8
	Lincs Cup	~	2
	Total	~	44

Born 09/02/1938 at Chingford. Paddy was already well known to Grantham sporting fans, although probably due to his service as an Essex County cricketer between 1958 and 1965. Football-wise, he was a defender who had spent time on the books at Southend United and came to Grantham following a transfer from Chelmsford City. Paddy made his debut in the September 1968 league game at Skegness Town and for the rest of the season played in most of the club's matches, including the FA Cup Proper tie against his old side, Chelmsford City, and the following round versus Swindon Town. In the Midland League Cup Paddy helped Grantham in every round to progress to the Final, but he was to miss out on both the decisive legs against Arnold with his final appearance for the club coming in April 1969 when he came off the substitute's bench in the Stamford fixture to replace Tony Farmer.

Philips

Seasons Played			
	F.A. Cup	~	
	Lincs Cup	~	
1884/85	Other	~	1
	Total	~	1

Made just one appearance for Grantham in the October 1884 friendly against Notts Rangers at London Road.

Pickard

Seasons Played			
	League	~	1
	F.A. Cup	~	
1933/34	Lincs Cup	~	
	Other	~	
	Total	~	1

Defender with experience at Grantham Amateurs who played only once for our team, the December 1933 Central Combination game at Chesterfield Reserves. He was however described in the *Grantham Journal* as a 'lusty full-back', presumably a compliment!

Pickering

Seasons Played			
	League	~	9
	F.A. Cup	~	
1945/46	Lincs Cup	~	1
	Total	~	10

Former Ransome & Marles midfielder who first played for Grantham in the March 1946 league match at Scunthorpe & Lindsey United and although there were only a couple of months left in the season, he did get the opportunity to play in the Lincolnshire Senior Cup Final against Boston United. His final appearance for the club came in the closing Midland League fixture at Rotherham United Reserves.

Sammy Pigott

Seasons Played			
	League	~	8 (2)
	F.A. Cup	~	
1995/96	F.A. Trophy	~	1
	League Cup	~	1
	Lincs Cup	~	
	Total	~	10 (2)

Born 15/01/1971 in Grantham. Christened 'Simon', but known to everyone as 'Sammy'. Former Grantham Amateurs and Harrowby United striker who progressed through the Reserves into the First team, making his debut in the October 1995 Dr Marten's League Cup tie against Ilkeston Town. Sammy had a good run in the side at the start of the New Year, scoring against Bilston Town and Paget Rangers, but made his final appearance in February 1996 at Nuneaton Borough. He also had a trial with Brighton around this time, but it was to Harrowby that he eventually returned. Sammy still lives locally and works as a greenkeeper on a local golf course.

Trevor Pike

Seasons Played			
	League	~	5
	F.A. Cup	~	1
1977/78	F.A. Trophy	~	
	League Cup	~	2 (1)
	Lincs Cup	~	
	Total	~	8 (1)

Forward who made his debut for The Gingerbreads in the September 1977 league fixture at home to Redditch United, but after scoring at Cambridge City played his last game for the club at the start of November in the FA Cup defeat at Burton Albion.

Arthur Pinchbeck

Seasons Played			
	League	~	4
	FA Amt. Cup	~	
1909/10-10/11	League Cup	~	
	Lincs Cup	~	1
	Other	~	1
	Total	~	6

Born 02/04/1888 in Grantham. In adult life was nicknamed 'Cully', a deviation from 'Curly' due to his loss of hair at an early age. Arthur was a moulder at Ruston & Hornsby who played centre-half for both Grantham Avenue and The Town. He was more evident in Grantham's matches in the latter half of the 1909/10 season, which included the March friendly against Queen's Park, and most likely played an important role in the following season's championship winning team, although little information is available on specific games. Arthur is also an ancestor of future Grantham Director and current journalist and local author, John Pinchbeck. Died 1969 at Grantham.

Pitts

Seasons Played			
	League	~	17 (4)
	Lincs Cup	~	
1931/32	Other	~	
	Total	~	17 (4)

Former Peterborough & Fletton United player who made his Grantham debut in the opening league game of the 1931/32 season at Loughborough Corinthians and scored his first goal for the club a month later against Boston. Unfortunately no data is available to show his final appearance.

Andy Plant

Seasons Played			
	League	~	31
	F.A. Cup	~	1
1989/90-90/91	F.A. Trophy	~	1
	League Cup	~	2
	Lincs Cup	~	
	Total	~	35

Born 30/11/1967 at Doncaster. Goalkeeper signed from Armthorpe Welfare who first played for Grantham in the Boxing Day 1989 fixture at home to Tamworth and became the club's first choice 'keeper during their last few months at London Road. Andy played in that final game against Dudley Town in October 1990, but was forced to quit through injury, with his last appearance at the end of the same month in the Larchimage Windows League Cup defeat at Rushden Town. Despite returning to the club in the 1996/97 pre-season, he was unable to regain his full match fitness and failed to make any more First team appearances.

David Platt

Seasons Played			
	League	~	84 (32)
	F.A. Cup	~	2
1975/76-77/78	F.A. Trophy	~	3 (3)
	League Cup	~	10 (5)
	Lincs Cup	~	4 (1)
	Other	~	1
	Total	~	104 (41)

Born 18/11/1956 at Leicester. Signed from Leicester City and made his debut for Grantham in the February 1976 league fixture at Wimbledon, finally splitting up the Nixon/Norris strike partnership. His first goal came in the match at Maidstone United the following month, but the following 1976/77 season he showed his quality by finishing as the Southern League's top goal-scorer, scoring hat-tricks against Weymouth and Burton Albion, despite missing several of the games towards the end of the campaign. David continued to knock in the goals after the Summer interval, even for a team that was struggling at the bottom of the table, but his last strike came in March 1978 at home to Worcester City, with his final appearance at the end of the same month against Kettering Town. The lure of a large transfer had become too great to a club that was struggling financially and he moved to Yeovil Town after a £4,000 fee was paid. He was soon lined up by The Glovers for a £20,000 move to Hereford United, but the deal fell through, most likely due to Dave suffering from terrible luck with ankle injuries during his time with the Somerset side. He eventually went on to play for Weymouth, Bath City, Trowbridge, Salisbury City, Poole Town, Minehead, Paulton Rovers, Chard Town and then even twenty years after leaving London Road, he was still regularly playing for Frome Town in the Western League. But this still wasn't the end of his career as intermittent appearances followed for Wimborne Town, Shaftesbury and finally Westland Sports. He is currently a painter and decorator around the Yeovil area and enjoys spending much of his free time on the golf course after recently recovering from serious illness.

Platts

Seasons Played			
	League	~	11 (7)
	F.A. Cup	~	
1935/36	Lincs Cup	~	1 (1)
	Other	~	1
	Total	~	13 (8)

Centre-Forward who had also played for Basford United and made his debut for Grantham in the March 1936 game at home to Barnsley Reserves. He then netted a hat-trick two weeks later against Mexborough Athletic and just to emphasize his quality in the side, he also scored single strikes in both the County Cup and Grantham Hospital Cup Finals during that period as well. His last game for the club though, came just over a month after his debut, at Lincoln City Reserves, but that highlights what a hectic period it must have been for the club, with him having made 13 appearances during that short time.

Calvin Plummer

Seasons Played			
	League	~	7 (4)
	F.A. Cup	~	3 (1)
1996/97	F.A. Trophy	~	1
	League Cup	~	2
	Lincs Cup	~	
	Total	~	13 (5)

Born 14/02/1963 at Nottingham. Previously scored 42 goals in over 250 First team appearances for Nottingham Forest, Chesterfield, Derby County, Barnsley and Plymouth, with spells playing on-loan in Finland for Reipas Lahden and Derry City in Ireland in 1987. He then returned to England to play non-league football for Gainsborough Trinity, Shepshed Albion, Corby Town, Nuneaton Borough and Birstall United. His initial game for Grantham came in the September 1996 FA Cup tie against Boston Town, with his first goal in the following fixture at home to Evesham United. Calvin's last appearance was in the November match at home to Bedworth United and he then had a spell on-loan at Arnold Town, before moving to Shepshed Dynamo and Kirby Muxloe. After the end of his playing career he became Manager of Notts Alliance side, Bilborough.

Dave Pollard

Seasons Played			
	League	~	29
	F.A. Cup	~	2
1969/70	F.A. Trophy	~	5
	League Cup	~	4
	Lincs Cup	~	1
	Other	~	1
	Total	~	42

Born circa 1940. Former Norwich City Reserves, Corby Town and Banbury United defender who played in the first home game of the 1969/70 season against Boston FC and most of the other Midland League fixtures that year as well, generally as the team's Captain. In the other competitions, Dave appeared in the FA Cup tie against Oldham Athletic and the FA Trophy match at Worcester City which was played in front of close to 7,000 supporters. His final appearance for the club came in the Champions Versus Runners-Up game at the end of April.

Pond

Seasons Played			
	League	~	2
	F.A. Cup	~	
1945/46	Lincs Cup	~	
	Total	~	2

Played just twice for the First team, in October 1945 at Denaby United and then the final Midland League fixture of the season at Rotherham United Reserves.

George Poole

Seasons Played			
	League	~	4
	F.A. Cup	~	1
1948/49	Lincs Cup	~	
	Total	~	5

Made three appearances for the club during September 1948, beginning with the Midland League fixture at home to Goole Town, and then twice more at the end of March 1949, ending in the match at Bradford City Reserves.

Poole

Seasons Played			
	League	~	9 (6)
	FA Amt. Cup	~	
1907/08	League Cup	~	
	Lincs Cup	~	4 (3)
1909/10-10/11	Other	~	5 (2)
	Total	~	18 (11)

Midfield player who began his Grantham career in the 1907/08 season, but due to the lack of information still in existence on this period, it is very difficult to tell how prominent he was in the team. We do know though that he played many games during the 1909/10 season, including the March friendly at home to Queen's Park, although the following championship winning year he seems to be less conspicuous. His last two goals for the club came in the February 1911 league game against Old Loughburians.

C. Pope

Seasons Played			
	League	~	8 (5)
	F.A. Cup	~	
1921/22-22/23	Lincs Cup	~	
	Other	~	
	Total	~	8 (5)

Centre-Forward who also played for Babbington Colliery and made his Grantham debut soon after the 1922 New Year, scoring his first goal for the club in the Central Alliance fixture at Heanor Town. Unfortunately many of his appearances from that season have only been discovered from score-sheets, so he most likely played in several further games than those quoted above. He continued to play for the club after the Summer break, but apparently for only a short period.

Jeff Potts

Seasons Played			
	League	~	31 (6)
	F.A. Cup	~	1
1993/94-94/95	F.A. Trophy	~	3
	League Cup	~	1
	Lincs Cup	~	
	Total	~	36 (6)

Striker who made his Grantham debut in the September 1993 Dr Marten's League Cup tie at Rushden & Diamonds and scored his first goal for the club against RC Warwick the following month. Jeff played in more than half of the fixtures from that season, but the following campaign made only six more appearances, the majority of which came around the Christmas period. The last of those was in the demoralising 5-0 home defeat against King's Lynn on Boxing Day and he soon left The Meres to play for Skegness Town and Bourne Town.

Powell

Seasons Played			
	League	~	5
	F.A. Cup	~	2
1933/34	Lincs Cup	~	
	Other	~	
	Total	~	7

Former Shirebrook half-back who first played for Grantham in the opening match of the 1933/34 season at Loughborough Corinthians, but despite playing in all of those first few games, there are no records that show him still playing after the October FA Cup replay against Sutton Town.

Tim Preece

Seasons Played			
	League	~	18 (1)
	F.A. Cup	~	
1993/94	F.A. Trophy	~	2
	League Cup	~	
	Lincs Cup	~	
	Total	~	20 (1)

Born 21/10/1966 at Halifax. Defender who previously played for Cambridge United Reserves, Newmarket Town, Thetford, Alfreton Town, Hucknall Town and Boston United. His first game for Grantham was in the January 1993 FA Trophy game at home to Witton Albion and he then played in all but two of the remaining fixtures, scoring against Stourbridge in April and ending his Grantham career by coming off the bench to replace Glenn Pearson in the closing match at Dudley Town. Tim was released by Grantham in the Summer and returned to, first Hucknall, and then Alfreton. He still lives in Nottingham and works as a General Manager for a furniture manufacturer.

Llewellyn Price

Seasons Played			
	League	~	21 (2)
	F.A. Cup	~	
1928/29	Lincs Cup	~	
	Other	~	
	Total	~	21 (2)

Born 12/08/1898 at Caersws. 'Lew', as he was known, was a midfielder who had previously played for Barmouth, Hampstead Town, Mansfield Town, Aston Villa, (during which time he was awarded Welsh Amateur International honours), Notts County, (including their 1922/23 Division Two Championship winning year), and Queen's Park Rangers, finishing his professional career with seven goals to his name in 83 senior appearances. He played in the majority of Grantham's games in the second half of the 1928/29 season, scoring his two goals for the club against Shirebrook in

February and the Reserve side of his old team, Notts County, at the end of April. No details are known about the end of his Grantham career or subsequent clubs, other than the knowledge that in 1935 he joined Basford United. Died 1969.

Priestley

Seasons Played			
	League	~	1
	F.A. Cup	~	
1914/15	Lincs Cup	~	
	Total	~	1

Played in the September 1914 Central Alliance fixture against Loughborough Corinthians, but it is not known how many other appearances, if any, he made that year.

Harry Pringle

Seasons Played			
	League	~	44 (17)
	F.A. Cup	~	3 (2)
1934/35-37/38	Lincs Cup	~	6 (3)
	Other	~	1
1939/40	Total	~	54 (22)

Born 08/04/1900 at Perkinsville. Began his career at Craghead United, before spending time on the books at Arsenal and then moving to Chester-le-Street. 1922 saw the start of the most successful spell of his career, when he joined Lincoln City, and Harry spent twelve seasons there, scoring 64 goals in 315 appearances. He became Grantham's first ever Player/Manager in the Summer of 1934 and got off to the best possible start when he scored on his debut in the opening Midland League match at Boston United. Only weeks later the club started their FA Cup run with a record 13-0 victory against Rufford Colliery, with Harry getting a brace in that match as well. He played in over half of that season's games and at the end, although missing out on the County Cup Final, he played in the replay when the club returned to Boston. The following season, although Harry played only occasionally, he took the team to the FA Cup First Round, when Notts County came over to London Road, another Lincolnshire Senior Cup Final and victories in the Grantham Hospital and Wilson Cups. Finally a year later in April 1937 the team at long last managed to defeat The Pilgrims in the County Cup Final to win Grantham the trophy for only the second time in their history. However, at the start of the 1937/38 season Harry had been forced out of the managerial position due to the club's financial difficulties, but he remained as the team's trainer and held that position for the next fourteen years. He continued to make appearances for the club as and when needed, with his final game for Grantham coming in May 1940 at Peterborough United. In the 1950's Harry became the trainer of the Aveling Barfords works team. Died 08/01/1965 in Grantham.

Nathan Proctor

Seasons Played			
	League	~	2
	F.A. Cup	~	
1989/90	F.A. Trophy	~	
	League Cup	~	
	Lincs Cup	~	
	Total	~	2

Born 1956 at Sheffield. Goalkeeper who began his career on Sheffield United's books, before making appearances for Boston United, Skegness Town and Mossley on-loan. He played in two fixtures for Grantham during February 1989 when Andy Plant was unavailable, against RC Warwick and Willenhall Town, ending up on the winning side both times.

Proctor

Seasons Played			
	F.A. Cup	~	
	Lincs Cup	~	
1888/89	Other	~	3
	Total	~	3

First played for the club in a friendly against Mapperley in January 1889 and then appeared in games at London Road versus Sphinx and finally Radcliffe in March.

Bob Puplett

Seasons Played			
	League	~	50 (39)
	F.A. Cup	~	3 (1)
1952/53-53/54	Lincs Cup	~	1 (1)
	Total	~	54 (41)

Former Kettering Town centre-forward who made his debut for Grantham in the opening league fixture of the 1952/53 season at Mansfield Town Reserves and scored his first goal for the club only two days later at Peterborough United. At the end of that season he played in the Final of the County Cup at Spalding United and seemed destined to become the club's top scorer until a final rally from Jack Macartney dashed Bob's hopes. Sadly for the club, by November 1953 Bob had left after scoring another 15 goals in 15 appearances, the last of which was at Doncaster Rovers Reserves.

Josh Quaily

Seasons Played			
	League	~	10
	F.A. Cup	~	
2004/05	F.A. Trophy	~	
	League Cup	~	1
	Lincs Cup	~	1 (1)
	Total	~	12 (1)

Born 1987 at Leicester. Striker who joined Grantham's Under-18 Academy at the start of the 2004/05 season, but was soon brought into the First team squad. Josh made his debut by coming off the bench to replace Peter Sutton in the Southern League fixture against Solihull Borough at the end of August. His first goal for the club came in the March 2005 Lincolnshire Shield tie at home to Stamford, and he remains with The Gingerbreads.

Mark Quayle

Seasons Played			
	League	~	6 (4)
	F.A. Cup	~	
1998/99	F.A. Trophy	~	
	League Cup	~	
	Lincs Cup	~	
	Total	~	6 (4)

Born 02/10/1978 at Liverpool. Began his career at Everton, but signed for Grantham on-loan from Notts County. He scored on his debut for The Gingerbreads in the February 1999 league fixture at King's Lynn, scored again in the following match at home to Gresley Rovers and then netted a brace against Rothwell Town. His period with the club ended in March at Merthyr Tydfil and after his release from Notts County he went on to play for Leigh RMI, Ilkeston Town, Altrincham, Morecambe, Telford United, Nuneaton Borough, Chester City, Scarborough and Northwich Victoria.

Cyril Quinn

Seasons Played			
	League	~	98 (32)
	F.A. Cup	~	16 (7)
1928/29	Lincs Cup	~	8 (1)
	Other	~	2 (1)
1934/35-37/38	Total	~	124 (41)

Born circa 1908 in Grantham. Started his career with Albion Rovers and then made eight appearances for Grantham at the start of the 1928/29 season, scoring his first goal for the club in September at Staveley Town. Cyril went on to play for Blackpool, Swindon Town and Fleetwood Town, scoring nine goals in his 67 Football League appearances. He returned to London Road in the Summer of 1934 and not surprisingly this time played a much more prominent role in the team, including appearances in the record 13-0 victory over Rufford Colliery, where he scored twice, and both the Lincolnshire Senior Cup Final and the replay against Boston United. The following season Cyril played in the FA Cup game against Notts County, a repeat of the previous County Cup Final, the Wilson Cup and the Grantham Hospital Cup, where he scored one of the goals that secured victory over Doncaster Rovers. By the 1936/37 campaign though, his appearances had dipped down to only nine during the whole season, but luckily for him one of those was the County competition final when Grantham finally defeated Boston United. His last goal for the club came in his final appearance, the entertaining October 1937 FA Cup tie against Boots Athletic that ended in an 8-3 victory for Grantham.

Walter Raby

Seasons Played			
	League	~	1
	F.A. Cup	~	
1920/21	Lincs Cup	~	
	Other	~	
	Total	~	1

Born 23/09/1902 at Lincoln. Forward who had previously spent time at Lincoln Robeys, Lincoln City and appeared for Grantham in the March 1921 fixture against Gresley Rovers, but it's not known if this was his only game for the club. He went on to play for Grimsby Town, scoring a single goal in his two First team appearances,

Clapton Orient, Scunthorpe & Lindsey United, Gainsborough Trinity, Poole Town and Doncaster Rovers. Died 09/03/1973 at Lincoln.

Andy Radford

Seasons Played			
	League	~	7
	F.A. Cup	~	
1989/90	F.A. Trophy	~	
	League Cup	~	2
	Lincs Cup	~	
	Total	~	9

Goalkeeper who made his debut for Grantham in the November 1989 Westgate Insurance League Cup tie against Atherstone United and played in the next seven matches, before making a lone and final appearance in February 1990 at home to Leicester United.

Peter Radford

Seasons Played			
	League	~	13 (1)
	F.A. Cup	~	1
1988/89-89/90	F.A. Trophy	~	1
	League Cup	~	4 (1)
	Lincs Cup	~	1
	Total	~	20 (2)

Born 03/05/1968 at Heanor. Former England Schoolboy International with experience at Kettering Town, Shepshed Charterhouse, Long Eaton and Alfreton Town. Peter first played for Grantham in the October 1988 league fixture at home to Nuneaton Borough and scored his initial goal in the same month at Stourbridge, with his only other strike the following month in the League Cup tie against Atherstone United. He went on to make a total of 16 appearances that season, which also included a spell on-loan at Ilkeston Town. Peter failed to make any more appearances though for the club after the September 1989 FA Cup tie at Boston FC due to breaking his arm, although he returned to the game with Ripley Town the following season.

Radford

Seasons Played			
	League	~	1
	F.A. Cup	~	
1926/27	Lincs Cup	~	
	Other	~	
	Total	~	1

Outside-Right who made just one appearance for Grantham, the Midland League game at Long Eaton in January 1927.

Bob Raine

Seasons Played			
	League	~	3
	F.A. Cup	~	
1954/55	Lincs Cup	~	
	Total	~	3

Born 17/11/1927 at Chesterfield. Former Newbold Colliery, Chesterfield, Kidderminster Harriers and Aldershot striker who scored 20 goals in his 49 Football League appearances. Bob played for Grantham in three consecutive Midland League fixtures during January and February of 1955, against Denaby United, Goole Town and Frickley Colliery.

Craig Ramsay

Seasons Played			
	League	~	8 (3)
	F.A. Cup	~	
1985/86-86/87	F.A. Trophy	~	4 (1)
	League Cup	~	3 (1)
	Lincs Cup	~	
	Total	~	15 (5)

Born 19/09/1962 at Dunfermline. Former Scottish Under-18 International, Dunfermline Athletic and Lincoln City player, who scored twice in his five appearances at Sincil Bank. After a spell at FC Jaro, where he finished the 1981/82 season as top scorer in the Finnish Division One League, he returned to England with Heanor Town and Alfreton Town. Craig then joined Grantham, making his debut in the November 1985 league match against VS Rugby, but only played in the next four games, plus another ten appearances in the middle of the 1986/87 season. In a sudden burst of scoring ability, Craig netted his first strike against VS Rugby in the November 1986 Bill Dellow League Cup, scored against Macclesfield Town and finished with a hat-trick less than a month later as The Gingerbreads demolished Rushden Town 8-0. His last appearance for the club came in the January 1987 League Cup tie at Woodford Town and he went back to Alfreton Town, before returning to Finland with Kokkolan PV and later rejoining FC Jaro, eventually spending time in the managerial seat there. Craig still lives in Finland and now works for the national FA there.

John Ramsden

Seasons Played			
	League	~	78 (1)
	F.A. Cup	~	6
1952/53-57/58	Lincs Cup	~	
	Total	~	84 (1)

Born 06/09/1932 in Grantham. Played for a West Bromwich Albion side during the late 1940's in a Midland Cup match against Aston Villa, but after coming out of the Armed Forces soon joined his home team. He made his debut for Grantham in the March 1953 league game at Nottingham Forest Reserves and missed only two of the remaining fixtures from that season. The following year though, John seldom played as Freddie Martin was preferred in the defensive position, but in the 1954/55 campaign he was back to a fairly regular place in the team and scored his one and only goal for the club at the end of August when Notts County Reserves came to London Road. His final three seasons with the team saw his appearances gradually diminish and his last game came on Christmas Day 1957 when Wisbech Town thrashed Grantham 7-0. Other than football, John also played for Grantham Cricket Club and was a well known local tennis player as well. He is now retired and still lives in the town.

Mark Ramsden

Seasons Played			
	League	~	24 (2)
	F.A. Cup	~	3
1984/85-85/86	F.A. Trophy	~	2
	League Cup	~	4
	Lincs Cup	~	3
	Other	~	
	Total	~	36 (2)

Born circa 1964. Started out as an Apprentice at Rotherham United, but was released by them after suffering a serious injury and joined Oughtibridge He came to Grantham in the Summer of 1984, making his debut in the opening County Cup tie of the new season at Boston United. Mark scored his first goal for the club the following month in a surprising 4-0 win at home to Morecambe and played in about half of the fixtures that term as the club struggled to avoid relegation. The following campaign he played in the first eight fixtures, but the September 1985 game against Gloucester City was his last for the club.

Paul Ramsey

Seasons Played			
	League	~	12 (1)
	F.A. Cup	~	
1997/98	F.A. Trophy	~	
	League Cup	~	
	Lincs Cup	~	
	Total	~	12 (1)

Born 03/09/1962 at Derry, NI. Former Northern Ireland International, with 16 caps, who previously played for Leicester City and Cardiff City, earning around 400 appearances during his time with those two clubs. He then moved to St Johnstone in Scotland, before signing for Barry Town, Telford United and then returning back to The Football League with Torquay United in 1995, making another 18 senior appearances. Paul then played for Merthyr Tydfil, TPV in Finland and Rothwell Town, before joining Grantham. Although he had only a short spell at The Meres, it was to be at a hugely successful time, making his debut in the February 1998 league victory at Redditch United and his first home game was played in front of a stadium record attendance for a league fixture, as Grantham thrashed their nearest rivals, Ilkeston Town, 6-0. Paul was unable to play in the FA Trophy tie against Southport, but helped Grantham in many of the remaining league matches, scoring against Blakenhall and playing his final appearance in the closing game at home to Stourbridge, which secured the league title. He left at the end of the season to join King's Lynn, where he also spent time as Manager of their Reserve team.

John Randall

Seasons Played			
	League	~	1
	F.A. Cup	~	
1974/75	F.A. Trophy	~	
	League Cup	~	
	Lincs Cup	~	
	Total	~	1

Former Grantham United goalkeeper who replaced Chris Gardiner for the January 1976 league fixture at home to Dover. John now lives in the Nottingham area.

Jack Ranshaw

Seasons Played			
	League	~	40 (20)
	F.A. Cup	~	7 (4)
1939/40	Lincs Cup	~	2
	Other	~	7 (3)
1945/46	Total	~	56 (27)

Born 19/12/1916 at Lincoln. Right-winger who had previously spent time at Lincoln Corinthians, Gainsborough Trinity, Newark Town, Lincoln City and Mansfield Town, before he scored on his Grantham debut in the first Midland League match of the 1939/40 season at Bradford Park Avenue Reserves. Of course this was a competition that would be abandoned after only three games because of European conflict, but by then Jack had already notched up five goals to his name. He played in most of the Midland 'War-Time' League fixtures and the Lincolnshire Senior Cup Final against Scunthorpe & Lindsey United. With Jack Macartney unavailable for large periods of time Ranshaw was able to finish as the club's joint highest scorer along with Jack Fahy. He played for Grimsby Town, Chesterfield, Mansfield Town and Lincoln City during The War, but after the end of hostilities he returned to London Road where he continued to be an important member of the side and appeared in every round of that season's FA Cup run, including both legs against Kettering Town and Mansfield Town. Jack's final goal for the club came in his last appearance for Grantham, in February 1946 at home to Bradford Park Avenue Reserves, and he then returned to Lincoln City, making three appearances for their First team, before joining Peterborough United, Boston United, March Town and Nettleham United. For many years after the end of his playing career he was groundsman at Sincil Bank and ran a newsagents at Nettleham. Died May 2003.

Rick Ranshaw

Seasons Played			
	League	~	133 (44)
	F.A. Cup	~	9 (6)
1993/94	F.A. Trophy	~	6 (2)
	League Cup	~	8 (4)
1999/00-02/03	Lincs Cup	~	6 (2)
	Total	~	162 (58)

Born 17/04/1970 at Sleaford. Began his career at Lincoln City, making one First team appearance, before moving to Bridlington Town, Gainsborough Trinity, Louth United, Harrowby United and Lincoln United. He played for Grantham in the first two County Cup games of the 1993/94 season, scoring on his debut as The Gingerbreads defeated Lincoln City, but soon rejoined Lincoln United. However, he came back to The Meres in August 1999 and was later followed by his former Manager, John Wilkinson, and several of his team-mates. Rick played in most of the games over the next year or so, including the October 2000 FA Cup tie at Rushden & Diamonds, where he scored one of the goals as Grantham bravely succumbed to a 5-4 defeat. He left for a brief spell at Gainsborough Trinity at the start of the 2001/02 season, but resumed his usual place in the side upon his return, soon scoring a hat-trick against Banbury United and finishing with 40 appearances as Grantham gained promotion back to the Dr Marten's Premier League. Rick then played in the October 2002 FA Cup final qualifying round at Morecambe and the April 2003 County Cup Final against Gainsborough Trinity. He scored his last goal in the closing fixture at home to Moor Green, but then left to join Lincoln United, signing dual forms that allowed him to also play for Harrowby United. Rick had a brief spell at Gedling Town in February 2004, but soon returned to Harrowby.

C. Ratcliffe

Seasons Played			
	League	~	1 (1)
	F.A. Cup	~	
1933/34	Lincs Cup	~	
	Other	~	
	Total	~	1 (1)

Centre-Half who had previously played for Lincoln Burton Road and whose surname is sometimes spelt 'Radcliffe'. Unfortunately the evidence for his only goal comes in end of season records, so no information is available to show the particular game.

Paul Raven

Seasons Played			
	League	~	1
	F.A. Cup	~	
1981/82	F.A. Trophy	~	
	League Cup	~	
	Lincs Cup	~	
	Other	~	
	Total	~	1

Former Gresley Rovers and Barry Town player who made just one appearance for Grantham when he came off the bench in the February 1982 league match at Workington to replace Alan Jones.

Chris Rawlinson

Seasons Played			
	League	~	1
	F.A. Cup	~	
1994/95	F.A. Trophy	~	
	League Cup	~	
	Lincs Cup	~	
	Total	~	1

Born 04/12/1975 at Newcastle. Former Lincoln City Trainee who appeared on Grantham's substitutes bench for many of the first matches during the 1994/95 season, but progressed to the field only once in September to replace Warren Ward as Grantham defeated Stourbridge with an unbelievable 7-2 score-line. Chris still lives in the Lincoln area and recently was playing for Alstom in the Lincolnshire League.

Rawlinson

Seasons Played			
	League	~	12 (13)
	F.A. Cup	~	
1925/26-26/27	Lincs Cup	~	
	Other	~	
	Total	~	12 (13)

Centre-Forward who was in the Armed Forces and stationed near to Grantham. His first two goals for the club came in the February 1926 Midland League game at Boston, but unfortunately only those games in which he scored are known for that season. The following campaign though, we know that he made only four appearances, with his final one in December at home to Lincoln City Reserves.

Rawlinson

Seasons Played			
	League	~	5 (1)
	F.A. Cup	~	1 (1)
1932/33	Lincs Cup	~	
	Other	~	
	Total	~	6 (2)

Most likely played all of his games for the club towards the beginning of the 1932/33 season, with his goals coming in October 1932 against Sutton Junction in the FA Cup and Gainsborough Trinity in the league.

Rawlinson

Seasons Played			
	League	~	21 (5)
	F.A. Cup	~	1
1946/47	Lincs Cup	~	3
	Total	~	25 (5)

Scored on his debut in the September 1946, 6-0 thrashing of Boston United and then played in most of Grantham's games over the next few months. He played in the April 1947 County Cup Final against Gainsborough Trinity, with his final appearance for the club coming two weeks later in the replay.

Paddy Phelan

Harry Pringle

John Ramsden

Rick Ranshaw

Chris Rawlinson

Rawlinson (1946/47)

Jimmy Rayner

Shaun Reddington

Stuart Reddington

Kevin Rimmington

Lee Rippin

John Robertson

Dave Robinson

George Robinson

Nick Robinson

Ralph Robinson

Jimmy Rayner

Seasons Played			
	League	~	83 (108)
	F.A. Cup	~	4 (3)
1957/58	Lincs Cup	~	4 (4)
1963/64-64/65	Total	~	91 (115)

Born 31/03/1935 at Cornsay, near Durham. Began his career at Langley Park Juniors and Grimsby Town, before moving to Bury, Hartlepool United, Barrow and Corby Town. He played for Grantham in October 1957 in a Midland League fixture against Goole Town and scored his first goal for the club only two weeks later at Bradford City Reserves. Jimmy played in every one of the remaining season's games, including the County Cup Final at home to Gainsborough Trinity and easily finished as the club's highest scorer, aided by four hat-tricks against Corby Town, Nottingham Forest Reserves, Spalding United and Gainsborough Trinity. By the time he returned to London Road in the summer of 1963 as Grantham's Player/Manager, his Football League experience had now widened to include his most successful spell so far, with Peterborough United. The season of 1963/64 was to be Grantham's first Midland League Championship and for Jimmy personally there was to be so many highlights. A club record of 71 goals for one season included six against Sutton Town and Retford Town, four put past Gainsborough Trinity and Denaby United, plus another five hat-tricks. The title was secured at their closest rivals, Scarborough, in April and only a few days later Jimmy was able to lift the trophy in front of 2,616 spectators after the Belper Town fixture. His goal-scoring skills continued into the following season, but after eight goals in only six games he was transferred back into The League when Notts County came up with a £2,500 fee. His final appearance for Grantham had been in September 1964 at London Road against Skegness Town. Following the end of his professional career, which saw him make over 150 appearances in The Football League, Jimmy went on to become Player/Manager at Ilkeston Town, before having a successful couple of seasons at Boston United, scoring 55 goals in the 1965/66 campaign, still a club record for The Pilgrims. He then returned to the North-East, had a short spell with Durham City, became Player/Manager at Gateshead, scouted for several Football League sides including Coventry City, before returning to Durham City as Chairman. Jimmy is now retired and still lives within a few miles of his home town.

Steve Raynor

Seasons Played			
	League	~	3 (3)
	F.A. Cup	~	
1990/91	F.A. Trophy	~	
	League Cup	~	
	Lincs Cup	~	
	Total	~	3 (3)

Previously played for Oldham Athletic Reserves and was brought to Grantham on the recommendation of Mick McGuire. He promptly scored twice on his debut in February 1991 at Newport AFC, again in the following match against RC Warwick, but the next Saturday he made his last appearance for the club at Bilston Town.

Leonard Raysen

Seasons Played			
	League	~	12 (2)
	F.A. Cup	~	
1926/27	Lincs Cup	~	
	Other	~	
	Total	~	12 (2)

Born 1908. Generally played in a forward role and made one First team appearance for Lincoln City at the start of the 1926/27 season, before coming to Grantham. Len made his debut in February 1927 at Denaby United, with his first goal coming a month later in the home game versus Frickley Colliery. His only other strike for the club was in April against Heanor Town, but his final appearance is not known. His surname is sometimes spelt 'Rayson'.

Sean Reddington

Seasons Played			
	League	~	1
	F.A. Cup	~	
2003/04	F.A. Trophy	~	
	League Cup	~	
	Lincs Cup	~	
	Total	~	1

Born circa 1984. Former Southwell City goalkeeper who played instead of Mario Ziccardi in the final league match of the 2003/04 season at Weymouth and was released by the club soon after the Summer break.

Stuart Reddington

Seasons Played			
	League	~	19 (2)
	F.A. Cup	~	1
2004/05	F.A. Trophy	~	2
	League Cup	~	1
	Lincs Cup	~	1
	Total	~	24 (2)

Born 21/02/1978 at Lincoln. Began his career at Lincoln United and in 1997 joined Chelsea after a £10,000 transfer, but failed to make their First team. His time there included loan spells at Kalmar FF (Sweden) and Mansfield Town, before joining the latter team permanently in 2001 for £20,000. After a total of 57 appearances, including assisting The Stags to promotion, Stuart joined Burton Albion and in 2003 moved to Gainsborough Trinity, scoring a goal against Grantham in the Lincolnshire Shield Final at the end of that campaign. Only months later Dave Norton had signed him for Grantham, where he made his debut in the opening match of the 2004/05 season at Brigg Town in the County competition. Stuart's two goals for the club came in consecutive fixtures during October 2004, against King's Lynn and Chesham United. His final appearance was at Merthyr Tydfil in February 2005 and at the end of the following month he left and took his career full circle by returning to Lincoln United.

Redhead

Seasons Played			
	Lincs Cup	~	2
	Other	~	8 (1)
1890/91	Total	~	10 (1)

Made his debut in the November 1890 friendly at home to Boston NE and straight away became a near constant member of the team that was involved not only in the Lincolnshire Senior Cup, but both Charity competitions based at Kettering and Newark. The latter of those saw his only goal for the club in January 1891 as Grantham progressed past Rovers Colts.

W. Reek

Seasons Played			
	League	~	1 (2)
	F.A. Cup	~	
1920/21	Lincs Cup	~	
	Other	~	
	Total	~	1 (2)

Inside-Right who also made appearances for Newark but evidently played only once for Grantham, against RAF Cranwell in September 1920, although he scored twice in the 3-1 win.

Nick Reeson

Seasons Played			
	League	~	
	F.A. Cup	~	
1999/00	F.A. Trophy	~	
	League Cup	~	
	Lincs Cup	~	1
	Total	~	1

Born 05/05/1980 at Boston. Former Boston Town and Lincoln City winger who made just one appearance for Grantham in the 1999/00 season's opening County Cup tie at home to Scunthorpe United. He went on to play for Boston United and Wisbech Town.

Jack Reeves

Seasons Played			
	League	~	55
	F.A. Cup	~	
1931/32-32/33	Lincs Cup	~	
	Other	~	1
1934/35-35/36	Total	~	56

Goalkeeper who had previously spent time at Nottingham Forest and made his Grantham debut at the start of the 1931/32 season against Loughborough Corinthians. Jack played in every game that season, but the following one seems to have been relegated to the Reserves team, although he was the unfortunate individual to have to face the Arsenal forwards during the friendly fixture of March 1933. In the 1934/35 season he deputised for Stan Walker in seven of the league games, whilst a year later, and the arrival of Arthur Jepson, left Jack with just two appearances in the Lincolnshire League game against Scunthorpe & Lindsey United and finally in March 1936 when the team lost 6-1 at Boston United.

Peter Reeves

Seasons Played			
	League	~	9
	F.A. Cup	~	1
1955/56	Lincs Cup	~	
	Total	~	10

Defender who made his debut in the September 1955 league fixture at home to Notts County Reserves, but then appeared only occasionally for the First team apart from a respectable run at the end of the campaign which finished at York City Reserves.

Reeves

Seasons Played			
	Other	~	4 (4)
1878/79-79/80	Total	~	4 (4)

Scored a hat-trick on his debut in the March 1879, 9-3 thrashing of Boston and then played in the final two friendlies of the season. He scored his only other goal in his last appearance for the club, the January 1880 match at home to Notts County.

Reeves

Seasons Played			
	League	~	1
	F.A. Cup	~	
1928/29	Lincs Cup	~	
	Other	~	
	Total	~	1

Known to have played in one Midland League fixture from the 1928/29 season, although no details are available on the actual game. This means that no information is even known as to his position, so there is always the possibility that it could be Jack Reeves covering one of the games for Stan Walker, who we know missed some of the fixtures that season.

Mark Renshaw

Seasons Played			
	League	~	3
	F.A. Cup	~	
1985/86	F.A. Trophy	~	
	League Cup	~	
	Lincs Cup	~	
	Total	~	3

Born circa 1963. Local player and former Gonerby Excelsior member who signed from Harrowby United and made his Grantham debut when he came on as substitute in the February 1986 fixture at home to Redditch United. Mark made just two more appearances for the team though, the following month against Gloucester City and Oldbury United, but continued to play for the Reserves side. He still lives and works locally.

Stanley Rhodes

Seasons Played			
	League	~	7 (3)
	F.A. Cup	~	1
1958/59	Lincs Cup	~	
	Total	~	8 (3)

Born 19/04/1929 at Sheffield. Began his career at Leeds United, before moving to Worksop Town and then making one First team appearance for Sheffield United. He played for Grantham in the opening Midland League match of the 1958/59 season at home to Goole Town and scored his first goal for the club a week later at North Shields. After a decent run in the initial month of the campaign, Stanley then had to wait until the end of November to make his final appearance for the club at Worksop Town. The following year he had moved on to Matlock Town, although a serious car accident in the Summer of 1959 led to the end of his career with their Reserves side.

Steve Richards

Seasons Played			
	League	~	32 (2)
	F.A. Cup	~	1
1983/84-84/85	F.A. Trophy	~	7
	League Cup	~	3
	Lincs Cup	~	2
	Other	~	
	Total	~	45 (2)

Born 24/10/1961 at Dundee. Defender with League experience at Hull City, making 58 appearances, who then played in the Belgian League with Lierse SK, before returning to England with Bridlington Trinity. He made his Grantham debut in the October 1983 fixture at Macclesfield Town and played in most of the remaining games, scoring against Rhyl and Witton Albion as the club finished fourth in the Northern Premier League. However, his last appearance came in September 1984, at home to Halesowen Town in the FA Cup, and he soon moved on to Goole Town and Gainsborough Trinity, before returning to The Football League to make appearances for York City, Lincoln City, Cambridge United, Scarborough, Halifax Town and Doncaster Rovers. By the end of his professional career, Steve had scored 26 goals in 380 senior appearances. His managerial career took him back to Gainsborough and to date he has also spent time at the helm of Guiseley, Frickley Athletic, Goole Town and Ossett Town.

Richardson

Seasons Played			
	Lincs Cup	~	
	Other	~	1
1889/90	Total	~	1

Made just one appearance for Grantham in the October 1889 friendly at home to Radcliffe.

Kevin Rimmington

Seasons Played			
	League	~	2
	F.A. Cup	~	2
1985/86	F.A. Trophy	~	
	League Cup	~	3
	Lincs Cup	~	2 (1)
	Total	~	9 (1)

Born 1961 at Rotherham. Full-Back signed from Rotherham United who scored from the penalty spot on his debut in the opening County Cup game of the 1985/86 season at home to Boston United. After only nine appearances though, the last of which came in October against Merthyr Tydfil, he left London Road and went on to play for Spalding United, Armthorpe Welfare, Brodsworth Colliery and Armthorpe Colliery Reserves. Kevin currently lives in Wales and is a Fibre Optic Designer for a national telecommunications company.

Lee Rippin

Seasons Played			
	League	~	47 (4)
	F.A. Cup	~	1
1991/92-93/94	F.A. Trophy	~	2
	League Cup	~	2
	Lincs Cup	~	1
	Total	~	53 (4)

Born 19/05/1965 at Boston. Started out as an Apprentice at Arsenal, before making moves to Spalding United, where he won a league winners medal, King's Lynn and Boston FC, who awarded him the honour of being the club's youngest ever Captain at the age of 21. He scored on his debut for Grantham in March 1991 at Redditch United and then played in every match up to the financial problems of the 1992/93 winter which led to his departure from The Meres and a return to Boston FC. He was brought back to the club by Allen Crombie in February 1994 and missed only one game up to the end of the season. Lee's last goal for Grantham came in the March fixture at Armitage, with his final appearance in the closing victory at Dudley Town. He returned to Boston once more and went on to make over 400 appearances for them, helping the club to two United Counties Championships, until his retirement at the end of the 2004/05 season.

Thomas Rippon

Seasons Played			
	League	~	8 (4)
	F.A. Cup	~	2 (4)
1926/27	Lincs Cup	~	
	Other	~	
	Total	~	10 (8)

Born 04/02/1888 at Beighton. 'Pip', as he was known, had started his career in 1911 at Grimsby Town and ten years later moved to Lincoln City, finishing with ten goals in a professional career that had lasted 151 Football League games. He then moved on to Worksop Town, York City and Wath Athletic, before making his Grantham debut in the opening fixture of the 1926/27 season at Sutton Town and scoring four goals a month later in the FA Cup match against New Hucknall Colliery. The following week saw another goal in the league fixture at home to York City and a hat-trick against Sutton Town, but he was soon to become missing from the team-sheets for some reason. He returned to make his final two appearances for the club in the New Year, with the trip over to Ilkeston United being the concluding one. Died 1950 at Sheffield.

D. Roberts

Seasons Played			
	League	~	2
	Lincs Cup	~	
1939/40	Other	~	1
	Total	~	3

Born circa 1923. Sixteen year-old goalkeeper from Sleaford who played in the March 1940 Midland 'War-Time' League game at Newark Town, (where he let in nine goals), a friendly against an Army XI a few days later, and finally the fixture against a powerful Scunthorpe & Lindsey United side where he probably did well to restrict the opposing forwards to only eight strikes. Could very easily be Donald Roberts, born 1923 at Sleaford.

Roberts

Seasons Played			
	League	~	1
	F.A. Cup	~	
1922/23	Lincs Cup	~	
	Other	~	
	Total	~	1

Local goalkeeper who played in the home game against Sutton Town in April of 1923 and managed to keep a clean sheet as Grantham ran out 2-0 winners.

Roberts

Seasons Played			
	League	~	6 (2)
	F.A. Cup	~	
1933/34	Lincs Cup	~	1 (1)
	Other	~	1 (1)
	Total	~	8 (4)

Reserves player who was given the opportunity to play in the November 1933 Central Combination fixture at home to Ilkeston United after scoring twice in a friendly against Newark Town. He then kept the place and scored his first goal for the club in a competitive match a week later at Kettering Town. Most likely he made more appearances than those shown above, with his last goals for the club coming in the April 1934 local Hospital Cup replay against RAF Grantham played at Harlaxton Road.

Alf Robertson

Seasons Played			
	League	~	49
	F.A. Cup	~	
1929/30	Lincs Cup	~	
	Other	~	
	Total	~	49

Born 02/07/1908 at Sunderland. Goalkeeper who had previously spent time at local side Bank Head, plus Newcastle United and Notts County. He first played for Grantham in the opening Midland League fixture of the 1929/30 season at Mansfield Town and missed only one league fixture that season, but there are no records to show the amount of cup appearances he made. Alf went on to play for Bradford Park Avenue, Clapton Orient, Bristol Rovers, Accrington Stanley and Dunkenhalgh, finishing at the start of the Second World War with 184 Football League appearances behind him. Died 1984 at Hyndburn, Lancashire.

John Robertson

Seasons Played			
	League	~	12 (4)
	F.A. Cup	~	2
1987/88	F.A. Trophy	~	1
	League Cup	~	4 (1)
1990/91	Lincs Cup	~	2
	Total	~	21 (5)

Born 20/1/1953 at Uddingston, Scotland. Began his career with local side Drumchapel Amateurs, but was soon snapped up by Nottingham Forest in May 1970. He was once described by Brian Clough as "a genius" and seems to have had as many nick-names as games, generally along the lines of 'Twinkletum', or rather more scathing comments about his weight. Yet despite being known to sneak in a crafty fag during the half-time break, here is one of the games greatest players. Former colleague, Larry Lloyd, later remarked on Nottingham Forest's tactics of that time. "Robbo would shuffle that fat arse of his, the full-back and 30,000 spectators would go one way.. then he'd cross and Forest would score - simple as that!". He laid on the cross for Trevor Francis to score the only goal in Nottingham Forest's first European Cup Final and scored the winner himself a year later. He also won medals for the Division One Championship, the League Cup and the Super Cup, making over 400 appearances for Forest, 243 of them consecutively. Robbo also played for Derby County and represented Scotland 28 times, scoring 8 International goals. After a short spell at Corby Town, he came to Grantham, where he made his debut in the opening County Cup tie of the 1987/88 season against Scunthorpe United. Amazingly though this wasn't Robbo's first appearance for a Grantham team. Back in the mid-1970's he and Tony Woodcock had guested for the Aveling Barford's works team that perhaps unsurprisingly won the 5-a-side tournament! Of course he was soon joined at London Road by Manager, Martin O'Neill, and John made 19 appearances that season, scoring his first goal for the club at home to Moor Green in September. In the Summer of 1989 he followed Martin O'Neill to Shepshed Charterhouse, but continued to play for local sides, including Parliament Street Methodists and Thringstone. With his thoughts turning towards a managerial career of his own, he sold the public house that he was running and as luck would have it, it was a return to Grantham that brought about that first post. He took over the managerial position from Danny Anderson in February 1990, spanning the period from the end of London Road, the tenancy at Spalding, where he played twice against Hinckley Town and Willenhall Town in the final two 'home' fixtures, and the first few months at The Meres. After a disappointing string of results, he left the club in the Spring of 1992 and soon returned to his job as Martin O'Neill's right-hand man, firstly at Wycombe Wanderers and Norwich City as Coach/Scout, before moving on to Leicester City and Glasgow Celtic as Assistant Manager/Coach.

Steve Robertson

Seasons Played			
	League	~	4
	F.A. Cup	~	
1988/89	F.A. Trophy	~	3
	League Cup	~	2
	Lincs Cup	~	1
	Total	~	10

Born 18/02/1964 at Newcastle. Former Melton Town and Stamford Town player who progressed through the Reserves, winning a Midland Regional Alliance Championship medal at the end of the 1987/88 season with them. Steve's First team debut came in the opening County Cup tie of the following season at home to Gainsborough Trinity, with his final appearance in November against Atherstone United in the Westgate Insurance League Cup. With his failure to maintain a First team place, Steve soon returned to Melton Town.

Darren Robinson

Seasons Played			
	League	~	4
	F.A. Cup	~	2 (1)
1996/97	F.A. Trophy	~	
	League Cup	~	
	Lincs Cup	~	1
	Total	~	7 (1)

Former Grimsby Town and Hull City player who was also a qualified FA Coach and Director of Sheffield United's Academy of Excellence. After leaving Hull, Darren made appearances for Burton Albion, Nuneaton Borough, Corby Town, Armitage, Leicester United and Shepshed Dynamo, before joining Grantham in the Summer of 1996. He made his debut in the opening County Cup tie of the season at home to Grimsby Town and scored his only goal for the club in the Preliminary Round of the FA Cup at Witham Town. However, Darren's last appearance came in the following round against Boston Town in September and he then returned to Shepshed. His career finished with Leicestershire side, Barrow, before he took up the position of Director of Football at Loughborough University.

Dave Robinson

Seasons Played			
	League	~	23 (3)
	F.A. Cup	~	1
1997/98	F.A. Trophy	~	
	League Cup	~	
2004/05	Lincs Cup	~	1
	Total	~	25 (3)

Born 14/07/1975 at Nottingham. Defender who started his career at Heanor Town, before moving to Ilkeston Town, winning a Dr Marten's Midland Division winner's medal in 1995, a year which also saw trials for him at Middlesbrough. After a spell at Gresley Rovers, he made his Grantham debut in the February 1998 league fixture at Redditch United and only days later was playing in the 6-0 thrashing of Ilkeston Town. Apart from the FA Trophy matches against Southport, which he was cup-tied for, Dave played in all of the remaining games, scoring against RC Warwick and Solihull Borough. He appeared in the closing match at home to Stourbridge, which secured the League Championship for Grantham, and then went on to play for King's Lynn and Tamworth. Whilst with The Lambs he was part of the team that won the Dr Marten's Premier League in 2002/03 and reached the Final of the FA Trophy. Dave returned to Grantham in the Summer of 2004, soon scoring his other goal for the club at home to Hemel Hempstead. However, the disastrous FA Cup exit at the hands of Shepshed Dynamo saw not only the departure of Dave Norton, but also Dave Robinson, and he soon rejoined Tamworth.

George Robinson

Seasons Played			
	League	~	254 (1)
	F.A. Cup	~	17
1948/49-54/55	Lincs Cup	~	8
	Total	~	279 (1)

Born 17/06/1925 at Melton Mowbray. Former Melton Town and Holwell Works defender who made 29 appearances for Notts County during the 1946/47 season. His Grantham debut came in the opening match of the 1948/49 season at Scarborough and George played in the majority of that season's games, scoring his only goal for the club in November at home to Mansfield Town Reserves. A year after this he played in the FA Cup First Round at Wrexham and although later that season he missed many of the games during the Spring period, he was back in time for the County Cup Final replay at Boston United, which ended in defeat for the team. As the club entered the new decade, George continued to be a near constant member of the team's defence and in March 1953 he once again appeared in the County Cup Final, with another defeat inflicted upon Grantham by The Pilgrims. A year later though, the team went one better and actually won the competition after defeating Gainsborough Trinity. Although George's final season with the club saw Charles Aley fighting for his position, he continued to play in many of the games right up until the end of the campaign, with his final appearance coming in April 1955 at Peterborough United.

Nick Robinson

Seasons Played			
	League	~	10 (1)
	F.A. Cup	~	2 (1)
1994/95	F.A. Trophy	~	
	League Cup	~	1
	Lincs Cup	~	1
	Total	~	14 (2)

Made his Grantham debut in the 1994/95 season's opening match in the County Cup against Grimsby Town and scored his first goal in the FA Cup tie at home to Leicester United in August. His other goal came in the 7-2 win at Stourbridge, but his final appearance was against Redditch United in November 1994.

Peter Robinson

Seasons Played			
	League	~	18 (2)
	F.A. Cup	~	1 (1)
1946/47-48/49	Lincs Cup	~	
	Total	~	19 (3)

Forward who first played for the team in the October 1946 league fixture at Frickley Colliery and scored his initial goal for the club two months later as Notts County Reserves were defeated 6-1. Peter kept his place in the side until the New Year and then had another three game spell towards the end of the season. The following campaign though, he made just five appearances and his last game, which also saw his final goal for the club, came in the October 1948 FA Cup win over Raleigh Athletic. Peter also played for the Lincolnshire FA representative side just after The War.

Ralph Robinson

Seasons Played			
	League	~	7
	F.A. Cup	~	
1957/58	Lincs Cup	~	
	Total	~	7

Born 12/11/1929 at Worsborough Dale, near Barnsley. Defender who previously played for Barnsley, Southport and Boston United. Ralph played for Grantham in the opening match of the 1957/58 season against Worksop Town and the following six games as well, but after losing his place to Alan Gee made no further appearances and went on to play for Sutton Town.

Robinson

Seasons Played			
	Other	~	1
1875/76	Total	~	1

Made just one appearance for the club in the December 1875 friendly against the Conservative Working Mens Club.

Robinson

Seasons Played			
	F.A. Cup	~	
	Lincs Cup	~	
1884/85-86/87	Other	~	3
	Total	~	3

Played in the first friendly of the 1884/85 season at home to the Grantham Volunteers, the November 1885 match at Sleaford and the initial game of the following season, once more against The Volunteers.

Rockley

Seasons Played			
	League	~	1
	F.A. Cup	~	
1932/33	Lincs Cup	~	
	Other	~	
	Total	~	1

Local full-back who also played for Grantham Amateurs, but details of the game in which he played for our club are not known.

Nick Roddis

Seasons Played			
	League	~	23
	F.A. Cup	~	
1992/93-93/94	F.A. Trophy	~	2
	League Cup	~	
	Lincs Cup	~	
	Total	~	25

Born 18/02/1973 at Rotherham. Previously spent time at Nottingham Forest, Aston Villa, both Boston clubs and Mansfield Town. He took over Andy Bullimore's defensive position for eight consecutive appearances at the end of 1992, starting with the league game at Rushden & Diamonds. He returned to the side once more in October 1993 and made his last appearance for the club in the January 1994 home game against Leicester United. After leaving Grantham, he relocated to the London area and played for Yeading, Hayes and Woking, during which time he also captained Great Britain in the 2001 World University Games in China. It was because of this dual arrangement, that didn't suit the Woking Manager, that Nick moved on to Margate and then Aldershot in the Conference, although lack of First team football due to injuries forced a move to Farnborough Town in the Summer of 2004. Transfers then followed to Crawley Town, AFC Wimbledon and St Alban's City. Nick has also been awarded England Semi-Professional International caps and is currently head of physical education at a London Prep school.

Dave Rogers

Seasons Played			
	League	~	25
	F.A. Cup	~	2
1994/95-95/96	F.A. Trophy	~	
	League Cup	~	1
	Lincs Cup	~	
	Total	~	28

Born circa 1969. 'Dodge', as he was known, was a local player who progressed through the Reserves to make his debut in the January 1995 league defeat at home to Hinckley Town and then played in the final four fixtures of the season. Dave then played in about half of the league games in the following campaign, with his last appearance in the closing match at Sutton Coldfield Town. For the last few years Dave has been living and working in Spain, helping with the family business of holiday villa sales and property developing.

Lee Rogers

Seasons Played			
	League	~	13
	F.A. Cup	~	1 (1)
1999/00	F.A. Trophy	~	
	League Cup	~	1
	Lincs Cup	~	1
	Total	~	16 (1)

Born 28/10/1966 at Doncaster. Former Doncaster Rovers, Chesterfield, (where he played in a total of 393 games, scoring once), and Gainsborough Trinity defender. He made his Grantham debut in the first league game of the 1999/00 season at Gloucester City and scored his only goal for the club in the 6-0 FA Cup victory over Northampton Spencer in September. Lee's last appearance for Grantham came in the November 1999 league fixture at home to Gloucester City and he then moved on to Barrow where he stayed until his retirement at the end of the 2002/03 season.

Rogers

Seasons Played			
	League	~	1
	F.A. Cup	~	
1930/31	Lincs Cup	~	
	Total	~	1

Former Shirebrook inside-forward who made one Midland League appearance for Grantham, but there is no information available to indicate the specific match.

Andy Rolph

Seasons Played			
	League	~	27 (1)
	F.A. Cup	~	1
1991/92	F.A. Trophy	~	1
	League Cup	~	7 (1)
	Lincs Cup	~	1
	Total	~	37 (2)

Born 28/10/1969 at Meriden. Former Birmingham City, Mile Oak Rovers and Chesterfield winger, with one goal to his name in 39 First team appearances during his time with the last of those clubs. His first game for The Gingerbreads came in the 1991/92 season's opening County Cup tie at Grimsby Town and he then played in the inaugural match at The Meres against Ilkeston Town in the FA Cup. His goals came in games against Leicester United and Dudley Town, but after playing in every fixture so far during that campaign, his career was cut short due to an injury sustained in the January 1992 match against Bedworth United.

A. Rooksby

Seasons Played			
	League	~	6
	FA Amt. Cup	~	
1907/08	League Cup	~	
	Lincs Cup	~	3 (1)
1909/10-10/11	Other	~	5
	Total	~	14 (1)

Individual who was certainly playing for the club by the November 1907 Grantham Minor Cup tie against Barrowby. In the 1909/10 season he was a near ever present member of the Grantham defence, sometimes playing in the same side as the following entry, probably his brother. He was certainly a valued member of the team in the following Championship winning season, with his only known goal for the club coming in the October 1910 County competition against Gonerby Athletic. For the start of the following season he is listed as the club's captain, although unfortunately no records exist of any games that he may have played in.

D. Rooksby

Seasons Played			
	League	~	
	Lincs Cup	~	
1909/10	Other	~	2 (1)
	Total	~	2 (1)

Known to have played and scored in the Grantham Minor Cup tie against Gonerby Town in December 1909 and the following round at home to Grantham Avenue. He is probably the brother of the previous entry.

Rooney

Seasons Played			
	League	~	1
	F.A. Cup	~	
1945/46	Lincs Cup	~	
	Total	~	1

Goalkeeper who played in the final Midland League fixture of the 1945/46 season at Rotherham United Reserves, taking over from that year's first choice player, Mick Brannan.

Ian Roscrow

Seasons Played			
	League	~	13
	F.A. Cup	~	
1989/90	F.A. Trophy	~	
	League Cup	~	
	Lincs Cup	~	
	Total	~	13

Born 31/12/1963 at Sheffield. Midfielder who previously played for Alfreton Town, Shepshed Charterhouse, Worksop Town and had also spent three years in New Zealand playing for Palmerston. He made his Grantham debut in the December 1989 league fixture at Bilston Town and played in many of the games over the next couple of months, returning to the side at the end of April to make his final appearance against Barry Town. Ian went on to make appearances for Gainsborough Trinity and Armthorpe Welfare. He then moved into a junior coaching position at Mansfield Town, plus scouted for several Football League sides, and in April 2004 was awarded the Assistant Manager's position at Bradford Park Avenue, but was released from that role at the end of the 2004/05 season.

Eric Ross

Seasons Played			
	League	~	5 (1)
	F.A. Cup	~	1
1937/38	Lincs Cup	~	
	Other	~	
1945/46	Total	~	6 (1)

Local player who also spent time with Grantham St John's and made four appearances for our club in September and October 1937. His first game was against Bradford Park Avenue Reserves in the Midland League and he scored his only goal for the club two days later at Denaby United. Eric returned to London Road after the Second World War, but made only two more appearances, with his final game coming in April 1946 at Mansfield Town Reserves.

Rossington

Seasons Played			
	League	~	5
	F.A. Cup	~	2
1948/49	Lincs Cup	~	
	Total	~	7

Defender who played in seven fixtures at the beginning of the 1948/49 season, starting with the September game at home to Goole Town and ending two months later against Bradford Park Avenue Reserves.

Rowbrey

Seasons Played			
	League	~	1
	F.A. Cup	~	
1929/30	Lincs Cup	~	
	Other	~	
	Total	~	1

Made one appearance for Grantham during the 1929/30 season, but there are no details of the actual fixture.

James Rowe

Seasons Played			
	League	~	5 (1)
	F.A. Cup	~	
2004/05	F.A. Trophy	~	
	League Cup	~	
	Lincs Cup	~	
	Total	~	5 (1)

Born 23/07/1983 at Derby. Former Ilkeston Town, Histon, Heybridge Swifts and Stamford striker. James made his Grantham debut replacing Jason Turner during the January 2005 league fixture at home to Merthyr Tydfil and scored his only goal the following month against Banbury United. A week later he made his final appearance for The Gingerbreads, down at Tiverton Town, and rejoined Stamford in time to play in their biggest game for several years, against Exeter City in the FA Trophy.

Shaun Rowlands

Seasons Played	League	~	3
	F.A. Cup	~	
1981/82-82/83	F.A. Trophy	~	
	League Cup	~	
	Lincs Cup	~	2
	Other	~	
	Total	~	5

Forward who came through the Reserves to make three appearances during the 1981/82 season, starting with the February 1982 league clash at Gainsborough Trinity. He played in the opening two County Cup ties of the following season, but after being replaced by Rob Smith, coincidentally during the Gainsborough Trinity tie, he made no further senior appearances.

George Rudkin

Seasons Played	League	~	40 (8)
	F.A. Cup	~	2 (1)
1935/36-36/37	Lincs Cup	~	5 (1)
	Other	~	3
	Total	~	50 (10)

Born 01/03/1912 at Horncastle. Inside-Left who took over George Dooley's position for the April 1936 Midland League fixture at Lincoln City Reserves and scored his first goal for the club the following week at home to Frickley Colliery. He played in all of the remaining games, including the Grantham Hospital Cup victory over Doncaster Rovers and the final match of the season when the team beat a Lincoln League XI in the Wilson Cup. George kept his place the following season and in April 1937 scored one of the goals in the 2-2 County Cup Final draw against Boston United, whilst at the end of the month he appeared in the successful replay. The following season he joined Mansfield Town, but made just one First team appearance, later scoring one goal in 16 games for Carlisle United in the 1938/39 campaign and then moving on to Boston United. After The War George signed for Chesterfield, but he failed to make another senior appearance.

George Russell

Seasons Played	League	~	25 (9)
	F.A. Cup	~	8 (8)
1945/46	Lincs Cup	~	1
1948/49-49/50	Total	~	34 (17)

Local player who had previously been appearing for the Aveling Barfords works team and scored twice on his Grantham debut in the first Midland League game after the Second World War, at London Road against Gainsborough Trinity. He continued to play in many of the games in the first few months of that season, including both the legs in the FA Cup Proper rounds against Kettering Town and Mansfield Town. George returned to the team in the 1948/49 season, but made only nine appearances that year, followed by another three in the next campaign. His final game was in the April 1950 Midland League fixture at Gainsborough Trinity.

Andy Ryder

Seasons Played	League	~	220 (27)
	F.A. Cup	~	14
1980/81	F.A. Trophy	~	17 (1)
	League Cup	~	33 (1)
1982/83-88/89	Lincs Cup	~	10
	Other	~	2 (1)
1991/92	Total	~	296 (30)

Born 29/06/1963 in Grantham. Progressed through the Youth and Reserve teams, plus had a brief spell at Sleaford Town, and made his debut by coming off the bench in the November 1980 league fixture at Lancaster City, although he did appear in a Midland Floodlit League game for Grantham during the 1979/80 season. However, Andy had to wait a further two years before he was able to make another appearance and even then only finished with three more games under his belt by the end of the 1982/83 season. He played in about half of the fixtures the following term, scoring his first goal in March 1984 at Burton Albion, but by the start of the 1984/85 season Andy had become a near constant member of the side. Sadly for him though, he was amassing appearances, including 178 consecutively, during a time when there are precious little highlights to report on, apart from the two years when Martin O'Neill came close to taking The Gingerbreads to promotion. It was towards the end of that time, in April 1989, that Andy scored what would turn out to be his final goal for the club, against Banbury United. He had a two season spell at Spalding United in the late 1980's/early 1990's, but returned to make another ten appearances at the start of the 1991/92 season. He played in the first match at The Meres, against Ilkeston Town in the FA Cup, coming off the bench to replace Tony Marsden, but made his final appearance for the club at the start of October against Bedworth United. After leaving Grantham, Andy later played for Harrowby United, but he now lives in Ashbourne and is the Head Green-keeper at the local golf club.

Arnold Rylott

Seasons Played	Other	~	1
1874/75	Total	~	1

Born 18/02/1839 in Grantham. Played for Arthur Hutchinson's team in the very first club match and Grantham's initial game against the Third Lincolnshire Volunteer Rifles in October 1874. He was better known though for his cricketing skills, playing for England, with clubs represented including Birkenhead, Grantham, Marleybone, during which time he was also head of ground staff at Lord's, Leicestershire and Staffordshire. In the Winter, Arnold earned his living as a game-keeper, whilst in the Summer months he was able to supplement his income by selling a potent home-made snuff to his fellow cricketers. He also published a book of verse, entitled *Our Bobby Rykitt When A Boy*. Died 17/04/1914 at Sandy.

Dave Saddington

Seasons Played	League	~	
	F.A. Cup	~	
1999/00	F.A. Trophy	~	
	League Cup	~	
	Lincs Cup	~	1
	Total	~	1

Young central defender who was signed from Leicester City, but played just once for Grantham in the July 1999 County Cup tie at home to Scunthorpe United before breaking his arm and being released by the club. After recovering from the injury, Dave went on to play for Holwell Sports.

Saddington

Seasons Played	F.A. Cup	~	2
	Lincs Cup	~	
1884/85-86/87	Other	~	2
	Total	~	4

Made one appearance for Grantham in the 1884/85 season at Notts Rangers in January, played once more in the following campaign and then appeared in the two FA Cup games during the Autumn of 1886, ending his career at home to Redcar.

Salew

Seasons Played	League	~	3 (2)
	F.A. Cup	~	
1885/86-86/87	Lincs Cup	~	
	Other	~	8 (4)
1891/92	Total	~	11 (6)

Scored on his debut in the March 1886 friendly against Notts Waverley and despite playing in the closing fixture of the season as well, made only a handful of appearances in the next term. He returned to London Road halfway through the club's first league competition, but played more often in the Charity Cup games rather than the Midland Amateur Alliance fixtures.

Alfie Sams

Seasons Played	League	~	200 (27)
	F.A. Cup	~	18 (3)
1935/36-36/37	Lincs Cup	~	12 (3)
	Other	~	2
1945/46-48/49	Total	~	232 (33)

Born 1912 at Lanchester. Left-sided forward who had previously played for Whitby United, Shildon, Trimdon Grange Colliery, before returning to Shildon. Alfie then made his Grantham debut in the opening league fixture of the 1935/36 season at Burton Town and scored his first goal for the club in the return match a week later. He straight away became a valuable member of the team and played in the FA Cup tie against Notts County, the Finals of the Grantham Hospital Cup and the Wilson Cup, but missed out on the conclusion to the season's County Cup. A year later though, he did appear in the Lincolnshire Senior Cup Final against Boston United, but by the time of the replay he was missing from the team. In the

Summer of 1937 he joined Mansfield Town and before The War also made appearances for Reading and Accrington Stanley, finishing with two goals in a total of 22 Football League appearances. Alfie returned to London Road though after Christmas 1945 and slotted into a midfield position in the team. Over the next two years he appeared twice more in losing County Cup Final teams, but in November 1947 he played in the FA Cup First Round Proper at Stockton. In his final season with the club he played in about half of the fixtures and scored his last goal in April 1949 at home to Frickley Colliery, a fortnight before his final appearance against Rotherham United Reserves. Died in the Summer of 1990 in Australia.

Jerome Samuels

Seasons Played			
	League	~	5
	F.A. Cup	~	
1998/99	F.A. Trophy	~	
	League Cup	~	
	Lincs Cup	~	
	Total	~	5

Born 08/03/1976 in Jamaica. Former Jamaican Under-18 International who had a period playing in the USA with Lightning SC, before joining Notts County where he made just one full appearance coming off the bench. His Grantham debut came in March 1999 at Merthyr Tydfil and he then played four more times before his final appearance in the closing fixture of the season at Weymouth.

Sanderson

Seasons Played			
	League	~	7 (8)
	FA Amt. Cup	~	
1909/10-10/11	League Cup	~	1 (1)
	Lincs Cup	~	1 (2)
	Other	~	3 (1)
	Total	~	12 (12)

Centre-Forward who was scoring for Grantham by the February 1910 fixture at home to West Bridgford Albion and most likely played in most of the remaining games from that season, with definite evidence of his appearance in the March friendly against Queen's Park. He was still a prominent member of the team after the Summer break, a season which would see Grantham's first league championship win, but with most of his appearances only being recognised from score-sheets, the end of his Grantham career is not known.

Sandy

Seasons Played			
	F.A. Cup	~	
	Lincs Cup	~	1
1887/88	Other	~	1
	Total	~	2

Made his debut in the March 1888 Lincolnshire Senior Cup semi-final against Gainsborough Trinity and also appeared in a friendly at Rotherham Town two weeks later.

Phil Saunders

Seasons Played			
	League	~	16 (1)
	F.A. Cup	~	
1986/87	F.A. Trophy	~	
	League Cup	~	
	Lincs Cup	~	
	Total	~	16 (1)

Former Mansfield Town Reserves, Arnold Town, Burton Albion and Bulwell player who first played for Grantham in the January 1987 league fixture at home to Forest Green Rovers. His only goal for the club was scored against Halesowen Town and his last appearance came in the closing match at Banbury United, following which Phil went on to play for Kimberley Town.

Saunders

Seasons Played			
	F.A. Cup	~	4 (1)
	Lincs Cup	~	3 (2)
1886/87-87/88	Other	~	7 (1)
	Total	~	14 (4)

Played in at least two of the 1886/87 season's FA Cup games, beginning at London Road in the tie against Lincoln Lindum and then scoring his first goal for Grantham in the next round at home to Redcar. He played in most of the competitive games the following season, with his final appearance in a friendly at home to Notts Jardine in March 1888.

Steve Saxby

Seasons Played			
	League	~	32 (1)
	F.A. Cup	~	1
1984/85-85/86	F.A. Trophy	~	1
	League Cup	~	5 (1)
	Lincs Cup	~	2
	Other	~	
	Total	~	41 (2)

Born 06/01/1964 at Melton Mowbray. Former Leicester City Reserves, Melton Town, Leicester United and Nuneaton Borough player who made his Grantham debut in the March 1985 league draw at Mossley. During the Summer break he went over to Finland, playing for Grankulla, but upon his return Steve played in many of the games over that following season, scoring against VS Rugby and Moor Green, with his last appearance at Coventry Sporting in March 1986. He went on to play for Skegness Town, Spalding United, Friar Lane Old Boys, then returned to Melton Town and finally managed Holwell Sports. Steve still lives in the Melton area and runs his own window cleaning company.

Schofield

Seasons Played			
	Other	~	2
1874/75	Total	~	2

Original club committee member who played in the first ever game in October 1874 when the Third Lincolnshire Volunteer Rifles came to London Road, followed by the friendly against Peterborough three weeks later.

Charlie Scoffield

Seasons Played			
	League	~	106 (23)
	F.A. Cup	~	9 (1)
1957/58	League Cup	~	1
	Lincs Cup	~	6 (3)
1959/60-64/65	Total	~	122 (27)

Born 16/03/1939 at Denton. Left-winger who first played for Grantham in the April 1958 Midland League fixture at Grimsby Town Reserves. He scored his first goal for the club three days later when Lincoln City Reserves came over to London Road and although Charlie played in most of the games left in that season, he then had to wait until the start of the 1959/60 campaign to play for the First team again. He was a prominent member of the side that season, but after only four matches the next year he was back to an almost constant position in the team for the 1961/62 season. Charlie played in the FA Cup First Round tie at Brierley Hill Alliance and the triumphant County Cup Final against Boston United the following April. The next season saw him playing in every single one of that year's games, including the December fixture at home to Retford Town during which he scored what would turn out to be his final two goals. As Grantham entered into their first successful Midland League Championship in 1963/64, he was forced to cover for first Bob Fry and then Ronnie Harbertson, severely limiting the appearances that he could make. Charlie played once more for Grantham, in the September 1964 FA Cup tie at Holbeach United, before joining Grantham St John's. He still lives in the town and is now retired, having been employed virtually all his working life for one of the town's senior engineering companies.

Scoffield

Seasons Played			
	League	~	2
	F.A. Cup	~	
1928/29	Lincs Cup	~	
	Other	~	1 (1)
1933/34	Total	~	3 (1)

Full-Back who had previously played for Basford United and made two appearances for Grantham at the start of 1929 in the league games at Denaby United and Barnsley Reserves. He is known to have returned to London Road in October 1933 to play and score in the local Hospital Cup tie against Grantham St John's, but no details are available to show whether this was an isolated appearance or not.

Gary Scotcher

Seasons Played	League	~	2 (1)
	F.A. Cup	~	
1992/93	F.A. Trophy	~	
	League Cup	~	
	Lincs Cup	~	
	Total	~	2 (1)

Born 05/08/1957 at Peterborough. 'Scotch' previously played for New England, Baker Perkins, Ramsey, St Ives, Parson Drove, Bourne Town, March Town, Mirlees Blackstone and Harrowby United. He scored in his first game for Grantham in March 1993 at home to Nuneaton Borough, but played only once more a month later against King's Lynn. He still lives in the Peterborough area and is a Contracts Manager for a construction company.

A. Scothern

Seasons Played	League	~	2
	Lincs Cup	~	
1931/32	Other	~	
	Total	~	2

Local player who also made appearances for Grantham Amateurs and end of season data shows that he played in two games for our club during the 1931/32 season, but the particular fixtures are not known.

Scothern

Seasons Played	League	~	2 (2)
	FA Amt. Cup	~	
1910/11	League Cup	~	
	Lincs Cup	~	
	Other	~	
	Total	~	2 (2)

Either A. Scothern (surely a different player to the previous entry) or H. Scothern, brothers who were both training with the club during the Summer of 1911. He scored twice in Grantham's first ever league title winning season, against Long Eaton YMCA in December 1910 and three months later at London Road in the match against Old Loughburians.

Scott

Seasons Played	League	~	2
	F.A. Cup	~	
1929/30	Lincs Cup	~	
	Other	~	
	Total	~	2

Former Ilkeston United forward who played in the opening league fixture of the 1929/30 season at Mansfield Town plus one other game, although it is not known which one.

Scott

Seasons Played	League	~	1
	F.A. Cup	~	
1932/33	Lincs Cup	~	
	Other	~	
	Total	~	1

Goalkeeper who had also played for Bolton Wanderers and made just one appearance for Grantham in an unknown fixture.

Seaney

Seasons Played	League	~	1 (1)
	F.A. Cup	~	
1922/23	Lincs Cup	~	
	Other	~	
	Total	~	1 (1)

Known from end of season data to have scored one goal for the First team, but no details are available to show which particular fixture this was in.

George Searby

Seasons Played	League	~	188 (67)
	F.A. Cup	~	20 (16)
1945/46-47/48	Lincs Cup	~	12 (3)
1949/50-51/52	Total	~	220 (86)

Born 21/03/1919 at Nuneaton. Right-sided player who began his career with local Newark sides, before moving on to Ransome & Marles and an Army XI during The War. George made his debut for Grantham in the September 1945 Midland League fixture at Shrewsbury Town, scoring his first goal for the club the following month at Boston United. He played in both legs of the FA Cup tie against Kettering and scored both consolation goals in the following round against Mansfield Town. The New Year saw more highlights as George netted his first hat-trick for Grantham in the 8-0 thrashing of Nottingham Forest Reserves. The season rounded off with an appearance in the Lincolnshire Senior Cup Final at Boston United, although it ended in a 3-1 defeat for the team. The following season George continued to play an important role in the side and made another County Cup Final appearance, although sadly for him he was unavailable for the replay. The 1947/48 FA Cup competition was to be one full of highlights for George as he appeared in all but one of Grantham's games, scoring four past the poor Basford United goalkeeper, playing in the 11-1 demolition of Ilkeston Town and then scoring in the First Round Proper tie up at Stockton. He returned to the club after another spell at Ransome & Marles for the start of the 1949/50 season and played in one more First Round FA Cup tie, this time at Wrexham, and another Lincolnshire County Cup Final, although, unfortunately, with the usual outcome of a runners-up medal. After one further full season with the club, George's appearances became infrequent in the 1951/52 campaign and he scored his final goal for the club in his last appearance, the closing fixture at Goole Town. He then retired from the game and worked for the family undertaking business. Died 03/08/1993 at Newark.

Searby

Seasons Played	League	~	2 (1)
	F.A. Cup	~	
1926/27	Lincs Cup	~	
	Other	~	
	Total	~	2 (1)

Centre-Forward who had also played for the Reserve sides of Manchester United and Brentford, plus spent time at Wath Athletic and Castleford. He scored in his first game for Grantham, the opening league fixture of the 1926/27 season at Sutton Town and played once more for the team a week later at Worksop Town.

Segar

Seasons Played	F.A. Cup	~	12
	Lincs Cup	~	20 (2)
1881/82	Other	~	47 (4)
1883/84-89/90	Total	~	79 (6)

Was certainly playing for Grantham by the time of the November 1881 FA Cup tie against Brigg Town, but it wasn't until the start of the 1883/84 season that he had established himself in the side. His first known goal for the club was in the January 1885 County Cup semi-final draw at Horncastle and he played in the Final against Gainsborough Trinity which saw Grantham win their first ever trophy. He continued to be a valued member of the team for the next few years, until his final appearance in January 1890 when the team were defeated 5-0 by Grantham Rovers in the Newark Charity Cup. Bearing in mind the unusual surname, this player could possibly be John Segar, (born circa 1864 in Ceylon), a member of a wealthy Swinegate family in town.

Sellers

Seasons Played	F.A. Cup	~	
	Lincs Cup	~	
1886/87	Other	~	1
	Total	~	1

Made just one appearance for the club in the January 1887 friendly against Grantham Volunteers.

Senior

Seasons Played	League	~	1 (1)
	F.A. Cup	~	
1922/23	Lincs Cup	~	
	Other	~	
	Total	~	1 (1)

Former Ilkeston United player who scored for Grantham in the September 1922 Central Alliance fixture at Heanor Town, but no other instances of him playing can be found.

Terry Sewell

Seasons Played	League	~	114 (33)
	F.A. Cup	~	11 (8)
1954/55-57/58	Lincs Cup	~	3
	Total	~	128 (41)

Inside-Right from Notts County who first played for Grantham in the November 1954 Midland League fixture at home to Scunthorpe & Lindsey United Reserves and netted his first two goals on New Year's Eve to help secure a 2-2 draw at Doncaster Rovers Reserves. As the years progressed Terry became more and more prominent in the team, although it was a barren period for the club with few games of any note until the April 1958 Lincolnshire Senior Cup 'A' Final against Gainsborough Trinity. This was only a few weeks before Terry's final goal for the club, at London Road versus Denaby United, and his Grantham career ended with the closing Midland League match at Scarborough.

Sewell

Seasons Played	F.A. Cup	~	
	Lincs Cup	~	1
1884/85	Other	~	1
	Total	~	2

Played in the second replay of the County Cup semi-final at Horncastle in February 1885, but sadly for him missed out on selection for the Final itself. He then made one other appearance for the club in the closing fixture of the season at home to Newark.

Seymour

Seasons Played	League	~	
	F.A. Cup	~	
1933/34	Lincs Cup	~	
	Other	~	1
	Total	~	1

Made just one appearance for Grantham in the 1933/34 season, but no details are known of the actual match.

Shannon

Seasons Played	F.A. Cup	~	7
	Lincs Cup	~	12
1881/82	Other	~	4
1883/84-86/87	Total	~	23

Was playing for the club by the time of the Second Round FA Cup tie against Staveley in November 1881, but despite appearing in the national competition once more two years later, it seems to have been the start of the 1884/85 season before he was consistently in the side for Grantham. He played in every one of the County Cup games that year, ending with an appearance in Grantham's first ever trophy winning final, as Gainsborough Trinity were defeated. The following two seasons though, his appearances were generally limited to the competitive competitions and his final game for the club came in February 1887 when Grantham were knocked out of the County Cup by Grimsby Town.

Kevin Sharp

Seasons Played	League	~	10
	F.A. Cup	~	
1989/90-90/91	F.A. Trophy	~	
	League Cup	~	
	Lincs Cup	~	
	Total	~	10

Nottingham Forest Reserves player who had two spells at Grantham on-loan, the first of which began with the March 1990 fixture at home to Redditch United and included the four following games, plus the closing match against Halesowen Town. Kevin returned to the club a year later and played in the final four fixtures of the 1990/91 season, ending at Redditch United in May.

Sharp

Seasons Played	League	~	1
	Lincs Cup	~	1
1894/95	Other	~	
	Total	~	2

Played in the November 1894 Grantham & District League fixture against Woolsthorpe and the following game when the club were knocked out of the Lincolnshire Shield by Grantham Rovers Colts. His surname is sometimes spelt 'Shape'.

Sharp

Seasons Played	League	~	15 (7)
	F.A. Cup	~	5 (3)
1919/20	Lincs Cup	~	
	Total	~	20 (10)

Centre-Forward who had previously played for Grantham Avenue and made his debut for our club in the opening fixture of the 1919/20 season at Long Eaton. He scored his first goal for Grantham in the FA Cup at Arnold St Mary's three weeks later, but despite missing many of the games over the Winter period, he was still with the team by the final fixture at Shirebrook.

Sharpe

Seasons Played	F.A. Cup	~	5
1877/78-78/79	Other	~	1
1880/81	Total	~	6

Played in the club's first ever FA Cup game against Clapham Rovers in October 1877 and seems to have been unique in that he only appeared in the FA Cup fixtures the following season and once again in the Autumn of 1880. However, he returned to London Road the following February to make one final appearance when Notts County came over to Grantham for a friendly.

Aubrey Shaw

Seasons Played	League	~	20
	F.A. Cup	~	2
1932/33-33/34	Lincs Cup	~	1
	Other	~	
	Total	~	23

Born 17/10/1912 at Grantham. Local Goalkeeper who also played for Grantham Amateurs and Grantham St John's, but unfortunately there are no details to show when he first played for our club. End of season data shows that he made five appearances in the 1932/33 season, but by the start of the next campaign he had become the club's first choice 'keeper. Died 14/10/1971 at Grantham.

Barry Shaw

Seasons Played	League	~	112
	F.A. Cup	~	6
1971/72	F.A. Trophy	~	7
	League Cup	~	11
1974/75-79/80	Lincs Cup	~	5
	Other	~	2
1981/82	Total	~	143

Born 07/12/1950 at Grantham. Local player with previous experience at Harrowby United and Sleaford Town who made a lone appearance for Grantham in the March 1972 Midland League Cup quarter-final tie at Retford Town. He returned to the First team at the end of 1974 and finished that season with another 16 appearances to his name. The arrival of John Bower at London Road though, in the Summer of 1975, severely limited Barry's appearances the following year, but he did come on as substitute in the November FA Cup replay at Port Vale. The next few campaigns continued to see him making only occasional appearances, but the 1978/79 season saw him at long last firmly established in Grantham's defence. Barry played in 30 league games that year, including the closing fixture at home to Merthyr Tydfil which saw a 3-0 win for The Gingerbreads secure the league title by one point over their opponents. Grantham's first season in the Northern Premier League was to be his last full season with the team, although he returned to make a sole appearance in the November 1981 Redmayne Trophy tie against Nottingham Forest when he came off the bench to replace Nick Jarvis. Barry continued his involvement with local football at Grantham Youths and Grantham United, before taking over the club's managerial position during the Autumn of 1985. He stayed at the London Road helm until the end of the 1986/87 season, over-seeing two mid-table league positions. Barry then returned to Harrowby United, the first of three periods as Manager there, eventually leading them to a Midland Regional League and Cup double and promotion into the United Counties League, before joining Cottesmore Amateurs. Barry still lives in Grantham and after many years in the double glazing business, is now involved in conservatory sales.

Dave Rogers

Ian Roscrow

Eric Ross

Alfie Sams

George Searby

Terry Sewell

Barry Shaw

Chris Shaw

Harry Siddall

Tony Simmons

Kevin Slinn

Fabien Smith

Jack Smith

Rob Smith

Aubrey Southwell

Neal Spafford

Chris Shaw

Seasons Played			
2000/01-01/02	League	~	2
	F.A. Cup	~	2
	F.A. Trophy	~	
	League Cup	~	1
	Lincs Cup	~	
	Total	~	5

Grantham born Reserves player who was forced to have the worst possible debut when he came on as substitute in the 6-0 loss at Newport County in February 2001. He played once more that season, against Sittingbourne, and then appeared in three cup games the following term, the last of which was in the November 2001 Dr Marten's League Cup tie at home to King's Lynn. Chris went on to make appearances for Gainsborough Trinity, Hucknall Town, Ilkeston Town and Eastwood Town.

Don Shaw

Seasons Played			
1962/63-63/64	League	~	39
	F.A. Cup	~	3
	Lincs Cup	~	
	Total	~	42

Defender who made his Grantham debut in the first Midland League game of the 1962/63 season at Holbeach United, but despite missing only one game that season lost his place to Ray Barnard after the Summer interval. This meant that Don, in Grantham's Championship winning season, was only able to make three appearances, with his final one against Arnold in November 1963.

Jim Shaw

Seasons Played			
1992/93	League	~	4
	F.A. Cup	~	
	F.A. Trophy	~	
	League Cup	~	
	Lincs Cup	~	1
	Total	~	5

Former Grimsby Town and Immingham Town player who made his Grantham debut in the opening County Cup tie of the 1992/93 season at Lincoln City. He then played in the first four league fixtures, with the September game at home to Bedworth United his final one.

Terrance Shaw

Seasons Played			
1955/56	League	~	2
	F.A. Cup	~	
	Lincs Cup	~	
	Total	~	2

Goalkeeper who covered for Ron Hewitt in the two league fixtures just after the 1956 New Year against Nottingham Forest Reserves and Scarborough. Sadly for Terrance, he finished on the losing side both times, and even worse for him was that in the latter fixture he had to pick the ball out of the net nine times.

T. Shaw

Seasons Played			
1921/22-22/23	League	~	20
	F.A. Cup	~	
	Lincs Cup	~	
	Other	~	3
	Total	~	23

Goalkeeper who played for Grantham towards the end of the 1921/22 season, probably after Bunting had been transferred to Leicester City. He kept the position for the following season as well, but no details are available to indicate his final appearance. During his time at London Road though, he was picked to play for the Lincolnshire representative side. He could very easily be Thomas Shaw (born circa 1900), a goalkeeper who was known to have started his career at Nottingham Forest, but by February 1923 was playing for Newark Town and a year later Mansfield Town.

Shaw

Seasons Played			
1890/91	Lincs Cup	~	
	Other	~	1
	Total	~	1

Made only one appearance for the club in the November 1890 friendly against Boston NE.

Shaw

Seasons Played			
1891/92	League	~	12
	F.A. Cup	~	1
	Other	~	4 (1)
	Total	~	17 (1)

Goalkeeper for Grantham during their first venture into league competition, the Midland Amateur Alliance in 1891, who played in the opening fixture at home to Notts County Rovers. He was noted though for scoring a goal during the 12-0 rout of Radcliffe in the January 1892 Newark Charity Cup tie. He may be Wainwright Shaw (born 1870 at Sheffield) who kept goal for Basford Wanderers, Mansfield, Bulwell, Grantham Rovers and Lincoln City during that decade.

Shaw

Seasons Played			
1891/92	League	~	
	F.A. Cup	~	1
	Other	~	
	Total	~	1

The second 'Shaw' that played in the October 1891 FA Cup defeat against Gainsborough Trinity, but for this individual it was to be his only appearance for the club.

Sheilton

Seasons Played			
1909/10	League	~	1
	Lincs Cup	~	
	Other	~	
	Total	~	1

Played in the April 1910 Midland Amateur Alliance fixture against West Bridgford Friary, but it is not known whether this was his only appearance or just one of many from that season.

Shelbourne

Seasons Played			
1886/87-87/88	F.A. Cup	~	
	Lincs Cup	~	
	Other	~	2
	Total	~	2

Known to have played in the November 1886 friendly against Boston and the March 1888 game at Rotherham Town.

Wilf Sheldon

Seasons Played			
1928/29	League	~	2
	F.A. Cup	~	
	Lincs Cup	~	
	Other	~	
	Total	~	2

Born 1908 at Bulwell. Outside-Right player who had previously played for Hawley's Dye Works FC, Bulwell Wesleyan Mission and Mansfield Town. Wilf made just two appearances for Grantham in the January 1929 fixture at home to Mexborough Athletic and a week later when the team travelled up to Barnsley Reserves. The following season he played in two First team games for Luton Town, but then moved on to Shirebrook, Sutton Town and Nottingham Water Department FC.

Shelley

Seasons Played			
1923/24	League	~	1
	F.A. Cup	~	
	League Cup	~	
	Lincs Cup	~	
	Other	~	
	Total	~	1

Midfielder with only one known appearance for the club, the February 1924 match at Retford Town.

George Shepherd

Seasons Played			
1947/48-48/49	League	~	15
	F.A. Cup	~	
	Lincs Cup	~	
	Total	~	15

Defender who played his first game for the club in the March 1948 Midland League fixture against Scunthorpe & Lindsey United and kept the place for most of the remaining games. However, after the September match against Boston United, with both Robinson and Hunt back in the side, George wasn't able to make another appearance.

Shepherd

Seasons Played	Lincs Cup	~	
	Other	~	1
1889/90	Total	~	1

Made just one appearance for Grantham in the 1889 Boxing Day friendly against Notts Rangers.

Shepherd

Seasons Played	League	~	1
	Lincs Cup	~	
1909/10	Other	~	
	Total	~	1

Goalkeeper who covered for the club's first choice player, Lee, in the January 1910 fixture at home to Nottingham University, but no information is available to show whether this was just an isolated game, or if he played in the position for any other matches.

Shepherd

Seasons Played	League	~	8 (3)
	F.A. Cup	~	
1922/23	Lincs Cup	~	
	Other	~	1 (1)
1924/25	Total	~	9 (4)

Former Notts County Reserves and Ilkeston United player who made a few appearances for Grantham towards the start of the 1922/23 season. He then returned to the club two years later and scored four goals during that spell, including a single strike in the March 1925 Grantham Hospital Cup semi-final victory over Lincoln Robey's.

Shepherd

Seasons Played	League	~	44 (1)
	F.A. Cup	~	4 (2)
1932/33	Lincs Cup	~	1
	Other	~	1
	Total	~	50 (3)

Player with experience at Lincoln City and Loughborough Corinthians who made his Grantham debut in the opening game of the 1932/33 season at Scarborough. He then went on to play in nearly every single match of that season, scoring goals against Sutton Junction and Boston United in the FA Cup, and Newark Town during the December 1932 league fixture.

Rob Shippey

Seasons Played	League	~	1
	F.A. Cup	~	
1979/80	F.A. Trophy	~	
	League Cup	~	
	Lincs Cup	~	
	Total	~	1

Born 08/04/1956 at Acaster Malbis, near York. Began his career with Grantham Reserves and the Sheffield Wednesday Youth side, but made just one full appearance for The Gingerbreads when he came on as substitute in the March 1980 Northern Premier League fixture at Worksop Town, replacing Barry Shaw. Rob went on to play for Melton Town and then returned to Grantham Reserves. He still lives near to the town and works in the construction industry.

Garry Shore

Seasons Played	League	~	39 (3)
	F.A. Cup	~	3
1978/79-80/81	F.A. Trophy	~	2
	League Cup	~	3 (1)
	Lincs Cup	~	3 (3)
	Other	~	1
	Total	~	51 (7)

Born 1958 at Nottingham. Forward signed from Radcliffe Athletic after previously having trials with Notts County, Aston Villa, West Bromwich Albion and Wolverhampton Wanderers. He made his debut for Grantham by coming on as a substitute in the November 1978 league fixture at Tamworth, scored his first goal in January 1979 at Weymouth in the Southern League Cup and then netted a hat-trick in the next match at home to Wellingborough. Garry played in half of the games the following season, but even the departure of Robbie Cooke couldn't guarantee a place up front for him. He did play in the December 1980 Redmayne Trophy tie against Nottingham Forest, but only three days later he made his final appearance against Workington. Garry then returned to Radcliffe and later signed for Long Eaton United. He still lives in the Nottingham area and currently runs his own engineering sales consultancy business. He is also a proficient croquet player, making appearances for Nottingham at a national level.

Short

Seasons Played	League	~	8 (2)
	F.A. Cup	~	
1926/27	Lincs Cup	~	1
	Other	~	
	Total	~	9 (2)

Centre-Forward from Ilkeston who played all his games for Grantham during January and February of 1927, scoring against his home team, Ilkeston United, and Gainsborough Trinity at London Road. He could be James Short (born ??/04/1896 at Hucknall), a forward who was playing for Ilkeston United at the start of the decade and also had Football League experience with Birmingham, Watford and Norwich City to his name.

Short

Seasons Played	League	~	
	F.A. Cup	~	
1936/37	Lincs Cup	~	
	Other	~	1
	Total	~	1

Made only one appearance for the First team in the Wilson Cup victory over RAF Cranwell at the end of the 1936/37 season.

T. Shreeves

Seasons Played	League	~	1
	Lincs Cup	~	
1939/40	Other	~	
	Total	~	1

Outside-Right with experience at Grimsby Town, Scunthorpe & Lindsey United and Grimsby Nomads, but played only once for Grantham in the November 1939 defeat at Peterborough United.

Shumach

Seasons Played	League	~	1
	Lincs Cup	~	
1939/40	Other	~	
	Total	~	1

Surely a story here, bearing in mind this goalkeeper's rather Germanic sounding surname who played in the club's final Midland 'War-Time' League game at Scunthorpe & Lindsey United and let in five as well!

Harry Siddall

Seasons Played	League	~	121 (57)
	F.A. Cup	~	10 (5)
1936/37-38/39	Lincs Cup	~	9 (6)
	Other	~	5 (3)
	Total	~	145 (71)

Forward who during his career also spent time at Chesterfield, Grimsby Town and Denaby United. Harry first played for Grantham in the opening league game of the 1936/37 season at Nottingham Forest Reserves, netting one of the goals, and then went on to play in all but one of the season's matches. Highlights at the end of that first campaign, which saw him finish as the club's highest scorer, included an appearance in the local Hospital Cup Final, a goal to help secure victory against Boston United in the County Cup, plus another strike in the Wilson Cup although this time it was sadly just a consolation effort. The following season he missed only two games as Grantham secured a runners-up position in the Midland League, whilst the 1938/39 campaign saw Harry still playing virtually every week, but with less goals to his name after the arrival of Jack Macartney. His final goal for Grantham came in April 1939 at Mansfield Town Reserves, a week before his last appearance and the club's closing fixture of the season at Nottingham Forest Reserves.

Harry Sillito

Seasons Played			
	League	~	9 (4)
	F.A. Cup	~	
1928/29	Lincs Cup	~	
	Other	~	
	Total	~	9 (4)

Born 10/07/1901 at Chester-le-Street. Forward who began his career with his local team and Washington Colliery, before signing for Chelsea, although he failed to break into their First team. In 1922 he transferred to Lincoln City and two years later joined Merthyr Town, who at that time were playing in Division Three (South) and managed by former Grantham player, Thomas Jones. After two goals in a total of 67 Football League appearances, Harry joined Grantham at the start of the 1928/29 season. He scored his first goal for the club in the September Midland League fixture at Worksop Town, but after those first few games his appearances became infrequent and his last goal came in the January 1929 draw at Grimsby Town Reserves. Died 1993 at Lincoln.

Sills

Seasons Played			
	League	~	2
	F.A. Cup	~	
1933/34	Lincs Cup	~	
	Other	~	
	Total	~	2

Right-Half who had previously played for Newark Town and appeared for Grantham in the December 1933 league fixture against Chesterfield Reserves and the Christmas Day match at his old club, Newark Town.

Tony Simmons

Seasons Played			
	League	~	19 (2)
	F.A. Cup	~	3 (1)
1999/00-02/03	F.A. Trophy	~	
	League Cup	~	1
	Lincs Cup	~	
	Total	~	23 (3)

Born 09/02/1965 at Sheffield. Former England Youth International who made over 130 League appearances for Sheffield Wednesday, Queen's Park Rangers, Rotherham United, Lincoln City and Cardiff City. After dropping into non-league football, Tony then appeared for Gainsborough Trinity, Spalding United, Holbeach United and Lincoln United. He teamed up with John Wilkinson there, before coming to Grantham as his assistant in December 1999 and making his debut in the home fixture against Dorchester Town. Tony scored his first goal in the January 2000 league match at Atherstone United and made a total of twelve appearances before the end of that season, but played only a handful of other times over the next few years, scoring his other goals against Langney Sports and Glapwell. His final appearance came in the December 2002 defeat at Weymouth and he returned to Lincoln United at the end of the 2002/03 season along with John Wilkinson and many of the players.

John Simpson

Seasons Played			
	League	~	6 (6)
	F.A. Cup	~	
1922/23	Lincs Cup	~	
	Other	~	1
	Total	~	7 (6)

Former Lincoln Rovers, Lincoln City, (with four First team appearances), and Scunthorpe & Lindsey United forward. John scored his first goal for Grantham in the September 1922 Central Alliance game against Coalville Swifts, yet despite scoring a brace in the games versus New Hucknall Colliery and Ilkeston United there is no evidence of him playing after the end of that year.

John Simpson

Seasons Played			
	League	~	5
	F.A. Cup	~	
1954/55	Lincs Cup	~	
	Total	~	5

Defender who played in the first five fixtures of the 1954/55 season, beginning at London Road versus Nottingham Forest Reserves and ending against Wisbech Town, but made no other appearances for the club after John Little returned to the side.

Tony Simpson

Seasons Played			
	League	~	47 (5)
	F.A. Cup	~	6
1988/89-89/90	F.A. Trophy	~	6
	League Cup	~	3
	Lincs Cup	~	2
	Total	~	64 (5)

Born 29/11/1969 at Nottingham. Nick-named 'Simmo the garden gnome', although more prominently after his move from the club! He began his career at Nottingham Forest, playing in a Dutch tournament for the club, and also had a brief spell at Notts County. His Grantham debut came in the opening County Cup tie of the 1988/89 season at home to Gainsborough Trinity and he missed only three games all season, scoring his first goal on New Year's Eve against Coventry Sporting. Tony was once more a valuable member of the side the following campaign, although only up to October, with his last goal coming that month at Stourbridge and his final appearance a week later in the FA Cup defeat at Goole Town. Tony went on to have two spells at Nuneaton Borough, followed by appearances for Tamworth, Ilkeston Town, Gresley Rovers and Arnold Town. He combined his footballing career with day jobs of teaching and guiding guests around The City Ground, Nottingham.

Simpson

Seasons Played			
	F.A. Cup	~	
	Lincs Cup	~	
1887/88-88/89	Other	~	2
	Total	~	2

Played in just one game for Grantham during the 1887/88 season, the November friendly at home to Lincoln Rangers, plus the match against Boston just over a year later.

Sindall

Seasons Played			
	League	~	14 (4)
	F.A. Cup	~	
1925/26-26/27	Lincs Cup	~	1
	Other	~	
	Total	~	15 (4)

Player whose surname is sometimes spelt 'Siddall' and scored his first goal for the club in January 1926 at Ilkeston United. He played only occasionally the next season, generally in the Autumn period, although details of his final appearance are not available.

Skaith

Seasons Played			
	League	~	6
	F.A. Cup	~	
1939/40	Lincs Cup	~	1
	Other	~	
	Total	~	7

Newark Town player, possibly based at Lincoln, who made a guest appearance for Grantham when the club made the short trip up the A1 on Christmas Day 1939 and found themselves a man short. He returned to Grantham in February and March of 1940, but following the 9-0 defeat at Newark Town, perhaps unsurprisingly played no more for The Gingerbreads and was kindly returned to his original team.

Colin Skeith

Seasons Played			
	League	~	1
	F.A. Cup	~	
1971/72	F.A. Trophy	~	
	League Cup	~	
	Lincs Cup	~	
	Other	~	
	Total	~	1

Born 15/10/1937 in Grantham. Nephew of Dick Skeith and brother-in-law of Cyril Brown. Colin was a goalkeeper who had previously played for Grantham St Anne's and St John's, with a dream move to Arsenal then wrecked by a torn cartilage injury. Upon recovery his career continued at Grantham Amateurs, then Ropsley and it was during this time he was called upon by Terry Bly to cover for Chris Gardiner in the March 1972 fixture at home to Frickley Colliery, keeping a clean sheet as Grantham ran out 3-0 winners. Colin went on to play for Woolsthorpe, Harlaxton and Croxton Kerrial, who he also managed. Other than football, Colin was an engineering draughtsman who worked in Grantham. Died 02/01/1997 in Grantham.

Dick Skeith

Seasons Played	League	~	2
	F.A. Cup	~	
1949/50	Lincs Cup	~	
	Other	~	
	Total	~	2

Born 22/06/1922 in Grantham. Christened Harold Skeith but known by everyone as Dick and started out with the Aveling Barfords works team, before joining Grantham St John's, (during which time he also made a guest appearance for Arsenal in a friendly at London Road), and Peterborough United Reserves. He then made two appearances for The Gingerbreads at the start of the 1949/50 season, against the Reserve sides of Nottingham Forest and Scunthorpe & Lindsey United, following which he joined Bourne Town. Dick later moved to Gainsborough to run a Post Office, then worked at Cottam Power Station, but is now retired and lives close to Lincoln. His nephew, Colin Skeith, also played for the club in the early 1970's.

Alfred Skerritt

Seasons Played	League	~	15 (1)
	F.A. Cup	~	
1922/23	Lincs Cup	~	
	Other	~	3 (1)
	Total	~	18 (2)

Born 1897 at Grantham. Centre-Half, previously with Grantham St John's, who was certainly playing for our club by the September 1922 fixture against Coalville Swifts and scored goals against Welbeck Colliery in February 1923 and a month later in the local Hospital Cup victory over Spalding United. Died 04/01/1945 at Grantham.

Skillington

Seasons Played	League	~	
	Lincs Cup	~	
1894/95	Other	~	1
	Total	~	1

Defender who played in the April 1895 Grantham Minor Cup tie at home to Newark Reserves, but no available data shows any league appearances for him. There is the possibility that he may be George Skillington, born circa 1869.

Slater

Seasons Played	F.A. Cup	~	3 (1)
	Lincs Cup	~	7 (1)
1885/86-90/91	Other	~	52 (15)
	Total	~	62 (17)

Made his debut in the December 1885 friendly at home to Lincoln City, but it wasn't until the start of the 1887/88 season that he became a regular player in the team. Over the next few years he played in many of those early cup competitions, including scoring the winning goal in the 1889 Kettering Charity Cup Final against Cambridge Granta, with the end of his career coming towards the close of the following year.

Slater

Seasons Played	League	~	1
	F.A. Cup	~	
1949/50	Lincs Cup	~	
	Total	~	1

Defender who played in the April 1950 Midland League game at Lincoln City Reserves after Eric Hunt became unavailable.

Kevin Slinn

Seasons Played	League	~	22 (5)
	F.A. Cup	~	2
2003/04	F.A. Trophy	~	1
	League Cup	~	
	Lincs Cup	~	2 (1)
	Total	~	27 (6)

Born 02/09/1974 at Northampton. Previously played for Cogenhoe United, Corby Town, Stockport County, Watford, Raunds Town, Boston United, Bedford Town, where he was their top scorer during the 2001/02 season, Wootton Blue Cross, St Alban's and Stamford. He made his Grantham debut in the opening County Shield tie of the 2003/04 season at home to Stamford and scored his initial goal in the first league game of the season against Dover Athletic. After 11 games though, many of his remaining appearances came from the substitute's bench, the last of which was in January 2004 at home to Crawley Town and soon after this he left Grantham to play for Brackley Town.

John Small

Seasons Played	League	~	46
	F.A. Cup	~	4
1966/67-67/68	Total	~	50

Born 14/01/1945 at Billingham. Goalkeeper who began his career at local side, Head Wrightson, before making two appearances for Hartlepool United in the 1965/66 season. He took over the role from George Crawford in time for the 1966 Christmas Eve fixture against Gainsborough Trinity and two weeks later was playing in the FA Cup Second Round against Oldham Athletic. The following season he played in the majority of the games, including the FA Cup tie against Altrincham, and his final game came in the closing fixture of the season at Lockheed Leamington. John's goalkeeping skills attracted a string of Football League scouts to London Road and yet he was never able to return to the top levels of the game.

H. Smalley

Seasons Played	League	~	1 (2)
	FA Amt. Cup	~	
1910/11	League Cup	~	1 (1)
	Lincs Cup	~	
	Other	~	
	Total	~	2 (3)

Former Lincoln City Reserves player who scored twice for Grantham in the November 1910 Midland Amateur League match against South Nottingham and the League Cup semi-final victory over Derby YMCA. It is not known how many, if any, other appearances he made for the club in this league title winning season

Smalley

Seasons Played	League	~	2 (1)
	F.A. Cup	~	
1927/28	Lincs Cup	~	
	Total	~	2 (1)

Previously played for Sutton Junction, scoring 60+ goals in one season, but made only a few appearances for Grantham at the end of the 1927/28 season, with his only goal for the club coming in the April game at Heanor Town.

Eric Smallwood

Seasons Played	League	~	2
	F.A. Cup	~	
1947/48	Lincs Cup	~	
	Total	~	2

Made only two appearances for Grantham at the start of the 1947/48 season, which were both Midland League fixtures against Boston United.

A. Smith

Seasons Played	League	~	4 (4)
1911/12	Total	~	4 (4)

Former Grantham Avenue player who scored in games against Derby County Reserves, Sutton Junction, Long Eaton and Sutton Town during the 1911/12 season. These facts are taken from incomplete score-sheets from that year, therefore he most likely scored more goals than just those, in many more matches.

Charles Smith

Seasons Played	League	~	16
	F.A. Cup	~	
1929/30	Lincs Cup	~	
	Other	~	
	Total	~	16

Born circa 1904 at Sheffield. Centre-half who had previously spent time at Barnsley, Doncaster Rovers, where he made one full appearance, Notts County and Scunthorpe & Lindsey United, where he won a Midland League Championship medal in 1927. Charles made his debut for Grantham in the opening match of the 1929/30 season at Mansfield Town, but left the club only a few months later.

E. Smith

Seasons Played			
	League	~	1
	F.A. Cup	~	
1924/25	Lincs Cup	~	
	Other	~	
	Total	~	1

Former Newark Town and Grantham St John's goalkeeper. Available records show just the one First team appearance for him, in the home game against Heanor Town in March of 1925.

Fabien Smith

Seasons Played			
	League	~	33 (2)
	F.A. Cup	~	1
2004/05	F.A. Trophy	~	3
	League Cup	~	1
	Lincs Cup	~	3 (3)
	Total	~	41 (5)

Born 17/01/1985 at Nottingham. Midfielder who began his career as a Trainee at Scunthorpe United, before moving on to Ilkeston Town and Gedling Town (on-loan). Fabien joined The Gingerbreads in the Summer of 2004 and scored on his debut in the opening County Shield game at Brigg Town. He played in many of the fixtures during the 2004/05 season and although initially starting the April County Final at Gainsborough Trinity viewing from the bench, came on with ten minutes left and scored his most important goal to date that secured The Gingerbread's monopoly over the competition. An important member of Lee Glover's team, Fabien remains with the club.

F. Smith

Seasons Played			
	League	~	3
	F.A. Cup	~	
1920/21	Lincs Cup	~	
	Other	~	
1922/23	Total	~	3

Full-Back who also played for Grantham St John's and made his Grantham debut in April 1921 during the Central Alliance game at New Hucknall Colliery. There are no records of him playing the following season, but during the 1922/23 campaign he made at least two appearances towards the beginning.

Gavin Smith

Seasons Played			
	League	~	5
	F.A. Cup	~	
1985/86	F.A. Trophy	~	
	League Cup	~	
	Lincs Cup	~	
	Total	~	5

Former Lincoln City Reserves and Boston FC full-back who made five appearances for Grantham at the start of 1986, beginning with the league fixture against Leicester United and ending with the match at Oldbury United in March, a fixture that attracted only 38 spectators. Gavin went on to play for Spalding United and Bourne Town.

G. Smith

Seasons Played			
	League	~	7 (8)
	F.A. Cup	~	
1926/27-27/28	Lincs Cup	~	
	Other	~	1 (1)
	Total	~	8 (9)

Centre-Forward who had also played for the Reserves side and Players Athletic, making only four league appearances for the First team at the end of the 1926/27 season, but netting six goals, including a hat-trick in the April Midland League game against Wombwell. His last goal for the club came in January 1928 at the London Road visit of Denaby United, but it is not known whether he made any appearances for the club after that date.

Jack Smith

Seasons Played			
	League	~	43 (20)
	F.A. Cup	~	2
1953/54	Lincs Cup	~	2
	Total	~	47 (20)

Inside-Right player from Bradford City who scored on his Grantham debut in the opening league match of the season at Peterborough United and then played in all but three of that year's games, including the County Cup Final win over Gainsborough Trinity. Jack finished the season as the club's second highest goal-scorer, behind Jack Macartney, and also broke a Midland League scoring record by netting a hat-trick in three minutes, which must have been either in the October 1953 match at Gainsborough Trinity or possibly the earlier game against Halifax Town Reserves when he finished the game with four goals to his name. The following season he played for Goole Town, but nothing is known of him after that.

J. Smith

Seasons Played			
	League	~	45 (31)
	F.A. Cup	~	3 (2)
1921/22	Lincs Cup	~	2
1923/24	Other	~	4 (3)
1925/26-26/27	Total	~	54 (36)

Versatile player to say the least, who made appearances both for the First team and also the Reserves in positions ranging from goalkeeper to centre-forward and most in-between. There is the possibility that he could be the same individual as some of the other 'Smith' entries where no Christian names are available and of particular note would be the individual who was scoring for Grantham in the 1920/21 season. The first definite evidence that we have of this individual is him scoring for Grantham in August 1921 during the Central Alliance game at Chesterfield Reserves, but despite playing many of that season's games there are no records of him appearing the following year. He scored on his return in August 1923 at Gresley Rovers and netted his first hat-trick a few weeks later when Sutton Junction played at London Road. He then seems to be missing from the Grantham team again for the following season, but by late 1925 team-sheets show him scoring goals once more. He played only intermittently for Grantham during his last season, although he helped secure victory in the local Charity Cup Final of April 1927 with a hat-trick against Grantham St John's.

Mark Smith

Seasons Played			
	League	~	13
	F.A. Cup	~	
1991/92	F.A. Trophy	~	
	League Cup	~	3
	Lincs Cup	~	
	Total	~	16

Born 02/01/1973 at Birmingham. In a publication of this nature you are bound to have players of the same name, but in the same season! This Mark was a goalkeeper signed on-loan from Nottingham Forest who made his debut for Grantham in the September 1991 league match at Hednesford Town and then played in a total of 16 consecutive games, with the December fixture against Hinckley Town his final appearance. After his release from Forest, he went on to play for Crewe Alexandra where he unfortunately set a British record in 1994, being dismissed from the field after only 19 seconds of the league fixture against Darlington. Mark then went on to make appearances for Walsall, Rushden & Diamonds, Bedford Town, Morecambe, Eastwood Town, Scarborough and Ilkeston Town.

Mark Smith

Seasons Played			
	League	~	1
	F.A. Cup	~	
1991/92	F.A. Trophy	~	
	League Cup	~	
	Lincs Cup	~	
	Total	~	1

Defender who made just one appearance for Grantham in the closing fixture of the 1991/92 season at Solihull Borough.

Ray Smith

Seasons Played			
	League	~	46 (30)
	F.A. Cup	~	1
1958/59-60/61	League Cup	~	2
	Lincs Cup	~	3 (3)
	Total	~	52 (33)

Striker from Bottesford who signed for Grantham from Holwell Works and scored twice in his first game, the December 1958 match at home to Gainsborough Trinity. He finished that first campaign only two goals short of the club's highest scorer, Bernard Weakley, in a poor year for the club, with one hat-trick to his name after the January game at home to Worksop Town. As Grantham moved into the Central Alliance (South) League, Ray appeared in most of those fixtures as well and scored another hat-trick against Rushden Town. However, the 1960/61 season saw only six appearances for him, with his final goal in his last game for the club, against Bourne Town in February 1961.

Rob Smith

Seasons Played			
1981/82-82/83	League	~	19
	F.A. Cup	~	2
	F.A. Trophy	~	1
	League Cup	~	2
	Lincs Cup	~	3
	Other	~	2
	Total	~	29

Made his debut in the first County Cup match of the 1981/82 season against Boston United and played in about half of the fixtures that year, but made only nine more appearances at the start of the 1982/83 season, the last of which was at Chorley in November.

Smith

Seasons Played			
1876/77	Other	~	1
	Total	~	1

Known to have played in the October 1876 friendly at Peterborough, but no records are available that show any other appearances for him.

Smith

Seasons Played			
1886/87	F.A. Cup	~	
	Lincs Cup	~	
	Other	~	1
	Total	~	1

Made just one appearance for Grantham in the October 1886 game against Brentwood.

Smith

Seasons Played			
1904/05	League	~	1
	Lincs Cup	~	
	Other	~	
	Total	~	1

Played in the March 1905 game at Huntingtower Road against Derby Thornhill, but it's not known whether he made any other appearances during that season.

Smith

Seasons Played			
1913/14-14/15	League	~	2
	F.A. Cup	~	
	Lincs Cup	~	
	Total	~	2

With very few full records available for this period, it is difficult to validate any players appearances if they were not scoring. We know that this defender played in the December 1913 Central Alliance fixture at Holwell Works and the Loughborough Corinthians game the following September, but there is no evidence to show how many other matches that he may have played in.

Smith

Seasons Played			
1919/20	League	~	3
	F.A. Cup	~	4 (1)
	Lincs Cup	~	
	Total	~	7 (1)

Sergeant in the Army who played at the inside-left position and also spent time at Liverpool at some point during his career. He could therefore be Wally Smith (born 1885 at Bootle) who had a trial with Liverpool in 1907 and gained Football League experience just before World War One with Bury and Birmingham City, or possibly more likely, George Smith who was at Liverpool in 1922 and also played for Gillingham, Tranmere Rovers and Coventry City in the first half of the decade. Both these players played in the appropriate position, but there is obviously also the chance that he may not have been an established player at all. Whoever he may have been, he played for Grantham in the first league match of the 1919/20 season at Long Eaton and scored his only goal for the club at the end of the same month in the FA Cup tie against Arnold St Mary's. However, there is no evidence of him playing after the FA Cup defeat at home to Sutton Town the following month.

Smith

Seasons Played			
1920/21	League	~	22 (22)
	F.A. Cup	~	2 (2)
	Lincs Cup	~	2 (1)
	Other	~	
	Total	~	26 (25)

Prolific centre-forward who scored two goals on his debut at Sutton Junction in August 1920, four goals on their return visit to London Road only a few weeks later and went on to finish with a 25 goal tally for that season. He could possibly be J. Smith who was playing for Grantham the following season.

Smith

Seasons Played			
1931/32	League	~	11 (1)
	Lincs Cup	~	
	Other	~	
	Total	~	11 (1)

Scored in his first game for Grantham, the opening Midland League fixture of the 1931/32 season at Loughborough Corinthians, but little is known about other games that he played in due to his appearance total being established from end of season data.

Smith

Seasons Played			
1945/46	League	~	4
	F.A. Cup	~	
	Lincs Cup	~	
	Total	~	4

Defender who played four games for Grantham in the 1946 New Year against the Reserve sides of Notts County, Nottingham Forest, Mansfield Town, plus Scunthorpe & Lindsey United.

Kamar Smithen

Seasons Played			
2004/05	League	~	1
	F.A. Cup	~	
	F.A. Trophy	~	
	League Cup	~	1
	Lincs Cup	~	1
	Total	~	3

Born circa 1986. Spent time in the Youth teams at Burton Albion and Gresley Rovers, then joined Grantham following time at South Normanton. He came off the bench to make his debut during the November 2004 league fixture at home to Hednesford Town, but played only twice more, in January 2005 at King's Lynn and against Stamford in the Lincolnshire Shield. Kamar remains with the club.

Smithson

Seasons Played			
1921/22	League	~	1
	F.A. Cup	~	
	Lincs Cup	~	
	Total	~	1

Former Grantham St John's and Newark Athletic player who appeared in the December 1921 Central Alliance fixture against Shirebrook, but it is not known if he made any other appearances for the club that season.

Smyth

Seasons Played			
1933/34	League	~	
	F.A. Cup	~	
	Lincs Cup	~	
	Other	~	1 (1)
	Total	~	1 (1)

Scored in the local Hospital Cup semi-final victory over RAF Grantham in April 1934, but no information is available that shows any other games that he may have played in.

Michael Sneddon

Seasons Played			
2004/05	League	~	7 (1)
	F.A. Cup	~	
	F.A. Trophy	~	
	League Cup	~	
	Lincs Cup	~	1 (1)
	Total	~	8 (2)

Born 07/10/1984 at Kettering. Striker who started at Leicester City, before a broken leg obstructed his career progression. He later had a trial at Boston United, but eventually joined S&L Corby and then Corby Town. Upon the arrival of Lee Glover at The Meres, Michael was one of the first targets for the new manager, but had to wait until March 2005 before he was able to sign for The Gingerbreads. Michael replaced Josh Quailey during that month's league fixture at Gloucester City to make his debut and only had to wait a matter of weeks before he was rewarded for his move, as he played in the victorious Lincolnshire County Shield Final against Gainsborough Trinity, scoring the first goal in the 2-1 win. Michael remains with the club.

Roy South

Seasons Played			
	League	~	113 (38)
	F.A. Cup	~	11 (5)
1964/65-66/67	Total	~	124 (43)

Born circa 1943. Former Heanor Town right-winger who made his Grantham debut in the opening fixture of the 1964/65 season at Loughborough United and scored his first goal for the club two days later at Sutton Town. Roy missed only one game that season and his prominence continued the following year as well, including FA Cup Proper appearances against Hendon and Swindon Town. His final season with the club included FA Cup encounters with Wimbledon and Oldham Athletic, before his final goal and appearance in the closing Midland League fixture at Retford Town.

Aubrey Southwell

Seasons Played			
	League	~	17 (1)
	F.A. Cup	~	1
1939/40	Lincs Cup	~	
1945/46	Other	~	1
1958/59	Total	~	19 (1)

Born 21/08/1921 in Grantham. Educated at the Boy's Central School in town and also played for Grantham St John's. His first appearance for 'The Town' came in a friendly against an RAF XI in September 1939, but he made only one more appearance that season, against Denaby United in February 1940. After the end of The War Aubrey joined Nottingham Forest, but returned to London Road at the end of the 1945/46 season to play in three more games for his home team. Only months later he joined Notts County, where a long and illustrious career included his rise to Club Captain and 358 appearances. He then stepped back into non-league football with Boston United, but returned again to Grantham in the Summer of 1958. The bulk of his appearances for the club came that season, with his only goal coming in March 1959 against South Shields and his last match the following month at Sutton Town. Following the end of his footballing career Aubrey became a salesman for a national brewery and later a wine merchant in Nottingham. Died 09/02/2005 in Nottingham.

Southwell

Seasons Played			
	League	~	2
	Lincs Cup	~	1
1893/94-94/95	Other	~	2
	Total	~	5

Played in the April 1894 Grantham Minor Cup Final and many of the games in the following season's Grantham & District League.

Neal Spafford

Seasons Played			
	League	~	5
	F.A. Cup	~	
2004/05	F.A. Trophy	~	1
	League Cup	~	
	Lincs Cup	~	1
	Total	~	7

Born 07/10/1986 at Rotherham. Joined Grantham in the Summer of 2004 and made his debut in the opening Lincolnshire County Shield fixture of the season at Brigg Town. However, Neal found himself sitting out many of the fixtures over the next few months, with his final appearance at the end of December against Havant & Waterlooville in the FA Trophy. The following month he was released by the club and joined Bourne Town.

Sparrow

Seasons Played			
	League	~	1 (2)
	F.A. Cup	~	
1913/14	Lincs Cup	~	
	Total	~	1 (2)

Scored twice in the January 1914 Central Alliance fixture at Leicester Fosse Reserves, but no details are known of any other appearances that he may have made for Grantham.

Jack Spaven

Seasons Played			
	League	~	103 (60)
	F.A. Cup	~	13 (14)
1926/27-29/30	Lincs Cup	~	4 (2)
	Other	~	3 (4)
	Total	~	123 (80)

Born 22/11/1891 at Scarborough. 'Spav' was a former Goole Town and Scunthorpe & Lindsey United player who also spent time at Scarborough, plus local sides St James and North End during his career. Those first years saw medals won in the West Riding Cup, Yorkshire County Cup, Yorkshire Combination, Castleford & District Cup, Boston Hospital Cup and RAF Shield. In 1919 he joined Nottingham Forest and in a successful six season spell there, with 46 goals in 157 games, he won a Division Two Championship medal, plus was highest scorer for three consecutive years. Jack made his Grantham debut in the opening league game of the 1926/27 season at Sutton Town and scored his first goal for the club a week later against Worksop Town. He played in the majority of the season's matches, including the April 1927 local Charity Cup Final when he scored a hat-trick in the 12-0 demolition of Grantham St John's, helping him finish the campaign as the club's top scorer. Jack continued to be a valuable member of the team the following season and in November 1928 scored the only goal in the FA Cup First Round Proper against Rhyl Athletic and netted the consolation strike in the following round at Wigan Borough. His final season playing for the club saw only two appearances for Jack, with the conclusion to his career coming in the September 1929 Midland League fixture at home to Mansfield Town. He was a popular player with the supporters, probably aided by the fact that he ran the Blue Horse pub situated next to the ground! In 1931 he moved back to Nottingham to take over the Lord Nelson on Carlton Street and retired in 1954. Died 29/08/1971 at Nottingham.

Adrian Speed

Seasons Played			
	League	~	511 (65)
	F.A. Cup	~	30 (2)
1990/91-04/05	F.A. Trophy	~	35 (4)
	League Cup	~	39 (3)
	Lincs Cup	~	18 (2)
	Total	~	633 (76)

Born 31/01/1971 at Nottingham. 'Speedie' began his career as an apprentice at Peterborough United, making one First team appearance against Fulham, before moving to Holbeach United, where he won a United Counties League winner's medal. He made his Grantham debut in the opening Lincolnshire County Senior Cup tie of the 1990/91 season at home to Grimsby Town, with his first goal for the club coming a month later at RC Warwick. Ady played in the final league match at London Road in October 1990 against Dudley Town and continued to appear in every game whilst the club shared grounds with Spalding United. August of 1991 saw him play in the inaugural game at The Meres, against Ilkeston Town in the FA Cup, but although the following few years saw him maintain his almost permanent place in the side, highlights for the team were few and far between. Of course things changed upon the arrival of Gary Mills as Manager at Grantham and Speedie played in more games than any of his colleagues in the 1997/98 Championship winning season, including the awesome 6-0 victory over Ilkeston Town in March 1998 and the FA Trophy ties against Conference sides, Hednesford Town and Southport. He was then one of only a handful of players that continued on at The Meres as the club was taken over by Antrac and professional contracts were offered. He played in the October 1998 FA Cup final qualifying round at Tamworth, whilst just over a year later, at the end of 1999, he was awarded the position of Caretaker Manager for two matches before the arrival of John Wilkinson, winning one of the games against Cambridge City and losing the other at Ilkeston Town. October of 2000 saw another appearance for Ady, albeit from the substitute's bench, in the thrilling, yet disappointing, 5-4 defeat in the FA Cup final qualifying round at Rushden & Diamonds. He then played in every league match of the promotion winning 2001/02 season, but the following campaign made only 19 appearances, including the April 2003 County Cup Final at Gainsborough Trinity. Speedie also missed many of the games at the start of the 2003/04 season, including the FA Cup First Round tie at home to Leyton Orient, which he was forced to view from the bench for the entire match, a point which he still considers to be one of the lowest moments in his Grantham career. By the end of the year though he was back at the heart of defence and in March 2004 played in the victorious Lincolnshire County Shield Final at home to Gainsborough Trinity.

In February 2005 Adrian finally matched Chris Gardiner's record number of appearances and was presented with a commemorative plate by the former goalkeeper before the home fixture against Banbury United. A week later, the long trip down to Tiverton Town saw Ady make the record his own, having pulled on the black and white shirt for the 625th time. Two months later Speedie played in a repeat of the previous year's County Shield, with another medal won as The Gingerbreads were this time victorious at The Northolme. He remains at the club, still clocking up the appearances, and rightly goes into the record books as not only a player of great loyalty, a rarity these days, but a true Gingerbread legend.

Mick Spencer

Seasons Played			
	League	~	36 (1)
	F.A. Cup	~	
1984/85-85/86	F.A. Trophy	~	2
	League Cup	~	4
1992/93	Lincs Cup	~	
	Other	~	1
	Total	~	43 (1)

Former Grantham United defender who came through the Reserves set-up, spending time as Captain, to make his First team debut in the October 1984 league fixture at home to Burton Albion. Mick played in many of the remaining games from that season, but turned out only five times towards the end of the following campaign. He rejoined Grantham from Dunkirk in January 1993, after the departure of many of that year's players, and scored his only goal for the club in the March draw at Weston-Super-Mare, with his final appearance a month later at home to Stourbridge.

Spikins

Seasons Played			
	F.A. Cup	~	
	Lincs Cup	~	
1888/89	Other	~	1
	Total	~	1

Played in the February 1889 friendly at Boston, but this is his only known appearance for Grantham.

Paul Spriggs

Seasons Played			
	League	~	1
	F.A. Cup	~	
1971/72	F.A. Trophy	~	
	League Cup	~	
	Lincs Cup	~	
	Other	~	
	Total	~	1

Born 29/10/1950 in Grantham. Began his career with the Notts County Youth team, but a serious ankle injury forced him into local football and Harrowby United. Paul then joined The Gingerbreads, but made just one appearance for the First team when he came off the substitute's bench in the February 1972 game against Gateshead to replace Mike Farmer. He continued to play for the Reserves side, although a broken leg during his time at London Road caused a halt to his career. He returned to the game in the latter half of the 1970's to make appearances for Grantham United. Paul still lives in the town and works as a Civil Servant.

Squires

Seasons Played			
	League	~	1 (1)
	F.A. Cup	~	
1925/26	Lincs Cup	~	
	Total	~	1 (1)

Inside-Right, originally from the Nottingham area, who scored in the club's first ever Midland League fixture in August 1925 at Mansfield Town, but sadly it's not known if he made any other appearances for the club.

George Stafford

Seasons Played			
	League	~	6
	F.A. Cup	~	1
1960/61	League Cup	~	
	Lincs Cup	~	
	Total	~	7

Former Boston United and March Town United full-back who played in the first game of the 1960/61 season at home to Kettering Town Reserves, but only a month later after the match at Potton United he lost his place to Barry Harbershon.

Carl Stahlberger

Seasons Played			
	League	~	3
	F.A. Cup	~	
1998/99-99/00	F.A. Trophy	~	
	League Cup	~	
	Lincs Cup	~	1
	Total	~	4

Reserves team player, and brother of Michael Stahlberger, who made three appearances towards the end of the 1998/99 season in both the fixtures against Tamworth and the closing match at Weymouth. The start of the following season saw him come on as substitute to replace Jim Neil in the opening County Cup tie at home to Scunthorpe United, but he played no further games for the First team. He continued to make appearances though for the Reserves, before leaving The Meres and later moving on to Radcliffe Olympic.

Michael Stahlberger

Seasons Played			
	League	~	29
	F.A. Cup	~	1
1998/99-99/00	F.A. Trophy	~	2
	League Cup	~	6
	Lincs Cup	~	1
	Total	~	39

Brother of Carl Stahlberger and a former Harrowby United and Grantham Reserves player who first played for the senior side in the October 1998 FA Trophy replay at home to Burton Albion. Michael went on to make a total of 17 appearances that year and then had his best run in the side towards the end of 1999. He made his final appearance in February 2000 at Tamworth, although he was forced to spectate in many of the following games from the bench. Michael later went on to join his sibling at Radcliffe Olympic and then moved to Southwell City and Gedling Town.

Les Stancer

Seasons Played			
1945/46-46/47	League	~	41 (13)
1948/49-50/51	F.A. Cup	~	1
1952/53	Lincs Cup	~	1
	Total	~	43 (13)

Born 16/04/1925 in Grantham. Played for Notts County during World War 2 friendlies, plus made one FA Cup appearance for them in the Autumn of 1945. Les was soon playing for Grantham though and scored on his debut in January 1946 against Mansfield Town Reserves. He made seven appearances for the club that term, one of which was in the Lincolnshire Senior Cup Final against Boston United, and only five in the subsequent season. The majority of his games came in the 1948/49 campaign, although after this his appearances came infrequently, with the end of his Grantham career in March 1953 when he covered for an unavailable Jack Macartney in the Midland League fixture at Nottingham Forest Reserves. Les later spent nearly 20 years as the landlord of the Cherry Tree public house on Harrowby Lane and although now retired, still lives in the town.

Darren Standage

Seasons Played			
	League	~	2
	F.A. Cup	~	1
2004/05	F.A. Trophy	~	
	League Cup	~	
	Lincs Cup	~	
	Total	~	3

Born circa 1986. Former Sandiacre Town midfielder who signed for Grantham in the Summer of 2004. After sitting out the first two games of the season he made his debut in the August Southern League match at home to Rugby United. He made just two more substitute appearances though over the next few weeks, against Hemel Hempstead and Shepshed Dynamo, and was released by the club in November.

Chris Staniforth

Seasons Played			
	League	~	16 (4)
	F.A. Cup	~	
1930/31	Lincs Cup	~	
	Total	~	16 (4)

Born 26/09/1895 at Carrington. Experienced forward who had previously played for Notts County 'A', Cresswell Athletic, Chesterfield Municipal, during their 1919/20 Midland League Championship winning year, Cresswell Colliery, Mansfield Town, the first of four spells there which saw another two Midland League winner's medals, Oldham Athletic, Notts County, twice, and Shirebrook. He remains Mansfield Town's leading club goal-scorer and played in many of the team's great games in the late 1920's, including FA Cup ties at Wolverhampton Wanderers and Arsenal. Chris made his debut for Grantham in the Spring of 1931, scoring in the league game at Grimsby Town Reserves in March, the two fixtures against Scunthorpe & Lindsey United and finally Hull City Reserves in April 1931. The following season he returned to Mansfield Town once more, who by then had been elected into The Football League, and he finally finished with a total of 32 goals in his 112 senior appearances. He went on to join Sutton Town, Worksop Town and then returned to Cresswell Colliery as Player/Manager. A dedicated footballer all his life, Chris fathered 12 children and named all of his eight boys after colleagues in the game that he respected. His playing career had seen a total of 226 goals in the 321 games that we have records of, with obviously his time at Field Mill resulting in his legendary status there. At one time whilst at Mansfield Town he was even challenged to a race around the pitch with a greyhound. The dog, called Krassin, managed to beat him, but afterwards Chris claimed that he had lost due to looking around to see where the dog was before he crossed the line! Following the end of his playing career, Chris continued to work at Cresswell Colliery, ran a public house in the area and worked in Ordnance stores during The War. Died 24/12/1954 at Carrington, although some publications list his place of death as Cresswell.

Staniforth

Seasons Played			
1946/47-47/48	League	~	12 (3)
	F.A. Cup	~	
	Lincs Cup	~	1
	Total	~	13 (3)

Scored in his first game for Grantham in November 1946 against Hull City Reserves, but then made only two more appearances which didn't come until the end of that season. The following year his appearances continued to arrive sporadically and his final game for the club was at the end of April 1948 at Notts County Reserves.

Stanton

Seasons Played			
1894/95	League	~	
	Lincs Cup	~	
	Other	~	1
	Total	~	1

Played in the April 1895 Grantham Minor Cup semi-final tie at home to Newark Reserves, but no information is available to show if he played in any other games.

Staples

Seasons Played			
1953/54	League	~	1
	F.A. Cup	~	
	Lincs Cup	~	
	Total	~	1

Played in only one game for Grantham, the January 1954 league match at Worksop Town.

John Steeples

Seasons Played			
1985/86	League	~	
	F.A. Cup	~	2
	F.A. Trophy	~	
	League Cup	~	1
	Lincs Cup	~	
	Total	~	3

Born 28/04/1959 at Doncaster. Forward, previously with Pilkington, Grimsby Town, Torquay United and Scarborough, who made 12 appearances in his Football League career. He played just three times for Grantham though, in September 1985 against Corby Town and the two FA Cup ties against Oldbury United.

Geoff Stephenson

Seasons Played			
1992/93	League	~	21 (5)
	F.A. Cup	~	1
	F.A. Trophy	~	1
	League Cup	~	2
	Lincs Cup	~	1
	Total	~	26 (5)

Born 28/04/1970 at Tynemouth. Defender who made 21 appearances for Grimsby Town, before moving into non-league football with Boston United, Eastwood Town and King's Lynn. He made his debut for Grantham in the opening County Cup tie of the 1992/93 season at Lincoln City, with his first goal for the club a month later at home to Bedworth United. Geoff played in every game up to the financial problems of January 1993, leading to his departure from The Meres, with his last appearance at home to Barri Town seeing his final goal scored from the penalty spot. He went on to play for Whitley Bay, Harrogate Town, Durham City, Morpeth Town, South Shields, Dunstan FB and Consett.

Jackie Stephenson

Seasons Played			
1930/31	League	~	34 (11)
	F.A. Cup	~	
	Lincs Cup	~	1 (1)
	Total	~	35 (12)

Born 01/06/1899 at Ryton-on-Tyne. Forward who began his career at Kettering Town, but moved into The Football League with Durham City, Norwich City and Hartlepools United, finishing with 23 goals in 152 senior appearances. Jackie was playing for Grantham by the November 1930 league match against Loughborough Corinthians and scored his first goal for the club at the end of that month at home to Denaby United. Although no details are available to indicate the end of his Grantham career, it is known that he finished the season as the second highest scorer behind James Sullivan. He went on to play for Crawcrook Albion, Cork and Wallsend.

Joseph Stephenson

Seasons Played			
1932/33	League	~	10
	F.A. Cup	~	
	Lincs Cup	~	
	Other	~	
	Total	~	10

Former Frickley Colliery, Huddersfield Town and Sheffield Wednesday player whose Grantham appearances have been found in end of season data, so unfortunately no information is available on the games that he played in.

Mark Steptoe

Seasons Played			
1994/95	League	~	2
	F.A. Cup	~	
	F.A. Trophy	~	
	League Cup	~	1
	Lincs Cup	~	
	Total	~	3

30/01/1963 at Grantham. 'Rab', as he was known, was a cousin of Nick Steptoe, and a goalkeeper who had previously played for Ancaster, Harrowby United, Grantham United, Croxton Kerrial, Mirlees Blackstone and Grantham Reserves. He covered for the unavailable Guy Hardcastle in the October 1994 games against Cambridge City, Bilston Town and RC Warwick. Mark went on to play for Cottesmore Amateurs, before returning to the Reserves, but a broken leg forced him to give up the game at the end of the decade. He still lives in the town and works as a gas engineer.

Nick Steptoe

Seasons Played			
1985/86	League	~	22
	F.A. Cup	~	
	F.A. Trophy	~	1
	League Cup	~	
	Lincs Cup	~	
	Total	~	23

Born 22/02/1962 at Grantham. Cousin of Mark Steptoe and a local defender who had previously turned out for Barkston, Ancaster and Grantham United. He made his First team debut in the November 1985 league fixture at Leamington and played in many of that season's games, up to his final appearance in April 1986 against Redditch United. Nick went on to play for Melton Town and Spalding United. He still lives in the area and for many years has worked as a bricklayer.

Athur Stevenson

Seasons Played			
1950/51	League	~	10
	F.A. Cup	~	3
	Lincs Cup	~	
	Total	~	13

Born 02/03/1924 at Lanchester, Durham. Defender previously with Denaby United who made 14 appearances for Doncaster Rovers at the end of the 1940's. He made his Grantham debut in the first match of the 1950/51 season at Bradford City Reserves and despite playing in many of the early games from that campaign, he was soon to lose his place to Eric Hunt. After this, he made only a couple of more appearances for the First team, with the final one coming in February 1951 in the match against Grimsby Town Reserves.

Stevenson

Seasons Played			
	League	~	1 (2)
	F.A. Cup	~	
1925/26	Lincs Cup	~	
	Total	~	1 (2)

Known to have scored a brace in the March 1926 game against Frickley Colliery, but no other information is known about him.

Stevenson

Seasons Played			
	League	~	2
	F.A. Cup	~	
1932/33	Lincs Cup	~	
	Other	~	
	Total	~	2

Could possibly be the same player as the previous entry, but this individual's two games are only known from end of season totals so it is impossible to verify this. It does however confirm that he is not the same person as Joseph Stephenson, who also made appearances that season. The only details that are available of him are that he played in the left-half position and was replaced in the team by Albert Sykes.

Dave Stewart

Seasons Played			
	League	~	60 (14)
	F.A. Cup	~	3
1983/84-85/86	F.A. Trophy	~	7 (1)
	League Cup	~	9 (1)
	Lincs Cup	~	1
	Other	~	1
	Total	~	81 (16)

Born 20/05/1958 in Belfast. Known by everybody as 'Sammy', he began his career at Bangor, Northern Ireland, but by the age of sixteen he was making appearances for Hull City. It was not long before he was also making his International debut, taking over from George Best when he was awarded a Northern Ireland cap for the 1977/78 International against Belgium. Club transfers then followed to Chelsea, Scunthorpe United, Hartlepool United, Canberra in Denmark, before moving into non-league football with Bridlington Trinity and Goole Town. His time in the Football League had seen 28 goals to his name in a total of 178 league and cup fixtures. Sammy scored on his debut for Grantham in the October 1983 league match at Southport and then netted goals in the next two games as well. He missed only three matches that season, which finished with Grantham in fourth place in the Northern Premier League, and his prominence continued the following year, although for a team that was now battling at the opposite end of the table. He made just seven appearances at the start of the 1985/86 season though, with his final goal at Forest Green Rovers and his last appearance in the October league game against Bromsgrove Rovers, before his return to Goole. Sammy currently lives in Hull, running his own insurance agency.

George Stillyards

Seasons Played			
	League	~	1
	F.A. Cup	~	
1953/54	Lincs Cup	~	
	Total	~	1

Born 29/12/1918 at Whisby, near Lincoln. Former Botolph United, Lincoln Rovers and Lincoln City player who made exactly 100 League appearances during his time at Sincil Bank. He also spent time on-loan at Stalybridge Celtic, before signing for Skegness Town. George made only one appearance for Grantham though, in the September 1953 Midland League fixture against Frickley Colliery, before joining Brigg Town. He was also a well known cricketer, playing many games for the Lincolnshire County side and the Ruston's team, where he worked for many years. George is now retired and still lives close to Lincoln.

Gorden Stimpson

Seasons Played			
	League	~	39 (4)
	F.A. Cup	~	3
1937/38-38/39	Lincs Cup	~	3 (1)
	Other	~	3
	Total	~	48 (5)

Outside-Left player who also made appearances for the now sadly defunct Rauceby Mental Hospital FC, with his Grantham debut in the November 1937 clash against Nottingham Forest Reserves. He scored his first goal for the club a month later at home to Lincoln City Reserves and was a valuable member of the Grantham team that finished in the runners-up position in the Midland League. But the following season his appearances came much less frequently, with his last game for Grantham in April 1939 when Frickley Colliery came to London Road for a league fixture.

Stoakes

Seasons Played			
	League	~	1
	F.A. Cup	~	
1919/20	Lincs Cup	~	
	Total	~	1

Only one known appearance for this player, the November 1919 Central Alliance game against Sutton Junction. He may be Henry Stoakes (born 17/12/1895 at Newark) who played for Newark Athletic, Notts County and Norwich City around this time.

Cyril Stocks

Seasons Played			
	League	~	219 (76)
	F.A. Cup	~	19 (12)
1934/35-39/40	Lincs Cup	~	16 (7)
	Other	~	13 (8)
1945/46	Total	~	267 (103)

Born 03/05/1905 at Pinxton, Derbyshire. Right-sided player who had previously played for South Normanton Amateurs, South Normanton Colliery and Nottingham Forest, taking over the position from Jack Spaven. He scored 79 goals in his 257 appearances there and upon joining Grantham it was reported in the press that "news of his transfer caused a lot of heartache in Nottingham". He made his debut in the opening match of the 1934/35 season at Boston United and scored his first two goals for the club in the record 13-0 victory in the FA Cup against Rufford Colliery a month later. Cyril played in every game in his first season at London Road, scoring five goals in the County Cup tie against Frodingham & Appleby United on the way to appearances in both the final and replay of the same competition against Boston United. The following season he played in the FA Cup First Round encounter against Notts County, another Lincolnshire Senior Cup Final, the Grantham Hospital Cup and finally the Wilson Cup played at Sincil Bank where he netted one of the goals in the 4-1 victory over a Lincoln League XI. The end of the 1936/37 season saw more cup final appearances for Cyril, in the Lincolnshire competition and both the local Hospital and Wilson Cups. The following season saw him finish as the club's highest scorer in the campaign that finished with Grantham as runners-up in the Midland League and he then continued to be one of the most prominent and valuable members of the team right up until the end of the decade. He returned to London Road after The Second World War, but only to make one more appearance in the FA Cup when Ollerton Colliery came to Grantham in October 1945 for a 3rd Qualifying Round tie.

Craig Stones

Seasons Played			
	League	~	7 (1)
	F.A. Cup	~	
1999/00	F.A. Trophy	~	
	League Cup	~	
	Lincs Cup	~	
	Total	~	7 (1)

Born 31/05/1980 at Scunthorpe. Midfielder who started out at Scunthorpe United and joined Grantham on-loan from Lincoln City. He played in the final seven fixtures of the 1999/00 season in an attempt to aid the club's escape from relegation, starting at home to Burton Albion, with his only goal scored against Atherstone United, and ending with the disappointment in the closing fixture against Crawley Town. Craig was soon released from Lincoln City, with 27 First team appearances to his name, and went on to play for Spalding United, Brigg Town and Gainsborough Trinity, before returning to Brigg where he was a member of their 2003 FA Vase winning side.

Luke Storey

Seasons Played			
1949/50	League	~	17 (6)
	F.A. Cup	~	
	Lincs Cup	~	3 (2)
	Total	~	20 (8)

Born 17/12/1920 at Dawdon. Former Blackhall Colliery and Lincoln City midfielder who made his Gingerbread debut in the September 1949 fixture against Halifax Town Reserves, but didn't score his first goal until the following January at Grimsby Town Reserves. He made the majority of his appearances after this date and scored both goals in the County Cup semi-final at Gainsborough Trinity, followed by an appearance in the Final, although Luke missed out on the replay. His last game for Grantham came in the Midland League fixture against York City Reserves at the end of April 1950 and he went on to play for Stalybridge Celtic and Corby Town.

Marshall Storey

Seasons Played			
1955/56-59/60	League	~	30
	F.A. Cup	~	2
	League Cup	~	
	Lincs Cup	~	1
	Total	~	33

Born 01/07/1933 at Warrington. Former Meadows Old Boys (Nottingham) player who made one appearance for the Grantham First team in April 1956 at Hull City Reserves and then played occasionally over the next few years as defensive cover. He played his last game for Grantham in the September 1959 league fixture at Corby Town Reserves and went on to Alfreton Town and then returned to Meadows Old Boys. Marshall worked as a Textiles Manager, but is now retired, still living in the Nottingham area. He is also a proficient Tennis and Badminton participant, playing to National level in Veteran competitions.

Storey

Seasons Played			
1925/26	League	~	1
	F.A. Cup	~	
	Lincs Cup	~	
	Total	~	1

Available team-sheets show just one appearance for this half-back in the club's first ever Midland League game against Mansfield Town at the start of the 1925/26 season. It is known that during his career he also played for Lincoln City Reserves and Boston.

Storey

Seasons Played			
1932/33	League	~	4
	F.A. Cup	~	
	Lincs Cup	~	
	Other	~	
	Total	~	4

Outside-Left player who also made appearances for Grantham Amateurs and is known to have played four times for our team during the 1932/33 season, although no details are available as to the actual matches.

Brian Storrow

Seasons Played			
1960/61-64/65	League	~	124 (39)
	F.A. Cup	~	9 (4)
	League Cup	~	
	Lincs Cup	~	6 (1)
	Total	~	139 (44)

Signed from Lincoln City School Old Boys FC and made his debut in the December 1960 Central Alliance (South) fixture against Anstey Nomads, scoring his first goal for the club a month later at home to Potton United. Brian played in most of the remaining games, but one of those that he missed out on was the Lincolnshire Senior Cup 'A' Final. The following season though, he was a near ever present member of the team, playing in the FA Cup First Round tie at Brierley Hill Alliance and the County Cup Final victory over Boston United. The 1962/63 season would prove to be the final campaign where Brian was a first choice member of the team, as the following season, Grantham's Midland League Championship winning year, saw him playing in about half of the total number of games. His final game for the club came in February 1965 when the team travelled up to Worksop Town for a Midland League fixture.

Steve Stoutt

Seasons Played			
1994/95-95/96	League	~	42 (9)
	F.A. Cup	~	2
	F.A. Trophy	~	2
	League Cup	~	2
	Lincs Cup	~	2
	Total	~	50 (9)

Born 05/04/1964 at Halifax. Previously played for Bradley, Huddersfield Town, Wolverhampton Wanderers, Grimsby Town, Lincoln City and Boston United, accumulating over 150 appearances during his time in The Football League. The 1993/94 season saw Steve as Team Manager for the Lincoln City Youth side, before his arrival at The Meres. His Grantham debut came in the January 1995 league fixture at Armitage, with his first goal for the club only a few weeks later against Ilkeston Town. He continued to play a prominent role in the side after the Summer interval, but the January 1996 game at Bedworth United was to be his last for the team, although he did have a brief spell as the club's caretaker manager around this time, in between Warren Ward and John Barnwell. Steve was last known to be working as a milkman in the Halifax area.

Strang

Seasons Played			
1911/12	League	~	2
	Total	~	2

Former Grantham Avenue half-back who played in the December 1911 Central Alliance fixture against Peterborough Loco and the match at home to Sutton Junction two months later, but it is not known how many other appearances he made for the club.

James Straughton

Seasons Played			
1919/20	League	~	1
	F.A. Cup	~	
	Lincs Cup	~	
	Total	~	1

Born circa 1892 at Workington. Inside-Right player who had scored twice in 15 appearances for Leicester Fosse, (renamed 'City' by the time of his arrival at London Road), just before World War One and then went on to play for Pontypridd and Leicester Imperial. James made just one appearance for Grantham in the November 1919 match at Hucknall Byron.

Street

Seasons Played			
1887/88-89/90	F.A. Cup	~	3
	Lincs Cup	~	3 (3)
	Other	~	40 (1)
	Total	~	46 (4)

Made his Grantham debut in the October 1887 friendly at Notts Olympic and scored his first two goals for the club in the County Cup against Boston at the end of the same month. He was a valuable member of the side during that period and played in the final of the Kettering Charity Cup against Cambridge Granta in March 1889. He made only one appearance for Grantham in the following season though, the Boxing Day victory over Notts Rangers.

Stanley Streets

Seasons Played			
1923/24	League	~	22 (22)
	F.A. Cup	~	1
	League Cup	~	1 (2)
	Lincs Cup	~	2 (1)
	Other	~	3 (3)
	Total	~	29 (28)

Born 25/06/1901 in Grantham. Exceptional centre-forward who first played for Grantham in the opening Central Alliance fixture of the 1923/24 season and although he didn't score his first goal for the club until his sixth match, he made up for lost time by netting four times in that game at home to Hucknall Byron. Stanley played in nearly every game that season and easily finished the campaign as the club's highest scorer. His skills had soon attracted the Football League scouts to London Road and in the Summer of 1924 he moved to Blackpool, followed by a transfer to Clapton (Leyton) Orient for £500, with £20 of this fee generously being forwarded to Grantham. He finished his professional career at Exeter City in 1929, with five goals scored in a total of 37 Football League appearances, and went on to play for Cork and West Stanley. Died 1961 at Newark.

Adrian Speed

Darren Standage

Chris Staniforth

Dave Stewart

Gorden Stimpson

Cyril Stocks

Brian Storrow

Steve Stoutt

Strang (1911/12)

Bill Stubley

Adam Sturgess

James Sullivan

Peter Sutton

Harry Swaby

Dave Swainston

John Tandy

Streets

Seasons Played			
	Lincs Cup	~	
	Other	~	1
1890/91	Total	~	1

Made only one appearance for Grantham in the January 1891 friendly at home to Nottingham Forest Reserves.

Striction

Seasons Played			
	F.A. Cup	~	
	Lincs Cup	~	
1887/88	Other	~	1
	Total	~	1

Played in just one game for the club, the October 1887 match at Notts Olympic.

Alistair Struthers

Seasons Played			
	League	~	1
	F.A. Cup	~	
1966/67	Total	~	1

Midfielder who made just one appearance for the club in the final Midland League fixture of the 1966/67 season at Retford Town.

Brian Stubbs

Seasons Played			
	League	~	30 (3)
	F.A. Cup	~	4
1981/82-82/83	F.A. Trophy	~	1
	League Cup	~	3
	Lincs Cup	~	1
	Other	~	1
	Total	~	40 (3)

Born 08/02/1950 at Keyworth. Began his career at Loughborough United, before spending the next 12 years at Notts County where he was renowned for his hard tackling and is still remembered today by the older generation of Magpies fans. As one recalls, "He was the only defender that in a clearance situation could get the ball and the opponent over the main stand!". After 486 appearances whilst at Meadow Lane and 27 goals, he signed for The Gingerbreads after turning down an offer from Bradford City and accepting some persuasion from his former team-mate and then Grantham Manager, Jon Nixon. He made his debut in the November 1981 league fixture at Burton Albion, with his first goal coming only weeks later against South Liverpool. Brian played in 20 games that season, a figure that was matched in the next campaign, with his final appearance in December 1982 at Workington. He went on to become Player/Manager at Calverton Miners Welfare and Keyworth United, but was last known to be working as a painter and decorator around the Nottingham area.

Bill Stubley

Seasons Played			
	League	~	4 (1)
	F.A. Cup	~	
1932/33	Lincs Cup	~	
	Other	~	
	Total	~	4 (1)

Born 11/061912 at Woolsthorpe. Had previously captained the Woolsthorpe Rovers side to Grantham League success in 1931/32, played for Grantham Amateurs, Grantham Thursday and trialed with Notts County. Bill scored for Grantham in the April 1933 Midland League game against Hull City Reserves but no details are known of his other three appearances. A noted cricketer, he also played for Woolsthorpe and Belvoir Estates. Bill worked all his life as a signalman on the railways and was also a noted baritone singer, gaining the nick-name the 'Singing Signalman'. In the late 1930's Bill moved to the South Yorkshire area, before returning home during The War and finally moving to Bottesford in 1970. Died 1999.

Adam Sturgess

Seasons Played			
	League	~	31 (1)
	F.A. Cup	~	
2004/05	F.A. Trophy	~	3 (1)
	League Cup	~	1
	Lincs Cup	~	2
	Total	~	37 (2)

Born 03/09/1980 at Kettering. Former Wellingborough Town, Rothwell Town and Corby Town midfielder who soon followed his Manager, Lee Glover, to The Meres in October 2004. His first game for the club came at the start of that month at home to Gloucester City and he played in all but one of the remaining fixtures during that campaign, scoring against Havant & Waterlooville and Banbury United. Adam also played in the April 2005 Lincolnshire Shield Final victory against Gainsborough Trinity. A vital element in Grantham's team, he remains with the club.

Sturtivant

Seasons Played			
	League	~	10
	F.A. Cup	~	
1891/92	Other	~	3
	Total	~	13

Defender who played in the club's inaugural league match in September 1891 at home to Notts County Rovers and many of the following games as well. Although his final appearance cannot be pinpointed, he seems to be missing from the team towards the end of that first season.

Sub

Seasons Played			
1879/80-80/81	F.A. Cup	~	
1886/87	Lincs Cup	~	
1889/90-90/91	Other	~	5
	Total	~	5

Assuming that he was just one individual, played very infrequently for the club with only a single game each season being able to be found. His debut for Grantham was in the March 1880 friendly at Sleaford and his last appearance in November 1890 at Kettering Town. However, not a single family what that surname, or any obvious deviation, exists in the 1881 census and my own theory is that here in the team-sheets are substitute players, possibly non club members, who turned out to make up the team.

Suddaby

Seasons Played			
	League	~	2
	F.A. Cup	~	
1950/51	Lincs Cup	~	
	Total	~	2

Forward who played in just the opening two fixtures of the 1950/51 season at Bradford City Reserves and Boston United. Possibly has the Christian name 'George'.

James Sullivan

Seasons Played			
	League	~	89 (88)
	F.A. Cup	~	7 (8)
1928/29-30/31	Lincs Cup	~	
	Other	~	1 (1)
	Total	~	97 (97)

Born 14/11/1904 at Burnley. Centre-Forward who began his career at Burnley, Barrow and Crewe College, before scoring 32 goals in 60 appearances for Crewe Alexandra and Notts County between 1924 and 1928. James scored twice on his Grantham debut in the opening league fixture of the 1928/29 season at Mansfield Town and appeared in the FA Cup Proper rounds against Rhyl Athletic and Wigan Borough. In his first year at London Road he scored three hat-tricks and even found the net five times in the games at Mexborough Athletic and Loughborough Corinthians to leave him with a final tally of 44 goals to his name. The following season saw him missing from more than half of the games, yet he still finished as the club's highest scorer, with one of those goals coming in the April 1930 Grantham Hospital Cup Final when Mansfield Town were defeated. Sadly no details are known as to his final appearance for the club, or even his concluding goal, but he was certainly still scoring up to the 6-2 defeat against Hull City Reserves at the end of April 1931. The following season he is known to have played for Loughborough Corinthians and later he joined Gainsborough Trinity. The figures quoted above are to the best of our knowledge accurate, meaning a tally of a goal a game for three complete seasons. James was one of the club's greatest centre-forwards, but with the passage of time seems to have been largely forgotten. He was also employed as a teacher and spent time at various East Midlands schools, including Southwark Street and Cottesmore.

Summerby

Seasons Played			
1890/91	League	~	4
1892/93	Lincs Cup	~	1
1894/95	Other	~	3
	Total	~	8

Played in the March 1891 friendly at home to Notts St George and then returned to the club at the worst possible moment, to appear in the October 1892 16-0 defeat at the hands of Notts County Rovers. He then played in many of the Grantham & District League fixtures of the 1894/95 season, but his final appearance for the club is not known. He may be Charles Summerby (born circa 1867 in Grantham), the only individual of that surname and of the right age group that was living in the County during the 1881 census.

Justin Sumner

Seasons Played			
1989/90	League	~	16 (1)
	F.A. Cup	~	
	F.A. Trophy	~	
	League Cup	~	
	Lincs Cup	~	
	Total	~	16 (1)

Born 19/10/1970 at Harrogate. Started his career as a Trainee at Leeds United, before moving to Doncaster Rovers, from where he joined Grantham on-loan after making just two appearances for their First Team. He made his debut for The Gingerbreads in the February 1989 league match at home to Bedworth United and only days later scored his only goal for the club at Stroud, with his final appearance in April against Barry Town. Justin later went on to play for Harrogate Town and Goole Town, but currently works as a football agent in London.

John Sutton

Seasons Played			
1973/74-76/77	League	~	13
	F.A. Cup	~	
	F.A. Trophy	~	1
	League Cup	~	1
	Lincs Cup	~	1
	Other	~	
	Total	~	16

Born 22/05/1951 at Nottingham. Goalkeeper, previously with Radcliffe Olympic and Nottingham Travellers, who covered for the unavailable Chris Gardiner in the April 1974 County Cup tie at home to Gainsborough Trinity, but then played up front in the league fixture against Dartford at the end of the season. He returned to his usual position to make a handful of appearances over the next few years, with his final game in September 1976 at home to Telford United. John then continued to play Sunday League football with Radcliffe Athletic and, until comparatively recently, occasionally turned out for the Radcliffe Veterans football team. He still lives just outside of Nottingham, working for a German lift company, but also runs his own on-course bookmakers.

J. Sutton

Seasons Played			
1919/20	League	~	4
1922/23	F.A. Cup	~	
	Lincs Cup	~	
	Other	~	
	Total	~	4

Former Arnold St Mary's and Hucknall Byron player who made his debut for Grantham in the January 1920 fixture at home to Mansfield Town. However he made only a couple of appearances for the club both that season and on his return in the 1922/23 campaign.

Peter Sutton

Seasons Played			
2003/04-04/05	League	~	23 (3)
	F.A. Cup	~	1
	F.A. Trophy	~	1
	League Cup	~	
	Lincs Cup	~	2
	Total	~	27 (3)

Born 02/09/1983 at Boston. Spent two years as a schoolboy at Lincoln City and previously played for Harrogate Town, plus was a member of the Armed Forces who spent time in Iraq. He made his debut for Grantham in the January 2004 league game at Crawley Town and scored his first goal for the club in the following match against Newport County. He then played for The Gingerbreads in the Lincolnshire County Shield Final victory over Gainsborough Trinity during March. The following season Peter found himself sat on the bench for many of the games and following his final appearance in the FA Trophy defeat at Havant & Waterlooville he was released by the club and joined Harrowby United.

Steve Sutton

Seasons Played			
1997/98	League	~	21
	F.A. Cup	~	
	F.A. Trophy	~	6
	League Cup	~	
	Lincs Cup	~	
	Total	~	27

Born 16/04/1961 at Hartington. Goalkeeper who made 257 appearances for Nottingham Forest during a 13 year spell, which also saw loan periods at Mansfield Town, Derby County, Coventry City and Luton Town. He played in Forest's 1989 and 1990 Littlewoods Cup winning sides, plus the Simod Cup winning team from the same era, before making a permanent move to Derby County in 1992 after a £300,000 transfer. Appearances then followed for Reading, on-loan, Birmingham City and Notts County with his professional appearance tally finally reaching 385. His first game for Grantham came in the December 1997 league fixture at Stafford Rangers, taking over the position from Peter Bulliman, and he went on to miss just one of the remaining games from that season. This meant that he played in some of the classic games during that Spring, including the fixtures against Hednesford Town, Ilkeston Town and Southport. His final appearance for The Gingerbreads came in the closing game at home to Stourbridge, with the resulting draw ensuring the League Championship for Grantham. Steve later went on to become Goalkeeping Coach at Leeds United and Notts County.

W. Sutton

Seasons Played			
1919/20	League	~	21 (3)
	F.A. Cup	~	2 (1)
	Lincs Cup	~	4
	Total	~	27 (4)

Made his Grantham debut in the opening Central Alliance fixture of the 1919/20 season at Long Eaton and scored his first goal for the club in the FA Cup replay against Boots Athletic which was played on Notts County's ground. He appeared in many of that season's games right up to the concluding one at Shirebrook.

Sutton

Seasons Played			
1884/85-89/90	F.A. Cup	~	6 (2)
	Lincs Cup	~	5 (3)
	Other	~	52 (16)
	Total	~	63 (21)

First played for the club in the friendly at Notts Rangers in January 1885, but as a new member of the team was not picked for the victorious County Cup Final a few months later. His first appearance for the club in the following season saw him score twice in the February 1886 game at home to Sleaford and this was soon followed by four goals in the 11-0 thrashing of Peterborough. It was therefore no surprise when he became a more prominent member of the side for the start of the 1886/87 campaign and he continued to be over the next few years, with the highlight of an appearance in the Kettering Charity Cup Final in March of 1889. His final season with the club saw him restricted to just one appearance though, the Boxing Day 1889 clash against Notts Rangers.

Sutton

Seasons Played			
1914/15	League	~	1
	F.A. Cup	~	
	Lincs Cup	~	
	Total	~	1

Known to have played in the first home league fixture of the 1914/15 season against Loughborough Corinthians, but there are no details as to any other appearances that he may have made.

Harry Swaby

Seasons Played			
1934/35-37/38	League	~	140 (1)
	F.A. Cup	~	16 (1)
	Lincs Cup	~	12 (2)
	Other	~	5
	Total	~	173 (4)

Born 22/01/1906 at Grimsby. Defender who previously played for Grimsby YMCA, Cleethorpes Town, Grimsby Town, Barnsley and

Scarborough, (where he was Club Captain), scoring twice in his 62 Football League appearances. He made his Grantham debut in the club's first Midland League fixture of the 1934/35 season at Boston United and highlights soon included an appearance in the 13-0 record FA Cup win over Rufford Colliery, plus games in both the County Cup Final and replay. The 1935/36 season saw Harry promoted to Captain at Grantham and this was followed by an appearance in the FA Cup First Round encounter against Notts County and his first goal for the club in the 7-0 January defeat of Hull City Reserves. However, with him absent from several of the games at the end of the season it meant that he missed out on the Lincolnshire Senior Cup Final and the local Hospital Final, but he was back in time for the concluding Wilson Cup fixture, which saw Grantham run out 4-1 winners against a Lincoln League XI. Finally in April of 1937 Harry played in a winning County Cup Final team, when Grantham beat Boston United and his last season with the club saw the team finish as runners-up in the Midland League. Harry played right up until the end of that campaign, with his final league fixture at Scunthorpe & Lindsey United in April 1938, just before appearances in the Spalding Victory Cup and the finale of the Champions versus Runners-Up trophy. Harry also played for Gainsborough Trinity at some point in his career, possibly in the season between leaving London Road and the start of World War Two. Died 03/11/1982 at Grimsby.

Paul Swaby

Seasons Played	League	~	2 (3)
	F.A. Cup	~	
1962/63	Total	~	2 (3)

Scored a hat-trick on his debut in the November 1962 defeat of Skegness Town, but then made only one more appearance for the team a week later at Ilkeston Town.

Dave Swainston

Seasons Played	League	~	147 (4)
	F.A. Cup	~	5
1988/89-91/92	F.A. Trophy	~	3
	League Cup	~	20 (1)
	Lincs Cup	~	2
	Total	~	177 (5)

Born 07/11/1962 at Chelmsford. Former British Students representative who previously played for Ilkeston Town, Heanor Town, Eastwood Town and Alfreton Town.. He made his Grantham debut by coming off the bench during the November 1988 league fixture at home to Gloucester City and remained in the side for many of the subsequent games as well, scoring his first goal in January 1989 against Rushden Town. Dave missed just one game during the 1989/90 season and three games the following year, with an appearance in the final league game at London Road against Dudley Town at the end of September 1990. Just under a year later, Dave played in the first game at the new Meres stadium, as Grantham played hosts to Ilkeston Town in the FA Cup and his final game for the club came in March 1992 at home to Hinckley Town. The following season he went on to play for Gresley Rovers and later moved to Belper Town.

Carl Swan

Seasons Played	League	~	13 (1)
	F.A. Cup	~	
1982/83	F.A. Trophy	~	
	League Cup	~	2
	Lincs Cup	~	
	Other	~	
	Total	~	15 (1)

Born 12/12/1957 at Sheffield. Son of the former England player, Peter Swan, who was banned for seven years by The FA after being jailed for match fixing. Carl previously played for Matlock Town, Buxton, Burton Albion, Doncaster Rovers after a £7,000 transfer and Rochdale, making a total of 18 League appearances. His Grantham debut came in the February 1983 league fixture at home to Marine and he played in all but two of the remaining games, scoring against Burton Albion, with his final appearance in the closing match at Matlock Town. He went on to play for Chesterfield Reserves, Goole Town, Worksop Town, plus made returns to Matlock Town and Buxton.

Swann

Seasons Played	League	~	1
	F.A. Cup	~	
1936/37	Lincs Cup	~	
	Other	~	
	Total	~	1

Goalkeeper who also played for Mowbray's Sports and covered for the unavailable Arthur Jepson in the final match of the 1936/37 season at home to Denaby United.

Ben Sweet

Seasons Played	League	~	4
	F.A. Cup	~	
1998/99	F.A. Trophy	~	
	League Cup	~	
	Lincs Cup	~	
	Total	~	4

Born 27/07/1978 at Huddersfield. Midfielder who after being released by Huddersfield Town, was spotted practising in a local park by a photographer talent-spotting for Sony. His overhead kicks were then soon filmed at the McAlpine Stadium and used in trailer advertisements for Playstation during televised coverage of Champions League matches on *ITV* and *Sky Sports*. Ben's football career then took him to Caernarfon Town and Cambridge City, before his arrival at Grantham, although he made just four consecutive appearances during January and February 1999 against Hastings Town, Burton Albion, Bath City and Gloucester City. He left both The Meres and England for the chance to play football in America, but soon returned to the country. After Ben's starring role in the TV commercial, he also appeared in *A Touch of Frost*, modelled for *Umbro*, and appeared on a fashion show televised on *Sky*. He is currently working as a First Director in the Film and TV industry and has also recently turned out for Wakefield & Emley FC.

Swindall

Seasons Played	League	~	2 (2)
	F.A. Cup	~	
1933/34	Lincs Cup	~	
	Other	~	
	Total	~	2 (2)

Scored in the Central Combination fixtures against Matlock Town in March 1934 and the closing game at RAF Cranwell, but no information is available to show any other appearances he may have made for the club.

Kevin Swinscoe

Seasons Played	League	~	19
	F.A. Cup	~	2
1980/81	F.A. Trophy	~	1
	League Cup	~	1
	Lincs Cup	~	3
	Other	~	1
	Total	~	27

Former regular in the Nottingham Forest Reserves team, before spending a period playing for Frankston City in Australia. He made his debut for Grantham in the opening County Cup tie of the 1980/81 season and played in most of the games in the first half of that season, including the Lincolnshire Senior County Cup Final against Lincoln City and the Redmayne Trophy game at home to Nottingham Forest. Kevin made his last appearance for the club in December 1980 at Lancaster City.

Albert Sykes

Seasons Played	League	~	38 (1)
	F.A. Cup	~	2
1932/33	Lincs Cup	~	2
	Other	~	2
	Total	~	44 (1)

Born 29/09/1900 at Shirebrook. Experienced left-half who had previously played for Maltby Victoria, Maltby Main Colliery Welfare, before making his League debut with Birmingham City in 1924. Transfers then followed to Brighton & Hove Albion, Lincoln City, Peterborough & Fletton United and Luton Town, with one goal to his name in a professional career total of 61 appearances. Albert appeared for Grantham in most of the 1932/33 season's fixtures after taking over the role from Stevenson, including the

March friendly against Arsenal. His only goal for the club came in the November 1932 Midland League match against Doncaster Rovers Reserves. Died 1994 at Rotherham.

Sykes

Seasons Played			
	League	~	1
	F.A. Cup	~	
1945/46	Lincs Cup	~	
	Total	~	1

Made just one appearance for Grantham in the October 1945 league defeat at Denaby United.

Taft

Seasons Played			
	Lincs Cup	~	1
	Other	~	2
1889/90	Total	~	3

Made his Grantham debut in the October 1889 friendly at home to Long Eaton Midland and then played in the following two games against Radcliffe and Lincoln Rangers in the County Cup. Possibly Harry Taft (born circa 1869 in Grantham), the son of a Bridge End Road shopkeeper.

Kyle Talbot

Seasons Played			
	League	~	17 (3)
	F.A. Cup	~	
1992/93	F.A. Trophy	~	1
	League Cup	~	1
	Lincs Cup	~	1
	Total	~	20 (3)

Born 12/01/1974 at Rotherham. Began his career as a Trainee at Grimsby Town and then made his debut for Grantham in the opening County Cup tie of the 1992/93 season at Lincoln City, scoring his first goal in November at Gresley Rovers. Kyle netted a brace in the fixture against Yate Town a month later, but left The Meres along with many of his team-mates and Manager after the January 1993 home game against Barri Town. He went on to play for Gainsborough Trinity, Maltby Main and Parkgate.

John Tandy

Seasons Played			
	League	~	29 (1)
	F.A. Cup	~	2
1981/82	F.A. Trophy	~	1
	League Cup	~	2
	Lincs Cup	~	2
	Other	~	1
	Total	~	37 (1)

Former Retford Town, Mossley, Worksop Town and Corby Town full-back whose first game for Grantham came in the August 1981 County Cup tie against Boston United. John played in many of the games during that season, including the November match against Nottingham Forest, with his only goal for the club at the end of March 1982 in the 4-0 win at Oswestry Town. His final appearance for Grantham was in the April defeat at Bangor City, with him viewing from the substitute's bench in the one remaining fixture at Macclesfield Town.

J. Tarrant

Seasons Played			
	League	~	1
	F.A. Cup	~	
1921/22	Lincs Cup	~	
	Total	~	1

Available records show him playing just the one game for Grantham in the April 1922 Central Alliance fixture at Ilkeston United. He was unfortunately killed sometime later in a mining accident.

E. Tasker

Seasons Played			
	League	~	2
	F.A. Cup	~	
1921/22	Lincs Cup	~	1
	Total	~	3

Reserves player who had also made appearances for Ilkeston United and played in the First team fixture against Grimsby Haycroft Rovers in December 1921 and most probably many of the following games as well. He was certainly still playing for the side by the league match at New Hucknall Colliery in April.

Dave Taylor

Seasons Played			
	League	~	11
	F.A. Cup	~	2
1970/71-72/73	F.A. Trophy	~	
	League Cup	~	1
	Lincs Cup	~	1
	Other	~	
	Total	~	15

Brother of Gerry Taylor and goalkeeper who first covered for Chris Gardiner in the December 1970 league fixture against Skegness Town, whilst the same month he also played in the FA Cup Second Round tie at home to Rotherham United. Obviously his appearances were limited during his time with the club, with his last game at the end of December 1972 at home to Bury Town. Dave worked in the financial industry in town for many years, but is thought to be now in the Nottingham area.

Dave Taylor

Seasons Played			
	League	~	121 (46)
	F.A. Cup	~	8 (5)
1996/97-01/02	F.A. Trophy	~	14 (6)
	League Cup	~	11 (5)
	Lincs Cup	~	6
	Total	~	160 (62)

Born 25/09/1969 at Nottingham. Previously played for Dunkirk, before the first of three spells at Ilkeston Town, followed by GPT Plessey, Arnold Town and Gresley Rovers. Dave arrived at Grantham on-loan in the Spring of 1996 from Ilkeston and made his debut in the March defeat at home to Tamworth, with his first goal the following week at Stourbridge. He netted a hat-trick against Hinckley Town, but after seven appearances he returned to Ilkeston. He was then signed by the club for £2,500 at the start of the following season and immediately continued his striking partnership with Dave King. He played in the majority of that Championship winning campaign and also scored the last minute winner against Hednesford Town to send Grantham into the Quarter-Final of the FA Trophy, where he again played in both the ties against Southport. April of 1998 saw a hat-trick for him in the 5-0 victory over Solihull Borough and he then played in the closing fixture of the season at home to Stourbridge as the team secured the necessary draw for the title. Dave was playing for Stamford Town at the start of the 1998/99 campaign, then joined King's Lynn and Wollaton, but soon returned to Grantham where he finished the season with 26 appearances to his name, including the October 1998 FA Cup final qualifying tie at Tamworth. Although Dave made only 11 appearances in the 1999/00 season, he was back as a near permanent member of the side after the Summer interval and scored one of the goals in the 5-4 defeat at Rushden & Diamonds in the FA Cup. Dave continued to score several important goals in Grantham's promotion winning year, although by now his appearances were starting to diminish. His final goal came in the April 2002 fixture at Dartford, with his last appearance in the closing game at Banbury when he came off the bench to replace Rick Ranshaw. He went on to play for Barwell, Gedling Town, Radcliffe Olympic and Arnold Town, before retiring through injury in October 2004.

David Taylor

Seasons Played			
	League	~	4
	F.A. Cup	~	
1992/93	F.A. Trophy	~	
	League Cup	~	
	Lincs Cup	~	
	Total	~	4

Lincoln United player who made four appearances towards the end of the 1992/93 season, in both fixtures against Hinckley Town, plus the game versus Sutton Coldfield Town and the closing match at home to Bridgnorth Town, before returning to Lincoln.

D. Taylor

Seasons Played			
	League	~	1
	F.A. Cup	~	
1932/33	Lincs Cup	~	
	Other	~	1 (1)
	Total	~	2 (1)

Former Grantham Amateurs player who made just one league appearance for our club, but also scored in the local Hospital Cup tie against Grantham St John's in January 1933.

Gerry Taylor

Seasons Played			
	League	~	348 (4)
	F.A. Cup	~	25 (2)
1970/71-80/81	F.A. Trophy	~	24
	League Cup	~	33 (1)
	Lincs Cup	~	13
	Other	~	4
	Total	~	447 (7)

Born 1946 at Sleaford. Brother of Dave Taylor. Gerry signed for Grantham from Sleaford Town after previously being on the books of Lincoln City and also playing Sunday League football for Sleaford Rangers. He made his Grantham debut in the October 1970 league fixture at Long Eaton United and scored his first goal for the club the following month at The City Ground, Nottingham, in the FA Cup second replay tie against Gainsborough Trinity. Only two days later Gerry played in the club's first ever victory over a Football League side in the Cup, when Stockport County came away from London Road with a 2-1 defeat. Just to cap an interesting first couple of months with Grantham he then appeared in the following round against Rotherham United. The end of that first season saw a Midland League Championship medal and Gerry also played in the first leg of the League Cup final, although Andy Crawford took his place in the return match against Arnold. The 1971/72 season saw another league title for the club, and for Gerry there was an appearance in the FA Trophy Quarter-Final tie against Yeovil Town, but the County Cup Final in May saw Crawford once more replacing him. As Grantham progressed into the Southern League, he finished that first season having missed only four games, with another League title winner's medal, plus an appearance in the FA Cup First Round against Bradford City. A year later he played in both the Cup ties against Rochdale and January 1974 saw his appearance in the biggest game in the club's history as Second Division leaders, Middlesbrough, came to London Road for a Third Round Proper tie. He continued to make many appearances over the next couple of years, although by comparison highlights are hard to find and Gerry himself was injured just before the FA Cup game against Port Vale in November 1975. His prominence in the side then continued to the 1978/79 season, when the team won the Southern League, Division One North Championship, whilst the club's entrance into the Northern Premier League coincided with Gerry's promotion to Club Captain. His final goal came in the September 1980 FA Cup replay against Long Eaton United, whilst the end of that year saw his appearance in the Redmayne Trophy tie against Nottingham Forest. However, his last appearance for Grantham was at one of the lowest points during that era, the February 1981 7-0 defeat at Marine. It was a sad end to such a long career with The Gingerbreads.

Jim Taylor

Seasons Played			
	League	~	16 (9)
	F.A. Cup	~	
1945/46	Lincs Cup	~	1 (1)
1947/48	Total	~	17 (10)

Played in four of the final league fixtures of the 1945/46 season, beginning with a goal at Mansfield Town Reserves, but Jim had to wait nearly two years before his next appearance for the club. He scored again on his return in the entertaining January 1948 league fixture at Gainsborough Trinity, although the team came away with a 10-6 defeat. He then played in many of the remaining fixtures, up to the concluding one at Bradford Park Avenue Reserves, which also saw his final goal for the club.

Paul Taylor

Seasons Played			
	League	~	38 (3)
	F.A. Cup	~	
1987/88	F.A. Trophy	~	
	League Cup	~	8 (1)
1990/91-91/92	Lincs Cup	~	
	Total	~	46 (4)

Born 20/12/1966 at Leith. Former Mansfield Town, Chesterfield Reserves, Matlock Town and Belper Town player who made his Grantham debut in the March 1988 league game at home to Buckingham Town and, after spending the following match viewing from the substitute's bench, started in all of the remaining fixtures of that season. After making appearances for Sutton Town and playing the game in Finland, he rejoined Grantham in the Autumn of 1990 just as the club began their spell sharing with Spalding United, scoring his first goal in December 1990 at Corby Town. A year later he scored again versus Corby and netted a brace past the Hinckley Town goalkeeper, but the league game at Tamworth just before Christmas 1991 was to be his last for the club and he then returned to Finland, although by 1995 he was back in this country and playing for Frickley Athletic.

'Pim' Taylor

Seasons Played			
	League	~	197 (2)
	F.A. Cup	~	23 (1)
1945/46-54/55	Lincs Cup	~	11
1958/59	Total	~	231 (3)

Christened Leslie Taylor and came from the Lincoln area, but it seemed sensible to keep his nickname as the above heading due to the fact that very few people actually knew what his real name was! He made his debut in the September 1945 match against Shrewsbury Town and in a season that saw many different players pull on the Grantham shirt, Pim was a near constant member of the side, missing only one of the remaining league games. He played in both the legs of the FA Cup ties against Kettering Town and Mansfield Town, plus the County Cup Final against Boston United in April of 1946. Just under a year later Pim scored his first goal for the club at Scarborough, shortly before another appearance in the Lincolnshire Senior Cup Final, this time against Gainsborough Trinity. November of 1947 saw him play in the FA Cup First Round against Stockton and two years later he appeared in the same stage of the competition at Wrexham. At the end of that season he played in another County Cup Final, but by now Pim's appearances were becoming more infrequent and he was missing from the replay against Boston United at the end of April. Over the next few years he continued to make a handful of appearances each season for the club, although two came unexpectedly in August 1952. The league match at Peterborough United was about to commence with a near 9,000 crowd eagerly awaiting the teams entrance. Unfortunately, Ron Hewitt, Grantham's goalkeeper, still hadn't turned up so Pim was asked to take over the important role! The following week at London Road, Ron *did* arrive, but Pim was still told to keep the position, possibly as a punishment to the AWOL 'keeper. However after this game against Halifax Town Reserves and another loss for the club, Ron was allowed to resume his customary position for the following match. Pim continued to notch up occasional appearances for the next few years, with his last game not coming until the April 1959 fixture at Blyth Spartans. He is also known to have played for Lincoln City at some point in his career, possibly at the start, but remained at London Road after the end of his playing days as the club's trainer. Pim was awarded a joint testimonial with Ronnie Harbertson in May 1967 when Nottingham Forest sent a side to London Road and he continued in his trainer's capacity until 1978.

Sam Taylor

Seasons Played			
	League	~	21 (13)
	F.A. Cup	~	
1928/29	Lincs Cup	~	
	Other	~	1 (1)
	Total	~	22 (14)

Born 17/09/1893 at Sheffield. Forward with a long footballing career behind him, with clubs previously represented including Atlas & Norfolk Steelworks, Silverwood Colliery and Huddersfield Town (with guest appearances for Rotherham County and Bradford Park Avenue during World War One), with the highlight of an FA Cup Final appearance in 1920 at Stamford Bridge. Sam then signed for Sheffield Wednesday, Mansfield Town, Southampton and Halifax Town, before coming to London Road. He played for Grantham in the second half of the 1928/29 season, scoring his first goal for the club in February 1929 against Shirebrook. Although Sam was a long way behind the club's highest scorer, James Sullivan, he did finish with the second best record of the year, a remarkable achievement considering the amount of games that he had missed. During the Summer though, he was transferred to Chesterfield and in 1931 finally finished his Football League career with 113 goals scored in 315 games, before joining Llanelli. Died March 1973 at Sheffield.

Scott Taylor

Seasons Played			
	League	~	29 (8)
	F.A. Cup	~	1
1995/96	F.A. Trophy	~	1
	League Cup	~	1
	Lincs Cup	~	2 (1)
	Total	~	34 (9)

Born 23/12/1970 at Dunfermline. Previously with Lincoln United, RAF Waddington and the RAF representative side, before joining Grantham. He scored on his debut in the opening County Cup tie of the 1995/96 season against Lincoln City and also scored in his final appearance at home to Bridgnorth Town at the end of April 1996. Scott went on to play for Cambridge City, Charterton, Hayes, Banbury United and Harrowby United.

Taylor

Seasons Played			
	F.A. Cup	~	
	Other	~	1
1880/81	Total	~	1

Made just one appearance for the club in November 1880 during a friendly held at Gainsborough.

Taylor

Seasons Played			
	League	~	3 (1)
	F.A. Cup	~	
1919/20	Lincs Cup	~	
	Total	~	3 (1)

Centre-Forward who had also played for Lincoln City and scored on his Grantham debut in January 1920 at Gresley Rovers, but then only played in the following two games against New Hucknall Colliery and Hucknall Byron. Assuming that he had made at least one First team appearance during his time at Sincil Bank, he may be either Frank Taylor (1887-1928) or James Taylor, both strikers there in the early 20th Century.

Taylor

Seasons Played			
	League	~	2
	F.A. Cup	~	1 (1)
1930/31	Lincs Cup	~	
	Total	~	3 (1)

Scored in the FA Cup tie against Boots Athletic in October 1930, but only came into the First team a couple of other times during that year.

Andy Teare

Seasons Played			
	League	~	1
	F.A. Cup	~	
2003/04-04/05	F.A. Trophy	~	
	League Cup	~	
	Lincs Cup	~	1
	Total	~	2

Former Grantham Youths and Reserves player and also the son of the club's Director, Paul Teare. Andy came off the substitute's bench to replace Jamie Clarke in the final league match of the 2003/04 season at Weymouth. In February 2005 he signed dual forms allowing him to also play for Shepshed Dynamo Reserves, whilst the following month he was able to gain another appearance for The Gingerbreads, replacing Adam Sturgess during the County Shield victory over Stamford.

Teesdale

Seasons Played			
	F.A. Cup	~	
	Lincs Cup	~	
1878/79	Other	~	10 (1)
1880/81-81/82	Total	~	10 (1)

Made his debut in the opening match of the 1878/79 season at Sleaford and despite playing in many of the early games from that year, was limited to friendly appearances only. He returned to the club two years later, scoring in the October 1880 fixture at Huntingdon County and although we know he was still occasionally playing a year later, the exact date of his final game is not known.

Mick Tennant

Seasons Played			
	League	~	1
	F.A. Cup	~	
1969/70	F.A. Trophy	~	
	League Cup	~	
	Lincs Cup	~	
	Other	~	
	Total	~	1

Born 06/05/1943 at Lincoln. Goalkeeper who made just one appearance for the First team, covering for Chris Gardiner in the August 1969 Midland League fixture at Long Eaton United and kept a clean sheet in the 4-0 win. Died 22/07/2004.

Tim Thacker

Seasons Played			
	League	~	118 (2)
	F.A. Cup	~	10
1980/81-82/83	F.A. Trophy	~	2
	League Cup	~	9
	Lincs Cup	~	7
	Other	~	5
	Total	~	151 (2)

Born 19/06/1962 at Nottingham. Former regular in Notts County's Reserve side who made his debut for Grantham in the second County Cup tie of the 1980/81 season at home to Gainsborough Trinity. Tim's first goal for the club came a month later against Macclesfield Town and the next couple of months saw appearances for him against Lincoln City in the County competition final and Nottingham Forest in the Redmayne Trophy. In October 1982 he played in the Lincolnshire County Senior Cup Final at Scunthorpe United and the FA Cup final qualifying round tie against Telford United. His only other goal for Grantham was in the April 1983 league match at Netherfield, with his final appearance in the following closing game at Matlock Town. Tim went on to join Shepshed Charterhouse and Kettering Town, although he broke his leg in a match there at the start of the 1986/87 season. He currently lives in Bath and owns two greeting card shops in Somerset.

Thomas

Seasons Played			
	Other	~	1
1875/76	Total	~	1

Made only one appearance for the club in the November 1875 game at home to the Third Lincolnshire Volunteer Rifles.

Thomas

Seasons Played			
	League	~	
	Lincs Cup	~	
1909/10	Other	~	1
	Total	~	1

Played in the December 1909 Grantham Minor Cup tie against Gonerby Town, but no information exists to show any league appearances that he may have made for the club.

Brian Thompson

Seasons Played			
	League	~	27
	F.A. Cup	~	
1964/65-65/66	Total	~	27

Born 20/10/1938 in Grantham. Goalkeeper with previous experience at Brush Sports, Kettering Town, Peterborough United Reserves, Wisbech Town and Lockheed Leamington. Brian took over the role from Graham Clarke for the January 1965 match at Scarborough, but despite playing in every one of the remaining fixtures that season, had to cover for Jim McDowall in the following campaign. His final appearance for Grantham came in March 1966 at home to Alfreton Town and despite being offered a contract by Stamford decided to give up the game. Various professions continued, ending with a family fashion business, although he is now retired and living in Nottingham.

Colin Thompson

Seasons Played			
	League	~	245 (80)
	F.A. Cup	~	21 (4)
1960/61-63/64	F.A. Trophy	~	16 (3)
	League Cup	~	16 (1)
1970/71-74/75	Lincs Cup	~	10 (4)
	Other	~	2 (1)
	Total	~	310 (93)

Born 25/07/1942 in Mombassa, Kenya. Scored on his debut in the final league fixture of the 1960/61 season at Spalding United and then, in his first game after the Summer break at Skegness Town, netted four more goals as well. Colin played in that season's FA Cup First Round tie at Brierley Hill Alliance and the victorious Lincolnshire Senior Cup Final at home to Boston United. The following season he made only ten appearances, but by the 1963/64 campaign, Colin was playing some of his best football and helped put Grantham well on their way to the Midland League Championship, before his final match at Long Eaton United in March. He soon signed for Peterborough United for what was described by the club as "a quite reasonable fee" and had a successful spell there making 94 appearances and scoring 18 goals, using his first Christian name of Peter, until the end of the decade. He was back in the Grantham team after a brief spell at Nuneaton Borough for the start of the 1970/71 season at Belper and Colin was soon awarded the position of Club Captain. Within a couple of weeks he had shown the fans that he was still as good as ever by putting four goals past the Retford Town 'keeper, but despite playing in most of that season's games, Colin was forced to spectate from the substitutes bench at the two FA Cup games against Stockport County and Rotherham United. Compensation arrived the following Spring though, with appearances in both legs of the Midland League Cup Final, plus the season finished with a League Championship medal. In the 1971/72 campaign he played in the FA Trophy Quarter-Final match at home to Yeovil Town and won a County Cup winner's medal after the team defeated Scunthorpe United, to go with his award for the team's second consecutive Midland League title. His prominence continued in the side as they progressed into the Southern League, winning another League Championship, and he also played in the November 1972 FA Cup First Round Proper at Bradford City. Colin missed just two League Cup ties during the 1973/74 season, giving him more FA Cup memories as the club beat Hillingdon Borough and Rochdale in the Proper rounds, before finally going out to Jack Charlton's Middlesbrough side. He scored his final goal for the club in March 1975 at home to Stourbridge, with his last appearance at the end of the same month at Burton Albion when he suffered a broken leg. Colin now lives in the Peterborough area and has returned to his original career as a Motor Vehicle Technician.

G. Thompson

Seasons Played			
	League	~	2
	F.A. Cup	~	
1932/33-33/34	Lincs Cup	~	
	Other	~	2
	Total	~	4

Local young goalkeeper who also turned out for Barkston, but sadly there is no information which shows the particular games he played in for Grantham.

Kenneth Thompson

Seasons Played			
	League	~	35 (17)
	F.A. Cup	~	6 (4)
1947/48	Lincs Cup	~	1
	Total	~	42 (21)

Forward, possibly from Doncaster Rovers, who first played for Grantham in the opening league match of the 1947/48 season at Scarborough. He scored his first goal for the club a few days later at London Road against Boston United and the following month, at Bradford City Reserves, he netted his only hat-trick for the club. In that season's FA Cup Kenneth played in the 11-1 thrashing of Ilkeston Town, the First Round Proper match at Stockton and missed only seven matches all season, playing right up until the closing fixture at Bradford Park Avenue Reserves.

Thompson

Seasons Played			
	League	~	2 (2)
	F.A. Cup	~	1 (1)
1914/15	Lincs Cup	~	
	Total	~	3 (3)

Was playing for Grantham by the time of the first home match of the 1914/15 season against Loughborough Corinthians, but other than the FA Cup tie against Basford United and the Boxing Day clash against Kettering Town, both games which saw him scoring, little is known about any other appearances that he may have made.

Thompson

Seasons Played			
	League	~	1
	F.A. Cup	~	
1921/22	Lincs Cup	~	
	Total	~	1

Available match reports show him playing just the one game, the April 1922 Central Alliance fixture at New Hucknall Colliery.

Kevin Thomson

Seasons Played			
	League	~	
	F.A. Cup	~	
1999/00	F.A. Trophy	~	
	League Cup	~	2
	Lincs Cup	~	
	Total	~	2

Made just two appearances for the First team by coming off the bench to play in the Dr Marten's League Cup ties against Rothwell Town and Cambridge City in November and December of 1999.

Thornton

Seasons Played			
	League	~	1
	F.A. Cup	~	
1946/47	Lincs Cup	~	
	Total	~	1

Played only once for Grantham in the September 1946 draw at Boston United.

Adrian Thorpe

Seasons Played			
	League	~	10 (1)
	F.A. Cup	~	
1997/98	F.A. Trophy	~	4 (1)
	League Cup	~	1
	Lincs Cup	~	
	Total	~	15 (2)

Born 25/11/1963 at Chesterfield. Began his career at Mansfield Town and Heanor Town, before making over 150 League appearances for Bradford City, Tranmere Rovers (on-loan), Notts County, where he played alongside Gary Mills, Walsall and Northampton Town. After a period playing in Hong Kong for Instant Dict, Adrian then turned out for Kettering Town and Arnold Town, before joining Grantham. He scored on his debut in the January 1998 FA Trophy tie against Leigh RMI and although several of his appearances then came from the substitute's bench, they did include some classic games like the 6-0 demolition of Ilkeston Town and both matches against Southport. Adrian's other goal came in the April defeat at Moor Green, with his final appearance in the next fixture against Blakenall. After leaving The Meres he went on to return to Arnold.

Len Thorpe

Seasons Played			
	League	~	123 (47)
	F.A. Cup	~	11 (4)
1948/49-51/52	Lincs Cup	~	7
	Total	~	141 (51)

Born 07/06/1924 at Warsop. Former Nottingham Forest and Mansfield Town right-winger who made his debut in the opening game of the 1948/49 season at Scarborough and scored his first goal a couple of weeks later in the home match against Boston United. He played in the majority of that season's fixtures, as he did the following year, but that campaign included appearances for Len in the FA Cup First Round at Wrexham and both the County Cup Final and the replay against Boston United. The opening fixture of the 1950/51 season at Bradford City Reserves saw his first hat-trick for the club, but a year later he was scoring in his final game for Grantham at the London Road visit of Worksop Town. Len was forced to retire from the game after that due to a dislocated knee.

Dave Taylor

Gerry Taylor

Paul Taylor

'Pim' Taylor

Andy Teare

Tim Thacker

Colin Thompson

Keith Tomlinson

Paul Tomlinson

Tonge (1912/13-13/14)

Arthur Treadgold

Ian Turner

Jason Turner

Phil Turner

Gary Twynham

Alan Wade

Tilford

Seasons Played			
1910/11	League	~	1
	FA Amt. Cup	~	
	League Cup	~	
	Lincs Cup	~	
	Other	~	
	Total	~	1

Forward who appeared in the January 1911 Midland Amateur Alliance game at West Bridgford Albion, but it is not known whether he played in any other games for the club.

Bert Tinklin

Seasons Played			
1931/32	League	~	39 (10)
	Lincs Cup	~	1 (1)
	Other	~	1 (1)
	Total	~	41 (12)

Born 16/06/1910 at Nottingham. Outside-Left player who made his debut for Grantham in the opening match of the 1931/32 season at Loughborough Corinthians and scored his first two goals for the club the following month at home to Doncaster Rovers Reserves. He is known to have played in most of that season's games, but no information is available to show the end of his Grantham career. Bert went on to play for Nuneaton Town and Folkestone, before moving into The Football League with Aldershot and Watford, where he scored a total of eight goals in 41 First team matches between 1934 and 1937. His career is also known to have taken him to Heanor Town, Loughborough Corinthians and Brierley Hill, although at what point is not known.

Pete Tobin

Seasons Played			
1973/74	League	~	
	F.A. Cup	~	
	F.A. Trophy	~	
	League Cup	~	1
	Lincs Cup	~	
	Total	~	1

Born 22/06/1953 in London. Previously played for Lincoln United, Lincoln City Reserves and Grantham Reserves. Pete made just one appearance for the First team when he started the February 1974 Southern League Cup tie at home to Nuneaton Borough, but was replaced during the game by Mick Farmer. He went on to return to Lincoln United, moved to Lincoln Claytons and then became Manager of Hop Pole Celtic. Pete still lives in the Lincoln area, works as a refuse collector and is recognised as somewhat of a local character, gaining the nickname 'The Flying Dustman'!

Bob Todd

Seasons Played			
1981/82-82/83	League	~	10 (1)
	F.A. Cup	~	
	F.A. Trophy	~	
	League Cup	~	1
	Lincs Cup	~	2
	Other	~	1
	Total	~	14 (1)

Midfield player who started out as an Apprentice at Liverpool, before moving to Scarborough. After a lengthy lay-off due to injury he joined Grantham, where his first match came in the January 1982 league game at home to King's Lynn. He made occasional appearances as cover over the next few months, with his only goal scored in the March 1982 fixture at Lancaster City. His last game for Grantham, against Marine at the end of August, saw Bob carried off the pitch and detained in Grantham Hospital with concussion. He soon recovered though and was back playing, this time for Gainsborough Trinity.

Keith Tomlinson

Seasons Played			
1968/69-71/72	League	~	102 (24)
	F.A. Cup	~	11 (2)
	F.A. Trophy	~	5 (1)
1974/75	League Cup	~	19 (5)
	Lincs Cup	~	4
	Other	~	2
	Total	~	143 (32)

Born circa 1942. Former Sheffield United Reserves, Worksop Town and Retford Town player who first appeared for Grantham in the opening match of the 1968/69 season at Sutton Town and scored his initial goal for the club just over a month later at Heanor Town. Keith played in that season's FA Cup Proper Rounds against Chelmsford City, (during which he scored one of the goals), and Swindon Town. He was also one of the few players to appear in every round of the Midland League Cup and scored in the first leg of the Final against Arnold. He continued to play in most of the games the following season, including another FA Cup First Round appearance, this time at Oldham Athletic, and also played in the FA Trophy replay at Worcester City in front of 6,700 spectators. The 1970/71 season saw more Cup highlights as Keith scored the first goal against Stockport County to set Grantham on their way to a maiden victory over a Football League side, plus an appearance in the following round at home to Rotherham United. Other than the Midland League Championship and another League Cup winner's medal, Keith played in the January 1971 FA Trophy Quarter-Final tie against Yeovil Town. After the Summer break he made only six appearances at the start of the campaign, although he did return to the team in January 1975 to make a lone appearance in the County Cup tie at Grimsby Town. Keith was last known to be working as an Accountant, based near to Sheffield.

Paul Tomlinson

Seasons Played			
1993/94-94/95	League	~	54 (23)
	F.A. Cup	~	2
	F.A. Trophy	~	4 (1)
	League Cup	~	2 (1)
	Lincs Cup	~	1 (2)
	Total	~	63 (27)

Born 23/12/1969 at Brierley Hill. Striker who had previously played for Hucknall Town and scored the winning goal that knocked Grantham out of the FA Cup in 1992. Allen Crombie seemed to have found a prolific striker when Paul scored on his debut for The Gingerbreads in the October 1993 league game at home to Hinckley Town, netted a brace only days later at RC Warwick and scored three more times before the end of the month. Sadly though, the goal ratio soon began to slip, although he continued to play in the majority of the games until his last goal in his final appearance at Armitage in January 1995. That game was a defeat for the struggling Grantham side against an already doomed team who managed only two victories all year. Paul went on to play for Arnold Town, before the first of five returns to Hucknall, followed by Shepshed Albion, Eastwood Town, Kettering Town, Alfreton Town, Lincoln United, Ossett Town, Gresley Rovers, Leek Town and Rolls Royce Leisure.

David Tonge

Seasons Played			
1996/97	League	~	2
	F.A. Cup	~	
	F.A. Trophy	~	
	League Cup	~	
	Lincs Cup	~	
	Total	~	2

Leicester born midfield player who at one point had a trial with Notts County and had previously played for St Andrews and Oadby Town in the Leicestershire Senior League, before moving to Leicester United, Hinckley Town, Corby Town and VS Rugby. He made just two appearances for Grantham, at Raunds Town at the end of August 1996 and against Shepshed Dynamo a week later. David soon returned to Hinckley Town, before joining Shepshed Dynamo, Friar Lane Old Boys, Thringstone and Coalville Town, where he helped them win the Leicestershire Senior League.

Tonge

Seasons Played			
1912/13-13/14	League	~	20 (30)
	F.A. Cup	~	6 (7)
	Lincs Cup	~	1 (1)
	Other	~	
	Total	~	27 (38)

Talented striker, although the above figures have been noted from score-sheets so he most likely played in many more games than those quoted. His first known goal for the club comes in the September 1912 FA Cup replay against Sneinton and his initial hat-trick was two months later in the league fixture at home to Sutton Town. He battled all season along with Bullivant for the title of the club's highest scorer and put himself into pole position after scoring five times against Gresley Rovers in March, although, sadly, final figures are not known. He began the following season where he had left off, scoring four goals past the Notts Rangers 'keeper, but from then on the goal quota began to decline, not only for him but for the whole team. Sadly no details are known about the end of his career, although he was still scoring for the club against Shirebrook at the end of March 1914.

Toplan

Seasons Played	League	~	
	Other	~	1
1893/94	Total	~	1

Played for Grantham in the April 1894 Minor Cup Final, but no details are known about any other appearances he made.

Kevin Topliss

Seasons Played	League	~	16
	F.A. Cup	~	
1992/93	F.A. Trophy	~	
	League Cup	~	
	Lincs Cup	~	1
	Total	~	17

Born 05/04/1967 at Grimsby. Was on the books of Grimsby Town, Scunthorpe United and Crewe Alexandra as a youngster, before making appearances for Brigg Town, North Ferriby United, Spalding United and King's Lynn. He made his debut for Grantham in the opening County Cup tie of the 1992/93 season at Lincoln City and was promptly sent off in the first league game at home to Yate Town, earning himself the distinction of becoming the first Grantham player to be banished from The Meres. His final appearance came in the January 1993 match against Barri Town and then Kevin, along with many of his colleagues, left The Meres due to the club's financial problems. He went on to play for Bourne Town and Wisbech Town.

Towers

Seasons Played	League	~	
	Lincs Cup	~	
1904/05	Other	~	1 (1)
	Total	~	1 (1)

Scored for the club in the October 1904 Grantham Minor Cup tie against Little Gonerby Swifts, but it is not known if he played in any other games for Grantham.

Phil Towle

Seasons Played	League	~	11
	F.A. Cup	~	
1990/91	F.A. Trophy	~	1
	League Cup	~	
1993/94	Lincs Cup	~	1
	Total	~	13

Born circa 1965. Joined Grantham from Hucknall Town and made his debut in the first match of the 1990/91 season at home to Grimsby Town in the County Cup. After only four games though, he returned to Hucknall and then spent time at Ilkeston Town. Phil rejoined Grantham in December 1993 and played in nine consecutive appearances, including the FA Trophy win over Conference side Witton Albion, before his last game against RC Warwick in February 1994. He returned once more to Hucknall and later, in August 2003, was appointed Assistant Manager at Ilkeston Town, but was sacked little more than two months into this job.

Steve Towle

Seasons Played	League	~	33 (4)
	F.A. Cup	~	5
1982/83	F.A. Trophy	~	1
	League Cup	~	3
	Lincs Cup	~	3 (1)
	Other	~	4 (1)
	Total	~	49 (6)

Full-Back who started out on the books at Notts County, but then moved on to Boston United, (winning a Northern Premier League winners medal), and Matlock Town. On his Grantham debut he scored from the penalty spot to help secure a County Cup victory over his old club, Boston United. A couple of months later he played in the Final of the same competition against Scunthorpe United, plus the final qualifying FA Cup tie at Telford United. Steve scored his last goal for the club in March 1983 at home to Workington, with his concluding appearance the following month against Gateshead. He went on to play for Alfreton Town, Heanor Town, Arnold Town and GPT Plessey.

Toynbee

Seasons Played	F.A. Cup	~	
	Other	~	3 (1)
1877/78-78/79	Total	~	3 (1)

Scored on his debut in the October 1877 friendly at Retford Rovers, but made only one other appearance for the club that season in the following match against Sleaford. He returned to London Road in March 1879 to make a final appearance for Grantham, again in a friendly at home to Sleaford.

Carl Tranter

Seasons Played	League	~	2
	F.A. Cup	~	
1999/00	F.A. Trophy	~	
	League Cup	~	
	Lincs Cup	~	
	Total	~	2

Born 04/10/1978 at Birmingham. Began his career as a Trainee at West Bromwich Albion, before moving to Bridgnorth Town and Kingstonian, where he received an FA Trophy winner's medal after their 1999 victory at Wembley. He signed for Grantham after periods training with Peterborough United and Oldham Athletic, but made just two appearances when he came off the bench in the first league games of the 1999/00 season against Gloucester City and King's Lynn. Carl went on to play for Stafford Rangers, Worcester City, Halesowen Town, Bromsgrove Rovers, twice, Bridgnorth Town, Colwyn Bay, Brierley Hill Town, Stourbridge and AFC Telford United.

Arthur Newton Treadgold

Seasons Played	F.A. Cup	~	1
	Lincs Cup	~	11 (3)
1883/84-85/86	Other	~	19 (9)
1887/88-89/90	Total	~	31 (12)

Born August 1863 at Great Gonerby. Educated at the King's School in town like his ancestor Isaac Newton, followed by a period at Oxford. 'Treaders' as he was known, first played for Grantham in the December 1883 friendly at Spilsby and by the following season had become a near ever present member of the team, with his first two goals for the club in October 1884 against Sleaford. At the end of that season he appeared in the Lincolnshire Senior Cup Final against Gainsborough Trinity, which saw Grantham lift a trophy for the first time. The season of 1885/86 though, was to be his final one as a prominent member of the club, with him missing completely the following year. From then until the end of the decade he made only occasional appearances due to his profession as a schoolmaster at St Leonard's, Hastings and then Bath College. His last game for Grantham was in January 1890 when they were knocked out of the Newark Charity Cup by Grantham Rovers. At the end of the decade the lure of gold took him and in 1898 he sailed to North America to join other prospectors, a move that was paid for with the aid of articles written for the *Manchester Guardian* during his travels. A year later he published a report on the Klondike and was granted a charter to supply electricity and water to the area. After a string of ventures and financial disasters that involved both individuals, high ranking financiers and even Governments, Arthur became somewhat of a legend in the area, earning the distinction of being "the man of diminutive stature and big ideas". He still features prominently in many historical publications that are written about the Klondike goldmines. Died 23/03/1951 in London.

Roy Trimbell

Seasons Played	League	~	2
	F.A. Cup	~	
1953/54	Lincs Cup	~	
	Total	~	2

Defender who played in the final two league fixtures of the 1953/54 season at the Reserve teams of York City and Hull City.

Truelove

Seasons Played	League	~	1
1905/06	Total	~	1

Goalkeeper who was playing for the club towards the start of the 1905/06 season, but no details are available as to just how many appearances he made.

Tucker

Seasons Played	Lincs Cup	~	3
	Other	~	13
1890/91	Total	~	16

Made his debut in the first friendly of the 1890/91 season at home to Notts Amateurs United and then played in the majority of the following games, with his last known appearance for the club coming in March 1891 against Notts St George.

Eddie Turner

Seasons Played	League	~	17
	F.A. Cup	~	
1980/81-81/82	F.A. Trophy	~	
	League Cup	~	1
1985/86-86/87	Lincs Cup	~	
	Other	~	
	Total	~	18

Born 06/01/1963 at Nottingham. Former Parkhead United, Nottingham Forest Colts, Dunkirk and Ruddington full-back who progressed through the Reserves side to make his First team debut in the April 1981 league game at home to Oswestry Town. He kept the place for the final three fixtures as well, but made only two appearances the following season and soon went on to play for Shepshed Charterhouse. He returned to London Road in March 1986 and played in the closing nine fixtures of the campaign, with his final three games after the Summer interval. His last appearance for the First team came in the October 1986 league draw against Rushden Town and upon leaving the club, he returned to Dunkirk.

Ian Turner

Seasons Played	League	~	27 (5)
	F.A. Cup	~	2
1985/86-86/87	F.A. Trophy	~	1
	League Cup	~	2
	Lincs Cup	~	1
	Total	~	33 (5)

Born 03/10/1963 at Quorn. Previously played for Burton Albion, Kettering Town, Shepshed Charterhouse, Ruddington and made his debut for Grantham in the January 1986 league game against Bridgnorth Town, with his first goal a week later at Leicester United. Ian continued to play in many of the games for Grantham over the next year or so, with his last goal coming as the equaliser in his final appearance against Hednesford Town in March 1987. He left the club soon after this and returned to Shepshed.

Jason Turner

Seasons Played	League	~	28 (14)
	F.A. Cup	~	
2004/05	F.A. Trophy	~	3 (1)
	League Cup	~	1
	Lincs Cup	~	2 (2)
	Total	~	34 (17)

Born 01/08/1981 at Nottingham. Striker with experience at Rothwell Corinthians, an extended trial at Oxford United, followed by spells at Rothwell Town and Kettering Town. An unsettled start to the 2004/05 season saw Jason spend time at Histon, Rothwell Town, again, and Stamford, before he joined Grantham in October. He scored on his debut in a disappointing defeat at Cirencester Town and over Christmas became the first Grantham player to score hat-tricks in consecutive games since Bob Norris back in 1971.In April 2005 he played in the Lincolnshire Shield Final, which saw The Gingerbreads maintain their dominance in the competition. Jason finished his first season at The Meres as Grantham's highest scorer, with 17 goals, and remains at the club.

Phil Turner

Seasons Played	League	~	1
	F.A. Cup	~	
2004/05	F.A. Trophy	~	
	League Cup	~	
	Lincs Cup	~	
	Total	~	1

Born 12/02/1962 at Sheffield. Began his career at Lincoln City, before moving to Grimsby Town and Leicester City. March 1989 saw his move to Notts County, after a £125,000 transfer fee was paid, with Phil already having 391 senior career appearances (and 30 goals) to his name. What was to follow was not only highlights for Phil personally, but for all concerned with The Magpies. The 1989/90 and 1990/91 seasons saw successive Play-Off promotions, the latter at Wembley into what would turn out to be the final Division One Championship before the introduction of The Premiership. Despite the disappointment of just one campaign in the English top flight, as Club Captain, Phil lifted the Anglo-Italian Cup in 1995, the last Englishman to do so with the demise of the competition a year later. He retired from the professional game at the end of the 1995/96 season due to injuries, with another 309 First team matches (and 22 goals) whilst at Meadow Lane, but in the Summer of 2004 joined Grantham as Assistant Manager to Dave Norton. Remarkably, at the age of 42, he was able to gain one more appearance to his name when he came on as substitute in the opening league fixture of the season at Chesham United. At the same time he was also able to take the record of the oldest Grantham player in the modern era, beating Mark Wallington by a couple of months. Following his departure from The Meres, at the same time as Norton, Phil has failed to be enticed into another footballing position and is currently concentrating on his career working in a secure hospital at Ilkeston.

Turtill

Seasons Played	F.A. Cup	~	1
	Lincs Cup	~	2
1885/86	Other	~	23 (16)
1888/89	Total	~	26 (16)

Made his debut for Grantham in the County Cup tie against Grimsby Town in January 1886 and scored his first goal a few days later at home to Notts County Reserves. However, after only one other appearance he seems to have left the club, although he returned a couple of years later to London Road. He played in the majority of the 1888/89 season's games, including the final of the Kettering Charity Cup and finished as one of the club's highest scorers. His final goal for Grantham came in the concluding friendly of the season against Grantham Rovers.

Gary Twynham

Seasons Played	League	~	16 (1)
	F.A. Cup	~	3 (2)
1998/99	F.A. Trophy	~	1
	League Cup	~	2
	Lincs Cup	~	1
	Total	~	23 (3)

Born 08/02/1976 at Manchester. Began his career at Manchester United, but then played for Darlington, (including their 1996 Division Three Play-Off Final at Wembley), and Gateshead. His Grantham debut came in the opening County Cup tie of the 1998/99 season at home to Scunthorpe United, with his first goal in the August league match at home to Bromsgrove Rovers. He played in the October FA Cup final qualifying round match at Tamworth, scoring Grantham's only goal, and by then Gary was one of Antrac's biggest hopes for a large transfer fee to offset some of their investments. But despite several rumours, his last game for the club came in the January 1999 match at Gloucester City and he left The Meres without any funds coming to the club. Gary went on to play for Bangor City and Hednesford Town, before returning to The Football League with Macclesfield Town. After finally finishing with a total of just three goals in 47 senior appearances during his professional career, he went on to play for Haverfordwest, Port Talbot, Barry Town and then returned to Haverfordwest in the Summer of 2004.

Vale

Seasons Played	League	~	
	Other	~	1
1893/94	Total	~	1

Played for Grantham in the April 1894 Minor Cup Final, but no information is available to show any league appearances that he may have made for the club.

Bob Vallance

Seasons Played	League	~	79 (3)
	F.A. Cup	~	13 (1)
1927/28-28/29	Lincs Cup	~	
	Other	~	
1930/31	Total	~	92 (4)

Born 19/09/1901 at Stanley Common. Former Heanor Town and Ilkeston United (or Town) player who made his Grantham debut in the opening match of the 1927/28 campaign at York City and played the majority of his games that season in the first half of the year. He was back in the team though at the start of the following campaign and scored his first goal for the club in the October 1928 FA Cup tie at Sutton Junction. He also played in the following rounds of that competition, including the First Round game against Rhyl Athletic and the trip up to Wigan Borough in December. Bob joined Notts County in the Summer of 1929, but refused a professional contract due to him running a successful coal business near Ilkeston. After only eight appearances there, he returned to London Road for the commencement of the 1930/31 season. Although end of season data shows that he played in half of the league fixtures, it is not known which was his final one. Following this second spell with Grantham, he moved on to Gainsborough Trinity, Stanley Common Miners Welfare, Smalley United and Stanley Excelsior, where he played well into the latter part of the decade. Died 28/02/1980 at Stanley Common.

Andrew Vangasse

Seasons Played			
	League	~	1
	F.A. Cup	~	
1992/93	F.A. Trophy	~	1
	League Cup	~	
1998/99	Lincs Cup	~	
	Total	~	2

Local player who made one appearance for Grantham in the January 1993 league game at Bilston Town and the October 1998 FA Trophy replay at home to Burton Albion. Andrew made appearances for several other local sides and was known to be playing for Harrowby United after his second spell at The Meres.

Nigel Vince

Seasons Played			
	League	~	46
	F.A. Cup	~	4
1989/90-90/91	F.A. Trophy	~	1
	League Cup	~	7
	Lincs Cup	~	
	Total	~	58

Full-Back who arrived at Grantham from Boston FC and made his debut in the August 1989 fixture at Bedworth United. Nigel played in just over half of that season's games and after a brief period in New Zealand returned to The Gingerbreads and played in a similar amount of games the following season, the last of which was in April 1991 at Barry Town. He then spent time at Cambridge United, before returning to Boston FC, followed by appearances for Spalding United, Wisbech Town and Holbeach United, where he won a United Counties Championship winner's medal in 2003. Another was won a year later after Nigel had returned to Spalding United and he then moved to Bourne Town in the Summer of 2004, but only months later had returned to Spalding.

D. Vincent

Seasons Played			
	Other	~	1
1875/76	Total	~	1

First of four possible Vincent brothers who played for the club during those first years. This individual made just one appearance though, in the final friendly of the 1875/76 season at Nottingham Lace.

Ernie Vincent

Seasons Played			
	League	~	3
	F.A. Cup	~	
1945/46	Lincs Cup	~	
	Total	~	3

Born 28/10/1907 at Washington. Began his career with local colliery sides at Dawdon, Ryhope, Seaham and Washington, before signing for Southport in 1930. A year later he moved to Manchester United, scoring a single goal in 64 games, and then transferred to Queen's Park Rangers, Doncaster Rovers and finally Stamford at the end of the decade, with a total of 151 Football League appearances to his name. Ernie played for Grantham in the first three Midland League fixtures after the end of The Second World War, two games against Gainsborough Trinity and the visit of the Reserves team of his old club, Doncaster Rovers, to London Road. Died 1978 at Worksop.

P. Vincent

Seasons Played			
	Other	~	1
1876/77	Total	~	1

Played in only one game for Grantham, the January 1877 friendly at home to Nottingham Castle, which was played to raise funds for the local hospital.

R. Vincent

Seasons Played			
	F.A. Cup	~	
1874/75	Other	~	3
1878/79	Total	~	3

First played for Grantham in the December 1874 match against Sleaford and then appeared in the friendlies at home to Bourne a month later and finally at Southwell in March 1879.

T. Vincent

Seasons Played			
	F.A. Cup	~	3
	Other	~	45 (8)
1874/75-78/79	Total	~	48 (8)

Original Grantham committee member who played in the very first club match for Mr Gamble's side, plus the earliest game against the Third Lincolnshire Volunteer Rifles in October 1874. Despite being a prominent member in those initial years, his first recorded goal does not come until the January 1877 match at Bourne. The following season he played in the club's inaugural FA Cup match against Clapham Rovers in October 1877 and continued in the side right up to the end of the 1878/79 season at home to Spilsby.

Vincent

Seasons Played			
	F.A. Cup	~	
	Lincs Cup	~	
1886/87	Other	~	1
	Total	~	1

Made just one appearance for the club in the October 1886 friendly at Notts Olympic, although there is always the possibility that this individual could be one of the previous 'Vincents' who was simply returning to help out his old club.

Simon Waby

Seasons Played			
	League	~	1
	F.A. Cup	~	
1996/97	F.A. Trophy	~	
	League Cup	~	
	Lincs Cup	~	
	Total	~	1

Born 1963 at Lincoln. Vastly experienced goalkeeper who was one of Lincoln United's longest serving players, with time also spent at Sleaford Town. Simon helped out The Gingerbreads by covering for the unavailable Peter Bulliman in the November 1996 league match at home to Bedworth United. He went on to continue his career with Lincoln United, also returned to Sleaford, but is now living in Spain working as a Property Estates Manager.

John Waddicor

Seasons Played			
	League	~	11
	F.A. Cup	~	
1984/85	F.A. Trophy	~	
	League Cup	~	
	Lincs Cup	~	
	Other	~	1
	Total	~	12

Born circa 1956 in Lancashire. Began his career at Blackburn Rovers and after a period playing football in Australia joined Bourne Town and then Stamford Town, playing and scoring for them in the 1984 FA Vase Final at Wembley. He made his Grantham debut in the August 1984 league fixture at home to Gainsborough Trinity, but played his final game in the November President's Cup tie at home to Matlock Town. John returned to Stamford and then signed for Wisbech Town.

Alan Wade

Seasons Played			
	League	~	37 (1)
	F.A. Cup	~	4
1956/57	Lincs Cup	~	1
	Total	~	42 (1)

Centre-Half who made his Grantham debut in the opening league fixture of the 1956/57 season at Scarborough and then played in most of that year's games. His only goal for the club was in April 1957 at Bradford City Reserves and his final appearance came in the concluding league fixture at Lincoln City Reserves. During his career he also spent time at Notts County and after the end of his playing days he worked at Loughborough University, coaching Bob Wilson and Dario Gradi amongst others, before moving to The FA, where he later became their Director of Coaching.

Wagg

Seasons Played			
	League	~	7 (1)
	F.A. Cup	~	2
1920/21	Lincs Cup	~	
	Other	~	
	Total	~	9 (1)

Player whose surname is sometimes spelt 'Wragg' and who appeared for the club at the start of the 1920/21 season. His only goal for Grantham came in his last known appearance, the November 1920 Central Alliance fixture at home to Derby County Reserves.

Keith Wain

Seasons Played			
	League	~	3 (1)
	F.A. Cup	~	
1958/59	Lincs Cup	~	
	Total	~	3 (1)

First played for Grantham in the August 1958 league fixture at North Shields, but failed to make the First team again until October, with his only goal for the club coming in his final appearance at Goole Town that month.

Wainwright

Seasons Played			
	League	~	2
	Lincs Cup	~	
1904/05	Other	~	
	Total	~	2

Known to have played in the two league games against Notts Magdala and Notts Magdala Amateurs during the 1904/05 season, but no data exists to show any other games he may have played in.

Wainwright

Seasons Played			
	League	~	10
	F.A. Cup	~	
1928/29	Lincs Cup	~	
	Other	~	
	Total	~	10

Forward who made his debut at Scunthorpe & Lindsey United in December 1928, only days after the club's FA Cup Second Round tie against Wigan Borough. Most of his appearances for Grantham came in the following couple of months, although there are no details known as to the end of his career.

Mick Waitt

Seasons Played			
	League	~	17 (7)
	F.A. Cup	~	1
1990/91-91/92	F.A. Trophy	~	1
	League Cup	~	1 (1)
	Lincs Cup	~	1
	Total	~	21 (8)

Born 25/06/1960 at Hexham. Previously played for Keyworth United, Arnold Kingswell, Notts County, Lincoln City, including their GM Vauxhall Conference winning season of 1987/88, Boston United, Lee Sang FC in Hong Kong and Nuneaton Borough, scoring 28 goals during his near 100 Football League appearances. He made his Grantham debut in the March 1991 game versus Sutton Coldfield Town played at The Halley Stewart Stadium, Spalding, and scored his first goal in the following fixture at Bridgnorth Town. Mick played in the opening match at The Meres, against Ilkeston Town in August 1991, but made his final appearance less than a month later in the FA Trophy tie at home to Buxton. After leaving Grantham he had spells at Gedling Town and Ilkeston Town, followed by his emigration to New Zealand to take up the Player/Coach position at Napier City FC. In 1993 he took them to a National League and Chatham Cup double and won the league again there in 1997/98. After promotion to the coaching staff of the National side, Mick was awarded the New Zealand Manager's position in 2002, with a contract up to the next World Cup. However this looks tenuous at present with the side already out of contention for the Finals.

Paul Waldron

Seasons Played			
	League	~	
	F.A. Cup	~	
1986/87	F.A. Trophy	~	
	League Cup	~	1
	Lincs Cup	~	
	Total	~	1

Made just one appearance for Grantham in the Bill Dellow League Cup tie against Shepshed Charterhouse at the end of October 1986.

Charles Walker

Seasons Played			
	League	~	38 (15)
	F.A. Cup	~	2 (1)
1948/49	Lincs Cup	~	
	Total	~	40 (16)

Forward who previously played for Doncaster Rovers Reserves and made his debut in the club's opening fixture of the 1948/49 season at Scarborough, with his first goal scored for Grantham only days later at Boston United. Charles appeared in the majority of that season's matches, up to the conclusion of the season at Mansfield Town Reserves, a game which also saw his final goal for the club.

Darren Walker

Seasons Played			
	League	~	
	F.A. Cup	~	
2001/02	F.A. Trophy	~	
	League Cup	~	
	Lincs Cup	~	1
	Total	~	1

Reserves team striker who made just one senior appearance in the opening County Cup tie of the 2001/02 season at Gainsborough Trinity.

Stan Walker

Seasons Played			
	League	~	101
	F.A. Cup	~	13
1926/27-28/29	Lincs Cup	~	5
1934/35	Other	~	
1937/38	Total	~	119

Born circa 1901 at Waddington. Goalkeeper who had previously played for Waddington, Lincoln City, Gainsborough Trinity and made 13 appearances for Grantham in his first season with the club, mainly towards the end of the campaign, although it is not known which game he made his debut in. He was once more in the side after the Summer interval, whilst the season of 1928/29 saw his first full year with the club and included appearances in the FA Cup Proper rounds against Rhyl Athletic and Wigan Borough. In April 1929 he was sold to Wolverhampton Wanderers, where he made one full appearance, before playing a total of 65 times for New Brighton and Doncaster Rovers. Stan returned to London Road for the start of the 1934/35 season and again played in the majority of the matches, including the club's record 13-0 victory in the FA Cup against Rufford Colliery and the County Cup Final at Boston United. After a period at Peterborough United, Stan then rejoined Grantham once more, but with Arthur Jepson in the side now he was only awarded another three appearances, the last of which came in the October 1937 8-3 FA Cup defeat of Boots Athletic. He continued to live in the area and several years later became the landlord of The Earlsfield Hotel on Dysart Road.

Steve Walker

Seasons Played			
	League	~	21
	F.A. Cup	~	
1982/83	F.A. Trophy	~	
	League Cup	~	2
	Lincs Cup	~	
	Other	~	1
	Total	~	24

Born 25/12/1963 at Ilkeston. Former Ilkeston Town midfielder who made one appearance for Halifax Town during the 1981/82 season. Unfortunately Steve's professional career was cut short after he suffered a broken leg, but it was hoped that his move to Grantham would be the first step back into The Football League. He made his debut in the league game at home to King's Lynn just after Christmas 1982 and missed only three fixtures before his final one in the closing match at Matlock Town. Steve's hoped for return to senior football failed to materialise and he went on to play for Shepshed Charterhouse, Heanor Town and Matlock Town. Several years later he was still playing, firstly for Bulwell, before being reunited with Bill Brindley upon his return to Heanor Town.

Walker

Seasons Played			
	Lincs Cup	~	2
	Other	~	
1890/91	Total	~	2

Made just two appearances for the club in the County Cup Second Round and replay against Grantham Rovers in January 1891.

Walker

Seasons Played			
	League	~	3 (1)
1911/12	Total	~	3 (1)

Most probably a regular player from the 1911/12 season, who scored at least one goal for the club in the March 1912 Central Alliance fixture at home to Ilkeston United.

Walker

Seasons Played			
	League	~	1
	F.A. Cup	~	
1930/31	Lincs Cup	~	
	Total	~	1

Centre-Forward who previously played for Sneinton Imperial, but made only one appearance for Grantham in the January 1931 league match at Notts County Reserves.

Tommy Walkerdine

Seasons Played			
	League	~	53 (17)
	F.A. Cup	~	5 (1)
1919/20	Lincs Cup	~	4
1922/23	Other	~	4 (3)
1924/25	Total	~	66 (21)

Born 1894 at Basford. Individual who could play as either a full-back or in a forward position and also made appearances for Norwich City Reserves, Netherfield, Boots Athletic, Peterborough & Fletton United and Stamford Town during his career. His Grantham debut came in the opening league match of the 1919/20 season at Long Eaton, with his first goal for the club the following month in the FA Cup tie against Boots Athletic. Although many team-sheets are missing from this period, there is no evidence of him playing for the club again until the start of the 1922/23 season, followed by his return once more a year later. Unfortunately no details are known about the end of his career either, although he was still scoring for Grantham by the April 1925 Central Alliance game at Hucknall Byron. Off the field, it is known that Tommy married into the Eatch family, - his Chairman and colleagues Edgar and Ernie's sister.

Dave Wall

Seasons Played			
	League	~	1
	F.A. Cup	~	
1991/92	F.A. Trophy	~	
	League Cup	~	
	Lincs Cup	~	1
	Total	~	2

Former Telford United midfielder who made just two appearances for Grantham at the start of the 1991/92 season against Grimsby Town and Bridgnorth Town.

Doug Wallace

Seasons Played			
	League	~	19
1945/46	F.A. Cup	~	3
1948/49	Lincs Cup	~	1
1954/55-55/56	Total	~	23

Previously played for Doncaster Rovers and made his Grantham debut in goal, when Mick Brannan was unavailable for the September 1945 match at Gainsborough Trinity. However, in his next two matches he reverted to his more usual out-field position, with the latter one being in the FA Cup Second Round, second leg, at Mansfield Town. Doug returned to the First team three years later and then again in the mid 1950s, after a spell at Boston United, to make occasional appearances, with his final game coming in November 1955 at Corby Town.

Wallatt

Seasons Played			
	League	~	1 (1)
	F.A. Cup	~	3 (4)
1912/13	Lincs Cup	~	
	Other	~	
	Total	~	4 (5)

Very little information known on this player, other than his goals in the FA Cup ties against Sneinton, New Hucknall Colliery and Stanton Hill Victoria and in the Central Alliance match at home to Leicester Fosse Reserves, all of which occurred during either September or October of 1912.

Mark Wallington

Seasons Played			
	League	~	2
	F.A. Cup	~	
1994/95	F.A. Trophy	~	
	League Cup	~	
	Lincs Cup	~	
	Total	~	2

Born 17/09/1952 in Grantham. Goalkeeper who began his career on Schoolboy forms at Lincoln City, before playing for Heckington United in the Grantham League. He gained various England caps at Schoolboy and Youth levels and moved into The Football League with Walsall in 1971. Mark then signed for Leicester City and made 467 appearances at Filbert Street, including seven years without missing a single game, and winning a Second Division Championship medal. Transfers then followed to Derby County and a return to Lincoln City, taking the number of senior appearances for him to 668. He made two appearances for Grantham against RC Warwick and Evesham United at the end of September 1994 and the beginning of October as cover for the unavailable Guy Hardcastle. After the New Year, Mark was awarded the position of Assistant to Manager, Warren Ward, but although being nominated as a substitute in a few of the following games, he made no further appearances. He then returned to his home town of Sleaford to become a secondary school teacher and also spent time coaching with the England Under-18 set-up.

Walton

Seasons Played			
	League	~	14
	F.A. Cup	~	5
1927/28	Lincs Cup	~	
	Total	~	19

Half-Back who had also played for Derby County Reserves and made his Grantham debut in the first Midland League match of the 1927/28 season at York City. Most of his appearances for the club came at the start of the season and although it's known that he returned to the side after the Winter, no information is available about his final game.

Warburton

Seasons Played			
	League	~	2
	F.A. Cup	~	1
1892/93	Total	~	3

Played for Grantham during the disastrous 1892/93 season against Sheffield, Belper and finally in the October 16-0 defeat at Notts County Rovers.

Alan Ward

Seasons Played			
	League	~	8
	F.A. Cup	~	1
1990/91	F.A. Trophy	~	1
	League Cup	~	5 (1)
	Lincs Cup	~	
	Total	~	15 (1)

First played for Grantham by coming off the bench to replace Peter Whitehurst in the August 1990 league fixture at home to Stourbridge. Apart from a spell at the start of the 1991 New Year, which included his only goal, at Chelmsford City, most of his appearances came from the substitute's position, with the last of those in March 1991 against Nuneaton Borough.

Kevin Ward

Seasons Played			
2000/01	League	~	15
	F.A. Cup	~	4
	F.A. Trophy	~	1
	League Cup	~	1
	Lincs Cup	~	
	Total	~	21

Born circa 1977 in Yorkshire. Winger who had previously made appearances for Barnsley and Cove Rangers, before playing in Sweden for MP IFK, Var TP and BK IFK. Returning to England, Kevin signed for Halifax Town, but soon moved on to Gainsborough Trinity, Goole Town, Harrogate Town and Lincoln United. He joined Grantham in the Summer of 2000, making his debut in the September league match at home to Histon, but then played only occasionally until his last game in March 2001 at home to Erith & Belvedere. Kevin soon returned to Lincoln, before making appearances for Spalding United, Holbeach United, Harrowby United, then having a spell in Finland, before returning to the country to play for Barwell and Kings Lynn.

Michael Ward

Seasons Played			
2000/01	League	~	1 (1)
	F.A. Cup	~	
	F.A. Trophy	~	
	League Cup	~	1
	Lincs Cup	~	1
	Total	~	3 (1)

Born 28/07/1978 at Lincoln. Brother of Paul Ward. Michael came to The Meres from Sleaford Town and played twice for the club in November 2000 against Wisbech Town and Boston United. He returned to the First team in May 2001 to make one more appearance, during which he scored, at Sittingbourne in the penultimate league game of the season. After leaving The Meres, Michael went back to Sleaford Town, where he still plays.

Paul Ward

Seasons Played			
1989/90-90/91	League	~	92 (4)
1993/94	F.A. Cup	~	3
	F.A. Trophy	~	2
	League Cup	~	12
	Lincs Cup	~	4
	Total	~	113 (4)

Born 15/10/1965 at Ely. Elder brother of Michael Ward. Paul previously played for Lincoln City Youths, Lincoln United, Sleaford Town and signed for Grantham from Grimsby Town. He made his debut in the 1989/90 season's County Cup game at home to Spalding United and played in most of that campaign's fixtures, scoring his first goal in December against Rushden Town. October of 1990 saw Paul playing in the final league fixture at London Road, against Dudley Town, and he finished that season missing just three matches all year. He went on to have a successful spell at Lincoln United, where he appeared in the FA Cup First Round Proper, and at one point seemed destined to join their neighbours Lincoln City. However, he returned to Grantham in the Summer of 1993 and continued to be a prominent member of the side over the next few months, but his final goal came in November at Leicester United, with his last appearance in January 1994 at home to Bridgnorth Town. After leaving The Meres, Paul went on to play for Boston Town, Lincoln United once more, and Sleaford Town where he remains.

Warren Ward

Seasons Played			
1993/94-95/96	League	~	92 (25)
	F.A. Cup	~	6 (4)
	F.A. Trophy	~	7 (2)
	League Cup	~	4 (1)
	Lincs Cup	~	5 (1)
	Total	~	114 (33)

Born 25/05/1962 at Plympton. Originally played for Yorkshire Amateurs and Guiseley, before making 39 League appearances for York City, Exeter City and Lincoln City. Warren then returned to the non-league scene, firstly with Boston United, followed by King's Lynn, Spalding United, Lincoln United and Wisbech Town. He scored on his Grantham debut, in a personally satisfying 3-2 Lincolnshire County Senior Cup victory against his old club at Sincil Bank and became a near constant member of the side that season. But the following year saw the departure of Manager, Allen Crombie, combined with a change in financial direction for Grantham and with Warren employed as a Professional coach and Football Development Officer with the Lincolnshire FA, it was thought that he would be the ideal person to step into the helm for the start of the 1994/95 season. The financial constraints proved to be too much for the team though and the club finished in the relegation zone and had to apply for re-election to stay in the Southern League. Despite an improvement the following year, it turned out to be not enough and after his final goal at the end of October 1995 in the Dr Marten's League Cup tie against Ilkeston Town, what would prove to be his last appearance came the following month at Solihull Borough when he came off the bench to replace Alec Leonce. Just after Christmas the inevitable happened and he was relieved of his duties, before moving on to Boston Town and then Wisbech Town in 1996, taking them into the Dr Marten's League. Warren has recently qualified as a PE Teacher, works for Leeds United in their Football in the Community programme and now runs his own corporate events company.

Ward

Seasons Played			
1945/46	League	~	7
	F.A. Cup	~	
	Lincs Cup	~	
	Total	~	7

A post-war problem in that according to end of season records, two 'Ward's' played for The Gingerbreads during the 1945/46 season. My only doubt is that despite them seemingly playing in different positions, they didn't play together in any games and no Christian initial is listed at any time that year, something which usually occurs when players of the same surname were at the club. Therefore this player and the following entry could possibly be just one individual and just to compound the problem, one of them is known to have previously spent time at Arsenal.

Ward

Seasons Played			
1945/46	League	~	4 (1)
	F.A. Cup	~	
	Lincs Cup	~	
	Total	~	4 (1)

See notes for previous entry. The only thing that can be said with certainty is that this 'Ward' scored for Grantham in the February 1945 Midland League fixture at home to Lincoln City Reserves.

Ward

Seasons Played			
1959/60	League	~	2
	F.A. Cup	~	
	League Cup	~	
	Lincs Cup	~	
	Total	~	2

Played just twice for the First team, in the November 1959 game at Nuneaton Borough Reserves as a replacement for Tommy Deans and the January 1960 home fixture against Wellingborough Town when Bernard Weakley became unavailable.

Warren

Seasons Played			
1921/22	League	~	1
	F.A. Cup	~	
	Lincs Cup	~	
	Total	~	1

Only one known appearance for this midfielder, the February 1922 Central Alliance match at Hucknall Byron.

Tony Warrington

Seasons Played			
1957/58-58/59	League	~	63
	F.A. Cup	~	6
	Lincs Cup	~	3
	Total	~	72

Born 12/02/1934 at Ecclesfield. Member of the RAF and a former Lincoln City goalkeeper, (with two First team appearances to his name), who took over the role from David Brown in time for the September 1957 match against Corby Town. He then appeared in every one of the remaining games from that season, including the Lincolnshire Senior Cup 'A' Final at home to Gainsborough Trinity. Tony remained the club's first choice 'keeper after the Summer break, although he was forced to have a lengthy spell away from the team towards the end of the year. His final appearance for the club came in the 1958/59 season's closing league fixture at Ashington.

Paul Waldron

Stan Walker

Tommy Walkerdine

Kevin Ward

Paul Ward

Warren Ward

F. Watchorn

Dale Watkins

Jim Watson

Richard Weale

Steve Wenlock

Jason White

Peter Whitehurst

Harry Wilbourn

Tim Wilkes

Kev Wilkin

F. Watchorn

Seasons Played			
	League	~	1
	F.A. Cup	~	
1922/23	Lincs Cup	~	
	Other	~	
	Total	~	1

Former Reserves player who had helped them win the Grantham League Division One title. As for the First team, he played in the March 1923 match against Shirebrook, but it is not known whether this was his sole appearance for the club.

Albert Waterall

Seasons Played			
	League	~	82 (4)
	F.A. Cup	~	11
1926/27-28/29	Lincs Cup	~	1
	Other	~	
	Total	~	94 (4)

Born 01/03/1887 at Radford, Nottingham. Previously played for Radford Institute, Sneinton and Notts County, (along with his brother, Ike), before joining Stockport County in 1913. He spent thirteen years there, five as Club Captain, and despite missing many games due to World War One, finished with 35 goals to his name in 289 appearances. His professional career ended in 1926 after short spells at Queen's Park Rangers and Clapton Orient, with 37 goals in 319 senior games. Albert scored on his Grantham debut in the December 1926 league game at home to Ilkeston United, but it would prove to his only goal during that maiden campaign. Over the next couple of years he played in the majority of Grantham's games, including the FA Cup matches against Rhyl Athletic and Wigan Borough towards the end of 1928. No details are available to show the end of his Grantham career, although it's known that he made few, if any, appearances for the club after January 1929. The end of his playing career saw his return to Nottingham, where he became licensee of a public house in the city. Died 08/03/1963 at Nuthall, Nottingham.

Watkin

Seasons Played			
	League	~	4 (4)
1911/12	Total	~	4 (4)

Forward who scored for Grantham in both the 1911/12 season's Central Alliance fixtures against Sutton Junction and netted a brace during the visit of Mansfield Town. He most probably was a regular player from that campaign, who made considerably more appearances and most likely had more goals to his name as well.

Dale Watkins

Seasons Played			
	League	~	23 (10)
	F.A. Cup	~	1 (1)
1992/93	F.A. Trophy	~	1 (1)
	League Cup	~	2
2003/04	Lincs Cup	~	
	Total	~	27 (12)

Born 04/11/1971 at Peterborough. Former England Under-15 Representative who played for Sheffield United, Grimsby Town, Rotherham United, Peterborough United, where he made his Football League debut and 13 senior appearances, and Wisbech Town, before joining Grantham. He scored on his debut in the 1992/93 season's opening league fixture at home to Yate Town and a month later had firmly established himself as a favourite with the fans by scoring seven goals in his first seven matches. Dale helped Grantham to climb into a promotion challenging position, but after the financial problems of the New Year he left The Meres along with many of his team-mates. He moved on to Rushden & Diamonds, helping them to win the Dr Marten's League Championship and Nationwide Conference, at the same time also being awarded England Semi-Professional honours. A £10,000 transfer then took Dale to Gloucester City and after this, appearances followed for Cheltenham Town, nine whilst in The Football League, Kettering Town and Chelmsford Town, from where he returned to Grantham for a one month loan period in November 2003. He failed to find his old form though and after his final appearance at Dover Athletic in December, he went on to play for King's Lynn, again on-loan, before joining Stamford Town in the Summer of 2004. A few months later another loan spell took him to Yaxley and a final transfer saw him move to Mirlees Blackstone.

Alan Watson

Seasons Played			
	League	~	2
	F.A. Cup	~	
1958/59	Lincs Cup	~	
	Total	~	2

Made just two appearances for the First team towards the end of the 1958/59 season. Firstly he replaced an unavailable Roger Carter for the March fixture at home to Horden Colliery and his only other appearance was against Blyth Spartans a month later.

C. Watson

Seasons Played			
	F.A. Cup	~	
	Lincs Cup	~	5
1888/89-90/91	Other	~	30 (12)
	Total	~	35 (12)

Made his debut in the October 1888 friendly against Nottingham Forest Reserves and scored his first two goals for the club a week later at home to Lincoln Ramblers. He played in many of that season's games, including the Kettering Charity Cup Final in March 1889 which saw Grantham defeat Cambridge Granta. His prominence in the side continued over the next couple of years, with his last known appearance coming in March 1891 when Notts Olympic knocked Grantham out of the Newark Charity Cup.

C. Watson

Seasons Played			
	League	~	
	F.A. Cup	~	1
1924/25	Lincs Cup	~	
	Other	~	
	Total	~	1

Former Newark Town and Newark Castle Rovers half-back with only one known appearance for Grantham, the September 1924 FA Cup game against his home club, Newark Town.

Frank Watson

Seasons Played			
	League	~	101 (34)
	F.A. Cup	~	9 (9)
1926/27-30/31	Lincs Cup	~	2 (1)
	Other	~	2 (2)
	Total	~	114 (46)

Born 15/11/1902 at Nottingham. Experienced player who had previously spent time at Ilkeston United, Aston Villa, Blackpool, making two First team appearances, Leeds United, Brentford, where he played in another seven senior fixtures, Southend United and Ilkeston Town. Frank made his Grantham debut in the February 1927 Midland League clash against Gainsborough Trinity and scored his first goal for the club a month later in the RAF Shield at home to Boston. He straight away became a prominent member of the team and continued to play in many of the matches up until the end of the following season. The 1928/29 season saw him trying to break back into The Football League with Crewe Alexandra, but after only one First team appearance he returned to London Road. There is no definite evidence to show the end of his Grantham career, although no records can be found of his name after the November 1930 defeat of Denaby United and after leaving London Road he joined Mansfield Town.

Gary Watson

Seasons Played			
	League	~	3
	F.A. Cup	~	
1989/90	F.A. Trophy	~	
	League Cup	~	
	Lincs Cup	~	
	Total	~	3

Former Eastwood Town player who made appearances for Grantham in the first three league games of the 1989/90 season against Dudley Town, Bedworth United and Nuneaton Borough. After losing his place in the side though, Gary returned to Eastwood.

Jim Watson

Seasons Played			
	League	~	88
	F.A. Cup	~	5 (1)
1992/93-94/95	F.A. Trophy	~	5 (1)
	League Cup	~	4
	Lincs Cup	~	3
	Total	~	105 (2)

Born 08/08/1971 at Lincoln. Defender who had previously played for Lincoln City, Wimbledon, Fulham, Aldershot and Wealdstone. He made his debut for Grantham in the February 1993 league fixture at Evesham United and was one of the few successes that came to the club during this time when the team was being made up of many local players. Although not being renowned for his goals, Jim will be best remembered for his fantastic free-kick in the January 1994 FA Trophy game against Witton Albion, with his only other strike for the club coming in the September 1994 FA Cup defeat at the hands of Burton Albion. His last game for Grantham came at the end of March 1995 at home to Redditch United and he soon went on to play for Lincoln United. Jim now lives in the Staffordshire area and works as a Prison Officer.

W. Watson

Seasons Played			
	F.A. Cup	~	
	Lincs Cup	~	1
1886/87-89/90	Other	~	15 (6)
	Total	~	16 (6)

Scored in his first game for the club, the January 1887 friendly against Grantham Volunteers, but it was not until the end of the decade that he began to play more regularly. This time coincided with the arrival of C.Watson into the team, possibly an indication of them being related in some way. His final game for Grantham was in February 1890 when Notts County Reserves drew at London Road.

Watson

Seasons Played			
	League	~	2 (2)
	F.A. Cup	~	1 (1)
1892/93	Total	~	3 (3)

Played in the 1892/93 season's league games against Sheffield and Matlock, where he netted a brace, and also the FA Cup game at home to Belper where he scored one of the consolation goals. Luckily for him he departed the club before the record defeat at the hands of Notts County Rovers and Grantham's subsequent demise. Of course there is always the possibility that he could be the same individual as either 'C' or 'W' Watson who were both playing only a few years previously.

Watton

Seasons Played			
	F.A. Cup	~	
	Lincs Cup	~	
1887/88	Other	~	1
	Total	~	1

Made just one appearance for Grantham in the November 1887 friendly against Lincoln Rangers, although when you bear in mind that W. Watson was playing in the side during the 1887/88 season, could this be simply a typing error in the match report of the time.

Paul Watts

Seasons Played			
	League	~	15 (5)
	F.A. Cup	~	
1995/96	F.A. Trophy	~	
	League Cup	~	1
	Lincs Cup	~	
	Total	~	16 (5)

Born 11/04/1978 at Pontefract. A former Lincolnshire County Schoolboy player who was promoted from the Reserves to the First team to make his debut in the August 1995 league fixture at Hinckley Town. Paul scored his first goal for the club at the end of the following month against Tamworth and made a total of 16 appearances, the majority of which came towards the end of the campaign. He scored in his final appearance at home to Bridgnorth Town in the penultimate game of the season. Paul later played for Boston United, (where he won a Dr Marten's Championship winning medal), Gainsborough Trinity, King's Lynn, Lincoln United, Holbeach United and Spalding United, the last four of which were during 2003.

Bernard Weakley

Seasons Played			
	League	~	86 (52)
	F.A. Cup	~	2 (1)
1957/58-60/61	League Cup	~	2 (2)
	Lincs Cup	~	5 (1)
	Total	~	95 (56)

Born 20/12/1932 at Rotherham. Made two appearances for Rotherham United during the mid 1950s and first played for Grantham in the October 1957 league fixture at Peterborough United in front of over 9,000 spectators. He then scored his first two goals for the club the following month at home to Mansfield Town Reserves, netted his initial hat-trick for Grantham against Rotherham United Reserves and in April 1958 appeared in the County Cup Final at home to Gainsborough Trinity. The following season he was missing from many of the matches and yet still finished what was a poor season for Grantham as the club's highest scorer with twelve goals, including another hat-trick, this time against Scarborough. As the club entered the Central Alliance (South) League, Bernard was back to playing most weeks for the team and it was therefore no surprise when he easily continued his role as the team's top scorer. For the 1960/61 season though, Bernard's appearances became scarce and his last game for Grantham, and his final goal, came in the January 1961 league fixture at Loughborough United.

Richard Weale

Seasons Played			
	League	~	22
	F.A. Cup	~	
2004/05	F.A. Trophy	~	1
	League Cup	~	
	Lincs Cup	~	2
	Total	~	25

Born 30/10/1980 at Leicester. Left-sided player who began his career as a Trainee at Leicester City, before moving to Stamford, Mirlees Blackstone, Kettering Town, Rothwell Town, Harrow Borough and Bedford Town. After joining The Gingerbreads he maintained his place on the substitute's bench during the November 2004 FA Trophy tie at Weston-Super-Mare, but was able to gain his debut in the resulting replay a few days later, replacing Jim Neil. Richard became a consistent part of Lee Glover's team, eventually playing in the April 2005 Lincolnshire Shield Final victory over Gainsborough Trinity, and remains with the club.

Adam Webster

Seasons Played			
	League	~	1
	F.A. Cup	~	
1999/00	F.A. Trophy	~	
	League Cup	~	
	Lincs Cup	~	
	Total	~	1

03/07/1980 at Leicester. Began his career with Thurmaston Town and Barwell, before joining Grantham on-loan from Notts County. He made just one appearance for The Gingerbreads, in the September 1999 league game at Clevedon Town, the team's first point of the season under the new leadership of Matt Carmichael. After being released by The Magpies, with just one substitute's appearance to his name, Adam went on to play for Bedworth United and then Worcester City, following a £8,000 transfer.

Ronnie Webster

Seasons Played			
	League	~	18 (5)
	F.A. Cup	~	
1966/67-68/69	League Cup	~	
	Lincs Cup	~	
	Total	~	18 (5)

Melton Mowbray based centre-forward who scored on his Grantham debut in the March 1967 Midland League fixture at home to Grimsby Town Reserves and after finding the net in his next game at Matlock Town, continued to play in many of the remaining games from that season. The following campaign though, Ronnie made only three more appearances and then, after he was substituted in the September 1968 match at Heanor Town, he played no further part in Grantham's progress.

Wells

Seasons Played			
	League	~	2
	F.A. Cup	~	1
1892/93	Total	~	3

First played for the club in the October 1892 Midland Amateur Alliance match at Sheffield and then appeared in the games against Belper and the final fixture at Notts County Rovers, Grantham's record defeat, before the club's demise.

Gervas Wells-Cole

Seasons Played			
	F.A. Cup	~	
	Lincs Cup	~	
1886/87	Other	~	1
	Total	~	1

Born 26/12/1860 or 26/10/1860 at Brigg. A former Cambridge University Football 'Blue' who made one appearance for Grantham in the closing friendly of the 1886/87 season, the 3-2 defeat of Derby County at London Road. He also played cricket for Lincoln Lindum and the Lincolnshire County side, as his three sons would also do in the early 20th Century. Gervas went on to become a member of the Kesteven County Council, landowner and agent. Died 02/03/1917 at Skellingthorpe.

Steve Wenlock

Seasons Played			
	League	~	35
	F.A. Cup	~	5
2002/03-03/04	F.A. Trophy	~	1
	League Cup	~	1
	Lincs Cup	~	6
	Total	~	48

Born 11/03/1978 at Peterborough. Defender, nick-named 'Wenners', who began his career as a Trainee at Leicester City, playing alongside Emile Heskey and Stuart Wilson and at one point was awarded the Captain's position for their Reserve side. He then had a three year spell at Cambridge City, before joining Grantham, making his debut in the August 2002 County Cup tie at Lincoln City. Steve played in just over half the fixtures that year, one of which was the Final of the County competition against Gainsborough Trinity at the end of April 2003. Just under a year later he played in a repeat of that game in the inaugural Lincolnshire Shield Final, with Grantham getting revenge on their rivals after a penalty shoot-out. However, after being substituted in the March 2004 league game at Weston-Super-Mare, he made no more appearances for the club and moved on to Rothwell Town for the start of the 2004/05 season.

Craig Weston

Seasons Played			
	League	~	48 (1)
	F.A. Cup	~	5
1989/90-90/91	F.A. Trophy	~	2
	League Cup	~	4
	Lincs Cup	~	2
	Total	~	61 (1)

Born 04/09/1969 at Burton. Previously played for Burton Albion, Belper Town and made his Grantham debut in the opening County Cup tie of the 1989/90 season at home to Spalding United. Craig played in the majority of that season's games, scoring what would turn out to be his only goal for the club in March 1990 against Stroud. At the end of September he played in the final league fixture to be held at London Road, against Dudley Town, and became the last Grantham player to be substituted there, when Spadge Farrow took over his position. However, the following week's return match in the West Midlands was his final one for the club and he went on to play for Gresley Rovers, appearing in their 1991 FA Vase Final at Wembley and winning two West Midlands League Championship winner's medals. Clubs represented after this include Belper Town and Alfreton Town, followed by a spell as Manager at Belper and playing once more, this time for Leek Town and Long Eaton United during the 2003/04 season.

Paul Weston

Seasons Played			
	League	~	8
	F.A. Cup	~	
1995/96	F.A. Trophy	~	
	League Cup	~	
	Lincs Cup	~	
	Total	~	8

Born 02/10/1972 in Grantham. Former Ancaster, Caythorpe, Croxton Kerrial, Harrowby United and Grantham Reserves player who was promoted to the First team for the final eight league fixtures of the 1995/96 season, starting at home to Corby Town and ending at Sutton Coldfield Town. Paul still lives in the town and works for the electricity board.

Whatford

Seasons Played			
	League	~	1
	F.A. Cup	~	
1952/53	Lincs Cup	~	
	Total	~	1

Played just once for the team in April 1953 when Nottingham Forest Reserves came over to London Road for a league fixture.

Wheat

Seasons Played			
	League	~	8
	F.A. Cup	~	
1946/47-47/48	Lincs Cup	~	
	Total	~	8

Defender who made his first appearance for Grantham in the April 1947 league match at home to Scunthorpe & Lindsey United and then played in most of the remaining fixtures from that season. However, he played in only one more game after the Summer break, in October when Scarborough came to London Road.

Wheatley

Seasons Played			
	Lincs Cup	~	
	Other	~	2
1889/90-90/91	Total	~	2

Played in the final friendly of the 1889/90 season at home to Notts County Reserves and the opening match of the following season against Notts Amateurs United.

Wheeler

Seasons Played			
	Lincs Cup	~	
	Other	~	2 (1)
1890/91	Total	~	2 (1)

Made his debut for Grantham in the October 1890 friendly against Notts St John's and scored in the club's next game at home to Notts St Luke's, but it appears that he made no further appearances after this.

S. Wheelhouse

Seasons Played			
	League	~	13 (2)
	F.A. Cup	~	2 (1)
1929/30-30/31	Lincs Cup	~	
	Other	~	
	Total	~	15 (3)

Outside-Left player who had also made appearances for Grimsby Town Reserves and scored for Grantham in the two February 1930 Midland League fixtures against Wath Athletic and Hull City Reserves. After playing in several of the matches in the first few months of the 1930/31 season he fails to appear in any more of the team line-ups. He is most likely a relative, possibly the son, of the former Grimsby Town Captain, Sid Wheelhouse, who died in The First World War.

Whetton

Seasons Played			
	League	~	7 (6)
	F.A. Cup	~	
1930/31-31/32	Lincs Cup	~	
	Total	~	7 (6)

Former Bentinck Colliery (Nottinghamshire) player who made just five appearances for Grantham towards the end of the 1930/31 season, but managed to score five goals as well. He is known to have made two more appearances the following season, although no details are available on these.

Whillock

Seasons Played	League	~	2
	F.A. Cup	~	1 (2)
1932/33	Lincs Cup	~	
	Other	~	
	Total	~	3 (2)

End of season data shows that this player made two appearances for Grantham during the 1932/33 season, but it is not known which particular matches these were in.

Whipple

Seasons Played	F.A. Cup	~	
	Other	~	2
1877/78	Total	~	2

Played twice for the club in friendlies during February 1878 against Stamford and Retford Rovers. He is probably George Ernest Whipple, the only individual with that surname and of the correct age residing in Grantham during the 1881 census.

Devon White

Seasons Played	League	~	
	F.A. Cup	~	
1987/88	F.A. Trophy	~	
	League Cup	~	
	Lincs Cup	~	1
	Total	~	1

Born 02/03/1964 at Nottingham. Began his career as an Apprentice at Notts County, before moving to Arnold Town, Lincoln City, plus Boston United and Naxxar Lions (Malta) on-loan. Shortly after a brief spell at Shepshed Charterhouse, Devon came to Grantham, although he made just one appearance in the opening County Cup fixture of the 1987/88 season against Scunthorpe United. His subsequent progression into The Football League remains open to debate as to whether he signed from Shepshed or Grantham, with the possibility that his sole appearance at London Road was treated as a trial, or he could even have signed dual-forms. One thing that is certain though is that following his game for Grantham he moved to Bristol Rovers, where he later went on to score a brace in the May 1990 local derby against Bristol City that clinched their Division Three promotion, and a goal in the Leyland Daf Cup Final at Wembley a few weeks later. Devon went on to make appearances for Cambridge United, Queen's Park Rangers, Notts County, (scoring the winning goal during their 1995 Anglo-Italian Cup Final victory at Wembley), Watford, Shrewsbury Town, Ilkeston Town and Stafford Rangers, scoring 125 goals in 494 senior games. Devon is now a qualified electrician and runs his own company in Nottingham.

Frank White

Seasons Played	League	~	5 (2)
	F.A. Cup	~	
1938/39	Lincs Cup	~	
	Total	~	5 (2)

Born 30/06/1910 at Warwick. Inside-Right who had previously played for Warwick Town, West Bromwich Albion, Coventry City, Newport County, Dudley Town and Racing Club (Paris), scoring 29 goals in a total of 136 Football League appearances. Frank made all of his appearances for Grantham consecutively during October and November 1938, starting at Scunthorpe & Lindsey United, with his two goals for the club coming during the Midland League fixture at Hull City Reserves. His Grantham career ended at Peterborough United and whether it was just coincidence, or a particular impression he made during that match, it was The Posh that he soon transferred to, making his debut in their FA Cup First Round tie at Bristol Rovers at the end of the month. Died 1981.

Jason White

Seasons Played	League	~	20 (10)
	F.A. Cup	~	
2004/05	F.A. Trophy	~	
	League Cup	~	
	Lincs Cup	~	1
	Total	~	21 (10)

Born 19/10/1971 at Meriden. Experienced striker who began his career as a Trainee at Derby County, before making Football League appearances at Scunthorpe United, Darlington, (on-loan), Scarborough, Northampton Town, Rotherham United, (initially on-loan), where he helped them to promotion out of Division Three, Cheltenham Town and Mansfield Town (again on-loan). His professional career had seen 45 goals scored in a total of 299 senior appearances. After spending time abroad, he joined Grantham in December 2004, coming off the bench to make his debut during the Southern League fixture at Hednesford Town. His first goal for the club came two weeks later as The Gingerbreads demolished Dunstable Town, whilst April of 2005 saw Jason play in the victorious Lincolnshire Shield Final at Gainsborough Trinity. He finished the season as the club's second highest goal-scorer, just behind Jason Turner, and remains at The Meres.

Stuart White

Seasons Played	League	~	13 (1)
	F.A. Cup	~	
1999/00	F.A. Trophy	~	
	League Cup	~	2
	Lincs Cup	~	
	Total	~	15 (1)

Former Doncaster Rovers, Lincoln United and Lincoln Moorlands midfielder who made his debut for Grantham in the October 1999 league fixture at King's Lynn. He scored his only goal for the club in the January 5-1 victory at home to Salisbury City, but at the start of the following month, against Tamworth, he made his final appearance. Stuart is currently in Australia, having retired from the game and deciding to travel around the world.

White

Seasons Played	F.A. Cup	~	2
1876/77	Lincs Cup	~	
1879/80-81/82	Other	~	18 (3)
1883/84-86/87	Total	~	20 (3)

First played for Grantham in the December 1876 friendly at home to Notts County, but it wasn't until the very end of the decade that he established himself in the side. His first known goal for the club came in January 1880 against Burghley Park, but after the following season his appearances became infrequent, although his final one didn't come until December 1886 against Louth.

White

Seasons Played	League	~	23 (19)
	F.A. Cup	~	5 (7)
1927/28	Lincs Cup	~	
	Total	~	28 (26)

Centre-Forward who also played for Stourbridge and Loughborough Corinthians and made his Grantham debut in the opening league fixture of the 1927/28 season at York City, with his first goal coming a week later at Ilkeston United. He battled all season with Jack Spaven for the position of club's highest scorer but lost out at the end of the campaign, with his final goal coming in the April match at Loughborough Corinthians.

White

Seasons Played	League	~	8
	F.A. Cup	~	
1951/52	Lincs Cup	~	
	Total	~	8

Forward who first played for the club in the August 1951 fixture at Boston United and continued to maintain his place in the side for several of the following games, but his final appearance came in January 1952 at home to Nottingham Forest Reserves.

Whitechurch

Seasons Played	League	~	3 (4)
1911/12	Total	~	3 (4)

Scored in the 1911/12 Central Alliance games against Walsall Reserves, Peterborough Loco, where he netted a brace, and Nottingham Forest Reserves, but no information is available to show any other appearances that he may have made.

Dean Whitehouse

Seasons Played			
	League	~	4
	F.A. Cup	~	
1984/85	F.A. Trophy	~	1
	League Cup	~	
	Lincs Cup	~	
	Other	~	1
	Total	~	6

Born 03/10/1963 at Mexborough. Midfield player with 14 appearances during a Football League career that had taken him to Barnsley, Oldham Athletic and Torquay United. Dean then joined North Ferriby United and Grantham, making six consecutive appearances for The Gingerbreads at the end of 1984, starting at South Liverpool and ending with the Boxing Day trip up to Goole Town. Following this fixture he went on to play for Alfreton Town.

Peter Whitehurst

Seasons Played			
	League	~	237 (110)
	F.A. Cup	~	12 (6)
1985/86-91/92	F.A. Trophy	~	13 (3)
	League Cup	~	37 (18)
	Lincs Cup	~	5 (2)
	Total	~	304 (139)

Born 25/04/1961 at Nottingham. Previously played for Bestwood Miners Welfare, Players, Nuthall, Ilkeston Town and Eastwood Town, with the majority of that time also seeing him playing for Sunday side, AD Bulwell. He scored a brace on his competitive Grantham debut in April 1986 against Leamington, although he had netted a hat-trick for the club in a Midland Floodlit League match against Peterborough United a few days before. Peter played in the final eight league fixtures and then completed the following season by finishing as the club's highest scorer, netting hat-tricks against Rushden Town and Hednesford Town, without missing a single game. March of 1988 saw Peter's injury in the game against Trowbridge, (caused by his ear-ring in a clash of hands with a member of the opposition), directly lead to The FA advising all players to either remove or tape up any items of jewellery. After a brief spell with Glenn Beech as the club's highest scorer, the 1988/89 season saw Peter back in his usual position, although what followed was appearances for a mediocre team that was sticking to mid-table performances and early Cup exits. He became Assistant Manager to John Robertson towards the end of the 1989/90 season, whilst his appearance in the club's final league fixture at London Road, against Dudley Town in September 1990, ensured that he would be remembered as the last great striker that played for the club at the ground. That 1990/91 season would be his final full year with the club and he finished with 33 strikes to his name, including another hat-trick against Spalding United, a remarkable achievement considering it was from a team that finished only ninth in the league and effectively played away from home for the majority of the season. Peter came on as substitute during the club's inaugural match at The Meres in August 1991 against Ilkeston Town in the FA Cup and after scoring his final goal from the penalty spot in the March 1992 league fixture at home to Bilston Town, he once more came on as substitute in the closing fixture of the 1991/92 season at Solihull Borough to make his last appearance. He was rewarded with a Testimonial match against Grimsby Town in October 1992 and went on to have a brief return playing at Ilkeston Town. With 110 goals to his name, he remains the highest scorer for the club in Southern League fixtures.

Ivan Whittaker

Seasons Played			
	League	~	4
	F.A. Cup	~	
1958/59	Lincs Cup	~	1
	Total	~	5

Former Holwell Works player who made his Grantham debut in the January 1959 match against Denaby United and then played in the next four games as well, with the County Cup tie at home to Gainsborough Trinity being his final one.

Widdowson

Seasons Played			
	F.A. Cup	~	
	Lincs Cup	~	
1886/87	Other	~	3 (1)
	Total	~	3 (1)

Played in the first friendly of the 1886/87 season against Grantham Volunteers, scored in the November fixture at home to Newark Town and made his final appearance in the return match against The Volunteers in the New Year.

Tommy Wield

Seasons Played			
	League	~	1
	F.A. Cup	~	
1922/23	Lincs Cup	~	
	Other	~	
	Total	~	1

Born 1886 at Lincoln. Half-Back who had previously played for St Catherine's, before joining Lincoln City in 1904, where he went on to score six goals in 137 appearances split over two spells with a period at Grantham Avenue in-between. After The First World War he played for Scunthorpe & Lindsey United and Gainsborough Trinity, before coming to Grantham. To the best of our knowledge though, he made only one appearance in the September 1922 Central Alliance fixture against Coalville Swifts. Tommy then went on to play for Horncastle Town and Lincoln Claytons. Died 1963 at Lincoln.

Searson Wigginton

Seasons Played			
	League	~	41 (7)
	F.A. Cup	~	
1931/32	Lincs Cup	~	
	Other	~	
1933/34	Total	~	41 (7)

Born 26/03/1909 at Leicester. Previously played football for Leicester Pharmacy, but was also an accomplished County cricketer for his home team. He played for Grantham in many of the 1931/32 season's games with his first *four* goals for the club coming in the November Midland League fixture at home to Denaby United. It is not known whether he made any appearances the following season, but evidence shows that he occasionally played for Grantham a year later, with his final goal coming in the January 1934 defeat of Sutton Town. Died 15/09/1977 at Bulawayo in Rhodesia.

Harry Wilbourn

Seasons Played			
	League	~	199 (3)
	F.A. Cup	~	20
1934/35-38/39	Lincs Cup	~	13
	Other	~	7
	Total	~	239 (3)

Born 10/02/1905 at Eckington. Left-Back who had a long footballing career behind him, with clubs represented including Anston Athletic, Sheffield United, Watford, Halifax Town, Mexborough Athletic and Gainsborough Trinity, although he made only nine First team appearances during his time with the three League sides. He first played for Grantham in the opening fixture of the 1934/35 season at Boston United and immediately became a valuable member of the side. One of his easiest games though, must have been the September 1934 FA Cup tie against Rufford Colliery as the opponents posed little threat to the Grantham defence with the home side running out 13-0 winners. Harry scored all three of his goals for the club within a month of each other around the 1935 New Year period, against Mexborough Athletic, Bradford City Reserves and Scarborough. Although he missed only a few games that season, two of those were the County Cup Final and replay against Boston United at the end of the campaign. The following season he played in the FA Cup First Round tie at home to Notts County, the Lincolnshire Senior Cup Final and the Grantham Hospital and Wilson Cup Finals as well. In April of 1937 Harry played his part in the defeat of Boston United in the County competition final and then missed only one league match the following season as Grantham finished in the runners-up position in the Midland League to Shrewsbury Town. He continued to be a near ever present member of the side, right up until the end of the 1938/39 season with his final appearance coming in the closing fixture at Nottingham Forest Reserves. Died 1991 at Poole.

Wilcockson

Seasons Played			
	League	~	5 (3)
	Other	~	1
1905/06-06/07	Total	~	6 (3)

Known to have played several games towards the end of the 1905/06 season and scored in the first two matches after the Summer interval against Long Eaton St Lawrence and Derby Thornhill. He most probably played in many other fixtures from that season, with more goals to his credit as well.

Paul Wilkin

Ian Wilkins

John Wilkinson

Ian Williams

Jim Williams

Hugh Wilson

Marc Wilson

Stuart Wilson

C. Winfield

Tim Wooding

Martin Wormall

Rick Wright

Henry Yaldren

Kelvin Yeomans

Tommy Young

Mario Ziccardi

Tim Wilkes

Seasons Played			
	League	~	77 (15)
	F.A. Cup	~	8 (7)
1996/97	F.A. Trophy	~	2
	League Cup	~	4
1999/00-00/01	Lincs Cup	~	2
	Total	~	93 (22)

Born 07/11/1977 at Nottingham. Nick-named 'Oliver' and joined Grantham on-loan from Notts County after playing just three First team games there. He made his debut in the February 1997 league match at Tamworth and played seven times over the next month, scoring three goals against Stourbridge, Solihull Borough and Sutton Coldfield Town. He returned to Notts County, but soon went on to play for Kettering Town and Telford United, with time at Gainsborough Trinity and Rothwell Town on-loan. He rejoined Grantham for the start of the 1999/00 season and played in the majority of the games over the next two seasons, including the October 2000 classic FA Cup encounter at Rushden & Diamonds, during which he scored. Tim's final goal for the club came in the 5-0 thrashing against a proficient Hastings United side in April 2001, with his last appearance in the closing fixture at home to St Leonards when he came off the substitutes bench. He went on to make appearances for Hinckley United, Barwell, Coalville Town, Shepshed Dynamo and then returned to Coalville.

Kevin Wilkin

Seasons Played			
	League	~	30 (6)
	F.A. Cup	~	4 (3)
2003/04	F.A. Trophy	~	1 (1)
	League Cup	~	1
	Lincs Cup	~	1
	Total	~	37 (10)

Born 01/10/1967 at Cambridge. Brother of Paul Wilkin. Kevin previously played for Great Shelford, Histon, Cambridge City and Northampton Town, after a £15,000 transfer, where he finished with 17 goals to his name after 101 appearances. Transfers then followed to Rushden & Diamonds, Nuneaton Borough and then a return to Cambridge City, where he finished as the club's highest scorer for the 2001/02 season and held the position of Player/Coach. He came to Grantham as Assistant Manger to Roger Ashby in the Summer of 2003 and made his debut in the club's first ever Lincolnshire Shield tie, at home to Stamford, at the start of the season, scoring his first goal at the end of the same month in the 2-2 draw at Merthyr Tydfil. It will be his goals in that season's FA Cup run that Kevin will be best remembered for though, as he netted both in the final qualifying round tie at Ashton United, plus the opening strike in the televised FA Cup First Round match at home to Leyton Orient. He is therefore the only Grantham player to score a goal on *Match Of The Day*, a scene that was later repeated on *A Question Of Sport*, with reference to the ensuing 'sprint-start' celebrations. His last goal for the club came in the February 2004 league defeat of Dorchester Town, with his final appearance two weeks later at Chippenham Town. He left, with Roger Ashby, to become Assistant Manager at Nuneaton Borough only days later.

Paul Wilkin

Seasons Played			
	League	~	24 (1)
	F.A. Cup	~	4 (1)
2003/04	F.A. Trophy	~	1
	League Cup	~	1
	Lincs Cup	~	
	Total	~	30 (2)

Born 22/04/1969 at Cambridge. Brother of Kevin Wilkin and a former Histon and Cambridge City player who then spent eight years with Hong Kong FC whilst working in the former colony. His first game for Grantham came in the August 2004 league fixture at home to Cambridge City, when he came off the bench to replace Jason Minett. Although he only scored two goals for Grantham, the first of which was against Havant & Waterlooville, his second was a stunning 25 yard effort in the FA Cup third qualifying round at Ashington. Paul then played in the First Round Proper tie at home to Leyton Orient, but his last appearance for Grantham came in the March 2004 defeat at Worcester City.

Ian Wilkins

Seasons Played			
	League	~	83 (1)
	F.A. Cup	~	6
1998/99	F.A. Trophy	~	6
	League Cup	~	7
2000/01-02/03	Lincs Cup	~	4
	Total	~	106 (1)

Born 03/04/80 at Lincoln. Defender who was signed on-loan from Lincoln City, where he made ten First team appearances, after having short spells at Scunthorpe United and Ballymena. He made his Grantham debut in the November 1998 league fixture at home to Cambridge City and played in a total of six games in that first spell with the club. After being released by Lincoln City he went on to play for Spalding United, but returned to The Meres towards the end of the 2000/01 season. Ian played in most of the fixtures the following year when Grantham won promotion back to the Dr Marten's Premier League and scored his only goal for the club in February 2002 at home to Burnham. The 2002/03 season saw appearances for Ian in the County Cup Final against Scunthorpe United, the FA Cup final qualifying tie at Morecambe and the April 2003 Lincolnshire County Senior Cup Final defeat against Gainsborough Trinity, which was his final appearance for the club. Ian left at the end of the season, along with his Manager and many of his colleagues, to play for Lincoln United.

Bert Wilkinson

Seasons Played			
	League	~	15
	F.A. Cup	~	1
1953/54-54/55	Lincs Cup	~	
	Total	~	16

Born 02/08/1922 at Sunderland. Defender who had previously played for Murton Colliery, Charlton Athletic, Lincoln City and Frickley Colliery. Bert made his Grantham debut in the September 1953 Midland League fixture at Nottingham Forest Reserves, but his appearances were generally limited to covering for either Eric Hunt or John Little. His final game for the club came in the October 1954 FA Cup clash at home to Boston United.

Gary Wilkinson

Seasons Played			
	League	~	1
	F.A. Cup	~	
1983/84	F.A. Trophy	~	
	League Cup	~	
	Lincs Cup	~	
	Total	~	1

Made just one appearance by coming off the bench to replace Gary Hooley in the February 1984 league fixture at Morecambe.

John Wilkinson

Born 12/08/1952 at Lincoln. Had previously played for several local Lincoln sides, before taking his coaching badges whilst at Rustons. In 1991 he was awarded the position of First team Coach at Lincoln United and a year later was promoted to the Assistant Manager's post, working with Allen Crombie and Gary Goddard, before becoming Manager of the club himself. Meanwhile, at Grantham Town, December 1999 was certainly a busy month for the club. Following the arrival of Dr Gordon Hotson as Chairman, he promptly sacked the Manager, Matt Carmichael, and after two games with Adrian Speed in temporary control, he appointed Wilkinson to the position. Despite a near impossible task, with Grantham firmly rooted to the bottom of the table, BFJ (an amiable nick-name reference to his figure!) turned the club around and came so close to performing 'The Great Escape' when the team were finally relegated on goal-difference after the concluding game of the season. By the start of the 2000/01 season, John had put together a squad that was capable of achieving success and in October the club were rewarded with a huge day at the biggest non-league club of the era, Rushden & Diamonds, in the FA Cup. Despite narrowly missing out on promotion, that crucial top-two position was achieved in 2002, with the club also winning the Dr Marten's Merit Cup and earning an appearance in the Lincolnshire County Senior Cup Final against Scunthorpe United. Grantham struggled back in the Premier Division and didn't secure their future until the final day of the season, although another FA Cup final qualifying round appearance and County Cup Final place were achieved. Only a few weeks after the end of the 2002/03 season, a disagreement between Wilkinson and Grantham's Board of Directors led to his return to Lincoln United, where he still remains.

Sam Wilkinson

Seasons Played			
	League	~	1
	F.A. Cup	~	
2000/01	F.A. Trophy	~	
	League Cup	~	
	Lincs Cup	~	
	Total	~	1

Born 30/06/1978 at Lincoln. Son of Grantham Manager, John Wilkinson, and a former Sleaford Town and Grantham Reserves player who stepped up to make a lone appearance for the First team in the May 2001 league game at Sittingbourne. After a return to Sleaford, in the Summer of 2004 Sam joined his father back at Lincoln United.

Wilkinson

Seasons Played			
	F.A. Cup	~	
	Lincs Cup	~	
1887/88	Other	~	1
	Total	~	1

Made only one appearance for the club in the November 1887 friendly at Lincoln Rangers.

Wilkinson

Seasons Played			
	League	~	2
1905/06	Total	~	2

Known to have played in the Midland Amateur Alliance games against Bridgford Athletic and Derby YMCA during the 1905/06 season, but no information is available to show any other games that he may have appeared in.

Wilkinson

Seasons Played			
	League	~	4 (5)
	F.A. Cup	~	
1925/26	Lincs Cup	~	1 (1)
	Total	~	5 (6)

Local player who also appeared for the Ruston & Hornsby's works side and scored twice for Grantham in the December 1925 match at home to Shirebrook. Other goals followed in the games against Boston, Newark Town, Mexborough Athletic and Castleford Town over the next few weeks, but no data exists to show his total appearances for that season.

Willerton

Seasons Played			
	Lincs Cup	~	
	Other	~	1
1889/90	Total	~	1

Made just one appearance for Grantham in the January 1890 friendly at home to Newark.

Ian Williams

Seasons Played			
	League	~	64 (24)
	F.A. Cup	~	5 (2)
1993/94-94/95	F.A. Trophy	~	6 (3)
	League Cup	~	4 (1)
	Lincs Cup	~	3
	Total	~	82 (30)

Born circa 1971 at Lincoln. 'Willo', as he was known, was a striker who began his career as a Trainee at Leicester City, before moving onto Holbeach United, winning United Counties League and Cup winners medals, Spalding United and Wisbech Town. His Grantham debut came in the opening County Cup tie of the 1993/94 season at Lincoln City, with his first goal in the maiden league fixture at Forest Green Rovers. He missed just one game that season, finishing as the club's top scorer, and played in every match in the following campaign, up to his final appearance in January 1995 at home to Evesham United, with his last goal coming from the penalty spot the previous week at Hinckley Town. Ian then went back to Wisbech, before joining Stamford Town, Lincoln United, a return to Spalding United, another spell at Lincoln starting in July 2000 and then a dual form contract at Harrowby United in the Summer of 2004 allowing him to play for both clubs.

Jim Williams

Seasons Played			
	League	~	116 (14)
	F.A. Cup	~	11 (2)
1955/56-57/58	Lincs Cup	~	4
	Total	~	131 (16)

Right-sided midfielder who began his Grantham career in the opening match of the 1955/56 season at Boston United and played in the majority of that year's games. He started the following season in a more defensive role, but scored his first goal for the club in September 1956 when Goole Town came to London Road for a league fixture. The 1957/58 season saw Jim still playing a prominent role in the side and towards the end of that campaign he played in the County Cup Final against Gainsborough Trinity. His final appearance for the club came in the closing fixture of the season at Scarborough.

Robbie Williams

Seasons Played			
	League	~	
	F.A. Cup	~	
1996/97	F.A. Trophy	~	
	League Cup	~	1
	Lincs Cup	~	
	Total	~	1

Born 30/12/1974 at Grantham. Reserves player who made just one appearance for the First team in the October 1996 Dr Marten's League Cup tie at home to Corby Town, during which he was replaced by Calvin Plummer from the substitutes bench. Robbie went on to play for Cottesmore Amateurs, Harrowby United, Bourne Town, Deeping Rangers, Boston Town, Spalding United and still plays at a local level.

Tony Williams

Seasons Played			
	League	~	1
	F.A. Cup	~	
1962/63	Total	~	1

Made just one appearance for Grantham in the October 1962 Midland League game at Spalding United.

Williamson

Seasons Played			
	F.A. Cup	~	1
	Lincs Cup	~	1
1883/84-84/85	Other	~	9
1886/87	Total	~	11

Made his first appearance for Grantham in the opening friendly of the 1883/84 season against the Grantham Volunteers and was most probably a regular player for the club in that season. The following year his appearances became more infrequent, although he did return to the side in the opening match of the 1886/87 season, again versus The Volunteers, for his final game.

Charlie Wilson

Seasons Played			
	League	~	37
	F.A. Cup	~	5
1934/35	Lincs Cup	~	4
	Total	~	46

Born 10/02/1904 at Cleethorpes. Full-Back who had previously played for Cleethorpes Town, before spending nine seasons at Grimsby Town, where he scored twice in 292 appearances. In 1933 Charlie joined Bournemouth & Boscombe Athletic, but played in just 11 First team games and came to Grantham in the Summer of 1934. He made his debut in the opening league match of the season at Boston United and within a few weeks was playing in the FA Cup tie against Rufford Colliery, although he presumably had little to do with Grantham running up a record score-line of 13-0. At the end of the season he also appeared in both the Lincolnshire Senior Cup Final and the replay at Boston United, a match which was to be his final game for the club. In October 1935 Charlie made his debut for Peterborough United, where he spent a successful year and a half with the fledgling club. Died 1994 at Grimsby.

E. Wilson

Seasons Played			
	League	~	
	F.A. Cup	~	1
1938/39	Lincs Cup	~	
	Total	~	1

Goalkeeper who at one time was being watched by Aston Villa scouts, but made just one appearance for the First team when

Maurice Healey was unavailable for the October 1938 FA Cup tie at home to Ollerton Colliery.

Hugh Wilson

Seasons Played			
	League	~	16
	F.A. Cup	~	1
1965/66-67/68	F.A. Trophy	~	
	League Cup	~	2
1969/70	Lincs Cup	~	
	Other	~	
	Total	~	19

Born circa 1938. Brother of former Arsenal goalkeeper and TV personality, Bob Wilson. Hugh was recruited from Fulbeck United and made his First team debut in the October 1965 Midland League game against Stamford. Although he spent several years at London Road, Hugh made only occasional appearances, with his final game coming in the Midland League Cup semi-final against Warley in April 1970.

Laurie Wilson

Seasons Played			
	League	~	3
	F.A. Cup	~	
2004/05	F.A. Trophy	~	
	League Cup	~	1
	Lincs Cup	~	
	Total	~	4

Born 05/12/1984 at Sheffield. Son of the current MK Dons Manager, Danny Wilson. Laurie worked his way through Sheffield Wednesday's Youth Academy to make two First team appearances, before being released at the end of the 2003/04 season. He then joined Burton Albion and came to Grantham on-loan in January 2005, making four appearances, starting with the King's Lynn League Cup tie and ending against Chippenham Town at the start of the following month. A couple of weeks later Laurie moved to Belper Town, again on-loan, then returned to Burton, but was released by them at the end of the 2004/05 season.

Lee Wilson

Seasons Played			
	League	~	15 (5)
	F.A. Cup	~	
1997/98	F.A. Trophy	~	
	League Cup	~	
	Lincs Cup	~	
	Total	~	15 (5)

Born 23/05/1972 at Mansfield. Began his career at Clipstone Miners Welfare, before making Football League appearances with Mansfield Town. Lee then moved on to Telford United, Halifax Town, Dagenham & Redbridge and Tamworth, where he won a Dr Marten's Midland Division League winner's medal. He made his debut for Grantham in the February 1998 league match at home to Brackley Town and scored his first two goals in the win over Redditch United at the end of the same month. Although Lee was unable to play in the following FA Trophy ties against Hednesford Town and Southport, he did manage a substitute's appearance in the memorable 6-0 win over Ilkeston Town. His final appearance for the club came in the closing fixture at home to Stourbridge, where a 1-1 draw ensured the league title for Grantham. He went on to play for Solihull Borough, King's Lynn, where he suffered a broken leg, Spalding United, Tamworth, Sutton Town, Clipstone again, and Glapwell, where he eventually became their Player/Manager.

Marc Wilson

Seasons Played			
	League	~	2
	F.A. Cup	~	
2003/04	F.A. Trophy	~	
	League Cup	~	
	Lincs Cup	~	1
	Total	~	3

Began his career playing for Grantham in the Youth and Reserves sides, before joining Harrowby United in the Summer of 2003. Marc returned to The Meres in the 2004 New Year, making his First team debut in the February league match at home to Merthyr Tydfil and then played against Chippenham Town plus Gainsborough Trinity in the Lincolnshire Shield Final of March 2004, his final appearance for the club. He then went back to Harrowby, but soon moved on to Bourne Town.

Richard Wilson

Seasons Played			
	League	~	6
	F.A. Cup	~	
1987/88	F.A. Trophy	~	
	League Cup	~	2
	Lincs Cup	~	
	Total	~	8

Born 10/04/1966. Nephew of Bob Wilson. Richard played in the same position as his uncle and had previously spent time at Notts County, Chesterfield and Lincoln City. He made eight appearances for Grantham, starting with the September 1987 Westgate Insurance League Cup tie against VS Rugby and ending in November at home to Wellingborough Town. Richard then returned to Lincoln City, playing in their GM Vauxhall Conference winning side, followed by moves to Kettering Town, Spalding United and Eastwood Town.

Simon Wilson

Seasons Played			
	League	~	5
	F.A. Cup	~	
1992/93	F.A. Trophy	~	
	League Cup	~	
	Lincs Cup	~	
	Total	~	5

Spalding based full-back who had previously spent time as an Apprentice at Sheffield Wednesday and first played for The Gingerbreads in the January 1993 league game at home to Dudley Town. Simon then made appearances in the final four matches of the season, ending against Bridgnorth Town and after the Summer break moved on to Spalding United.

Stuart Wilson

Seasons Played			
	League	~	93 (23)
	F.A. Cup	~	8
2001/02-03/04	F.A. Trophy	~	6 (2)
	League Cup	~	5 (5)
	Lincs Cup	~	6 (1)
	Total	~	118 (31)

Born 16/09/1977 at Leicester. Scored four goals, plus made 34 senior appearances for Leicester City, one of which was the 1-0 victory over Manchester United at Old Trafford, and also netted four strikes at The Meres in a pre-season friendly against Grantham in 1997. After a period on-loan at Sheffield United, Stuart joined Cambridge United, finishing with a total of another 12 First team appearances to his name, before moving into non-league football with Anstey Nomads, Cambridge City and Shepshed Dynamo. His Grantham debut came in the September 2001 league fixture at home to Histon, with his first two goals for the club coming a month later in the 6-0 demolition of VS Rugby. Stuart was an important member of the side that won promotion in the Spring of 2002, whilst the following season saw appearances for him in the Lincolnshire County Cup Final against Scunthorpe United, the final qualifying round FA Cup tie at Morecambe and the County Final defeat at Gainsborough Trinity. His prominence continued in the side for the 2003/04 season, with an appearance in the FA Cup First Round tie against Leyton Orient. Stuart scored in his final game for the club, in February 2004 at Newport County, although he did spectate from the substitutes bench in a couple of fixtures over the next month. He then followed former Grantham Manager, Roger Ashby, to Nuneaton Borough, but was released by them in May 2005.

Wilson

Seasons Played			
	F.A. Cup	~	
	Lincs Cup	~	1 (1)
1884/85	Other	~	
	Total	~	1 (1)

Scored in his only game for Grantham, the Lincolnshire Senior Cup victory against Lincoln Lindum in January 1885 that sent the club into the semi-final of the competition.

Wilson

Seasons Played			
	Lincs Cup	~	
	Other	~	3
1889/90	Total	~	3

Made his first appearance for the club in the December 1889 friendly at home to Mapperley and then played in the games against Newark and Grantham Rovers over the next month.

Harold Windle

Seasons Played			
	League	~	18 (5)
	F.A. Cup	~	3 (2)
1948/49	Lincs Cup	~	
	Total	~	21 (7)

Scored twice on his debut in the opening Midland League game of the 1948/49 season at Scarborough and missed very few of the games over the following few months, until his final appearance against Ransome & Marles in the Christmas 1948 period.

Windus

Seasons Played			
	League	~	9 (6)
	FA Amt. Cup	~	
1909/10-10/11	League Cup	~	1 (1)
	Lincs Cup	~	2
	Other	~	5 (4)
	Total	~	17 (11)

Scored his first goal for Grantham in the October 1909 Midland Amateur Alliance match at home to Derby YMCA and despite many team-sheets missing from this period, I have little doubt that he was a prominent player both that season and the following Championship winning one as well. His final goal for the club came in the important victory over West Bridgford Albion in April 1911 which clinched the Midland Amateur League title. Most likely to have been either Robert Windus (Born circa 1880 - Died March 1916 at Grantham) a local blacksmith's striker, or Alfred Windus (Born circa 1883 - Died 21/12/1943 at Grantham).

C. Winfield

Seasons Played			
	League	~	22
	F.A. Cup	~	2
1926/27	Lincs Cup	~	1
	Other	~	1
	Total	~	26

Six foot, five inch tall goalkeeper who had also played for the Aston Villa third team, Nottingham Forest Reserves and Newark Town, with his Grantham debut coming in the first league match of the 1926/27 season at Sutton Town. His final match for the club was in February 1927 at Scunthorpe & Lindsey United, with him having played in every match of the season up to that point.

Steve Wing

Seasons Played			
	League	~	2
	F.A. Cup	~	
1987/88-88/89	F.A. Trophy	~	
	League Cup	~	
	Lincs Cup	~	
	Total	~	2

Born 06/01/1968 in Grantham. Successful local player who had previously played for Harlaxton, Grantham Amateurs and Grantham Reserves, amongst others. He made appearances for The Gingerbreads in the January 1988 league match against Hednesford Town and the October match at home to Bridgnorth Town. Steve still lives in Grantham and works for a distribution company situated opposite the club's stadium.

Walter Winnell

Seasons Played			
	League	~	2
	F.A. Cup	~	
1930/31	Lincs Cup	~	
	Total	~	2

Born ??/02/1908 at Sheffield. Former Park Labour, Luton Town, Bristol Rovers, (with one goal to his name in four First team appearances), and Chesterfield player. He made only two appearances for Grantham though, in November 1930 against Denaby United and Loughborough Corinthians. His surname is sometimes spelt 'Wimmell'.

Witham

Seasons Played			
	League	~	3 (3)
	F.A. Cup	~	
1926/27	Lincs Cup	~	
	Other	~	
	Total	~	3 (3)

Centre-Forward who also played for Boston, Scunthorpe & Lindsey United and made his Grantham debut in the February 1927 league fixture at home to Gainsborough Trinity. He scored his first goal for the club in his next game against Denaby United, then netted a brace in the London Road defeat of Shirebrook, but no information shows him playing in any of the subsequent games for the club.

Jim Witherford

Seasons Played			
	League	~	1
	F.A. Cup	~	
1954/55	Lincs Cup	~	
	Total	~	1

Born 16/04/1930 at Sheffield. Former Norton Woodseats and Chesterfield midfielder who made just one appearance for Grantham in the August 1954 fixture at Notts County Reserves.

Wollatt

Seasons Played			
	League	~	7 (9)
1911/12	Total	~	7 (9)

The club's top goal-scorer from the 1911/12 season, who netted his first two goals for the club in the December 1911 Central Alliance fixture. He obviously made many other appearances that season than those known from the above figures, but data does exist to show that he scored in his final appearance in the club's closing fixture against Sutton Town. Despite the slight difference in surnames, there is the possibility that he could be Leslie Woollatt, who played for Grantham Avenue and Mansfield Town just before The War.

Wolmington

Seasons Played			
	F.A. Cup	~	
	Lincs Cup	~	
1887/88	Other	~	3
	Total	~	3

Made his debut in the October 1887 friendly against Nottingham Forest Reserves, but then only appeared in the matches at home to Lincoln Rangers and Notts Rangers over the next couple of months.

Andy Wood

Seasons Played			
	League	~	
	F.A. Cup	~	
1988/89	F.A. Trophy	~	
	League Cup	~	
	Lincs Cup	~	1
	Total	~	1

Forward who made just one appearance for Grantham in the opening County Cup tie of the 1988/89 season at home to Gainsborough Trinity.

Arthur Wood

Seasons Played			
	F.A. Cup	~	
	Lincs Cup	~	
1881/82	Other	~	1
	Total	~	1

Born 1855 in Grantham. A Wine Merchant by profession, which does beg the question as to whether he was introduced to the club by Arthur Hutchinson who was in the same trade. He is the first of three 'Woods' who played for the club that season, but Arthur is only known to have made one appearance, in the December 1881 friendly against Peterborough.

Barrie Wood

Seasons Played			
	League	~	96 (18)
	F.A. Cup	~	9 (1)
1964/65-66/67	Total	~	105 (19)

Born 05/12/1936 at Doncaster. Former Wolverhampton Wanderers, Doncaster Rovers, Scunthorpe United, South Shields, Barnsley and Goole Town player whose father, Willie Wood, had once played for Oldham Athletic. During his professional career Barrie had scored three goals, but made only ten First team appearances for the previously mentioned sides. His Grantham debut came in the opening match of the 1964/65 season at Loughborough United, but it wasn't until October that he made the position his own, at the expense of Alfie Gibbons, with his first goal coming in the December Midland League match at home to Bourne Town. The following season he appeared in the FA Cup Proper rounds against Hendon and Swindon Town and a year later in matches against Wimbledon and Oldham Athletic in the same competition. The start of that 1966/67 season had also seen the introduction of the new law allowing substitutions and the opening fixture at Goole Town saw Barrie as the first one named by the club, although his failure to progress into play meant that the honour went to Neil Marshall the following week. Barrie's final goal for Grantham was at the London Road game against Stamford in January 1967, with his concluding appearance two months later at Gainsborough Trinity.

Dennis Wood

Seasons Played	F.A. Cup	~	6
	Lincs Cup	~	7 (1)
1877/78-81/82	Other	~	30 (5)
1883/84-85/86	Total	~	43 (6)

First played for the club in the February 1878 friendly at Sleaford, followed by many of the games during this period. His initial goal came in the March 1879 match at home to Boston, but his most important one came towards the end of his career, six years later, when Grantham beat Gainsborough Trinity in the County Cup Final to win the club's first ever trophy. This was despite there being doubts as to his ability to play after spraining his ankle that morning. His final appearance for Grantham was in the January 1886 game at home to Grimsby Town.

Frederick Wood

Seasons Played	F.A. Cup	~	4
	Lincs Cup	~	
1880/81-81/82	Other	~	9
1885/86	Total	~	13

Made his first appearance for Grantham in the November 1880 friendly at Gainsborough, but it was the middle of the decade when he had his most consistent period in the team. However, his final game for the club came just after Christmas 1885 when the Grantham Volunteers played a friendly at London Road.

Huw Wood

Seasons Played	League	~	54 (4)
	F.A. Cup	~	3
1978/79-80/81	F.A. Trophy	~	6 (1)
	League Cup	~	6 (1)
	Lincs Cup	~	4
	Other	~	
	Total	~	73 (6)

Born 16/11/1960 at Bellshill. Former England Schoolboy International and Nottingham Forest Reserves player who made his Grantham debut in the August 1978 Southern League Cup tie at home to Corby Town whilst still attending school. He scored his first goal for the club in November at Telford United and finished his first season, a Championship winning one for the club, having played in just over half of the games, including the crucial decider against Merthyr Tydfil. Huw also joined the England Youth squad that year, the only player to do so from outside the Football League. By Grantham's entrance into the Northern Premier League he had firmly established himself in the side, but after playing in the first two County Cup games of the 1980/81 season, the last of which was against Gainsborough Trinity, he was transferred to Scunthorpe United. However, he made only one league appearance there, coming off the substitute's bench, and soon moved on to play for Shepshed Charterhouse, Arnold Town and in the late 1980's, Radcliffe. Huw is now a successful businessman, living just outside of Nottingham, dealing in property and pensions and still plays for the Radcliffe Veterans football team.

William Wood

Seasons Played	League	~	6
	F.A. Cup	~	5 (1)
1883/84-92/93	Lincs Cup	~	10 (4)
	Other	~	57 (26)
	Total	~	78 (31)

Made his debut in the November 1883 game at Gainsborough Trinity and scored his first goal for the club towards the end of the 1884/85 season in the County Cup semi-final at Horncastle, although he failed to make the Final itself. It wasn't until the 1887/88 season that William really established himself in the side, but by the end of that campaign he had become the club's highest scorer, a role that he kept for the next couple of years. Towards the end of his career he had the distinction of playing in Grantham's first ever league game, the September 1891 visit of Notts County Rovers to London Road, but following that his appearances became infrequent. It should have been a fitting end to a successful career, but unfortunately he was to tarnish his record in October 1892. With the club in turmoil he very graciously offered to return as goalkeeper, a role he had played a couple of times previously, for the Midland Amateur Alliance fixture at Notts County Rovers. Sadly for him the game resulted in the club's record defeat, with William picking the ball out of the net sixteen times.

Wood

Seasons Played	League	~	7
	F.A. Cup	~	4 (1)
1945/46	Lincs Cup	~	
	Total	~	11 (1)

Played in the first game after The Second World War, the Midland League fixture at London Road against Gainsborough Trinity, and many of the following games as well. His only goal for the club was in the FA Cup First Round, first leg, at Kettering Town, with his final appearance coming in the following round against Mansfield Town in December 1945.

Woodcock

Seasons Played	F.A. Cup	~	1
	Lincs Cup	~	1
1887/88-90/91	Other	~	22 (3)
	Total	~	24 (3)

Made a sole appearance for the club in the 1887/88 season, a March friendly at home to Newark, but by the following season he had established himself in the side, with his first goal for the club coming in November 1888 against Beeston St Johns. His prominence in the team lasted until the end of the next season, although he returned in January 1891 to help out in the County Cup replay against Grantham Rovers.

Woodcock

Seasons Played	League	~	2
1905/06	Total	~	2

Played in the two Midland Amateur Alliance fixtures against Bridgford Athletic in the 1905/06 season, but no information is available to show any other appearances that he may have made.

John Woodger

Seasons Played	League	~	21 (3)
	F.A. Cup	~	
1961/62-62/63	Lincs Cup	~	
	Total	~	21 (3)

Scored on his debut in the March 1962 league fixture against Retford Town and then replaced Alan Clay at the end of that season. The following campaign began with him out of the side once more, but at the end of the term he had returned to have his best run in the team, up until his final appearance in the concluding match at Boston United.

Woodhead

Seasons Played	League	~	1
	F.A. Cup	~	
1936/37	Lincs Cup	~	
	Other	~	
	Total	~	1

Forward who made just one appearance for Grantham in the March 1937 Midland League game at home to Grimsby Town Reserves.

Tim Wooding

Seasons Played	League	~	70 (1)
	F.A. Cup	~	5
2003/04-04/05	F.A. Trophy	~	4
	League Cup	~	2
	Lincs Cup	~	4
	Total	~	85 (1)

Born 05/07/1973 at Wellingborough. Started his career at Rushden Town Youths and then Norwich City as a Trainee. A devout Liverpool fan, Tim's career came to a temporary halt whilst he recovered from injuries sustained during the 1989 Hillsborough disaster. Another Trainee position was then gained at AFC Bournemouth, before he joined Rushden & Diamonds, Boston United, (during their 2000/01 Conference season), and Cambridge

City. He made his Grantham debut in the first league game of the 2003/04 season at home to Dover Athletic and then missed just one match until the following Spring, gaining appearances in the FA Cup First Round tie against Leyton Orient and the Lincolnshire Shield Final victory over Gainsborough Trinity. Tim was an almost constant member of the Grantham side in the 2004/05 season, scoring his first goal for the club in August at home to Bath City, and remains with the club.

Charles Woodruff

Seasons Played			
	F.A. Cup	~	
	Other	~	2
1879/80-80/81	Total	~	2

Born circa 1849 in Grantham. Individual who has only two known appearances for the club, the January 1880 friendly against Notts County, which ended with a 7-0 Grantham victory, and the match at home to Nottingham Park in November. Died 01/11/1926 in Grantham.

Charlie Woodruff

Seasons Played			
	League	~	3 (2)
	F.A. Cup	~	2 (1)
1913/14	Lincs Cup	~	
	Total	~	5 (3)

Born 19/01/1884 in Grantham. Most likely the son of the former entry. Charlie had previously played for Grantham Avenue, Tottenham Hotspur, with one goal scored in ten appearances, and Doncaster Rovers. He scored on his debut for Grantham in the September 1913 FA Cup tie at Notts Rangers and although many team-sheets are missing from this period he seems to have been a prominent member of that season's team. His surname is sometimes spelt 'Woodruffe'. Died 1943 in Grantham.

W. Woods

Seasons Played			
	F.A. Cup	~	
	Other	~	1
1877/78	Total	~	1

Made only one appearance for Grantham in the February 1878 friendly at home to Retford Rovers.

Woods

Seasons Played			
	League	~	1
	F.A. Cup	~	
1930/31	Lincs Cup	~	
	Total	~	1

Inside-Right who also made appearances for Grantham St John's and played just once for our club in the January 1931 league match at Chesterfield Reserves.

Woodward

Seasons Played			
	League	~	1
	F.A. Cup	~	
1951/52	Lincs Cup	~	
	Total	~	1

Goalkeeper who played in the December 1951 Midland League game at Scarborough, with Horace Hinton unavailable, but it was a match which saw Grantham lose by a 7-0 score-line.

Woodwiss

Seasons Played			
	Other	~	1
1876/77	Total	~	1

Only one known appearance for this player in the November 1876 match at Sleaford.

John Woolley

Seasons Played			
	League	~	1
	F.A. Cup	~	
1969/70	F.A. Trophy	~	
	League Cup	~	
	Lincs Cup	~	
	Other	~	
	Total	~	1

Played just once for Grantham in the closing Midland League fixture of the 1969/70 season at Stamford.

Nigel Woolley

Seasons Played			
	League	~	1
	F.A. Cup	~	
1991/92	F.A. Trophy	~	
	League Cup	~	
	Lincs Cup	~	
	Total	~	1

Came on as substitute in the March 1992 league match at RC Warwick, replacing John O'Hare.

Martin Wormall

Seasons Played			
	League	~	
	F.A. Cup	~	
2004/05	F.A. Trophy	~	
	League Cup	~	
	Lincs Cup	~	1 (1)
	Total	~	1 (1)

Born 1979 in Grantham. Local player who began his career in the Grantham League with St Anne's and Three Gables, before moving on to IPP Newark and Harrowby United. Despite various Football League scouts watching him there, he had trials with several local sides, including Grantham in their Lincolnshire Shield tie at Brigg Town at the start of the 2004/05 season, during which he scored. Despite being offered a place in the side, Martin decided to return to Harrowby.

Arthur Worrall

Seasons Played			
	F.A. Cup	~	
	Lincs Cup	~	1
1886/87-88/89	Other	~	9 (5)
	Total	~	10 (5)

Born 1868 at Nottingham. Former King's School, Grantham, and Oxford student who made his debut for the club in the opening match of the 1886/87 season at London Road against the Grantham Volunteers. His first goal came in the December 1886 friendly against Louth, but after this date his appearances became rare, with his final game two years later against Ecclesfield. Arthur went on to become a Schoolmaster in Louth.

Dave Worthington

Seasons Played			
	League	~	1
	F.A. Cup	~	
1985/86	F.A. Trophy	~	
	League Cup	~	1
	Lincs Cup	~	
	Total	~	2

Born 19/04/1955 at Boston. Previously played for several East Midlands sides, including Ruskington, Boston FC, Boston United, Sutton Town, Bridlington Town and Spalding United. He made two appearances for Grantham during October 1985 against VS Rugby and Bilston Town. Dave still lives in the Boston area and currently runs his own roofing company.

Doug Wragg

Seasons Played			
	League	~	5
	F.A. Cup	~	2 (1)
1965/66	Total	~	7 (1)

Born 12/09/1934 at Nottingham. Former England Schoolboy International who made a total of 203 appearances, scoring 34 goals whilst at West Ham United, Mansfield Town, Rochdale, (including their 1962 League Cup Final appearance at Wembley), and Chesterfield. He first played for Grantham in the August 1965 league match at Worksop Town and scored his only goal for the club in the FA Cup tie against Boston FC a month later. With most of his appearances coming in the first few months of that season, Doug then had to wait until the following February to make what turned out to be his final appearance in the game against Arnold.

Derek Wright

Seasons Played			
	League	~	11 (1)
	F.A. Cup	~	
1956/57	Lincs Cup	~	
	Total	~	11 (1)

The above figures are quoted from the end of season data, but unfortunately the same season saw Richard Wright also appearing and as they didn't play in the same games together it means that team-sheets do not differentiate between the two by printing Christian name initials. The only fact that can be quoted with any certainty is his only goal for the club, which came in the January 1957 game against Denaby United.

Fred Wright

Seasons Played			
	League	~	47
	F.A. Cup	~	2
1929/30-30/31	Lincs Cup	~	
	Other	~	
	Total	~	49

Born 1908 at Ruddington. Full-Back who for some reason also seems to have been known as 'Danny' and had previously played for Ruddington and Notts County, although he had made just one First team appearance there in the 1928/29 season. His Grantham debut came in the opening league fixture of the 1929/30 season at Mansfield Town, but little is known about other specific games that he played in. The following year he is known to have made only 11 appearances, all of which were at the start of the campaign. He was then transferred to Hull City for £350, but once again failed to impress and after only two outings in their senior side moved to Loughborough Corinthians.

Jack Wright

Seasons Played			
	League	~	10 (4)
	F.A. Cup	~	3 (3)
1934/35	Lincs Cup	~	
	Total	~	13 (7)

Born at North Wingfield, Derbyshire. Forward who had previously played for Alfreton Town, Staveley Town, Matlock Town, Notts County, scoring the winning goal in his only First team appearance, Ilkeston United and Sutton Town. He made his Grantham debut in the opening match of the 1934/35 season at Boston United and scored his first goal in the FA Cup tie against Sutton Town in October. Grantham had a strong attacking line-up that year though and Jack struggled to make a consistent number of appearances, with his final one coming in February 1935 when Gainsborough Trinity came over to London Road.

Richard Wright

Seasons Played			
	League	~	3 (2)
	F.A. Cup	~	
1956/57	Lincs Cup	~	
	Total	~	3 (2)

See notes for Derek Wright. Known to have scored twice for Grantham on his debut, the September 1956 win over Scarborough.

Rick Wright

Seasons Played			
	League	~	39 (1)
	F.A. Cup	~	2 (1)
1999/00-01/02	F.A. Trophy	~	
	League Cup	~	3
	Lincs Cup	~	1
	Total	~	45 (2)

Born 1973 at Lincoln. Defender who started out his career as an Apprentice at Lincoln City, before making appearances for Harby and Lincoln United. He followed Manager, John Wilkinson, to The Meres at the end of 1999 and made his debut in the home fixture against Dorchester Town. His first goal for the club came in the September 2000 FA Cup tie at home to Bedworth United, but he finished that campaign with just 19 appearances to his name. Rick returned to the side at the start of the 2001/02 season, but was forced to quit The Gingerbreads due to injury, with the September league fixture at Rugby United his final appearance.

Wright

Seasons Played			
	F.A. Cup	~	
	Lincs Cup	~	2
1879/80-80/81	Other	~	7 (1)
1883/84-86/87	Total	~	9 (1)

First played for Grantham in the December 1879 friendly at Boston and scored his solitary goal for the club the following December at Gainsborough. He made only a handful of appearances each year though, with his final game for Grantham coming on New Year's Day 1887 in a Lincolnshire Senior Cup tie at Market Rasen Town.

Wright

Seasons Played			
	League	~	1
	F.A. Cup	~	
1892/93	Total	~	1

Made just one appearance for the club in the October 1892 record defeat at the hands of Notts County Rovers in the Midland Amateur Alliance, although it is always possible that he could be the same individual as the previous entry.

Wright

Seasons Played			
	League	~	11
	F.A. Cup	~	3
1919/20	Lincs Cup	~	2
	Total	~	16

Half-Back who also played for Radcliffe and made his Grantham debut in the September 1919 match at Derby County Reserves. He seems to have been cover for a strong defence that included 'Tiny' Yaldren and Tommy Walkerdine that year. Unfortunately no details are known about the end of his Grantham career.

Wright

Seasons Played			
	League	~	3 (2)
	F.A. Cup	~	
1926/27	Lincs Cup	~	1 (1)
	Other	~	
	Total	~	4 (3)

Former Lincoln City Reserves player who scored for Grantham in one of his first matches for the club, on Boxing Day 1926 at Newark Town. However, despite scoring again a couple of days later in the home fixture against Denaby United he made only a couple of other appearances.

Bernard Wrigley

Seasons Played			
	League	~	15
	F.A. Cup	~	
1926/27	Lincs Cup	~	
	Other	~	
	Total	~	15

Born 1894 at Clitheroe. Experienced goalkeeper who had previously played for Clitheroe Royal Blues, Clitheroe Amateurs, Great Harwood, Blackburn Rovers and Lincoln City, making a total of ten Football League appearances. Bernard replaced the club's first choice 'keeper, Winfield, for the February 1927 Midland League clash at home to Gainsborough Trinity and kept the place for the rest of the season. After leaving London Road, he returned to Great Harwood. Died 1965.

Alan Wycherley

Seasons Played			
	League	~	14
	Lincs Cup	~	
1939/40	Other	~	6 (1)
	Total	~	20 (1)

First played for the club in the opening match of the 1939/40 season at Bradford Park Avenue Reserves and scored his only goal for Grantham against an RAF XI as the cancellation of the Midland League led to a series of friendlies being played. He then continued to play in the team in every one of the club's fixtures in the first of the 'War-Time' league competitions, with his final appearance against Gainsborough Trinity in January 1940.

Ken Wycherley

Seasons Played			
	League	~	6
	F.A. Cup	~	1
1946/47	Lincs Cup	~	
	Total	~	7

Made his debut in the September 1946 game at Boston United, but played only occasionally, the final time being in the April 1947 league fixture at Peterborough United.

Wyles

Seasons Played			
	F.A. Cup	~	
1874/75	Other	~	5 (1)
1876/77-77/78	Total	~	5 (1)

Played in the club's first ever game, as the Third Lincolnshire Volunteer Rifles came to London Road in October 1874, but made infrequent appearances after this. His only goal for the club arrived two years later at Peterborough and his final appearance was in the London Road visit of Bourne in March 1878.

Henry Yaldren

Seasons Played			
	League	~	145 (3)
	F.A. Cup	~	12
1919/20-23/24	League Cup	~	1
	Lincs Cup	~	8
1925/26-28/29	Other	~	5
	Total	~	171 (3)

Born 1894 at Southampton. With a height of 6'6" he could only have the nick-name 'Tiny'. He was a Corporal in the Army and also played for Loughborough Corinthians during his footballing career. He first played for Grantham in the October 1919 FA Cup tie against Sutton Town and his first goal for the club came in September 1921 at Coalville Swifts. Sadly so many of the team-sheets are missing from the decade that 'Tiny' played and yet that simply highlights the following fact. Bearing in mind that the above figures are quoted from those matches where evidence still exists that he played, his true appearance figures could be vast, certainly to the point where he should still be considered as one of the most prominent players in the club's history. Many older Granthamians will remember him though for his later position as Head Park Keeper at Dysart Park, a post he held certainly well into the 1950's. Died 13/07/1964 in Grantham.

Eddie Yeardley

Seasons Played			
	League	~	79
	F.A. Cup	~	4
1952/53-53/54	Lincs Cup	~	4
	Total	~	87

Centre-Half from the North-East who possibly played for Willington in the 1949/50 FA Amateur Cup Final. He began his Grantham career in the August 1952 league match against Halifax Town Reserves and immediately made the position his own, playing in the majority of that season's games including the Lincolnshire Senior Cup 'A' Final at Spalding United. The following year he once again played in the County Final, although this time Eddie finished with a winner's medal after the team beat Gainsborough Trinity at London Road. He played right up until the closing league fixture of the 1953/54 campaign at Hull City Reserves and a week later appeared in the Stamford Invitational Cup against the host side, but the Summer saw his transfer to Boston United.

Yeatman

Seasons Played			
	F.A. Cup	~	
	Lincs Cup	~	
1879/80	Other	~	9 (3)
1881/82	Total	~	9 (3)

Made his debut in the opening friendly of the 1879/80 season at home to Newark and scored his first goal the following February against Sleaford. He returned to the team at the end of 1881 to make his final appearance in the home match against Peterborough.

Kelvin Yeomans

Seasons Played			
	League	~	47 (4)
	F.A. Cup	~	6
1968/69-69/70	F.A. Trophy	~	5
	League Cup	~	13
	Lincs Cup	~	3
	Other	~	
	Total	~	74 (4)

Born 25/08/1947 at Nottingham. Former Beeston, Notts County and Ilkeston Town defender who first appeared for Grantham in the October 1968 league fixture against Long Eaton United. Kelvin played in every one of the remaining matches from that season, including the FA Cup ties against Chelmsford City and Swindon Town, and both legs of the Midland League Cup Final. The following season saw his first goal for Grantham in the September game at home to Heanor Town, followed by an appearance in the FA Cup First Round at Oldham Athletic. His final game for the club came in March 1970 in a Midland League Cup tie against Worksop Town, with his whole career at London Road completed without missing a single game.

Steven Young

Seasons Played			
	League	~	
	F.A. Cup	~	
2002/03	F.A. Trophy	~	
	League Cup	~	
	Lincs Cup	~	1
	Total	~	1

Joined Grantham in the Summer of 2001 from Lincoln City and spent the following year in the Reserves and Youth Teams. He made just one appearance for the First team, coming off the bench to replace Stuart Wilson in the opening County Cup tie of the 2002/03 season at home to Scunthorpe United, confusingly the Final of the previous season's competition. Steven left the club soon after to tour around Australia.

Tommy Young

Seasons Played			
	League	~	38 (13)
	F.A. Cup	~	3 (1)
1981/82-82/83	F.A. Trophy	~	1
	League Cup	~	2 (1)
	Lincs Cup	~	1
	Other	~	
	Total	~	45 (15)

Born 24/12/1947 at Glasgow. Striker with experience at Falkirk, Tranmere Rovers and Rotherham United, making nearly 200 appearances in the English Football League. Tommy then signed for Runcorn, where he won a Northern Premier League Cup winners medal, followed by moves to Buxton and Corby Town. He made his Grantham debut in the opening County Cup game of the 1981/82 season against Boston United with his first goal coming from the penalty spot a couple of weeks later at home to Goole Town. He played in most of the fixtures that season, scoring a total of 13 goals, one of which is thought to be the quickest at London Road, officially timed at 8 seconds, with Morecambe being the victims in the April 1982 League fixture. He scored in his final game for Grantham, again from the penalty spot, in the September 1982 FA Cup tie at home to Hinckley Athletic. After spending many years working in Maltby Colliery, he was made redundant in 1993 and was last known to be working as a plate-layer a few years after that.

Young

Seasons Played			
	League	~	1
	F.A. Cup	~	
1923/24	League Cup	~	
	Lincs Cup	~	
	Other	~	
	Total	~	1

Only one known appearance for this midfielder, the January 1924 Central Alliance match at home to Retford Town.

Zemontas

Seasons Played			
	League	~	1
	F.A. Cup	~	
1953/54	Lincs Cup	~	
	Total	~	1

Played only once for Grantham, although it was one of the highlights of the season, the November 1953 home league fixture against Boston United, which that year ended in a 2-2 draw.

Mario Ziccardi

Seasons Played			
	League	~	214
	F.A. Cup	~	18
1999/00-04/05	F.A. Trophy	~	10
	League Cup	~	9
	Lincs Cup	~	14
	Total	~	265

Born 01/12/1977 at Aylesbury. Spent time as a youngster at Nottingham Forest and Scunthorpe United, but was signed for Grantham by his ex-manager, John Wilkinson, from Lincoln United. The transfer was officially for an undisclosed sum, but thought to be around £3,000, which would be a club record fee. His first game for The Gingerbreads came in the January 2000 league match at home to Merthyr Tydfil and he was an important signing as the club desperately attempted to prevent, ultimately unsuccessfully, the threat of relegation. He played in the October 2000 FA Cup final qualifying round tie at Rushden & Diamonds and was seen as a crucial element for the club's attempt to gain promotion straight back up to the Dr Marten's Premier League. But Mario was sent off three times during the 2000/01 season, including the 6-0 defeat at Newport IOW, and the subsequent suspensions caused Wilkinson severe problems. He did however play in every fixture of the following season, which finished with the important promotion, whilst a year later saw him miss just one league game, plus appearances were gained in the County Cup Final at home to Scunthorpe United, the FA Cup tie at Morecambe and the Lincolnshire Final against Gainsborough Trinity at the end of April. November 2003 saw his appearance in the FA Cup First Round Proper tie at home to Leyton Orient, but an unfortunate tackle out of the area on an opposing forward heading goal-bound resulted in another red card, this time in front of *Match Of The Day* cameras. He also played in the March 2004 Lincolnshire Shield Final victory over Gainsborough Trinity, with another appearance just over a year later in a corresponding County Final as The Gingerbreads retained their position as Lincolnshire's premier non-league team. Mario remains with the club and is one of Grantham's longest serving goalkeepers now, second only to Chris Gardiner in number of games played.

~~~~~

Club Officials

The following list is made up almost entirely from Grantham match-day programmes. Therefore, for the majority of the seasons, whilst the information will be correct for the start of that particular campaign, it does not necessarily include any mid-season additions and departures.

Grantham / Grantham Town FC Presidents

1945/46 - 1947/48 Bill Durance

1976/77 - 1977/78 The Hon. Edward Cust

1978/79 - 1980/81 Rt Hon. The Lord Brownlow

1982/83 - 1996/97 Rt Hon. Margaret Thatcher, Prime Minister
later ~ Rt Hon. Margaret Thatcher, MP
later ~ Baroness Thatcher of Kesteven

1999/00 - 2001/02 Michael Bird

2003/04 - To Date George Freeston

Grantham / Grantham Town FC Chairmen

1945/46 R. Cooper
1945/46 Freddie Poole
1946/47 George Pestell
1947/48 Reg Maycroft
1950/51 - 1956/57 Bill Durance
1957/58 - 1971/72 Frank Baxter
1972/73 - 1977/78 Fred Goodliff
1978/79 Peter Rawlinson
1979/80 Frank Baxter
1980/81 - 1982/83 David Boothman
1983/84 - 1984/85 John Toon
Circa 1984/85 Colin Lamb
1985/86 John Moore
1987/88 - 1990/91 Tony Balfe
1991/92 Geoff Charnock
1991/92 Tony Balfe
1992/93 Gordon Watson
1994/95 - 1999/00 Alan Prince
1999/00 - 2000/01 Gordon Hotson
2001/02 - 2004/05 Barry Palmer
2004/05 - To Date Roger Booth
~~~~~

Grantham / Grantham Town FC Secretaries

1945/46 - 1946/47 H. Cartwright
1947/48 G. Sumner
1950/51 - 1952/53 J. Carmen
1953/54 - 1955/56 A. Spencer
1956/57 C. Hatton
1957/58 D. Wallace
1958/59 -1959/60 R. Lawrence
1960/61 - 1961/62 J. Pinner
1962/63 - 1965/66 J. Hanson
1966/67 - 1974/75 F. Ilott
1975/76 - 1978/79 J. Toon
1979/80 - 1984/85 H. Kilbourn
1985/86 R. Crutcher
1987/88 R. Adams
1988/89 - To Date P. Nixon

Grantham / Grantham Town FC Treasurers

1945/46 S. Gamage
1946/47 C. Hunt
1947/48 L. Bacon
1966/67 - 1978/79 J. Hanson
1979/80 L. Selby
1980/81 - 1983/84 W. Parkinson
1984/85 D. Britton
1994/95 - 1997/98 Mrs E. Prince

Grantham / Grantham Town FC Directors

1950/51 G. Pestell, H. Leek, W. Kirby, F. Harrison
1952/53 G. Pestell, H. Leek, W. Gillison, T. Cadwallader
1953/54 - 1954/55 G. Pestell, A. Spencer, H. Leek, W.Gillison, T. Cadwallader, E. Eatch
1955/56 G. Pestell, A. Spencer, H. Leek, W. Gillison, E. Eatch, F. Baxter, W. Kirby
1956/57 F. Baxter, G. Pestell, A. Spencer, H. Leek, W. Gillison, W. Kirby, J. Fisher, G. Hockley
1957/58 W. Kirby, A.Spencer, W. Gillison, H. Leek, G. Hockley, J. Fisher, S. Richardson
1958/59 W. Kirby, A. Spencer, W. Gillison, G. Hockley, J.Fisher, S. Richardson
1959/60 W. Kirby, A. Spencer, W. Gillison, S. Richardson
1960/61 - 1961/62 W. Kirby, W. Gillison, S. Richardson, F. Goodliff
1962/63 W. Kirby, W. Gillison, S. Richardson, F. Goodliff, J. Pinner
1963/64 W. Kirby, S. Richardson, F. Goodliff, J. Pinner, J. Hanson
1964/65 F. Goodliff, S. Richardson, J. Pinner, J. Hanson, G. Foster
1965/66 F. Goodliff, S. Richardson, J. Pinner, J. Hanson, G. Foster, H. Pearse, T. Scott
1966/67 F. Goodliff, J. Pinner, J. Hanson, G. Foster, H. Pearse, T. Scott, H. Smalley
1967/68 F. Goodliff, J. Pinner, J. Hanson, G. Foster, T. Scott, E. Smalley, N. Key
1968/69 - 1969/70 F. Goodliff, J. Pinner, J. Hanson, G. Foster, T. Scott, N. Key, N. Pinchbeck
1970/71 - 1971/72 F. Goodliff, J. Pinner, J. Hanson, T. Scott, N. Key, N. Pinchbeck, J. Lambley
1972/73 J. Hanson, F. Baxter, J. Pinner, T. Scott, J. Lambley
1973/74 - 1974/75 J. Hanson, F. Baxter, J. Lambley, N. Johnson, L. Selby
1975/76 J. Hanson, P. Rawlinson, F. Baxter, J. Lambley, N. Johnson, L. Selby, T. Scott, R. Castle
1976/77 P. Rawlinson, F. Baxter, R. Castle, J. Kerr
1977/78 P. Rawlinson, F. Baxter, R. Castle
1978/79 F. Baxter, J. Pinchbeck, A. Day, A. Barnbrook, C. Blankley
1979/80 G. Corton, I. Saddington, A. Day, A. Barnbrook, C. Blankley
1980/81 G. Corton, C. Blankley, A. Day, W. Parkinson, J. Toon, S. Dryden, F. Baxter
1981/82 J. Toon, C. Blankley, W. Parkinson, H. Kilbourn, S. Dryden, F. Baxter
1982/83 J. Toon, C. Blankley, W. Parkinson, H. Kilbourn, S. Dryden, F. Baxter, K. Gillison
1983/84 C. Blankley, K. Gillison, H. Kilbourn, W. Parkinson, P. Southerington, K. Walker, J. Wilks, A. Day
1984/85 W. Parkinson, M. Blankley, W. Britton, K. Cullington, K. Gillison, H. Kilbourn, J. Moore, P. Southerington, K. Walker, J. Wilks, A. Day, P. Gottlieb
1985/86 W. Parkinson, W. Britton, K. Cullington, K. Gillison, P. Credland, J. Toon, P. Southerington, P. Gottlieb
1987/88 J. Burns, K. Green, G. Watson
1988/89 J. Burns, G. Charnock, K. Green, G. Watson, R Whatton
1989/90 G. Charnock, B. Gustar, G. Watson
1990/91 G. Charnock, B. Gustar
1991/92 B. Gustar
1992/93 T. Balfe, P. Elliot, B. Duller, P. Nixon
1993/94 M. Pearce, P. Credland, P. Elliot, B. Duller
1994/95 - 1995/96 B. Duller
1996/97 A. Davidson, G. Freeston, B. Palmer
1997/98 G. Freeston, B. Palmer
1998/99 P. Nixon, G. Freeston, B. Palmer
1999/00 B. Palmer, K. Roe, K. Healey, P. Day, G. Freeston
2000/01 B. Palmer, J. King, G. Freeston, Mrs S. Hayes, G. Charles
2001/02 P. Teare, K. Healey, P. Day, T. Harrison
2002/03 P. Teare, K. Healey, P. Day, D. Bullock, N. Podam
2003/04 P. Teare, D. Bullock, J. Gilbert
2004/05 B.Palmer, P. Teare, D. Bullock, R. Booth, S. Boam, J. Gilbert